Global Transformations

In memory of Gisela Held and Margaret McGrew

Global Transformations

Politics, Economics and Culture

David Held and Anthony McGrew,
David Goldblatt and Jonathan Perraton

Stanford University Press
Stanford, California
1999

Stanford University Press
Stanford, California
© 1999 David Held, Anthony G. McGrew, David Goldblatt
   and Jonathan Perraton
Originating publisher Polity Press, Cambridge
   in association with Blackwell Publishers Ltd, Oxford
First published in the U.S.A. by Stanford
   University Press, 1999
Printed in Great Britain
Cloth ISBN 0–8047–3625–1
Paper ISBN 0–8047–3627–8
LC 98–61263
This book is printed on acid-free paper.

Contents

6   People on the Move   283

Conclusion: the Shape of Contemporary Globalization   414

Grids

Figures and Maps

Figures

Maps

Tables

Boxes

Preface

This volume is a product of nearly a decade of research and an unusual confluence of interests.

In the mid-1980s David Held and Anthony McGrew had a number of extended conversations about the changing nature and form of established liberal democratic nation-states in the context of intensifying regional and global relations. The result was too often mutual incomprehension! As a student of political theory, David Held had tended to regard the world of regional and global relations as outside the sphere of political theory, while Anthony McGrew, as an international relations theorist, had tended to analyse domestic politics as a marginal element of the interstate system. Many excellent conversations and discussions revealed that neither position, as it stood, engaged sufficiently with the changing nature of politics in a more interconnected world – and that the traditions and conceptual tools of both parties to the dialogue could very usefully be developed.

An application to the Economic and Social Research Council followed. At issue was an attempt to create a framework for an extended encounter between political theory and international relations focused on pressing issues related to the changing role of the modern state. In particular, the research set out to investigate the extent to which regionalization and globalization are transforming the nature of world order and the position of national sovereignty and autonomy within it.

The research was funded by the ESRC (award no. R000 23 3391) and we are extremely grateful for the opportunity this provided, as well as for the excellent research guidance that came from several anonymous referees.

After the funding of the project was secured, the conversation between David Held and Anthony McGrew was extended further across disciplinary boundaries to cope with the range of pressing problems which the research agenda created. David Goldblatt brought to the project a background in social theory and environmental politics while Jonathan Perraton joined as the project's economist. Both made contributions to the intellectual framework of the project as well as to every aspect of the research programme. This was a truly collective effort and the result is a synthesis of our collective expertise.

Many people have contributed to the production of the volume. Anne Hunt provided outstanding support in the processing and reprocessing of the enormous manuscript; Ray Munns drew and redrew the maps and figures with exceptional patience in the face of changing specifications; Rebecca Hunt provided invaluable assistance helping to create the databases for the book; Brenda Martin offered much needed research assistance during the final stages of the project; Julia Harsant, Sue Pope and Gill Motley furthered the process of the manuscript's publication with great conscientiousness and care; Ann Bone copy-edited the text with extraordinary patience and diligence; Serena Temperley eased the book through the production process with great skill; and Jane Rose helped set down the plans to bring the volume to the attention of a wide readership. We are extremely grateful to all these people and to the many colleagues, friends and family members who have provided support, advice and (usually!) constructive criticism.

Acronyms and Abbreviations

A&A	arms and armaments
AIC	advanced industrialized country
AIDS	Acquired Immune Deficiency Syndrome
AMRAAM	advanced medium-range anti-aircraft missile
APEC	Asia-Pacific Economic Cooperation
APT	Asia-Pacific Telecommunity
ARF	ASEAN Regional Forum
ASEAN	Association of South East Asian Nations
BIS	Bank for International Settlements
BSE	Bovine Spongiform Encephalopathy
BWC	Biological Weapons Convention
BWS	Bretton Woods system
CAFOD	Catholic Fund for Overseas Development
CENTO	Central Treaty Organization
CEPT	Conference of European Postal and Telecommunications Administrations
CFCs	chlorofluorocarbons
CFE	Conventional Forces in Europe Treaty
CITEL	The Inter-American Telecommunications Commission
CITES	Convention on International Trade in Endangered Species
COMECON	Council for Mutual Economic Assistance
CTBT	Comprehensive Test Ban Treaty
DIB	defence industrial base
DOD	Department of Defense (US)
ECHR	European Commission on Human Rights
EEC	European Economic Community
EFTA	European Free Trade Association
EMS	European Monetary System
ERM	European exchange rate mechanism
EU	European Union
EUROCORPS	European Multilateral Force
FAO	Food and Agriculture Organization
FDI	foreign direct investment
FRG	Federal Republic of Germany
FSX	US-Japanese Advanced Fighter
GATS	General Agreement on Trade and Services
GATT	General Agreement on Tariffs and Trade
GCD	general and complete disarmament

GDP	gross domestic product
GDR	German Democratic Republic
GNP	gross national product
G5	Group of Five
G7/G8	Group of Seven/Eight (leading industrial nations)
G10	Group of Ten
IAEA	International Atomic Energy Agency
IBRD	International Bank for Reconstruction and Development
ICAO	International Civil Aviation Organization
ICJ	International Court of Justice
ICTU	International Confederation of Trade Unions
IDA	International Development Agency
IFC	International Finance Corporation
IFPI	International Federation of Phonographic Industries
IGO	intergovernmental organization
ILO	International Labour Organization
IMCO	International Maritime Consultancy Organization
IMF	International Monetary Fund
INF Treaty	Intermediate-Range Nuclear Force Treaty
INGO	international non-governmental organization
INTELSAT	International Telecommunications Satellite Organization
IPCC	International Panel on Climate Change
IRBM	Intermediate Range Ballistic Missile
ISDN	International Services Digital Network
ITU	International Telecommunication Union
LIFFE	London International Financial Futures Exchange
M&A	mergers and acquisitions
MERCOSUR	Southern Cone Common Market (Latin America)
MFN	most favoured nation
MNC	multinational corporation
MNE	multinational enterprise
MTCR	Missile Technology Control Regime
MTR	military-technological revolution
NACC	North Atlantic Council for Cooperation
NAFTA	North American Free Trade Agreement
NATO	North Atlantic Treaty Organization
NIE	newly industrializing economy(ies)
NGO	non-governmental organization
NPT	Treaty on the Non-Proliferation of Nuclear Weapons
NSG	Nuclear Suppliers Group
NWFZ	nuclear weapon-free zone
OAS	Organization of American States
OAU	Organization of African Unity
ODA	Official Development Assistance
OECD	Organization for Economic Cooperation and Development
OPEC	Organization of Petroleum Exporting Countries
OSCE	Organization for Security and Cooperation in Europe

OTA	US Congress Office of Technology Assessment
OTC	over the counter
PATU	Pan African Telecommunications Union
PCB	polychlorinated biphenyls
PFP	Partnership for Peace
PTT	Post, Telegraph and Telephone Administrations
R&D	research and development
RCC	Regional Commonwealth for Communications
SALT	Strategic Arms Limitation Talks
SAM	surface-to-air missile
SEATO	South East Asia Treaty Organization
SIACS	states in advanced capitalist societies
SIPRI	Stockholm International Peace Research Institute
SMEs	small and medium-sized enterprises
SOPEMI	Système d'observation permanente des migrations (Continuous Reporting System on Migration)
START	Strategic Arms Reduction Talks
SU	Soviet Union
SWIFT	standardized world interbank and financial transactions
TRIMS	trade related investment measures
TRIPS	trade in intellectual property rights
UAE	United Arab Emirates
UK	United Kingdom
UN	United Nations
UNCD	United Nations Conference on Disarmament
UNCHR	United Nations Commission on Human Rights
UNCTAD	United Nations Conference on Trade and Development
UNCTC	United Nations Center for the Study of Transnational Corporations
UNDP	United Nations Development Programme
UNEP	United Nations Environment Programme
UNESCO	United Nations Educational, Scientific and Cultural Organization
UNFPA	United Nations Fund for Population Activities
UNHCR	United Nations High Commission for Refugees
UNICEF	United Nations Children's Fund
UNIDO	United Nations Industrial Development Organization
UPU	Universal Postal Union
US	United States
UV	ultraviolet
WASP	white Anglo-Saxon Protestant
WCED	World Commission on Environment and Development
WEU	Western European Union
WFP	World Food Programme
WHO	World Health Organization
WMO	World Meteorological Organization
WRI	World Resources Institute
WTO	World Trade Organization

Introduction

Globalization is an idea whose time has come. From obscure origins in French and American writings in the 1960s, the concept of globalization finds expression today in all the world's major languages (cf. Modelski, 1972). Yet, it lacks precise definition. Indeed, globalization is in danger of becoming, if it has not already become, the cliché of our times: the big idea which encompasses everything from global financial markets to the Internet but which delivers little substantive insight into the contemporary human condition.

Clichés, nevertheless, often capture elements of the lived experience of an epoch. In this respect, globalization reflects a widespread perception that the world is rapidly being moulded into a shared social space by economic and technological forces and that developments in one region of the world can have profound consequences for the life chances of individuals or communities on the other side of the globe. For many, globalization is also associated with a sense of political fatalism and chronic insecurity in that the sheer scale of contemporary social and economic change appears to outstrip the capacity of national governments or citizens to control, contest or resist that change. The limits to national politics, in other words, are forcefully suggested by globalization.

Although the popular rhetoric of globalization may capture aspects of the contemporary zeitgeist, there is a burgeoning academic debate as to whether globalization, as an analytical construct, delivers any added value in the search for a coherent understanding of the historical forces which, at the dawn of the new millennium, are shaping the socio-political realities of everyday life. Despite a vast and expanding literature there is, somewhat surprisingly, no cogent theory of globalization nor even a systematic analysis of its primary features. Moreover, few studies of globalization proffer a coherent historical narrative which distinguishes between those events that are transitory or immediate and those developments that signal the emergence of a new conjuncture; that is, a transformation of the nature, form and prospects of human communities. In acknowledging the deficiencies of existing approaches, this volume seeks to develop a distinctive account of globalization which is both historically grounded and informed by a rigorous analytical framework. The framework is explicated in this introduction, while subsequent chapters use it to tell the story of globalization and to assess its implications for the governance and politics of nation-states today. In this respect, the introduction provides the intellectual foundation for addressing the central questions which animate the entire study:

- What is globalization? How should it be conceptualized?
- Does contemporary globalization represent a novel condition?

- Is globalization associated with the demise, the resurgence or the transformation of state power?
- Does contemporary globalization impose new limits to politics? How can globalization be 'civilized' and democratized?

As will soon become apparent, these questions are at the root of the many controversies and debates which find expression in contemporary discussions about globalization and its consequences. The subsequent pages offer a way of thinking about how these questions might be addressed.

The Globalization Debate

Globalization may be thought of initially as the widening, deepening and speeding up of worldwide interconnectedness in all aspects of contemporary social life, from the cultural to the criminal, the financial to the spiritual. That computer programmers in India now deliver services in real time to their employers in Europe and the USA, while the cultivation of poppies in Burma can be linked to drug abuse in Berlin or Belfast, illustrate the ways in which contemporary globalization connects communities in one region of the world to developments in another continent. But beyond a general acknowledgement of a real or perceived intensification of global interconnectedness there is substantial disagreement as to how globalization is best conceptualized, how one should think about its causal dynamics, and how one should characterize its structural consequences, if any. A vibrant debate on these issues has developed in which it is possible to distinguish three broad schools of thought, which we will refer to as the *hyperglobalizers*, the *sceptics*, and the *transformationalists*. In essence each of these schools may be said to represent a distinctive account of globalization – an attempt to understand and explain this social phenomenon.

For the hyperglobalizers, such as Ohmae, contemporary globalization defines a new era in which peoples everywhere are increasingly subject to the disciplines of the global marketplace (1990; 1995). By contrast the sceptics, such as Hirst and Thompson, argue that globalization is essentially a myth which conceals the reality of an international economy increasingly segmented into three major regional blocs in which national governments remain very powerful (1996a; 1996b). Finally, for the transformationalists, chief among them being Rosenau and Giddens, contemporary patterns of globalization are conceived as historically unprecedented such that states and societies across the globe are experiencing a process of profound change as they try to adapt to a more interconnected but highly uncertain world (Giddens, 1990, 1996; Rosenau, 1997).

Interestingly, none of these three schools map directly on to traditional ideological positions or worldviews. Within the hyperglobalist's camp orthodox neoliberal accounts of globalization can be found alongside Marxist accounts, while among the sceptics conservative as well as radical accounts share similar conceptions of, and conclusions about, the nature of contemporary globalization. Moreover, none of the great traditions of social enquiry – liberal, conservative and Marxist – has an agreed perspective on globalization as a socio-economic phenomenon. Among Marxists globalization is understood in quite incompatible ways as, for instance, the extension of monopoly capitalist imperialism or, alternatively, as a radically new form of globalized capitalism

(Callinicos et al., 1994; Gill, 1995; Amin, 1997). Similarly, despite their broadly orthodox neoliberal starting points, Ohmae and Redwood produce very different accounts of, and conclusions about, the dynamics of contemporary globalization (Ohmae, 1995; Redwood, 1993). Among the hyperglobalizers, sceptics and transformationalists there is a rich diversity of intellectual approaches and normative convictions. Yet, despite this diversity, each of the perspectives reflects a general set of arguments and conclusions about globalization with respect to its

- conceptualization
- causal dynamics
- socio-economic consequences
- implications for state power and governance
- and historical trajectory.

It is useful to dwell on the pattern of argument within and between approaches since this will shed light on the fundamental issues at stake in the globalization debate.[1]

The hyperglobalist thesis

For the hyperglobalizers, globalization defines a new epoch of human history in which 'traditional nation-states have become unnatural, even impossible business units in a global economy' (Ohmae, 1995, p. 5; cf. Wriston, 1992; Guéhenno, 1995). Such a view of globalization generally privileges an economic logic and, in its neoliberal variant, celebrates the emergence of a single global market and the principle of global competition as the harbingers of human progress. Hyperglobalizers argue that economic globalization is bringing about a 'denationalization' of economies through the establishment of transnational networks of production, trade and finance. In this 'borderless' economy, national governments are relegated to little more than transmission belts for global capital or, ultimately, simple intermediate institutions sandwiched between increasingly powerful local, regional and global mechanisms of governance. As Strange puts it, 'the impersonal forces of world markets ... are now more powerful than the states to whom ultimate political authority over society and economy is supposed to belong ... the declining authority of states is reflected in a growing diffusion of authority to other institutions and associations, and to local and regional bodies' (1996, p. 4; cf. Reich, 1991). In this respect, many hyperglobalizers share a conviction that economic globalization is constructing new forms of social organization that are supplanting, or that will eventually supplant, traditional nation-states as the primary economic and political units of world society.

Within this framework there is considerable normative divergence between, on the one hand, the neoliberals who welcome the triumph of individual autonomy and the market principle over state power, and the radicals or neo-Marxists for whom

---

[1] The approaches set out below present general summaries of different ways of thinking about globalization: they do not represent fully the particular positions and many differences among the individual theorists mentioned. The aim of the presentation is to highlight the main trends and faultlines in the current debate and literature.

contemporary globalization represents the triumph of an oppressive global capitalism (cf. Ohmae, 1995; Greider, 1997). But despite divergent ideological convictions, there exists a shared set of beliefs that globalization is primarily an economic phenomenon; that an increasingly integrated global economy exists today; that the needs of global capital impose a neoliberal economic discipline on all governments such that politics is no longer the 'art of the possible' but rather the practice of 'sound economic management'.

Furthermore, the hyperglobalizers claim that economic globalization is generating a new pattern of winners as well as losers in the global economy. The old North–South division is argued to be an increasing anachronism as a new global division of labour replaces the traditional core–periphery structure with a more complex architecture of economic power. Against this background, governments have to 'manage' the social consequences of globalization, or those who 'having been left behind, want not so much a chance to move forward as to hold others back' (Ohmae, 1995, p. 64). However, they also have to manage increasingly in a context in which the constraints of global financial and competitive disciplines make social democratic models of social protection untenable and spell the demise of associated welfare state policies (J. Gray, 1998). Globalization may be linked with a growing polarization between winners and losers in the global economy. But this need not be so, for, at least in the neoliberal view, global economic competition does not necessarily produce zero-sum outcomes. While particular groups within a country may be made worse off as a result of global competition, nearly all countries have a comparative advantage in producing certain goods which can be exploited in the long run. Neo-Marxists and radicals regard such an 'optimistic view' as unjustified, believing that global capitalism creates and reinforces structural patterns of inequality within and between countries. But they agree at least with their neoliberal counterparts that traditional welfare options for social protection are looking increasingly threadbare and difficult to sustain.

Among the elites and 'knowledge workers' of the new global economy tacit transnational 'class' allegiances have evolved, cemented by an ideological attachment to a neoliberal economic orthodoxy. For those who are currently marginalized, the worldwide diffusion of a consumerist ideology also imposes a new sense of identity, displacing traditional cultures and ways of life. The global spread of liberal democracy further reinforces the sense of an emerging global civilization defined by universal standards of economic and political organization. This 'global civilization' is also replete with its own mechanisms of global governance, whether it be the IMF or the disciplines of the world market, such that states and peoples are increasingly the subjects of new public and private global or regional authorities (Gill, 1995; Ohmae, 1995; Strange, 1996; Cox, 1997). Accordingly, for many neoliberals, globalization is considered as the harbinger of the first truly global civilization, while for many radicals it represents the first global 'market civilization' (Perlmutter, 1991; Gill, 1995; Greider, 1997).

In this hyperglobalist account the rise of the global economy, the emergence of institutions of global governance, and the global diffusion and hybridization of cultures are interpreted as evidence of a radically new world order, an order which prefigures the demise of the nation-state (Luard, 1990; Ohmae, 1995; Albrow, 1996). Since the national economy is increasingly a site of transnational and global flows, as opposed to the primary container of national socio-economic activity, the authority and legitimacy of the nation-state are challenged: national governments become increasingly unable either to control what transpires within their own borders or to fulfil by themselves the

demands of their own citizens. Moreover, as institutions of global and regional governance acquire a bigger role, the sovereignty and autonomy of the state are further
eroded. On the other hand, the conditions facilitating transnational cooperation between
peoples, given global infrastructures of communication and increasing awareness
of many common interests, have never been so propitious. In this regard, there is
evidence of an emerging 'global civil society'.

Economic power and political power, in this hyperglobalist view, are becoming
effectively denationalized and diffused such that nation-states, whatever the claims of
national politicians, are increasingly becoming 'a transitional mode of organization
for managing economic affairs' (Ohmae, 1995, p. 149). Whether issuing from a liberal
or radical/socialist perspective, the hyperglobalist thesis represents globalization as
embodying nothing less than the fundamental reconfiguration of the 'framework of
human action' (Albrow, 1996, p. 85).

The sceptical thesis

By comparison the sceptics, drawing on statistical evidence of world flows of trade,
investment and labour from the nineteenth century, maintain that contemporary levels
of economic interdependence are by no means historically unprecedented. Rather
than globalization, which to the sceptics necessarily implies a perfectly integrated
worldwide economy in which the 'law of one price' prevails, the historical evidence
at best confirms only heightened levels of internationalization, that is, interactions
between predominantly national economies (Hirst and Thompson, 1996b). In arguing
that globalization is a myth, the sceptics rely on a wholly economistic conception of
globalization, equating it primarily with a perfectly integrated global market. By contending that levels of economic integration fall short of this 'ideal type' and that such
integration as there is remains much less significant than in the late nineteenth century
(the era of the classical Gold Standard), the sceptics are free to conclude that the extent
of contemporary 'globalization' is wholly exaggerated (Hirst, 1997). In this respect, the
sceptics consider the hyperglobalist thesis as fundamentally flawed and also politically
naive since it underestimates the enduring power of national governments to regulate
international economic activity. Rather than being out of control, the forces of internationalization themselves depend on the regulatory power of national governments to
ensure continuing economic liberalization.

For most sceptics, if the current evidence demonstrates anything it is that economic
activity is undergoing a significant 'regionalization' as the world economy evolves in
the direction of three major financial and trading blocs, that is, Europe, Asia-Pacific
and North America (Ruigrok and Tulder, 1995; Boyer and Drache, 1996; Hirst and
Thompson, 1996b). In comparison with the classical Gold Standard era, the world
economy is therefore significantly less integrated than it once was (Boyer and Drache,
1996; Hirst and Thompson, 1996a). Among the sceptics, globalization and regionalization
are conceived as contradictory tendencies. As both Gordon and Weiss conclude, in
comparison with the age of world empires, the international economy has become considerably less global in its geographical embrace (Gordon, 1988; Weiss, 1998).

Sceptics tend also to discount the presumption that internationalization prefigures
the emergence of a new, less state-centric world order. Far from considering national

governments as becoming immobilized by international imperatives, they point to their growing centrality in the regulation and active promotion of cross-border economic activity. Governments are not the passive victims of internationalization but, on the contrary, its primary architects. Indeed, Gilpin considers internationalization largely a by-product of the US-initiated multilateral economic order which, in the aftermath of the Second World War, created the impetus for the liberalization of national economies (Gilpin, 1987). From a very different perspective, Callinicos and others explain the recent intensification of worldwide trade and foreign investment as a new phase of Western imperialism in which national governments, as the agents of monopoly capital, are deeply implicated (Callinicos et al., 1994).

However, despite such differences of emphasis, there is a convergence of opinion within the sceptical camp that, whatever its exact driving forces, internationalization has not been accompanied by an erosion of North–South inequalities but, on the contrary, by the growing economic marginalization of many 'Third World' states as trade and investment flows within the rich North intensify to the exclusion of much of the rest of the globe (Hirst and Thompson, 1996b). Moreover, Krugman questions the popular belief that a new international division of labour is emerging in which deindustrialization in the North can be traced to the operation of multinational corporations exporting jobs to the South (Krugman, 1996). Similarly Ruigrok and Tulder, and Thompson and Allen seek to demolish the 'myth' of the 'global corporation', highlighting the fact that foreign investment flows are concentrated among the advanced capitalist states and that most multinationals remain primarily creatures of their home states or regions (Ruigrok and Tulder, 1995; Thompson and Allen, 1997). Accordingly, the sceptical thesis is generally dismissive of the notion that internationalization is bringing about a profound or even significant restructuring of global economic relations. In this respect, the sceptical position is an acknowledgement of the deeply rooted patterns of inequality and hierarchy in the world economy, which in structural terms have changed only marginally over the last century.

Such inequality, in the view of many sceptics, contributes to the advance of both fundamentalism and aggressive nationalism such that rather than the emergence of a global civilization, as the hyperglobalizers predict, the world is fragmenting into civilizational blocs and cultural and ethnic enclaves (Huntington, 1996). The notion of cultural homogenization and a global culture are thus further myths which fall victim to the sceptical argument. In addition, the deepening of global inequalities, the realpolitik of international relations and the 'clash of civilizations' expose the illusory nature of 'global governance' in so far as the management of world order remains, as it has since the last century, overwhelmingly the preserve of Western states. In this respect, the sceptical argument tends to conceive of global governance and economic internationalization as primarily Western projects, the main object of which is to sustain the primacy of the West in world affairs. As E. H. Carr once observed: 'international order and "international solidarity" will always be slogans of those who feel strong enough to impose them on others' (1981, p. 87).

In general the sceptics take issue with all of the primary claims of the hyperglobalizers pointing to the comparatively greater levels of economic interdependence and the more extensive geographical reach of the world economy at the beginning of the twentieth century. They reject the popular 'myth' that the power of national governments or state sovereignty is being undermined today by economic internationalization or global governance (Krasner, 1993, 1995). Some argue that 'globalization' more often than not reflects a politically convenient rationale for implementing unpopular orthodox neoliberal economic strategies (Hirst, 1997). Weiss, Scharpf and Armingeon, among others, argue that the available evidence contradicts the popular belief that there has been a convergence of macroeconomic and welfare policies across the globe (Weiss, 1998; Scharpf, 1991; Armingeon, 1997). While international economic conditions may constrain what governments can do, governments are by no means immobilized. The internationalization of capital may, as Weiss argues, 'not merely restrict policy choices, but expand them as well' (1998, pp. 184ff.). Rather than the world becoming more interdependent, as the hyperglobalizers assume, the sceptics seek to expose the myths which sustain the globalization thesis.

The transformationalist thesis

At the heart of the transformationalist thesis is a conviction that, at the dawn of a new millennium, globalization is a central driving force behind the rapid social, political and economic changes that are reshaping modern societies and world order (Giddens, 1990; Scholte, 1993; Castells, 1996). According to the proponents of this view, contemporary processes of globalization are historically unprecedented such that governments and societies across the globe are having to adjust to a world in which there is no longer a clear distinction between international and domestic, external and internal affairs (Rosenau, 1990; Cammilleri and Falk, 1992; Ruggie, 1993; Linklater and MacMillan, 1995; Sassen, 1996). For Rosenau, the growth of 'intermestic' affairs define a 'new frontier', the expanding political, economic and social space in which the fate of societies and communities is decided (1997, pp. 4–5). In this respect, globalization is conceived as a powerful transformative force which is responsible for a 'massive shake-out' of societies, economies, institutions of governance and world order (Giddens, 1996).

In the transformationalist account, however, the direction of this 'shake-out' remains uncertain, since globalization is conceived as an essentially contingent historical process replete with contradictions (Mann, 1997). At issue is a dynamic and open-ended conception of where globalization might be leading and the kind of world order which it might prefigure. In comparison with the sceptical and hyperglobalist accounts, the transformationalists make no claims about the future trajectory of globalization; nor do they seek to evaluate the present in relation to some single, fixed ideal-type 'globalized world', whether a global market or a global civilization. Rather, transformationalist accounts emphasize globalization as a long-term historical process which is inscribed with contradictions and which is significantly shaped by conjunctural factors.

Such caution about the exact future of globalization is matched, nonetheless, by the conviction that contemporary patterns of global economic, military, technological, ecological, migratory, political and cultural flows are historically unprecedented. As Nierop puts it, 'virtually all countries in the world, if not all parts of their territory and all segments of their society, are now functionally part of that larger [global] system in one or more respects' (1994, p. 171). But the existence of a single global system is not taken as evidence of global convergence or of the arrival of single world society. On the contrary, for the transformationalists, globalization is associated with new patterns of global stratification in which some states, societies and communities are becoming increasingly enmeshed in the global order while others are becoming increasingly marginalized. A new configuration of global power relations is held to be crystallizing as the North–South division rapidly gives way to a new international division of labour such that the 'familiar pyramid of the core–periphery hierarchy is no longer a geographic but a social division of the world economy' (Hoogvelt, 1997, p. xii). To talk of North and South, of First World and Third World, is to overlook the ways in which globalization has recast traditional patterns of inclusion and exclusion between countries by forging new hierarchies which cut across and penetrate all societies and regions of the world. North and South, First World and Third World, are no longer 'out there' but nestled together within all the world's major cities. Rather than the traditional pyramid analogy of the world social structure, with a tiny top echelon and spreading mass base, the global social structure can be envisaged as a three-tier arrangement of concentric circles, each cutting across national boundaries, representing respectively the elites, the contented and the marginalized (Hoogvelt, 1997).

The recasting of patterns of global stratification is linked with the growing deterritorialization of economic activity as production and finance increasingly acquire a global and transnational dimension. From somewhat different starting points, Castells and Ruggie, among others, argue that national economies are being reorganized by processes of economic globalization such that national economic space no longer coincides with national territorial borders (Castells, 1996; Ruggie, 1996). In this globalizing economy, systems of transnational production, exchange and finance weave together ever more tightly the fortunes of communities and households on different continents.

At the core of the transformationalist case is a belief that contemporary globalization is reconstituting or 're-engineering' the power, functions and authority of national governments. While not disputing that states still retain the ultimate legal claim to 'effective supremacy over what occurs within their own territories', the transformationalists argue that this is juxtaposed, to varying degrees, with the expanding jurisdiction of institutions of international governance and the constraints of, as well as the obligations derived from, international law. This is especially evident in the EU, where sovereign power is divided between international, national and local authorities, but it is also evident in the operation of the World Trade Organization (WTO) (Goodman, 1997). However, even where sovereignty still appears intact, states no longer, if they ever did, retain sole command of what transpires within their own territorial boundaries. Complex global systems, from the financial to the ecological, connect the fate of communities in one locale to the fate of communities in distant regions of the world. Furthermore, global infrastructures of communication and transport support new forms of economic and social organization which transcend national boundaries without any consequent diminution of efficiency or control. Sites of power and the subjects of power may be literally, as well as metaphorically, oceans apart. In these circumstances, the notion of the nation-state as a self-governing, autonomous unit appears to be more a normative claim than a descriptive statement. The modern institution of territorially circumscribed sovereign rule appears somewhat anomalous juxtaposed with the transnational organization of many aspects of contemporary economic and social life (Sandel, 1996). Globalization, in this account, is therefore associated with a transformation or, to use Ruggie's term, an 'unbundling' of the relationship between sovereignty, territoriality and state power (Ruggie, 1993; Sassen, 1996).

Of course, few states have ever exercised complete or absolute sovereignty within their own territorial boundaries, as the practice of diplomatic immunity highlights (Sassen, 1996). Indeed the practice, as opposed to the doctrine, of sovereign statehood has always readily adapted to changing historical realities (Murphy, 1996). In arguing that globalization is transforming or reconstituting the power and authority of national governments, the transformationalists reject both the hyperglobalist rhetoric of the end of the sovereign nation-state and the sceptics' claim that 'nothing much has changed.' Instead, they assert that a new 'sovereignty regime' is displacing traditional conceptions of statehood as an absolute, indivisible, territorially exclusive and zero-sum form of public power (Held, 1991). Accordingly, sovereignty today is, they suggest, best understood 'less as a territorially defined barrier than a bargaining resource for a politics characterized by complex transnational networks' (Keohane, 1995).

This is not to argue that territorial boundaries retain no political, military or symbolic significance but rather to acknowledge that, conceived as the primary spatial markers of modern life, they have become increasingly problematic in an era of intensified globalization. Sovereignty, state power and territoriality thus stand today in a more complex relationship than in the epoch during which the modern nation-state was being forged. Indeed, the argument of the transformationalists is that globalization is associated not only with a new 'sovereignty regime' but also with the emergence of powerful new non-territorial forms of economic and political organization in the global domain, such as multinational corporations, transnational social movements, international regulatory agencies, etc. In this sense, world order can no longer be conceived as purely state-centric or even primarily state governed, as authority has become increasingly diffused among public and private agencies at the local, national, regional and global levels. Nation-states are no longer the sole centres or the principal forms of governance or authority in the world (Rosenau, 1997).

Given this changing global order, the form and functions of the state are having to adapt as governments seek coherent strategies of engaging with a globalizing world. Distinctive strategies are being followed from the model of the neoliberal minimal state to the models of the developmental state (government as the central promoter of economic expansion) and the catalytic state (government as facilitator of coordinated and collective action). In addition, governments have become increasingly outward looking as they seek to pursue cooperative strategies and to construct international regulatory regimes to manage more effectively the growing array of cross-border issues which regularly surface on national agendas. Rather than globalization bringing about the 'end of the state', it has encouraged a spectrum of adjustment strategies and, in certain respects, a more activist state. Accordingly, the power of national governments is not necessarily diminished by globalization but on the contrary is being reconstituted and restructured in response to the growing complexity of processes of governance in a more interconnected world (Rosenau, 1997).

The three dominant tendencies in the globalization debate are summarized in table I.1. To move beyond the debate between these three approaches requires a framework of enquiry through which the principal claims of each might be assessed. But to construct such a framework demands, as an initial condition, some understanding of the primary faultlines around which the debate itself revolves. Identifying the critical issues in the debate creates an intellectual foundation for thinking about how globalization might

Table I.1 Conceptualizing globalization: three tendencies

	Hyperglobalists	Sceptics	Transformationalists
What's new?	A global age	Trading blocs, weaker geogovernance than in earlier periods	Historically unprecedented levels of global interconnectedness
Dominant features	Global capitalism, global governance, global civil society	World less interdependent than in 1890s	'Thick' (intensive and extensive) globalization
Power of national governments	Declining or eroding	Reinforced or enhanced	Reconstituted, restructured
Driving forces of globalization	Capitalism and technology	States and markets	Combined forces of modernity
Pattern of stratification	Erosion of old hierarchies	Increased marginalization of South	New architecture of world order
Dominant motif	McDonalds, Madonna, etc.	National interest	Transformation of political community
Conceptualization of globalization	As a reordering of the framework of human action	As internationalization and regionalization	As the reordering of interregional relations and action at a distance
Historical trajectory	Global civilization	Regional blocs/clash of civilizations	Indeterminate: global integration and fragmentation
Summary argument	The end of the nation-state	Internationalization depends on state acquiescence and support	Globalization transforming state power and world politics

best be conceptualized and the particular grounds on which any assessment of competing claims about it might be pursued.

Sources of Contention in the Globalization Debate

Five principal issues constitute the major sources of contention among existing approaches to globalization. These concern matters of

- conceptualization
- causation
- periodization
- impacts
- and the trajectories of globalization.

In exploring each of these in turn a cumulative picture will develop of the requirements of a rigorous account of globalization, a picture which will help move us beyond the debate between the three approaches outlined above.

Conceptualization

Among both the sceptics and hyperglobalizers there is a tendency to conceptualize globalization as prefiguring a singular condition or end-state, that is, a fully integrated global market with price and interest rate equalization. Accordingly, contemporary patterns of economic globalization are assessed, as previously noted, in relation to how far they match up to this ideal type (Dore, 1995; Hirst and Thompson, 1996b). But even on its own terms this approach is flawed, since there is no a priori reason to assume global markets need be 'perfectly competitive' any more than national markets have ever been. National markets may well fall short of perfect competition but this does not prevent economists from characterizing them as markets, albeit markets with various forms of 'imperfections'. Global markets, as with domestic markets, can be problematic.

In addition, this 'ideal type' approach is both unacceptably teleological and empiricist: unacceptably teleological in so far as the present is (and apparently should be) interpreted as the stepping stone in some linear progression towards a given future end-state, although there is no logical or empirical reason to assume that globalization – any more than industrialization or democratization – has one fixed end condition; and unacceptably empiricist in that the statistical evidence of global trends is taken by itself to confirm, qualify or reject the globalization thesis, even though such a methodology can generate considerable difficulties (Ohmae, 1990; R. J. B. Jones, 1995; Hirst and Thompson, 1996b). For instance, the fact that more people in the world speak (dialects of) Chinese than English as a first language does not necessarily confirm the thesis that Chinese is a global language. Likewise, even if it could be shown that trade–GDP ratios for Western states in the 1890s were similar to, or even higher than, those for the 1990s, this evidence by itself would reveal little about the social and political impacts of trade in either period. Caution and theoretical care are needed in drawing conclusions from seemingly clear global trends. Any convincing account of globalization must weigh the significance of relevant qualitative evidence and interpretative issues.

In comparison, socio-historical approaches to the study of globalization regard it as a process which has no single fixed or determinate historical 'destination', whether understood in terms of a perfectly integrated global market, a global society or a global civilization (Giddens, 1990; Geyer and Bright, 1995; Rosenau, 1997). There is no a priori reason to assume that globalization must simply evolve in a single direction or that it can only be understood in relation to a single ideal condition (perfect global markets). Accordingly, for these transformationalists, globalization is conceived in terms of a more contingent and open-ended historical process which does not fit with orthodox linear models of social change (cf. Graham, 1997). Moreover, these accounts tend also to be sceptical of the view that quantitative evidence alone can confirm or deny the 'reality' of globalization since they are interested in those qualitative shifts which it may engender in the nature of societies and the exercise of power; shifts which are rarely completely captured by statistical data.

Linked to the issue of globalization as a historical process is the related matter of whether globalization should be understood in singular or differentiated terms. Much of the sceptical and hyperglobalist literature tends to conceive globalization as a largely singular process equated, more often than not, with economic or cultural interconnectedness (Ohmae, 1990; Robertson, 1992; Krasner, 1993; Boyer and Drache, 1996; Cox, 1996; Hirst and Thompson, 1996b; Huntington, 1996; Strange, 1996; Burbach et al., 1997). Yet to conceive it thus ignores the distinctive patterns of globalization in different aspects of social life, from the political to the cultural. In this respect, globalization might be better conceived as a highly differentiated process which finds expression in all the key domains of social activity (including the political, the military, the legal, the ecological, the criminal, etc.). It is by no means clear why it should be assumed that it is a purely economic or cultural phenomenon (Giddens, 1991; Axford, 1995; Albrow, 1996). Accordingly, accounts of globalization which acknowledge this differentiation may be more satisfactory in explaining its form and dynamics than those which overlook it.

Causation

One of the central contentions in the globalization debate concerns the issue of causation: what is driving this process? In offering an answer to this question existing accounts tend to cluster around two distinct sets of explanations: those which identify a single or primary imperative, such as capitalism or technological change; and those which explain globalization as the product of a combination of factors, including technological change, market forces, ideology and political decisions. Put simply, the distinction is effectively between monocausal and multicausal accounts of globalization. Though the tendency in much of the existing literature is to conflate globalization with the expansionary imperatives of markets or capitalism this has drawn substantial criticism on the grounds that such an explanation is far too reductionist. In response, there are a number of significant attempts to develop a more comprehensive explanation of globalization which highlights the complex intersection between a multiplicity of driving forces, embracing economic, technological, cultural and political change (Giddens, 1990; Robertson, 1992; Scholte, 1993; Axford, 1995; Albrow, 1996; Rosenau, 1990, 1997). Any convincing analysis of contemporary globalization has to come to terms with the central question of causation and, in so doing, offer a coherent view.

But the controversy about the underlying causes of globalization is connected to a wider debate about modernity (Giddens, 1991; Robertson, 1992; Albrow, 1996; Connolly, 1996). For some, globalization can be understood simply as the global diffusion of Western modernity, that is, Westernization. World systems theory, for instance, equates globalization with the spread of Western capitalism and Western institutions (Amin, 1996; Benton, 1996). By contrast, others draw a distinction between Westernization and globalization and reject the idea that the latter is synonymous with the former (Giddens, 1990). At stake in this debate is a rather fundamental issue: whether globalization today has to be understood as something more than simply the expanding reach of Western power and influence. No cogent analysis of globalization can avoid confronting this issue.

Periodization

Simply seeking to describe the 'shape' of contemporary globalization necessarily relies (implicitly or explicitly) on some kind of historical narrative. Such narratives, whether they issue from grand civilizational studies or world historical studies, have significant implications for what conclusions are reached about the historically unique or distinctive features of contemporary globalization (Mazlish and Buultjens, 1993; Geyer and Bright, 1995). In particular, how world history is periodized is central to the kinds of conclusions which are deduced from any historical analysis, most especially, of course, with respect to the question of what's new about contemporary globalization. Clearly, in answering such a question, it makes a significant difference whether contemporary globalization is defined as the entire postwar era, the post-1970s era, or the twentieth century in general.

Recent historical studies of world systems and of patterns of civilizational interaction bring into question the commonly accepted view that globalization is primarily a phenomenon of the modern age (McNeill, 1995; Roudometof and Robertson, 1995; Bentley, 1996; Frank and Gills, 1996). The existence of world religions and the trade networks of the medieval era encourage a greater sensitivity to the idea that globalization is a process which has a long history. This implies the need to look beyond the modern era in any attempt to offer an explanation of the novel features of contemporary globalization. But to do so requires some kind of analytical framework offering a platform for contrasting and comparing different phases or historical forms of globalization over what the French historian Braudel refers to as the *longue durée* – that is, the passage of centuries rather than decades (Helleiner, 1997).

Impacts

There is an extensive literature implicating economic globalization in the demise of social democracy and the modern welfare state (Garrett and Lange, 1991; Banuri and Schor, 1992; Gill, 1995; Amin, 1996; J. Gray, 1996; Cox, 1997). Global competitive pressures have forced governments, according to this view, to curtail state spending and interventions; for, despite different partisan commitments, all governments have been pressed in the same direction. Underlying this thesis is a rather deterministic conception of globalization as an 'iron cage' which imposes a global financial discipline on governments, severely constraining the scope for progressive policies and undermining the social bargain on which the post-Second World War welfare state rested. Thus there has apparently been a growing convergence of economic and welfare strategies among Western states, irrespective of the ideology of incumbent governments.

This thesis is contested vociferously by a plethora of recent studies which cast serious doubt on the idea that globalization effectively 'immobilizes' national governments in the conduct of economic policy (Scharpf, 1991; R. J. B. Jones, 1995; Ruigrok and Tulder, 1995; Hirst and Thompson, 1996b). As Milner and Keohane observe, 'the impact of the world economy on countries that are open to its influence does not appear to be uniform' (1996, p. 14). Such studies have delivered significant insights into how the social and political impact of globalization is mediated by domestic institutional structures, state strategies and a country's location in the global pecking order (Hurrell and Woods, 1995; Frieden and Rogowski, 1996; Garrett and Lange, 1996). A number of authors have also contributed to a greater awareness of the ways in which globalization is contested and resisted by states and peoples (Geyer and Bright, 1995; Frieden and Rogowski, 1996; Burbach et al., 1997). In so doing, such studies suggest the need for a sophisticated typology of how globalization impacts on national economies and national communities which acknowledges its differential consequences and the signal importance of the forms in which it is managed, contested and resisted (Axford, 1995).

Trajectories

Each of the three 'schools' in the globalization debate has a particular conception of the dynamics and direction of global change. This imposes an overall shape on patterns of globalization and, in so doing, presents a distinctive account of globalization as a historical process. In this respect, the hyperglobalizers tend to represent globalization as a secular process of global integration (Ohmae, 1995; R. P. Clark, 1997). The latter is often associated with a linear view of historical change; globalization is elided with the relatively smooth unfolding of human progress. By comparison, the sceptical thesis tends to a view of globalization which emphasizes its distinct phases as well as its recurrent features. This, in part, accounts for the sceptics' preoccupation with evaluating contemporary globalization in relation to prior historical epochs, but most especially in relation to the supposedly 'golden age' of global interdependence (the latter decades of the nineteenth century) (R. J. B. Jones, 1995; Hirst and Thompson, 1996b).

Neither of these models of historical change finds much support within the transformationalist camp. For the transformationalists tend to conceive history as a process punctuated by dramatic upheavals or discontinuities. Such a view stresses the contingency of history and how epochal change arises out of the confluence of particular historical conditions and social forces. And it informs the transformationalist tendency to describe the process of globalization as contingent and contradictory. For, according to this thesis, globalization pulls and pushes societies in opposing directions; it fragments as it integrates, engenders cooperation as well as conflict, and universalizes while it particularizes. Thus the trajectory of global change is largely indeterminate and uncertain (Rosenau, 1997).

Clearly, a convincing attempt to construct an analytical framework which moves the globalization debate beyond its present intellectual limits has to address the five major points of contention described above. For any satisfactory account of globalization has to offer: a coherent conceptualization; a justified account of causal logic; some clear propositions about historical periodization; a robust specification of impacts; and some sound reflections about the trajectory of the process itself. Confronting these tasks is central to devising and constructing fresh ways of thinking about globalization.

The five tasks inform the chapters that follow, and we return to them again in the conclusion. What follows immediately is an attempt to address the first of the concerns – the nature and form of globalization.

Rethinking Globalization: an Analytical Framework

What is globalization? Although in its simplest sense globalization refers to the widening, deepening and speeding up of global interconnectedness, such a definition begs further elaboration. Despite a proliferation of definitions in contemporary discussion – among them 'accelerating interdependence', 'action at a distance' and 'time-space compression'[2] (see, respectively, Ohmae, 1990; Giddens, 1990; Harvey, 1989) – there is scant evidence in the existing literature of any attempt to specify precisely what is 'global' about globalization. For instance, all the above definitions are quite compatible with far more spatially confined processes such as the spread of national or regional interconnections. In seeking to remedy this conceptual difficulty, this study commences from an understanding of globalization which acknowledges its distinctive spatial attributes and the way these unfold over time.

Globalization can be located on a continuum with the local, national and regional.[3] At the one end of the continuum lie social and economic relations and networks which are organized on a local and/or national basis; at the other end lie social and economic relations and networks which crystallize on the wider scale of regional and global interactions. Globalization can be taken to refer to those spatio-temporal processes of change which underpin a transformation in the organization of human affairs by linking together and expanding human activity across regions and continents. Without reference to such expansive spatial connections, there can be no clear or coherent formulation of this term.

Accordingly, the concept of globalization implies, first and foremost, a *stretching* of social, political and economic activities across frontiers such that events, decisions and activities in one region of the world can come to have significance for individuals and communities in distant regions of the globe. In this sense, it embodies transregional interconnectedness, the widening reach of networks of social activity and power, and the possibility of action at a distance. Beyond this, globalization implies that connections across frontiers are not just occasional or random, but rather are regularized such that there is a detectable *intensification*, or growing magnitude, of interconnectedness, patterns of interaction and flows which transcend the constituent societies and states of the world order. Furthermore, growing extensity and intensity of global interconnectedness may also imply a *speeding up* of global interactions and processes as the development of worldwide systems of transport and communication increases the potential velocity of the global diffusion of ideas, goods, information, capital and people. And the growing *extensity*, *intensity* and *velocity* of global interactions may also be associated with a deepening enmeshment of the local and global such that the *impact* of distant events is magnified while even the most local developments may come to have enormous global consequences. In this sense, the boundaries between domestic matters and global affairs may be blurred. A satisfactory definition of globalization must capture each of these elements: extensity (stretching), intensity, velocity and impact. And

[2] By 'accelerating interdependence' is understood the growing intensity of international enmeshment among national economies and societies such that developments in one country impact directly on other countries. 'Action at a distance' refers to the way in which, under conditions of contemporary globalization, the actions of social agents (individuals, collectivities, corporations, etc.) in one locale can come to have significant intended or unintended consequences for the behaviour of 'distant others'. Finally, 'time-space compression' refers to the manner in which globalization appears to shrink geographical distance and time; in a world of instantaneous communication, distance and time no longer seem to be a major constraint on patterns of human social organization or interaction.

[3] Regions refer here to the geographical or functional clustering of states or societies. Such regional clusters can be identified in terms of their shared characteristics (cultural, religious, ideological, economic, etc.) and high level of patterned interaction relative to the outside world (Buzan, 1998).

a satisfactory account of globalization must examine them thoroughly. We shall refer to these four elements henceforth as the 'spatio-temporal' dimensions of globalization.

By acknowledging these dimensions a more precise definition of globalization can be offered. Accordingly, globalization can be thought of as

> *a process (or set of processes) which embodies a transformation in the spatial organization of social relations and transactions – assessed in terms of their extensity, intensity, velocity and impact – generating transcontinental or interregional flows and networks of activity, interaction, and the exercise of power.*

In this context, flows refer to the movements of physical artefacts, people, symbols, tokens and information across space and time, while networks refer to regularized or patterned interactions between independent agents, nodes of activity, or sites of power (Modelski, 1972; Mann, 1986; Castells, 1996).

This formulation helps address the failure of existing approaches to differentiate globalization from more spatially delimited processes – what we can call 'localization', 'nationalization', 'regionalization' and 'internationalization'. For as it is defined above, globalization can be distinguished from more restricted social developments. Localization simply refers to the consolidation of flows and networks within a specific locale. Nationalization is the process whereby social relations and transactions are developed within the framework of fixed territorial borders. Regionalization can be denoted by a clustering of transactions, flows, networks and interactions between functional or geographical groupings of states or societies, while internationalization can be taken to refer to patterns of interaction and interconnectedness between two or more nation-states irrespective of their specific geographical location (see Nierop, 1994; Buzan, 1998). Thus contemporary globalization describes, for example, the flows of trade and finance between the major regions in the world economy, while equivalent flows within them can be differentiated in terms of local, national and regional clusters.

In offering a more precise definition of these concepts it is crucial to signal that globalization is not conceived here in opposition to more spatially delimited processes but, on the contrary, as standing in a complex and dynamic relationship with them. On the one hand, processes such as regionalization can create the necessary kinds of economic, social and physical infrastructures which facilitate and complement the deepening of globalization. In this regard, for example, economic regionalization (for instance, the European Union) has not been a barrier to the globalization of trade and production but a spur. On the other hand, such processes can impose limits to globalization, if not encouraging a process of deglobalization. However, there is no a priori reason to assume that localization or regionalization exist in an oppositional or contradictory relationship to globalization. Precisely how these processes interrelate in economic and other domains is more an empirical matter, and one which is dealt with in subsequent chapters.

Historical forms of globalization

Sceptics of the globalization thesis alert us to the fact that international or global interconnectedness is by no means a novel phenomenon; yet they overlook the possibility that the particular form taken by globalization may differ between historical eras. To distinguish the novel features of globalization in any epoch requires some kind of analytical framework for organizing such comparative historical enquiry. For without such a framework it would be difficult to identify the most significant features, continuities or differences between epochs. Thus the approach developed here centres on the idea of *historical forms of globalization* as the basis for constructing a systematic comparative analysis of globalization over time. Utilizing this notion helps provide a mechanism for capturing and systematizing relevant differences and similarities. In this context, historical forms of globalization refer to

> *the spatio-temporal and organizational attributes of global interconnectedness in discrete historical epochs.*

To say anything meaningful about either the unique attributes or the dominant features of contemporary globalization requires clear analytical categories from which such descriptions can be constructed. Building directly on our earlier distinctions, historical forms of globalization can be described and compared initially in respect of the four spatio-temporal dimensions:

- the extensity of global networks
- the intensity of global interconnectedness
- the velocity of global flows
- the impact propensity of global interconnectedness.

Such a framework provides the basis for both a *quantitative* and a *qualitative* assessment of historical patterns of globalization. For it is possible to analyse (1) the extensiveness of networks of relations and connections; (2) the intensity of flows and levels of activity within these networks; (3) the velocity or speed of interchanges; and (4) the impact of these phenomena on particular communities. A systematic assessment of how these phenomena have evolved provides insights into the changing historical forms of globalization; and it offers the possibility of a sharper identification and comparison of the key attributes of, and the major disjunctures between, distinctive forms of globalization in different epochs. Such a historical approach to globalization avoids the current tendency to presume either that globalization is fundamentally new, or that there is nothing novel about contemporary levels of global economic and social interconnectedness since they appear to resemble those of prior periods.

Of course, the very notion of historical forms of globalization assumes that it is feasible to map, in an empirical sense, the extensity, intensity, velocity and impact propensity of global flows, networks and transactions across time. In subsequent chapters we seek to operationalize each of these dimensions by using various statistical and other indicators to assess, for instance, the geographical scope of trade flows – their magnitude, velocity, impact and so on. But one particular dimension of globalization is especially difficult to operationalize: the impact propensity of global flows, networks and transactions. Yet without some clear understanding of the nature of impact, the notion of globalization would remain imprecise. How should impact propensity be conceived?

For the purpose of this study, we distinguish between four analytically distinct types of impacts: *decisional, institutional, distributive* and *structural*. Decisional impacts refer to the degree to which the relative costs and benefits of the policy choices confronting governments, corporations, collectivities and households are influenced by global forces and conditions. Thus globalization may make some policy options or courses of action more or less costly and, in so doing, condition the outcome of individual or organizational decision-making. Depending on decision-makers' and collectivities' sensitivity or vulnerability to global conditions, their policy choices will be constrained or facilitated to a greater or lesser degree.[4] Decisional impacts can be assessed in terms of high impact (where globalization fundamentally alters policy preferences by transforming the costs and benefits of different courses of action) and low impact (where policy preferences are only marginally affected).

But the impact of globalization may not always be best understood in terms of decisions taken or forgone, since it may operate less transparently by reconfiguring the agenda of decision-making itself and, consequently, the available choices which agents may or may not realistically make. In other words, globalization may be associated with what Schattschneider referred to as the 'mobilization of bias' in so far as the agenda and choices which governments, households and corporations confront are set by global conditions (1960, p. 71). Thus, while the notion of decisional impacts focuses attention on how globalization directly influences the preferences and choices of decision-makers, the notion of institutional impact highlights the ways in which organizational and collective agendas reflect the effective choices or range of choices available as a result of globalization. In this respect, it offers insights into why certain choices may never even be considered as options at all.

Beyond such considerations, globalization may have considerable consequences for the distribution of power and wealth within and between countries. Distributional impacts refer to the ways in which globalization shapes the configuration of social forces (groups, classes, collectivities) within societies and across them. Thus, for instance, trade may undermine the prosperity of some workers while enhancing that of others. In this context, some groups and societies may be more vulnerable to globalization than others.

Finally, globalization may have discernible structural impacts in so far as it conditions patterns of domestic social, economic and political organization and behaviour. Accordingly, globalization may be inscribed within the institutions and everyday functioning of societies (Axford, 1995). For instance, the spread of Western conceptions of the modern state and capitalist markets have conditioned the development of the majority of societies and civilizations across the globe. They have forced or stimulated the adaptation of traditional patterns of power and authority, generating new forms of rule and resource allocation. The structural consequences of globalization may be visible over both the short and the long term in the ways in which states and societies accommodate themselves to global forces. But such accommodation is, of course, far

---

[4] 'Sensitivity involves degrees of responsiveness within a policy-framework – how quickly do changes in one country bring costly changes in another and how great are the costly effects ... Vulnerability can be defined as an actor's liability to suffer costs imposed by external events even after policies have been altered' (Keohane and Nye, 1977, p. 12).

from automatic. For globalization is mediated, managed, contested and resisted by governments, agencies and peoples. States and societies may display varying degrees of sensitivity or vulnerability to global processes such that patterns of domestic structural adjustment will vary in terms of their degree and duration.

In assessing the impact of globalization on states and communities, it is useful to emphasize that the four types of impact can have a direct bearing on them, altering their form and modus operandi, or an indirect bearing, changing the context and balance of forces with which states have to contend. Decisional and institutional impacts tend to be direct in this regard, although they can have consequences for the economic and social circumstances in which states operate. Distributional and structural impacts tend to be indirect but, of course, none the less significant for that.

There are other important features of historical forms of globalization which should be distinguished. In addition to the spatio-temporal dimensions which sketch the broad shape of globalization, there are four dimensions which map its specific organizational profile: *infrastructures, institutionalization, stratification* and *modes of interaction.* Mapping the extensity, intensity, velocity and impact propensity of networks of global interconnectedness necessarily involves mapping the *infrastructures* which facilitate or carry global flows, networks and relations. Networks cannot exist without some kind of infrastructural support. Infrastructures may be physical, regulative/legal, or symbolic, for instance, a transportation infrastructure, the law governing war, or mathematics as the common language of science. But in most domains infrastructures are constituted by some combination of all these types of facility. For example, in the financial realm there is a worldwide information system for banking settlements, regulated by a regime of common rules, norms and procedures, and working through its own technical language via which its members communicate.

Infrastructures may facilitate or constrain the extensity and intensity of global connectedness in any single domain. This is because they mediate flows and connectivity: infrastructures influence the overall level of interaction capacity in every sector and thus the potential magnitude of global interconnectedness. Interaction capacity, understood as the potential scale of interaction defined by existing technical capabilities, is determined primarily, but not exclusively, by technological capacity and communications technology (see Buzan et al., 1993, p. 86). For instance, the interaction capacity of the medieval world system, constrained as it was by limited means of communication, among other things, was considerably less than that of the contemporary era, in which satellites and the Internet facilitate instant and almost real-time global communication (Deibert, 1997). Thus changes in infrastructure have important consequences for the development and evolution of global interaction capacity.

Infrastructural conditions also facilitate the *institutionalization* of global networks, flows and relations. Institutionalization comprises the regularization of patterns of interaction and, consequently, their reproduction across space and time. To think in terms of the institutionalization of patterns of global connections (trade, alliances, etc.) is to acknowledge the ways in which global networks and relations become regularized and embedded in the practices and operations of the agencies (states, collectivities, households, individuals) in each social domain, from the cultural to the criminal (see Giddens, 1979, p. 80). Institutionalization, therefore, constitutes a further significant dimension of historical forms of globalization.

Discussion of infrastructures and institutionalization links directly to the issue of power. By power is meant the capacity of social agents, agencies and institutions to maintain or transform their circumstances, social or physical; and it concerns the resources which underpin this capacity and the forces that shape and influence its exercise. Accordingly, power is a phenomenon found in and between all groups, institutions and societies, cutting across public and private life. While 'power', thus understood, raises a number of complicated issues, it usefully highlights the nature of power as a universal dimension of human life, independent of any specific site or set of institutions (see Held, 1989, 1995).

But the power of an agent or agency or institution, wherever it is located, never exists in isolation. Power is always exercised, and political outcomes are always determined, in the context of the relative capabilities of parties. Power has to be understood as a relational phenomenon (Giddens, 1979, ch. 2; Rosenau, 1980, ch. 3). Hence, power expresses at one and the same time the intentions and purposes of agencies and institutions and the relative balance of resources they can deploy with respect to each other. However, power cannot simply be conceived in terms of what agents or agencies do or do not do. For power is also a structural phenomenon, shaped by and in turn shaping the socially structured and culturally patterned behaviour of groups and the practices of organizations (Lukes, 1974, p. 22). Any organization or institution can condition and limit the behaviour of its members. The rules and resources which such organizations and institutions embody rarely constitute a neutral framework for action, for they establish patterns of power and authority and confer the right to take decisions on some and not on others; in effect, they institutionalize a power relationship between 'rulers' and 'ruled', 'subjects' and 'governors' (McGrew, 1988, pp. 18–19).

Globalization transforms the organization, distribution and exercise of power. In this respect, globalization in different epochs may be associated with distinctive patterns of global *stratification*. In mapping historical forms of globalization, specific attention needs to be paid to patterns of stratification. In this context, stratification has both a social and a spatial dimension: hierarchy and unevenness, respectively (see Falk, 1990, pp. 2–12). Hierarchy refers to asymmetries in the control of, access to and enmeshment in global networks and infrastructures, while unevenness denotes the asymmetrical effects of processes of globalization on the life chances and well-being of peoples, classes, ethnic groupings and the sexes. These categories provide a mechanism for identifying the distinctive relations of global domination and control in different historical periods.

There are important differences too in the dominant *modes of interaction* within each epoch of globalization. It is possible to distinguish crudely between the dominant types of interaction – imperial or coercive, cooperative, competitive, conflictual – and the primary instruments of power, for example, military vs economic instruments. Thus, arguably, in the late nineteenth-century era of Western expansion, imperialism and military power were the dominant modes and instruments of globalization, whereas in the late twentieth century economic instruments, competition and cooperation appear to take precedence over military force (Morse, 1976).

All in all, historical forms of globalization can be analysed in terms of eight dimensions: see box I.1. Collectively, they determine the shape of globalization in each epoch.

Box I.1 Historical forms of globalization: key dimensions

Spatio-temporal dimensions
1   the extensity of global networks
2   the intensity of global interconnectedness
3   the velocity of global flows
4   the impact propensity of global interconnectedness

Organizational dimensions
5   the infrastructure of globalization
6   the institutionalization of global networks and the exercise of power
7   the pattern of global stratification
8   the dominant modes of global interaction

Determining the Shape of Contemporary Globalization

Building on the framework above, a typology of globalization can be constructed. Global flows, networks and relations can be mapped in relation to their fundamental spatio-temporal dimensions: extensity, intensity, velocity and impact propensity. Figures I.1 and I.2 set out the relations between these four dimensions. In these figures high extensity refers to interregional/intercontinental networks and flows, and low extensity denotes localized networks and transactions. Accordingly, as figure I.3 indicates, there are different possible configurations of these dimensions; the four uppermost quadrants in this figure represent, at one spatial extreme, different types of globalized worlds (that is, different configurations of high extensity, intensity, velocity and impact) while the lower quadrants represent, at the other spatial extreme, different configurations of localized networks. This simple exercise delivers the groundwork for devising a more systematic typology of globalization which moves the debate beyond the economistic ideal type and 'one world' models of the sceptics and hyperglobalizers. For the four upper quadrants of figure I.3 suggest that there are a multiplicity of logical shapes which globalization might take since high extensity can be combined with different possible values for intensity, velocity and impact.

Four of these potential shapes are of particular interest since they represent the outer limits of this typological exercise, combining high extensity with the most extreme values of intensity, velocity and impact. In this regard, figure I.4 identifies four discrete logical types of globalization which reflect very different patterns of interregional flows, networks and interactions. They constitute a simple typology of globalization which shows that it has no necessarily fixed form:

- Type 1 represents a world in which the extensive reach of global networks is matched by their high intensity, high velocity and high impact propensity across all the domains or facets of social life from the economic to the cultural. This might be labelled *thick globalization*. For some sceptics the late nineteenth-century era of

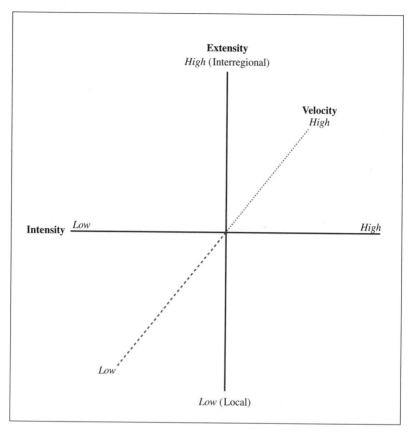

Figure I.1   Spatio-temporal dimensions of globalization 1

global empires comes close to this type. But, as figure I.4 indicates, there are other potential shapes to globalization, among which this is only one.

- Type 2 refers to global networks which combine high extensity with high intensity and high velocity but in which impact propensity is low. This might be labelled *diffused globalization* in so far as its impacts are highly mediated and regulated. While it has no historical equivalents, it is a state of affairs which, normatively speaking, many of those critical of the excesses of contemporary economic globalization might find desirable.
- Type 3 is characterized by the high extensity of global interconnectedness combined with low intensity, low velocity but high impact propensity. This might be labelled *expansive globalization*; for it is defined more by its reach and impact than the velocity of flows. The early modern period of Western imperial expansion in which European empires had acquired a tentative global reach with considerable intercivilizational impacts comes closest to this type.
- Type 4 captures what might be labelled *thin globalization* in so far as the high extensity of global networks is not matched by a similar intensity, velocity or impact, for these all remain low. The early silk and luxury trade circuits connecting Europe with China and the East have close parallels with this type.

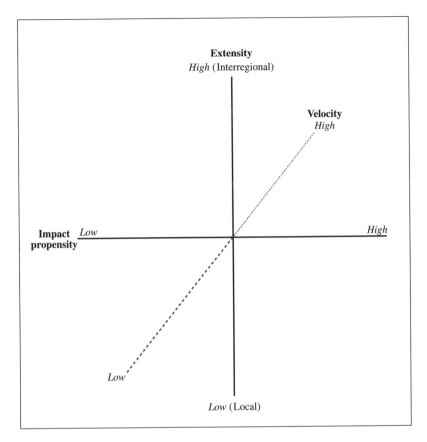

Figure I.2 Spatio-temporal dimensions of globalization 2

The typology presents four alternative ways of conceiving of globalization, but there are many other possible configurations. The 'thought experiment' which generates these four types can yield a range of other possible outcomes, depending on the values given for each spatio-temporal dimension. Which (if any) type most appropriately describes actual historical forms of globalization is the task of subsequent chapters to pursue.

Globalization is, we have sought to argue, neither a singular condition nor a linear process. Moreover, it is best thought of as a highly differentiated phenomenon involving domains of activity and interaction as diverse as the political, military, economic, cultural, migratory and environmental. Each of these domains involves different patterns of relations and activities. These can be thought of as 'sites of power' – interaction contexts or organizational milieux in and through which power operates to shape the action capacities of peoples and communities; that is, to mould and circumscribe their effective opportunities, life chances and resource bases. Elements of the interaction context of a particular site may operate largely autonomously; that is to say, the relations and structures of power on that site may be internally created and applied. Examples of this include aspects of military organization in which internal hierarchies can generate resources, entrench authority and develop clear powers of intervention

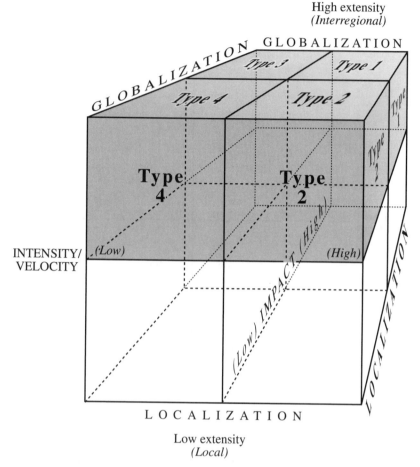

Figure I.3 Logical types of globalization

in tightly circumscribed realms. However, some sites of power may generate pressures and forces which extend beyond their boundaries, and shape and limit other sites. Certain networks of interaction have greater capacity than others for organizing intensive and extensive, authoritative and diffused social relations (see Mann, 1986, ch. 1). These sites of power become to a degree the sources of power for other sites. The reach of the medieval church into economic life, or the influence of powerful corporations, productive and financial, on governments in the contemporary era are cases in point.

The political, military, economic and cultural domains and those of labour and migratory movements and of the environment are the central sites of power that will be explored below. We do not claim that this is a definitive set of possible sites or sources of power (cf. Mann, 1986; Held, 1995, pt 3). It clearly excludes a singular focus on areas which could be a key part of the narrative of the book, for instance, technology. But it is our claim here that the domains we cover are necessary and indispensable to an account of the development of globalization; other domains, including technology, will be threaded through the story we present, but they will not be the focus of individual

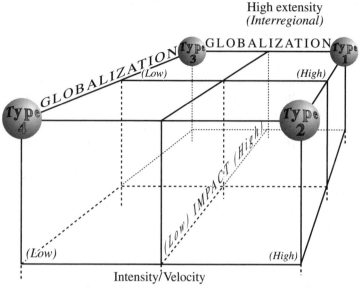

Type 1 = thick globalization
    (high extensity, high intensity, high velocity, high impact)

Type 2 = diffused globalization
    (high extensity, high intensity, high velocity, low impact)

Type 3 = expansive globalization
    (high extensity, low intensity, low velocity, high impact)

Type 4 = thin globalization
    (high extensity, low intensity, low velocity, low impact)

Figure I.4 A typology of globalization

chapters. The main point to emphasize is the necessity of examining globalization through a series of central domains of human activity, and to recognize that a general account of globalization cannot simply read off or predict from one domain what has occurred or might occur in another. To date, the debate about globalization has too often been weakened by contributions which take, for instance, changes in the world economy (in relation to global financial markets or global competitive forces), or in the interstate system (in relation to changing patterns of regional and global governance), or in the environment (in relation to global warming) as typical of changes occurring across other domains of human interaction. But there is no justified reason to assume that any one domain can necessarily exemplify activities and patterns of change in others. It is extremely important to keep these distinctive domains separate and to construct an account of globalization and its impact from an understanding of what is happening in each and every one of them.

This book, then, analyses processes of globalization in terms of a theoretical model based on examining a number of deeply embedded processes of change taking place in different domains and in different historical periods. It does not collapse these into a single process, but treats them as different processes, working according to different possible historical time-scales, whose interaction needs careful consideration, for it can lead to variable and contingent outcomes. The stress is on processes, factors and distinctive causal patterns, rather than on the presumption of a monocausal explanation. We return to the implications of this differentiated and multicausal approach later in the volume, and sum up its significance in the conclusion.

The typology of globalization (figures I.1–4) delivers a method for describing globalization which avoids both the simplicity of sceptical and hyperglobalist accounts and also the pitfalls of more speculative analysis about the direction of global trends. In this respect the typology acknowledges the complexity of globalization as well as its historical contingency. But while such a typology helps create a basis for understanding contemporary globalization, it will only make full sense in the context of – and after – systematic comparative enquiry into the historical forms of globalization.

Subsequent chapters utilize the broad elements of this framework for describing and explaining the historical patterns of globalization in each of the key domains of human activity. They do so by comparing four great epochs of globalization: the premodern period; the early modern period of western expansion; the modern industrial era; and the contemporary period from 1945 to the present. The leading processes of globalization, it will be seen, unfolded across several centuries in a slow and uneven manner, and it is difficult, if not impossible, to identify any single starting point. There are interesting continuities across different historical periods as well as breaks, ruptures and reversals. Different processes of globalization have developed at different times, followed different trajectories and tempos. This is reflected in somewhat different periodizations used in each chapter of this book. For example, chapter 1 takes the history of political globalization back to the ancient empires. Chapter 2 on organized violence and the military begins by reflecting on key changes in the early modern period. Chapters 3–5 also start from the early modern period, exploring the globalization of trade, finance and production. Chapter 6 on migration begins with the earliest migratory movements which peopled the planet, but examines, in particular, movements which followed from the expansion of Europe. Chapter 7 starts with the globalization of culture from the spread of the Roman Empire and world religions, while it puts special emphasis on developments from the late nineteenth century. And chapter 8 focuses on environmental degradation in the second half of the twentieth century, although earlier significant periods are mentioned. The conclusion pulls these different historical narratives together, examining disjunctures and confluences of change across earlier periods and domains. It brings the story of the different temporalities together, exploring some of their main connections and articulations. The latter is an important exercise since the potential synergy between processes of globalization in each domain may produce its own systemic logic. While it is essential to map globalization in each domain it is also crucial not to neglect the ways in which the totality of these flows, networks, interactions and interconnections generates its own imperatives. The conclusion will, therefore, seek to integrate the narratives of globalization in each domain into a more comprehensive comparison of the main historical forms of globalization.

It is important to stress that it is only after the mapping of historical forms of globalization, with respect to the key domains of human activity, that it is possible to identify the extent to which there is a clustering of patterns of global interconnectedness across all these areas. Only from an analysis of such clustering will it be feasible to deduce the overall shape of contemporary globalization; that is, whether contemporary patterns of global change can most appropriately be described as thick, thin, expansive, diffused, or by some other potential shape.

In sum

The account of globalization developed in subsequent chapters reflects and builds on a number of points made so far in the introduction:

1 Globalization can best be understood as a process or set of processes rather than a singular condition. It does not reflect a simple linear developmental logic, nor does it prefigure a world society or a world community. Rather, it reflects the emergence of interregional networks and systems of interaction and exchange. In this respect, the enmeshment of national and societal systems in wider global processes has to be distinguished from any notion of global integration.

2 The spatial reach and density of global and transnational interconnectedness weave complex webs and networks of relations between communities, states, international institutions, non-governmental organizations and multinational corporations which make up the global order. These overlapping and interacting networks define an evolving structure which both imposes constraints on and empowers communities, states and social forces. In this respect, globalization is akin to a process of 'structuration' in so far as it is a product of both the individual actions of, and the cumulative interactions between, countless agencies and institutions across the globe (Giddens, 1981; Buzan et al., 1993; Nierop, 1994; Jervis, 1997). Globalization is associated with an evolving dynamic global structure of enablement and constraint. But it is also a highly stratified structure since globalization is profoundly uneven: it both reflects existing patterns of inequality and hierarchy while also generating new patterns of inclusion and exclusion, new winners and losers (Hurrell and Woods, 1995). Globalization, thus, can be understood as embodying processes of structuration and stratification.

3 Few areas of social life escape the reach of processes of globalization. These processes are reflected in all social domains from the cultural through the economic, the political, the legal, the military and the environmental. Globalization is best understood as a multifaceted or differentiated social phenomenon. It cannot be conceived as a singular condition but instead refers to patterns of growing global interconnectedness within all the key domains of social activity. To understand the dynamics and consequences of globalization, therefore, demands some knowledge of the differential patterns of global interconnectedness in each of these domains. For instance, patterns of global ecological interconnectedness are quite different from the patterns of global cultural or military interaction. Any general account of the processes of globalization must acknowledge that, far from being a singular condition, it is best conceived as a differentiated and multifaceted process.

4 By cutting through and across political frontiers globalization is associated with both the deterritorialization and reterritorialization of socio-economic and political

space. As economic, social and political activities are increasingly 'stretched' across the globe they become in a significant sense no longer primarily or solely organized according to a territorial principle. They may be rooted in particular locales but territorially disembedded. Under conditions of globalization, 'local', 'national' or even 'continental' political, social and economic space is re-formed such that it is no longer necessarily coterminous with established legal and territorial boundaries. On the other hand, as globalization intensifies it generates pressures towards a re-territorialization of socio-economic activity in the form of subnational, regional and supranational economic zones, mechanisms of governance and cultural complexes. It may also reinforce the 'localization' and 'nationalization' of societies. Accordingly, globalization involves a complex deterritorialization and reterritorialization of political and economic power. In this respect, it is best described as being *aterritorial*.

5   Globalization concerns the expanding scale on which power is organized and exercised, that is, the extensive spatial reach of networks and circuits of power. Indeed, power is a fundamental attribute of globalization. In an increasingly interconnected global system, the exercise of power through the decisions, actions, or inactions, of agencies on one continent can have significant consequences for nations, communities and households on other continents. Power relations are deeply inscribed in the very processes of globalization. In fact, the stretching of power relations means that sites of power and the exercise of power become increasingly distant from the subjects or locales which experience their consequences. In this regard, globalization involves the structuring and restructuring of power relations at a distance. Patterns of global stratification mediate access to sites of power, while the consequences of globalization are unevenly experienced. Political and economic elites in the world's major metropolitan areas are much more tightly integrated into, and have much greater control over, global networks than do the subsistence farmers of Burundi.

The points set out above help clarify the meaning of globalization in very specific ways. In particular, they draw attention to the dangers of eliding globalization with concepts such as interdependence, integration, universalism and convergence. Whereas the concept of interdependence assumes symmetrical power relations between social or political actors, the concept of globalization leaves open the possibility of hierarchy and unevenness; that is, a process of global stratification. Integration too has a very specific meaning since it refers to processes of economic and political unification which prefigure a sense of community, shared fortunes and shared institutions of governance. As previously noted, the notion of globalization as the precursor to a single world society or community is deeply flawed. So too is the association of globalization with 'universalism' for clearly the global is not a synonym for the universal; global interconnectedness is not experienced by all peoples or communities to the same extent or even in the same way. In this respect, it is also to be distinguished from convergence since it does not presume growing homogeneity or harmony. On the contrary, as both Bull and Buzan have argued, growing interconnectedness may be both a source of intense conflict (rather than cooperation) as well as a product of shared fears and deeply held animosities (Bull, 1977; Buzan, 1991).

The Book Ahead

The volume begins by exploring political globalization (see chapter 1). There are several reasons for this starting point. In the first instance, expansionist states and empires have been active in creating regional and global links and they are important elements of the changing historical forms of globalization. Second, different types of states have created distinctive forms of territorial space – from loose frontiers to tightly organized boundaries – which have shaped and mediated patterns of regional and global relations, networks and flows. Third, one particular form of political rule – the modern and contemporary nation-state – profoundly altered the nature, form and prospects of globalization; for it was with the development of the modern nation-state that the focal point of rule became national governments and their claim to sovereignty, autonomy and distinctive forms of accountability within a bounded territory. It is worth dwelling on this latter point for a moment.

Modern nation-states, as will be seen from chapters 1 and 2, distinguish themselves from previous forms of political rule by claiming a proper symmetry and correspondence between sovereignty, territory, legitimacy and, with the passage of the nineteenth and twentieth centuries, democracy. The concept of sovereignty lodges a distinctive claim to the rightful exercise of political power over a circumscribed realm (see Skinner, 1978, vol. 2; Held, 1995, ch. 2). It seeks to specify the political authority within a community which has the right to determine the framework of rules, regulations and policies within a given territory and to govern accordingly. However, in thinking about the impact of globalization on the modern nation-state, one needs to distinguish the claim to sovereignty – the entitlement to rule over a bounded territory – from state autonomy – the actual power the nation-state possesses to articulate and achieve policy goals independently. In effect, state autonomy refers to the capacity of state representatives, managers and agencies to articulate and pursue their policy preferences even though these may on occasion clash with the dictates of domestic and international social forces and conditions (Nordlinger, 1981). Moreover, to the extent that modern nation-states are democratic, sovereignty and autonomy are assumed to be embedded within, and congruent with, the territorially organized framework of liberal democratic government: 'the rulers' – elected representatives – are accountable to 'the ruled' – the citizenry – within a delimited territory. There is, in effect, a 'national community of fate', whereby membership of the political community is defined in terms of the peoples within the territorial borders of the nation-state; this community becomes the proper locus and home of democratic politics.

For many of those involved in the debate about globalization and its consequences, the sheer density and scale of contemporary economic, social and political activity appear to make territorial forms of politics increasingly impotent. Within Western societies this perception is linked to anxieties about the declining effectiveness of government, the growing fragmentation of civic communities and, despite the end of the Cold War, growing personal insecurity. Whether real or imagined, these anxieties reflect a 'fear that, individually and collectively, we are losing control of the forces that govern our lives' (Sandel, 1996, p. 3). Thus it is argued by hyperglobalizers and transformationalists that globalization weaves together, in highly complex and abstract systems, the fate of households, communities and peoples in distant regions of the globe such that 'communities of fate' cannot be identified in exclusively national or territorial terms. The implication is that, under conditions of globalization, one cannot understand the nature and possibilities of political community by referring merely to national structures.

Of course, it is essential to recognize that sovereignty, particularly in its legal sense, is eroded only when it is displaced by forms of independent and/or 'higher' legal or juridical authority which curtail the rightful basis of decision-making within a national polity. But for the hyperglobalizers and transformationalists, the very idea of the sovereign state as an independent unit which governs itself and directs its own future sits uneasily alongside the globalization of economic production and exchange, the growing significance of international regimes, legal interaction and global institutions, the internationalization of domestic policy and the domestication of international policy. Globalization poses the question as to whether global and regional patterns of enmeshment are displacing 'notions of sovereignty as an illimitable, indivisible and exclusive form of public power' such that 'sovereignty itself has to be conceived today as already divided among a number of agencies – national, regional and international – and limited by the very nature of this plurality' (Held, 1991, p. 222).

However, while globalization may constrain what governments can do, governments are, the sceptics retort, by no means necessarily immobilized nor is their sovereignty necessarily eroded. Moreover, globalization has differential impacts; its political consequences vary considerably between different states as well as across different policy sectors. Whether globalization entails a general diminution, an enhancement or a transformation of the sovereignty and autonomy of states remains a controversial matter. Subsequent chapters will, therefore, return repeatedly to this theme.

Mapping the shape and political consequences of globalization is the key objective of the chapters that follow. But the range of states which will be considered will be restricted first and foremost to states in advanced capitalist societies (SIACS). There are two justifications for narrowing the enquiry in this way. First, if globalization does impact on sovereign statehood it is the SIACS, as the principal model and locus of modern statehood, which provide the strongest test of its political ramifications. Second, in the globalization debate the hyperglobalizers, the transformationalists and the sceptics make radically different claims about the fate of SIACS. This study seeks to evaluate these competing claims. However, it does so by concentrating the enquiry on six specific SIACS, namely the US, UK, Sweden, France, Germany and Japan. This particular configuration of states has been selected because of the differences and commonalities between them along a range of variables including their positions in the interstate hierarchy, domestic political structures and cultures, foreign and defence policy postures, levels of global enmeshment, industrial and economic structures and performance and strategies for adjusting to globalization (see the Methodological Appendix). Accordingly, the penultimate and concluding sections of subsequent chapters will seek to relate the analysis of the shape and history of globalization in each domain to the fate of the six SIACS. This will involve a specific exploration of their differential levels of global enmeshment in each domain and an examination of its implications for state sovereignty and autonomy. The primary purpose of this analysis is to deliver a more systematic understanding of the nature and differential political consequences of contemporary globalization. For comparative purposes, other individual states – particularly those with developing economies – will be referred to and discussed only where relevant.

The threads of the volume will be drawn together in the last chapter, which will seek, as noted previously, to deliver a systematic description and assessment of the shape of contemporary globalization. This chapter will conclude with an assessment of the implications of globalization for the sovereignty and autonomy of SIACS. But it will also take the globalization debate into normative territory in exploring some of the key intellectual, institutional and political challenges it generates. In particular, it will confront directly the political fatalism which surrounds much discussion of contemporary globalization with a normative agenda which elaborates the possibilities for democratizing and civilizing the unfolding 'global transformation'.

1

The Territorial State and Global Politics

The objective of this chapter is to provide an account of the changing historical forms of political globalization; that is, the shifting reach of political power, authority and forms of rule. The chapter shows, to anticipate the argument which follows, how the earliest phases of political globalization were accompanied by a slow and largely haphazard development of territorial politics. The emergence of the modern nation-state and the incorporation of all civilizations within the interstate system, however, created a world organized and divided into domestic and foreign realms – the 'inner world' of territorially bounded national politics and the 'outer world' of diplomatic, military and security affairs. While these realms were by no means hermetically sealed, they were the basis on which modern nation-states built political, legal and social institutions. From the early twentieth century this division became more fragile, and increasingly mediated by regional and global flows and processes. The contemporary era is marked by a deterritorialization of politics, rule and governance, although new forms of territorialization, such as regionalism, are evident as well.

The chapter has six main parts. In the first part, changing forms of political rule and, in particular, the rise of the modern nation-state are explored. In the second part, the growth of transboundary, transnational and intergovernmental political processes and problems is examined. The focus of the third part is on the development of international mechanisms, institutions and rules of political decision-making which have generated new forms of global and regional governance. The main historical forms of modern political globalization are summarized in the fourth section. In the fifth part, the differential enmeshment of the six SIACS or case study countries in global processes is reviewed. And in the sixth and final part, the implications of changing forms of political globalization are explored for the nature of state sovereignty, autonomy and accountability.

1.1 From Empires to Modern Nation-States

Conventional political maps of the contemporary world disclose a very particular conception of the geography of political power; for there are clearly demarcated territorial areas within which there is assumed to be a singular state which possesses internationally recognized borders. Only the polar regions appear to stand outside of this patchwork, though some maps show the segmented claims of some states to these areas as well. At the turn of the first millennium this cartography would have appeared both astonishing and incomprehensible. The limited cartographic knowledge of even the most cosmopolitan civilizations of the time would have been overwhelmed by the details of the known world today. The existence of the otherwise isolated Americas and Australia from Eurasia-Africa would have surprised those in each of these spheres. Were they to have had even an inkling of the ease and speed of travel and the degree of interconnections and exchange between the contemporary world's regions, they would have been truly astonished.

At the beginning of the second millennium, human civilizations developed in relative isolation. The most deeply rooted ancient civilizations, particularly the Chinese, Japanese and Islamic, were quite 'discrete worlds' (Fernández-Armesto, 1995, ch. 1). While they were, of course, highly sophisticated and in many respects culturally complex worlds, they had relatively little contact with one another, although they were not without some forms of direct interchange (Mann, 1986; Watson, 1992; Fernández-Armesto, 1995; Ferro, 1997). For example, trade flowed across cultures and civilizations, linking the economic fortunes of different societies together as well as acting as a conduit for ideas and technological practices. Extensive trading networks often connected the ancient civilizations in great loops of cause and effect (see chapters 3 and 4; Abu-Lughod, 1989). One of the most remarkable examples of this was the Chinese development of ocean-going fleets which, from the thirteenth century, were able to explore vast sections of the seas, making possible an extensive pattern of trade with India, Western Asia and East Africa in luxury goods such as silk, silver and slippers (Kennedy, 1988, p. 7; see also chapter 3 below). But in spite of these interchanges, the ancient civilizations developed largely as a result of internal forces and pressures; they were separate and to a large extent autonomous civilizations, shaped by imperial systems which stretched over scattered populations and territories (Fernández-Armesto, 1995, ch. 1).

1.1.1 Early state forms: the shifting extensity of political rule

Early imperial systems

Imperial systems or empires have dominated the history of state formation over the centuries, particularly in their size and grandeur. Some, notably the Chinese, retained identifiable institutional forms over long periods. They required an accumulation and concentration of coercive means – above all, of military and war-making ability – to sustain themselves. When this ability waned, imperial systems disintegrated. All 'traditional' empires developed as a result of expansion from initially more restricted power bases and confined states. Moreover, the deployment of military strength was uppermost in the creation and maintenance of frontiers or territorial boundaries, though the latter were often in flux and shifted according to patterns of alliances, rebellion and invasion (Giddens, 1985, pp. 80–1).

While imperial systems were frequently crossed by long-distance trading routes, their economic requirements were largely met through the exaction of tribute, some of which was used to buy off threatened assaults if military power fell short. The tribute system supported the emperor, his administrative apparatus and the military. But however powerful empires might have been relative to rival power centres, they could sustain only limited administrative authority. Empires stretched over a plethora of communities and societies which were culturally diverse and heterogeneous. Empires were *ruled* but they were not *governed*; that is to say, emperors dominated a limited social and geographical space, but lacked the administrative means – the institutions, organizations, information, personnel and so on – to provide regularized administration over the territories they claimed as their own. Although the intensity of political power may have been considerable, the extensity of political authority was circumscribed. Nonetheless, through intermarriage and cultural or religious assimilation between the emperor's inner circle and local elites, bonds were extended to help integrate the reach of imperial authority (see chapter 7). The polities of empires busied themselves with intrigue and conflicts within dominant groups or classes and within local urban centres; beyond that the resort to military force was the prime mechanism for binding and integrating peoples and territories. Although force was frequently effective, its significance should not be exaggerated. For the size, mobility and deployment of armies depended on the availability of water and local harvests to plunder. The military depended on the countryside and could move no more quickly than its men could march in a day, subject to food availability.

Representing the geography of such states on a contemporary map runs into considerable difficulties. First, the reach of military power and political power were not identical. Most empires could project military power and military threats further than they could regularize political power and administrative control. Political power and control were themselves uneven over territories. Political control varied along transportation routes; it tended to be more regular close to main roads and rivers, and irregular further from them. It also varied with the emergence of alternative power centres within core territories, and the overlapping claims to legal authority of theocratic institutions and local aristocracies. Furthermore, as the military and political power of states diminished at the periphery of their realm they might overlap with more local systems of political rule or the peripheries of other empires. In these frontier regions fixed boundaries could not be drawn and the overlapping hues of local polities and adjacent empires would shift and change over time.

In the following section we chart some of the key processes by which these early discrete and polymorphous worlds were slowly altered and enveloped by changing European political and economic structures – structures which engendered a very particular conception of political rule and community which later came to dominate the political imagination.

Systems of divided authority in medieval Europe

The major power divisions which emerged across the European land mass a thousand years ago – the Kingdom of France, the Germanic Empire, the Principality of Poland, for example – helped disguise the area's fragmented and divided political terrain. Those who prevailed over territories did so above all as military victors and conquerors, exacting tribute and rent; they were far from being heads of state governing clearly demarcated territories and peoples (Tilly, 1990, pp. 38–9). To the extent that we can talk of a political order in Europe at all at this time, it was one marked by interlocking ties and obligations, with networks of rule fragmented into many small, autonomous parts (Poggi, 1978, p. 27). Political power tended to be local and personal in focus, generating a world of 'overlapping claims and powers' (P. Anderson, 1974a, p. 149). Some of these claims and powers conflicted. The principle of territorial political rule was not yet privileged over other principles of political order and, accordingly, no ruler or state was sovereign in the sense of being supreme over a given territory and population (Bull, 1977, p. 254). Against this background, tensions were rife and war was frequent.

Economic life in medieval Europe was dominated by agriculture, and any surplus generated within the economy was subject to rival claims. A successful claim helped constitute a basis to build and sustain political power. The sites of power which developed, crystallized into a web of kingdoms, principalities, duchies and other power centres. This web was complicated further by the emergence of alternative political structures in the cities and towns. Cities and urban federations depended on commerce and manufacture, and frequently enjoyed an independent resource base and autonomous systems of rule specified by charters. Among the best known were the Italian city-states, but across Europe numerous urban centres formed, asserting diverse claims to political authority. Nowhere, however, did they, alongside the web of feudal relations in the countryside, alone determine the pattern of rule or political control. For in the Middle Ages 'Europe' more accurately meant 'Latin Christendom', and the papacy and the Holy Roman Empire gave Christendom what general unity it enjoyed. The latter order has been referred to as 'the order of international Christian society' (Bull, 1977, p. 27). For it was Christian first and foremost; it looked to God for the authority to resolve disputes and conflicts; its primary political reference point was religious doctrine, and it was overlaid with assumptions about the universal nature of human community.

1.1.2   Early modern states: absolutism and the emergence of the interstate system

The developments that led to the erosion of medieval notions of politics were complex and many. Among these were struggles between monarchs, princes and barons over the domain of rightful authority; peasant rebellions against the weight of taxation and obligation; the spread of trade, commerce and market relations; the flourishing of Renaissance culture with its renewed interest in classical political ideas; transformations in technology, especially in military technology; the consolidation of national monarchies; religious strife and the challenge to the universal claims of Catholicism; and the struggle between church and state. In the sections that follow, a number of these changes will be dwelt on, but it is important to clarify first the type of state that emerged during this period.

Two dominant forms of political regime can be distinguished in Europe from the fifteenth to the eighteenth century: the 'absolute' monarchies found in France, Prussia, Spain, Austria, Russia and Sweden, among other places, and the 'constitutional' monarchies and republics found in England and Holland (Mann, 1986, p. 476). There are important differences between these regime types, although in terms of the history of state/society relations some of the differences have been more matters of appearance than substance. The focus here will be on absolutism, which played a pivotal role in the shaping of the modern polity and the interstate system.

Absolutism involved the development of a form of state based on a number of elements: the absorption of smaller and weaker political units into larger and stronger political structures; a strengthened ability to rule over a unified territorial area; a tightened system of law and order enforced throughout a territory; the application of a more unitary, centralized and calculable rule by a single, sovereign head; and the emergence of a relatively small number of states engaged in an 'open-ended, competitive, and risk-laden power struggle' (Poggi, 1978, pp. 60–1). While the actual power of absolutist rulers has often been overstated, these changes marked a substantial increase in public authority from above.[1] Certainly, the absolutist monarch claimed to be the ultimate authority on all matters of human law, although it is important to note that this broad writ was understood to derive from, and was legitimated in relation to, the law of God.

The proximate sources of the modern political world – that is, of the modern nation-state system itself – were European absolutism and the interstate order it initiated. For in condensing political and military power in its own hands, and in seeking to create a central system of rule, absolutism paved the way for the emergence of a secular and national system of power. The concentration of power set in motion a series of developments that were of great significance to the history of political communities, including the growing coincidence of territorial boundaries with a uniform system of rule; the concentration and extension of fiscal management; the centralization of administrative power; the gradual monopolization of military power by the state; the introduction of standing armies; the creation of new mechanisms of law making and enforcement; and the formalization of relations among states through the development of diplomacy and diplomatic institutions (see P. Anderson, 1974b, pp. 15–41; Giddens, 1985, ch. 4; Mann, 1986, chs 12–15). Absolutism helped initiate a process of state-making which began to reduce the social, economic and cultural differences *within* states and expand the differences *among* them, that is, it helped to forge political communities with a clearer and growing sense of identity – national identity (Tilly, 1975, p. 19).

The nature and form of the interstate system crystallized at the intersection of 'international' and 'national' conditions and processes. (These terms are in inverted commas because they did not take on their full contemporary meaning until the era of fixed borders, that is, the era of the nation-state.) It was at this intersection, in fact, that the shape of the state was largely determined – its size, external form, ethnic composition, organizational structure, material infrastructure and so on (see Hintze, 1975, chs 4–6, 11). At the heart of this process was the ability of states to secure and strengthen their power bases and, thereby, to order their affairs, internally and externally. This, in turn, depended on their capacity to organize the means of coercion (armies, navies and other forms of military might) and to deploy them when necessary (see chapter 2 below). Those states, in particular, able to draw on the resources of a large population, a relatively robust commercial economy and a tradition of technological innovation became the dominant political forces, laying down the rules of the political game for others and, wherever possible, expanding the reach of their political jurisdiction (Tilly, 1975).

---

[1] Interesting contrasts can be drawn between absolutism in the West and East; see P. Anderson, 1974b.

1.1.3   The European 'society of states'

By the end of the seventeenth century Europe was no longer simply a mosaic of polities, but an evolving 'society of states' in which the principles of sovereignty and territoriality became supreme. The consolidated power of each individual state was at the same time part of the process of overall interstate formation (Giddens, 1985, p. 91). For a concomitant of each and every state's claim to uncontestable authority was the recognition that such a claim gave other states an equal entitlement to autonomy and respect within their own borders. The development of state sovereignty was central to the process of mutual recognition whereby states granted each other rights of jurisdiction in their respective territories and communities. Sovereignty established an entitlement to rule over a bounded territory, although whether such rule was effective – that is, whether a state possessed sufficient autonomy to articulate and achieve its objectives in relation to other key agencies and social forces – was always another matter (Krasner, 1995). But in the world of relations among states, the principle that all states had equal rights to self-determination became paramount in the formal conduct of states towards one another. Of course, at issue was largely the formal relations among the most powerful states – the rights and privileges of sovereignty were by no means granted to all those peoples and communities with whom these states came into contact (see below).

The emergent European society of states was articulated by a new conception of international law which has been referred to as the 'Westphalian model' (after the Peace Treaties of Westphalia of 1648, concluded after the Thirty Years' War) (Falk, 1969; Cassese, 1986). The model covers the period of international law and regulation from 1648 to 1945 (although some would contend it still holds today). While it can be disputed that all the elements of the model (as described below) were intrinsic to the treaties signed at Westphalia, this dispute need not be examined here (see Krasner, 1995; Keohane, 1995). For the model should be taken to depict a *normative trajectory* in international law which did not receive its fullest articulation until the late eighteenth and early nineteenth centuries when territorial sovereignty, the formal equality of states, non-intervention in the domestic affairs of other recognized states and state consent as the basis of international legal obligation became the core principles of international society (see Crawford and Marks, 1998).

The model depicts the development of a world order consisting of territorial, sovereign states in which there is no supreme authority: states settle their differences privately and by force if necessary; they engage in diplomatic relations but otherwise there is minimal cooperation; they seek to place their own (national) interest above all others; and they accept the logic of the principle of effectiveness, that is, the principle that might eventually makes right in the international world – appropriation becomes legitimation. The model of Westphalia can be summarized by the following points (see Falk, 1969; Cassese, 1986, pp. 396–9; Held, 1995, p. 78):

1   The world consists of, and is divided into, sovereign territorial states which recognize no superior authority.
2   The processes of law-making, the settlement of disputes and law enforcement are largely in the hands of individual states.

3   International law is oriented to the establishment of minimal rules of coexistence; the creation of enduring relationships among states and peoples is an aim, but only to the extent that it allows state objectives to be met.

4   Responsibility for cross-border wrongful acts is a 'private matter' concerning only those affected.

5   All states are regarded as equal before the law: legal rules do not take account of asymmetries of power.

6   Differences among states are often settled by force; the principle of effective power holds sway. Virtually no legal fetters exist to curb the resort to force; international legal standards afford minimal protection.

7   The minimization of impediments to state freedom is the 'collective priority'.

This new order of states, while providing a framework for the expansion of the state system, simultaneously endorsed the right of each state to autonomous and independent action. States were conceived as 'separate and discrete political orders' with no common authority to shape or curtail their activities (Beitz, 1979, p. 25). In this conception, the world consists of separate political powers pursuing their own interests, backed by diplomatic initiatives and, in the last instance, by their organization of coercive power.

The pursuit and management of interstate relations through diplomacy dates back to Italian city-states in the fifteenth century, although the origins of diplomacy lie much earlier (Bull, 1977; Derian, 1987; Watson, 1992). After the Peace of Westphalia, however, the exchange of diplomats as officially accredited state agents, the creation of permanent diplomatic missions and the codification of diplomatic immunities gradually became entrenched throughout Europe. Two legal rules, in particular, were taken to uphold national sovereignty in international affairs: 'immunity from jurisdiction' and 'immunity of state agencies'. The former prescribed that 'no state can be sued in the courts of another state for acts performed in its sovereign capacity'; and the latter stipulated that 'should an individual break the law of another state while acting as an agent for his country of origin and be brought before that state's courts, he is not held "guilty" because he did not act as a private individual but as the representative of the state' (Cassese, 1988, pp. 150–1). The underlying purpose of these rules was to protect a government's autonomy in all matters of foreign policy and to prevent domestic courts from ruling on the behaviour of foreign states (on the understanding that all domestic courts everywhere were so prevented). And the upshot has traditionally been that governments and their diplomats have been left free to pursue their interests subject only to the constraints of the 'art of the possible'. In this context, states could interact with each other on the basis, in principle, of a predictable framework of relations. Embassies remained inviolable and acts of intrusion were interpreted as a violation of sovereignty and risked a major diplomatic incident. Accordingly, states enjoyed relatively safe niches in each other's territory for the representation and pursuit of their interests. As a result, the diplomatic importance of all states in the interstate system (measured by the number of diplomatic missions sent or received) steadily grew (see Small and Singer, 1973; Nierop, 1994).

Of course, the principles and rules of the Westphalian political order did not simply translate into one conception of international affairs (see chapter 2 below; Hall, 1996). And the consolidation of the nation-state system has not been a uniform process, affecting each region and country in a similar way. From the outset this process has involved great costs for the autonomy and independence of many, especially in non-European civilizations. In fact, the spread of the interstate system has been consistently characterized by both hierarchy and unevenness as Europe burst outwards across the world (see Falk, 1990, pp. 2–12).

1.1.4 Changing forms of political globalization: infrastructures, velocity and stratification

The growth of the interconnections between states became progressively shaped by the expansion of Europe, although imperial expansion elsewhere, for instance from Russia, ran concurrent with it (Ferro, 1997, ch. 2). The expansion of Europe led also to the dismantling of older, non-European interstate connections. Key features of the modern states system – the centralization of political power, the expansion of state administration, territorial rule, the diplomatic system, the emergence of regular, standing armies – which existed in Europe in embryo in the sixteenth and seventeenth centuries were to become prevalent features of the global order. The main vehicle for this was, to begin with, the European states' capacity for overseas operations by means of military and naval forces capable of long-range navigation.

The early leaders in exploration were the Spanish and Portuguese. While the Iberian monarchies led the first two centuries of European expansion, they met increasingly strong competition. Their position was eroded in the seventeenth century by the Dutch and subsequently by the British and French: see map 1.1. British and French influence were ascendant in the eighteenth century, and Britain was quite dominant in the nineteenth. 'Perhaps because it was so largely built round Britain,' as Hobsbawm put it, 'the world economy of nineteenth-century capitalism developed as a single system of free flows, in which the international transfers of capital and commodities passed largely through British hands and institutions, in British ships between the continents, and were calculated in terms of the pound sterling' (1969, p. 14, cf. p. 314). British naval and military power reinforced London's position as the centre of world trade and finance (see chapters 3 and 4). However, until this moment no one single power was hegemonic; at least two powerful states were always contending for dominance in Europe itself, and their interests constantly clashed in colonial territories. In addition, the expansion of world commerce drew non-state actors into these struggles (Tilly, 1990, p. 189). The colonies became the 'jewels in the crown' of the new empires (see Furnivall, 1948; Spear, 1960; Fieldhouse, 1966; Pakenham, 1992; Ferro, 1997). Through the imposition of trade monopolies and special commercial arrangements, each empire tried to secure exclusive control of the flow of trade and resources for its own enrichment. The enhancement of national prestige was also, of course, another motivating factor in these processes.

The expansion of Europe across the globe, as one observer has noted, 'enhanced the demand for organizations that would be capable of operating on such a scale. All the basic types of organization of modern society – the modern state, modern corporate enterprise, modern science – were shaped by it and benefited greatly from it' (Modelski, 1972, p. 37). Imperial expansion, in particular, became a major source of growth of state activity and power. While the process of equipping, planning and financing overseas

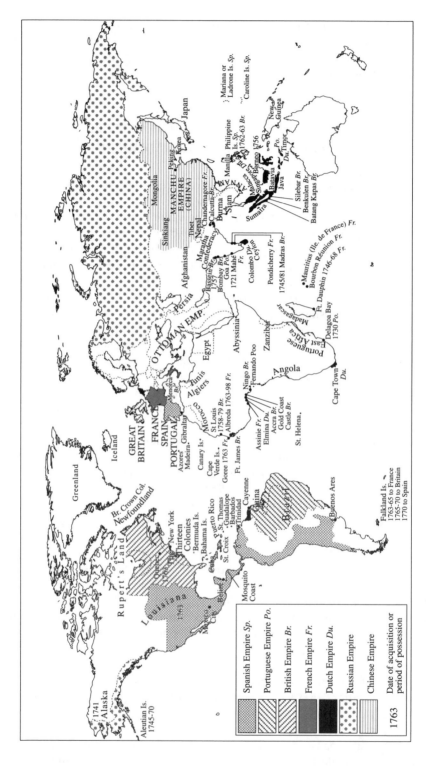

Map 1.1 Global empires, 1763 (*Source:* Adapted from Black, 1994)

exploration sapped national resources, as did the management of newly acquired posts and territories, governments reaped some of the fruits of the 'discovery' and exploitation of non-European lands. Executive powers and state bureaucracies frequently gained both in experience and assets, and this enhanced their autonomy in the face of local assemblies and groups. Those states which were able to call on a sound administrative infrastructure, a substantial population and a wide tax base, alongside arms and ship-building industries, gained an advantage. This advantage was enjoyed by absolutist and constitutional governments in the seventeenth and eighteenth centuries; in the nineteenth century it was enjoyed by the emergent modern nation-states.

While early modern colonialism criss-crossed many parts of the world, and the expansion of the European-Atlantic maritime empires forged deep connections between regions, the historical watershed in the growing enmeshment of political communities probably lies in the last half of the nineteenth century. The impetus to the formation of global processes, both in terms of extensity and intensity, was provided by the rapid expansion of European powers during this period, and by the contest over the terms of this expansion and the struggle by various regional centres to contain it (Geyer and Bright, 1995; Ferro, 1997, pp. 345–50). Undoubtedly, the rapidly developing empires of Britain and of other European states were the most powerful agents of globalization in the late nineteenth century. By the end of this century the spread of the British Empire had been so great that it comprised nearly a quarter of the land surface of the world and included more than a quarter of the population: see map 1.2. The British Empire, to borrow a phrase, 'stretched long fingertips over the world' (Fernández-Armesto, 1995, p. 264). At issue was not simply an intensification of European expansion along a continuum that ran back through earlier centuries, but a new ordering of relations of domination and subordination among the major regions of the world, aided by new communications and transport infrastructures which facilitated new mechanisms of political control.

European colonialism had often been propelled by a spirit of 'pioneering expansionism', aided and abetted by an interest in the exploitation of local conditions and infrastructures. In Africa, for example, the imperialists succeeded best when they followed the recommendations of a British parliamentary committee: 'adopt the native government already existing; being content with controlling their excesses and maintaining peace between them' (quoted in Fernández-Armesto, 1995, p. 419; see Pakenham, 1992). The management and control of massive overseas territories was extraordinarily expensive and deeply impractical unless use was made, wherever possible, of existing political structures and resources. Until innovatory developments in the infrastructure of communication and travel were widely available in the late nineteenth century – new breeds of fast steamers, Morse code, the telegraph, cable links and so on – highly dispersed territories remained hard to communicate with and were vulnerable to independently minded colonial administrators and/or shifting local circumstances about which the imperial centres might know too little, too late. Although changes in the technology of communication and travel were far from a panacea for the political elites and classes in London, Paris and Washington, without investing in them and deploying them wherever practicable they thought they could not fully manage their expanding overseas interests and personnel (see, for example, Pakenham, 1992, ch. 3).

But perhaps more than anything else, this period of expansion marks, somewhat paradoxically, the beginnings of a shift from imperial and territorial forms of control,

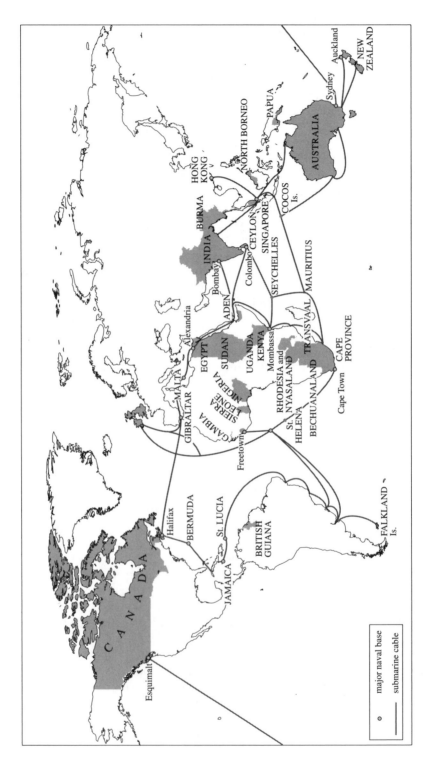

Map 1.2 The British Empire, 1900: colonies and infrastructure (*Source*: Adapted from Kennedy, 1988)

which were deeply contested and fought over, to new, distinctive non-territorial forms of power and domination. Slowly, during the late nineteenth century and early twentieth century, European empires supplemented their modes of control involving direct access or direct administration with new forms of infrastructural interaction and control. Geyer and Bright put the point thus: 'through spatial expansion and occupation . . . a new effort, with new capabilities, to synchronize global time and co-ordinate interactions within the world . . . [was] made possible by the formation of communications-based systems of control . . . that began to . . . [enmesh] the world in global circuits of power by the end of the century' (1995, p. 1047). European states moved beyond the extension of their power over others to the formation of mechanisms and organizations which might give them some infrastructural control of others. Over time, regimes of personal order and direct control, with their haphazardness and uncertainties, gave way to new transnational forms of organization and activity. These were often marked by more anonymous systems of power – managed and controlled by new transnational organizations and/or multinational corporations – which began to develop a life of their own independently of the nation-states that initiated them. Instead of territorial empires stretching over many regions and seeking to subject them to a single political system, a new political order began to unfold based on a proliferation of governmental organizations, transnational practices and networks of exchange – in industry and banking, in information and communication, in travel and cultural interchange. The influence of Western commerce, trade and political organization was to outlive direct rule, giving rise to new patterns of non-territorial globalization – globalization without territory (see Pieterse, 1997). Powerful national economic interests were often able to retain hegemonic positions over former colonial territories through the replacement of 'a visible presence of rule' with the 'invisible government' of banks, companies and international organizations (Ferro, 1997, pp. 349–50: see chapters 3–5 below). Of course, in many cases, this process would have to wait until after the Second World War and the formal initiation of decolonization to be finally completed.

Nonetheless, from the foundation of the International Telegraph Union in 1865, a plethora of intergovernmental organizations developed with responsibility for regulating and ordering diverse domains of activity. At issue was not the creation of a single authority to manage world affairs, but rather the establishment of regulatory regimes for, in principle, the predictable and orderly conduct of pressing transnational processes. By 1914, as table 1.1 indicates, significant aspects of global affairs were already subject to international regulation by world organizations, thus creating a new infrastructure for the transnational management and control of economic, social and cultural processes. Throughout this formative phase of international governance, regulatory activity gradually extended beyond the boundaries of Europe to embrace a more global jurisdiction. The expansion of these distinctive forms of public and private international regulation had significant consequences:

Telegrams, letters and packages flooded the international networks. . . . The tonnage of goods – especially of industrial products – shipped along European railways and roads constantly increased. National courts defended foreign holders of copyrights, patents and trademarks. Producers increasingly employed the same standards. The benefits received by Europe's most privileged workers converged. The slave trade waned. Fewer epidemics crossed national frontiers. (Murphy, 1994, p. 106)

Table 1.1 World organizations in 1914 (by main area of responsibility and date of founding)

FOSTERING INDUSTRY

Infrastructure

1865	International Telegraph Union
1874	Universal Postal Union
1884	International Railway Congress Association
1890	Central Office of International Railway Transport
1894	Permanent International Association of Navigation Congresses
1905	Diplomatic Conference on International Maritime Law
1906	Universal Radiotelegraph Union
1909	Permanent International Association of Road Congresses

Industrial standards and intellectual property

1875	International Bureau of Weights and Measures
1883	International Union for the Protection of Industrial Property
1886	International Union for the Protection of Literary and Artistic Works
1912	International Bureau of Analytical Chemistry of Human and Animal Food

Trade

1890	International Union for the Publication of Customs Tariffs
1893	Hague Conference on Private International Law
1913	International Bureau of Commercial Statistics

MANAGING POTENTIAL SOCIAL CONFLICTS

Labour

| 1901 | International Labour Office |

Agriculture

1879	International Poplar Commission
1901	International Council for the Study of the Sea
1902	International Sugar Union
1905	International Institute of Agriculture

STRENGTHENING STATES AND THE STATE SYSTEM

Public order and administration

| 1875 | International Penitentiary Commission |
| 1910 | International Institute of Administrative Sciences |

Managing interstate conflicts

| 1899 | Permanent Court of Arbitration |
| 1907 | International Court of Justice |

STRENGTHENING SOCIETY

Human Rights

| 1890 | International Bureau against the Slave Trade |

Relief and welfare

| 1907 | Bureau for Information and Enquiries regarding Relief to Foreigners |

continued

Table 1.1 *continued*

Health	
1900	Commission on Revision of the Nomenclature of the Causes of Death
1907	International Office of Public Hygiene
1912	International Association of Public Baths and Cleanliness
Education and research	
1864	International Geodetic Association
1903	International Association of Seismology
1908	International Commission for the Teaching of Mathematics
1909	Central Bureau for the International Map

Source: Murphy, 1994, pp. 47–8

By creating a form of international order conducive to stability and the expansion of industrial capitalism, the new international organizations laid the foundations of a more comprehensive, albeit still fragmented, system of global regulation in the twentieth century.

1.1.5 The modern nation-state and world order

Central to this emerging new international order was the modern nation-state. Modern states are nation-states – political apparatuses, distinct from both ruler and ruled, with supreme jurisdiction over a demarcated territorial area, backed by a claim to a monopoly of coercive power, and enjoying legitimacy as a result of a minimum level of support or loyalty from their citizens. Like all definitions in political analysis, this one is controversial (see Held, 1995, ch. 3). But for our purposes here, it is particularly useful because it underscores a number of the actual innovations of the modern state itself and the international society of states. These include territoriality, monopolistic control of the means of violence, an impersonal structure of power and a distinctive claim to legitimacy, all of which should be clarified briefly.

First, while all states have made claims to territories, it is only with the modern nation-state system that exact borders have been gradually fixed. Postwar decolonization was especially important to this process. Second, the claim to hold a monopoly on force and the means of coercion (sustained by a standing army and the police) became possible only with the 'pacification' of peoples, the breaking down of rival centres of power and authority within the nation-state. This element of the modern state was not fully achieved until the nineteenth century in Europe, and it has remained a remarkably fragile achievement in many countries. Third, the idea of an impersonal and sovereign political order – that is, a legally circumscribed structure of power – with supreme jurisdiction over a territory could not prevail while political rights, obligations and duties were conceived as closely tied to religion and the claims of the traditionally privileged, such as the monarchy and nobility. This matter still remained in contention in the eighteenth and nineteenth centuries in Europe and still remains so in those countries today where the 'rule of law' is in question. Fourth, when claims to 'divine right' or 'state right' were challenged and eroded, the loyalty of citizens became something that had to be won by modern states: invariably this involved a claim by the state to be legitimate because it reflected and/or represented the needs, wishes and interests of its citizens.

Since the Second World War the modern nation-state has become the principal type of political rule across the globe. With decolonization and the collapse of the Soviet empire the number of nation-states has grown rapidly (see figure 1.1 below, p. 54). Moreover, the modern nation-state has acquired a particular political form – its main variant has crystallized as *liberal* or *representative democracy*. Liberal democracy means, of course, that decisions affecting a community are taken by a subgroup of representatives who have been chosen, that is legitimated, through the electoral process to govern within the framework of the rule of law. In the arena of national politics, liberal democracy is distinguished by the presence of a cluster of rules and institutions all of which are necessary to its successful functioning; without any of these, liberal democracy cannot be fully realized. The rules and institutions are (1) the constitutional entrenchment of control over governmental policy in elected representatives; (2) the establishment of mechanisms for the choice and peaceful removal of elected representatives in frequent, fair and free elections; (3) the right to vote for all adults in such elections (unless legitimately disbarred due to severe mental illness or criminal conviction); and (4) the right to run for public office. In addition, there must be (5) an effective right for each citizen to freedom of expression, including to criticize the conduct of government and the socio-economic system in which it is embedded; (6) accessible sources of information other than those controlled by government or by any other single body or group; and, finally (7) an established right to form and join independent associations, whether they be political, social or cultural, that could shape public life through legitimate, peaceful means (Dahl, 1989, pp. 221, 223). The number of countries with these rules and institutions has increased greatly in the nineteenth and twentieth centuries, consolidating liberal democracy as the dominant type of the modern nation-state (see Ware, 1992; Held, 1993; Potter et al., 1997).

It is possible to distinguish three 'waves' of democratization (with some notable concomitant setbacks) which have marked out the consolidation and reach of liberal democracy over time; the first from the early nineteenth century to the mid-1920s; the second from the Second World War to the early 1960s; and the third from 1974 onwards (see box 1.1; Huntington, 1991). The most recent wave helped secure a dominant position for liberal democracy across many of the world's regions. In 1974 at least 68 per cent of all countries could reasonably be called authoritarian; by the end of 1995, nearly 75 per cent of all countries had established procedures for competitive elections and adopted some formal guarantees of political and civil rights. At the current juncture, the number of liberal democracies appears to be still growing. The 'third wave' began in southern Europe and spread to Latin America, parts of Asia and sub-Saharan Africa, Eastern Europe and the former Soviet Union in the 1980s and early 1990s. Table 1.2 sets out these changes by world region and by reference to three regime types: authoritarianism (marked by a dominant state, no competitive elections and severe restrictions on civil and political rights); partial democracy (with some accountability of government to citizens through elections, but with curtailed election procedures, rights and associational autonomy); and liberal democracy (with accountable governments, free and fair competitive elections, civil and political rights, associational autonomy and so on). Of course, there is no necessary evolutionary path

---

Box 1.1 Waves of democratization according to Samuel Huntington (1991)

First, long wave 1828–1926
Examples: USA, Britain, France, Italy, Argentina, the overseas British dominions.

First, reverse wave 1922–42
Examples: Italy, Germany, Argentina.

Second, short wave 1943–62
Examples: West Germany, Italy, Japan, India, Israel.

Second, reverse wave 1958–75
Examples: Brazil, Argentina, Chile.

Third wave 1974–
Examples: Portugal, Spain, numerous others in Latin America, Asia, Africa, Eastern Europe.

Source: Potter et al., 1997, p. 9

Table 1.2 Evidence of democratization, 1975 and 1995

	Countries in 1975 (N = 147)			Countries in 1995 (N = 164)		
	Authoritarian	Partial democracy	Liberal democracy	Authoritarian	Partial democracy	Liberal democracy
Western Europe, North America and Australasia	2	0	22	0	0	24
Latin America	15	2	5	2	5	15
Asia	18	4	3	11	5	9
Sub-Saharan Africa	43	2	3	12	16	20
Middle East and Persian Gulf	14	3	2	13	3	2
Eastern Europe and the USSR/ former USSR	9	0	0	5	14	8
Total	101	11	35	43	43	78
Percentage	68.7%	7.5%	23.8%	26.2%	26.2%	47.6%

Source: Potter et al., 1997, p. 9

from authoritarianism to liberal democracy; the hold of liberal democracy on political communities has often been tentative and capable of reversal.

Built as it was on an emerging conception of the modern nation-state, the development of liberal democracy has taken place within a fairly delimited political space (cf. Walker, 1988; Connolly, 1991; McGrew, 1997). For modern democratic theory and practice was constructed on Westphalian foundations. National communities, and theories of national communities, were based on the presupposition that political communities could, in principle, control their destinies and citizens could come to identify sufficiently with each other such that they might think and act together with a view of what was best for all of them, that is, with a view of the public good (Sandel, 1996, p. 202). It was taken for granted that, bar internal difficulties, the demos, the extent of the franchise, the form and scope of representation and the nature and meaning of consent – in fact all the key elements of self-determination in politics – could be specified with respect to geography: systems of representation and democratic accountability could be neatly meshed with the spatial reach of sites of power in a circumscribed territory. Moreover, as a consequence of this, clear-cut distinctions could be elaborated – and national institutions built on – the difference between 'internal' and 'external' policy, between domestic and foreign affairs.

Of course, the construction of a national democratic community was often deeply contested as different social, economic and cultural groups fought with each other about the nature of this community and about their own status within it. If it had not been for the extensive and often violently suppressed struggles of working-class, feminist and civil rights activists in the nineteenth and twentieth centuries a genuinely universal suffrage would not have been created in many countries (see Potter et al., 1997). The construction of nations and national identities has been equally harshly contested. We return to the cultural politics of nation-building and nationalism in chapter 7, but it is worth dwelling for a moment on the complex relationships between these phenomena and the process of modern state-making. States are institutions, nations are cross-class collectivities which share a sense of identity and collective political fate on the basis of real, imagined and constructed cultural, linguistic and historical commonalities. Nationalism describes both the emotive allegiance of individuals to that identity and community, and the political project of acquiring a state in which that nation is dominant. The fixed borders of the modern territorial state have almost invariably encompassed a diversity of ethnic, cultural and linguistic groups with mixed identities and allegiances; and the relationship between these entities – the nations and nation-state – have been variable and sharply contested. Some nationalisms have supported and been mobilized by the project of successful state formation – the French and France are an example. Some nations and nationalisms have emerged in opposition to other national projects – Catalonian nationalism in Spain; some have emerged in opposition to multiethnic imperial states – Hungarian nationalism versus the Austro-Hungarian Empire; and some have emerged in opposition to foreign colonial powers – Indian nationalism, for instance.

Nonetheless, despite the diversity of nationalisms and their frequently ambiguous relationships to states, the theory of democracy took for granted, particularly as it developed in the nineteenth and twentieth centuries, the link between the demos, citizenship, electoral mechanisms, the nature of consent, and the boundaries of the nation-state. The fates of different political communities may be contested and intertwined, but the appropriate place for determining the foundation of 'national fate' was the territorially based, political community itself. In the contemporary world the key principles and practices of liberal democracy remain associated almost exclusively with the principles and institutions of the sovereign nation-state. Further, modern democratic theory and democratic politics assumes a symmetry and congruence between citizen-voters and national decision-makers. Through the ballot box, citizen-voters are, in principle, able to hold decision-makers to account; and, as a result of electoral consent, decision-makers are able to make and pursue law and policy legitimately for their constituents, ultimately the people in a fixed, territorially based community.

Accordingly, the heart or 'deep structure' of the modern system of democratic nation-states can be characterized by a number of striking features, broadly: democracy in nation-states and non-democratic relations among states; the entrenchment of accountability and democratic legitimacy inside state boundaries and the pursuit of the national interest (and maximum political advantage) outside such boundaries; democracy and citizenship rights for those regarded as 'insiders' and the frequent negation of these rights for those beyond their borders. However, these distinctions themselves may no longer appear so clear-cut as political globalization itself has encouraged the growth of a 'global politics'.

1.2 The Emergence of Global Politics

Today, virtually all nation-states have gradually become enmeshed in and functionally part of a larger pattern of global transformations and global flows (Nierop, 1994, p. 171). Transnational networks and relations have developed across virtually all areas of human activity. Goods, capital, people, knowledge, communications and weapons, as well as crime, pollutants, fashions and beliefs, rapidly move across territorial boundaries (McGrew, 1992). Far from this being a world of 'discrete civilizations', or simply an international society of states, it has become a fundamentally interconnected global order, marked by intense patterns of exchange as well as by clear patterns of power, hierarchy and unevenness.

In order to grasp the transformations which have affected and continue to affect the state and political decision-making, a number of concepts need to be clarified, including those of global politics, global governance, international regime, and state sovereignty. Without clarity about these terms, it is hard to understand the numerous global processes and structures that have altered the nature of politics and, in particular, the nature of the modern political community. For these terms help specify the dimensions of the globalization of politics.

1.2.1 The globalization of politics

'Global politics' is a term which usefully captures the stretching of political relations across space and time; the extension of political power and political activity across the boundaries of the modern nation-state. Political decisions and actions in one part of the world can rapidly acquire worldwide ramifications. In addition, sites of political action and/or decision-making can become linked through rapid communications into complex networks of decision-making and political interaction. Associated with this 'stretching' is a frequent 'deepening' impact of global political processes such that, unlike in ancient and modern empires, 'action at a distance' permeates with greater intensity the social conditions and cognitive worlds of specific places or policy communities. As a consequence, developments at the global level frequently acquire almost instantaneous local consequences and vice versa.

The idea of 'global politics' challenges the traditional distinctions between domestic/international, inside/outside, territorial/non-territorial politics, as embedded in conventional conceptions of 'the political' (see Walker, 1993). It also highlights the richness and complexity of the interconnections which transcend states and societies in the global order. Although governments and states remain, of course, powerful actors, they now share the global arena with an array of other agencies and organizations. The state is confronted by an enormous number of intergovernmental organizations (IGOs), international agencies and regimes which operate across different spatial reaches, and by quasi-supranational institutions, like the European Union. Non-state actors or transnational bodies, such as multinational corporations, transnational pressure groups, transnational professional associations, social movements and so on, also participate intensively in global politics. So too do many subnational actors and national pressure groups, whose activities often spill over into the international arena. Accordingly, the global arena can be conceived of as a polyarchic 'mixed actor system' in which political authority and sources of political action are widely diffused (Mansbach et al., 1976; Rosenau, 1997). This conception alone challenges the conventional Westphalian, state-based or realist characterization of the global political order.

Global politics today is anchored not only in traditional geopolitical concerns involving security and military affairs, but also in a large diversity of economic, social and ecological questions. Pollution, drugs, human rights and terrorism are among an increasing number of transnational policy issues which cut across territorial jurisdictions and existing global political alignments, and which demand international cooperation for their effective resolution. Defence and security issues no longer dominate the global agenda or even the political agendas of national governments. The concept of 'global governance' helps articulate this matter.

By global governance is meant not only the formal institutions and organizations through which the rules and norms governing world order are (or are not) made and sustained – the institutions of state, intergovernmental cooperation and so on – but also all those organizations and pressure groups – from MNCs, transnational social movements to the plethora of non-governmental organizations – which pursue goals and objectives which have a bearing on transnational rule and authority systems (see Rosenau, 1997). Clearly, the United Nations system, the World Trade Organization and the array of activities of national governments are among the central components of global governance, but they are by no means the only components. If social movements, non-governmental organizations, regional political associations and so on are excluded from the notion of global governance, its form and dynamics will not be properly understood. Global politics presupposes a broad notion of global governance as a necessary element in the changing constellation of political life.

The growth in the number of new forms of political agency and organization reflects the rapid expansion of transnational links, and the corresponding desire by most states for some form of international governance to deal with collective policy problems (see Luard, 1977; Krasner, 1983). It also reflects, as will be shown below, the growing pressure of non-governmental bodies for the development of new forms of accountability in international political life. In order to grasp some of the changes underway in this domain, it is important to understand the concept of international regime.

An international regime can be defined in terms of 'implicit or explicit principles, norms, rules, and decision-making procedures around which actor expectations converge in a given issue area of international relations' (Krasner, 1983, p. 2). Regimes are not merely temporary or ad hoc agreements; rather, they can be thought of as 'intervening variables' between the basic power and economic structures of the international system, and definite outcomes. The failure, for example, of markets to regulate the supply and distribution of goods and services, or to resolve pressing transnational problems, may provide incentives for states and political actors to establish distinct regimes. Regimes can provide a framework of legal liability, improve available information, reduce the transaction costs of cooperation and inject a degree of predictability into otherwise 'anarchic' relations (see Keohane, 1984a). International regimes are an expression of the necessity to find new modes of cooperation and regulation for collective problems.

International regimes mark out the growing institutionalization of global politics (Young, 1989, p. 11). They constitute forms of global governance, distinct from traditional notions of government conceived in terms of the specific sites of sovereign political power. In the contemporary international system there is, of course, no single political authority above the state. But despite this, international regulatory regimes have developed rapidly, reflecting the intensification of patterns of global and regional enmeshment. As Young remarks:

> International regimes cover a wide spectrum in terms of functional scope, geographical domain, and membership. Functionally, they range from the narrow purview of the polar bear agreement to the broad concerns of the arrangements for Antarctica and outer space. The geographical area covered may be as limited as the highly restricted domain of the regime for fur seals in the North Pacific or as far flung as that of the global regimes for international air transport (the International Civil Aviation Organization/International Air Transport Association system) or for the control of nuclear testing. With respect to membership, the range runs from two or three members, as in the regime for high-seas fishing established under the International North Pacific Fisheries Convention, to well over a hundred members, as in the nuclear non-proliferation regime. What is most striking, however, is the sheer number of international regimes. Far from being unusual, they are common throughout international society. (1989, p. 11)

International regimes embrace a wide range of political actors, including governments, governmental departments and subnational governing authorities. Moreover, while several regimes have at their core an intergovernmental organization, many are much more fluid arrangements, arising from specific treaties, collective policy problems or transnational communities of interest. Thus the international security regime in Europe is constructed around complex relations among several institutions, such as the North Atlantic Treaty Organization (NATO), the EU, the Western European Union (WEU: a collective defence organization of nine West European states formed in 1948) and the Organization for Security and Cooperation in Europe (OSCE: a grouping of fifty states, all European but for the USA and Canada, whose main function is to foster political stability and military security in Europe). In comparison, the international nuclear non-proliferation regime has no formal international organization at its core, but instead an international treaty combined with rolling international conferences at which key decisions are taken. This is very similar to the law of the sea regime governing the exploitation of resources on the seabed. In addition, international regimes have many different core functions. Some simply engage in monitoring activities, as is the case for many arms control regimes, such as those regulating arms reductions in Europe (the Conventional Forces in Europe Treaty, or CFE), while others constitute forums for taking collective decisions on international property rights, as in the allocation of radio frequencies or satellite orbits. Despite this diversity in forms, functions and constitutions, international regimes articulate a system of governance – or, perhaps better still, a system of 'governance without government' – in the contemporary world order (Rosenau, 1992, p. 5).

At this juncture, a fundamental note of caution needs to be inserted into the discussion of global politics, global governance and international regimes. When assessing their impact, particularly their relationship to states and world order, it is important to reflect on two issues raised in the introduction. First, that the sovereignty of an individual nation-state is eroded only when it is displaced by forms of 'higher' and/or independent and/or deterritorialized and/or functional forms of authority which curtail the rightful basis of decision-making within a national framework. For as indicated earlier, national sovereignty connotes the entitlement to rule over a bounded territory, and the political authority within a community which has the right to determine the framework of rules, regulations and policies and to govern accordingly. Second, in thinking about the impact of globalization on the nation-state, one needs to distinguish sovereignty from state autonomy – the capacity the state possesses to articulate and achieve policy goals independently. Accordingly, it is essential to ask: has the sovereignty of the nation-state remained intact while the autonomy of the state has altered, or has the modern state actually faced a diminution of sovereignty in the face of the globalization of politics? This question will be fundamental to the arguments that follow in many chapters – and we will return to it in the concluding chapter of the book. In the meantime, it is important to emphasize that to explore the globalization of politics is not necessarily to conclude that the modern nation-state has withered away, or that the sovereignty of the modern state is fundamentally eroded, or that the autonomy of the state has been radically cut short. These are fundamental questions which remain to be explored. In exploring them, the subsequent sections will trace out the emergence of global politics, the changing pattern of institutionalization and the development of the infrastructure of political decision-making at international, transnational and global levels.

1.2.2 Internationalization and transnationalization: extensity, intensity and institutionalization

In 1997 the finance and employment ministers of the world's leading capitalist states (the G7 or Group of Seven) met in London to discuss the problem of unemployment. The principal object of this G7 'summit for jobs' was to review how international coordination of national economic strategies might assist job growth across the G7 nations. This summit had a symbolic importance at the time in bringing unemployment to the top of the Western political agenda. Indeed, the annual G7 summits have focused their attention increasingly on issues which might previously have been regarded as primarily 'domestic' or welfare issues. In effect, this represents an attempt to manage or 'govern' those aspects of political life which escape the control of any single state. This has meant an increasing focus on questions of economic, ecological and social security, rather than on traditional geopolitics and military security. The G7 summits highlight what has been evident for some time: a growing 'institutionalization' of global politics as governments and their citizens come to terms with a world of transnational flows and connections.

This kind of institutionalization is not simply a twentieth-century phenomenon. As highlighted previously, international mechanisms to 'govern' aspects of global affairs have been in evidence since the middle of the nineteenth century (and long before that if one counts the 'balance of power' as such a mechanism: see chapter 2). However, especially since the Second World War, there has been an extraordinary expansion of such mechanisms. Along with substantial increases in flows of trade, foreign direct investment (FDI), financial commodities, tourism, cultural links, hazardous waste and knowledge (all documented in later chapters), there has been a corresponding intensification of forms of international cooperation to manage, regulate, facilitate and sometimes prevent these burgeoning flows and connections. This is not to argue that such regulation is simply the product, or consequence, of these new flows, since there are strong reasons to believe it may have been an important underlying contributory cause (see Murphy, 1994). Rather, it is simply to hold that there is a distinct connection between historical patterns of socio-economic globalization and historical patterns of political globalization.

The development of international agencies and organizations has led to significant changes in the decision-making structure of world politics. New forms of multilateral and multinational politics have been established involving governments, IGOs and a wide variety of transnational pressure groups and international non-governmental organizations (INGOs). In 1909 there were 37 IGOs and 176 INGOs, while in 1996 there were nearly 260 IGOs and 5,472 INGOs. Some indication of the scale of the transformation in progress since 1945 is evident in figure 1.1. In addition, it is interesting to note that during the period 1946–1975 the number of international treaties in force between governments more than doubled from 6,351 to 14,061, while the number of such treaties embracing intergovernmental organizations expanded from 623 to 2,303.

Such evidence suggests that a rapid process involving the 'internationalization' of political decision-making has been underway in recent times. Not surprisingly, these developments have been accompanied by the growth of diplomatic connectedness. Since the end of the Second World War, this growth has been especially rapid: the average diplomatic connectedness of states has nearly doubled, while the total number of diplomatic missions has more than trebled (see table 1.3), although the spread of diplomatic relations remains uneven. For instance, recent data show that 21 states host between 0 and 10 ambassadors; 79 host 11–50; 46 host 51–100 while 9 host 101–150 (Kidron and Segal, 1995, pp. 76–7).

But even these figures conceal the explosive growth of governmental and transgovernmental communication and interaction – that is, policy networks or communications networks connecting officials in departments in one state with their opposite numbers in other states or with an IGO. These policy networks are extensive and highly active on a day-to-day basis, facilitated increasingly by electronic communications. As Clarke observes in relation to the UK, 'domestic departments are increasingly having to come to operate in the international environment in order to fulfil their

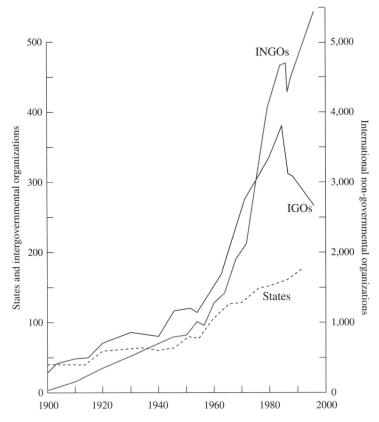

Figure 1.1 The growth of states, IGOs and INGOs in the twentieth century (*Source*: Union of International Associations, 1996)

Table 1.3 Diplomatic connectedness of states, 1950–1991 (number of other states linked to by at least one resident emissary)

	1950	1960	1970	1980	1991
Number of states	81	90	134	159	167
Total connectedness	2,140	3,566	5,388	7,163	7,762
Average connectedness	26	40	40	45	46
Connectedness for selected states					
USA	70	80	115	136	150
France	70	75	117	133	142
Federal Republic of Germany	[a]	69	99	125	135[b]
UK	67	80	115	131	132
Japan	[a]	65	90	104	111
Sweden	50	73	73	86	94

[a] FRG and Japan not yet allowed to engage in diplomatic relations in 1950.
[b] FRG in 1991 is Germany.
Source: Nierop, 1994, app. 2

responsibilities. Every month some two hundred officials from the Ministry of Agriculture, Fisheries and Food alone are required to travel to Brussels' (1992, p. 96). This creates enormous problems of policy coordination such that often the state appears not so much as a single actor on the world stage but as a multiplicity of actors in many different forums. In 1989, for instance, the UK Department of Health and Social Security found itself agreeing to a World Health Organization (WHO) charter on environmental issues, unaware that it undermined the Department of the Environment's negotiating position within the EU in opposition to tougher environmental standards (Clarke, 1992, p. 165).

While traditionally a Ministry of Foreign Affairs has been primarily responsible for all aspects of international relations and foreign policy, this responsibility is today increasingly diffused among different ministries and departments. This has brought with it not only a rapid acceleration in the number and forms of agencies making international agreements, but also in the number and forms of agreements made between states. Indeed, officials in many ministries today find it extremely difficult to decide what is and what is not a domestic matter; they find it hard to monitor the range of agreements being made at different regional and international levels; and they find it practically impossible to keep track of all the different international meetings that have substantial implications for their understanding of their respective policy domains. To some extent this is not a new phenomenon. For instance, the Universal Postal Union was founded in 1874 as a union of postal administrations, with the purpose of creating, establishing and monitoring agreements among governmental departments which had responsibility for the efficient and effective delivery of the post. But with the sheer growth in the number of organizations operating in the international and transnational sphere, and with the spread of ministries and agencies engaged in international affairs, the whole system of international decision-making and diplomacy has become much more complex and diversified. Departments or ministries of foreign affairs become but one set of agencies in this complex system, such that even diplomats have come to contemplate 'the end of foreign policy' (Talbott, 1997, p. 81).

If one were to add to this extensive intergovernmental and transgovernmental activity the key multilateral conferences of the postwar period, the annual G7, EU, IMF, APEC, ARF and MERCOSUR summits and the many other official and unofficial summits, an image of extremely intense and overlapping networks of global, regional and multilateral governance appears. As an illustration of this, it can be noted that in the middle of the nineteenth century there were two or three conferences or congresses per annum sponsored by IGOs; today the number totals close to 4,000 annually (Zacher, 1993). Such conferences, meetings and related policy networks are highly uneven in terms of their spatial reach, functional embrace, jurisdiction, power and political salience (see, for example, map 1.3). Nevertheless, a very clear pattern emerges in respect of the internationalization of the institutions, practices and policy-making processes of the modern nation-state. National government is locked into an array of global, regional and multilateral systems of governance.

This tendency is exemplified further by the growing enmeshment of international rules with national legislation and national legal processes. Research on the proportion of national legislation which incorporates or reflects international standards has generated some interesting findings. By surveying the references, direct and indirect, to international law in the twentieth-century statutes of the United Kingdom and

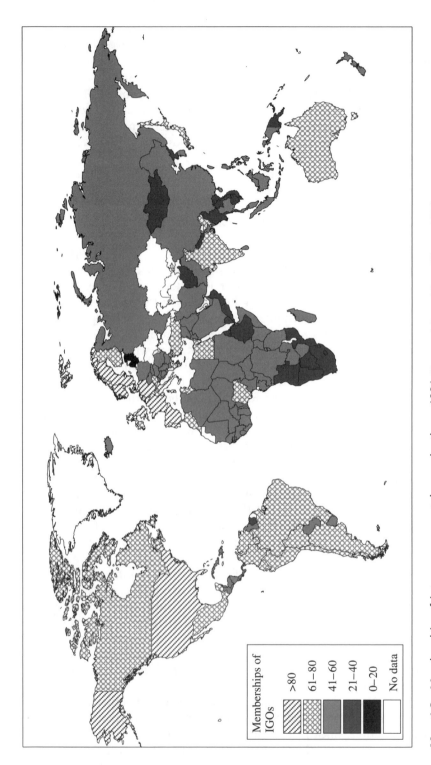

Map 1.3 Membership of intergovernmental organizations, 1991 (*Source*: Adapted from Nierop, 1994)

Memberships of IGOs

>80

61–80

41–60

21–40

0–20

No data

Australia, it has been shown that the proportion of national legislation which reflects or incorporates international legal standards has increased significantly during the century. And the research concludes: 'the extent of the references to international legal rules and instruments in the legislation of these two countries is impressive; it refutes simplistic versions of the separation of municipal from international law' (Crawford, 1979b, p. 646; see also Alston and Chiam, 1995). There is also evidence of a growth in the extent to which international law has become an important point of reference in national courts. At stake is the number of cases in national courts in which issues of international law have been raised, whether involving the interpretation of treaties or other international legal documents. The evidence available indicates a significant increase in such cases since the early 1970s (see Crawford 1979a). In this respect, there is no longer a strict separation between domestic and international legal rules.

Accordingly, international engagement today is not something that a particular state, or its Ministry of Foreign Affairs, can simply choose to pursue or disregard. For at the level of international law alone, international engagement is not an option. The activities of an increasing number of government departments, national courts and legislatures reflect the politics, standards and concerns of international rule-making, formal and informal.

The institutionalization of global politics and global governance is not restricted to the internationalization of governmental and state activities. Alongside the latter can be charted a corresponding transnationalization of economies, civil societies and national communities. In almost every sphere of social activity, from the economic to the cultural, there has been a significant institutionalization of transnational relations and networks – that is, those relations and activities cutting across national territorial boundaries. New transnational organizational forms have emerged, organizing people and coordinating resources, information and sites of social power across national borders for political, cultural, economic, technological or social purposes (Lash and Urry, 1994).

This transnationalization is most conspicuous in relation to the globalization of finance and production and the development of MNCs (see chapters 4–5 below). For example, in 1973, 239 national banks established the SWIFT (standardized world interbank and financial transactions) system, creating a worldwide framework for rapid interbank communications; by 1989 SWIFT had 1,000 members in 51 states (Ward, 1989, p. 263). But it is evident in many other domains as well. In the domain of politics there exist scores of transnational pressure groups and international non-governmental organizations, from Greenpeace to the International Confederation of Trade Unions (ICTU); in the cultural sphere there are groups such as the World Muslim Congress and diverse Christian associations; in the social domain there are numerous organizations like the International Red Cross, the Catholic Fund for Overseas Development (CAFOD) and OXFAM; and in the scientific domain professional organizations proliferate, such as the International Association of Nutritional Sciences and the International Political Science Association. Since the 1950s the growth of transnational organizations – that is, non-governmental organizations (excluding corporations and companies) which have members in more than two countries – has been explosive: from a total of 832 in 1951 to 5,472 in 1996 (see figure 1.1 above).

Even though such figures may not be entirely accurate in all respects (there are definitional problems and problems of data collection), they indicate a trend in most parts of the globe towards the institutionalization of social, cultural and political relations which transcend national frontiers. Many of these transnational organizations function to coordinate action at a distance, organizing communities of interest across territorial boundaries and across the world's major regions (see, for instance, the discussion of environmental groups in chapter 8 below). Some represent particular transnational communities, for example, the Catholic Church, or social movements such as that of ecology or the women's movement. Others are less benign forms of transnational organization such as terrorist and criminal organizations. Despite conflict between smugglers and political authorities over many centuries, the growth in recent years of transnational criminal organizations related to the trade in narcotics (now estimated to be worth over 300 billion dollars a year), and of wide-reaching organized crime (the Triads, Cosa Nostra, etc.) in general, have become a major concern to governments and police forces across the globe (see chapter 3 below; Williams, 1994; Castells, 1998).

Whatever the underlying causes of this dramatic internationalization of state activity and the transnationalization of social and political relations, there is little doubt that there has been a growing internationalization of political decision-making and of diverse aspects of global governance – that is, there has been a marked extension in the infrastructures and institutions of global political networks, rule-making and activity.

1.2.3 Mediating global politics: developing infrastructures and the velocity of political interaction

Nations, peoples and organizations are linked by many new forms of communication and media which range across borders. The revolution in microelectronics, in information technology and in computers has established virtually instantaneous worldwide links which, when combined with the technologies of the telephone, television, cable, satellite and jet transportation, have dramatically altered the nature of political communication. The new forms of communication enable individuals and groups to overcome geographical boundaries which once might have prevented contact; and they create access to a range of social and political experiences which the individual or group may never have had an opportunity to engage with directly (see Giddens, 1991, pp. 84–5). The intimate connection between 'physical setting', 'social situation' and politics which has distinguished most political associations from premodern to modern times has been ruptured; the new communication systems create new experiences, new modes of understanding and new frames of political reference independently of direct contact with particular peoples or issues (Meyrowitz, 1985, p. 7; and see chapter 7 below). At the same time, unequal access to these new modes of communication has created novel patterns of political inclusion and exclusion in global politics.

The development of new communication systems generates a world in which the particularities of place and individuality are constantly redisplayed and reinterpreted by regional and global communication networks. But the relevance of these systems goes far beyond this, important though this is; for the new communication systems are a means, if not the means, for the enhancement of many of the processes of political change documented in the previous section and in the sections which follow; that is to say, they are fundamental to the possibility of organizing political action and exercising political power across vast distances, and to transforming modern political communities and the territorial states system more generally (Deibert, 1997). For example, the expansion of international and transnational organizations, the extension of international rules and legal mechanisms – their construction and monitoring – have all received an impetus from the new communication systems and all depend on them as a means to further their aims (see chapters 2, 4 and 7 below).

Contemporary telecommunications reconstitute the nature and shape of political organizations, and connect communities together in novel frameworks of interchange (see chapter 7 for an elaboration and refinement of this argument). However, they do not merely serve to stretch political relations across space or extend the links between political communities; they have a role in intensifying the velocity of political interaction as well. The rapid reporting of events, incidents and catastrophes can generate almost immediate regional or global ramifications. Tens of millions of people, across every continent, witnessed what was happening in China in Tiananmen Square in 1989, in the siege of the Russian White House in 1991, and in the North Sea in 1995 when Greenpeace successfully challenged the UK Shell Corporation's bid to scuttle a giant oil storage and loading buoy (the Brent Spar). The fact that television cameras recorded these events as they were unfolding created access to, and involvement with, events which, although they took place in a specific locality, came to impinge quickly and directly on many parts of the world. This, in turn, formed the basis of complex and diverse reactions by agencies of the state and civil society.

Today's global telecommunications network embraces every country, although not yet significant sections of the world's population. It reflects, like many other global networks, the geography of power and privilege; the person-to-person, or point-to-point, international telephonic or fax service found in the advanced capitalist world is not yet available in many places. For instance, in the small town of Villes de Bravo, west of Mexico City, most of the population rely on communal telephonic services, while in other parts of the country even those services are sparse. Asymmetries of access and opportunity pervade the global telecommunications network.

Interestingly, the global network itself is one of the most highly regulated sectors of transnational activity. It is governed by the international telecommunications regime, embracing the International Telecommunication Union (ITU) (which in turn embraces a Radiocommunication Sector, the World Radiocommunication Conferences and the International Satellite Organization) and various regional organizations (see box 1.2). Between them, these organizations provide the mechanisms of international coordination which facilitate the operation of the entire system of worldwide telephonic, telegraphic, radio and satellite communication. Each time an international telephone call is made, or an international fax is sent, it relies not just on the technical hardware and software of the global communications infrastructure, but also indirectly on the effective application of the rules and regulations of the international telecommunications regime.

Since the formation of the International Telegraph Union in 1865, international communication has been the subject of intense European and, later, global control. Jealous of their national sovereignty, while also wishing to protect national military and commercial security, European governments vigorously policed their 'telegraphic ports' in the early days of the telegraphic revolution. The complexity of establishing, on a bilateral basis, rights of passage for telegraphic traffic created serious barriers to an internationally connected network. This in turn created the absurdity of telegrams

Box 1.2   Regional intergovernmental telecommunications organizations

The *Asia-Pacific Telecommunity (APT)*, founded in 1979, is based in Bangkok with 26 member countries.

In Africa, the *Pan-African Telecommunications Union (PATU)* was established in 1977 based on the desire to have a continental institution coordinate the development of telecommunications in Africa.

The Arab *Telecommunications Permanent Committee* of the Arab League groups the ministers of communications in the Arab-speaking world.

The *Conference of European Postal and Telecommunications Administrations (CEPT)* began as a consultative group of Western European PTTs (Post, Telegraph and Telephone administrations); it recently admitted members from Eastern Europe. With structural reform taking place in many countries in the region, CEPT has evolved into a grouping of ministries of communications and regulatory agencies, and operators have created their own group.

The *Inter-American Telecommunications Commission (CITEL)* is a branch of the Organization of American States; all countries in the region except Cuba are members.

The *Regional Commonwealth for Communications (RCC)*, based in Moscow, groups the posts and telecommunications ministries of the Commonwealth of Independent States.

Source: Extract from ITU, 1994b, p. 93, box 5.9

being decoded at national boundaries, walked through customs where a tariff was imposed, and then literally handed over to the telegraph office on the other side of the customs post (Cowhey, 1990). With the establishment of the ITU regime in 1865, international coordination and cooperation facilitated the more familiar practice of uninterrupted flow dependent on 'an international telegraph regime requiring its members to accept all international messages and to link the wires of the separate national systems into a single network' (Murphy, 1994, pp. 86–7). The advantages of this system meant that by the turn of the century the ITU's European regime had become global.

By the late twentieth century the problems of maintaining an effective global communications network have become much more complex and more highly politicized. The stakes are very high since the global market for the provision of communication services is huge: an estimated US$600 billion per annum in 1997. The implications for national sovereignty and autonomy are also considerable in that, unlike the early days of the telegraph, no state can effectively police or control the transnational flows of electronic mail, images, data, broadcasts and so on which cross its boundaries. A particularly interesting case in this regard is the Internet (see chapter 7).

The sheer scale of telecommunications activity is impressive: in 1980 there were 240,000 million international calls made from Germany, but by 1988 the figure was 600,352 million; and for Thailand and China the respective figures are 873 million to 12,646 million, and 1,075 million to 45,030 million (Zacher, 1992; and see chapter 7). In the six-year period from 1990 to 1996, the number of telephone lines alone increased from 520 million to 718 million, with the biggest growth coming from Asia (ITU estimates, *Financial Times*, 17 Mar. 1998, p. 1). Moreover, as the world's airwaves and satellite orbits have become more crowded, the role of the international telecommunications regime has become increasingly important in allocating international rights to exploit usable frequencies and satellite orbital slots free from undue interference. Without this kind of international regulatory activity, the entire system of global communications would become increasingly fragmented and, arguably, increasingly inefficient. Even countries such as Japan, the USA and the UK, which could opt out of aspects of the regime, have not done so because of the overall benefits of international coordination in such a crucial commercial sector.

The politics of the international telecommunications regime is significant for what it reveals about the shifting balance of state and corporate power in global politics. Until the 1970s the regime operated with little controversy. Since the global financial services revolution and the deregulation of the telecommunications business in the USA and the UK, however, the regime has become highly politicized. The basic norms of the regime – standardization of networks, collective decision-making over global commons issues (broadcast spectrum and satellite orbital slots), jointly provided services and multilateral coordination – remain intact. So too, for the most part, do the regime's rules and decision-making mechanisms. The result has been to ensure that all states have minimal levels of access to the system, particularly satellite-based communications, which a purely market-driven regime would not have provided. The regime has, in some sense, introduced elements of global equity into aspects of its international decision-making. Conditioning this approach is the distinctive institutional politics of the regime. This gives 'Third World' states and their national communications monopolies greater voting power than might be warranted by their economic status, although most decisions are taken by consensus.

However, as deregulation of the communications sectors in advanced economies has proceeded apace, a transnational coalition of multinational corporations has emerged to press for a more liberal international telecommunications regime. Backed also by a transnational community of finance and banking interests, which are reliant on cheap communications, the pressures for liberalization of the global communications market – to move further away from equity in decision-making – remain intense. These pressures reached their clearest expression in the run-up to the WTO agreement to liberalize international trade in basic telecommunications services which came into effect on 5 February 1998. Yet, even the USA, the most resolute proponent of global deregulation, has been prepared to date to accept 'the principle of planning a fixed satellite services system which allows each nation its own orbital position' in order to avoid the breakdown of the entire regulatory order (Vogler, 1992, p. 13).

The politics of the regime is shaped effectively by the interplay of a relatively small coalition of governments, corporate interests and technical specialists pressing for greater liberalization, and a much larger group of states, with their respective national communications monopolies and technical specialists, desiring to limit, but not necessarily prevent, further liberalization. The result is the complex interaction of international and transnational political forces in which political outcomes are mediated by the institutional dynamics of the regime itself.

The nature of the contemporary telecommunications regime illustrates the dynamic interplay between the domestic and the international domains. Furthermore, it reinforces the notion of global politics in so far as political space can no longer simply be conceived as coterminous with the boundedness of the territorial nation-state: politics and governance spill across national boundaries, such that there is no simple inside/outside or domestic/external duality. The telecommunications regime represents a type of functional political space which transcends national territorial boundaries and which articulates, in this case, a sense of political community not anchored in a territorial logic *per se*, but rather in a transnational community of interests whose commonality resides in members' positions as providers, consumers or regulators of international telecommunications services. In this respect, the global telecommunications infrastructure mediates the Westphalian order of states and rearticulates political interests, structures and outcomes.

1.3 Multilayered Governance and the Diffusion of Political Authority

The First and Second World Wars led to a growing acknowledgement that international governance could not rely on the balance of power if the most extreme forms of violence against humanity were to be outlawed, and the growing interconnectedness and interdependence of nations recognized. Slowly, the subject, scope and very sources of the Westphalian conception of international regulation, particularly its conception of international law, were all challenged (see Bull, 1977, ch. 6). It is useful to summarize some of the main legal transformations that have taken place, since these are indicative of underlying changes in global politics.

First, there has been a challenge mounted to the doctrine that international law, as Oppenheim put it, is a 'law between states only and exclusively' (see 1985, ch. 1). Individuals and groups have become recognized as subjects of international law on the basis of such innovatory agreements as the charters of the Nuremberg and Tokyo war crimes tribunals (1945), the Universal Declaration of Human Rights (1948), the Covenant on Civil and Political Rights (1966), and the European Convention on Human Rights (1950).

Second, opinion has moved against the doctrine that international law is primarily about political and geopolitical affairs. According to this new conception, international law is concerned increasingly with coordinating and regulating economic, social, communication and environmental matters. Linked to the substantial expansion in the number of actors and agencies in world politics – for example, the United Nations itself, the World Bank, the International Telecommunication Union, the Food and Agricultural Organization and the World Health Organization – there have been many pressures to increase the scope of international law. In line with this development, there are those who characterize the changing reach of international law as being ever less concerned with the freedom of states, and ever more with the general welfare of all those in the global system who are able to make their voices heard, such as corporations, pressure groups and so on (cf., for example, Röling, 1960; Friedmann, 1964; Cassese, 1986, esp. chs 7–9).

Third, the influential legal view that the only true source of international law is the consent of states – either their expressed consent, or their implied consent – has been called into question. Today, a number of sources of international law compete for recognition. These include the traditional sources such as international treaties or conventions which are recognized by states; international custom or practice which provides evidence of an accepted rule or set of rules; and the underlying principles of law recognized by 'civilized nations'. However, alongside these sources can now be found the 'will of the international community', which can assume the 'status of law' or which can become the 'basis of international legal obligation' under certain conditions (cf. Bull, 1977, pp. 147–58; Jenks, 1963, ch. 5; Falk, 1970, ch. 5). This notion represents a break in principle with the requirement that every individual state must offer its consent in the making of international rules and responsibilities. Furthermore, the vast array of formal and informal standards and rules agreed or adhered to in and through intergovernmental and transnational activities creates a dense patchwork of regulatory mechanisms which have far-reaching organizational consequences (see, for instance, sections 1.2.2 and 1.3.2 of this chapter).

1.3.1   The United Nations system

While the Westphalian model of international law had critics throughout the modern era, it was not until after the Second World War that a new model of international regulation was widely advocated and accepted, culminating in the adoption of the UN Charter. The changes introduced by the Charter raised fundamental questions about the nature and form of international law, questions which point to the possibility of a significant disjuncture between the law of nation-states – of the states system – and of the wider international community. For at the heart of these changes lies a conflict between claims made on behalf of individual states and those made on behalf of an alternative organizing principle of world affairs: ultimately, a community of states, with equal voting rights in the General Assembly of nation-states, openly and collectively regulating international life while constrained to observe the UN Charter and a battery of human rights conventions. However, this conflict is far from settled, and it would be misleading to conclude that the era of the UN Charter model simply displaced the Westphalian logic of international governance.

The image of international regulation projected by the Charter (and related documents) was one of 'states still jealously "sovereign"', but linked together now in a 'myriad of relations'; subject in principle to tight restrictions on the resort to force; under pressure to resolve disagreements by peaceful means and according to legal criteria; and constrained to observe 'certain standards' with regard to the treatment of all persons on their territory, including their own citizens (Cassese, 1991, p. 256). Of course, just how restrictive the provisions of the Charter have been to states is an important issue. Before addressing it, leading elements of the Charter model should be outlined: see box 1.3.

The organizations and procedures of the UN were designed partly to avoid the weakness that had been evident in the League of Nations (see Zimmern, 1936; Osiander, 1994, ch. 5), and to accommodate the international power structure as it was understood in 1945. The political division of the globe into powerful nation-states, with distinctive sets of geopolitical interests, was built into the Charter system. One of the most obvious manifestations of this was the special veto power accorded to the Permanent Members of the UN Security Council. This privileged political status added authority

Box 1.3 The UN Charter model

1   The world community consists of sovereign states, connected through a dense network of relations, both ad hoc and institutionalized. Individuals and groups are regarded as legitimate actors in international relations (albeit with limited roles).

2   Certain peoples oppressed by colonial powers, racist regimes or foreign occupying forces are assigned rights of recognition and a determinate role in articulating their future and interests. The principle of self-determination is legitimized.

3   There is a gradual acceptance of standards and values which call into question the principle of effective state power; accordingly, major violations of given international rules are not in theory to be regarded as legitimate. Restrictions are placed on the resort to force, including the unwarranted use of economic force.

4   New rules, procedures and institutions designed to aid law-making and law enforcement in international affairs are created.

5   Legal principles delimiting the form and scope of the conduct of all members of the international community, and providing a set of guidelines for the structuring of international rules, are adopted.

6   Fundamental concern is expressed for the rights of individuals, and a corpus of international rules is created seeking to constrain states to observe certain standards in the treatment of all, including their own citizens.

7   The preservation of peace, the advancement of human rights and the establishment of greater social justice are the stated collective priorities; 'public affairs' include the whole of the international community. With respect to certain values – peace, the prohibition of genocide – international rules now provide in principle for the personal responsibility of state officials and the attribution of criminal acts to states.

8   Systematic inequalities among peoples and states are recognized and new rules – including the concept of 'the common heritage of mankind'* – are established to create ways of governing the distribution, appropriation and exploitation of territory, property and natural resources.

* First propounded in the late 1960s, the concept of 'the common heritage of mankind' was proposed as a device to exclude a state or private right of appropriation over certain resources and to permit the development of those resources, where appropriate, for the benefit of all, with due regard paid to environmental protection.

Source: Extract from Held, 1995, p. 86, adapted from Cassese, 1986, pp. 398–400

and legitimacy to the position of each of the major powers; for although they were barred in principle from the use of force on terms contrary to the Charter, they were protected by their veto against censure and sanctions in the event of unilateral action. As a result, the UN was virtually immobilized during the Cold War as an autonomous actor on many pressing issues (see Falk, 1975a, pp. 169–96, 1975b, pp. 69–72; Cassese, 1986, pp. 142–3, 200–1, 213–14, 246–50). Moreover, the Charter gave renewed credence (through Article 51) to unilateral military action if it was necessary in 'self-defence', since there was no clear delimitation of the meaning of this phrase. In certain respects, therefore, the Charter framework represents an extension of the interstate system.

However, the UN Charter system has also been distinctively innovative and influential in a number of ways. It has provided an international deliberative forum in which, in principle, all states are equal in certain respects, a forum of particular value to many developing countries and to those seeking a basis for 'consensus' solutions to international problems. It has provided a formal framework for decolonization, and for the pursuit of the reform of international institutions. Moreover, it has aided the development of an elaborate system of governance for the provision of 'international public goods', from international air traffic control, telecommunications and posts (bringing some of the earlier established international organizations under its auspices) to the control of contagious diseases, humanitarian relief for refugees and victims of natural disasters, and the protection of the environmental commons (especially the ozone layer and climate alteration) (see Imber, 1997; and see chapters 2 and 8 below). All these 'goods' require international cooperation in order to deliver and safeguard them effectively. This requirement has, in turn, helped engender an extensive system of global governance (see box 1.4), albeit one which has evolved piecemeal over time and been subject to intense political conflict and financial pressure (see Childers, 1993).

Further, the UN has provided a vision, valuable in spite of all its limitations, of alternative principles of global governance to those of traditional geopolitics, principles based on collective decision-making between governments and non-governmental organizations, and, under appropriate circumstances, of a supranational presence in world affairs championing human rights. Indeed, this vision, if carried to its logical extreme, challenges the whole principle that humankind can or should be organized as a society of sovereign states above all else. This development needs further consideration (see below, chapter 2 and the conclusion).

1.3.2   The human rights regime

Changes in international law have placed individuals, governments and non-governmental organizations under new systems of legal regulation. International law recognizes powers and constraints, and rights and duties, which have qualified the principle of state sovereignty in a number of important respects; sovereignty *per se* is no longer a straightforward guarantee of international legitimacy. Entrenched in certain legal instruments is the view that a legitimate state must be a democratic state that upholds certain common values (see Crawford, 1994). One significant area in this regard is human rights law and human rights regimes.

'The defence of human dignity knows no boundaries,' observes Emilio Mignone, an Argentinean human rights campaigner (quoted in Brysk, 1993, p. 281). This statement captures important elements of the international human rights regime as a global political and legal framework for promoting rights. It also highlights the potential conflict which can exist between a universal understanding of human rights and the political organization of the world into sovereign nation-states. Human rights activists, like Mignone, vigorously reject the notion of the nation-state as a bounded political space within which political authorities can treat their citizens as they wish. Sovereignty, by contrast, involves not just supreme power over a political community within a delimited territory, but also a claim by the state to withstand – as a matter of right – intervention in its domestic affairs by external agencies. The very existence of international human rights, therefore, can be considered (and is by many governments) as an unwarranted intrusion into the internal affairs of states. Yet, in the post-Second World War era, a

Box 1.4 United Nations organizations and specialized agencies

UN organizations

Created by the General Assembly after 1945, these organizations are funded from the UN's own budget raised by membership contributions and by additional voluntary contributions. Taken together, they embrace the social and economic functions of the UN.

Acronym	Name	HQ
UNCTAD	UN Conference on Trade and Development	Geneva
UNICEF	UN Children's Fund	New York
UNHCR	UN High Commission for Refugees	Geneva
UNDP	UN Development Programme	New York
UNEP	UN Environment Programme	Nairobi
WFP	World Food Programme	Rome
UNFPA	UN Fund for Population Activities	New York

UN specialized agencies

Legally separate organizations, many of which predate the UN, with their own membership, budgets and programmes. Nominally, the specialized agencies are subject to coordination by the UN via its Economic and Social Council, and an annual heads of agencies meeting, called the Administrative Committee on Coordination.

Acronym	Name	Founded	HQ
ITU	International Telecommunication Union	1865	Geneva
WMO	World Meteorological Organization	1873	Geneva
UPU	Universal Postal Union	1874	Bern
ILO	International Labour Organization	1919	Geneva
ICAO	International Civil Aviation Organization	1944	Montreal
IMF	International Monetary Fund	1944	Washington DC
IBRD	International Bank for Reconstruction and Development (World Bank)	1944	Washington DC
FAO	Food and Agriculture Organization	1945	Rome
UNESCO	United Nations Educational, Scientific and Cultural Organization	1945	Paris
WHO	World Health Organization	1946	Geneva
IMCO	International Maritime Consultancy Organization	1948	London
GATT (WTO)	General Agreement on Tariffs and Trade (now World Trade Organization)	1948	Geneva
IFC	International Finance Corporation (IBRD subsidiary)	1956	Washington DC
IAEA	International Atomic Energy Agency	1957	Vienna
IDA	International Development Association (IBRD subsidiary)	1960	Washington DC
UNIDO	UN Industrial Development Organization	1967	Vienna

Source: Adapted from Imber, 1997, pp. 206–7

substantial majority of states have either supported or acquiesced in the development of a comprehensive international human rights regime.

The contemporary human rights regime consists of overlapping global, regional and national institutions and conventions. At the global level, human rights are firmly entrenched in the International Bill of Human Rights, which comprises the UN Declaration of Human Rights of 1948 and the several conventions on civil, political and economic rights adopted predominantly in the 1960s and 1970s. These were complemented in the 1980s by the Convention on the Elimination of Discrimination against Women and the Convention on the Rights of the Child. The UN Commission on Human Rights (UNCHR) is responsible for policing this system and bringing persistent abuses to the attention of the UN Security Council. In addition, the International Labour Organization (ILO) is charged, in principle, with policing the area of workers' rights.

Within most of the world's regions there is an equivalent legal structure and machinery. In the case of Europe, the European Commissioner for Human Rights, the European Court of Human Rights and the Organization for Security and Cooperation in Europe (OSCE) oversee human rights issues and adjudicate on abuses. In Africa, the Banjul Charter, and in the Americas, the Inter-American Committee on Human Rights of the Organization of American States (OAS), have similar functions. But perhaps as significant in promoting human rights, if not more so, are the multiplicity of international non-governmental organizations such as Amnesty International, the League of Human Rights and the International Commission of Jurists.

Since the 1970s 'both the number of human rights NGOs and the level of their activity has increased dramatically' (Donnelly, 1993, p. 14). There are now over 200 US NGOs associated with human rights issues, a similar number in the UK and across Europe, and expanding numbers of such organizations within the developing world. The significance of these NGOs is not simply that they monitor and publicize human rights abuses, but that they also campaign on specific causes and, combined, form a global network of human rights organizations. They can operate transnationally with the consequence that they are able to bypass governments and establish vigorous global or regional networks of activists. In effect, these human rights NGOs represent a distinctive kind of transnational social movement which in many national contexts is regarded as radical both in terms of its espousal of individual rights and in its claim to defend the autonomy of civil society against the possible dictates of the state.

Each of the main UN human rights covenants has now been ratified by over 140 out of 190 states, and more are expected to ratify them. Increasing numbers of states appear willing to accept, in principle, general duties of protection and provision, as well as of restraint, in their own procedures and practices (see Beetham, 1998). While these commitments are rarely backed by coercive powers of enforcement, the demands of the new international human rights regimes – formal and informal – have created a plethora of groups, movements, agencies and lawyers all engaged in reworking the nature of national politics, national sovereignty and state accountability.

However, it would be wrong simply to conclude that the global human rights regime is a powerful deterrent to the violation of human rights. Even international action against Argentina in the late 1970s and early 1980s (see box 1.5) did not, by itself, bring about the termination of human rights abuses. Further, even the formal organs of the regime, such as the UNCHR, have no coercive powers to uphold rights. In addition, since states still claim sovereign immunity there is often little that can be done except

Box 1.5 The transnational struggle over human rights

A telling illustration of the global role of NGOs in the area of human rights issues concerns the case of Argentina in the late 1970s and early 1980s, following the military coup of 1976.

In 1977, during a visit to Argentina, US Secretary of State Cyrus Vance handed to the president of the military junta a list of 7,500 cases of unexplained 'political disappearances', a list prepared initially by Argentinean human rights activists and forwarded to Washington-based human rights NGOs. (This figure represents only about a quarter of the number of people who are estimated to have 'disappeared' during almost eight years of dictatorship.) By mobilizing the machinery of the international human rights regime and global networks of human rights NGOs, Argentinean activists were able to bring world media and political attention to focus on the country's human rights record. Concerted mobilization of international pressure through transnational networks, the UNCHR, OAS and individual governments involved intense global and regional political activity (see Fisher, 1989). Las Madres de Plazo de Mayo (the Mothers of the Plaza de Mayo), or Mothers of the Disappeared, one of the best-known human rights groups in Argentina:

> visited the United States, Canada and Europe in 1978 . . . were delegates to the Catholic Church's Pueblo Conference, the OAS and the United Nations in 1979, testified before the US Congress in the same year, and were nominated for three Nobel Prizes in 1980. When Las Madres toured Europe . . . they were received as visiting dignitaries by the Prime Minister of Spain, the French President, and the Pope. (Brysk, 1993, p. 265)

In turn, this activity focused bilateral and multilateral pressure from the US and European governments on the Argentinean state, including aid cut-offs, 'inspections' from the UN and OAS, and other sanctions. External assistance from such diverse sources as the Ford Foundation, the World Council of Churches, Amnesty International, the Norwegian Parliament, Dutch churches, the governments of the USA, France, Sweden, Denmark and Switzerland, and the UN, ensured, too, that the civil liberties and human rights movements in Argentina remained highly active throughout the entire period of the military dictatorship. As a consequence, it is possible to argue that the 'international human rights regime was both an ally and arena for the Argentine human rights movement' (Brysk, 1993, p. 266). In other words, it was in some sense an extension of national political space, and a new sphere in which the civil rights struggle could be advanced.

to publicize key cases and agitate for bilateral and multilateral action in international fora. Nevertheless, the political and legal significance of the regime, in qualifying the notion of the rightful authority of the state, should not be underestimated. In this regard, the European Convention for the Protection of Human Rights and Fundamental Freedoms (1950) is particularly noteworthy. In marked contrast to the Universal Declaration of Human Rights and the subsequent UN Covenants on Rights, the European Convention was concerned, as its preamble states, 'to take the first steps for the collective enforcement of certain of the rights stated in the Universal Declaration'. The European initiative was and remains a most radical legal innovation: an innovation which, against the stream of state history, allows individual citizens to initiate proceedings against their own governments. Within this framework, states are no longer free to treat their own citizens as they think fit (Capotorti, 1983, p. 977).

In regional and international law, accordingly, there has been a gradual shift – albeit unevenly experienced and reinforced – away from the principle that state sovereignty must be safeguarded irrespective of its consequences for individuals, groups and organizations. Respect for the autonomy of the subject, and for an extensive range of human rights, creates a new set of ordering principles in political affairs which can delimit and curtail the principle of effective state power. These developments are indicative of an alteration in the weight granted, on the one hand, to claims made on behalf of the state system and, on the other hand, to those made on behalf of an alternative organizing principle of world order, in which unqualified state sovereignty no longer reigns supreme.

A further telling example in this regard is the tendency in contemporary international law to entrench the notion that a legitimate state must be a state that upholds certain common democratic values (see Crawford and Marks, 1998). For instance, in Article 21 the Universal Declaration of Human Rights asserts the democratic principle along with enumerated rights as a 'common standard of achievement for all peoples and nations' (see UN, 1988, pp. 2, 5). However, the word 'democracy' does not itself appear in the Declaration and the adjective 'democratic' appears again only once (in Article 29). By contrast, the UN International Covenant on Civil and Political Rights (1966) (which came into force in 1976) elaborates this principle in Article 25, making a number of different rights agreements and conventions into a binding treaty (see UN, 1988, p. 28). According to Article 25 of the Covenant:

> Every citizen shall have the right and the opportunity, without . . . unreasonable restrictions:
> (a) to take part in the conduct of public affairs, directly or through freely chosen representatives;
> (b) to vote and to be elected at genuine periodic elections which shall be by universal and equal suffrage and shall be held by secret ballot, guaranteeing the free expression of the will of the electors;
> (c) to have access, on general terms of equality, to public service in his country.

The American Convention on Human Rights, along with other regional conventions, contains clear echoes of Article 21 of the Universal Declaration as well as of Article 25 of the Covenant on Civil and Political Rights, while the European Convention on Human Rights is most explicit in connecting democracy with state legitimacy, as is the statute of the Council of Europe, which makes a commitment to democracy a condition of membership. Although such commitments often remain fragile, they further signal the beginnings of a new approach to the concept of legitimate political power in international law; that is to say, they entrench in international law the notion that a legitimate political power must be, on the one hand, a form of political power that is accountable to the members of the political community in which it is embedded and, on the other, a promoter of fundamental human rights.

The challenge to the legal efficacy of state sovereignty is evidenced further in the recognition of the necessity to uphold certain rights of distinctive minority groups, or of persons belonging to such groups (see Crawford and Marks, 1998). Since 1989 concerns about interethnic conflict have created an urgent sense that specific minorities need protection. In 1992 the United Nations General Assembly adopted a Declaration on the Rights of Persons Belonging to National, Ethnic, Religious and Linguistic

Minorities. Proclaiming that states 'shall protect the existence and national, cultural, religious and linguistic identity of minorities', the Declaration sets out rights for members of minorities to be able 'to participate effectively in cultural, religious, social and public life'. While the Declaration is not yet legally binding, it is widely regarded as establishing a future trajectory of international law. In other contexts, the impetus to secure protection for minority rights is particularly noteworthy. Within the Council of Europe, a Charter for Regional and Minority Languages and a Framework Convention for the Protection of National Minorities have been elaborated. Moreover, the Organization for Security and Cooperation in Europe (the OSCE) has adopted a series of instruments affirming minority rights and has founded the office of High Commissioner for National Minorities to provide 'early warning' and 'early action' with respect to 'tensions involving national minority issues' (Crawford and Marks, 1998, pp. 76–7).

These developments are important signs of the shift away from the Westphalian, state-centric focus in international law to what amounts to a new tendency for the delimitation of state sovereignty. A final telling example to be mentioned in this context is the erosion of the traditional view that humanitarian intervention to prevent grave violations of human rights is unacceptable simply because it infringes the principle of national sovereignty. This is evident in UN-sponsored interventions in Iraq, Somalia and Bosnia. For instance, UN Security Council resolution 688 (5 April 1991), which legitimized the notion of safe havens for Kurds within Iraq, 'broke new ground in the degree to which it involved the Security Council in taking a stand against a state's ill treatment of its own people' (Greenwood, 1993, p. 36). As a consequence, the traditional priority accorded to state sovereignty over humanitarian demands is being reconsidered. Of course, the impact of this reconsideration is unevenly experienced across the globe. Nevertheless, it is reasonable to hold that 'there is now an area of domestic conduct in regard to human rights . . . that is under the scrutiny of international law. This does not issue a general licence for intervention . . . But it does expose the internal regimes of all the members of international society to the legitimate appraisal of their peers' (Vincent, 1986, p. 152). And it is reasonable to hold that, as Crawford and Marks remark, 'international law, with its enlarging normative scope, extending writ and growing institutionalization, exemplifies the phenomenon of globalization' (1998, p. 82).

1.3.3   From international to cosmopolitan law

By cosmopolitan law, or global law, or global humanitarian law, is meant a domain of law different in kind from the law of states and the law made between one state and another for the mutual enhancement of their geopolitical interests (see Held, 1995, ch. 10). Cosmopolitan law refers here to those elements of law – albeit created by states – which create powers and constraints, and rights and duties, which transcend the claims of nation-states and which have far-reaching national consequences. Elements of such law define and seek to protect basic humanitarian values which can come into conflict, and sometimes contradiction, with national laws. These values set down basic standards or boundaries which no political agent, whether a representative of a government or state, should, in principle, be able to cross.

Box 1.6 Rules of warfare

'Major instruments that set forth the "laws of war" and their main fields of application include (1) the Declaration of Paris of 1856, which limited sea warfare by abolishing privateering and specifying that a blockade had to be effective to be legally binding; (2) the Geneva Convention of 1864 (revised in 1906), which provided for humane treatment for the wounded in the field; (3) the Hague Convention of 1899, which codified many of the accepted practices of land warfare; (4) the Hague Convention of 1907, which revised the 1899 Convention concerning the rights and duties of belligerents and of neutral states and persons, and proclaimed rules governing such new weapons as dumdum bullets, poisonous gas, and the use of balloons for bombing; (5) the Geneva Conventions of 1929, which provided for decent treatment for prisoners of war and the sick and wounded; (6) the London Protocol of 1936, which limited the use of submarines against merchant ships; and (7) the Geneva Convention of 1949, which updated rules concerning the treatment of prisoners, the sick and wounded, and the protection of civilians. In addition to these and other minor conventions and regional treaties, belligerents in the contemporary world are bound by customary international law and a "law of humanity" forbidding unwarranted cruelty or other actions affronting public morality but not covered by either customary or treaty law.'

Source: Plano and Olton, 1988, p. 193

It has already been argued in the previous section that human rights regimes and human rights law sit uneasily with the idea of accepting state sovereignty alone as the proper principle for the organization of relations within and between political communities. They have been treated separately (section 1.3.2) because of their centrality to contemporary global politics. But they could be thought of as an element of cosmopolitan law, along with the law of war, the law governing war crimes and crimes against humanity, and environmental law. Together, these domains of law constitute a developing set of standards and constraints which bear upon and qualify the notion of an untrammelled principle of state sovereignty. While commitment to these standards often remains weak, they signal a further change affecting the concept of legitimate state power in regional and global law.

The formation of the rules of warfare has been based on the assumption that, while war cannot be completely abolished, some of its most appalling consequences, for soldiers and citizens alike, should be rendered illegal and, therefore, warfare should be made as humane as possible. The aim of the rules of warfare is to limit conduct during war to minimum standards of civilized behaviour that will be upheld by all parties to the armed conflict. While the rules of warfare are often violated during wars, they have served in the past to provide a break on some of the more indiscriminate acts of destruction that could in principle be perpetrated. The major multilateral conventions governing war are set out in box 1.6.

The rules of warfare form an evolving framework of regulations seeking to restrain the conduct of belligerents in the course of international armed conflicts. The rules are premised on the 'dual notion that the adverse effects of war should be alleviated as much as possible (given military necessities), and that the freedom of the parties to resort to methods and means of warfare is not unlimited' (Dinstein, 1993, p. 966). While most of the rules of warfare evolved as customary law these rules are now codified in numerous international agreements. These agreements mark, in principle, a significant change over time in the legal direction of the modern state, for they challenge the principle of military discipline and question national sovereignty at one of its most sensitive points: the relation between the military and the state and the capacity of the military to pursue 'reasons of state' irrespective of the consequences for other peoples. The use of state violence during interstate war is, in principle, circumscribed.

This process of the gradual 'legal circumscription' of the state is illustrated as well by the rights that some states themselves have conceded to individuals who refuse to serve in national armies. By recognizing legally the status of conscientious objection, many states have also accepted that there are clear occasions when an individual has a moral obligation beyond that of his or her obligation as a citizen of a state (see Vincent, 1992, pp. 269–92). These 'transcendent obligations' are exemplified further by the results of the International Tribunal at Nuremberg (and the parallel tribunal in Tokyo). The Tribunal laid down, for the first time in history, that when *international rules* that protect basic humanitarian values are in conflict with *state laws*, every individual must transgress the state laws (except where there is no room for 'moral choice') (Cassese, 1988, p. 132). Contemporary international law has generally endorsed the position taken by the Tribunal, and has affirmed its rejection of the defence of obedience to superior orders in matters of responsibility for crimes against peace and humanity.

> Since the Nuremberg Trials, it has been acknowledged that war criminals cannot relieve themselves of criminal responsibility by citing official position or superior orders. Even obedience to explicit national legislation provides no protection against international law. Additionally, war crimes are not subject to the application of ordinary rules of statutes of limitations. Hence, there is no time limit on the prosecutions, which can commence after many decades. (Dinstein, 1993, p. 968)

The rule systems governing warfare and crimes against humanity are mainly concerned with the perpetration of violence against people during war. However, many forms of violence perpetrated against individuals, and many forms of abuse of power, do not take place during declared acts of war. In fact, it has recently been argued that the distinctions between war and peace, and between aggression and repression, are eroded by changing patterns of violence (Kaldor, 1998). The kinds of violence witnessed in the Bosnian conflict in 1993–5 highlight the role of paramilitaries and of organized crime, and the use of parts of national armies which may no longer be under the direct control of a state. Such groups use forms of violence which are often dispersed, fragmented and directed against civilians. They commit atrocities and rape, and mount sieges. They often aim to pursue a form of identity politics or ethnic exclusion. What these kinds of 'warfare' signal is that there is a very fine line between explicit formal crimes committed during acts of national war, and often major attacks on the welfare and physical integrity of citizens in situations that may not involve a declaration of war by states. While many of the new forms of warfare do not fall directly under the classic rules of war, they are massive violations of international human rights. Accordingly, the rules of war and human rights law can be seen as necessarily *complementary* forms of international rules (see Kaldor, 1998). The ground which is being staked out now in international legal agreements suggests that the containment of armed aggression and abuses of power can only be achieved through both the control of warfare and the prevention of the abuse of human rights. The weaknesses in the enforcement of human rights regimes have already been discussed. The weaknesses in the enforcement of the rules of warfare are also only too apparent. Nonetheless, the rules of warfare and human rights regimes together lay down principles and norms about national and international political behaviour which, in principle, circumscribe the proper form and scope of sovereignty. For all the limitations of enforcement, these are significant changes. If the rules and rights discussed were enforced impartially, this would represent a very considerable development in international law and in the nature of the organizational principles governing the conduct of political communities towards one another.

The challenge to the efficacy of state sovereignty can be illustrated further by another arena of emerging regulation: the law governing the environment and the use of natural resources. In this domain there has been a questioning of the traditional principles regulating the appropriation of territory and resources. At the heart of classical Westphalian international law, the earth, sea and air were recognized as phenomena legitimately falling under the sovereign authority of states on the condition that 'whoever possessed a territory and exercised actual control over it successfully secured a legal title' (see Cassese, 1986, pp. 376–7). While the principle of state sovereignty has been extended in recent times to cover the control of resources in a variety of domains, including the continental shelf and exclusive 'economic zones' (areas which stretch up to 200 nautical miles from coastal states), a new concept was propounded in 1967 as a potential vehicle for rethinking the legal basis of the appropriation and exploitation of resources: the 'common heritage of mankind' (see box 1.3 above). Although the principle was subject to intensive discussion in the United Nations and elsewhere, it was eventually enshrined in two important treaties, the Convention on the Moon and Other Celestial Bodies (1979) and the Convention on the Law of the Sea (1982). First introduced as a way of thinking about the impact of new technologies opening up the possibility of the exploitation of natural resources – on the seabed or on the moon and other planets – which were beyond national jurisdiction, its early champions saw it as a basis for arguing that the vast domain of hitherto untapped resources should be developed for the benefit of all, particularly the poor and the developing nations.

Among the key elements of the concept of the common heritage are the exclusion of a right of appropriation; the duty to exploit resources in the interest of humankind; and the duty to explore and utilize resources for peaceful purposes only (Cassese, 1986, p. 390). The introduction of the concept of the common heritage points to the possibility of a legal order based on equity and cooperation. Although there is still a great deal of argument as to exactly where and how this principle should be applied, and how the benefits accruing from the exploitation of new resources should be distributed, the introduction of the concept was a turning point in international legal thinking.

In sum, the rules of war, laws governing crimes against humanity, the innovations in legal thinking on the use of resources and human rights regimes all mark a shift in direction so far as the subject and scope of international law are concerned. Opinion has moved against the doctrine that international law must be a law between states only and exclusively. At issue is the emergence of a vast body of rules, quasi-rules and legal changes which are beginning to alter the basis of coexistence and cooperation in the global order. The legal innovations referred to challenge the idea that the supreme normative principle of the political organization of humankind can and should remain simply that of sovereign statehood. Most recently, proposals put forward for the establishment of an international criminal court add further testimony to the gradual shift towards a 'universal constitutional order' (see Crawford, 1995; Dugard, 1997; Weller, 1997). The new legal frameworks set out to curtail and delimit state sovereignty, and set basic standards and values for the treatment of all during war and peace. These new standards and values are the basis of what is called here the emerging framework of cosmopolitan law. Of course, this body of law is by no means subscribed to systematically; but it points to the development of a post-Westphalian order – a new global politics setting down a new legal framework for the conduct and regulation of relations among political communities.

1.3.4 Regionalism: new layers of governance

The emergence of global politics and elements of cosmopolitan law has gone hand in hand with the development of new forms of regionalism. Many of these will be explored in later chapters (see chapters 2, 3 and 5). At issue here is the development of forms of *political* regionalism. By political regionalism is meant a geographical cluster of contiguous nation-states which share a number of common attributes, have significant levels of interaction, and which enjoy institutionalized cooperation through a formal multilateral structure. Thus within Europe it is possible to identify the European Union with the political and economic boundaries of a regional community of states and societies, while in South Asia the Association of South East Asian Nations (ASEAN) defines the boundaries of a developing regional political complex.

The EU is probably best described neither as an international regime nor as a federal state, but as a network of states involving the pooling of sovereignty (see Keohane and Hoffmann, 1990, p. 10). The EU was founded on a series of 'intergovernmental bargains', bargains which have more recently included the Single European Act (1986), the Maastricht Treaty (1991) and the Amsterdam Treaty (1997). More than any other kind of international organization, the political processes of the EU can be described by the term 'supranationality'. It is important to bear in mind that the Union's powers were gained by the 'willing surrender' of aspects of sovereignty by individual states – a 'surrender' which, arguably, has actually helped strengthen European nation-states in the face of the dominance of the US in the first three decades after the Second World War and the rise of the economic challenge of Asia-Pacific (see Wallace, 1994). Furthermore, the member states of the European Union retain the final and most general power in many areas of their affairs, while the entrenchment of the notion of 'subsidiarity' within the EU legal framework after Maastricht enhanced policy choices for states in certain spheres (see Neunreither, 1993). However, within the Union, sovereignty is now also clearly divided: any conception of sovereignty which assumes that it is an indivisible, illimitable, exclusive and perpetual form of public power – embodied within an individual state – is outmoded.

The member states of the European Union are no longer the sole centres of power within their own borders. As the European Court of Justice noted, 'by creating a Community of unlimited duration, having its own institutions, its own personality . . . and, more particularly, real powers stemming from a limitation of sovereignty or a transfer of powers from the States to the Community, the member States have limited their sovereign rights' (Mancini, 1990, p. 180). Within Union institutions, the Council of Ministers has a particularly significant position, for it has at its disposal powerful legal instruments which allow it to formulate and enact policy with a minimum of national democratic accountability. Of all these instruments, 'regulations' are the most notable because they have the status of law independently of any further negotiation or action on the part of member states. Disputes about national interpretations and applications of regulations (or directives) can be heard at the European Court of Justice; and the Court has taken on a major role in the harmonization of law within the Union. Moreover, with the passing of the Single European Act, unanimity within the Council of Ministers has been replaced by 'qualified majority voting' for a significant number of issue areas (see Noel, 1989). While there are certain safeguards to national sovereignty built into this change (decisions about which issues can be decided by majority voting must themselves be based on unanimity), policies can be adopted which are opposed by individual governments. The place of national sovereignty is, thus, no longer guaranteed.

The treaty agreed at the Maastricht summit of 1991 seeks, moreover, not only to extend the scope of economic and monetary union, but also to extend the framework of political integration to other spheres. In particular, it significantly advances the notion of EU citizenship: every national citizen of a member country of the EU is now also a citizen of the Union with the right to travel and reside anywhere within the EU and the right to vote and contest political office in the country of their residence. Accordingly, the importance of old political borders further declines and the process of deterritorialization continues. Freedom of movement and the right to political participation wherever one resides challenges a traditional basis of loyalty to a single state (see Khan, 1996). If the Maastricht treaty were to be fully implemented, along with the social terms and conditions of the Amsterdam treaty (concerned to outlaw discrimination based on gender, race, religion, nationality, among other categories), the member states would have taken several major steps towards becoming a highly integrated supranational political association (see Pinder, 1991; Ross, 1995).

The intensity of political interactions in Europe mark it off in important respects from the increasing intensity of international interactions in general. Wallace explains this in the following terms:

> What is distinctive about Europe is . . . the creation of a relatively stable institutional network for intergovernmental bargaining for the accommodation of shared interests across a very broad agenda; and . . . the existence of common traditions, history, culture and political values, to which political leaders and institution builders can appeal for support in legitimizing the rules they have agreed to implement and the burdens they have agreed to share. (1994, p. 20)

Thus the European region can be differentiated from more general processes of increasing global flows and interactions not only by the internal density of political interaction but also on the basis of shared cultural and historical connections. The existence and development of a formal intergovernmental institutional framework enables the further development of these interactions and common histories. However, it would be wrong to exaggerate the degree to which both geographically and functionally the European region represents a simple political, social and cultural unity.

The European region is made up of a number of subregions and regimes which stack up on top of each other to produce a patchwork effect. The fifteen EU members and their shared institutions provide a core around which the rest of European interaction is increasingly focused. However, even within the Union there are clearly differences between the original six members and the later members. Beyond the EU core, EFTA and NATO membership produces a second concentric ring of interaction and institutional forms in the European region: in the case of NATO institutions lock Europe into global military networks, while in the case of the Scandinavian countries institutions and interactions exist which cut across EU regimes. Finally, Eastern and Central Europe, the Balkans and the states of the ex-Soviet Union all maintain a variety of diverse relations and interactions with the European core.

Since the end of the Cold War, there has been a significant acceleration in the institutionalization of regional relations beyond Europe: in the Americas, Asia-Pacific and, to a lesser degree, in Africa. But the forms taken by this regionalism are radically different from the integrationist model of the EU. Indeed, to date the rest of the world has largely rejected the EU model as something to emulate directly. Unlike the Westphalian principle of sovereign statehood, the Brussels principle of 'pooled sovereignty' has found little resonance in Kuala Lumpur, Brazilia or Lagos. Instead, beyond Europe, a more open form of regionalism has developed, referred to by the notion of the 'new regionalism'. This is evident most explicitly in the Asia-Pacific.

Building on the relative success of the core subregional grouping of ASEAN, several nations of the Pacific Rim came together in late 1989 to establish a multilateral forum to enhance intergovernmental cooperation. APEC (Asia-Pacific Economic Cooperation), as it is known, was initially regarded as 'four adjectives in search of a noun'. But since its inception membership has expanded to include all the major states in the region and it has spawned a vast array of working groups and intergovernmental networks for the purposes of extending free trade and capital liberalization within the region. APEC is guided by regular ministerial meetings across a range of key policy domains, and annual summit meetings of heads of state which seek to set the regional agenda. Serviced by a small secretariat in Singapore, APEC represents a 'new regionalism' in the Asia-Pacific which, although restricted to economic matters, is evolving into a significant institutionalized forum for multilateral cooperation ('open regionalism') rather than regional political integration ('closed regionalism') (Ravenhill, 1998). While it does not involve legally binding agreements, APEC has agreed an action agenda for economic cooperation and the 'spirit of community in the Asia-Pacific' which includes specific commitments to regional free trade by 2010.

In addition to APEC, there is also an evolving regional security dialogue institutionalized in the ASEAN Regional Forum (ARF) (see chapter 2). In parallel with APEC and ARF there are also a range of region-wide transnational associations, such as PECC (Pacific Economic Cooperation Council), PBEC (Pacific Basin Economic Council), PAFTAD (Pacific Trade and Development) and CSCAP (Council for Security Cooperation Asia-Pacific) (Yamamoto, 1995). These elite associations are also mirrored by developing regional links and cooperation among social movements and citizen groups, from the women's movement, religious groups and environmental groups, to coalitions such as the 'People's Summit' held alongside the official APEC annual summit in Vancouver in November 1997 (Woods, 1998).

This 'new regionalism' is also evident in developments in Latin America, especially the creation of MERCOSUR (Southern Cone Common Market) in 1991. The principal aim of MERCOSUR is to encourage closer economic integration among Southern American states, partly in response to the development of NAFTA (North American Free Trade Agreement) (Grugel, 1996). Beyond Latin America too there are also more limited regional initiatives in the Arab Middle East, such as the GCC (Gulf Cooperation Council), AMU (Arab Maghreb Union) and ACC (Arab Cooperation Council) (Tripp, 1995). In addition, established regional initiatives in Africa, the Caribbean, Asia and the Pacific Islands have been reinvigorated as the Cold War has ended and regionalism elsewhere has become more intense.

Furthermore, there is a growing interregional diplomacy as these 'old' and 'new' regional groupings seek to consolidate their relationships with each other, whether in terms of access to markets or simply a diplomatic dialogue. Through ASEM (Asia-Europe Meeting), convened in 1996, the EU and ASEAN states have established a diplomatic dialogue on areas of common concern from economics to human rights, while the EU has signed agreements with MERCOSUR and entered into discussions with NAFTA on creating an AFTA (Atlantic Free Trade Area). Similarly the US, as the principal agent of NAFTA, has entered a dialogue with MERCOSUR with respect to encouraging closer cooperation. In this respect, the 'new regionalism' is not a barrier to political globalization but, on the contrary, entirely compatible with it – if not an indirect encouragement.

1.4   Historical Forms of Political Globalization: the Transformation of Political Community

The fundamental transformations described so far are set out in grids 1.1 and 1.2, which summarize the shift, first, to the development of territorially based political communities and, second, to an emerging era of global politics and multilayered global and regional governance. The first shift is marked by the growing centralization of political power within Europe, the sedimentation of political rule into state structures, the territorialization of politics, the spread of the interstate order, the development of forms of accountability within certain states and, at the same time, the denial of such accountability to others through colonial expansion, conquest and war. The second shift by no means replaces the first in all respects; layers of governance emerge both within and across political boundaries creating a new, multilayered system of governance. However, the second shift is marked by the internationalization and transnationalization of politics, the deterritorialization of aspects of political decision-making pertinent to states, the development of regional and global organizations and institutions, the emergence of regional and global law and a multilayered system of global governance, formal and informal. This complex, contested, interconnected order has profound implications for the nature of the democratic political community.

At the end of the second millennium, as indicated previously, political communities and civilizations can no longer be characterized simply as 'discrete worlds'; they are enmeshed and entrenched in complex structures of overlapping forces, relations and

Grid 1.1 World political order: historical comparisons

	Early modern (14th–18th century)	Modern (19th–20th century)	Contemporary (1945 on)
Changing state forms	Fragmented political associations – overlapping authority structures Growing political centralization in Europe: constitutional monarchies and absolutism Empires, city-states, dispersed/fragmented power elsewhere	Consolidation of modern nation-state and liberal democratic regimes in Europe and USA Spread of nationalism	Further spread of liberal democratic states in Latin America, Asia, Africa and Eastern Europe Consolidation of nation-state form
Interstate system	Intraterritorial rivalries Intraregional rivalry Minimal international regulation and constraints on state violence Balance of power	Global empires Development of multilateral diplomatic and legal regulation Geopolitics	Decolonization Rapid expansion of multilateral diplomatic interchange Regionalism: EU, APEC, NAFTA Global political institutions develop: UN system
Emergence of global politics	Initial European imperialist expansion – stretching of political rule	Beginnings of global political interchange: initial institutionalization of international and transnational political decision-making, especially concerning issues of trade, war and peace	Growing internationalization and transnationalization of politics, governance and authority Proliferation of international and transnational regulatory regimes Multilayered governance Emergence of elements of cosmopolitan law Global politics: neo-medieval order?

Grid 1.2 Historical forms of political globalization

	Early modern (14th–18th century)	Modern (19th–20th century)	Contemporary (1945 on)
Extensity	Largely intraterritorial and intraregional, but beginnings of imperial expansion	Global empires Global system of nation-states emerges	Global states system Global political order emerges Regionalization of politics and interregionalism
Intensity	Low-volume, but nodes of intensity when political and/ or economic competitors meet and clash	Increasing volume and expansion of flows/connections	Unprecedented level of flows, agreements, networks (formal and informal) and connections
Velocity	Limited, sporadic	Increasing	Speeding up of global political interaction as 'real time' communication emerges
Impact propensity	Low, but with concentrated nodes of impact	Increasing institutional and structural consequences	High: interconnectedness, sensitivity and vulnerability
Infrastructures	Minimal; very slow emergence of multilateral frameworks, from treaties to conference organizations	Emergence of international and transnational organizations and regimes	Extensive change in size, form and range of regimes and international and transnational organizations and legal mechanisms Real-time global communication and media infrastructures
Institutionalization	Minimal – but beginnings of diplomacy and regularization of interstate networks	Tentative but fragile development of rules, regimes and international law	Marked development of regimes, international law, elements of cosmopolitan law, intergovernmental and transnational organizational structures *continued*

Grid 1.2 *continued*

	Early modern (14th–18th century)	**Modern (19th–20th century)**	**Contemporary (1945 on)**
Stratification	Development of Eurocentric world order Political organization weak, diffuse and unequal across territories	Political, military and economic power hierarchy concentrated in North/West Political capabilities develop but massive asymmetries are prevalent	From bipolar Cold War to multipolar world North/South hierarchy eroded as NICs and non-state actors alter power structure Political organizations in every part of globe but still very significant inequalities in capabilities
Modes of interaction	Rivalry, 'limited war' Conflictual/coercive Imperialist	Territorial Diplomatic Geopolitical/coercive Imperialist Conflict and competition Development of total war	Deterritorialization and reterritorialization 'Reasons of state' pursued within emerging framework of cooperative and collaborative endeavour Cooperation and competition Geo-economic End of empire

movements. Clearly, these are often structured by inequality and hierarchy. But even the most powerful among them – including the most powerful nation-states – do not remain unaffected by the changing conditions and processes of regional and global entrenchment. Five central points can be noted to help characterize the changing relations between political globalization and modern nation-states. All indicate an increase in the extensiveness, intensity, velocity and impact of political globalization. And all suggest important points about the evolving character of the democratic political community in particular.

First, the locus of effective political power can no longer be assumed to be national governments – effective power is shared and bartered by diverse forces and agencies at national, regional and international levels. Second, the idea of a political community of fate – of a self-determining collectivity – can no longer meaningfully be located within the boundaries of a single nation-state alone. Some of the most fundamental forces and processes which determine the nature of life chances within and across political communities are now beyond the reach of individual nation-states. The system of national political communities persists of course; but it is articulated and rearticulated today with complex economic, organizational, administrative, legal and cultural processes and structures which limit and check its efficacy.

Third, it is not part of the argument presented here that national sovereignty today, even in regions with intensive overlapping and divided political and authority structures, has been wholly subverted – not at all. But it is part of the argument that there are significant areas and regions marked by criss-crossing loyalties, conflicting interpretations of rights and duties, interconnected legal and authority structures, etc., which displace the notion of sovereignty as an illimitable, indivisible and exclusive form of public power. The operation of states in increasingly complex regional and global systems affects both their autonomy (by altering the costs and benefits of policies and influencing institutional agendas) and their sovereignty (by changing the balance between national, regional and international legal frameworks and administrative practices). While massive concentrations of power remain features of many states, these are frequently embedded in, and articulated with, fractured domains of political authority.

Fourth, the late twentieth century is marked by a significant series of new types of 'boundary problem'. We live in a world of 'overlapping communities of fate', where the trajectories of each and every country are more tightly entwined than ever before. Given this, new types of boundary problem follow. In the past, of course, nation-states principally resolved their differences over boundary matters by pursuing reasons of state backed, ultimately, by coercive means. But this power logic is singularly inadequate and inappropriate to resolve the many complex issues, from economic regulation to resource depletion and environmental degradation, which engender – at seemingly ever greater speeds – an intermeshing of 'national fortunes'. In a world where powerful states make decisions not just for their own people but for others as well, and where transnational actors and forces cut across the boundaries of national communities in diverse ways, the questions of who should be accountable to whom, and on what basis, do not easily resolve themselves.

Fifth, the distinctions between domestic and foreign affairs, internal political issues and external questions, the sovereign concerns of a nation-state and international considerations, are no longer clear cut. Governments face issues such as drugs, AIDS, BSE (Bovine Spongiform Encephalopathy), the use of non-renewable resources, the management of nuclear waste, the spread of weapons of mass destruction, and global warming which cannot meaningfully be categorized in these terms. Moreover, issues like the location and investment strategy of MNCs, the regulation of global financial markets, the threats to the tax base of individual countries in the context of a global division of labour and the absence of capital controls all pose questions about the continued value of some of the central instruments of national economic policy (see chapters 3–5). In fact, in all major areas of policy, as subsequent chapters make clear, the enmeshment of national political communities in regional and global flows and processes involves them in intensive transboundary coordination and regulation. Political space for the development and pursuit of effective government and the accountability of power is no longer coterminous with a delimited political territory. Contemporary forms of political globalization involve a deterritorialization of political authority, although exactly how far this process has gone remains to be specified further.

1.5 Differential National Enmeshment

From the period following the Second World War until 1989, the nature of world politics and of national security was shaped decisively by the 'great contest' between the United States and the Soviet Union. The bifurcation of West and East dominated global affairs. The Cold War international system had a strongly hierarchical structure (see chapter 2). The operation of the US and USSR as world powers, and the development of alliances like NATO and the Warsaw Pact, constrained decision-making for many states in the postwar years. A state's capacity to initiate particular foreign policies, pursue certain strategic concerns, choose between alternative military technologies and control certain weapons systems located on its own territory was limited by its place in the international system of power relations (see Herz, 1976; Kaldor and Falk, 1987).

The global rivalry between the Soviet Union and the USA mediated world politics for almost five decades. During this time the world became a unified strategic arena in which the struggle for ideological and military supremacy permeated every geographical region. As Waltz observed: 'in a bipolar world there are no peripheries. With only two powers capable of acting on a world scale, anything that happens anywhere is potentially of concern to both of them' (1979, p. 171). Even the political identity of those states that sought neutrality during the Cold War was defined in relation to the superpower competition; they became the 'non-aligned'. Nowhere was this impact of the Cold War felt more acutely than in Europe.

At the end of the Second World War, the six case study countries in this volume – the USA, the UK, France, Germany, Sweden and Japan – occupied very different starting points in the global political system. However, with the spread of liberal democratic regimes around the world and the entrenchment of liberal economic arrangements, there have been some notable points of convergence among these countries in the realms of interstate relations, geopolitics and global politics. In this regard it is interesting to look at table 1.4. It is readily apparent that the enmeshment of each of the six countries in global politics has changed shape and form over the last five decades. While each of the countries began life very differently in the immediate postwar years, they have practically all shed their previous colonial commitments, four are members of NATO and Sweden recently joined a linked NATO programme, the Partnership for Peace. In addition, four countries are now members of the European Union, and all are major players – albeit with somewhat different levels of enmeshment in IGOs and INGOs – in international and global politics.

Of course, significant differences remain. The USA's hegemonic military role continues, reinforced by the collapse of the Soviet Union in 1989. While Britain and France remain key permanent members of the Security Council of the United Nations, enjoying veto powers, their position as global actors has been subject to decline since 1945. Both countries once enjoyed primary geopolitical roles and now have secondary roles, albeit significant secondary roles, in interstate and UN affairs. The growing economic clout of Germany and Japan has also had significant consequences. As defeated states after the Second World War, both countries were prevented from military participation in international and global affairs. Both countries accepted constitutions which blocked them from participating in international military action, including UN-sponsored action. The growing economic strength of these two states, and the constant

Table 1.4 Contemporary patterns of differential national enmeshment in the world political order: some key comparisons

	USA	UK	France	Germany	Sweden	Japan
Prewar geopolitical role	Regional hegemon – isolationist	Global empire	Global empire	Revisionist/expansionist power	Independent neutral	Imperial power
Diplomatic connectedness						
1950	70	67	70	0	50	0
1991	150	132	142	135	94	111
Military alliances/cooperative security structures	NATO founder 1949 ANZUS 1951 US-Japan Mutual Security Treaty 1951 CSCE 1975–91 OSCE 1991– ARF 1994–	NATO founder 1949 WEU 1954 CSCE 1975–91 OSCE 1991–	NATO founder 1949 WEU 1954 CSCE 1975–91 OSCE 1991–	NATO member 1955 WEU 1954 CSCE 1975–91 OSCE 1991–	Formerly neutral, joined NATO Partnership for Peace Programme 1993 WEU observer (1995) CSCE 1975–91 OSCE 1991–	US-Japan Mutual Security Treaty 1951 ARF 1994–
IGO memberships						
1950	59	62	67	25	35	14
1996	64	71	87	83[a]	87	63
UN role	Permanent member of Security Council	Permanent member of Security Council	Permanent member of Security Council	Seeking permanent membership of Security Council	Leading member of non-aligned movement	Seeking permanent membership of Security Council
UN budget contribution (%)						
1984–5	25	4.46	6.26	8.31	1.31	9.58
1997	25	5.32	6.42	9.06	1.23	15.65

continued

Table 1.4 *continued*

	USA	UK	France	Germany	Sweden	Japan
Key multilateral economic fora	WTO OECD G7 IMF/IBRD	WTO OECD G7 IMF/IBRD	WTO OECD G7 IMF/IBRD	WTO OECD G7 IMF/IBRD	WTO OECD IMF/IBRD	WTO OECD G7 IMF/IBRD
Regional engagements	NAFTA/APEC OAS	Joined EU 1973	EU founder member 1958	EU founder member 1958	EU member 1995 Nordic Council 1952 Nordic Council of Ministers 1971	APEC
INGO participation 1960	612	742	886	841	651	412
1996	2418	3031	3255	3204[a]	2733	1970
International legal connectedness	ICJ	ICJ ECHR UNCHR	ICJ ECHR UNCHR	ICJ ECHR UNCHR	ICJ ECHR UNCHR	ICJ UNCHR
Present global role	Hegemonic military power Primary role in geopolitics and diplomacy	From global power to middle-ranking power	From global power to middle-ranking power	Dominant EU power Major global role	Independent medium-ranking power	Economic superpower Limited geopolitical role

[a] FRG data prior to 1996.
Sources: The 1950 IGO data and the data on diplomacy are drawn from Nierop, 1994, app. 2. The 1996 IGO data and 1960 and 1996 INGO data are drawn from Union of International Associations, *Yearbook of International Organizations*, 1983–4, 1996–7. Country shares in UN budget are taken from www.un.org

financial crisis of international institutions such as the UN, has meant that a larger role has beckoned for some time. Japan, in particular, has sought a growing role in international politics and has sought to link its growing financial contribution to international institutions to a more significant political – and perhaps soon military – role.

1.6   Conclusion: Political Globalization and Structural Impacts

This chapter has focused on two quite distinct conceptions of world order and political organization in the modern world: that associated with traditional interstate or geopolitical relations, and that associated with the emergent framework of global politics and global governance. It has been argued that the contemporary globalization of politics is transforming the very foundations of world order by reconstituting traditional forms of sovereign statehood and reordering international political relations. But these transformative processes are neither historically inevitable nor by any means fully secure. As a result, the contemporary world order is best understood as a highly complex, contested and interconnected order in which the interstate system is increasingly embedded within evolving regional and global political networks. The latter are the basis in and through which political authority and mechanisms of governance are being articulated and rearticulated.

To refer to the contemporary world order as a complex, contested, interconnected order is to acknowledge the 'messy appearances' which define global politics at the turn of the new millennium (Mann, 1993, p. 4). But certain trends are identifiable, and these have been highlighted through an exploration of the changing form of international and transnational organizations, the substantial growth of IGOs and INGOs, the rapid development of different forms of regime, the changing structure of the form, scope and subject of international law, the emergence of regional organizations and institutions, and so on. All these developments illuminate a shift away from a purely state-centric politics to a new more complex form of multilayered global governance. There are multiple, overlapping political processes at work at the present historical conjuncture.

This conjuncture is not without some interesting historical parallels. In particular, the late medieval era in Europe has some resonance with current developments. The existence in medieval times of an array of authority structures from the local to the transnational and supranational, coexisting with an evolving system of territorially defined political units, has similarities to the contemporary period. This is not to argue that nothing has fundamentally changed. Rather, it is to suggest that a 'new medievalism' may be a useful metaphor for thinking about the present era. As Bull describes it, the 'new medievalism' represents 'a modern and secular equivalent of the kind of universal political organization that existed in Western Christendom in the Middle Ages. In that system no ruler or state was sovereign in the sense of being supreme over a given segment of the Christian population; each had to share authority with vassals beneath, and with the Pope and (in Germany and Italy) the Holy Roman Emperor above' (Bull, 1977, p. 254). It may seem fanciful to imagine a modern and secular counterpart to this world of overlapping authority and multiple loyalties. But this is similar in some respects to the kind of world order that has been described in the preceding pages. Moreover, as Bull goes on to remark:

It is familiar that sovereign states today share the stage of world politics with 'other actors' just as in medieval times the state had to share the stage with 'other associations' . . . If modern states were to come to share their authority over their citizens, and their ability to command their loyalties, on the one hand with regional and world authorities, and on the other hand with sub-state or sub-national authorities, to such an extent that the concept of sovereignty ceased to be applicable, then a neo-medieval form of universal political order might be said to have emerged. (1977, pp. 254–5)

While the concept of sovereignty has by no means been rendered redundant, state sovereignty today jostles for recognition alongside novel forms of political power and sites of authority. *Pace* Bull, a neo-medieval world order can be thought of as one in which political space and political community continue to be shaped by the territorial reach of state sovereignty, but not exclusively so. A prime illustration of this is the European Union, which is constituted by overlapping authorities and contested loyalties. In this sense, the EU represents a continuous struggle or 'search for new political spaces' and poses rather dramatically the question of where the proper place lies for political authority, action and accountability: the nation-state or the international body? (see Pattie, 1994, p. 1010.) However, this question, alongside further exploration of the nature of the contemporary world order, is addressed more substantively in the following chapters.

2
The Expanding Reach of Organized Violence

For many historians the twentieth century is defined above all else by the experience of total war. Since 1914, observes Hobsbawm, humankind has 'lived and thought in terms of world war, even when the guns were silent and the bombs were not exploding' (1994, p. 12). A combination of industrialized warfare and geopolitical competition fuelled an unprecedented globalization of military conflict and rivalry. Viewed from the perspective of a new millennium, historians may reflect on an 'age of catastrophe' in which two world wars, and the Cold War, claimed in excess of 187 million victims worldwide and ravaged societies across the globe (see Hobsbawm, 1994, p. 12). Modern warfare required the mobilization of entire societies and ensured that few states in the world system could isolate themselves from its prosecution or the political consequences of its resolution. With the arrival of the nuclear age the ever-present possibility that superpower military confrontation could result in the annihilation of the entire planet reinforced the notion of humanity as a single, global community of fate. In few other domains has globalization been so extensive, visibly encompassing the globe, or, conceived in human social and political terms, so (potentially) catastrophic.

2.1   Introduction

From the earliest civilizations to the present day, military power has been central to the globalization of human affairs. The formation of the first empires was decisively shaped by available military technology and organized violence (Mann, 1986). Historically, military power has been crucial to the territorial expansion of states and civilizations. Indeed, no account of globalization would be convincing if it failed to acknowledge the enormous violence and suffering which accompanied the formation of the modern interstate system.

Accordingly, one important task here is to examine the historical role of military power as a key mechanism through which human social relations have become globalized. Alongside this, the chapter seeks to review, as well as to assess, the historical evidence with respect to the expanding reach of organized violence. Simply put, the chapter attempts to map the major trends and distinctive patterns of military globalization from the early modern period to the present. This will embrace, in sections 2.3–5, an examination of the world military order (its evolution, structure, dynamics) specifically in respect of both its changing geography and historical patterns of global military relations. From this analysis it should be possible to construct a substantive comparison of the historical forms of military globalization (section 2.6). In this context, some observations will be made about the historical form and political significance of contemporary patterns of military globalization, addressing the question: what is new? Supplementing this broad historical sweep, section 2.7 will be devoted to assessing, for each of our six key states (namely the US, UK, Germany, France, Japan, and Sweden), the complex architecture of national enmeshment in the contemporary world military order. Section 2.8 will offer some qualified conclusions concerning the implications of military globalization for state sovereignty and the character of 'national' defence in the post-Cold War era. But to begin with, what are we to understand by the term military globalization?

2.2   What is Military Globalization?

Over the last century globalization in the military domain has been visible in, among other things, the geopolitical rivalry and imperialism of the great powers (above all, from the scramble for Africa circa 1890s to the Cold War), the evolution of international alliance systems and international security structures (from the Concert of Europe to the North Atlantic Treaty Organization), the emergence of a world trade in arms together with the worldwide diffusion of military technologies, and the institutionalization of global regimes with jurisdiction over military and security affairs, for example, the international nuclear non-proliferation regime. Indeed, it is possible to argue that all states are now enmeshed, albeit to varying degrees, in a world military order. This world military order is highly stratified and highly institutionalized: stratified, in that there is broadly a first tier (superpowers), second tier (middle-ranking powers), and third tier (developing military powers); institutionalized, in that military-diplomatic and multilateral arrangements define regularized patterns of interaction. At the same time it is shaped by a relatively autonomous arms dynamic.

Before exploring the nature of the contemporary world military order it is necessary to establish some conceptual clarity in the use of key concepts. In particular some clarification of the concepts *global militarization* and *military globalization* is required. While here the former loosely refers to a generalized process of global military build-up (measured by increased levels of total world military expenditures, armaments or armed forces), the latter concept refers exclusively to the process (and patterns) of military connectedness that transcend the world's major regions as reflected in the spatio-temporal and organizational features of military relations, networks and interactions. Although these two processes may, at particular conjunctures, be highly correlated, in that specific phases of global militarization (such as occurred in the early 1980s) appear to be closely associated with distinct phases of military globalization (in the 1980s, the resurgence of superpower global rivalry), the causal pathology is decidedly complex (see Ross, 1987; Shaw, 1991, esp. ch. 1). With this distinction in mind the primary focus of this chapter is on the process of military globalization.

Military globalization can be conceived very crudely as a process which embodies the growing extensity and intensity of military relations among the political units of the world system. (Military relations, and military power, refer here to forms of organized violence.) Understood as such, it reflects both the expanding network of worldwide military ties and relations, as well as the impact of key military technological innovations (from steamships to reconnaissance satellites) which, over time, have reconstituted the world into a single geostrategic space. Historically, this process of time-space compression has brought centres of military power into closer proximity and potential conflict, as the capability to project enormous destructive power across vast distances has proliferated. Simultaneously, military decision and reaction times have shrunk, with the consequence that permanent military machines, along with their permanent preparation for war, have become an integral feature of modern social life.

Various quantitative indicators may be utilized to help map the spatio-temporal and organizational dimensions of military globalization. These include the reach of imperial expansion; foreign military presence; military diplomatic representation; the arms trade; arms expenditure; defence expenditure; alliance membership; military cooperation agreements; defence industrial linkages; the incidence of military intervention; and patterns of military assistance. Indicators such as these make it feasible to track significant shifts in historical forms of military globalization and national profiles of enmeshment in the world military order. Such a systematic appraisal holds out the prospect of a more comprehensive mapping and representation of both historical forms of military globalization and historical world military orders.

Analytically, it is helpful to distinguish between three different facets of military globalization: the global reach of the war system (great power rivalry and conflict); the global arms dynamic (the military production system and trade in arms); and the expansion of geogovernance of security and military affairs, such as arms control agreements. Each of these facets tells one aspect of the story about military globalization, but in combination they offer a comprehensive account of the evolution of the world military order. The concept of a world military order is of relatively recent origin. It refers to the ways in which military relations and activities (from war to military production) between political entities (whether nation-states, city-states or empires) constitute a complex field of interaction which embodies its own structure and dynamics. Although for analytical purposes it is helpful to distinguish between these three facets – the war system, the arms dynamic, and geogovernance – it is crucially important to recognize that both historical world military orders and historical forms of military globalization are constituted by, and through, their interaction. Since the objective is to map historical forms of military globalization, this chapter commences by exploring these three facets in isolation before considering them together.

Accordingly, the analysis begins with a historical treatment of the three key mechanisms through which military globalization has been articulated:

1 the war system (that is, the geopolitical order, great power rivalry, conflict and security relations);
2 the arms dynamic (through which military capabilities and armaments production technologies are diffused throughout the globe); and
3 the geogovernance of organized violence (embracing the formal and informal international regulation of the acquisition, deployment and use of military power).

2.3 The Globalization of the War System: Geopolitics and the Evolution of a World Military Order

For much of humanity and in human history, the experience of globalization has been a bloody one. Writing in 1552, Bartolomé de Las Casas (among the first of the Europeans to bring to the attention of his masters the atrocities perpetrated in the earliest colonizization of the New World) observed: 'The common ways mainly employed by the Spaniards who call themselves Christian and who have gone there to extirpate those pitiful nations and wipe them off the earth is by unjustly waging cruel and bloody wars' (1992, p. 31). Far from being a benign process, globalization has been associated with extraordinary levels of organized violence.

At the beginning of the sixteenth century the world was separated largely by geography into several major military empires or civilizations among which there was limited political and military interaction. Apart from some significant trading links the interaction between each of these major power centres was mainly circumscribed by the 'friction of distance', reinforced by a growing political introversion in the most advanced civilizations (Black, 1998).

In 1418, almost a century before Columbus discovered the New World, the Chinese emperor's treasure fleet, commanded by Admiral Zheng He, had moored off the town of Malindi, not far from Mombasa on the eastern coast of Africa (Levathes, 1994, p. 19). As Levathes observes, 'while Europe was still emerging from the Dark Ages, China with her navy of giant junks, was poised to become the colonial power of the sixteenth century and tap the riches of the globe' (1994, p. 142). But a concern with the domestic problems of imperial rule brought with it the end of Chinese overseas expansion; by 1436, according to Kennedy, 'an imperial edict banned the construction of seagoing ships . . . China had decided to turn its back on the world' (1988, p. 7). Similarly in Japan, the shogunates adopted a 'closed country' – sakaku – policy which culminated in 1636 with the cessation of ocean-going ship construction (Kennedy, 1988, p. 14; Beasley, 1995). In many respects the Eurasian civilizations were less interconnected at the beginning of the fifteenth century than in the early Middle Ages (Hodgson, 1993, p. 123; Roberts, 1995, pp. 140, 305).[1] Indeed, in the late fifteenth century the world had yet to be circumnavigated, American civilization remained unknown in Europe, and 'the continent of Asia was in some respects less accessible to Europeans and Christians than it had been for several centuries' (Phillips, 1988, p. 246).

As the early modern era dawned, the world was organized politically into several largely autarchic civilizations, each with its own unique pattern of power politics and military relations. Although in the earlier centuries of the first millennium there had been considerable military interaction between the major civilizations, from the westward and eastward expansion of the Mongol Empire, the rise of Islam, and the Crusades, among other episodes, this did not constitute in any meaningful sense a world military order (Ferro, 1997; Phillips, 1988). On the contrary, the premodern world can be described as 'subsystem dominant' in that effectively there were several distinct, but circumspect world military orders (Black, 1998). The history of how these world orders became submerged within one global system of military relations, a single geopolitical order, is associated primarily with the history of European imperial expansion and its contestation.

---

[1] This is not to suggest that there was no significant interaction. On the contrary the long-standing conflict between the Ottoman Empire in the East and Europe in the West was of great importance in shaping the destiny of both civilizations. Nevertheless, as Watson observes, they remained quite separate world orders (see 1992, p. 216).

2.3.1   The growing extensity of European military power: early expansion, 1492–1800

Orthodox accounts of the 'rise of the West' tend to exaggerate Western military supremacy and the weakness of its victims (Watson, 1992, p. 214; Geyer and Bright, 1995). From the vantage point of the end of the twentieth century the diffusion of European civilization across the globe can too readily be represented as the smooth unfolding 'logic' of history. But such a narrative ignores the contingency, the discontinuities and the contestation of the process of European expansion. Implicit in the orthodox 'rise of the West' discourse is a Eurocentric conception of world history in which it was seen as predictable that European civilization, with its superior military capabilities, came to acquire global primacy. Such a view neglects the often tenuous grip of European power across the globe and the role of local forces in imperial expansion (Fernández-Armesto, 1995; Geyer and Bright, 1995). Since the nature of imperial expansion has been discussed in chapter 1, the narrative here concentrates on the historical pattern of military globalization and its connection with the discrete phases of European overseas expansion.

Three distinct phases in the military expansion of European international society can be identified: the age of 'discovery' covering the late fifteenth to the early seventeenth centuries; a period of consolidation from the seventeenth to the mid-nineteenth century; and the age of world empire from 1850 to the turn of the century (Howard, 1984, p. 124). During each of these phases a combination of military innovation, economic logic, domestic politics and great power rivalry conditioned the territorial expansion of European civilization. This expansionism was never preordained; for in the Middle Ages European civilization was somewhat precariously situated in respect of the balance of world military power. Contained by the considerable military might of the Ottoman Empire, the Mongols and Islam, Christian Europe had adopted a largely defensive military posture in the aftermath of the Crusades. Moreover, Europe's sovereigns were significantly exercised by domestic and continental power struggles. Yet, remarkably, by the close of the eighteenth century the major European powers together had acquired political control of 35 per cent of the world's land area (Headrick, 1981, p. 3).

This initial expansion was accompanied by an aggressive spirit of military conquest following closely on the successful early voyages of discovery. Facilitated by advances in navigational technologies and the construction of more powerful and robust warships, the major European powers quickly established settlements in the New World and Asia. Although military power was quite decisive to this, it was less the superiority of European military technology and more the calculated application of force (alongside the rapid spread of European diseases borne by invading armies) which contributed to the relative ease of conquest. In addition, local warlords and military forces, as in Cortes's startling military defeat of Montezuma, contributed significantly to this military conquest (Diaz, 1963; Fernández-Armesto, 1995). With the capability to construct and arm large ocean-going vessels came the beginnings of a significant shift in the balance of world military power; a shift which the more powerful European states sought to consolidate.

During the period 1500 to the late seventeenth century, war and military conflict had raged across continental Europe. A period of intensive innovation in military technology and organization ensued as each major power sought, by military means, to prevent potential rivals from acquiring continental hegemony. A qualitative arms race developed with advances in defensive military technologies (such as fortress construction) stimulating developments in offensive military technologies (such as bombardment techniques). The arrival of gunpowder and the musket transformed the character of land warfare as established forms of military organization, strategy and tactics became obsolescent. Standing armies developed and this imposed greater financial demands on the state. The costs, as well as the growing scale and sophistication of war, required an increasingly centralized and organized site of political authority, capable of raising the taxes and finance to conduct modern warfare. This emerged in the form of the increasingly centralized European absolutist state (see section 1.1.2 above).

In the competitive struggle to prevent their rivals from acquiring hegemony, Europe's great powers built up large and sophisticated military machines. These capabilities provided them with a significant military-technological advantage over other potential centres of world power. Whether or not this period is characterized as a 'military revolution', the late sixteenth through to the early eighteenth century witnessed the conjuncture of several major developments which altered, over the longer term, the balance of military power between the world's major civilizations (Parker, 1988; Black 1991, 1994).

This historic realignment of military power underwrote a further expansion of European overseas empires by the Dutch, Spanish, Portuguese and British in particular. Advanced warship design and construction facilitated the creation of large battle fleets capable of projecting power in distant waters. As Parker notes, 'the new ships of the line were able to operate by 1688 in the Caribbean, in the Indian Ocean, and in the Pacific, in order to gain both tactical and strategic advantage' (1988, p. 103). Despite many setbacks, the balance of military advantage on land too began to shift towards the West. Superior firepower, military organization, tactics and logistics contributed to Austria's decisive military defeat of the Ottoman Empire in 1718. The resulting Peace of Passarowitz witnessed the advent of 'the period when Europeans became militarily superior to peoples who in the past had been their equals or superiors, most notably the Turks' (Black, 1994, p. 14).

Beyond Europe, the world's major civilizations were increasingly put on the defensive against the advanced military capabilities and technologies of the European powers. In addition to the new territorial acquisitions, the geographical reach of existing colonial rule was pushed deeper into the hinterland of the world's continents (see map 1.2 above; Howard, 1984). Even so, some colonies were acquired only against enormous military odds, and because of severe military-logistical constraints many were only tenuously held (see Black, 1994, pp. 19–20). Nevertheless, by the late eighteenth century, the widening 'firepower gap' between the major European states and the rest of the world established the military conditions for the West's pursuit of 'the first global hegemony in history' (Parker, 1988, p. 154).

The struggle for European global hegemony had profound political and military consequences: a world military order was in the making. First, European powers sought to construct a new world order mirroring the political principles and standards of European civilization. A global set of rules and practices for the conduct of interstate relations slowly developed. This was loosely based on the 'Westphalian system' of 1648 which had defined the legal and institutional form of the post-medieval European states system (see chapter 1 above; Osiander, 1994). Second, the widening 'firepower gap' and the intercontinental reach of European empires stimulated many non-European states to acquire Western military technologies and to emulate, if they could, European forms of military organization. At stake was the perceived survival of other civilizations as independent political units. During this period, 'the great states of East Asia paid more attention to the military innovations of the Europeans than to any other aspect of Western culture' (Parker, 1988, p. 144). Military and political elites outside the West became increasingly sensitive to developments in European military institutions, technologies and modes of warfare. Third, as European empires stretched across continents, the fate of more and more of the world's peoples became entwined with the dynamic of European power politics. From the early eighteenth century 'wars among European great powers regularly included overseas combat and their settlement often included realignments of overseas empires' (Tilly, 1990, p. 168).

2.3.2 The emergence of geopolitics: military infrastructures and the stratification of military power

Despite American independence, the mid to late nineteenth century witnessed the consolidation of European imperial power. Regions and civilizations which had so far eluded European control experienced first-hand its military might. By 1878 the great powers had almost doubled the world land area under their dominion (Headrick, 1981, p. 3). This frenzied phase of expansion was influenced in part by the industrialization of warfare which transformed, as well as multiplied exponentially, the military capacity of all the major powers. The steamship, railroad, telegraph and systems of telegraphic communications revolutionized military force and the infrastructures of organized violence. Enormous military power could now be projected across greater and greater distances.

In India railway infrastructures transformed military logistics, allowing, as the Governor-General Lord Dalhousie explained in 1853, 'the concentration of . . . military strength on any given point, in as many days as it now requires months to effect' (quoted in Headrick, 1981, p. 82). In 1842 British sea-power extended no further than 200 miles into mainland China yet within a decade it had extended to Hankow, double the distance inland (Howard, 1984). McNeill observes that as 'steamships and railroads supplemented animal pack trains, natural obstacles of geography and distance became increasingly trivial. European armies and navies therefore acquired the capacity to bring their resources to bear at will even in remote and impenetrable places' (1982, p. 257).

New technologies of war, such as the breech-loading rifle, the Gatling gun, gunboats, the machine-gun and sophisticated artillery, together with the ability to mass produce military hardware, reinforced the growing 'firepower gap' between the West and the 'rest'. According to Kennedy, in terms of military capability 'the leading nations possessed resources 50 or 100 times greater than those at the bottom' (1988, p. 150).

The dramatic scale of this 'firepower gap' is illustrated by the occurrence, during this period, of some of the most lopsided military confrontations in world history.

During the 1841 Opium War with China the British steamship *Nemesis* single-handedly destroyed in one day '9 war junks, 5 forts, 2 military stations and 1 shore battery' (Parker, 1988, p. 154). Within a year the Chinese empire was defeated by the deployment of a few gunboats and superior military firepower. In Africa the 31,000-strong army of the Nupe Emirate of Sokoto was defeated in 1897 by the Royal Niger Company force of 539 men (Headrick, 1981, p. 117). Indeed, such was the scale of the military imbalance that in many contexts 'military power could be kept in reserve, if used at all' (Howard, 1984, p. 7).

The industrialization of war (that is, the application of industrial production methods and technologies to the instruments and techniques of warfare), combined with huge and increasingly well organized and disciplined armed forces, facilitated the most extensive phase of Western imperialism since the initial voyages of discovery. The 'new imperialism' of the late nineteenth century witnessed the colonization of Africa, the consolidation of European power in Asia and the Middle East, the subjugation of China, the forced end to Japanese isolationism, and the extension of US power into Latin America and the Pacific. As the twentieth century dawned, the world had been reconfigured and reconstituted into 'a single net of economic and strategic relations' (Watson, 1992, p. 265).

What had begun centuries before as a series of separate imperial adventures had evolved, by the end of the nineteenth century, into an intercontinental system of military and strategic relations dominated by Western powers laying down new infrastructures of influence and control. In the capitals of Europe the global (as opposed to simply the European) balance of power figured prominently in military and foreign policy calculations since the 'Great Power struggles were no longer over European issues . . . but over markets and territories that ranged across the globe' (Kennedy, 1988, p. 195). It is no historical coincidence that it was during this period that the discipline of geopolitics was established.

In capturing the strategic significance of new 'distance shrinking' technologies – which brought potential rivals closer together and made it easier to organize the deployment and use of military force in distant parts of the world – the discourse of geopolitics provided Western military and political elites with a rational interpretative framework through which to understand, and to act on, the world. Geopolitics equated state power with control over territorial space and redefined international politics in terms of the contest between the great powers for mastery of the world's oceans and land-mass. In this competition for political and military supremacy, imperial expansion – the mastery of space – was considered necessary not only to maximize national power (and thus security) but also to stabilize the fragile domestic social order (see Kearns, 1993; O'Tuathail, 1996, ch. 3). The discourse of geopolitics popularized and legitimized a conception of the world as a unified strategic space across which the great powers conducted their military and political rivalry. As the French statesman Leon Gambetta enthused at the turn of the twentieth century: 'to remain a great nation or to become one, you must colonize' (quoted in Joll, 1984, p. 148).

As European great power rivalry acquired a global character, so too did networks of military relations. All the great powers, to varying degrees, established a transcontinental military infrastructure. Military bases and outposts were constructed in strategic locations in distant points of the globe, partly for the purpose of defending the empire and partly to secure trade and supply routes. Foreign bases also guaranteed the logistical infrastructure necessary to project military power rapidly to crisis zones in strategic areas of the world. Worldwide communications networks were installed both over land and under the sea. By 1900 some 19,000 miles of underwater cable had been laid across the world's oceans and the entire British Empire was connected directly to its military command posts in London (Headrick, 1981, p. 162).

This period also witnessed a startling expansion in military diplomacy as military relations between states gained greater political salience. Governments began to collect more systematically than ever before data on foreign armed forces and military capabilities. Military, and especially naval, attachés became common in all major embassies from the 1850s onwards, although the practice of official accreditation of such attachés was not commonplace until the 1860s (see Hamilton and Langhorne, 1995, p. 120). The first British military attachés were appointed in 1855 to Paris, Turin and Constantinople; Sweden, France, and Italy had military attachés in a number of European capitals by the 1880s. And by 1914 there were approximately 300 worldwide (M. S. Anderson, 1993, pp. 129–30).

At much the same time as military diplomacy became institutionalized there was also a widening diffusion, as well as emulation, of European and American models of military organization, strategy and tactics (see Ralston, 1990). Throughout Latin America, Africa, and Asia, Western states trained and equipped indigenous military forces, either to supplement imperial forces or to cement informal military alliances in the struggle for global power. Even Japanese and Chinese military and political elites actively sought and acquired Western military assistance (Beasley, 1995, p. 64; Black, 1998). By the turn of the twentieth century the intensity of global military competition and the extensive reach of European networks of military power had compressed the globe into a single geopolitical space.

2.3.3 The age of global conflict, 1914–1990

With the consolidation of Europe's global reach, civilizations, empires and nations around the globe became significantly interrelated in terms of their security and survival. The prospects for peace in each part of the world were no longer determined solely by local circumstances or local decision-makers but were increasingly contingent on the complex dynamics of global power relations and developments across interconnected sites of military and political decision-making. While the great powers had the capacity to exercise greater control over their strategic environment than subordinate states, every region was enmeshed in a global system of military and security relations which, lacking effective mechanisms of conflict resolution, was subject to severe and uncontrollable crisis tendencies with potentially catastrophic consequences.

When war erupted in 1914 it very rapidly expanded beyond continental Europe. Three factors significantly influenced the extent of this military globalization. First, strategically significant imperial possessions were drawn into the conflict almost from the outset. Hostilities spread to Africa and the Middle East. Second, industrialization had transformed the nature of modern warfare. Huge war machines had been created. But in order to function efficiently they required the mobilization of entire nations and empires. The war effort depended on global sourcing of raw materials and food supplies. For the combatants, modern warfare demanded both a national and a transnational

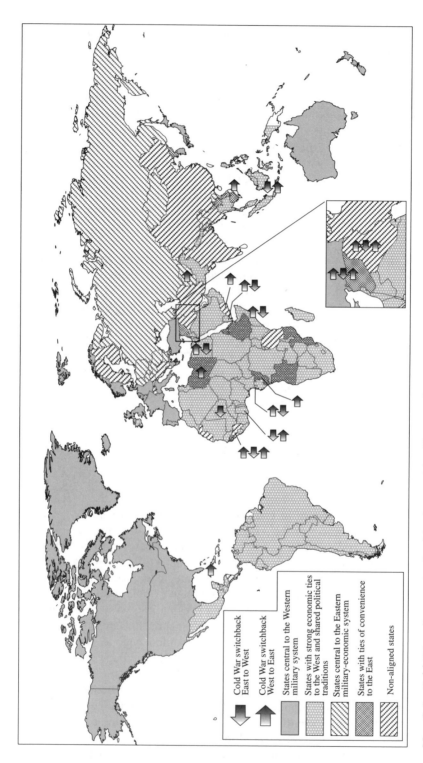

Map 2.1 Cold War alignments: the bipolar world military order (*Source*: Adapted from Kidron and Smith, 1983)

mobilization of all available industrial, technological, human and natural resources. Third, the scale and nature of industrialized war made international alliances essential since no state by itself had the resources necessary to achieve military victory or to avoid defeat. The Triple Entente (Britain, France and Russia) and the Triple Alliance (Germany, Italy and Austria-Hungary) functioned as institutional mechanisms for coordinating the prosecution of the war as well as organizing the war effort on an international scale.

The First World War demonstrated that war between great powers in the industrial age could no longer be confined exclusively to the combatants on the battlefield. Unlike fifteenth-century warfare, war in the twentieth century, in respect of both its prosecution and consequences, had acquired an extensive geographic reach: 'war, once conducted by military geniuses on a battlefield of limited scope, had come to embrace whole continents and to involve citizens at the home front in the era of total warfare' (Klein, 1994, p. 55). The age of global conflict had arrived.

The Second World War was, as Hobsbawm puts it, a 'global human catastrophe' (1994, p. 52). The scale of the war effort, of destruction and of human suffering were historically unprecedented. As war embraced Europe and the Far East, military hostilities raged across almost every single continent and ocean, excepting Latin America and Southern Africa. Few of those states not engaged directly or indirectly in military combat could effectively remain neutral since supplying the war effort of both the Axis (Germany, Italy and Japan) and the Allied powers (USA, Britain, France) required extensive sourcing. As McNeill notes, 'transnational organization for war . . . achieved a fuller and far more effective expression during World War II than ever before' (1982, p. 356). But the most profound consequence of the war was the resultant transformation in the structure of world power. The year 1945 marked the end of Europe's global hegemony and confirmed the US and the Soviet Union as global superpowers. This structural transformation heralded dramatic consequences for the pattern of postwar global military and security relations.

For nearly five decades following the termination of the Second World War international politics was dominated by the rivalry between the two superpowers, the US and the Soviet Union. Their visions of how the postwar world should be ordered were incompatible, and the pattern of geopolitics very rapidly settled into a Cold War confrontation between East and West. World politics was fractured into two rival blocs each dominated by competing systems of military alliances and regional security pacts. In addition, the US and the Soviet Union entered into scores of bilateral and multilateral military cooperation and security agreements with nations around the world.

Although the rivalry between the two superpowers was not experienced evenly across the globe, in that some regions, such as the Middle East, Central America and East Asia, became key arenas in which the 'great struggle' was played out, the ever-present possibility of nuclear Armageddon encouraged a strong awareness of humanity's collective fortunes (see map 2.1). While the nuclear arms race made war between the two superpowers rationally unthinkable (but not necessarily improbable), East–West rivalry was displaced into Africa, Asia and Latin America. In turn, the process of decolonization and the struggle for national liberation became imbued with a Cold War military dynamic. Where direct intervention was eschewed, war by proxy ensued. As Europe's foreign military presence was reduced, that of the two superpowers expanded (see Harkavy, 1989). Even outer space and the underwater world of the

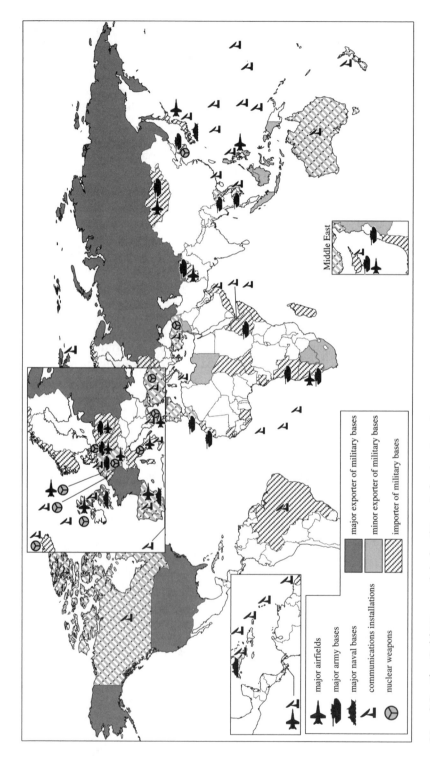

Map 2.2 The Cold War: a global military infrastructure (*Source: Adapted from Kidron and Smith, 1983*)

oceans began to be colonized for military purposes. Despite the dramatic technological advances in military logistics and communications systems, which one might expect to have reduced the demand for global military deployment, the demand actually increased. By 1982 the number of foreign military bases and installations numbered around 3,000. Moreover, in 1985 at the height of the 'second' Cold War, the US had close to 500,000 troops deployed worldwide in over 70 countries, while the Soviet Union had in excess of 600,000 troops abroad (Harkavy, 1989, ch. 4). Although direct historical comparisons are not entirely meaningful, the ratio of foreign troop deployments to total armed forces for most great powers was probably higher in the mid-twentieth century than in the nineteenth (see map 2.2).

The Cold War constituted a unique system of global power relations which, paradoxically, both divided the globe into rival camps and yet unified it within a strategically interconnected world military order. It involved extensive and intensive regional and global networks of military power and, for the superpowers at least, enormous military infrastructures to project unparalleled destructive power to almost any single site on the world's surface. It was also highly institutionalized and stratified (into the First World, Second World and Third World) (see map 2.3). When both superpowers signed the Charter of Paris in November 1990, following the collapse of the 'people's democracies', the Cold War ended as abruptly as it had begun. But its legacy continues to influence the contemporary geopolitical landscape.

2.3.4   Disorganized geopolitics: regionalization and global security

With the end of the Cold War the pattern of global military and security relations has been transformed. In some respects the structure of world military power at the end of the twentieth century reflects a return to a traditional pattern of multipolar power politics, but in other respects, especially the sole military superpower status of the US, it is historically unique (see Waltz, 1993). But three important qualifications need to be made.

First, in terms of military power the 'firepower gap' between the US and the rest is enormous. In military expenditure terms the US, even taking into account planned expenditure reductions, spends considerably more than other major powers combined. Moreover, in respect of military capability (excluding manpower), the technological and hardware gap between the US and the others remains considerable. Accordingly, the US remains a military superpower in a world of many middle-ranking military powers. Second, in comparison with previous historical epochs, not only is the rivalry between today's great powers relatively muted (only China could be described as a 'revisionist power') but it is no longer articulated primarily in military terms. Third, the primary security interests of today's great powers, apart from the US, are conceived overwhelming in regional (or local) terms. Global security and military relations may therefore be accorded declining significance in calculations of great power politics. These qualifications suggest that the present system, unlike the multipolar interstate system of the late nineteenth century in which great power rivalry was increasingly globalized, may be becoming more regionalized, more fragmented and therefore more disorganized.

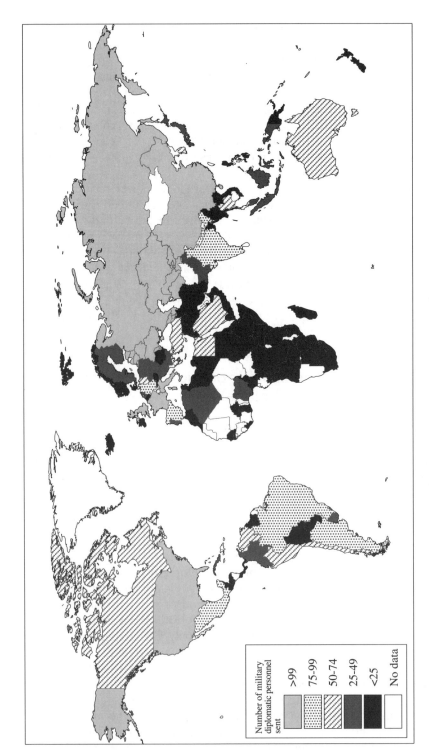

Map 2.3 Patterns of military diplomatic involvement, 1985–1986 (*Source*: Adapted from Nierop, 1994)

Number of military
diplomatic personnel
sent

>99
75–99
50–74
25–49
<25
No data

As the Cold War has ended and the foreign military presence of the US and Soviet Union has contracted (by quite spectacular proportions) the reassertion of regional and local patterns of interstate rivalry has been intense. One consequence of this is the visible tendency towards 'the decentralization of the international security system', the fragmentation of the world into relatively discrete (but not entirely self-contained) regional security complexes (Buzan, 1991, p. 208).[2] This is evident, among other cases, in the resurgence of nationalist conflicts and tensions in Europe and the Balkans, in the Indo-Pakistan rivalry in South Asia, and in the rivalry over the South China seas in South East Asia. As the overlay of Cold War conflict has been removed, a significant external restraint on regional conflicts (whose origins may often predate even the age of European empires) has disappeared. In some cases, such as South East Asia, the consequences to date have been relatively benign, but in many regions rivalries and tensions have escalated. This 'regionalization' of international security represents an important distinguishing feature of the post-Cold War world military and security order.

The significance of this regionalization, however, is contested by cross-cutting imperatives in the pattern of contemporary security relations. One highly debated interpretation is that the global security and military order is undergoing a process of 'structural bifurcation'; that is, fragmentation into two largely separate systems each with different standards, rules of conduct and interstate behaviour. The likely implications and costs of (conventional or nuclear) war among advanced industrial states, argues Mueller among others, are now so potentially overwhelming that major war has become obsolescent; it would be counterproductive either as a mechanism for resolving interstate conflicts or as a mechanism for transforming the international status quo (see Mueller, 1989). In contradistinction to this, states in the periphery (that is, those states in the developing world) operate within a system in which political instability, militarism and state expansion remain endemic and in which there is no effective deterrent to war as a rational instrument of state policy. Accordingly, patterns of international military and security relations are radically diverging as the post-Cold War world order becomes increasingly bifurcated (cf. McFail and Goldeier, 1992).

However, counterposed to these processes of fragmentation and regionalization are powerful centripetal forces reinforcing the unified character of the world military order. Four factors in particular deserve mention in this respect:

- First, in many global regions, there is a gradual shift taking place towards cooperative defence or multilateral security arrangements. The desire to avoid interstate conflict and the enormous costs, technological requirements and domestic burdens of defence are together contributing to the historic strengthening, rather than weakening, of multilateral and collective defence arrangements as well as international military cooperation and coordination. The end of the Cold War has not witnessed the demise of NATO, as many predicted in 1990, but rather its expanding role and significance. Moreover, in many of the world's key regions multilateral frameworks for security and defence cooperation are beginning to emerge alongside existing regional arrangements. These, like the ASEAN Regional Forum (ARF) in Asia-Pacific, may be at a very early stage of development and beset by all kinds of

[2] A regional security complex according to Buzan can be defined in terms of 'patterns of amity and enmity that are substantially confined within some geographic area' (Buzan, 1991, p. 190).

rivalries, but historically they represent a significant institutionalization of military and security relations. Furthermore, many of these arrangements are becoming less regionally specific as the US has strengthened its global engagements (for instance, with NATO and ARF). At the global level, too, the peacekeeping activities of the UN and its more general collective security functions have become more visible, although not necessarily more effective. These developments reflect a realization that with the end of the Cold War, and against the background of recent military technological change, 'the capacity of the state to defend territorial boundaries against armed attack' may have weakened (Cammilleri and Falk, 1992, p. 152). Certainly, many states now recognize that national security can no longer be achieved simply through unilateral actions alone.

- Second, the rising density of financial, trade and economic connections between states (see chapters 3, 4 and 5 below) has expanded the potential vulnerability of most states to crises in distant parts of the globe. Accordingly, many states, not simply just the world's major powers, remain acutely sensitive (if not vulnerable) to security and military developments in other regions. Such sensitivities may be highly selective, and certainly not all parts of the globe are perceived as of comparable strategic importance. Nevertheless, as the 1990 crisis in the Gulf demonstrated, military developments in strategically critical regions continue to be of global significance. Regionalization and globalization of military/security relations are by no means contradictory processes, and may be mutually reinforcing.

- Third, threats to national security are becoming both more diffuse and no longer simply military in character (Buzan et al., 1998). Thus the proliferation of weapons of mass destruction poses a potential threat to all states. But proliferation is in part a product of the diffusion of industrial and technological knowledge as well as hardware. Preventing proliferation is thus a classic collective action problem in that it demands worldwide action. Similarly, environmental, economic, narcotics, terrorist, cultural, criminal and other threats to national security cannot be resolved through either solely military or solely national means. Accordingly, there is a permanent demand for global mechanisms of coordination and cooperation to deal with the expanding penumbra of security threats.

- Fourth, in the global states system the military security of all nations is significantly influenced by systemic factors. Indeed, the structure of power and the actions of the great powers remain dominant influences on the military postures of each other and of all other states. At one level this is simply because the great powers set the standards, be it in military technology or force levels, against which all other states ultimately calibrate their defence capability. Thus US defence policy has more wide-ranging global effects than does that of Kiribati. How the great powers act affects the security of all the world's regions. Furthermore, given the lack of any overarching authority to impose global stability, most states will tend to seek peace through military strength. This creates a severe security dilemma in that through simply pursuing their own security, by adding to or improving their military capability, states 'can easily threaten the power and security aspirations of other states' (Buzan, 1991; and see sections 1.2 and 1.3 above). The consequence is a spiral of international insecurity as potential rivals respond in a like manner. Accordingly, national security, in an anarchic interstate system, can never be disentangled entirely from global systemic conditions.

All this suggests that the contemporary geopolitical order, far from simply fragmenting, remains beset by problems of global strategic interconnectedness. The lack of any serious global political and military rivalries of the kind represented by the Cold War, or the New Imperialism of the 1890s, should not be read as a process of military deglobalization. However, we will return to this issue after a fuller consideration of the other facets of the world military order: the global arms dynamic and international security regimes.

2.4 A Global Arms Dynamic?

At the height of the second Cold War, in the mid-1980s, world military expenditure (in constant 1987 US dollars) approached $1,000 billion per annum (almost $190 for every individual on the planet); spending on military hardware exceeded $290 billion, while the trade in arms amounted to over $48 billion (see Krause, 1992, p. 93; Sivard, 1991, p. 499). In this period, approximately 120 countries were engaged in producing, buying and transferring arms and military technology. It might therefore reasonably be concluded that a functioning global 'arms transfer and production system' existed with its own 'global arms dynamic' (Krause, 1992, p. 1).

The 'arms dynamic' refers to a process of quantitative and qualitative change in national and global military capabilities (Buzan, 1987, p. 73). Among the most significant forces driving this process, aside from geopolitical and domestic factors, is military technological innovation. Military technological innovation is central to the arms dynamic and has important global consequences. In particular, the worldwide standard of military technology is set by the most militarily advanced states, effectively those states with the scientific, industrial and technological capacity to innovate. As the innovators develop and deploy leading edge military technology, other states are confronted with a pronounced security dilemma: either they strive to acquire the latest hardware and systems or, failing to do so, their potential military power, and in consequence their military security, may be eroded. The operation of the arms dynamic therefore exhibits an inherent globalizing logic in that it directly encourages the transcontinental proliferation of military capabilities and technology. Indeed, it promotes a kind of military-technological chain reaction within and across the world's major regional security complexes, since as the frontier of military technology advances, states seek to maintain their relative position in the hierarchies of regional and global power. The term 'global arms dynamic' captures this relationship between the 'process of qualitative advance in military technology' and 'the spread of both technology, and knowledge about technology, ever more broadly throughout the international system' (Buzan, 1987, p. 36). One vivid illustration of the global arms dynamic occurred in the aftermath of the 1991 Gulf War. In the opening hours of that war, advances in the integration of C^3I technologies (that is, command, control, communications and intelligence), combined with new Stealth aircraft, were exploited to devastating effect in completely disabling the Soviet-built Iraqi air defence system. Having been proven in combat, advanced C^3I systems have become an increasingly essential requirement in all national military procurement programmes across the globe.

The global arms dynamic operates within a distinctly hierarchical arms transfer and production system, for there are major disparities between the military-technological capacities of different classes of states. Krause characterizes the hierarchical structure of this system in terms of four distinct tiers (or groupings) of states (1992, pp. 31–2):

- first-tier suppliers – the military-technological innovators;
- second-tier suppliers – major producers and adapters of weapons technology and systems;
- third-tier suppliers – those that reproduce and copy existing military technologies and hardware;
- fourth-tier recipients – primarily purchasers of arms.

This structure is largely self-reproducing since, as Buzan notes: 'The leading powers in the system have to keep close to the front edge of the technological advance unless they want to fall back into the second rank of power. Aspirants to the first rank power status must acquire the capability to compete at the leading edge of technological innovation' (1987, p. 37).

Although the specific occupants of these tiers have changed over time, the deep structure of the system has remained primarily intact since early modern times. So too (until the late twentieth century) has Western dominance of this structure; a situation signally consolidated by the industrialization of warfare in the nineteenth century. However, industrialization and modernization have challenged Western dominance as new arms suppliers and centres of military production beyond the West have emerged in the late twentieth century. By analysing the main expressions of this global arms dynamic, the arms trade and the diffusion of military technology, a more systematic picture of this facet of military globalization will emerge.

2.4.1   The early modern arms trade system: extensity, intensity and stratification

Accounts of the modern arms trade system almost overwhelmingly explain its development as a product of geopolitical conditions, processes of state expansion, the changing organizational forms of national military production and military-technological innovation (see McNeill, 1982; Creveld, 1989; Pearton, 1982; Krause, 1992). They also tend to emphasize the discontinuities and stratification of the process of global spread. The latter has been punctuated by discrete expansionary impulses, in which the scale and scope of arms transfers increase, followed by long periods of consolidation in the spatial pattern and scale of arms flows. The transition from the decentralized, fragmented, localized and delimited spatial reach of the premodern arms trade to the highly institutionalized, extensive and intensive contemporary trade in arms is explicable only in terms of a discontinuous series of transformations in the arms market, each driven by contingent developments rather than a single, secular process of historical change.

Although the evidence of a trade in arms during the premodern era is limited, it tends to confirm that the extensity, intensity and impact of arms transfers were highly circumscribed (Black, 1998). Krause notes that within the Roman Empire the main centres of arms production were located close to garrisons and were state controlled (1992, p. 35). There was no organized or institutionalized arms trade to speak of. Indeed, it was not until the early medieval period that any regularized arms trade began to emerge within Europe, let alone between Europe and the world beyond. In other regions such as the Chinese and Mongol empires, military innovations (crossbow, cavalry) diffused fairly rapidly, although this was not accompanied by a regularized arms trade *per se* (Pacey 1991; McNeill, 1982).

War and conquest between city-states and kingdoms in Europe accelerated the diffusion of arms, while the first crusades, with some assistance from merchant capitalists, spread European arms beyond the continent into the Middle East and, through trade networks, even more widely. Similarly, the clash of 'civilizations' on the boundaries of Western Christendom brought with it the diffusion of Mongol, Muslim and Chinese arms and military techniques, the best known being gunpowder (Contamine, 1984, p. 139).[3] However, the fact that it took two centuries for knowledge of gunpowder to reach Europe from China (via the Mongol and Islamic empires) underlines the characterization of the early arms trade as disorganized, sporadic, fragmented and localized, and the slow pace of diffusion of military innovation – developments within 'discrete worlds'. Indeed, the sporadic, circumscribed extensity and limited intensity of these early arms transfers are such that it is impossible to conceive them as, in any meaningful sense, constituting an arms trade 'system'.

In the premodern era the trade in arms occurred almost exclusively within the confines of separate world civilizations. Bartlett, for instance, describes how in the period 950–1350 Frankish arms and military technology (such as castles and bombardment techniques) spread across Europe (1994, pp. 70–84). By means of conquest and emulation, castles, siege machinery and crossbows became familiar instruments of medieval warfare within Europe. It was perhaps only with the invention of gunpowder and cannon that a more virulent arms trade developed, since both gunpowder and its associated artillery were produced on a significant scale. Even so, the nature of the technology was such that highly localized production tended to be the norm. Family-run local foundries, whose main business was making church bells, were easily adapted to become 'cannon factories'. The result was that by 1360–70 most towns and all major powers across Europe had acquired significant arsenals produced locally, or, alternatively, purchased from various sources in Italy, Germany, France and the Low Countries (see Contamine, 1984, pp. 139–50). This early arms trade was primarily regional, largely in private hands, and lacked state regulation (see Krause, 1992, p. 37; Harkavy, 1975, p. 35).

With the collapse of the medieval European order, the political foundations of this disorganized 'arms market' were undermined. As states began to develop more permanent forms of military organization, such as standing armies and navies, so the need for more rationally organized arms production grew. State authorities sought to

---

[3] According to Contamine the formula for gunpowder was first written down in the Wujumg Zongyao in 1044. It was not until 1267 that Roger Bacon produced the first 'Western' formula for gunpowder. This gap of over 200 years indicates the relatively low level of interaction between known civilizations in this period. Compare this with the late nineteenth century when the major European arms manufacturers, such as Whitworths and Krupps, were selling the most advanced arms abroad, straight from the production line, and sometimes even before they had been acquired by their own national armed forces (see Contamine, 1984, p. 139; and Krause, 1992, p. 66; McNeill, 1982, p. 241). Or compare it with the contemporary era when less than fifty years after the first rockets were constructed in Germany and the USA, states such as China, India, Brazil and many others now have access to missile technology.

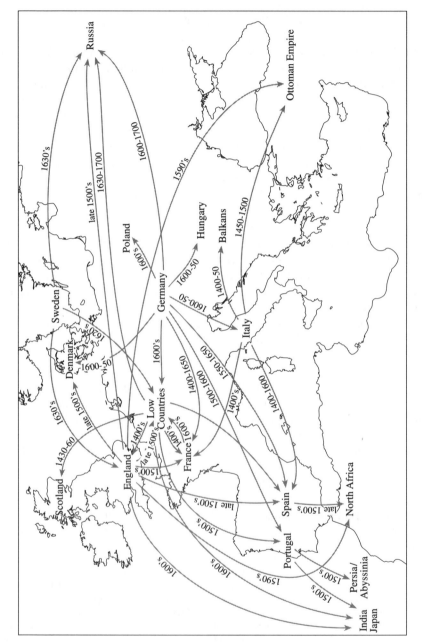

Map 2.4 The arms trade in the early modern period (*Source:* Adapted from Krause, 1992)

monopolize military-related production and commerce, developments legitimated by a policy of autarky. In the case of England, virtual dependence on foreign supplies of gunpowder in the fourteenth century was transformed effectively into outright autarky by the 1520s (Krause, 1992, p. 40). Similarly in Sweden, France, Prussia, Spain and Portugal the process of early modern state formation was associated with the drive for substantive autarky in arms procurement. But, paradoxically, with the huge growth in levels of permanent armed forces during the sixteenth and seventeenth centuries, domestic production by itself became insufficient to fulfil most national requirements (Parker, 1988, p. 61; Black, 1994, p. 9; Krause, 1992, pp. 42–7). Even first-tier arms producers, such as Britain and Sweden, imported some arms, while second-tier producers, such as France, Russia and Spain, experienced significant arms shortages.

The establishment of government arsenals, such as that designed by Colbert in France during the eighteenth century, did not resolve the problem of arms supply since traditional craft production technologies placed severe physical limits on maximum attainable output (see Krause, 1992, pp. 39–47). Russia, for instance, despite attempts to achieve self-sufficiency, had to import significant quantities of firearms, some 40,000 from Holland alone between 1653 and 1655. Major production centres, such as that at Liège, flourished by shipping huge quantities of cannon and muskets across Europe to France, Spain, Britain and Prussia, among other countries. Paradoxically, far from drastically curtailing the arms trade, the limitations of craft production contributed over the medium term to the emergence of an intense intra-European arms trade.

During this period European rulers began for the first time to view arms transfers as a potentially significant instrument in continental power politics. As Krause observes, supplying arms to other nations, both within and outside Europe, was used 'systematically in a positive way by states to influence alliances and the outcome of battles' (1992, p. 42). In addition, the early voyages of conquest and the establishment of worldwide empires created, for the first time, a potentially global arms market. Japan initially began importing firearms and cannon from Europe in the sixteenth century (in 1551 and 1543 respectively), establishing a stockpile of 300,000 units by 1556. By the eighteenth century, imperial conquest and the operation of traders had brought guns in large quantities to West Africa, the Ottoman Empire, India and the Americas. In the mid-seventeenth century the Dutch were exchanging twelve guns for every African slave and as a result it is estimated that approximately 180,000 guns were exported to Africa each year during the period 1658–1750 (Parker, 1988, p. 121; Krause, 1992, p. 56). Firearms also reached the most unlikely destinations. Black relates the story of an American force, at the turn of the nineteenth century, attacking a base of fugitive slaves and Creek Indians in the deepest reaches of Florida's Apalochicola River only to discover 'a regularly constructed fortification built under the direction of a British Colonel maintaining ten cannon with 3200 firearms in the arsenal' (1994, p. 21). A nascent global arms transfer system was taking shape with Europe at its core (see map 2.4).

2.4.2 The modern arms trade: the industrialization of warfare and the global arms market

Following the 'gunpowder revolution', weapons and arms production techniques evolved slowly: military-technological innovation was incremental rather than revolutionary.

When Napoleon invaded Italy in 1796 his soldiers bore arms which hardly differed 'from those with which Charles VIII had done the same almost exactly 300 years earlier' (Creveld, 1989, p. 87). Even at the turn of the nineteenth century arms were still being produced on a craft basis, in small workshops and foundries. However, the coming of industrialization fundamentally altered both the instruments of war and the nature of arms production. It triggered a military-technological revolution perhaps even more profound in its global consequences than the gunpowder revolution six centuries earlier.

With the industrialization of warfare in the nineteenth century came a distinctive new phase in the globalization of arms transfers. The trade in arms was transformed in terms of its extensity, intensity, velocity, impact, institutionalization, patterns of stratification, modes of transfer and the kinds of weapons traded. This transformation was driven by a constellation of factors, including: the process of continual weapons innovation (the Maxim-gun, steamship, the Mini bullet, etc.) which generated a progressively shifting military-technological frontier to which all states sought to aspire; the capability to mass produce weapons and thus to export arms in significant quantities; the emergence of a separate military-industrial sector of the economy which produced weapons largely for profit; a new and more intensive phase of imperial expansion; and the rapid development of a global communications and transport infrastructure facilitating trade of all kinds (see section 1.1.5 above). The result, as McNeill observes, was that by the 1860s 'a global, industrialized armaments business...emerged' (1982, p. 241). A regularized, institutionalized and largely privately run global arms trade system began to develop and function with minimal political interference (except for the period 1914–18) until the 1930s (Harkavy, 1975, p. 36).

Amongst the first-tier arms suppliers – Britain, Germany and France – the key agencies in the military-industrial sector were the large private corporations, such as Krupps, Vickers, Armstrong/Whitworths, Schneider, Creusot. These companies represented enormous concentrations of economic and industrial power and were effectively regarded as 'national champions' in the global arms export market. The combination of almost mass production technologies, international competition and a growing worldwide demand for arms created an arms export boom. In the late nineteenth century, Krupps exported 86.4 per cent of its arms output, while prior to the First World War Schneider was exporting 50 per cent and Vickers 33 per cent (McNeill, 1982, p. 302). As domestic defence markets became increasingly saturated, resulting in military-industrial overcapacity, the drive for exports became even more intense. Moreover, governments sanctioned a largely unregulated trade in arms.

One of the consequences of this free trade regime was that arms were diffused ever more widely throughout the interstate system. Imperial conquest, combined with an increasingly well-developed global trade and communication infrastructure, enhanced the global export prospects of private arms manufacturers. As a result, markets in South America, Asia, the Near East and Africa became increasingly accessible to European arms exporters. In the early twentieth century, Krupps was supplying around 52 states with arms, French manufacturers 23 states, while British companies exported arms to buyers on every continent (Krause, 1992, pp. 59–61). The scale of the arms trade was also considerable. While no systematic or reliable arms trade statistics exist for this period, some measure of transfers is evident from the following statistics: between 100,000 and 150,000 guns were exported annually from Britain to West Africa in the late nineteenth century; French arms sales doubled between 1895 and 1913; by 1914 Krupps had sold over 26,000 cannon (51 per cent of its total production) abroad; while the French company Schneider exported some 45,000 cannon between 1885 and 1914 (Headrick, 1981, p. 106; McNeill, 1982, p. 303; and Krause, 1992, pp. 59–60).

Throughout this period there was tremendous pressure to export in order to recoup the huge research and development (R&D) costs of new weapons systems. This resulted in some arms companies selling the latest high-tech arms on the world market before they had been purchased by their own national armed forces. Armstrongs, a British manufacturer, constructed and exported cruisers that were faster and outgunned those of the Royal Navy; it delivered its initial batch of advanced 8-inch guns to the Russians (Krause, 1992, p. 66). The first submarine constructed in Britain was exported to Greece before the Royal Navy had taken delivery of its own craft (Harkavy, 1975, p. 36). Well before the Great War engulfed Europe, the arms merchants, encouraged by their respective governments, had created a global arms trade system which operated on a largely commercial logic and was effectively beyond the control of governments. As Krause concludes, in the years 1860–1914, 'the international arms transfer system evolved from a hegemonic state in which the first tier monopolized modern weapons supplies to one in which modern arms were diffused throughout the globe' (Krause, 1992, p. 72).

In the aftermath of the Great War, patterns of global arms transfers and production adapted rapidly to the altered geopolitical and economic environment. Rather than defining a new historical discontinuity in respect of the evolution of the modern arms trade system, the war represented more of a temporary hiatus. To a large extent the diffusion of weapons and the commercialization of the arms trade resumed their nineteenth-century course. As more countries industrialized so new arms suppliers, such as Czechoslovakia and Poland, joined the ranks of established suppliers, while the war transformed the United States into a first-tier arms producer; at the same time Germany, under the Versailles settlement, became a non-player (officially at least) in the arms trade.

Political and economic instability during the interwar years encouraged a growth in world military spending which remained in excess of prewar levels (Sloutzki, 1941, p. 23). As military spending grew, so too, until the 1929 crash, did the trade in arms and armaments (A&A) (see figure 2.1). Even throughout the 1930s depression, arms exports fell much less sharply than did exports in general and they recovered much more rapidly (Sloutzki, 1941, p. 67). In comparison with the previous century, a significantly larger number of states were engaged in selling arms on the world market. As a consequence, the structure of the international arms market arguably became less concentrated and increasingly more oligopolistic. Although a global hierarchy of military-technological capabilities existed, the number of first-tier, second-tier and third-tier producers showed some increase (Harkavy, 1975, p. 90). Around twenty countries were involved in exporting arms with nine accounting for almost 90 per cent of world arms exports (Sloutzki, 1941, p. 72). While the major powers still dominated the arms business they had to confront many new competitors. Harkavy's comprehensive study of the interwar arms trade concludes that for virtually all classes of major weapons systems there existed a considerable multiplicity of potential suppliers (1975). Interestingly, production of the most advanced military technologies, such as combat aircraft or tanks, was even more widely diffused than it was to be in the post-1945

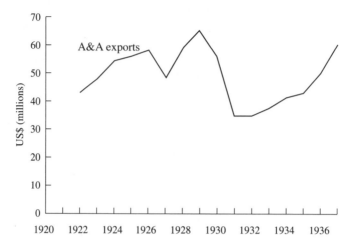

Figure 2.1 The global arms trade in the interwar period (*Sources:* Sloutzki, 1941; League of Nations, *Statistical Yearbook of the Trade in Arms and Ammunition*, Geneva, various years)

period. Three major political consequences flowed from this situation: procurement of even the latest weapons systems became relatively easy for any state with the necessary resources; arms purchasers constantly sought to diversify their sources of supply; and effective control of the arms trade came to require international cooperation.

Extremely complex webs of arms trading relations developed during this period. As governments sought to enhance their autonomy they acquired arms from many different suppliers. So evolved a multiple-supplier pattern of trade with the result that, by the late 1930s, the great majority of nations in all regions of the world were purchasing arms from the rival blocs of democracy and dictatorship (Harkavy, 1975, p. 127). In turn, these overlapping trade relations invited more intense military interconnections between, and across, the world's major regions. For, where multiple-supplier patterns existed, arms importers effectively mediated connections between competing supplier networks, generating greater complexity and interdependencies within the arms trading system. In this sense, the arms trade during the interwar period acquired a powerful systemic dynamic; it became more of a structured totality than was evident in previous historical periods.

In respect of the extensity of the trade, the number of states importing weapons approached sixty, plus a further sixty protectorates or colonies (Sloutzki, 1941, p. 72). Markets in China and Latin America, in particular, became increasingly salient in this period.

One distinctive feature of the interwar arms trade was the emergence of new mechanisms or modes of arms transfer, such as production licensing and transnational production. Following postwar demobilization, the restructuring of arms manufacturing across the globe, combined with the growth of international cartels more generally (see chapter 5), stimulated a significant transnationalization of the arms production business (Harkavy, 1975, p. 38). This took different commercial forms, from the existence of transnational interlocking directorates and stock ownership, to foreign licensing, to the establishment of corporate subsidiaries abroad. Licensed production, as opposed to direct sales, came to account for a significant slice of arms transfers. In comparison with traditional modes of arms supply, licensing created more institutionalized and regularized patterns of relations, since it involved the transfer of knowledge, techniques and production organization. In the most advanced sectors, such as combat aircraft, it also became the dominant mode of arms transfer. Licensees also tended to acquire multiple licences so as not to be dependent on any single company. In the 1930s Japan acquired production licences from British, German and US aero-engine companies while Sweden acquired production licences for combat aircraft from the UK, the US and German companies (Harkavy, 1975, p. 170).

Propelled by commercial competition and static domestic markets, many arms companies established subsidiaries abroad. British shipbuilding companies invested abroad in new production facilities while Junkers built bombers in Sweden and Krupps built submarines in Holland (Harkavy, 1975, p. 173; Krause, 1992, p. 77). Such developments represented the initial stages of a transnational restructuring of defence production which, in part, was a commercial response to a growing and largely unregulated global arms market. However, with the onset of war, arms production was decisively nationalized across the globe. In this respect, the Second World War defines a much greater discontinuity in the evolution of the global arms trade than did the Great War.

Although the 1939–45 war did not prefigure a complete cessation in the international trade in arms it did involve a dramatic reconfiguration of the existing interwar pattern. Arms production was dedicated solely to the war effort. In effect, the war transformed the established global structure of supply, acquisition patterns, and modes of arms transfers. It also required massive state intervention to organize and redirect huge scientific, financial and industrial resources to ensure a continuous flow of arms and military innovation (Pearton, 1982). Not surprisingly, the arms trade came to be dominated (until more recently) by the two superpowers, the US and the Soviet Union, as first-tier suppliers. It reacquired a global dimension as the Cold War ensured that arms transfers became a major instrument of East–West rivalry. But, in large measure, the Cold War arms transfer system can be viewed as something of a historical aberration since it was dominated by governments and decisively conditioned by the bipolar structure of world politics.

2.4.3 The contemporary arms trade: extensity, intensity and stratification

Before examining the distinctive features of the contemporary arms transfer system, it might be helpful to place this in the context of the key trends and patterns in postwar global military expenditure, military capabilities and arms sales. Following demobilization in 1945, world military expenditure grew fairly rapidly until the early 1950s, stabilized until the 1960s, and then resumed an upward trajectory. It peaked in 1987 at around US$1,000 billion, and since the end of the Cold War it has been in steady decline. Over the three decades 1960–90 total world military expenditure amounted to a staggering $21,000,000,000,000 (in 1987 US dollars) (Sivard, 1991, p. 11). Of course, these global trends disguise several important features of the distribution of arms spending. Over much of this period NATO and the Warsaw Pact states accounted for the largest proportion of world military spending, while spending by the two superpowers alone constituted by far the largest part of total world military spending. But

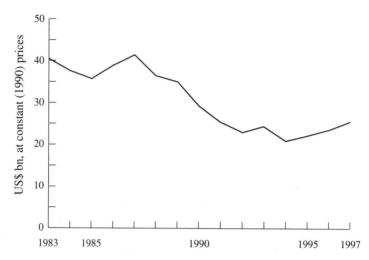

Figure 2.2   Global exports of major conventional weapons, 1983–1997 (*Source*: SIPRI, 1998, p. 292)

in the post-Cold War era the US and Russian share of world military spending has declined. However, Western military spending still accounts for the largest single proportion of the world total. Of growing significance is the expansion in defence spending within the developing world. Since the 1960s defence expenditure within the developing world has constituted an increasing share of total world military spending.

Parallel trends are evident in the world arms trade. While the intensity of arms transfers has increased dramatically since 1945 much of this growth is directly related to the military build-ups of the early 1960s, mid-1970s and mid-1980s. Arms exports reached a postwar peak of $48–50 billion in the mid-1980s after which they declined precipitately to below half that figure in 1991 (see figure 2.2). Even so, in the post-Cold War era the value of world arms exports remains above that of the 1960s. But global figures disguise a significant structural shift in the pattern of arms transfers. From the late 1960s onwards the developing world purchased the largest share of world arms imports, dwarfing the level of trade between the major OECD countries. (Interestingly, this situation is almost the inverse of the trend in the structure of merchandise trade and foreign direct investment over this period, see chapters 3 and 5 below.) Some indication of the scale of this shift is given by Brzoska and Ohlson, who note that between 1971 and 1985 arms purchases by the developing world totalled $286 billion (constant 1985 US dollars), four times the value of its total purchases in the period 1951–70 (1987, p. 1). But from the early 1990s, the combined consequences of the end of the Cold War and global recession resulted in arms purchases by the developing world declining both in absolute terms and as a proportion of total world arms imports. To date, this appears to be a cyclical rather than a structural trend (Laurance, 1992, p. 134).

Bound up with these shifts in the extensity and intensity of the global arms trade is a parallel shift in patterns of stratification. After the 1970s the number of countries supplying arms on the world market steadily increased to around forty in 1990 (Laurance, 1992, p. 103). This is a considerably greater number than in any previous epoch (see figures 2.3 and 2.4). Moreover, until recently, this expansion of suppliers was associated

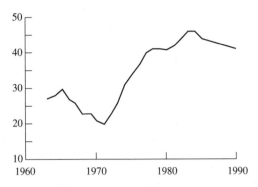

Figure 2.3 Numbers of countries supplying arms, 1960–1990 (*Source*: Laurance, 1992)

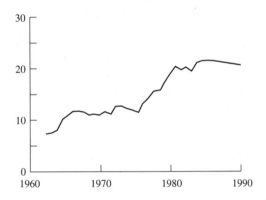

Figure 2.4 Numbers of countries supplying arms to the developing world, 1960–1990
(*Source*: Laurance, 1992)

with decreasing levels of concentration within the arms transfer market (measured in terms of supplier shares of the global arms trade) as new producers captured an increasing share of the world arms export market. Underlying this decreased concentration were the aggressive sales policies of second-tier producers, such as France, Britain, China and Germany, alongside the rapid emergence of third-tier producers, such as Israel, India, Brazil and South Korea (among others) (see Krause, 1992, p. 86; Brzoska and Ohlson, 1987, p. 112). Since 1990, when Russian arms exports collapsed and the end of the Cold War heightened international competition in the arms business, the trend towards lower levels of producer concentration has been temporarily reversed (Anthony, 1994a).

As the number of arms producers has grown over the postwar period, so too has the number of arms purchasers. From the 1970s onwards the total number of purchasers has remained pretty much stable at over a hundred countries (Laurance, 1992, p. 135). This is not so different from the interwar period, excepting that decolonization has swollen the number of independent states. But in terms of geographical scope, no world region or continent remains outside the contemporary arms transfer system, although there is considerable unevenness in respect of regional and national levels of enmeshment. Furthermore, this unevenness is evident particularly in relation to arms imports; the top ten arms importers have consistently accounted for around 50 per cent of total world arms imports throughout the postwar period. The diffusion of modern weapons is much more 'lumpy' than is suggested by any simple picture of progressive global militarization (Krause, 1992, p. 188).

With the demise of the Soviet Union the US now dominates, as in the immediate postwar period, the arms supply business. Even so, many more arms suppliers exist today than in 1945 and with defence expenditures in most parts of the world in decline the competition for arms exports is intense. The contemporary arms transfer system therefore remains very much a buyer's market, with the consequence that the US position today is quite markedly different from 1945 when it had an effective arms supply monopoly.

Although the trend over the postwar era has been towards greater diversity in terms of suppliers and purchasers, the system remains distinctly hierarchical. In this respect, the supplier market has become less concentrated (Laurance, 1992). Yet despite this, the top six arms suppliers (US, UK, France, China, Russia, Germany) continue to account for the bulk of world arms transfers. These patterns are replicated in respect of arms exports to the Third World even though the supply situation is a little more diverse (see Brzoska and Ohlson, 1987, app. 4A/B). There is also a clear hierarchy in the arms import market, although it is a considerably less concentrated one than the arms supply sector. As Anthony notes, in the early 1990s, 25 states accounted for 90 per cent of weapons imports, somewhat less than in earlier years (1994a). Associated with this hierarchical pattern is a distinctive geography: there is a tremendous unevenness in the spatial patterns of arms exports and imports. Over the postwar period there has been a detectable geographical shift in the locus of the arms trade away from the North (in the early postwar years), to the Middle East (late 1960s on), and more recently towards Asia (see Krause, 1992, p. 184).

In addition, Laurance observes that, in comparison with the period up to the 1960s, the arms market has become 'increasingly commercial in nature, as measured by the steady increase in the percentage of trade that does not directly involve the government as a contracting party' (1992, p. 147). This is unlikely to be simply a cyclical phenomenon. The dramatic downturn in the global defence market following the end of the Cold War is forcing all arms producers to compete increasingly in the export market, since governments view this as a strategy to sustain a national defence industrial base. Further, there is a growing trend towards the privatization and commercialization of defence production in all states, including China, thereby reinforcing export competition.

This brief discussion of key trends in the evolution of the postwar contemporary arms transfer system can be summarized in three key points:

- First, the extent of direct and indirect involvement in the arms trade (however unevenly experienced) is such that the term 'global' arms transfer system appears entirely warranted.
- Second, the extensity of the contemporary arms trade, along with the density and velocity of the associated transactions, are further evidence of the existence of a highly interconnected world military order. In these respects, the contemporary arms transfer system has come to assume some attributes characteristic of the late nineteenth century.
- Third, the contemporary arms trade involves the diffusion of advanced weapons systems and weapons of unprecedented destructive power. The proliferation of

advanced military capabilities is a product of both the arms competition and global patterns of industrialization. Most weapons now transferred to the developing world are new rather than refurbished (Brzoska and Ohlson, 1987, p. 11). Moreover, an increasing number of developing states continue to acquire advanced military capabilities. Between 1980 and 1990 the number of countries acquiring surface-to-air missile systems (SAMs) and advanced fighter aircraft (AFA) increased considerably (see Laurance, 1992). One of the military consequences of the proliferation of advanced technologies, such as ballistic missiles, advanced combat aircraft and surface ships, is to augment the capacity of some developing countries to project considerable strategic power over huge distances.

Contemporary arms transfers are therefore contributing to a redistribution of military capability in the global system. But the proliferation of advanced weapons can only be properly understood in the context of the worldwide diffusion of military-industrial production capabilities.

2.4.4 The global diffusion of arms production capability: the early modern and modern eras

In the early modern period, proximity to raw materials and to centres of military and political authority were the predominant determinants of the geography of arms production. Within the world's major civilizations, arms were undoubtedly produced on a significant scale. War, conquest and empire-building were the primary mechanisms by which military technologies in one locale were transferred to others. When, over a thousand years ago, the Franks expanded across Europe, they brought with them new kinds of castles and siege weapons (Bartlett, 1994). During the Middle Ages the crusades facilitated the diffusion of military technologies between East and West. Within medieval Europe cannon and artillery technology spread from Italy, such that within the space of twenty years all but the most peripheral regions had acquired (through emulation) their own production facilities (Contamine, 1984, pp. 139–50). Five decades after first appearing in Europe the technology had reached the Balkans and the Ottoman Empire. But the gunpowder revolution also represented a quite important stage in respect of the institutional mechanisms and infrastructures by which military-technological capability came to be spread. For the production of artillery and firearms required a highly skilled workforce. Accordingly, from the late medieval era throughout much of the early modern period, the diffusion of military technology 'primarily took the form of the migration of skilled workers' (Krause, 1992, p. 44). Prior to the Thirty Years' War, Gustav Adolphus made Sweden an advanced military power by acquiring Dutch military technology through the migration of Dutch arms makers (Parker, 1988, p. 23).

Within Europe, the transfer of military technology was effectively unregulated and there was considerable commerce in military technology. Weapons technology 'leaked' beyond Europe too, via trade networks, missionaries and the first empires, into Asia, Latin America and Africa. The Mughal army exploited Western military technology as did the Japanese, the Ottomans and the Chinese (Parker, 1988, pp. 126–9; Krause, 1992, pp. 48–53). Even so, the Indian artillery in the late eighteenth century still 'had not advanced upon the technologies of the fifteenth' (Krause, 1992, p. 52). Despite the diffusion of European military technology, Western Europe sustained its technological superiority until well into the twentieth century.

With the consolidation of the absolutist state, both the pace of military innovation and the diffusion of military technology slowed appreciably. Throughout Europe, rulers developed state owned and managed arsenals, effecting state control of all military production. With the Industrial Revolution, however, military-technological innovation came to be driven primarily by developments in the civil sector (Creveld, 1989, p. 220). The technologies and production methods which enabled the development of the steamship, railways and telegraphs transformed not only the actual instruments of warfare but their production. New forms of state-military-industry relations arose to exploit civil technologies both for military production and for the battlefield. As new civil industrial technologies and methods spread, so too did the capacity to produce both advanced weapons systems and armaments in vast quantities.

Following the Great Exhibition in 1851, Britain acquired American advanced production techniques and machinery specifically for the (yet to be constructed) Enfield armoury and by 1863 it was producing 100,370 rifles per annum (McNeill, 1982, pp. 233–5). By 1870 the rest of Europe was doing the same. Industrial capitalism was contributing to a significant diffusion of military productive capability as well as military-related technology. This process of diffusion was no longer, as it appeared to be in the absolutist era, under the direct control of governments. For the primary agents were the great private industrial concerns of the age, the Krupps, Vickers, Schneiders and Armstrongs, whose interests lay in expanding markets for their products and know-how. There were also a host of other smaller commercial concerns willing to export military production technology or civil technologies with military applications. Russia modernized its military production capability at the turn of the century with the direct assistance of the major European arms producers (Krause, 1992, p. 66). Likewise Japan, China, Italy, Austro-Hungary, the Ottoman Empire, Spain and newly independent nations in Latin America imported foreign military technology as part of a strategy of economic modernization (McNeill, 1982; Krause, 1992).

By the early twentieth century, all global regions were becoming integrated into a world military-technological order in which military-industrial developments within the first tier of producers (Britain, France, Germany and the USA) were quite rapidly diffused to second-tier (Russia, Austro-Hungary, Italy, Spain) and third-tier producers (Japan, China, Turkey) through emulation and transnational networks of military-technological innovation.

Although the 1914–18 war temporarily halted trade in military-industrial technologies, previous patterns quickly re-emerged during the interwar period. Well into the late 1930s, foreign licensed production 'accounted for a fairly significant proportion of the total arms transfers . . . averaging nearly 20 per cent for categories other than warships and submarines' (Harkavy, 1975, p. 150). In parallel, arms production became more internationalized through the operation of international cartels and the establishment of foreign production ventures by many of the leading arms companies. Through both these mechanisms, weapons technology and military production technology in key defence sectors, such as combat aircraft, dispersed beyond the primary first-tier producers to the second and third tiers. Even so, the hierarchy of military-productive capability altered little from the early interwar years. With the approach of war, the diffusion of military technology became increasingly regulated by governments, such that it was well into the postwar period before licensed production attained its prewar levels.

2.4.5 Contemporary patterns of global arms production: extensity, intensity, stratification and institutionalization

The structure of contemporary global military production is summarized in table 2.1. Five features are worth elaboration. First, the Soviet Union and the US, not surprisingly, dominated global arms production for much of the postwar period but today the US is, without doubt, the leading arms producer. Not since the military-industrial revolution of the early nineteenth century has the gap in military production capacity between the great powers and subordinate powers been so dramatic. Moreover, when military-technological capacity is taken into account (measured in terms of military R&D expenditure) the gap is even more remarkable. Second, despite this gap the number of states with significant military production capabilities in the second and third tiers is probably greater than at any time in the modern era. Third, the expansion in the number of second-tier states reflects a return to the prewar situation (and even further back perhaps, with some historical continuities with arms production centres in medieval times). Fourth, the third-tier arms producers are now predominantly to be found within the newly industrialized and industrializing regions of the globe. This defines a significant shift in the locus of arms production since in previous historical eras the third-tier countries were predominantly located on the European periphery. Finally, in terms of the extensity of arms production, the table reflects the rapid diffusion of military technological-productive capacity westwards, eastwards, and to the south. No global region is without at least two centres of indigenous military production and no regional power is without some domestic military production capability.

Since the close of the Second World War there has been a rapid and extensive diffusion of both military technology and the means to produce modern weapons systems. In his study of technology and warfare, Creveld concludes that the contemporary era 'differs from many previous ones in that a single, fairly homogeneous, military technology is recognized everywhere as dominant' (1989, p. 290). What have been the key processes underlying this historic shift?

From the 1970s the accelerating pace of capitalist industrialization in Asia, Latin America and the Middle East has facilitated a noticeable expansion in indigenous military production capabilities.[4] Between 1960 and 1980 the number of developing countries producing sophisticated military systems almost doubled (Brzoska and Ohlson, 1986; Newman, 1984). By exploiting their developing industrial infrastructure, states such as Brazil and Taiwan have been able to construct a significant defence industrial base. Such a base has enabled entry into the arms export market too. Of course, in most cases this transformation has not been achieved without external assistance, and

---

[4] Note that the term indigenous capabilities refers here to the capacity to produce domestically rather than (necessarily) an autonomous production capability. Only the US and Russia may claim to have an effectively autonomous (but not completely so) defence industrial base.

Table 2.1 The world military order: the structure of arms production

	1980	1993
First-tier arms producers	United States	United States
	Soviet Union	
Second-tier arms producers	Britain	Russia (CIS)
	France	Britain
	Germany	France
	Japan	Germany
	Poland	Japan
	Italy	China
	Canada	Italy
	Czechoslovakia	Canada
	Netherlands	Sweden
	Spain	Spain
	Sweden	Belgium
	Switzerland	Switzerland
	Belgium	Czech Republic
		Poland
		Netherlands
Third-tier arms producers	China	India
	India	Israel
	Israel	Brazil
	Yugoslavia	South Korea
	South Africa	Argentina
	Brazil	Taiwan
	South Korea	Turkey
	Argentina	Pakistan
	Taiwan	Greece
	Turkey	Singapore
	Egypt	South Africa
	Pakistan	Egypt
	North Korea	North Korea
	Singapore	Serbia
	Greece	Iran
	Iraq	Iraq
Fourth-tier arms purchasers	The rest	The rest

the direct transfer of military technology has played and continues to play (in many cases) an important role in nurturing indigenous military capability. Nevertheless, it is a startling fact that in 1950 the total value of indigenous arms production in the entire developing world was 'roughly equivalent to the cost in the mid-1980s of one main battle tank,' yet by 1984 it was nearly 500 times greater (Brzoska and Ohlson, 1986, p. 7).

Until the 1960s, most transfers of military technology were from the superpowers to their client states. The primary object of their transfers was to assist in the reconstruction and strengthening of the military industrial base within the core states of their respective alliance systems. By the 1970s, licensed production became a key institutional mechanism through which military technology was transferred not just within each alliance, but also between the major suppliers and Third World states. By far the largest single licenser of military technology is the US (see figure 2.5), while the largest licensees are Italy and Japan. But the largest single group of licensees are the newly industrializing nations. In those developing states engaged in military production, licensed production accounts for a significant proportion of total domestic arms output and is conspicuously more important in respect of advanced military systems. Moreover, a small number of Western companies dominate licensed arms production in the developing world.

As the growth in foreign licensing since the 1960s suggests, commercial forces rather than geopolitics have become increasingly powerful determinants of the global pattern of military technology transfer. This has become even more apparent since interbloc rivalry has been replaced by a more fluid international environment in which geopolitics takes second place to geo-economics. Moreover, the consequent collapse of world defence spending has triggered a major restructuring of indigenous defence industries on every continent. But the process of defence industrial restructuring also has its origins in the constantly rising costs of advanced military technologies and weapons production. Such costs have consistently outpaced the growth in defence procurement budgets. Declining defence spending since the late 1980s has forced national defence industries to confront both the problems of cost escalation and production overcapacity.[5] The demise of the Cold War has accelerated this process. Within Europe, transnational collaboration, co-development and co-production arrangements have emerged as solutions to cost escalation, but more recently they have been triggered by problems of overcapacity. From the 1980s a new trend developed within the Western defence industry: the transnationalization of defence production.

Alongside the expansion of licensed production, major American and European defence companies have engaged much more actively in novel forms of international collaboration. Subcontracting, global sourcing, co-production, multinational consortia, joint ventures, strategic alliances and co-development projects have all become more prevalent (see figures 2.6 and 2.7) (Bitzinger, 1994; Skons, 1993). International subcontracting is now extensive, while for many major arms projects forms of co-production (FSX US General Dynamics and Japan's Mitsubishi Company), co-development (FSX; Eurocopter; European Fighter Aircraft), multinational consortia (European Fighter Aircraft (Typhoon)) and joint ventures (Eurocopter) have acquired increasing importance. In addition, as the pressures for industrial restructuring have grown more intense, the number of cross-border mergers, acquisitions and corporate strategic alliances has increased significantly (Bitzinger, 1994). This is most transparent in the advanced defence sectors of aerospace and electronics.

Such developments represent a significant transnationalization of the Western defence industrial base, a process which is being driven by a commercial logic, as opposed to primarily domestic or national security requirements (Skons, 1993). But this transnationalization reflects too a more generalized pattern across all advanced capitalist economies which, since the 1970s, have witnessed a considerable expansion of

---

[5] Some indication of this cost escalation is provided by E. B. Kapstein who notes that in 1970 US firms sold 3,500 military aircraft for $4bn, by 1975 they sold half that number for the same price, by 1980 it was down to 1,000 at $6bn, and by 1985 919 at $18bn (1994a, pp. 13–19).

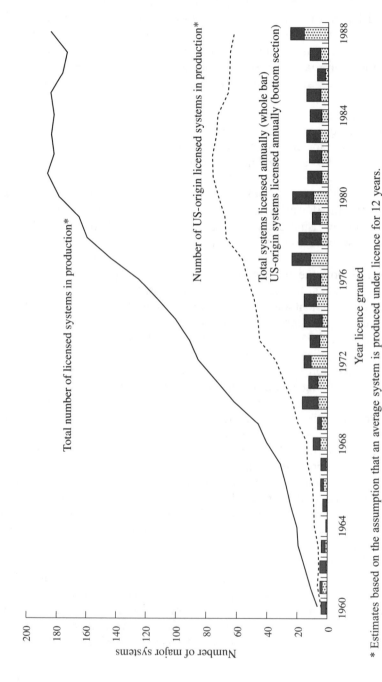

* Estimates based on the assumption that an average system is produced under licence for 12 years.

Figure 2.5 Estimated worldwide licensed production of major conventional weapons systems, 1960–1988
(*Source:* US Congress, 1991, from SIPRI data)

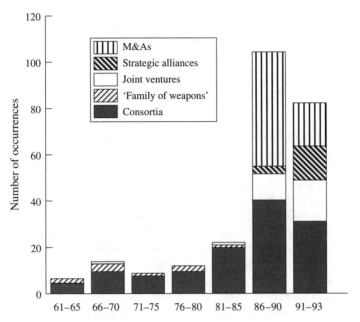

Figure 2.6 Interfirm linkages within the global defence industry, 1961–1993
(*Source*: Bitzinger, 1993)

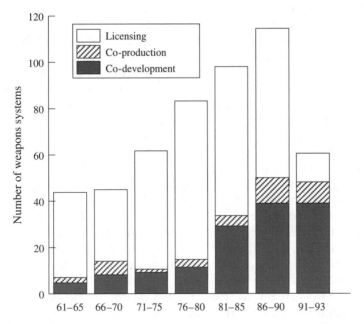

Figure 2.7 Globalization of arms production by production activity, 1961–1993
(*Source*: Bitzinger, 1993)

internationalized production (see chapter 5 below). However, some caution is required in interpreting these trends, since this transnationalization tends to be regionally concentrated rather than truly global. A more accurate description may therefore be cast in terms of regionalization, although a number of trans-Atlantic and trans-Pacific collaborative defence projects and corporate arrangements do exist (some would argue an increasing number). Nevertheless, as Taylor concludes, 'to think of defence corporations as national entities under the dominant influence of their home governments is less and less appropriate. The development and production of defence equipment is increasingly being organized on an international basis' (T. Taylor, 1990).

In the contemporary era of declining defence procurement budgets, the transnationalization of defence production provides one solution to the maintenance of a 'national' defence industrial capacity. Accordingly, this is not simply a process which is confined to Europe, or the transatlantic region, where it is most evident, but one which is a part of a secular trend in defence industrial restructuring (Bitzinger, 1994). This is largely because for many big defence companies 'internationalization is one strategy of consolidation for long-term survival in the market' (Skons, 1993, p. 160). Restructuring of the national defence industrial base unfolds alongside a global restructuring of defence production. In varying degrees, all countries engaged in defence production are gradually being touched by these twin developments. As a consequence, in parallel to many political phenomena discussed earlier (see chapter 1), the distinction between the foreign and the domestic is breaking down. Indeed, the enormous complexity of cross-border intercorporate and production networks involves a 'shift away from traditional, single-country patterns of weapons production towards more transnational development and manufacture of arms' (Bitzinger, 1993, p. 7). Volvo Aero Engines AB, for instance, produces engine parts for US Navy fighters while simultaneously being engaged in licensed production of an engine for the Swedish Gripen advanced fighter aircraft. As in the commercial sector, global sourcing of defence production is a growing practice as cost containment becomes more critical. For industrializing states with an indigenous defence production capability, global sourcing remains essential to meeting defence needs (Brzoska and Ohlson, 1986, p. 285). But it is also supplemented by other forms of collaboration, sometimes with the governments of other developing countries or advanced states, in the development or production of 'indigenous' military systems (Bitzinger, 1993, p. 35). In the post-Cold War era, the global diffusion of military technology and defence industrial capacity is becoming closely associated with a transnationalization of defence production.

The spread of both defence industrial capability and military technology is facilitated by the increasingly central role acquired by commercial (civil) technologies (and civil technological innovation) in the development and manufacture of advanced weapons systems. The military-technological revolution (MTR) of the late twentieth century is a product of the 'information age'. The same technologies which are revolutionizing aspects of everyday life, from the supermarket checkout to personal communications, are transforming the logistics of war and the modern battlefield, which, as the 1991 Gulf War demonstrated, is now 'constructed' as 'a blizzard of electronic blips' rather than a 'storm of steel' (Creveld, 1989, p. 282). Hardly surprising, then, that when Lieutenant-General Gus Pagonis, the officer responsible for US military logistics during the 1991 Gulf War, retired he was hired immediately by Sears Roebuck (the fourth largest retail business in the US) to take charge of their distribution system (Economist Intelligence Unit, 1995, p. 5).

Key technologies are today largely dual-use technologies. The traditional boundary between civil and military-industrial sectors appears to be crumbling. As Laurance observes, 'we are seeing the passing of the time when industry could be neatly divided into military and non-military compartments' (1992, p. 146). While these boundaries have always been blurred (witness the largely bogus distinction between 'civil' and 'military' nuclear technology) dual-use technologies have become both more prevalent and increasingly essential to the functioning of advanced military systems. Some argue that much military-technological innovation is now the product of a 'spin-on' effect, as advances in civil technologies are consciously exploited for military purposes (Stowsky, 1992). In 1990 one survey of twenty large US industrial corporations reported that spin-ons from commercial products accounted for 'the majority of goods that the firms produced for the military' (Economist Intelligence Unit, 1994, p. 13). This apparent 'civilianization' of the defence industrial base is reminiscent of the situation in the nineteenth century as the Industrial Revolution began to transform military production and arms technology. It may, in turn, also have equally profound global consequences.

Dual-use technologies are, by definition, commercial and the industries that produce them are considerably more globalized than the defence industrial sector. As a consequence, most dual-use technologies are intensively traded across the globe, while the capability to produce them is actively dispersed through the operations of transnational corporations. According to Carus, the 'result is that an increasingly large number of countries have access to many of the technologies needed to exploit the military technological revolution' (1994). This in turn is transforming the stratification of military-technological power within the global system. For the cohort of states and corporations at the leading edge of commercial technological innovation is no longer entirely synonymous with the cohort of today's great military powers or military-industrial corporations. In this respect, it is instructive to note that in 1989 38 per cent of US military semiconductors were imported while the Pentagon 'cannot put a single missile or aircraft up in the sky without the help of three Japanese companies that provide 95 per cent of the ceramic packages that protect their electronics' (OTA, 1991, p. 38; Economist Intelligence Unit, 1994, p. 18).

2.5 Emerging Forms of Geogovernance: Organized Violence

The regulation of military power articulates an important political, ethical and juridical interface between the war system and the global arms dynamic. Essentially it represents a process of primitive global governance of the world military order and a form of what was earlier called cosmopolitan law (see section 1.3.3 above). By mapping the attributes of historical patterns of the geogovernance of organized violence, a much richer understanding will be yielded of the process of military globalization. The analysis will concentrate on three domains: the emergence of international security regimes; the regulation of war and military conflict; and the regulation of the instruments of war.

2.5.1   Geogovernance of military power: international security regimes

Sir Robert Walpole was a strong believer in the value of international alliances, observing that the use of alliances 'has in the last age been too much experienced to be contested. It is by leagues, well concerted and strictly observed, that the weak are defended against the strong' (quoted in Kegley and Raymond, 1994, p. 93). Historically, alliances have been a traditional mechanism by which states have coordinated the use and deployment of military force. At a minimum, alliances involve interstate agreement on 'the conditions under which they [states] will or will not employ military force' (Russett quoted in Kegley and Raymond, 1994, p. 90). They have also tended to be of a rather pragmatic nature, devised to deal with immediate contingencies. But they can involve much greater degrees of military collaboration or coordination of defence and national security policies, and can be relatively permanent features of the geopolitical landscape. Compared to previous centuries the major alliance arrangements in the postwar era have been much more formal and institutionalized. Alliances represent one means by which the state's employment of military power is regulated at an interstate level. To varying degrees they also represent a process of the internationalization of military security.

Even before the early modern period, alliances and pacts were used by rulers and princes in all major civilizations as a means to deter or prosecute war (Watson, 1992). But with the evolution of the modern states system, alliances became the primary mechanism for regulating rivalries between European states. Early alliance formations were bilateral or trilateral pacts between the great powers designed to meet immediate threats. They tended to be very flexible arrangements in that states frequently changed alliance partners in response to new international conditions. Such pacts operated in secret or involved secret undertakings and were abhorred for that very reason by President Woodrow Wilson, the main architect of the League of Nations. But by the mid-twentieth century, with the onset of the Cold War, the form and the dynamics of alliance formations were significantly transformed.

Specifically, both superpowers established formal, quasi-permanent, regional and multilateral alliances. These effectively covered all the world's major regions, creating a global 'patchwork' of military and security arrangements. These arrangements were formal, legalized in treaties, and more institutionalized than comparable arrangements in previous epochs. New organizational structures, such as NATO and the Warsaw Pact, were established, requiring the coordination of national defence and security policies. In effect, the postwar system of global alliances defined a historically unique form of international security regime (those norms, rules and decision-making procedures which regulate the military/security domain) which locked member states into special kinds of collective defence arrangements. Those states outside these alliance arrangements were forced either into informal defence pacts with a superpower or alternatively to adopt a defensive strategy of non-alignment. In this sense, the existence of global alliance systems regulated (either directly or indirectly) the defence postures of all states in the interstate system.

In the post-Cold War world the trend towards institutionalized alliance arrangements has not abated. What has changed is the greater emphasis now placed on strengthening and extending regional cooperative security or multilateral defence mechanisms. This is particularly evident in the post-Cold War European security order. NATO still remains the key forum within which Western European defence strategies are formulated and agreed. Its day-to-day functioning has encouraged the creation of strong transgovernmental networks, or communities of interest, between national defence bureaucracies and military forces. Even the ending of the Cold War has not undermined it, since it has expanded to include some former Warsaw Pact members (such as Poland, Hungary and the Czech Republic) and, through the Partnership for Peace (PFP) arrangement, Russia, Sweden and other European states. In both the routine conduct of its affairs and in times of international crisis, NATO provides an institutional mechanism for multilateral decision-making and military cooperation which significantly qualifies the idea of national security and military autonomy. Security is no longer simply defined in terms of the defence of national territorial boundaries, but rather in terms of collective defence and international security.

The ending of the Cold War, combined with instabilities in Europe, has encouraged further this internationalization or, more accurately, regionalization of security affairs. Existing institutions such as the Western European Union and the Organization for Security and Cooperation in Europe have been given new responsibilities and functions. These have involved the creation of distinctive mechanisms of international consultation and coordination which reach deeply into the domestic affairs of member states. Europe, in effect, is witnessing the development of a new structure of collective security – a revised 'Concert of Europe' (see below) – which invites a tighter integration of military and security affairs. Collective defence rather than solely national defence is today a reality within the Atlantic arena. It is instructive to note that even traditionally neutral states such as Sweden no longer feel able to sustain their military independence and neutral posture. Moreover, given increasing budgetary constraints and the escalating costs of defence hardware, 'in the not too distant future, no European country will be able to mount a unilateral conventional military campaign that can defeat any adversary able to conduct modern military operations' (see Zelikow, 1992, pp. 12–30). Military-industrial factors reinforce the trend towards stronger collective organization of defence functions.

Beyond Europe, too, there are similar developments in the direction of the globalization and regionalization of security regimes in Asia (within ASEAN), Africa (OAU) and Latin America (OAS). Within ASEAN, the ASEAN Regional Forum (ARF) constitutes an evolving consultative arrangement between the Asia-Pacific nations and key global powers such as the US and EU in respect of regional security affairs (Leifer, 1996). As Snyder observes, it represents an important and novel step towards the institutionalization of security cooperation and multilateral dialogue in the Asia-Pacific (1996). But this trend is quite unevenly experienced and it is moderated by the weak norms of international society in some regions as well as existing regional rivalries and enmities.

In parallel with this regionalization and globalization of security is a developing recognition that traditional conceptions of security which privilege notions of 'national security' are no longer adequate in the post-Cold War context. In the 1990s the practice of collective security has been revised and rehabilitated following the legacy of the failure of the League of Nations 'experiment'.

The practice of collective security had its origins in the Concert of Europe (1815–70) which, through a system of institutionalized great power conferences, reinforced relative peace and security within Europe for much of the nineteenth century (I. Clark, 1989, ch. 6). The Concert system could be described as an international security regime. Zelikow argues that security arrangements in post-Cold War Europe are beginning to resemble a new Concert system (1992). But, unlike in the Concert era, the contemporary regionalization of security (within and beyond Europe) is also conjoined with international initiatives to re-establish a cooperative or common security regime at the global level within the context of a reformed United Nations.

In theory, membership of the United Nations involves participation in a global collective security regime since the Charter provides for the UN to act against aggressors and to restore the peace (see Chapters I and VII of the UN Charter). But the Cold War prevented the UN from developing its collective security function. However, the recent phenomenal growth in UN peacekeeping activities (see table 2.2) and the legitimacy accorded to evolving international norms of collective action imply some shift in the international community's attitudes to collective and cooperative security. This reflects a strong perception that, in an interconnected world order, effective security cannot be achieved merely through unilateral action. Rather, national and international security are considered in some degree indivisible. In the contemporary global system the resolution of the national security dilemma has acquired a significant regional and global dimension.

Table 2.2 UN peacekeeping activities

UN missions in Cold War period

MIDDLE EAST – UNTSO
United Nations Truce Supervision Organization
June 1948–present[a]

INDIA/PAKISTAN – UNMOGIP
United Nations Military Observer group in India and Pakistan
January 1949–present[a]

MIDDLE EAST – UNEF I
First United Nations Emergency Force
November 1956–June 1967

LEBANON – UNOGIL
United Nations Observation Group in Lebanon
June 1958–December 1958

CONGO – ONUC
United Nations Operation in the Congo
July 1960–June 1964

WEST NEW GUINEA – UNSF
United Nations Security Force in West New Guinea (West Irian)
October 1962–April 1963

YEMEN – UNYOM
United Nations Yemen Observation Mission
July 1963–September 1964

continued

Table 2.2 *continued*

CYPRUS – UNFICYP
United Nations Peacekeeping Force in Cyprus
March 1964–present[a]

DOMINICAN REPUBLIC – DOMREP
Mission of the Representative of the Secretary-General in the Dominican Republic
May 1965–October 1966

INDA/PAKISTAN – UNIPOM
United Nations India-Pakistan Observation Mission
September 1965–March 1966

MIDDLE EAST – UNEF II
Second United Nations Emergency Force
October 1973–July 1979

GOLAN HEIGHTS – UNDOF
United Nations Disengagement Observer Force
June 1974–present[a]

LEBANON – UNIFIL
United Nations Interim Force in Lebanon
March 1978–present[a]

AFGHANISTAN/PAKISTAN – UNGOMAP
United Nations Good Offices Mission in Afghanistan and Pakistan
April 1988–March 1990[a]

IRAN/IRAQ – UNIMOG
United Nations Iran-Iraq Military Observer Group
August 1988–February 1991[a]

Total: 15 UN missions in Cold War period

UN missions in post-Cold War period

ANGOLA – UNAVEM I
United Nations Angola Verification Mission I
January 1989–June 1991

NAMIBIA – UNTAG
United Nations Transition Assistance Group
April 1989–1990

CENTRAL AMERICA – ONUCA
United Nations Observer Group in Central America
November 1989–January 1992

IRAQ/KUWAIT – UNIKOM
United Nations Iraq-Kuwait Observations Mission
April 1991–present

ANGOLA – UNAVEM II
United Nations Angola Verification Mission II
June 1991–February 1995

continued

Table 2.2 *continued*

UN missions in post-Cold War period *contd*

EL SALVADOR – ONUSAL
United Nations Observer Mission in El Salvador
July 1991–April 1995

WESTERN SAHARA – MINURSO
United Nations Mission for the Referendum in Western Sahara
September 1991–present

CAMBODIA – UNAMIC
United Nations Advance Mission in Cambodia
October 1991–March 1992

CAMBODIA – UNTAC
United Nations Transitional Authority in Cambodia
March 1992–September 1993

FORMER YUGOSLAVIA – UNPROFOR
United Nations Protection Force
March 1992–December 1995

SOMALIA – UNSOM I
United Nations Operations in Somalia I
April 1992–March 1993

MOZAMBIQUE – ONUMOZ
United Nations Operation in Mozambique
December 1992–December 1994

SOMALIA – UNSOM II
United Nations Operation in Somalia II
March 1993–March 1995

RWANDA/UGANDA – UNOMUR
United Nations Observer Mission in Uganda-Rwanda
June 1993–September 1994

GEORGIA – UNOMIG
United Nations Observer Mission in Georgia
August 1993–present

LIBERAL – UNOMIL
United Nations Observer Mission in Angola
September 1993–present

HAITI – UNMIH
United Nations Mission in Haiti
September 1993–June 1996

RWANDA – UNAMIR
United Nations Assistance Mission for Rwanda
October 1993–March 1996

continued

Table 2.2 *continued*

CHAD/LIBYA – UNASOG
United Nations Aouzou Strip Observer Group
May 1994–June 1994

TAJIKISTAN – UMOT
United Nations Mission of Observers in Tajikistan
December 1994–present

ANGOLA – UNAVEM III
United Nations Angola Verification Mission III
February 1995–June 1997

CROATIA – UNCRO
United Nations Confidence Restoration in Croatia
March 1995–15 January 1996

FORMER YUGOSLAV REPUBLIC OF MACEDONIA – UNPREDEP
United Nations Preventive Deployment Force
March 1995–present

BOSNIA AND HERZEGOVINA – UNMIBH
United Nations Mission in Bosnia and Herzegovina
December 1995–present

CROATIA – UNMOP
United Nations Mission of Observers in Prevlaka
January 1996–present

CROATIA – UNTAES
United Nations Transitional Administration for Eastern Slavonia, Baranja and Western Sirmium
January 1996–present

HAITI – UNSMIH
United Nations Support Mission in Haiti
July 1996–July 1997

GUATEMALA – MINUGUA
United Nations Verification Mission in Guatemala
January 1997–May 1997

ANGOLA – MONUA
United Nations Observer Mission in Angola
July 1997–present

HAITI – UNTMIH
United Nations Transition Mission in Haiti
August 1997–present

Total: 30 UN missions in post-Cold War period to date

[a] Span Cold War and post-Cold War periods.
Source: UN – http://www.un.org/

The existence of overlapping regional and global security regimes defines a new conjuncture in the historical pattern of international security affairs. For few states, and certainly no major global regions, are excluded from participation in existing international (regional and global) security regimes. Moreover, the institutionalization of and mutual interaction between these diverse regimes have contributed to the formation of a global regulatory infrastructure which, irrespective of its limited authority, is embedded (however unevenly) in the military and security practices of the majority of the world's states.

2.5.2   Geogovernance of military power: war and conflict

Watson records that even in classical civilizations mechanisms existed for regulating interstate conflict short of war (1992, ch. 12). Nevertheless, war was largely conceived as a legitimate mechanism for the settlement of city-state and imperial disputes or rivalries. Over time, attitudes to the regulation of war have oscillated between the desire to inject morality into its conduct and the desire to abolish it altogether. What is evident is that since classical times the subject, the scope and the mechanisms of this regulation have markedly altered, as has the nature of warfare itself.

Attempts to regulate war have concentrated on three areas: the conduct of war; the prevention of war; and the abolition of war. Although from early modern times all three have been the object of political attention it was not until the modern era that the emphasis shifted decisively to prevention and abolition. However, while preventive measures, such as the superpower hot line, Cold War crisis prevention arrangements, and international legal mediation of disputes through the International Court of Justice (ICJ) have all played a role in international conflict management, this has been primarily on a bilateral or case-by-case basis. Moreover, initiatives to reduce war, such as the Locarno Treaty of 1925, or to abolish it, as in the Kellogg-Briand Pact of 1928, have proved of little enduring value. Much more significant throughout the postwar period, and latterly in the post-Cold War period, have been UN peacekeeping and peacemaking operations. The UN's role in both these domains has expanded enormously since the 1980s (table 2.2 above). Associated with this expansion is the development of new international norms concerning the right of the international community to intervene in the sovereign affairs of states where crimes against humanity are believed to have occurred or to be occurring (see section 1.3.3 above). In this sense, the war and conflict prevention role of the UN has acquired increasing global salience even if the UN has often failed to achieve positive results.

Of equal importance to the global regulation of military conflict has been the evolution, since the Middle Ages, of a universal code of conduct for the prosecution of war. In medieval times the Roman Catholic Church sought quite successfully to establish international rules to govern the resort to military force and the conduct of war. The doctrine of the just war became the moral standard of Christian civilization in its approach to war and also the foundation of much subsequent juridical thinking about the laws of war (Watson, 1992, pp. 144–8; Contamine, 1984, pp. 280–4). But the just war doctrine – *jus ad bellum* – had only limited impact on secular powers and was used to legitimize both intra-European and extra-European conquest. In part this was because states were still rather hollow shells, there were no standing armies and the conduct of war was a largely private affair. The development of formal systems of diplomacy and the consolidation of the states' monopoly over the means of violence provided the institutional infrastructure for more comprehensive and systematic attempts to regulate the conduct of war. The French Revolution and the subsequent Napoleonic Wars, which culminated in the Peace of Vienna, encouraged this process further.

The legislative foundations of the modern laws of war were laid in the period 1815 to 1914 (Best, 1980, p. 128). Driven in part by the arrival of industrial warfare, and by a large international peace movement, a series of international conferences legislated for the rules of conduct in modern war as opposed to the earlier focus on the rules defining the rightful use of military force (Best, 1980, p. 331). This process culminated in the Hague Conferences which established a more humane and codified international legal framework for the conduct of war and constraints on the use of force. What began in Europe spread much further afield as the standard set by European international law became a relevant criterion for membership of the international society of states in the twentieth century. Following the establishment of the League of Nations, and its successor the United Nations, the laws of war have been extended to new domains with the negotiation and ratification of stricter codes of conduct for states and soldiers (see box 1.6, p. 71). Moreover, in the postwar period international laws to protect civilians in the new conditions of total war have also been agreed. These developments constitute a universal set of principles and legal rules which have the force of international law, binding signatory states to observe internationally agreed standards of conduct in war. In the twentieth century, the international laws of war have come to acquire a universal jurisdiction. The unhappy fact that they are not universally or systematically observed reflects both the absence of any international authority with the power to ensure compliance and the changing nature of war itself (Kaldor, 1998).

2.5.3 Geogovernance of military power: the instruments of war

One of the earliest recorded arms control initiatives is the decision of the Lateran Council in 1139 to prohibit the use of crossbows between Christian armies (Contamine, 1984, p. 274). This prohibition, like most arms control and disarmament initiatives, proved to have a very temporary and limited impact. Nevertheless, it represents the beginning of a somewhat uninspiring history of interstate attempts to regulate (and prevent) the acquisition, diffusion, use and deployment of the instruments of war. This history also tends to confirm what the earlier discussion of war and security has highlighted, namely a significant transformation in the form, scope and intensity of interstate regulatory activity in the twentieth century. Indeed, it is arguably true to say that international arms control and disarmament are quintessentially modern phenomena.

Prior to the Hague Peace Conferences (1899 and 1907), attempts to regulate arms took the form of unilateral initiatives. For instance, in 1660 Britain imposed export controls on armaments (primarily, it must be said, to ensure domestic supplies)(Krause, 1992, p. 41). But by the late nineteenth century, the revolution in the instruments of warfare generated growing political demands, backed by a vociferous peace movement, for international 'legislation' to prohibit inhumane weapons and to regulate the growing arms trade (Howard, 1981). Although the Hague Conferences dealt almost solely with the former, their relative success created a political momentum for further controls which, following the carnage of the First World War, was articulated in the negotiations for general and complete disarmament in the 1930s. The Hague Conferences defined a significant watershed in the history of arms control since they represent the moment when arms control became a multilateral activity with a potential global jurisdiction. Whereas the first Hague Conference involved twenty-six (mainly European) states, the second was attended by forty-four states 'representing nearly all the recognized national governments of the world' (S. Brown, 1994, p. 220).

In the aftermath of the First World War the advocates of general and complete disarmament discovered, in the League of Nations, a new institutional forum within which to further the disarmament project (Howard, 1981). From 1932 to 1934 all the worlds sixty-four recognized states met in Geneva at the World Disarmament Conference to initiate the process of general and complete disarmament. But 'realism' triumphed over 'idealism', with the conference breaking up having achieved little. As the League returned to discussing the dangers of level-crossings in Europe, Germany invaded the Sudetenland, putting paid to the general and complete disarmament project.

With the onset of the Cold War a new impetus for disarmament arose in the form of the atomic bomb and other weapons of mass destruction. As a result, the postwar period has witnessed the most sustained, intensive – as well as frustrated – attempts at multilateral control, not just of weapons of mass destruction, but of conventional arms too. Arms control has become a permanent feature of international politics. Agencies for arms control and disarmament (or sections within foreign ministries) exist within all the worlds major states, managing what has become a continuous diplomatic process. A permanent UN Disarmament Conference in Geneva also ensures that arms control issues are kept high on the global security agenda.

Although the process of postwar arms control has involved the negotiation of global arms restraints and prohibitions, such as the Treaty on the Non-Proliferation of Nuclear Weapons (NPT), the majority of initiatives have been focused on regions, such as the Intermediate Nuclear Forces (in Europe) Treaty or the Pacific Nuclear Weapons Free Zone, or specific functional issues, such as the Comprehensive Test Ban Treaty (CTBT). And while some agreements have acquired almost universal ratification, such as the 1925 Geneva Protocol and the Biological Weapons Convention, many others, such as the Inhumane Weapons Convention or the Antarctica Treaty, have attracted very limited international support. Arms control has become a multilateral process reflecting the extensity and intensity of security and defence interconnections between states in the military domain. Even in the 'golden era' of superpower bilateral negotiations between 1968 and 1990, such as the Strategic Arms Limitation Talks (SALT) and Strategic Arms Reduction Talks (START), the formal diplomatic process was shadowed by both informal and formal multilateral discussions and negotiations with alliance partners.

The primacy attached to multilateralism arises simply because most of the key arms control problems arise today from the dense interconnectedness of the world military order and, as such, mostly require collectively agreed and implemented solutions. As already noted, the fact that there are many arms suppliers, combined with the growth of dual-use technologies, enormously complicate international attempts to regulate arms. For governments can acquire weapons from many potential sources, or manufacture them indigenously by purchasing technology or components from a multiplicity of suppliers. In addition, as the distinction between civil and military technologies erodes, attempts to control the diffusion of sensitive technologies necessarily demand expanded domestic and international regulation (as well as surveillance) of both domestic and international commerce. In this way, international arms control regimes invade both the domestic and the civil sphere.

Reliance on formal and informal multilateral regimes to deal with a variety of arms control issues has grown considerably in the postwar period. Informal regimes provide a mechanism for regulating a specific issue area without the distractions and complications of formal conference diplomacy and treaty-making. Thus, for instance, the Nuclear Suppliers Group and the Arms Control Middle East Group have evolved to regulate access to sensitive nuclear technology and the flow of arms to the Middle East respectively.

For much of the postwar period, arms control has promised more than it has delivered. But since the late 1980s it has begun 'to look like a vehicle to accomplish change rather than merely a vehicle to codify the status quo' (Sharp, 1991, p. 111). Many recent agreements involve methods of verification or commitments which intrude considerably on national sovereignty and national military autonomy. With the end of the Cold War the pace of change has accelerated considerably, and real disarmament, not simply arms control, has been effected. This is not to argue that in the post-Cold War era the regulation of arms is likely to be ultimately more successful than previously, but simply to recognize that it does now impinge in quite significant ways on the defence policy processes of many states. The international regulation of arms is not something which is carried on simply in UN forums but is constitutive of the military and arms procurement practices of many states. Over the postwar period, the cumulative effect of global, regional and functional patterns of international arms control activity has been to nurture a global infrastructure of armaments regulation.

2.6 Historical Forms of Military Globalization: a Comparison

Here a start is made on synthesizing the evidence and the arguments of the previous discussion to construct a profile of the dominant features of military globalization in the early modern, modern and contemporary periods. Although this periodization is somewhat arbitrary and imprecise, it nevertheless provides a simple framework for organizing initial thoughts about what, if anything, is distinctive about military globalization today.

Drawing on the previous discussion, grid 2.1 summarizes the key features of the evolving world military order according to this general periodization. The comparison between the early modern period and the contemporary era is particularly striking, whereas that between the modern and contemporary periods is more subtle, although by no means less profound. For instance, while in the interwar period the arms transfer system was undoubtedly global in scale, in the contemporary era it is much more intensive, the subject of considerable multilateral regulation, reflects distinctive mechanisms of arms diffusion, and is a highly institutionalized feature of interstate diplomacy and foreign policy.

Grid 2.1 The world military order: historical comparisons

	Early modern (14th–18th century)	**Modern (19th–20th century)**	**Contemporary (1945 on)**
Geopolitics	Intraregional rivalry Initial imperial expansion Limited war	Global empires Total war	Global rivalry Cooperative security and collective defence Rivalry and competition within institutionalized cooperative frameworks Overlapping regional and global security complexes
Arms transfer system	Localized, disorganized, craft production	Industrialization of war Emergence of global arms dynamic Unregulated private world market in arms Diffusion of defence productive capacity	Intensification of global arms dynamic Expanding scale and volume of trade in arms Transnationalization of arms production Commercialization of arms trade in regulated global market
Geogovernance	Largely absent: civilizational and religious restraints	Beginnings of multilateral and legal regulation Failure of collective security	Generalization, legalization, institutionalization of regulatory regimes

In order to comment more meaningfully on historical patterns of military globalization it is necessary to return to the conceptual framework developed in the introduction. This delivers a fairly systematic and rigorous method for comparing changing historical forms of military globalization. Grid 2.2 presents a summary of the dominant features of military globalization in each historical period.

The central question to be addressed here is: what, if anything, is distinctive about contemporary military globalization? This question can be answered by reflecting on some of the key comparisons revealed in grid 2.2:

● Contemporary military globalization in most key respects reflects more extensive patterns and systems of military/security interconnectedness than at any time since the late nineteenth century, excluding the periods of both world wars. Despite the ending of Cold War rivalry, there has not been a detectable return to earlier forms of national military autarky but rather the opposite; nor has the world broken up into discrete regional security complexes. Globalization and regionalization in the

Grid 2.2 Dominant features of military globalization

	Early modern	**Modern**	**Contemporary**
Extensity	Largely intraregional arms flows Age of Discovery and expansionism	Consolidation of global empires and rivalries Beginnings of global arms trade and multilateral regulation	Global states system Global arms dynamic Interpenetration of global and regional security complexes
Intensity	Low volume of flows/connections because of poor infrastructural capacity	High volume and velocity of flows/connections	Unprecedented level of flows/connectivity across all military/security domains
Velocity	Measured in centuries/decades	Low to high	High: rapid diffusion
Impact propensity	Low: mercantilism and autarky	High sensitivity/vulnerability	High sensitivity/growing vulnerability
Infrastructure	Limited: absence of regularized, reliable, effective, swift, global communication systems	Development of regularized, reliable global transport and communication systems	Advanced universal communications and transport systems, and military surveillance
Institutionalization	Extremely limited: absence of systems of military diplomacy, arms trade, regulation	Limited and fragile: evolution and collapse of global arms trade, collective security arrangements	Extensive but fragile: consolidation and extension of arms trade, collective defence and cooperative security arrangements, regulatory regimes
Stratification	European dominance and arms monopoly – Eurocentric order Highly unequal	Military power highly concentrated in Atlantic centric order Limited global diffusion of military capabilities and power	Dilution of Atlanticist global dominance – relatively decentralized Significant global diffusion of military capabilities and power
Modes of interaction	Imperialist/coercive	Imperialist, global rivalries, expansionist, total war	Rivalry, competition and conflict within cooperative, collective and collaborative structures

military domain appear to be mutually reinforcing rather than mutually exclusive processes.

- The intensity of global military expenditure, arms transfers and military-diplomatic connectedness is, by historical standards, remarkably high for an era distinguished by the prolonged absence of great power military conflict.
- In comparison with the late nineteenth century, the arms trade, arms production and networks of military/security relations have become much more institutionalized and regulated.
- The consequences of the emerging military-technological revolution have been to accelerate the global arms dynamic as the military standards set by the first-tier and second-tier states acquire, with greatly increased velocity, a global status (Buzan, 1987).
- The world military order has become more decentred as globalization and modernization have encouraged the emergence of new concentrations of military power. Whereas at the turn of the century Europe dominated the world military order, by the close of this century it has been eclipsed by the US, while enormous concentrations of military power and military productive potential have appeared in Asia, Latin America and the Middle East.
- Although the structure of world military power and capabilities (first to fourth tiers) has remained pretty much static, there have been fairly dramatic changes in the occupants of each tier. The patterns of stratification associated with contemporary military globalization are, therefore, quite distinct from those evident at the turn of the century or before. Of course, there are interesting continuities, but the global diffusion of military technology and capabilities has created a very different strategic environment – whereas, for instance, in 1897 India was a British colony, it now has a declared nuclear capability.
- Although the globalization of the contemporary arms trade has become increasingly driven by a commercial logic, it is still much more state managed, and subject to international monitoring and regulation, than in any previous epoch.
- In the contemporary era the diffusion of military technology, knowledge and practices has not been primarily a by-product of empire-building, military conquest or intercivilizational conflict, as in earlier phases of military globalization, but rather it has acquired its own dynamic.
- The existence of global and regional regulatory regimes/security structures of all kinds points to the highly institutionalized and regularized nature of contemporary military globalization. Associated with this too is the multilateralism and transnationalization of defence and security policy processes as bureaucrats, politicians, military personnel, non-governmental organizations and citizen groups seek to promote their interests.
- The notions of national and military security are undergoing a significant transformation as the emphasis shifts to cooperative or multilateral defence and security mechanisms, and the security agenda expands to incorporate a multiplicity of threats from the environmental to the cultural. This reflects the increasingly overlapping fortunes of national communities of fate (see chapter 1).
- In the wake of the ending of the Cold War there are growing (financial, technological, industrial and political) pressures on SIACS to engage in multilateral cooperative efforts to achieve the rationalization of their defence industrial bases.

This is contributing to the (admittedly slow) denationalization of defence industries in most advanced states, and to a globalization of defence production (Bitzinger, 1994).

- And finally, the presumed historical connection between societal militarization and military globalization appears no longer to hold, in as much as among leading states contemporary military globalization has gone hand in hand with the long-term demilitarization of domestic society (Shaw, 1991). In the contemporary era, military globalization and societal demilitarization may be becoming mutually reinforcing processes.

In the following section, many of these points are further elaborated in relation to the enmeshment of states in advanced capitalist societies (SIACS) in the contemporary world military order.

2.7   Contemporary Patterns of National Enmeshment in the World Military Order

In the preceding sections the analysis has concentrated exclusively on historical forms of military globalization. In the context of this, the position and role of those key states which inform this study – US, UK, Sweden, Germany, Japan and France – have been given considerable exposure. However, the emphasis has been on their significance at the level of the world military order. Here the analysis is reversed by developing, for each of these states, a profile of their enmeshment in the contemporary world military order from a national perspective. This will establish both a more systematic account of the comparative significance of military globalization for these SIACS and a more secure empirical base from which, in the final section of the chapter, to establish some general conclusions about its political consequences. But before launching into such profiling, some acknowledgement must be made of the structural trends in respect of the relationship between military power and state power among SIACS.

Shaw argues, based on a number of indicators, that advanced capitalist societies are evolving in the direction of 'post-military societies' (1991). What he means by this is not that these societies are necessarily more pacific *per se*, but rather that the structural balance between welfare and warfare in society has shifted decisively towards the former. In comparison with the modern era, when all capitalist societies were organized for total war, the military as a social institution (and by definition the military-industrial complex) 'exists ever more on the margins of post-military society' (Shaw, 1991, p. 134). Some indicators of this trend are evident in the decline in military personnel and the secular decline in state military expenditure (see figure 2.8 below). These trends, in most cases, have been reinforced by the end of the Cold War. As Shaw further observes, the contrast between the militarized societies of the era of industrialized warfare and today's post-military societies was vividly paralleled in the 1991 Gulf War: in that war the differences 'between the classically militarized Iraqi society, in which even old men and early teenagers were drawn into military service and military ideology pervaded everyday life, and the post-military societies of the West was sharp' (1991, p. 203).

This trend cannot be dissociated from the changing conditions, and technology, of warfare in the late twentieth century. The era of total war, according to Creveld, is being replaced by the era of regionalized and intrastate low-intensity conflict (1991). Moreover, the prosecution of war in the information age appears no longer to require the total mobilization of societies, merely their political acquiescence, since it is both more capital intensive and potentially more circumscribed (C. Gray, 1997). Indeed, as discussed earlier, it is arguably the case that the world is experiencing a new military-technological revolution (MTR) as information technologies transform existing military capabilities, the conduct of warfare and the ability to project military force over considerable distances with great precision (Carus, 1994). Paradoxically, the lethality of military power is increasing exponentially while simultaneously military establishments and military spending are in relative decline. The MTR is encouraging quite contradictory developments as it increases both the spectrum of possibilities for the use of military force while also reducing military autonomy in the conduct of war – the latter because real-time global communications systems enable direct political supervision and intervention in military operations to a degree which is quite unprecedented historically.

Finally, in the post-Cold War era, the traditional relationship between the military, the state and industry, epitomized in the institution of the military-industrial complex, is undergoing a significant transformation. As noted earlier, the defence industries in all major states are experiencing a major restructuring of production, patterns of ownership and corporate organization. The collapse in defence spending, combined with rising R&D and production costs, have generated powerful pressures for a comprehensive reorganization of the Cold War defence industrial base in all major powers. An interconnected process of national and transnational corporate restructuring of the defence sector is underway which, as noted earlier, is propelling a significant transnationalization of the Western defence industrial base (DIB). As Skons observes of Europe: 'In the 1990s, the large Western European companies are becoming more and more interconnected, not only at the level of joint development or production but also at the capital investment level' (1994).

Alongside this restructuring is an evolving privatization of the defence business and, as noted in the previous section, a growing civilianization of the DIB. Governments, most particularly second-tier suppliers such as the Europeans, are confronted by an acute defence production dilemma: namely, that in order to sustain a cost-effective military capability the national DIB has to be progressively transnationalized, so compromising the very notion of a national DIB and national defence (Buzan, 1991; see chapter 8). This is reinforced further by the impact of the MTR since 'newer and smarter conventional weapons . . . have the dual effect of raising the costs of defence and elevating . . . the security consequences of import-dependence' (Haglund, 1989, p. 245). The cumulative impact of these developments is to reconstitute the fundamental relations between the state, industry and the military. As Silverberg argues, the Cold War 'was unique in allowing managers, governments, and military planners to rationally plan, budget and steadily implement industrial policies and programmes on a predictable, orderly, and long term basis' (1994). With the end of the Cold War the latter mode of operation is being replaced by more flexible, short-term and commercial arrangements which have the effect of disrupting the traditional relations between the key stakeholders in the military-industrial-bureaucratic complex.

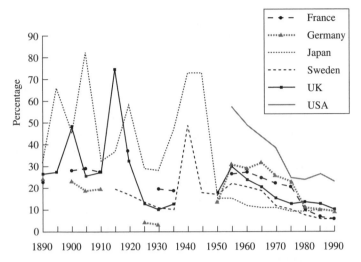

Figure 2.8   Military expenditure as a share of government expenditure, 1890–1990
(*Sources*: Calculated from Mitchell, 1983, 1992; SIPRI, 1991)

These three trends help define the historical context within which patterns of national enmeshment in the world military order among SIACS are to be interpreted. These patterns will be constructed from an examination of postwar trends in national resources devoted to defence; the DIB; the arms trade; membership of international security structures; and the external use or deployment of military force. For each of the countries in the study – US, Japan, Sweden, UK, Germany and France – an individual portrait will emerge of the structure of national enmeshment in the world military order. The analysis begins with the US as the only remaining first-tier arms producer and supplier.

2.7.1   First tier: the US

In their study entitled *Dismantling the Cold War Economy*, Markusen and Yudken assert that 'for the United States, the second half of the twentieth century has been a military-industrial era' (1992, p. xv). In many respects, both the size of and the trends in postwar defence expenditure tend to conceal the extent to which the US economy as a whole has been regulated through a policy of 'military-Keynesianism' or structurally conditioned by the 'industrial policy' of the Department of Defense (DOD). While defence spending has always constituted a significant slice of government expenditure, and a significant proportion of the budget is expended on military procurement and R&D, the general trend in defence spending, as a proportion of GNP, since the end of the Cold War has been downwards (see figure 2.8), as has the complement of military personnel. Despite this, the US maintains a massive conventional and nuclear military capability well beyond that of Russia or even the major middle-ranking powers combined.

With the end of the Cold War there is considerable overcapacity in the defence industrial sector (as much as 90 per cent in the missile industry). This has provoked an ongoing process of restructuring, most particularly in the aerospace sector (Brzoska and Pearson, 1994; Gansler, 1995). Associated with this is a growing move towards 'strategic corporate alliances and sub-contracting arrangements between US and European defence companies' (OTA, 1991, p. 24). Foreign defence companies have sought to buy into the US defence industrial base, as is evident from the increasing number of potentially sensitive foreign takeovers or mergers investigated by the US DOD (Friedberg, 1991). Combined with the growing attraction of co–production, co-development and collaborative ventures with partners abroad (mostly Europeans) these developments have provoked rising DOD and Congressional concern about the national security implications of the (largely exaggerated) transnationalization of the US defence industrial base. These concerns are reinforced further by the growing import-ance of dual-use technologies in meeting defence requirements. In those commercial sectors like electronics, on which the defence industry is totally dependent, the level of global sourcing and foreign investment is extremely high. As a result, it is not only the defence industrial base which is subject to a process of transnationalization but also indirectly the products themselves. Stowsky notes that 'many of America's most vaunted weapons – from the AMRAAM missile to the M-1 tank – literally could not be built without commercially developed Japanese machine tools' (1992, p. 137). It is important not to exaggerate the scale of this transnationalization for, although there are no comparative figures, it is probably the case that it is relatively less significant than in Europe, the developing world, or even Japan. Although qualifications are in order, a key point remains: the problem of transnationalization, as a recent OTA report observed, is a completely new experience for US defence planners and the defence industry (OTA, 1991, p. 38).

The US has always been a major exporter of arms, but its relative position in the global arms market and the destination of its arms deliveries have changed over time. In the early Cold War period it had a near monopoly in the world export market, but by the 1970s and 1980s it had been overtaken by the Soviets. In the post-Cold War period it is once again dominant. In the 1980s arms trade boom, the US exported $59,000 billion worth of military equipment to eighty-four countries in four years (Krause, 1992, p. 102). But this conceals important shifts in the geographical pattern, mode and industrial significance of its arms trade. For since the 1950s and 1960s the direction of trade has shifted away from Europe, to the Middle East in the 1970s and 1980s, and to Asia in the 1990s (Krause, 1992, p. 100). Of greater significance is the trend, which had slowed in the early 1980s, of increasing reliance by the major US arms manufacturers on foreign sales. Since 1983, direct commercial sales 'in which a US company delivers arms directly to a foreign corporation or government have expanded significantly' (OTA, 1991, p. 11). With the dramatic slowdown in the domestic arms demand from the late 1980s, dependence on foreign sales has increased quite markedly. This is a pronounced structural shift, since domestic procurement expenditure is set to decline permanently from its 1990 level by at least a third. As a result, those major companies which are significantly reliant on defence business are becoming more intensely engaged in the arms export market (see Gansler, 1995). Moreover, the costs of new weapons procurement programmes, combined with cuts in procurement budgets, means that export sales, or collaborative arrangements which involve a sharing of costs, may soon be preferable (or even essential) to the alternative of continuous 'downsizing' (OTA, 1991; Krause, 1992; Gansler, 1995). This represents a significant shift in the posture and corporate strategy of US defence contractors, who for most of the twentieth century have been largely content to rely on the domestic market alone.

Paradoxically, the greater emphasis on competing in the world arms market is paralleled by a significant retrenchment in the global deployment of US forces. In comparison with the 1980s the US global military presence has shrunk, although new technologies and massive airlift capabilities (as demonstrated in the 1991 Gulf War) have reduced the requirement for a large foreign presence. This retrenchment has not prevented the US from continuing to use military force where and when it has judged it necessary. Despite the ending of the Cold War, alliance entanglements remain just as extensive as five decades ago. Indeed, with the expansion of NATO and the developments in Asia-Pacific, the US role as a 'regional balancer' in all the world's major regional security complexes remains critical to the maintenance of global security and reinforces the integration of all regions within a single military security order.

The US continues, as it did in the Cold War period, to play a crucial role in processes of global arms control and military diplomacy. Even though the Cold War is at an end, US enmeshment in the world military order has not so much declined as undergone a significant restructuring.

2.7.2   The second tier: Japan, the UK, France, Sweden and Germany

During the postwar period, Japan's enmeshment in the world military order has been primarily as the industrialized world's largest arms importer. Although it is today one of the world's largest military spenders, Japan's defence expenditure has declined (as a proportion of GNP) since 1955 and has only recently begun to rise. Even though it has developed a significant indigenous DIB, defence production remains limited and largely dependent (but decreasingly so) on licensed production of arms from the US. Indeed, for major weapons systems it relies entirely on the US such that '60 per cent of [its] weapons are purchased off the shelf from the USA, and the remaining 40 per cent are produced in Japan' (Ikegami-Anderson, 1993, p. 339).

But since the 1980s there has been a strong emphasis on indigenous procurement. Even so this still requires significant foreign assistance in the form of technology transfer. The alliance relationship with the US, however, continues to constrain both how and what Japan produces as well as its more general defence posture. Thus the FSX fighter collaboration between Mitsubishi and General Dynamics arose in part because of US fears of an indigenous independent fighter capability in Japan. Arms exports remain prohibited by Article 9 of the Japanese constitution, but this does not apply to defence-related dual-use equipment. However, no official figures exist to gauge the size of this export trade (OTA, 1991, pp. 114–15). It is interesting to note that most electronics and semiconductor exports from Japan to US defence contractors are recorded as commercial sales (OTA, 1991, p. 116).

Despite the appearance of limited enmeshment in the world military order, it can be claimed that 'Japan plays a bigger role in international security today because it controls a resource that is critical to military strength: high technology' (Vogel, 1992, p. 56). Combined with its role in the UN, its more active military diplomacy in Asia with respect to regional security issues, and its more assertive military posture with respect to force projection in the South China seas, Japan is much more deeply enmeshed in the world military order than at any point since the interwar period.

Although European arms producers exhibit quite different patterns of enmeshment in the world military order, they also exhibit many common features. The obvious differences are in terms of military capabilities and security postures. All have a sizeable and advanced DIB but the size, deployment and composition of their military forces differ quite markedly. Moreover, while Sweden has a declared policy of neutrality, Germany, the UK and France are full members of NATO.[6] Since the end of the Cold War both France and Sweden have changed their postures with respect to NATO (Sweden by participating in the Partnership for Peace and France by rejoining the military side of the alliance). All in varying degrees are heavily engaged in global and regional military diplomatic networks. Sweden, Britain and France provide significant material and military assistance to UN peacekeeping operations, the latter two in line with their status as permanent members of the Security Council. In addition, Britain and France, as ex-colonial powers, still retain an extra-European military presence.

In relation to patterns of defence expenditure, Germany and Sweden, with their markedly lower propensity to devote resources to defence, are distinct from France and Britain where defence has tended to consume a significantly larger proportion of GNP. But the general trend in defence spending among all these European states has been downwards and this is particularly evident in respect of defence spending as a proportion of government expenditure (see figure 2.8 above). However, in the 1990s considerable divergences have emerged as France and Sweden have increased defence expenditure and Britain and Germany have reduced it, although at differential rates (T. Taylor, 1994b, p. 110). This divergence is also replicated in relation to reductions in armed forces. These divergences reflect different patterns of defence organization, military commitments, defence politics and the structure of the defence industrial base.

All four states share in common the problem of restructuring and adapting the national DIB to the post-Cold War security environment. While the structure of the DIB in each country is different in significant respects (Germany and Sweden are less dependent economically on arms production than either Britain or France) they nevertheless all have a significant aerospace, defence electronics and munitions sector. In all cases, determined attempts to establish 'national champions' in the main defence sectors have been pursued, with the consequence that the DIB in each state is heavily concentrated (OTA, 1991, p. 74).

For much of the early postwar period, up until the 1970s, all except Britain relied considerably on US licensed production for a range of military equipment. This was particularly the case in respect of France and Germany. As these states rebuilt their national DIB, indigenous defence production expanded, but as defence costs continued to rise and national procurements budgets were squeezed in the 1970s, the pressures for transnational arms collaboration increased considerably. This trend accelerated in the 1990s as it became clear that domestic production was insufficient to sustain a viable national DIB, such that discussion of the formation of a single European aerospace and defence company began in late 1998. For the major second-tier producers,

[6] Sweden's official policy has recently been called into question, see Commission on Neutrality Policy, 1994.

the postwar DIB has traversed a trajectory of dependence or semidependence, relative autonomy, and increasing functional interconnectedness.

As the DIB in all these states is becoming transnationalized, the trend is increasingly towards regional collaboration and cooperation (Bitzinger, 1994; Skons, 1993). In the 1980s France and the UK were spending 30 per cent of their defence procurement budgets on collaborative projects, Germany a huge 45 per cent (Bitzinger, 1993, p. 26). Encouraged by NATO policies, as well as by the shift towards a single European market, the regionalization of the European DIB has been reinforced further by the end of the Cold War. Alongside this regionalization, there has been a significant expansion in US-European defence industrial collaboration (Bitzinger, 1993; OTA, 1991). As Krause observes, these developments 'demonstrate that the advance of technology and the evolution of the arms production and transfer system have meant that leading second tier suppliers can no longer maintain independent, across-the-board, production of sophisticated weapons' (1992, p. 150).

Alongside the transnationalization of the DIB, all four European countries have become steadily more dependent on arms exports to maintain an indigenous defence production capacity. France and Germany especially became major arms exporters to the Third World in the 1970s and 1980s (Huebner, 1989; Brzoska and Ohlson, 1987) while the UK too expanded its arms exports significantly in the 1980s (Krause, 1992, p. 134). Even Sweden, which in the 1980s had one of the world's most restrictive arms export policies, has become more deeply engaged in the world arms market. As domestic demand for arms production has declined so the pressure to export has become more intense. Britain, France, and to a degree Germany, are now in direct and intense competition with the US in all the world's major arms export markets.

2.8   Contemporary Military Globalization and its Political Consequences

Military power has been fundamental to the evolution and the institutional form of the modern sovereign, territorial nation-state. The independent capacity to defend national territorial space by military means is at the heart of the modern conception of the institution of sovereign statehood. But, as discussed here, contemporary military globalization poses quite profound questions about the meaning and practice of state sovereignty and autonomy. For in the contemporary age, the traditionally presumed correspondence between the spatial organization of military power and the territorial nation-state appears to be changing. Among the six SIACS discussed in the previous section, enmeshment in the world military order has significant political consequences which strike at the heart of the notion of independent statehood.

Although there are significant variations among SIACS in terms of national enmeshment in the world military order, there is a shared experience in respect of how contemporary military globalization impacts on national security as both a doctrine and strategy; the organization and management of national defence; national defence procurement and production; and the politics of national security and 'postmilitary' society. These decisional, institutional, distributional and structural impacts will be explored in turn.

2.8.1   Decisional impacts: defence policy
and military force

The management of defence and the making of defence policy within SIACS is no longer primarily a national affair. The existence of NATO, with its many subsidiary organs and committees, and other multilateral defence related fora (OSCE, UNCD, MTCR, etc.), combined with the proliferation of transgovernmental or transnational bureaucratic, military, defence-industrial and expert networks, has contributed to the 'stretching' of the defence policy process and the task of defence management across national boundaries. Military globalization has stimulated the institutionalization, among these six Western SIACS, of a multilayered and multilateral system of governance for Atlantic defence and security matters complementing existing domestic structures and processes.

National defence policy-making, from decisions about defence strategy to the deployment and use of military force, is embedded in a matrix of institutionalized bilateral and multilateral consultative and cooperative mechanisms, both official and unofficial. Few aspects of national security policy remain totally untouched by these developments; even intelligence agencies have developed their own forms of interagency dialogue. Although, as a military superpower, the US appears to retain the greatest (relative) autonomy in the military domain, this is to overlook the simple fact that as the linchpin of European and Pacific military-security arrangements, its military autonomy is decidedly compromised by the web of military commitments and arrangements in which it has become entangled. Military might and national military autonomy are therefore not necessarily positively correlated. Among the European middle powers, the UK, France and Germany, defence cooperation and collaboration has extended even to the establishment of the Eurocorps, a multilateral military force. Within the military arm of NATO the emphasis on integrated military command, interoperability, standardization, joint military planning and multilateral military operations constitutes a significant departure from the traditional idea of national military autonomy. These developments, however, by no means prefigure the end of national armed forces *per se*, nor a shift towards some functional specialization in military roles, and certainly not international military integration. Nor are they uniformly experienced by all six SIACS, as the cases of Japan and Sweden, which are on the margins of these developments, testify.

In comparison with the early twentieth century when, as the catastrophe of the Great War demonstrated, decisions to (threaten to) use military force were the unquestioned preserve of national governments alone, the growth of multilateral defence and security arrangements complicates, if it does not compromise, government decision-making in this regard. Treaty obligations, military and defence commitments, the interlocking nature of military capabilities, logistics and forces, internationalized defence production and weapons procurement, among other factors, transform the political context and the politics of national decision-making with respect to the costs and benefits of all aspects of defence policy, but most especially the use of military force or the declaration of war. Although all SIACS ultimately retain the de jure sovereign power to declare war or to (threaten to) use military force, the costs and benefits of alternative courses of military action are circumscribed, in some key respects, by both formal and informal commitments. In this regard it is interesting to note that in the original US Congressional debate on ratification of the NATO Treaty in the late 1940s deep concern was expressed, by Senator Vanderberg among others, that the Treaty could usurp the sovereign right of the US, and the constitutional authority of Congress, with respect to the most sacred decisions over war and peace (Glennon, 1990, pp. 209–14). Such concerns became even more acute in the nuclear missile age when decision times about war and peace were reduced to minutes rather than weeks.

Among SIACS the intensity and institutionalized form of national enmeshment in the world military order raise serious questions about whether they have the capability to conduct independent military operations. For decades critics have questioned whether technically or politically Britain's 'independent' nuclear deterrent and the French 'force de frappe' could ever be used without consultation or even joint decision-making with Washington. Furthermore, in the post-Cold War era of shrinking defence budgets and defence rationalization there is also reasonable doubt about the ability of the European middle-ranking powers, in particular, to launch or conduct independent conventional military operations. As Shaw comments, the Falklands War of 1982 may represent the end of an era and the 'exception that proves the rule' (1997, p. 34). But even in the case of the US, which undoubtedly has the military capability to act independently, the complex web of global commitments in which it is entangled mediates the exercise of military power in respect of the use of force beyond its immediate territory, as the 1998 Iraq crisis demonstrated. Although for most SIACS national sovereignty with respect to the most critical decisions about national security has by no means been usurped by a higher authority, decision-making on military and security matters is, nevertheless, compromised by contemporary patterns of national enmeshment in the world military order to the extent that, in practice, existing military and security relations, obligations and commitments influence the costs and benefits of different policy choices, while they also presume multilateral consultation or even alliance co-decision.

2.8.2   Institutional impacts: national or cooperative security?

The doctrine of national security remains one of the essential defining principles of modern statehood. The autonomous capacity of the modern state to defend the nation against external threats is a crucial (to some the essential) ingredient of traditional conceptions of sovereignty. For if a state does not have the capacity to secure its territory and protect its people then its very *raison d'être* can be called into question. National security has, therefore, been understood traditionally in primarily military terms: as the acquisition, deployment and use of military force to achieve national goals (Buzan, 1991). Without such a capacity, the very essence of the institution of modern statehood would be decidedly altered.

Of course, the ideology of modern statehood has not always been replicated in the political practices of states (Krasner, 1995). But in the military domain, above all others, modern states have always sought to maintain their independence. However, in the contemporary era, military globalization and patterns of national enmeshment in the world military order have prompted a serious rethinking about the idea and the practice of national security. Although the discourse of national security dominates political and popular debate about military matters in all the six SIACS in this study, it is more of a simplified representation or legitimating device than a determinant of the actual behaviour of states. For most SIACS the strategy for achieving 'national security' has become almost indistinguishable from an international security strategy since, together with other advanced states, they collectively constitute a 'security community' within which military force plays no active role in the relations between member states (Deutsch and Burrell, 1957).

Within this 'security community', national defence and security strategy is constructed within institutionalized alliance systems in which consultation and cooperation complement national mechanisms of security policy. The development and pursuit of national security goals are therefore inseparable, in most respects, from the development and pursuit of alliance security. National security and alliance security might therefore be best conceived as mutually constituted (S. Weber, 1993). Even for states such as France, which has historically sought to pursue a highly autonomous defence posture, or Sweden, which retains a declared policy of neutrality, postwar national security policy has effectively always been shaped (and in the post-Cold War context increasingly so) by the functioning of this broader 'security community' (see Commission on Neutrality Policy, 1994; Ullman, 1989).

Moreover, for the United States, membership of NATO represents a historic shift in national security posture away from autarky, isolationism and the avoidance of external military commitments (Ruggie, 1996, p. 43). In 1949 NATO was the first peacetime alliance in US history. Indeed, for a nation which, in the post-Cold War era, does not have to contend with any direct military threats to its territorial integrity or its populace, the reaffirmed commitment to NATO (and its expansion), as well as to the US-Japan Security Alliance, signifies just how deeply postwar military globalization has transformed its historical security posture. As a military superpower, national security has become indivisible from the maintenance and pursuit of global security. For the US, along with other members of this 'security community', the practice of cooperative security is redefining the traditional agenda of national security (S. Weber, 1993).

2.8.3 Distributional impacts:
defence procurement and production

As earlier sections of this chapter have recounted, the contemporary era represents a significant transformation in the organization and nature of the global arms trade and of arms procurement. Among the six SIACS discussed here, the last two decades in particular have witnessed a notable transnationalization of the defence industrial base. Declining defence procurement budgets and defence industrial overcapacity have combined to produce a major (ongoing) restructuring of the defence industry both within and across all states. In comparison with the globalization of civil enterprises, the globalization and regionalization of the defence industrial business remains very much in its initial stages. But it is at its most intense within Europe and the Atlantic security community.

The transnationalization of the defence industrial base represents a distinctive new stage in the organization of defence production and procurement akin to (but on a very different scale from) the global restructuring of industrial production (Sassen, 1996; Moravcsik, 1991; Bitzinger, 1994; Skons, 1994; and see chapters 3 and 5 below). It is also reinforced by the fact that many of the most critical defence technologies are produced in those very civil industrial sectors, such as electronics or optics, which have been subject to increasing globalization. These developments have quite profound, although not necessarily completely novel, implications for the orthodox approach to defence-industrial organization, which traditionally has privileged – alongside national strategies of defence and procurement – the national defence industrial base above all else as the necessary underpinning to an 'autonomous' national defence capability. Both the regionalization and globalization of the defence-industrial sector compromise such autonomy in a fairly direct way since they make the acquisition (and crucially the use) of arms and weapons systems (not to mention defence industrial policy) potentially subject to the decisions and actions of other authorities or corporations beyond the scope of national jurisdiction.

In some contexts, however, such regionalization and globalization may be exploited to enhance defence industrial and military autonomy. Sweden, for instance, by engaging in collaborative and licensing arrangements with both American and European aerospace defence contractors, has been able to sustain a highly advanced defence industrial capability which it might otherwise have been unable to support. Japan too has reduced its military dependence on the US by exploiting an intensely competitive world market in military technology transfer and licensing. In the realm of defence production and procurement, globalization and regionalization by no means automatically prefigure the demise of a national defence industrial base but they do alter the strategies and policies that governments have to pursue in order to sustain it, as well as the patterns of industrial winners and losers. In the case of European states, the consolidation of 'national champions' through government supported (but not necessarily initiated) mergers and acquisitions has complemented the emergence of 'European champions' to compete in the global and regional arms market with their American rivals. Autonomy is thus sought through a strategy of internationalization rather than nationalization. This alone represents a significant departure from orthodox notions of military autonomy defined and pursued in exclusively national terms. And it has significant implications for mechanisms of national accountability and democracy, which are returned to below.

2.8.4 Structural impacts: from the national security state to 'postmilitary' society?

The Cold War was never solely an interstate phenomenon. On the contrary, its dynamics reached deep into the social and political institutions of domestic society, East and West, with profound consequences for many aspects of social life. In the case of the US the resultant militarization of society, the economy and the state apparatus represented a historic departure from normal peacetime conditions. When President Eisenhower warned of the dangers of the military-industrial complex he voiced the concerns of many who feared the corruption of American democracy and the American way of life from the unrelenting preparation for war (Brodie, 1973, p. 290). With the demise of the Cold War, American and European societies have experienced a significant demilitarization of social, economic and political life, the historical consequences of which are still far from completely evident.

What the Cold War demonstrated, among other things, was the dynamic interaction between superpower ideological rivalry and the conduct of political and social life within states, East and West. In some senses the Cold War system acted as a kind of disciplinary mechanism which helped to order political life in both the East and the West. This can be seen, most especially in the SIACS discussed here, in the very way in which political life was represented as a titanic struggle between the political pro-grammes of left and right (irrespective of how the labels were interpreted in specific national contexts). But in the post-Cold War era that 'discipline' has been removed. This, according to some, has contributed to the demise of the old left–right political alignments as well as to the emergence of a 'postmilitary' politics (Shaw, 1991; Giddens, 1995).

Within most SIACS, 'life politics' – preoccupations with the environment, identity, citizenship, welfare, education, health, etc. – has acquired a new dominance over the security politics associated with the Cold War era (and much of the twentieth century too). In this respect, the transformation in the geopolitical order is associated with what might arguably be considered a transformation of political life and the state within the West: from the national security state to the postmilitary state (Beck, 1997). Of course, this is not to argue that the end of superpower rivalry is the sole or even primary cause of this development, but merely to acknowledge that, because of their deep enmeshment in the world military order, the configuration of domestic politics in SIACS is certainly influenced by the prevailing pattern of military globalization.

Whether domestic politics in SIACS is undergoing a profound transformation remains a matter of debate. What is less controversial is the manner in which contem-porary military globalization has encouraged a global politics of security. The widening agenda of security, combined with the institutionalization of cooperative defence (and security) and the global regulation of military power, has contributed to a broadening of defence and security politics. The notion that the politics of defence and security issues are coterminous with national political space is belied by such diverse phenomena as the existence of global campaigns to ban landmines or to establish an international criminal court for crimes against humanity, and the lobbying by defence contractors within NATO and Europe for changes in defence industrial policy or government regulations on both sides of the Atlantic or in the East. Political activity on 'national security' matters is no longer simply a domestic affair.

There can be little doubt that contemporary military globalization has significant implications for the sovereignty, autonomy and politics of SIACS. Although the latter are differentially enmeshed in the world military order and retain differential capa-cities to manage military globalization, the institution of modern sovereign statehood is subject to powerful transformative forces. This is not to suggest that the end of the sovereign nation-state is nigh; on the contrary, the state remains central to the world military order. Rather, it is to argue that contemporary military globalization is con-tributing, along with other aspects of globalization, to the reconstitution of sovereignty, autonomy and democracy, that is, to the reconstitution of the modern nation-state. But developments in the military domain may not be replicated elsewhere, as the discussion of trade globalization in the next chapter demonstrates. Accordingly, this argument will be assessed more fully in the concluding chapter in relation to the historical evidence across all the key domains of power.

3
Global Trade, Global Markets

Today all countries trade internationally and, with the odd exception like North Korea, they trade significant proportions of their national income. Around 20 per cent of world output is traded and a much larger proportion is potentially subject to international competition: trade has now reached unprecedented levels, both absolutely and proportionate to world output. Trade is a key mechanism for moving goods, and increasingly services, around the globe, and it is also central to technology transfer. At the very least it connects domestic markets to international markets, while historically opening up national markets to trade has often had radical effects in unleashing new competitive forces and transforming domestic economies. If, in the past, trade sometimes formed an enclave largely isolated from the rest of the national economy, it is now an integral part of the structure of national production in all modern states.

3.1 Trade and Globalization

Trade links distant markets, so that, for example, the seasonality of fruit and vegetables has disappeared from Western supermarkets, since worldwide sourcing makes these products available throughout the year. Widely available technology means that a book published by a small company in Britain can be ordered in bookshops around the world. Trade has revolutionized the prospects of all industrial sectors – today few industries rely purely on domestic markets or domestically produced components and raw materials. For example, although the construction industry primarily uses domestic materials, employs local labour and satisfies domestic demand, capital equipment may be imported and, with increasing international ownership of construction firms, support services may also be traded.

Trade in the sense of the exchange of goods and services between people over distance has a long history. Great trading empires have arisen periodically ever since regular long-distance travel became possible. But international trade, the exchange of goods and services between nations, by definition only emerged with the establishment of the nation-state. Trade has been entwined with the rise of the modern state and its fortunes: states required revenues, above all to wage military campaigns, and trade offered an obvious source of funds. Identifying historical patterns of trade globalization is the primary objective of this chapter, and this entails deploying the analytical framework developed in the introduction.

3.1.1 Concepts

Trade globalization involves more than simply the exchange of goods and services between separate economies since it suggests the emergence of worldwide markets for traded goods and services. Of course, this does not presume that all countries trade with all others; rather it assumes the existence of a trading system in which trade activity between any two countries may affect trade relations between the rest. More specifically, trade globalization implies the existence of significant levels of interregional trade such that markets for traded goods function at a global rather than primarily intraregional level. Global trade therefore entails a system of regularized exchange of goods and services at the interregional level. Understood in these terms this chapter seeks to examine whether, in the contemporary era, a form of trade globalization exists.

Although for some products a global trading system has operated for centuries, both the hyperglobalizers and the transformationalists regard the contemporary era as unique in respect of the extensity and intensity of trading relations. How far contemporary flows of trade are consistent with this notion of trade globalization, and how far markets for goods and services now operate at the global level, constitute key questions which the analysis addresses. But what is a global market?

For a global market to exist there must be significant levels of regularized exchange of goods (or services) at the interregional level. Where barriers to trade, either in the form of transport costs or protection, have fallen sufficiently, foreign producers from one region may compete with domestic producers in another. As this transregional competition evolves, the demand and supply of goods increasingly operate at the global level: firms supply goods across the world and have to respond to competition from foreign firms. Of course, this competition can take various forms such that global markets may often reflect oligopolistic rather than perfectly competitive conditions, with a few major producers dominating a trading sector.

The most obvious examples of global markets are those for some primary commodities where trade is concentrated physically in a handful of locations, if not just one – for instance, bulk trading of produce from around the globe takes place in institutionalized and centralized exchanges. Even where significant proportions of a product are not physically traded within these markets, the exchanges fulfil the function of collecting and disseminating information about global demand and supply conditions, so setting benchmark world prices. For some primary commodities a world market emerged during the classical Gold Standard period. Although global markets for primary commodities still operate today, such as the Rotterdam spot market for oil, they are responsible for a declining proportion of international trade. It should be noted, too, that such markets do not necessarily operate as perfect markets: some have periodically been subject to intervention in the form of international commodity agreements, some have been manipulated by key players and some have been cartelized. Global markets for manufactured goods (and, latterly, tradable services) have emerged primarily in the postwar period mainly as the result of the interpenetration of national markets, creating dense networks of trade (Perraton, 1998). Thus many national and local firms respond to worldwide demand and face competition from firms based in other countries and regions.

3.1.2 Indicators

Applying the analytical framework from the introduction, the *extensity* of world trade is taken here to refer to regular intercontinental flows and networks of trade. Data for trade between geographical blocs provide a means of assessing whether there are trends towards *regionalization* or *globalization*. Regionalization here refers to the evolution of markets for traded goods involving geographically contiguous economies among whom levels of trade intensity are much greater than for trade with other countries.

The *intensity* of trade is a measure of the magnitude of global trading activity. It can be estimated by the ratio of world trade to world output, although global estimates of this are very crude. National trade to GDP measures are more accurate, and long-run estimates for the six countries in this study offer a detailed historical picture of the changing magnitude of trade. But trade–GDP estimates provide only a basic measure, since they suffer from two main limitations.[1] First, they do not reflect how much output is actually tradable; much of the postwar growth of GDP has been in non-tradables, particularly government activity and non-tradable services (personal services like hair-dressing, for instance). Accordingly, we also examine how trade has grown relative to *private GDP* (that is, GDP minus government spending) and review the evidence concerning trade in services. Secondly, since the prices of traded goods rise at a different rate from non-traded goods then trade–GDP ratios will be biased over time when measured in current prices, so we also provide estimates of these ratios in constant prices.

There are no simple indicators of *impact*, so trade–GDP ratios provide only the starting point for a more qualitative assessment. For instance, an industrialized economy with the same trade–GDP ratio as a developing economy may find it easier to absorb fluctuations in trade levels: thus there is a difference between sensitivity and vulnerability to external factors (see the introduction). At various times and in various countries marginal changes in trade relative to income have had a large impact on the fortunes of different groups. It may be that the smaller the trade–GDP ratio the more important the marginal effects: if a country's imports have been pared down to just those goods that are both vital and impossible to produce domestically, the trade–GDP ratio would be low but the effects of even a small disruption potentially large. For example, although East European countries had small trade shares in the 1970s and 1980s, they had to export to the West to pay for vital imports and this caused major domestic economic difficulties. Important distinctions therefore need to be made between the decisional, institutional, distributional and structural impacts of trade.

For trade to have a significant structural economic impact it must form a non-trivial proportion of output and have developed beyond an enclave to become integral to production in the economy as a whole. Trade globalization implies the existence of global markets for traded goods and services which transform national economies to the extent that production is conditioned increasingly by global competitive forces. National differences still influence what each country produces and how rapidly its production grows, but national economic activity is embedded within global networks

---

[1] Strictly speaking trade–GDP ratios are not appropriate because trade figures are gross and GDP measures value added. The most obvious problem is where imports are simply re-exported directly without further processing, but there are other complexities. Instead of using export figures, the import content of exports should be subtracted so that the domestic value added in producing exports is measured. By the same token, imports should be measured minus that proportion that is exported again either directly or through being used in the production of exports, so that only imports that are exchanged for domestic production are included. In practice, making these adjustments would require a detailed input-output model of each economy, something that is only available for some economies and even then not systematically.

of trading activity. Within economies trade also has distributional impacts in so far as it makes some groups richer and others poorer. We show how domestic distributional impacts have changed over time and how these are influenced by the nature of trade.

The countries linked by trade may also have widely different income levels, while the nature of trading markets and access to them vary widely. Hyperglobalist or sceptical accounts either simply assume that trade leads to global convergence in income levels or that it simply perpetuates or increases international inequality. The shifting patterns of *stratification* in international trade are examined here and the picture is shown to be often more complex than either of these accounts suggests.

Evolving transport *infrastructures* have facilitated trade greatly. Moreover, the difficulties of securing property rights in long-distance trade have also culminated in the establishment of a variety of institutionalized trade arrangements. Global trading networks and markets have emerged at various times, but they have taken a variety of historical forms. Trade relations too have been *institutionalized*, as global legal frameworks have emerged governing the conduct and trade policy of nations and firms.

3.2 Trade: From Antiquity to the Rise of the Nation-State

Intercontinental trade dates back to antiquity (Sabloff and Lamberg-Karlovsky, 1975). Early Mesopotamia, in the third millennium BC, was importing raw materials; Babylonian and Indian societies were engaging in trade as far back as 800 BC; while Hellenic civilization in the eastern Mediterranean was, from the fifth century BC, exploring trade routes to both its east and west (Curtin, 1984; Bentley, 1993; R. P. Clark, 1997). The extent of these ancient trading connections was always limited by geographical obstacles and lack of knowledge of what lay beyond, together with the limits of land and maritime transport technologies. Not surprisingly, Australia and the Americas remained outside Eurasian and African trading networks. Within the Americas the absence of any large domesticated animal and the failure to develop wheeled vehicles meant intercivilizational trade on the continent was limited. Although Mesoamerican civilization developed sophisticated road-building techniques, created a hereditary class of human porters and deployed river transport and canoes extensively, these were never sufficient to extend their trading network much beyond contemporary Mexico (Hassiz, 1985). Andean, Mesoamerican and Southern American societies of the pre-Colombian era remained, for the most part, quite discrete worlds.

In Eurasia the domestication of animals and improving technologies for harnessing their power, road-building, imperial security and improvements in shipping, cartography and navigation techniques made intercontinental and interregional trade more feasible. By 300 BC Greek traders were in contact with northern India via Arabia and trade between India and China was developing. When the Chinese Han dynasty (206 BC–AD 220) took control of the crucial land corridor between the Himalayas and the Steppes, an East–West corridor over the Eurasian land mass was effectively opened (Yü, 1997). The Silk Route, as it became known, was a complex patchwork of land and sea routes that linked the Roman Empire in the West with the Chinese Han empire in the East, by way of Anatolia, Mesopotamia, Persia, routes north and south of the

Talkiman Desert and into China itself. Branching off from this trade other routes connected up with northern India, South East Asia, Russia and Arabia. At either end of the route more local networks connected up the peripheral regions of Europe, Japan and Korea to the Silk Route. This trade was overwhelmingly in precious metals and luxury goods, and prospered until the fall of the Western Roman Empire and the Han empire. Trade was rekindled in the four centuries leading up to AD 1000 and blossomed between AD 1000 and 1350. As Deng concludes, 'China's long-distance staple trade reveals a system of international exchange . . . in fact . . . the existence of a China-centred trading system in pre-modern Asia' (1997).

Over the same period, seaborne networks of trade flourished between the Islamic lands of the fertile crescent and Arabia, the coastal city-states of India, African kingdoms and Arab entrepots on the east coast of Africa. In the fourteenth and early fifteenth centuries these trade networks connected directly with China itself so that in the premodern era trading networks had developed linking Europe, Asia and Africa (Abu-Lughod, 1989; Chaudhuri, 1985; Snow, 1988).

As European empires expanded into Asia from the sixteenth century, more extensive trading networks were established between the two continents through imperial trading companies. Throughout this period Europe consistently ran a payments deficit with Asia, financing it by gold and silver flows from the Americas following the Spanish conquest of the 'New World'. During the seventeenth and eighteenth centuries an Atlantic trading system – the slave triangle – evolved between the West Indies, Europe and Africa (see chapter 6). Although trading relations within this system rarely extended to include Asia, almost a quarter of British exports to Africa originated in India (Findlay, 1990). In this sense a world trading system can be said to have emerged around the sixteenth century (Braudel, 1984; A. Smith, 1991).

Long-distance trade flowed between entrepot ports, by both sea and overland caravan routes. Major trading cities such as Venice were also centres for regional trade and developed extensive links with local markets inland. In Europe a growing network of regular travelling fairs sustained markets trading local, regional and even non-European goods (Braudel, 1982). Luxury products predominated in intercontinental trade, although maximizing revenues from the Asian sea trade required carrying a mixed cargo of luxury and bulk goods (Chaudhuri, 1985, ch. 9). Trade grew within Europe as the Baltic regions supplied grain, cloth and iron to the rest of the continent. As with intercontinental trade, precious metals from the Americas financed the rest of Europe's deficit with the Baltic. Technological innovations, improved navigation and better organization of trade lowered transport costs, making it profitable to trade an increasing range of goods. But, in comparison with today, the *extensity* of trade activity was restricted.

Regular trade needs institutional structures to secure property rights in exchange. Entrepot ports were home to merchant communities which traditionally organized trade. Merchants made sophisticated judgements about current and future market conditions, leading to some convergence in the prices of commodities between areas. They relied on extensive but fragile networks of communication with other trading cities, enabling them to organize trade across frontiers. Banking systems evolved to finance this trade too (see chapter 4 below). Merchant courts developed wherein disputes between merchants were settled by a court of their peers. As this *lex mercatoria* evolved, an international legal framework for trade was institutionalized.

During this era trade played a significant role in the rise of cities and the emergence of the modern state. While certain trading cities had existed for centuries, outside of the relatively closed economies of China and Japan the growth and increased prosperity of other cities was often connected with rising trade. These cities developed an economic dynamic as industry and commerce flourished within them. Trade by its very nature tended to increase the extensity and intensity of market relations between different regions. With the emergence of the absolutist state in Europe (see chapter 1 above) governments began to play an active role in taxing commerce while also promoting and protecting their own merchants. Trade became a key source of revenue out of which military expenditure was funded.

Protectionism emerged in the late seventeenth century, not simply as an expedient device for raising state revenues, but also because mercantilist doctrines achieved political dominance (Magnusson, 1994). Mercantilism grew out of a belief that an economy could increase its wealth through a trade surplus and the consequent accumulation of precious metals. Trade was thus conceived as a zero-sum competition: one state's loss was another state's gain. It was not primarily an anti-trade strategy as such, but rather sought to maximize exports and minimize imports by promoting domestic industry while simultaneously limiting imports.

Not surprisingly, the *intensity* of trade and its *impact* on economies during this period was limited. At the start of the nineteenth century it is estimated by Kuznets (1967) that world exports amounted to only 1–2 per cent of world GDP, belying notions that an integrated capitalist world economy had emerged through trade in the sixteenth century (Wallerstein, 1974, 1980). Although Abu-Lughod (1989) indicates that there is some evidence that, as far back as the twelfth century, trade affected production in the European heartlands, it was largely confined to products unavailable in Europe and therefore did not involve direct competition. In this respect, apart from export development through slave labour in the Americas and the Caribbean, intercontinental trade during this early period did not lead to specialization in production: the vast majority of output and employment everywhere remained agricultural. Thus trade was not significant enough by itself to determine patterns of international inequality, as evidenced by the fact that several regions that were later to become peripheral to the world economy prospered through trade in this period. As Fernández-Armesto notes, until the eighteenth century both India and China outstripped Europe in terms of manufacturing and economic capacity (1995). Trade was essential to the economic prosperity of the major trading cities that comprised the world's trading posts, but its impact on economic activity more generally was limited.

3.3   From the Industrial Revolution to the Second World War: the Rise and Fall of World Trade

Foreign trade played a secondary role in Britain's industrial revolution. A key shift was political and intellectual as the climate gradually turned against mercantilism following the 1776 publication of Adam Smith's *The Wealth of Nations* (and subsequent tracts) showing the potential for mutual gains through freer trade. The triumph of the free traders and the era of British free trade can properly be dated from the mid-nineteenth century with the repeal of the Corn Laws (which placed tariffs on imported grain) in

1846; the 1849 repeal of the Navigation Acts; and the 1860 negotiation of an Anglo-French trade treaty. Other countries' desire to participate in trade as it grew led to the negotiation of bilateral treaties and similar reductions in protection levels. Although tariffs remained high generally, a fundamental change was signalled with the growing acceptance of the most favoured nation (MFN) principle (Bairoch, 1989).

Under the MFN principle, trade preferences granted by one state to its most favoured trading partner are applied equally to all other countries so that trade policy does not discriminate between countries. The effect of the MFN principle is that if one country negotiates a tariff cut with another, that reduction applies equally to all its other trading partners. In the latter part of the nineteenth century, when neighbouring countries and long-standing trading partners negotiated tariff reductions with each other, the application of the MFN principle meant that the benefits of such reductions effectively spread much more widely, reducing tariff levels more generally. Although protection levels varied after 1814 they declined generally as a consequence of the negotiation of several major trade treaties, particularly between 1860 and 1879.

From initially low and stable levels at the start of the nineteenth century, trade volumes grew at about 2.3 per cent annually from 1820 to 1850 and then accelerated to around 5 per cent between 1850 and 1870 (Rogowski, 1989). Although accurate figures for world income growth are lacking, trade generally grew faster than world income through the nineteenth century (Kuznets, 1967; Rogowski, 1989, ch. 2). For Western states as a whole exports rose to around 5 per cent of GDP by the middle of the century and to 10 per cent by 1880 (Krugman, 1995). Expanding trade, spurred by declining protection and falling transport costs, was consolidated as the Industrial Revolution took hold and communication infrastructures improved.

3.3.1 International trade during the classical Gold Standard, 1870–1914

The huge expansion of trade during the latter part of the nineteenth century up to the First World War was, in part, a product of industrialization. The application of steam power to railways and shipping greatly improved international transport. Foreign investment and the acquisition of technology ensured countries beyond Britain industrialized and so competed in international markets. Industrialization led to rising demand for raw materials. This created a more extensive trading order as an increasing number of countries and colonies sought to supply them. For the first time mass trade in basic commodities, not just luxuries, became profitable. The number of areas engaged in trade rose rapidly: by 1913 155 areas were registered as participating in international trade, while the figure for the early nineteenth century was probably less than half of that (Kuznets, 1967). An extensive international trading system was thus a reality by the early twentieth century.

Growing extensity was also associated with greater trade intensity. Developing areas used their receipts from exports of primary products to buy manufactures from the industrialized countries as exporters sought out new markets. This set the pattern for trade stratification before the Second World War, with trade between developed and developing economies constituting around half of the total (table 3.1). Through the classical Gold Standard and interwar periods, primary products – especially food and

Table 3.1 The direction of world trade, 1876–1928 (percentages)

	Between developed economies	Developed–developing	Between developing economies
1876	45.0	51.0	4.0
1913	43.0	52.0	5.0
1928	40.0	49.0	11.0

Source: Kuznets, 1967

raw materials – constituted the majority of world trade, with manufactures accounting for less than 40 per cent (Yates, 1959; Kuznets, 1967).

The Gold Standard, established in the 1870s, ensured a stable international payments system by fixing the price of the world's main currencies in terms of gold. Trade intensity (measured by volume) grew at around 3.5 per cent per annum over the period 1870–1914, as against world real output growth of around 2.7 per cent (Kitson and Michie, 1995). Kuznets (1967) estimates that by the eve of the First World War the value of world exports stood at 16–17 per cent of world income.[2] More recent estimates for the industrialized countries put this figure lower, at around 12 per cent, suggesting that the growth of trade relative to output slowed in the years leading up to the First World War (Krugman, 1995). This is more consistent with other developments at the time.

Transport costs for shipping freight fell steadily to half their mid-1870s rates by the early 1900s, and then started to rise again before the First World War (Isserlis, 1938). Protection levels fluctuated during 1879–92 and increased thereafter up to the First World War, so that for many countries tariff rates were higher in 1914 than in 1878 and discriminatory protection re-emerged as some countries retreated from the MFN principle (Bairoch, 1989). This was a return to protectionism: the German economist Friedrich List (1789–1846) developed the notion that emerging economies needed to shelter their industries until they developed to the levels of the leading economies. Several important economies adopted protectionist policies. Nevertheless, a recognizable global trading system emerged during this period such that a significant proportion of the world's output was exchanged.

Growing trade meant that domestic markets became increasingly linked and global markets for some goods emerged. For certain primary commodities, such as rice and wheat, formal global markets were instituted: large volumes of these commodities were traded through established centres in Europe and the US, setting benchmark prices for the entire world (Latham, 1986). There was extensive intercontinental trade between developed and developing areas and between Europe and North America. Although O'Rourke and Williamson (1994) point to evidence of international price convergence for certain basic manufactured goods, for the majority of other goods there is scant evidence of the existence of functioning global markets. Moreover, much intercontinental trade followed the existing preference systems of empires and their spheres of

---

[2] Such estimates make bold assumptions about the size of world trade and income and are thus subject to wide margins of error. They may overestimate this ratio through underestimating GDP, since much of the non-marketed GDP went unrecorded but trade was largely recorded.

influence. Trade flows were often concentrated particularly strongly between countries that had negotiated trade treaties (Irwin, 1993). These networks of trading relations expanded to incorporate more countries, but their limited geographical reach meant that while international markets for many traded goods emerged between groups of countries, these fell short of truly global markets.

Trade intensity among the developing economies rose considerably over this period. Beyond these economies there were huge variations in levels of trade: from autarky to some economies that were virtually export platforms. Among Latin American countries exports rose from approximately 10 per cent to 18 per cent of GDP over the period 1860–1900, while among Asian economies exports were much lower, rising from about 1 to 5 per cent of GDP over the same period (Hanson, 1980). Most African economies probably lay somewhere in between. Exports from developing areas tended to be concentrated among those countries with easily extractable minerals or with established commercial agriculture. Many developing economies had low export levels; in some the export sector formed an enclave. Indeed, the linkages between export activity and national economies varied widely (Morris and Adelman, 1988, chs 3 and 6). Thus, although the great majority of territories were trading by the First World War, many economies could scarcely be said to have been incorporated fully into an international trading system.

There was no institutionalized international trading regime during this period: as noted, international trade diplomacy was conducted largely through bilateral negotiations, as was the application of formal legal measures to secure contracts in exchange. Nevertheless, expanding trade led to pressures for the harmonization of standards and rules for trading. A range of international agreements were negotiated so that common trading standards and practices evolved at the international level (Murphy, 1994, chs 2–4). Sometimes these agreements were initiated by governments, but often they arose at least in part from private initiatives. Similarly, international arrangements were instituted to facilitate and regulate the expansion of international transport and communications infrastructures essential for the conduct of trade. The relative independence of these institutions from national governments meant that they continued to function after the First World War.

3.3.2   The interwar years: the breakdown of world trade

Trading networks disrupted by the Great War were frequently not re-established. From 1913 up to the crash of 1929 world trade volumes grew at 2.2 per cent per annum, roughly in line with output, while tariff levels were not much greater than before the war (Kitson and Michie, 1995). Following the 1929 crash, protectionism became widespread as countries raised their trade barriers and abandoned the MFN principle in favour of discriminatory measures. Tariffs and other barriers escalated as countries used 'beggar-my-neighbour' protection in self-defeating attempts to pass on the costs of recession to each other. Trade plummeted after 1929: between 1929 and 1937 world trade volumes actually fell by 0.4 per cent per annum, although this understates the initial fall. World output too grew slowly at 0.8 per cent per annum over the same period (Kitson and Michie, 1995). The falls in trade greatly exacerbated the downturn

Table 3.2 Tariff rates (%) for selected countries, 1820–1931

	1820[a]	1875[a]	1913	1926	1931
France	[b]	12–15	18	12	38.0
Germany	8–12	4–6	12	12	40.7
Japan	[b]	5	20	16	24.0
Sweden	[b]	3–5	16	13	26.8
Great Britain	45–55	0	0	4	10.0[c]
United States	35–45	40–50	33	29	53.0

[a] Manufactures only.
[b] Extensive restrictions on trade in force.
[c] 1932.
Sources: Bairoch, 1989; Panic, 1988, pp. 149–51; Pomfret, 1988, p. 25; Minami, 1994, ch. 7

in economic activity, an indication of the importance of trade to many economies. When growth did resume it was primarily generated domestically. Primary commodity exporters were particularly hard hit: just as growth had increased demand for these commodities, recession and protectionism led to falls in demand and, consequently, prices. Falling prices encouraged an expansion of supply to make up producer incomes, pushing prices down still further.

Where countries did reduce tariffs and trade did recover it was often inside regional or imperial trading arrangements, although even these sometimes increased protection overall by raising barriers against other countries while reducing barriers between members (Pomfret, 1988, ch. 2; Eichengreen and Irwin, 1995). The emergence of insulated imperial or regional blocs sharply reversed the trend towards a global trading system.

We can examine these developments in more detail in relation to the six countries in this study. This perspective is more reliable than global data since it avoids having to estimate the size of the world economy. The trends in protection shown in table 3.2 are consistent with the general picture of tariff rates falling until the 1870s, a tendency to rise thereafter, with significant rises coming after the crash of 1929 (with the exception of Britain). Using annual data we can trace trends in both exports and trade (calculated here as the value of exports plus imports) in relation to national income as an indicator of the intensity of trade relations for these countries. Moreover since government activity was (and is) overwhelmingly not traded it is important also to examine trade levels in relation to total private national economic activity.

During the classical Gold Standard era Britain had the highest level of trade to national income among developed economies. Britain's industrial supremacy and access to extensive colonial territories provided its exporters with ready markets. Exports of goods and services formed around 30 per cent of GDP and, as figure 3.1 shows, the value of trade reached almost 60 per cent of GDP. The value of exports stood at around 25–33 per cent of private GDP (for trade see figure 3.2). Initially Britain maintained these trade levels after the First World War, but they declined in the 1920s as export growth fell, both absolutely and relative to income growth, and then crashed in the 1930s. Tariff protection was reinstituted in the 1920s and increased in the 1930s. By the Second World War the British economy had become heavily oriented to domestic and imperial markets and faced increasing competition in the latter.

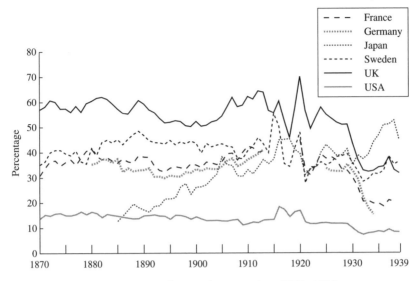

Figure 3.1 Trade as a percentage of GDP, six countries, 1870–1939 (*Sources*: For France, Mitchell, 1992; Lévy-Leboyer and Bourguignon, 1990; for Germany, Mitchell, 1992; for Japan, Ohkawa and Shinohara, 1979; for Sweden, Johansson, 1967; for the UK, Feinstein, 1972; for the US, Mitchell, 1983)

French trade grew significantly relative to income after 1860 (figure 3.1). Trade levels in France were high by developed country standards for much of the nineteenth century. Tariff levels rose in the 1880s and 1890s and then fell again in the first part of the twentieth century. Through the classical Gold Standard period the value of exports reached around 15 per cent of GDP while trade to private GDP ratios were higher (see figure 3.2). After the First World War trade levels relative to GDP recovered rapidly to reach classical Gold Standard levels by the mid-1920s; they subsequently declined as a consequence of the economic turbulence of the late 1920s and collapsed after 1929.

In the 1870s Germany had one of the most liberal trade regimes in the world. This was reversed in the 1880s and trade as a share of GDP fell, leading to declining trade levels, as figures 3.1 and 3.2 reveal. These recovered from the 1890s with rising exports, not simply because of the development of German industry but also because of aggressive export promotion policies. This new protectionism was an attempt both to ensure national self-sufficiency in agriculture and to construct an industrial base behind tariff barriers. Hyperinflation in the early 1920s severely disrupted trade, such that even in the late 1920s trade relative to GDP was still below those levels typical of the classical Gold Standard period. Trade fell sharply in the 1930s as a result of both the general decline in world trade and the protectionist policies of the Nazis.

By comparison the USA had relatively high trade–GDP levels in the early nineteenth century, similar to Britain's at the time, but as figures 3.1 and 3.2 indicate trade levels (as a share of GDP) fell sharply with the disruption of the Civil War and throughout the classical Gold Standard period exports remained below 10 per cent of GDP while total trade was approximately 15 per cent of GDP. Trade remained important and in absolute terms US exports grew strongly over this period, roughly in line with national income. The pattern continued after the First World War with exports continuing to

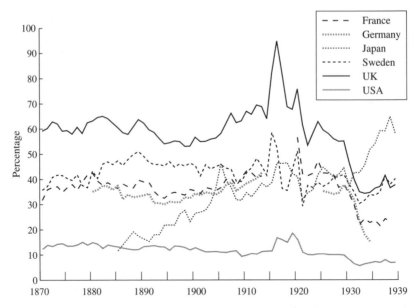

Figure 3.2 Trade as a percentage of private GDP, six countries, 1870–1939 (*Sources*: As figure 3.1)

grow, with the result that the US became established as a world trading power, but trade levels (as a share of GDP) fell in the early 1920s as income growth outstripped trade growth. Trade actually fell still further in the early 1930s; it was the USA's decision to increase tariffs in 1929 that marked the start of the 1930s protectionism.

As figure 3.1 reveals, Japan's trade rose steadily from negligible levels in the 1880s so that on the eve of the First World War exports of goods and services formed around 10 per cent of output while total trade amounted to over 20 per cent of GDP. In 1899 Japan asserted tariff autonomy, raising tariffs several times until 1911 as it used protectionism as a strategy for developing domestic industry. This did not prevent trade rising absolutely and relative to output, albeit from very low levels. After the First World War trade levels initially fell but then recovered in the late 1920s and continued to rise in the 1930s, peaking at around 25 per cent of GDP (as measured by exports only) or in excess of 50 per cent of trade to private GDP (see figure 3.2). Japan's rising trade in the 1930s resulted from a shift in both the structure and geography of its trade and from a massive initial devaluation (Minami, 1994, ch. 7). Japanese exports grew rapidly in the 1930s as a result of the expansion of its Greater East Asia Co-prosperity sphere.

Swedish trade–GDP levels in the classical Gold Standard era were, at around 40 per cent, generally higher than for any of the other countries noted above apart from Britain. As figures 3.1 and 3.2 show trade–GDP levels increased rapidly over the 1860s and early 1870s and then fluctuated such that exports of goods and services formed around 20 per cent of GDP while trade–GDP ratios were more than double that of the classical Gold Standard period. Sweden's trade–GDP ratios had recovered by the late 1920s to pre-First World War levels, and although its trade declined in the early 1930s it recovered partially thereafter so that trade–GDP levels in the late 1930s were comparable to the 1920s. Its high trade levels did not reflect low protectionism – Sweden raised tariffs in the 1890s to levels that were high by the standards of the smaller European countries (Bairoch, 1989).

3.3.3   The economic impact of trade

During the eighteenth and early nineteenth centuries trade was too small to have played more than a minor role in national economic development. Moreover, even during the Gold Standard era it has been debated how far trade was a cause or a consequence of rapid economic growth. Trade did contribute to economic growth since it provided larger markets and cheap raw material imports. That the 1930s depression hit countries worldwide illustrates both the global extent of the trading system and the economic significance of trade.

For the above six countries, trade was mostly a secondary factor in national economic growth during the period 1870–1939. Even in the British case high levels of trade were the product of economic success rather than its primary cause. Sweden was the closest case to export-led growth through natural resource exports. But the impact of the growing intensity of trade diffused ever more widely throughout these economies as national markets evolved and deepened (Schön, 1986).

Elsewhere demand for primary exports was a major source of growth for many developing countries rich in natural resources and for the more developed primary exporters of the time, notably Australia, Canada, Argentina and South Africa. Demand for their goods contributed directly to growth and stimulated the development of associated processing industries. Governments used export revenues to undertake major infrastructure projects, often supplemented by borrowing abroad against future export earnings. Nevertheless, although there are examples of successful export-led development in the classical Gold Standard period, high trade levels were neither necessary nor sufficient for growth. Morris and Adelman found that whether trade had a significant positive impact on developing economies depended on whether their domestic market structures were sufficiently advanced to realize the gains from trade and diffuse them throughout the national economy (1988, chs 3 and 6). Trade often had a significant impact in stimulating the development of market relations within an economy, but this was by no means automatic.

Trade, however, was a significant determinant of the incomes of different sectors within countries and ultimately had a key impact on domestic politics. Falling protection and transport costs led to a marked convergence in the prices of internationally traded goods so that countries became increasingly specialized in those sectors where they had a competitive advantage. This led to a pattern of trade stratification in which those countries notably rich in natural resources expanded exports of primary products while the industrializing countries specialized in manufactures. This international division of labour had profound effects on the fortunes of different sectors and groups in industrial and developing countries. Standard trade theory – see box 3.1 – predicts that as countries became more open to trade the returns to factors of production will converge internationally. Recent studies confirm that as a consequence of trade there was significant international convergence in wage, rent and profit rates during the classical Gold Standard period (O'Rourke and Williamson, 1994; O'Rourke et al., 1996). Trade, combined with migration and international capital flows, led to a significant

Box 3.1 Opening up to trade: economic and distributional impacts

The standard economic theory of trade makes a number of assumptions. Once a country opens up to trade the prices of its tradable goods are assumed to reflect world prices (adjusted for the exchange rate) rather than domestic prices. World prices reflect the relative costs of producing tradable goods in the global market rather than in the national economy. Depending on the structure of relative costs in each country this will make it profitable to expand the output of some goods, while for other goods that can be produced more cheaply abroad domestic output will be replaced by imports. Thus opening up to trade will lead to increased production of the tradable goods in which the country has a *comparative (competitive) advantage* and a fall in the production of goods in which it has a relative disadvantage, sometimes to zero production levels.

What determines relative costs in a country and thus its comparative advantage? In the textbook (Heckscher-Ohlin) approach cost differences reflect the relative supplies of factors of production, basically land, labour (of different skill levels) and capital, with the relatively abundant factor(s) being relatively cheap. Opening up to trade leads to each country specializing in goods that use the relatively abundant factor(s) intensively in their production, given that these are relatively cheap to produce domestically, and importing goods whose production uses the relatively scarce factor(s) intensively, making them relatively expensive to produce domestically.

Opening up to trade therefore affects the distribution of income between land, labour and capital. Under the Stolper-Samuelson theorem, opening up to trade will increase the income of abundant factors and reduce the income of scarce factors. Intuitively it can be seen that as trade increases the demand for products that use the abundant factor(s) intensively and reduces demand for goods that use the scarce factor(s) intensively, this would increase demand for the abundant factor(s), increasing its return, and decrease demand for the scarce factor(s), decreasing its return. The income of a country will still rise overall from the gains to trade but the distribution of such gains will be uneven. In principle the gainers could fully compensate the losers and still be better off than before but this assumes state intervention. However, under plausible conditions, the magnitude of the income distribution effect will be several times the size of the gain from trade.

The factor price equalization theorem goes further, showing that under certain conditions the returns to different factors, that is land rents, wage rates and profit rates, would converge worldwide. Intuitively it can be seen that trade will ensure that returns in each country to the relatively abundant factor(s) will rise and those to the relatively scarce factor(s) will fall. Since the abundant factor(s) is relatively cheap and the scarce factor(s) expensive this implies that prices of factors rise where previously they were relatively cheap and fall where previously they were relatively expensive so that they would tend to converge globally. Theoretically wages, or the returns to capital, will converge internationally if labour or capital is free to move from low to high wage or profit countries, but factor price equalization through trade indicates that it can occur even without such factor mobility. Factor price equalization still relies on a set of restrictive assumptions and in the absence of all the conditions holding there is more likely to be a tendency for international differences in factor prices to narrow rather than for there to be complete equalization.

narrowing of differences in wages between countries as they became subject to global competitive pressures (Williamson, 1995). Further, increasing agricultural trade lowered the cost of food and was thereby a major source of increases in real wages. Thus, while more efficient farmers in the Americas saw their incomes rise, in many European countries there was a prolonged agricultural decline as cheaper agricultural products from the US became available.[3] These movements stopped short of complete convergence as other factors modified or accentuated these trends. This tendency to global convergence ceased in the interwar years as protectionism increased, and wages, profits and rents actually diverged worldwide during the late 1930s. In labour-abundant European countries real wages fell, while the land-abundant USA experienced a severe agricultural depression.

3.3.4   Trade globalization: from the Gold Standard era to the Great Depression

During the period from 1870 to 1939 markets for key goods began to acquire a global dimension and, unlike earlier periods, this resulted in country specialization such that national patterns of production were increasingly influenced by global competition. One result of this, broadly in line with standard trade theory, was that income levels within those economies more fully enmeshed in the trade system were increasingly subject to global market disciplines and this had a key impact on domestic politics. Groups standing to gain from free trade mobilized in favour of it, those standing to lose organized for protectionism (Rogowski, 1989). But these trends largely ceased after the First World War and were eroded in the 1930s.

Although the *extensity* of trade for much of this period expanded to incorporate much of the globe, and significant global markets for some products did emerge, networks of trade for most goods were often geographically restricted. Since most countries had some degree of protection, even in the classical Gold Standard period, this further restricted the development of global markets and partially insulated economies from the impact of trade. The *intensity* of trade varied widely. For the developed countries and major primary exporters trade grew from negligible to significant proportions of their national income. For many other economies trade levels were often small and their impact on the rest of the economy limited. Thus the trade system was highly stratified, such that economies beyond Europe and the major primary exporters often played a negligible role in world trade.

3.4   The Rise of a Global Trading Order

Trade grew even more rapidly than output throughout the postwar period; during this 'golden age' (1950–73) trade volumes grew at 5.8 per cent per annum, much more

---

[3] Wages rose relative to rents in labour-abundant countries and rents rose relative to wages in land-abundant countries. This ratio doubled in France between 1870 and 1910, more than doubled in Britain and Sweden and rose by 40 per cent in Germany over the same period; these movements appear to be higher for the least protected countries, again in line with standard trade theory. In the land-abundant USA this ratio halved over the same period; this is indicative of the impact of trade since, as noted, US trade–GDP ratios remained low throughout this period.

rapidly than during the nineteenth century, while world output grew at an unprecedented rate of 3.9 per cent per annum (Kitson and Michie, 1995). Subsequently both declined and during 1973–96 on average trade grew at 4.1 per cent and output at 3.3 per cent per annum,[4] although this masks much more rapid rises in the late 1980s, resumed through the 1990s. But just how far contemporary levels and patterns of trade constitute a distinctive new phase of globalization remains to be determined.

3.4.1   The development of global free trade

The 1944 Bretton Woods agreement not only established a system of fixed exchange rates but also the basis for a multilateral trading order. In a conscious attempt to avoid the protectionism of the 1930s, the 1947 Havana Charter provided for an International Trade Organization to oversee the operation of the world trading system. President Truman abandoned the proposal when protectionists and staunch free traders (who feared it would regulate trade) united to oppose it in the US Congress. By default the weaker General Agreement on Tariffs and Trade (GATT), a multilateral forum for tariff negotiations, became the primary international trade agency. Effectively the GATT was little more than a trade agreement among the signatories, with a small secretariat overseeing observance of its rules and providing technical services for multilateral trade liberalization negotiations under its auspices. In 1995, however, it was superseded by the World Trade Organization (WTO), a much more powerful institution.

The GATT regime, on which the WTO is built, was based on four main principles:

- *non-discrimination* (the MFN principle);
- *reciprocity*, that tariff reductions in one country should be matched by reductions among its trading partners;
- *transparency*, that the nature of trade measures should be clear; and
- *fairness*, so that practices like dumping of goods at below market prices or predatory pricing by exporters were deemed unfair and countries were entitled to institute protection against them.

The Articles of the GATT provided for some exceptions to the rules in order to protect a country's balance of payments and industry. GATT formed the basis for the postwar trade regime and the framework for seven rounds of global tariff reduction negotiations. The number of countries involved rose progressively so that the 1967–70 Kennedy Round included over eighty countries, while the 1986–93 Uruguay Round embraced most countries in the world. These multilateral negotiations successively reduced tariffs, so that by the end of the Tokyo Round in 1979 they were lower among OECD countries than during the classical Gold Standard era, and reductions agreed during the Uruguay Round reduced them still further.

Although tariffs are now at their lowest level for centuries, it is sometimes claimed that the decline in tariff protection among OECD countries has been at the very least offset by the rise of various non-tariff barriers. Non-tariff barriers are, broadly speaking, any government measure that distorts the volume, composition or direction of

---

[4] Calculated from IMF, *International Financial Statistics Yearbook* for 1998.

trade; as such almost any government measure could affect trade and so estimates of their range and effects vary. There are direct barriers in the form of quotas on imports, negotiated restrictions on import quantities, support for exporters, customs delays and procedures, and government policies of buying from domestic producers; indirectly trade may also be affected by government support for industries and by regulation of products on, for example, health and safety or environmental grounds. Estimates indicate that these barriers affected only around 18 per cent of the world's exports in 1992 (Page, 1994, p. 51). It is difficult to assess the impact of non-tariff barriers, not least because the data usually refers only to the extent of their coverage and not to their actual implementation. Harrigan (1993), for instance, found that their impact on the trade of OECD countries was small. They are probably higher in developing countries and have a greater impact on their trade since they are particularly prevalent in agricultural, textiles and several other industrial sectors in which many developing countries have a comparative advantage (Page, 1994, ch. 3). Again, they appear to cover only a minority of the exports of developing countries and some of these barriers have been reduced as a result of the Uruguay Round, notably with the phasing out of the Multi-fibre Agreement which limits textiles trade.

Not only did the GATT produce large reductions in tariffs and thereby liberalize trade, but latterly it moved into other sectors, notably reducing barriers to trade in services. The WTO regime aims to reduce or eliminate a whole range of non-tariff barriers and differences in trading conditions between countries. Moreover, the WTO is a much more powerful institution in so far as its dispute panels have the authority to make binding judgements in cases where trade rules are subject to dispute or transgressed. In this respect the WTO is a significant institutional force for trade liberalization (Hoekman and Kostecki, 1995; Qureshi, 1996).

Until the 1980s the trend towards greater trade openness among industrialized countries was not generally matched in the developing world. Many developing countries emerged from the interwar years sceptical of the benefits of an open trading system and gave priority to building a national industrial base. The resultant protectionism may in practice have owed more to temporary expediency than coherent national goals, but it had a decisive impact on their trade policies. From the 1980s there has been a sea change among developing countries, with widespread reductions in trade barriers, undertaken both as a domestic strategy and under pressure from multilateral institutions like the World Bank, the IMF and WTO. Sachs and Warner (1995) found that from 1960 until the late 1980s the proportion of the world's economies that could be classed as operating broadly open trade policies was stable at below a quarter measured by population and less than a half measured by GDP. Since then the proportions have risen to over a half and around two-thirds respectively, figures that will rise still further when China is admitted to the WTO and so long as the trend towards trade liberalization continues.

Since Comecon's collapse most East European countries have liberalized their trade regimes so that their tariff levels are now little higher than OECD countries. Despite the collapse of regional trading arrangements among the former Comecon countries, the major countries have generally managed to expand their exports to the rest of the world, mostly to other European countries, often reaching trade–GDP levels of above 50 per cent, which is comparable to, or higher than, the average either for developed countries or for developing countries at similar income levels.

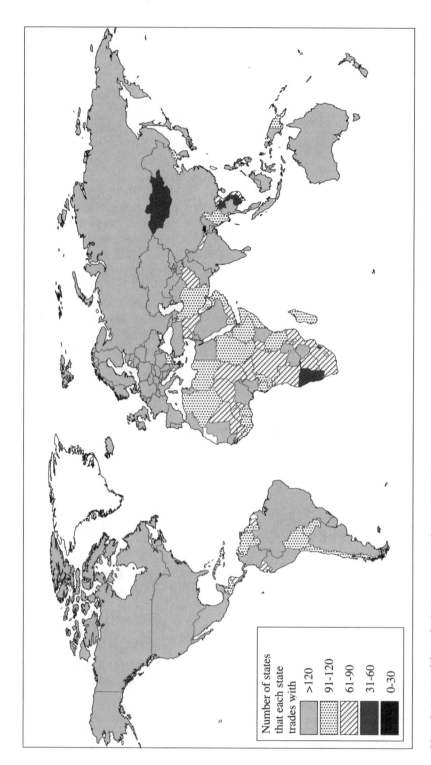

Map 3.1 World trade interconnectedness, 1990 (*Source:* Adapted from Nierop, 1994)

Number of states
that each state
trades with

>120

91–120

61–90

31–60

0–30

Table 3.3 Intensity of trade links, 1928–1990 (percentage of maximum possible trade links in each period)

	1928	1938	1950	1960	1970	1980	1990
Constant sample	–	–	64.4	74.4	83.8	89.6	95.3
Non-constant sample	55.4	53.5	64.4	62.2	55.5	56.2	66.2

The constant sample measures trade connectivity for a group of 68 countries over the period; the non-constant sample measures connectivity for all those countries for which trade data were available for that year.
Sources: Data for 1928–38 estimated from League of Nations, 1942; data for 1950–90 from Nierop, 1994, p. 41

By the 1970s a largely free trade order had been established among all the OECD countries and since the 1980s this has been extended to developing countries and countries formerly closed to trade under communism, with the result that a global trading system now exists. Historically, protection levels are lower than in previous eras while trade liberalization is likely to continue. Trade levels are higher, both absolutely and in relation to output, than ever before. Below we examine the growing *extensity* and *intensity* of this global trade system in more detail.

3.4.2 The extensity of trade and the emergence of global markets

The emergence of global free trade provided the basis for open worldwide markets. For such markets to emerge requires networks of trade between regions and countries. Over the postwar period trade has become much more extensive than ever before as a worldwide network of trading relations between regions and countries has developed. Nierop notes that by 1990 the majority of countries traded with the majority of others (1994, ch. 3; and see map 3.1). More precisely, table 3.3 shows trade relations between countries as a percentage of the maximum possible trade connectivity (every country trading with every other). For comparison, estimates for 54 territories using interwar data are also included. The data show a postwar rise in the intensity of trading relations towards the maximum possible. While the non-constant sample figures do not show a clear trend, nevertheless the latest figure is indicative of an extensive world trading system and suggests that the extensity of trading relations is higher than during the interwar period, consistent with the above evidence of the restricted extensity of trading networks in the interwar and classical Gold Standard periods. The expanding reach of trade relations since the 1980s is consistent with the increase in developing country participation.

Extensive as they are, trade networks still appear to be concentrated within certain geographical areas, crudely Europe, the Americas and Asia-Pacific, three trade blocs with some economic coherence and including most of the industrialized economies. To many sceptics such developments have been interpreted as evidence that trade is becoming regionalized rather than globalized.

Regionalization, as opposed to globalization, implies that trade flows are clustered between similar countries which tend to be geographically contiguous, and that markets within a region are (at least) partially insulated from the rest of the world. This is more likely to be so in a regional customs union, where members adopt a common trade policy towards the rest of the world, than with a regional free trade arrangement where members simply agree to reduce barriers against each other – 'open regionalism'. The EU is the only functioning customs union in the world. It has not adopted a protectionist stance towards the rest of the world, except in agricultural products, and trade with non-EU countries rose as a proportion of EU GDP in the period 1973–85 (Jacquemin and Sapir, 1988; Neven and Röller, 1991). NAFTA is a free trade area between the USA, Canada and Mexico, and has not increased protection against the rest of the world; nor has APEC or ASEAN (Petri, 1993). The evidence suggests that trade regionalization is complementary to, and has grown alongside, interregional trade.

Anderson and Norheim investigated the growth of intraregional and interregional trade for the world's major economic regions since the 1930s (1993a; 1993b). Their results show no strong move towards regionalization: trade has grown vigorously between regions as well as within them. While the intensity of intraregional trade rose in the postwar period (figures for Europe in the nineteenth century show virtually no intraregional bias), between 1979 and 1990 there was only a small rise in intraregional intensity within the EU and actual falls in Asia and America. Interestingly the intensity of intraregional trade is lower in Western Europe than in America or Asia, so that the institutionalization of regional markets does not necessarily appear to lead to closed regions. This is reinforced by other evidence, specifically indices for the propensity to trade extraregionally. These indices show a rising propensity for extraregional trade in America and Asia, and a fluctuating propensity in Europe over the postwar period. These figures, consistent with other estimates, do not support the regionalization thesis (cf. Lloyd, 1992).

Contemporary regional trading arrangements have been designed to liberalize trade not build protectionist fortresses, recognizing the potential benefits from freer trade but also the relative ease of reaching agreement at the regional, as opposed to the global, level. While open regionalism does not appear to be leading to mercantilist trading blocs, for smaller and developing economies it is partly driven out of fear of being left out of preferential trading arrangements (Perroni and Whalley, 1994). Paradoxically, negotiation of regional trade agreements is partly insurance against the possibility of regional trade blocs. The threat of regionalization has thus proved more potent than its reality.

3.4.3   The growing intensity of postwar trade

In the postwar period trade grew more rapidly than world income. World figures are crude, but they tell a simple story. In 1950 world exports amounted to 7 per cent of world output, but as figure 3.3 shows this rose gradually in the 1960s, more sharply in the early 1970s and some estimate the figure today is around 17 per cent (Krugman, 1995). The figures for OECD countries have been broadly similar, as would be expected from their dominant position in the world economy. For oil-importing developing countries the ratio of exports to GDP fell until the 1970s, reflecting protectionist policies, but rose in the 1970s and through the 1990s as a result of declining protectionism and the pursuit of export-oriented policies. For these countries exports are equivalent to

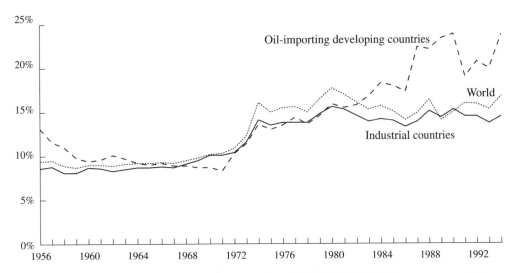

Figure 3.3 World exports as a percentage of world GDP, 1956–1994 (*Sources*: IMF, 1988; IMF, *International Financial Statistics*, various years)

Table 3.4 Trade–GDP percentages for developed countries (constant prices)

	1913	1950	1973	1985
Exports–GDP	11.2	8.3	18.0	23.1

	1880–1900	1901–1913	1948–1958	1959–1972	1973–1987
Imports–GDP	12.4	13.3	10.1	15.4	21.7

Sources: Maddison, 1991, p. 327; McKeown, 1991, p. 158

around 20 per cent of GDP. Much of this increase is accounted for by the Asian tiger economies (whose trade growth was disrupted following the 1997–8 crisis), although trade is on the rise for many developing countries.

These figures may appear little higher than those noted earlier for the classical Gold Standard era, leading the sceptics to claim that the postwar growth of trade is little more than a return to those levels after the disruption of the interwar years (for instance, Hirst and Thompson, 1996b, ch. 2). However, levels of trade to GDP and trade to private GDP for the major OECD economies demonstrate much greater trade intensity to date than during the classical Gold Standard era. Furthermore, direct comparison of figures between the two periods can be misleading: current price data understate the rise in trade–GDP ratios since the prices of traded goods tend to rise less rapidly than those for non-traded goods due to the greater competition such goods face and their greater potential for technical progress (Gregorio et al., 1994). Price data is also subject to considerable margins of error. At the same time, where the key OECD economies are concerned, the figures in table 3.4 do indicate that trade, as a proportion

Table 3.5 Falling transport and communication costs, 1920–1990 (constant 1990 US$)

	Sea freight[a]	Air transport[b]	Cross-Atlantic telephone call[c]
1920	95	–	–
1930	60	0.68	244.65
1940	63	0.46	188.51
1950	34	0.30	53.20
1960	27	0.24	45.86
1970	27	0.16	31.58
1980	24	0.10	4.80
1990	29	0.11	3.32

[a] Average ocean freight and port charges per short ton of import and export cargo.
[b] Average air transport revenue per passenger mile.
[c] Three-minute New York–London call.
Source: Hufbauer, 1991

of GDP (measured in constant prices), has been higher since the early 1970s than in any previous era. While only current price data are available for developing countries, trade as a percentage of GDP, at least since the 1970s, is also higher than during the classical Gold Standard period.

Of course, these figures refer only to trade in goods. Data on world trade in services only became available from 1980 onwards and are subject to a considerable margin of error. But services trade has more than doubled to over $1.3 trillion a year and now constitutes well over 20 per cent of total world trade (calculated from WTO, 1995). On this basis estimates of world exports as a percentage of world output should be revised upwards to around 21.8 per cent (calculating world income at 1996 market exchange rates) and 18.6 per cent (calculating it at purchasing power parity which adjusts for differences in price levels between countries) (IMF, 1997b). The data for services, according to Moshirian (1994), significantly underestimate trade in financial services and, by implication, world services trade in total. Services tend to be less traded and tradable relative to goods and so services trade–GDP ratios are typically lower than for an economy as a whole. But the share of services traded has risen over time and constitutes a significant shift in the character of global trade. Both OECD and developing countries trade a significant proportion of their services output and have done so at least since the mid-1970s (Hoekman and Karsenty, 1992). Indeed, some developing countries have a strong comparative advantage in labour-intensive services and export around a third of their commercial services output.

These developments are indicative of a qualitative shift in the intensity of postwar trade as national markets became increasingly enmeshed with each other such that trade is now integral to national economic prosperity. As noted, national barriers to trade have been sharply reduced. Transport costs have also fallen, reducing the costs of trading: as table 3.5 shows, through much of the postwar period transport costs have fallen considerably in real terms as a result of technical progress, containerization and cheap fuel. In this respect, falls in communications costs and the information revolution have played a central role in facilitating large volumes of trade in services. As tariffs and transport costs have declined they have become secondary or even negligible components of the price of traded goods. Under these circumstances global markets are evolving in so far as traditional barriers to trade no longer significantly limit foreign competition in national markets. Falls in tariffs and transport costs since the Second World War have encouraged the emergence of global markets for a much wider range of goods (and some services) than during the classical Gold Standard era.

It is not simply that a greater proportion of domestic output is traded than ever before, but it is also the case that a rising proportion of private domestic output is potentially tradable and therefore subject to international competition. Agricultural goods, though tradable, are usually protected in OECD countries, but they form a dwindling sector in these economies. Manufactured goods are generally tradable, even if the market for them varies with transport costs and the differences in national preferences. While personal services generally remain non-tradable, given limited protection and dwindling communications costs a growing proportion of business services have become tradable. As large and small companies from different countries increasingly penetrate each others' domestic markets and the intensity of trade flows increases, there is evidence of growing global competition and the evolution of a system of global market relations.

Trade too is becoming more deeply enmeshed with domestic economic activity. Not only are a greater number of goods and services becoming tradable but also the interconnections between tradable and non-tradable production are becoming deeper and denser: non-tradable production often requires tradable inputs and non-tradables output is often sold to the tradables sector. This interlocking relationship between the tradable and non-tradable sectors further deepens the reach of global market forces within national economies.

3.4.4 Shifting patterns of trade stratification

Although the vast majority of countries are incorporated into the contemporary global trading system, patterns of differential enmeshment and unevenness between regions illustrate the stratification of global trade. Developed states have dominated postwar trade. In 1950 they accounted for 64 per cent of world exports, in 1970 for 75 per cent and in 1996 70 per cent. From the 1950s until the 1980s any decline or fluctuation in their share of world trade (around 70 per cent) was closely mirrored by changes in the share attributed to oil-exporting developing countries. The share of other developing countries in world trade actually declined from the 1950s to the 1970s, under the influence of protectionist policies and slow growth in demand for their exports. Although some developing countries increased their shares of world trade in the 1960s and 1970s, it is only since the mid-1980s that oil-importing developing countries as a whole have expanded their share of world trade relative to both oil exporters and the developed economies. Moreover, much of this growth in trade shares is attributable to the rise of the East Asian tiger economies.

Although these figures refer to merchandise trade, the patterns are similar for services trade. While developing countries are presumed to have a comparative advantage in labour-intensive services, given their low wage levels, OECD countries' share of world services exports is similar to merchandise trade. In 1997 they accounted for 70.1 per cent of services exports and 66.8 per cent of world services imports; these shares were similar to a decade earlier, indicating that the largest part of services trade,

Table 3.6 Direction of world exports, 1965–1995 (percentage of world total)

	Between developed economies	Developed–developing	Between developing economies
1965	59.0	32.5	3.8
1970	62.1	30.6	3.3
1975	46.6	38.4	7.2
1980	44.8	39.0	9.0
1985	50.8	35.3	9.0
1990	55.3	33.4	9.6
1995	47.0	37.7	14.1

Totals do not sum to 100 due to trade with Comecon countries, countries not otherwise classified and errors.
Source: Calculated from IMF, *Direction of Trade Statistics Yearbook*, various years

like merchandise trade, is between industrialized countries (calculated from WTO, 1995; Daniels, 1993, p. 82).

As table 3.6 shows, for much of the postwar period, world trade has been concentrated among the developed economies. Only in the 1990s has non-oil trade between developed and developing countries risen as a proportion of total trade; there has also been some increase in trade between developing countries, in part reflecting new trade agreements between them. These shifts partly reflect the changing composition of world trade. Whereas primary goods made up the majority of trade before the Second World War, postwar trade has been dominated by manufactures along with increasing levels of services trade since the 1980s. But, as noted, developing states are no longer simply exporters of primary products but are engaged increasingly in trade in manufactures and services. A new international division of labour is evolving which has important consequences for the stratification of world trade.

Apart from trade in fuels, the trade in primary commodities has dwindled to relatively low levels. The share of manufactures in total world trade has risen continuously since the war. Since the mid-1960s this trade has accounted for the majority of world trade flows and today accounts for around three-quarters of all trade.[5] Until recently manufactures trade was dominated by the OECD countries, but there have been increases in the share of non-oil developing countries in world trade, largely due to their export of manufactures. By comparison, those developing countries which have continued to specialize in primary commodities have faced markets that have often grown slowly and at times declined. The growth of the share of developing countries in world manufactures exports (excluding China) is detailed in table 3.7. Without China, their share of exports of world manufactures is around 20 per cent, having risen from 10 per cent in 1980 and around half that a decade earlier (WTO, 1996). This growth is overwhelmingly due to the East Asian countries. Latin America's share of world exports has stagnated during the 1990s, while the shares of Africa and the Middle East have fallen. Similar trends can be seen with services exports of developing countries. By comparison with exporters of manufactures, only a handful of primary exporting countries have achieved rapid export growth and expanded their share of world markets.

[5] UNCTAD, *Handbook of International Trade and Development Statistics*, various issues.

Table 3.7 Developing countries' share of world manufactures exports, 1963–1995

1963	6
1973	7
1980	10
1985	13
1990	15.5
1995	20

Source: GATT/WTO, *International Trade Yearbook*, various years

East Asian manufactures exporters have achieved rapid economic growth so that most are now among the richest industrializing economies. The pattern of export for these countries is significantly different from other developing countries (Noland, 1997). They have relatively high levels of investment, both domestic and foreign. Although growth in these countries may not have been export-led as such, exporting to world markets is central to maintaining the profitability of investment and thus sustaining growth rates, especially following the 1997–8 crisis.

Trade has played a key role in the performance of individual developing countries, leading to differential performance among them so that in economic terms they can no longer be seen as a homogeneous bloc facing common external conditions. A group of NIEs, particularly in East Asia, grew rapidly throughout the 1980s and mid-1990s mainly by exporting manufactures to OECD economies. As the most successful NIEs have moved out of low wage production, other poorer economies have expanded exports of these products. Some of the latter have since prospered in the world economy. For others industrial growth slowed with exposure to global competition. Those low income countries, particularly in Africa, that failed to develop manufactured exports have remained exporters of primary commodities. Although trade conditions for these products have varied through the postwar era, these exporters have tended to face sluggish markets. In the early 1980s demand for most primary commodities fell sharply, and with it prices. These falls had a huge negative impact on primary exporters and in many cases growth rates and investment levels have still not recovered.

Trade competition in the world economy has led to diverging income levels, with the most successful NIEs achieving per capita income levels equivalent to some smaller developed economies, while many of the poorest states confront declining terms of trade. In this respect the new international division of labour embodies a polarization of economic fortunes in the global economy and new patterns of stratification.

As noted, the developed states still dominate world trade. But even here significant shifts are detectable. Rather than trading different goods between countries with very different industrial structures, increasingly developed countries have been trading similar goods. This intra-industry trade brings domestic producers into direct competition with foreign producers of the same products. This reinforces the dynamic of global competition and contributes to the evolution of global markets. Intra-industry trade on almost any measure forms the majority of developed countries' trade in manufactures and has been the most dynamic element for much of the postwar period (see table 3.8). However, it typically forms only a small fraction of developing countries' trade,

Table 3.8　Intra-industry trade indices for OECD states, 1964–1990

	1964	1970	1980	1990
Canada	37	52.1	51.5	60.0
USA	48	44.4	46.5	71.8
Japan	23	21.4	17.1	32.4
Germany	44	55.8	56.6	72.2
France	64	67.3	70.1	77.2
Italy	49	48.7	54.8	57.4
UK	46	53.2	74.4	84.6
Sweden	–	52.3	58.2	64.2

Source: OECD, 1987, p. 273; 1996a, p. 30

Table 3.9　Import content of finished manufactures (percentages), 1899–1985

	1899	1913	1950	1959	1963	1971	1985
UK	16	17	4	6	7	12	29
France	12	13	7	6	12	17	27
Germany	16	10	4	7	10	16	26
Italy	11	14	8	8	13	12	20
USA	3	3	2	3	3	9	24
Japan	30	34	3	4	6	4	6
Sweden	8	14	12	17	17	37	46
Canada	20	23	16	20	18	37	45

Source: OECD, 1987, p. 271

although for some NIEs it is now around a third of their total manufactures trade (Stone and Lee, 1995).

Intra-industry trade is important to understanding the new international division of labour. It also helps to explain the relative growth of contemporary trade and the relative rise in trade between developed states (Helpman and Krugman, 1985, ch. 8). Trade within a single industry implies product differentiation and economies of scale in production since firms reach a larger market enabling them to expand and reduce their unit costs. Moreover, as incomes rise, demand for differentiated goods tends to increase more than proportionately and part of this demand will be satisfied by importing such goods (Hunter and Markusen, 1988).

Trade has risen not just for finished goods, but also for semifinished manufactures and components. Falling trade costs have meant that production processes, once concentrated in one country, can be parcelled out and distributed around the globe, what Krugman dubs 'slicing up the value chain' (1995) or alternatively 'global commodity chains' (Gereffi and Korzeniewicz, 1994). The increased ability to slice up the value chain in this fashion leads to increases in trade relative to domestic production. Technological change, the global organization of production and the low costs of trade have made possible specialization in each segment of the production process (see chapter 5 below). This, as table 3.9 shows for the G7 countries and Sweden, has sharply raised the proportion of imported inputs included in the manufacturing process such that these national economies have become progressively more dependent on trade for domestic production.[6] The recent transformation of the US from virtual self-sufficiency to significant levels of import dependence comparable to other industrial countries is particularly striking.

Production processes now entail intensive and extensive trading relations (see chapter 5). Intrafirm trade now accounts for between a quarter and a third of total trade (UNCTAD, 1995). Slicing up the value chain has increased trade too between industrialized and developing countries, reinforcing the shift towards a new international division of labour (Castells, 1996; Hoogvelt, 1997, ch. 3). Whereas, in the past, advanced industrial processes tended to be concentrated in developed economies, companies now locate segments of the production process in lower wage countries or subcontract to local companies in Asia or Latin America, which leads to higher levels of trade between developed and developing countries. Many domestic production processes, wherever they are located, have thereby become increasingly enmeshed in global production chains.

Trade has expanded relative to output for most of the postwar period not just because of decreasing tariff barriers and transport costs (Rose, 1991), but also because of the changing structure of global production. The expansion of manufacturing in industrialized countries has been based on the growing enmeshment of national economies largely through intra-industry trade such that global markets have evolved both for many manufactured products and their inputs. Growing trade between developed and developing countries in the 1980s also reflects a shift in the nature of production. A new international division of labour with new patterns of global stratification is evolving. These developments are inseparable, however, from greater trade liberalization, a product, in part, of the growing institutionalization of the global trading system.

3.4.5   The infrastructure and institutionalization of global trade

Improved transport and communications networks have provided the *infrastructure* for a global trading system while the *institutionalization* of trade liberalization has contributed to the growing intensity of trade activity.

The nature of the GATT trading regime was crucial to postwar trade expansion even though its institutional failings were legion – it was not a formal international organization, nor was it powerful enough to act as one (Jackson, 1989). Although it had formal powers, in practice disputes were settled by negotiation and it proved largely powerless to resist the non-tariff barriers instituted by OECD countries particularly against agricultural products and textiles. Equally, many developing countries made broad interpretations of the provisions for exceptional protection in the GATT's Articles of Agreement. In this context what is remarkable is the success of the GATT system in

---

[6] This also raises the difficulty seen with trade–GDP figures above, that they do not measure the value added of traded goods. Slicing up the value chain increases the number of times a good is traded during the production process. Each time the good is traded, the measurement of trade rises by its gross value, rather than by the proportion of value added in the good that is traded.

developing and maintaining an open trading system (at least for manufactures) through the negotiation of the seven rounds of trade barrier reductions. It is probably reasonable to conclude that its structures played an important role in the postwar trading order but that the wider political commitment to trade liberalization was vital.

With the reduction of tariffs to minimal levels and the changing nature of trade, the skeleton framework of the GATT was insufficient, hence the creation of the World Trade Organization (Hoekman and Kostecki, 1995). As formal barriers to trade have been eliminated, interest has shifted towards differences in the domestic regulations and laws governing competition in different countries. Since domestic regulations can be seen to give competitive advantage to firms from one country over another they can be construed as potential barriers to trade. Whereas earlier phases of trade liberalization merely created moves to eliminate external trade barriers, the intensification of trade combined with the internationalization of production have led to pressures for a much deeper harmonization of domestic laws and regulatory structures governing business. Evolving global markets imply pressure for common rules to govern them. In the neoliberal view such markets are created simply through deregulation. In practice the complexity of modern trade requires a detailed set of common laws and regulations for global market relations to function. This is well illustrated by the extensive legal frameworks drawn up for regional markets, such as in the negotiation of the Single European Market or NAFTA. As the WTO and OECD states seek greater trade liberalization, the focus of their activity has shifted towards the harmonization of domestic competition and business rules in so far as these are perceived as the major remaining barriers to global free trade (Trebilcock, 1996; Jonquières, 1998).

3.5 Historical Forms of Trade Globalization: the Transformation of Global Trade

The historical evidence at both the world and country levels shows a trend towards higher levels of trade today than ever before, including during the classical Gold Standard period. The postwar growth of trade, at rates above those previously recorded, has been related to a liberalization of international trade relations that is unprecedented in the modern epoch. Today the world trading system is defined both by an intensive network of trading relations embracing virtually all economies and by evolving global markets for many goods and some services. This shift towards global markets has been facilitated by the existence of worldwide transport and communications infrastructures, the promotion of global trade liberalization through the institutionalization of a world trade system, and the internationalization of production (see chapter 5 below). National markets are increasingly enmeshed with one another as intra-industry trade has expanded and global competition transcends national borders, impacting directly on local economies. In these respects individual firms are confronted by a potential global marketplace while they simultaneously face direct competition from foreign firms in their own domestic markets.

In contrast, during the classical Gold Standard era, markets for manufactured goods tended to operate on a more spatially delimited scale (see grid 3.1). The stratification of the global trading system also reflects these developments as a new international division of labour emerges associated with the evolution of global markets. To talk of

North and South is to misrepresent contemporary patterns of stratification in respect of trade. For while a hierarchy of trading power remains, the North–South geographical divide has given way to a more complex structure of trade relations. Despite the historical concentration of trade among OECD states, global trade patterns have shifted during the contemporary era such that North and South, in this context, are becoming increasingly empty categories (cf. Castells, 1996; Hoogvelt, 1997). The composition of global trade is shifting too as trade in services becomes more significant (Strange, 1996; WTO, 1997). In all these respects the world trading system is undergoing a significant transformation.

3.6 National Enmeshment in the Global Trading System

The six SIACS in this study illustrate the above trends towards the greater extensity, intensity and impact of trade activity. The trend towards more open markets in the postwar period is evident in table 3.10. Tariffs among these countries have been progressively reduced to negligible levels and, except for the special case of Britain, are clearly lower than during the classical Gold Standard era.

As with the general picture noted earlier, table 3.11 shows that the export–GDP levels for the six countries are clearly higher in constant price terms than during the classical Gold Standard and have been so for over two decades, apart from the exceptional case of Britain. Even Britain in the 1980s surpassed the ratios it had achieved as a major trading power. Current price data enable us to trace the evolution of trade intensity for these countries in more detail, and these figures include exports of services, unlike the global and constant price data. For all these countries trade grew in absolute terms throughout the postwar period, except during the early 1980s; it is the growth of trade relative to GDP, and hence their openness to trade, that is of concern here.

By 1950 French exports had recovered to around 15 per cent of GDP (at current prices) while trade overall (figure 3.4) was about twice that, with the export–private GDP ratio comparable to levels reached during the classical Gold Standard period. Levels declined as economic difficulties led to the reintroduction of some protectionist measures, before stabilizing at around 12 per cent (exports to GDP) and twice that for trade to GDP. Both rates doubled in the early 1970s to reach levels relative to private output that were clearly higher than those of the classical Gold Standard era (figure 3.5). The importance of trade to French domestic economic policy is evident throughout the 1980s and 1990s when the policy of competitive disinflation aimed to squeeze inflation by maintaining a high value of the franc, forcing French companies to compete internationally. The result has been rising exports such that the intensity of trade (whether measured by trade to private GDP or exports to GDP) rose still further.

Postwar German data refers to the Federal Republic of Germany until unification, and is thus not strictly comparable to prewar German data. After initial postwar disruption trade recovered quickly so that by the late 1950s exports and trade as a percentage of GDP (figure 3.4) were comparable to levels reached before the First World War. In the postwar period, on average, trade grew faster than national income such that by the 1990s exports were almost 40 per cent of private GDP (for trade see figure 3.5). Germany succeeded in developing a range of competitive industries so that its exporters have continued to increase market shares. Moreover domestic macroeconomic

Grid 3.1 Historical forms of trade globalization

	Pre-Industrial Revolution	Classical Gold Standard	Interwar years	Bretton Woods period	Contemporary period
Extensity	Medium: long-standing links between Asia, Europe and Africa extended to Americas and then Australasia	High: most territories incorporated into international trade by early twentieth century	High number of countries participating in trade, but breakdown of earlier linkages into closed trading blocs	Communist countries largely excluded from world trade, universal participation among the rest	Almost universal participation and high level of linkages between countries; WTO membership 132 states in 1997
Intensity	Low for economies generally, but important for certain industries	Medium: very high for some countries but low for many	Initially lower than before World War I and falling sharply in the 1930s to low levels	Initially low, rising to levels comparable to the classical Gold Standard	High: levels relative to output unprecedented; more private output tradable than ever before
Velocity	Low	Medium–high	Low	Low	High: rapid technological change and global competition
Impact propensity	Low for most economies; important for a few industries and wider social change	High: central to the development of primary exporters and increasingly important in determining incomes in industrial states	High initial impact of trade downturn, becoming low	Increasing impact as trade grows; important for industrial growth	High: trade key part of economies and increasingly important in determining income and industrial structures
Infrastructure	Crude transport systems improving over the period with better ships and	Industrialized transport with the application of steam power; transport	Continued transport improvements, masked by other developments	Falling air and sea freight costs	Consolidation of earlier falls in costs

Dramatic advances in communications |

	navigation techniques	costs falling significantly; new communications technology			technology encourages trade in services
Institutionalization	Trading companies and merchant organizations Protection initially low, but rising with formation of nation-states Minimal international regulation	Increasing bilateral agreements on international market standards Variable levels of protection; sometimes high, but gradual acceptance of most-favoured-nation principle	Breakdown of international arrangements Rising protectionism in the 1930s and descent of trade into regionalism	Trade formalized under the GATT Multilateral management of trade Beginnings of liberalization	The World Trade Organization increasingly acting as global institution to ensure common rules worldwide and intensification of trade liberalization
Stratification Hierarchy	Initially low, but trade increasingly organized through empires from seventeenth century	Much trade organized through empire Trade dominated by key exporters	Major states able to organize regional arrangements as world trade collapses	Trade increasingly conducted between industrialized countries; US dominant trading country	Trade still predominately between OECD countries, but declining concentration of trade Increasing role of other countries, initially oil exporters and subsequently NIEs
Unevenness	Highly uneven: a few nodes of trade, other areas largely untouched by it	Trade important for leading economies and primary exporters, but other areas marginalized	Falling trade hits primary exporters particularly hard; some countries able to generate recovery domestically	Slow growing markets for some countries, but general world expansion partially compensates	Increased differentiation by trade; key element of growth for some economies, marginalization for some others

Table 3.10 Tariff rates for selected countries, 1965–1985 (percentages)

	1965	1970	1975	1980	1985
France	6.1	2.6	1.4	1.1	0.9
Germany	4.6	3.0	2.4	1.8	1.3
Japan	7.5	7.0	3.0	2.5	2.4
Sweden	6.3	4.0	2.4	1.7	2.5
UK	6.0	2.8	1.8	2.2	1.7
USA	6.7	6.1	4.4	3.1	3.5

Source: EPAC, 1996, p. 10

Table 3.11 Exports as a percentage of GDP (constant prices) for selected countries, 1913–1997

	1913	1950	1973	1987	1997
France	6.0	5.6	11.2	14.3	21.1
Germany	12.2	4.4	17.2	23.7	23.7[a]
Japan	2.1	2.0	6.8	10.6	11.0
Sweden	12.0	12.2	23.1	27.0	28.0
UK	14.7	9.5	11.5	15.3	21.0
USA	4.1	3.3	5.8	6.3	11.4

[a] 1995.
Sources: For 1913–87, Maddison, 1991, p. 327; for 1997, estimated from IMF, *International Financial Statistics Yearbook*, 1998

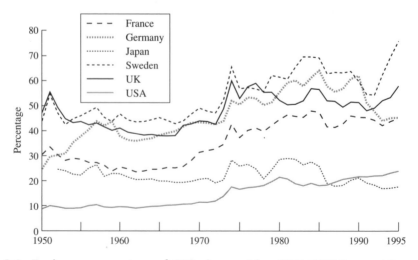

Figure 3.4 Trade as a percentage of GDP, six countries, 1950–1995 (*Source*: IMF, *International Financial Statistics*, various years)

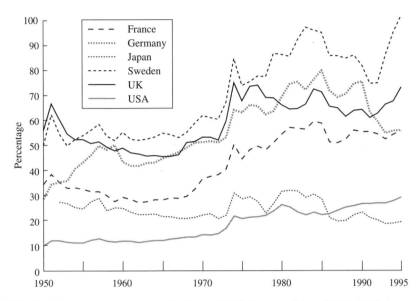

Figure 3.5 Trade as a percentage of private GDP, six countries, 1950–1995 (*Source:* IMF, *International Financial Statistics,* various years)

conditions have often been tight as part of a strong anti-inflation policy, so that external markets, particularly in the EU, have been an important source of demand for exports. As tight domestic conditions also limit the demand for imports, the result has been significant periods of trade surplus despite a strong currency.

Evidence for the primarily domestic roots of Japan's initial postwar growth is shown in figure 3.4; a conclusion in line with other studies (cf. Boltho, 1996b). Although trade–GDP levels were around 25 per cent in the early 1950s, they fell back to around 20 per cent soon after. They remained at these levels until the early 1970s. Although trade–GDP levels in the 1970s rose towards 30 per cent this has since fallen to around 20 per cent. Exports as a share of GDP stand at just over half this, reflecting Japan's persistent trade surplus and very low import ratio compared with other countries. Unlike other industrialized countries, Japan did not regain the trade–GDP levels achieved during the classical Gold Standard era in current price terms (although it did in constant price terms) or the even higher levels it achieved in the interwar period. Japan's postwar economic strategy entailed the construction of close relations between major corporations and their component suppliers. As a result demand for imports of consumer goods and intermediates was low, being met domestically. Japan's persistent trade surplus thus derives primarily from its very low import levels, since export levels are low relative to GDP by OECD standards. Partly as a result of government targeting, Japan's trade advantage evolved from labour-intensive manufactures towards heavy and technologically advanced goods. It has not achieved a general competitive advantage in all sectors, but has developed a strong advantage in certain electronics goods, semiconductors and cars, accounting for most of its trade surplus.

In the postwar period Sweden rapidly returned to trade levels relative to GDP achieved during the classical Gold Standard (see figure 3.4). As with other OECD states trade levels rose sharply in the 1970s, dipped in the 1980s and rose again in the

1990s, exports having recovered since the 1992 krona devaluation. As a small country Sweden's postwar economic policy relied on a strong export sector remaining competitive in several niche markets to generate prosperity for the economy as a whole.

By comparison, the United Kingdom, in the aftermath of the war, had a strong international trading position reflecting its past strengths, captive imperial markets and the devastation of continental European economies. Nevertheless, as figure 3.4 shows, even in the early 1950s trade–GDP levels were below those achieved during the classical Gold Standard era and declined during the late 1950s and early 1960s as the UK's international trading position was eroded. Imports showed a marked tendency to run ahead of exports throughout the postwar period. Export and trade intensity started to rise in the late 1960s following the 1967 sterling devaluation and subsequent EEC entry. Trade levels rose sharply in the early 1970s, aided by the floating of sterling. By the mid-1970s ratios of exports and trade to private GDP had reached classical Gold Standard levels (see figure 3.5). Over the past two decades exports as a percentage of private GDP have been around 33 per cent, again comparable to the levels achieved during the classical Gold Standard period.

The postwar trends for the USA appear paradoxical: during the 1950s and 1960s when the US had an indisputable technological lead over the rest of the world, trade levels were low; yet they rose in the 1970s when the US was losing this lead. This paradox is easily explained: in the immediate postwar period the US had little need to import beyond specific raw materials. Limited export prospects to a Europe with negligible foreign exchange led US companies to invest directly in production in these countries (see chapter 5 below). As the USA lost its technological lead in some sectors in the 1970s and 1980s it lost its comparative advantage in a range of products and so import penetration increased. At the same time it retained and increased its comparative advantage in other industries (such as computer software), reflected in rising exports. Overall levels of trade relative to GDP (and private GDP) have risen since the 1980s to exceed levels attained during the classical Gold Standard era (see figures 3.4 and 3.5).

3.7   The Impact of Global Trade Relations

The transformation of the global trading order has significant impacts on the management of national economies but most especially the capacity of governments to ensure national prosperity. Trade has distinct decisional, institutional, distributional and structural consequences for the developed OECD economies.

3.7.1   Decisional impacts: macroeconomic management

As trade has encouraged the development of global markets and economies have become more open, the impact of international conditions on national economies has intensified. Macroeconomic fluctuations in one state tend to spill over to other countries and higher export levels mean that external conditions have a greater impact on national output. The transmission of economic fluctuations reflects more than just the increasing intensity of trade, but also the way in which trade has become increasingly enmeshed with domestic economic activity. Of course, the impact of macroeconomic fluctuations depends not only on trade but also other economic linkages, notably financial globalization, and the success of national macroeconomic policy in offsetting such fluctuations. Nevertheless, for the major economies macroeconomic fluctuations are now more strongly correlated than in previous epochs, including the classical Gold Standard era; this despite the fact that in principle floating exchange rates can give greater national autonomy in macroeconomic policy (Eichengreen, 1994a). Adapting to such fluctuations is a central task of macroeconomic management.

While the increased intensity of trading relations makes national economies more sensitive to international fluctuations in the demand for and prices of goods, whether they become more vulnerable depends on the adaptability of the economy to external shocks, including the ability to use offsetting macroeconomic policies. As noted in the introduction, there is a distinction to be made between sensitivity and vulnerability to external developments, in terms of the costs and time-scales associated with adjustment to external shocks. Any definitive assessment of vulnerability would require direct modelling of each economy. In this context it is worth remembering that rises in the prices of imports in the 1970s, especially of oil, had a profound impact on macroeconomic policy.

3.7.2   Institutional impacts: trade politics and the welfare state

For its supporters, free trade is a fragile creation, its general benefits poorly understood by policy-makers and the populace at large, its existence under constant threat from protectionist groups. Given its significant domestic impacts, its persistence in the postwar period therefore requires some explanation. Part of the explanation is the desire of politicians to avoid the protectionism of the 1930s. But, crucially, the transformation of trade in the postwar period has also transformed the domestic politics of trade.

The decline of polarized pro- and anti-free trade politics is associated with the transformation of trade towards intra-industry trade where the distribution of gains and losses has become less politically tangible. This has underwritten a much wider constituency for free trade. Protectionist demands have become fragmented and focused on particular industries rather than driven by coherent class or sectoral interests such as labour, agriculture or heavy industry. Moreover, demand for imported products, dependence on open export markets and the internationalization of production have all provided important counterweights to protectionist pressure (Milner, 1989). These cross-cutting interests and constituencies make it difficult for old-style protectionism to achieve widespread public support despite its populist attractions. Protectionism is also more difficult to pursue in the context of multilateral constraints on trade policy and the global shift towards increased liberalization.

Moreover, since trade in principle produces a net welfare gain for a country, the gainers could compensate the losers and still be better off. In this light it is not surprising that more open economies generally have more extensive welfare states (Rodrik, 1997). Nevertheless, the growth of trade and changes in the structure of trade have placed increasing strains on the welfare role of SIACS. Although there is no systematic evidence that welfare provision harms trade performance (cf. Pfaller et al., 1991),

employers, in the tradable industries particularly, resist increases in their social security contributions, pressing for reductions on grounds of global competitiveness. But
erosion of the employment prospects for low-skilled workers as a result of trade
(discussed below) places a significantly higher burden on the welfare system. While it is
rarely strictly true that these welfare provisions cannot be afforded, the costs of social
protection have risen while political support for them has been undermined by changing patterns of trade. Thus global trade has had contradictory impacts in so far as it
has increased the demands on the welfare state while undermining the political basis
for funding it. As Kapstein asserts, 'Just when working people most need the nation-
state as a buffer from the world economy, it is abandoning them' (1996, p. 16).

3.7.3   Distributional impacts: labour

As trade has encouraged the evolution of global markets, demand for labour is coming to be significantly influenced by global competitive forces. Wages in the tradables
sector tend to play an important benchmark role for the rest of the economy. International competition through trade, especially from developing countries, is often
assumed to reduce wages and social and environmental standards to the lowest common
denominator (see, for instance, Hines and Lang, 1993). A little less dramatically, standard trade theory predicts that wages will converge between countries through trade,
rising in labour-abundant countries, where they are initially low, and falling in labour-
scarce countries, where they are initially high.

Trade is driven by technological differences, scale economies and differences in the
relative supplies of factors of production. During the classical Gold Standard period
there was a marked international convergence in wages. Such convergence arose from
increasing specialization as countries exchanged dissimilar goods produced with broadly
similar technology. The nature of postwar trade has modified these trends. As noted,
much of the postwar trade between developed countries has been in similar products,
while these countries have converged in productivity levels. Thus, although there has
been a marked convergence in postwar wage levels among developed countries, this
has been due to the convergence in productivity levels rather than to trade (Dollar
and Wolff, 1993; Wolff, 1997). Where countries have sustained specific technological
advantages this has enabled them to pay higher wages. Where these are spent on non-
tradables, and taxed to fund public services, they can help to maintain comparable wage
levels in the rest of the economy. Similar effects can arise with intra-industry trade
driven by economies of scale. Under plausible conditions, both capital and labour benefit
from increased intra-industry trade (Helpman and Krugman, 1985, ch. 9).

Although this implies that trade has a benign impact on labour, heightened competition can bring adverse pressure on wages and non-labour costs. The most radical
effects of trade on labour arise when technology has become widely diffused internationally and comparative advantage is largely determined by relative factor supplies.
If specific advantages are eroded and scale effects do not predominate, the basis for
sustaining higher wages falls and wage convergence may be expected. This can apply
to trade between developed countries as well as between developed and developing
countries. Where countries have similar access to technology, inter-industry trade can
be analysed in terms of relative differences in the supplies of skilled labour, as noted

above. The evidence from the postwar period is consistent with this: whereas rising intra-industry trade increased the incomes of labour and capital, inter-industry trade increased the incomes of skilled workers and reduced the incomes of others (Oliveira Martins, 1994). As developing countries have expanded their exports of low skill products and developed countries have become increasingly specialized in high skill goods, this has produced significant international convergence in wages for groups of workers with similar skill levels (Wood, 1994). The decline in low skill industries within developed economies has sharply reduced demand for unskilled workers, leading to falling wages and rising unemployment; in Wood's estimate, demand for unskilled labour has fallen by over 20 per cent compared to the hypothetical situation without such inter-industry trade (Wood, 1994, 1995).

Existing research indicates that the comparative advantage of developed economies is derived from both their relative abundance of skilled labour and their technological advantages – although the general convergence in productivity levels among these economies masks persistent differences between industries (Cörvens and Grip, 1997; Dollar and Wolff, 1993; Gustavsson et al., 1997; Wolff, 1997). Since the 1980s wage inequality has risen within developed countries: wages for highly skilled and educated workers have risen relatively while employment prospects for low-skilled workers in manufacturing particularly have worsened. The causes of this shift are the subject of intense debate most especially in relation to how far this trend is attributable to trade with (lower-wage) developing countries and how far to technological change (Lawrence, 1996; Leamer, 1996). Although some have doubted that the small rise in import penetration of developed economies by developing countries – of the order of 1 or 2 per cent of GDP – can explain these changes in employment and wage levels, Wood disagrees (1994; 1995). Wood's research suggests that these changes are attributable to trade. Other research indicates that trade and technological innovation have contributed roughly equally to these developments (Minford et al., 1997). Either way, contemporary patterns of trade do have important consequences for labour in developed states.

3.7.4   Structural impacts: global competition, deindustrialization and shifting patterns of industrial production

The evolution of global markets has led to specialization among countries so that what is profitable to produce, and what is not, is significantly influenced by global competitive conditions. Crucially the positions of countries are not static: as economies mature and acquire new technology their relative positions change. Since international patterns of comparative advantage are shifting over time, national economies face pressures to reallocate resources continually and not just as a one-off response to rising trade. In this sense trade has significant impacts on the structure of national economies.

With increasing export competition trade has induced structural shifts within developed economies. Throughout much of the postwar golden age many OECD countries lagged behind the USA technologically. They exported, largely to third countries and not the US, those products both where their technological inferiority was least and where this could be offset by lower costs, especially lower wages. From the 1970s Japan and Europe began to catch up with the USA technologically (Dollar and Wolff, 1993, chs 3–6; Hansson and Henrekson, 1994). Although national productivity levels are now broadly comparable among developed countries, this masks significant differences in productivity within particular sectors. Specific technological advantages continue to generate relative advantages in trade. However, technology is diffused internationally, not least through trade. Technical knowledge is therefore not an enduring source of relative advantage – although patterns of specialization arising from technical knowledge may persist where countries retain an advantage in generating it. As technology diffuses and productive conditions converge among the developed countries there is some evidence of convergence in trade specialization between them (Soete and Verspagen, 1994).

As economies develop the capacity to export within global markets, trade increases and competition intensifies. As technology is diffused internationally lower cost producers generate further competitive pressures. The emergence of lower cost producers reduces the ability of any single producer to pass on cost increases. This forces structural changes as some industries contract or are eliminated while others expand; countries cannot be competitive in everything or nothing, but the domestic social and economic adjustment entailed in shifting resources from declining to expanding sectors can be considerable. Precisely because competitive advantage is relative, changes in one country's competitive position impact directly on other countries. These points are well illustrated by the case of the USA in the 1980s as it moved from trivial trade shares to relative trade openness. Although technological catch-up meant that the US lost relative advantage in a range of industries, it still retained a clear advantage in many others. Some domestic industries boomed by exporting, but a range – notably the car industry – were forced into extensive restructuring. The point is that higher trade did not simply entail a general loss in the competitiveness of US industry, but a major structural change in the economy driven by greater vulnerability to global competition.

The most radical structural impact of trade on developed economies comes from low-cost producers acquiring production technology, as is evident in the rise of manufactures exporters in the NIEs. Again the effect of this is not to wipe out all producers in developed countries. Even the most advanced NIEs still lag behind the leading industrial nations technologically, giving them significantly lower productivity levels (Dollar and Wolff, 1993, ch. 8). As NIEs have acquired production technology the basis of competition in trade has shifted (as noted) from technological superiority to relative supplies of skilled and unskilled labour (Wood, 1994). Most OECD countries have become more specialized in products requiring intensive inputs of high-skilled labour, while the NIEs have expanded exports of products requiring relatively low-skilled labour. This has largely wiped out sections of industries in developed countries in certain textiles, leather goods, toys and sports goods. Note that this does not suggest a general loss of competitiveness among the developed economies; rather as trade with NIEs has increased they have become more specialized, expanding the output of some goods while contracting that of others.

This discussion introduces some caution into debates about national competitiveness and deindustrialization in developed economies. The global reorganization of industry through trade has led to profound structural changes within, and between, developed economies through specialization, rather than a general loss of national competitiveness. Even where technology has been diffused to developing countries the competitive advantage of developed economies has not been eliminated since the basis of competition has shifted towards the relative abundance (as noted) of skilled labour. In practice the developed countries have maintained much of their competitive and technological advantage.

Deindustrialization in advanced economies, that is, the decline of manufacturing industry as a share of total employment and output (at least when measured in current prices), has often been attributed to trade competition, particularly in the US and Britain. Some relative decline is an inevitable product of shifting trade patterns and the associated new international division of labour. Manufacturing's share of employment tends to decline at higher levels of development: as productivity rises in manufacturing, progressively fewer and fewer workers are needed to produce a given level of output. Some advanced economies have increased their shares of world manufactures exports at the expense of others, but even for poorly performing industrial economies like Britain this only accounts for a fraction of the decline of domestic manufacturing as a proportion of national output and employment (Rowthorn and Wells, 1987). More precisely, even if manufacturing exports had risen rapidly, the relative shift to services would have been broadly the same. Trade with NIEs, and other developing countries, has induced a domestic reorganization of production rather than a general decline in manufactured production (deindustrialization) within developed economies. Indeed developed countries have a trade surplus with developing countries as the latter's industrialization increases demand for machinery and other advanced goods. The global diffusion of technology and the emergence of new producers have speeded up the dynamics of global competition such that continuous structural adaptation has become a permanent feature of the operation of advanced economies.

3.8 Conclusion: State Autonomy and Sovereignty

Trade has been integral to postwar growth among OECD countries and trade levels today are historically unprecedented. An extensive and intensive network of trading relations operates creating the conditions for functioning global markets, the domestic impacts of which extend well beyond the traded sector into the economy as a whole. While institutionalized regional trading arrangements have evolved, they have tended to reinforce the trend towards freer trade – as the evolution of the WTO indicates.

From its inception the nation-state has used trade protection to raise revenues, manage balance of payments difficulties and promote domestic industry. By the late twentieth century institutional constraints, as well as economic costs, have severely limited the scope for national protectionism. Today, not only tariffs and quota restrictions, but also policies supporting domestic industry and even domestic laws with respect to business competition and safety standards are subject to growing international scrutiny and regulation. In addition, the historical experience of achieving economic development through protection, though mixed, is now a much diminished policy option, as the East Asian crisis of 1997 demonstrated. Autarky, or 'delinking', is also off the political agenda. Recent enthusiasm for human capital policies – education and training – reflects not only academic and political interest in the potential of these measures for ameliorating some of the adverse consequences of global free trade but also the apparent foreclosing of other policy options. In these respects, the contemporary globalization of trade has transformed state autonomy and induced shifts in state policy. Furthermore, the global regulation of trade, by bodies such as the WTO, implies a significant renegotiation of the Westphalian notion of state sovereignty. As the economic turmoil of the late 1990s demonstrated, for the foreseeable future the prosperity of SIACS, and communities within them, is likely to remain profoundly influenced by the dynamics of global trade. But trade globalization is only one strand in the overall story of the emergence of today's global economy: finance and production are the others and these are the subjects of subsequent chapters.

4

Shifting Patterns of Global Finance

There are few more pervasive images of globalization than men and women at their trading desks in the City of London or Wall Street frantically buying and selling currencies and assets from around the globe at the push of a button. Although heavily concentrated in the three main centres of London, Tokyo and New York, world foreign exchange trading averages a staggering $1,490 billion every working day. In addition billions of dollars of financial assets are traded daily across the globe. Besides current assets, the emergence of futures markets means that it is possible to buy and sell assets and currencies forward, that is into the future. The development of new financial instruments, the deregulation of national financial markets and the growth of international banks and other financial institutions have created a functioning global financial system. Today worldwide trading of currencies and government bonds means that exchange rates and interest rates, two critical variables in the formulation of national macroeconomic policy, are determined in the context of global financial markets.

4.1 Indicators of Financial Globalization and Financial Enmeshment

Cross-border financial flows have occurred for centuries and this chapter uses several indicators of international financial activity to map them over time and space. There are many ways of measuring the extensity and intensity of international finance and it is useful here to distinguish between financial openness, financial enmeshment and financial integration. The openness of national financial markets refers to the level of legal restrictions on international financial transactions. The level of enmeshment refers to the extent of national financial engagement in global financial activity: there is no single measure of this, but it is variously indicated by the turnover of overseas assets on national markets, the involvement of both foreign financial institutions in domestic financial markets and domestic financial institutions in overseas financial markets, and national shares of various global financial flows. Financial integration is used here only in the precise economic sense of the extent to which the prices of, and the returns to, assets are equalized between different national financial markets. In a completely integrated market the returns on identical financial assets are equalized, but of course many internationally traded assets are not identical. Measures of interest rate or asset price equalization fail to capture the complexity of financial globalization as a historical process. Thus a better indicator is the extent to which there is a convergence between returns to, or prices of, bundles of similar financial assets.

These various indicators provide a basis for describing historical forms of financial globalization and assessing precisely what is new about the contemporary era. By examining the geographical reach of world financial markets we can assess the *extensity* of international finance. Exploring the magnitude of global financial flows (both gross and net) delivers an insight into historical patterns of the *intensity* of financial globalization. The changing *velocity* of financial flows, which is related to infrastructural shifts in communication technologies, is significant in determining the impacts of such activity. That financial globalization can have profound *impacts* on the conduct of national economic policy is incontrovertible but the kinds of impacts (decisional, institutional, distributional and structural) may differ between eras, while the impact of global financial flows is mediated significantly by national economic conditions. World-wide financial flows are also predicated on various *infrastructures* and their *institutionalization*, both of which have varied across time and space. Finally, global finance shows clear patterns of *stratification*: as in the domestic economy, for example, different categories of borrowers confront different interest rates and borrowing conditions.

4.1.1   The structure of the argument

Global finance embraces flows of credit (such as loans and bonds), investment (FDI, equities) and money (foreign exchange). This broad conception of finance informs the subsequent story of shifting historical patterns of global financial activity. Relying on the framework elaborated in the introduction, this chapter explores the spatio-temporal and organizational forms of global finance as these have evolved since the early modern period. Accordingly, the analysis seeks to identify the key attributes of financial globalization in the early modern, classical Gold Standard, Bretton Woods and contemporary periods. Building on this discussion the novel attributes of contemporary financial globalization are identified. In addition, the enmeshment within the global financial system of the six SIACS, the focus of this study, is reviewed, as are the consequences of global financial activity for state autonomy and state sovereignty. In telling the story of financial globalization several technical terms are used frequently so these are elaborated in box 4.1.

4.2   Early Patterns of Global Financial Activity

Cross-border trade from the earliest of times has required some form of accepted currency. Initially this was usually precious metals such as gold. Transcontinental movements of gold and silver can be dated back to the twelfth century (Watson, 1967), and the rise of intercontinental trade from that time brought intermittent financial relations between traders. Organized international finance dates primarily from the fourteenth century when Florentine merchant banks, such as the famous Peruzzi Company, developed multinational links by establishing either 'foreign' operations or reciprocal arrangements with foreign banks (Abulafia, 1997; Hunt, 1994). From the sixteenth century Europe imported large quantities of precious metals, much of which were used

---

Box 4.1 Technical terms in financial globalization

International capital flows can be defined as cross-border flows of assets and loans, both long-term and short-term, and differentiated into several types:

- *foreign direct investment* ownership of or investment in overseas enterprises in which the investor plays a direct managerial role;
- *international bank lending* loans to foreign creditors in domestic or foreign currency;
- *international bonds* credit instruments issued by or to overseas creditors/debtors which include a promise to pay a specified amount of money on a fixed date and to pay interest periodically at stated intervals – bonds are therefore marketable securities denominated in standard units;
- *portfolio investment* investment in corporate shares or long-term bonds held simply for their return with the investor playing no managerial role;
- *international equities* shares in companies issued to foreigners;
- *'new' financial instruments* derivatives, options, swaps;
- *development assistance* official government-to-government aid flows;
- *international monetary flows* buying and selling of foreign currencies.

Gross capital flows measure total capital flows out of an economy or alternatively flows inwards.

Net capital flows measure gross outward flows minus gross inward flows – net flows indicate whether an economy is accumulating claims on the rest of the world or vice versa.

---

to finance trade with Asia. As a consequence monetary conditions in Europe and Asia became entwined (Vilar, 1991).

Although cross-border monetary flows have a long history, a European financial order, in the sense of regularized or institutionalized systems for organizing credit between the major economies, dates largely from the sixteenth century (Germain, 1997). During this period Antwerp developed as the primary centre for Europe-wide finance. Its ascendance reflected both its pivotal position in trade (both within Europe and between Europe and Asia) and its liberal financial policies: many foreign financiers operated openly in its markets. The growth of international finance at this time was fuelled by two main developments. First, growing trade networks increased the demand for cross-border financial services simply in order to overcome the costs and the dangers of transporting money. Second, the difficulties facing absolutist states in raising funds, especially for waging costly wars, created considerable pressures and opportunities for organized finance. The Bank of England, for example, was founded in 1694 as a private bank to finance Britain's war with France. In Europe the emergence of modern states was closely associated with the creation of unified currencies under central control (Goodhart, 1985).

As Germain notes, in this early modern period the key centres of financial activity were located generally in areas where commerce, and hence demand for financial services, were concentrated (1997, ch. 2). Accordingly, Europe's main financial centre shifted away from the Italian city-states to Antwerp, mirroring the shift in European commerce. With the rise of the Dutch and British economies in the seventeenth and eighteenth centuries, international financial activity moved to new centres in Amsterdam and London. Although these networks of international finance were initially confined to Europe, they expanded abroad alongside early European empires and their associated trading companies (see chapters 1 above and 5 below).

By the eighteenth century increased demand for international financial services led to the development of sophisticated markets (including, for example, some futures trading) in Amsterdam and London, servicing North European trade as well as providing domestic finance. Communications between these key nodes of financial activity took around a week, but the intensity of transactions was such that they constituted an integrated European financial market (defined in terms of a convergence in the price of and return on financial assets) (Neal, 1990; Zevin, 1992). Rising trade made the Amsterdam markets increasingly liquid: domestic demand for funds failed to keep pace with rising supply as Dutch industry experienced a relative decline. Over the eighteenth century the Amsterdam markets diversified, becoming major lenders to other European states (Riley, 1980).

Although relatively extensive, in respect of their intercontinental embrace, cross-border financial networks in this period were restricted to the reach of imperial systems. The magnitude of such flows was considerable and their impacts significant in so far as war-making and state-building created debts that had to be financed through a combination of domestic taxation and credit from both foreign and domestic sources (Tilly, 1990). Moreover, as noted, there was a convergence in interest rates and asset prices.

4.3 The Classical Gold Standard Period: 1870–1914

Britain's Industrial Revolution and rise to world trade dominance helped London to achieve and consolidate a primary position in international finance. By the late nineteenth century not only did London operate as the leading international financial market, but also British banks expanded and developed their global activities.

During the period from 1870 to the First World War cross-border financial flows became considerably more extensive and intensive. Developments in communications infrastructures meant that domestic financial markets became deeply enmeshed within international financial networks. Governments operated few, if any, restrictions on international financial flows, while the values of major currencies were regulated through the operation of the global Gold Standard system. As Sir Ernest Barker commented in 1915, 'Improved means of communication, and especially the telegraph, have created a single system of credit for all the world' (Barker, 1915). This period, it is often claimed, is the first in which a truly global financial system existed. Indeed, for the sceptics, the classical Gold Standard era prior to the First World War is taken as a benchmark for financial globalization, in so far as they argue that the scale of net flows was greater than at any time since and that adherence to the rules of the Gold Standard meant that countries had to subordinate their domestic economic policy to a rigid set of international rules (Zevin, 1992; Hirst and Thompson, 1996b, ch. 2). But this view is misleading, as the subsequent analysis demonstrates.

Table 4.1 Foreign investment stocks by investing country, 1825–1938, as percentage of world total

	Britain	France	Germany	Netherlands	United States	Total ($m)
1825	55.6	11.1		33.3		900
1840	58.3	25.0		16.7		1,200
1855	63.9	27.8		8.3		3,600
1870	62.0	31.6		6.3		7,900
1885	55.7	23.6	13.6	7.1		14,000
1900	51.1	21.9	20.3	4.6	2.1	23,700
1914	44.0	19.9	12.8	2.6	7.8	45,450
1938	41.7	7.0	1.3	8.7	21.2	54,950

Source: Estimated from Woodruff, 1966, pp. 150–7

4.3.1 International capital: the extensity, intensity and stratification of financial flows

Capital flowed across the globe in this period, while the intensity of foreign investment acquired major economic significance to investing and borrowing countries alike. Although estimates of cross-border capital flows vary, and are subject to wide margins of error, the broad patterns are clear. Table 4.1 shows a significant expansion in the magnitude of capital flows. Britain remained the dominant exporter of capital, although its leading position at the start of this period was eroded gradually. France was a significant exporter of capital, while Germany and the USA only emerged as significant exporters towards the end of this period. The overall share of Dutch foreign investment in the global total dropped rapidly as other investors entered the market.

Whereas foreign investment in the eighteenth and early nineteenth centuries largely went to other European countries, in this period it acquired a distinctive interregional or intercontinental dimension. As table 4.2 shows, although by the First World War 40 per cent of foreign investment was in the Americas there were large investments in Asia, Africa and Australia. These stocks were accumulated from the large-scale flows over this period. As the leading economies matured, their savings levels exceeded domestic demand for investment. Conversely, in many emerging economies demand for investment funds exceeded domestic savings levels: rapid urbanization combined with relatively young populations led to high demands for infrastructural investment. For a given level of risk, these overseas projects offered higher returns than those available domestically. British investment in particular flowed to the primary exporting countries to finance infrastructure projects; railways alone may have accounted for a third of all its foreign investment over this period. A much higher proportion of French and German lending financed foreign government deficits, as Dutch lending had in earlier centuries. Around a third of foreign investment was direct investment by private companies, much of it from the US (see chapter 5).

The increased intensity of these investment flows between the major creditor and debtor nations is evident from table 4.3. Britain invested on average 5 per cent of its

Table 4.2 Stocks of foreign investment by recipient area as percentage of global total, 1914 and 1938

	1914	1938
Americas	43.6	45.4
USA	15.8	12.7
Canada	8.2	12.1
Argentina	6.7	5.8
Brazil	4.9	3.6
Mexico	4.4	3.3
Europe	24.4	18.7
Asia	17.7	20.4
Near and Middle East	6.7	1.5
India and Ceylon	4.4	5.6
China	3.3	4.7
Africa	8.9	7.4
Union of South Africa	3.8	2.6
Oceania	5.3	8.1
Australia	3.8	6.9

Sources: Calculated from Cameron and Bovykin, 1991, p. 13; Woodruff, 1966, ch. 4

Table 4.3 Net foreign investment flows as a percentage of GDP, 1870–1920

	Britain	France	Germany	Japan	Sweden	USA
1870	+5.6		+0.6		−1.6	−2.7
1880	+3.2	−0.4	+1.9		−3.7	+0.1
1890	+5.8	+2.0	+2.0	+0.1	−2.5	−0.1
1900	+1.8	+3.8	+1.3	−4.2[a]	−2.7	+1.4
1910	+7.4	+3.6	+1.3	−2.8	+0.4	0
1920	+2.6			+2.2	+0.5	+2.4

+ = outflow.
− = inflow.
[a] 1899.
Sources: Green and Urquhart, 1976, p. 244, except Japan, calculated from Ohkawa and Shinohara, 1979

GDP abroad annually over this period compared with the other major investors at half or less of that level. Nevertheless, these foreign investments constituted a significant proportion of total national investment. For the emerging economies of Canada, Australia and Argentina foreign borrowing sometimes financed up to half of their total domestic capital investment (Vos, 1994, ch. 4). Such borrowing was central to their development: it financed much of the infrastructure that underlay their growth. In general, net flows of cross-border investment, relative to the incomes of lending and recipient countries, have rarely been matched since, nor over such a sustained period.

Since this borrowing was largely through government bonds, the European markets for international bonds (especially London) acquired a more global reach (Vos, 1994, ch. 4). With the international issuing and trading of government bonds, demand and supply for these financial instruments was determined increasingly in a global market. The global bond market was essentially privately organized, with governments placing few if any restrictions on trading. On the other hand they rarely intervened to support lenders when borrowing countries rescheduled or defaulted on their loans (although the British government did help rescue Barings Bank when it was bankrupted by the Argentine debt crisis of the 1890s).

From 1870 to 1914 London retained its position as the leading financial centre, followed by Paris, such that the value of foreign securities listed on the London and Paris markets typically exceeded the value of domestic securities (Morgenstern, 1959). Berlin and Amsterdam were the next largest centres in Europe, although New York had risen to prominence by the First World War. Just as there was a clear hierarchy among financial centres, the distribution of capital flows was similarly uneven. As the figures in table 4.2 above suggest, although foreign investment had an intercontinental reach it was concentrated in a small number of countries.

If the global financial system was highly stratified it also became increasingly organized throughout this period. There was a significant expansion and institutionalization of international banking activity, most especially in the case of Britain. By 1860 British banks had in excess of a hundred overseas branches, 700 by 1890 and almost 1,400 by 1914 (Jones, 1993). Moreover, Western banks expanded as far abroad as China (Nishimura, 1997). The development of global financial interconnectedness was facilitated further by the construction of intercontinental telegraph cables which linked major financial markets. Such infrastructures also encouraged the institutionalization and formalization of international monetary arrangements as embodied in the classical Gold Standard.

4.3.2   International money: the operation of the classical Gold Standard

In the latter part of the nineteenth century the values of major currencies were fixed to the price of gold, providing the basis for a system of fixed exchange rates: the classical Gold Standard. After the preliminary Paris International Monetary Conference (1867) the Gold Standard was established formally in 1878. Initially, participation was confined to the leading European economies, North America and Australia; it was only in the early twentieth century that membership expanded to include the bulk of the European and Latin American countries, Japan and the leading colonial territories, although some of the weaker economies later left and devalued their currencies. Membership of the Gold Standard system required that countries both convert their currency into gold on demand and did not restrict international gold flows.

The classical Gold Standard (see box 4.2) is often portrayed as a system embodying both globally integrated financial markets, unparalleled before or since, and mechanisms of automatic adjustment which ensured that national economies had to adjust to global financial disciplines. More critical accounts argue that adjustment may not have been automatic; although the openness of national economies meant that financial authorities had to adjust domestic policy, particularly interest rates, to world conditions so as to ensure compatibility with the Gold Standard, they had, in Keynes's phrase, to play by 'the rules of the game'.

Box 4.2   The operation of the Gold Standard in theory

There are several variants of the orthodox account of the automatic adjustment under the Gold Standard, but the principles are much the same. Exporters receive payment in foreign currency. Having no wish to hold foreign currency they convert it into gold and then present the gold to their own national bank for conversion into their domestic currency. Thus a country running a balance of payments deficit would experience a net outflow of gold and one running a balance of payments surplus would experience a net inflow. Since gold provides the money base – all domestic currency can be converted into gold on demand – this would determine each country's money supply. The adjustment process was assumed to follow automatically from this. Decreases in the money supply would lead to falling domestic prices, making exports cheaper and imports dearer, so rectifying the balance of payments deficit. The reverse process would operate with a balance of payments surplus.

In practice adjustment was rarely automatic and nor did governments necessarily play by the 'rules of the game', as the evidence of persistent balance of payments surpluses and deficits suggests (Bloomfield, 1959; Eichengreen, 1996, ch. 2; Ford, 1989; Panic, 1992). In this respect, domestic monetary policy was never solely determined by global financial markets since countries frequently did not adjust their economies in line with the implied rules. As noted, industrialized countries with a trade surplus invested heavily in developing economies, effecting huge transfers of capital which often covered the latter's deficits. Surplus countries in particular found it easy to sustain their position without the domestic economic adjustment implied by the operation of the Gold Standard system. But economies periodically faced pressure to adjust, although instead of adjusting automatically, monetary authorities typically responded by manipulating interest rates. A balance of payments deficit could be covered in the short term by raising domestic interest rates: money would flow into the country to take advantage of higher rates in the confidence that the absolute commitment of the authorities to the Gold Standard would require them to undertake the necessary domestic adjustment, that is, this commitment led to the stabilization of short-term capital flows. Higher interest rates would depress domestic demand and reduce import levels, correcting the deficit. Adjustment thus took place more by changes in output and employment levels than through changing prices.

Furthermore, given Britain's hegemonic position in the world economy and sterling's role as the leading international currency, the Bank of England played a central role in managing the Gold Standard. To this extent, rather than a self-organizing system of global adjustment, the operation of the Gold Standard was orchestrated from London. The Bank of England actively managed major disruptions to the system, often by taking the lead in collective intervention with other major central banks and coordinating financial policies to achieve stability (Eichengreen, 1992, ch. 2).

Domestic adjustment policies were thus engineered, rather than automatic. Further, national money supply, price levels and interest rates did not follow gold movements or adjust to balance of payments conditions in the simple way that orthodox accounts claim. Indeed, the money supply and price levels frequently did not move in line with international gold movements or national balance of payments conditions, since monetary authorities within the leading economies often adjusted the money supply in quite the opposite direction to that predicted by orthodox accounts (Bloomfield, 1959). This confirms that national monetary conditions and policies were determined as much by domestic as world financial markets, such that national monetary authorities retained considerably more autonomy in respect of the conduct of macroeconomic policy than orthodox accounts of the Gold Standard presume.

Nevertheless, differentials between the interest rates of major countries diminished sharply over this period as financial markets became more enmeshed (Morgenstern, 1959; Eichengreen, 1994a). However, interest rates were not equalized. Instead, persistent differences remained between them despite the Gold Standard system and the free flow of capital movements (Morgenstern, 1959). For Britain, France, the USA and Canada domestic priorities were as significant as international capital movements in determining domestic interest rates (Wallace and Choudhry, 1995; Lévy-Leboyer and Bourguignon, 1990). By comparison, German and Swedish monetary conditions and policy more closely resembled orthodox Gold Standard conditions. Beyond Europe, the rudimentary nature of financial systems in developing economies, and their peripheral involvement in the Gold Standard system, meant that international financial conditions tended to have only a limited impact on domestic monetary policy. Far from producing a convergence of national monetary conditions across the globe, as orthodox accounts of the classical Gold Standard era often presume, there was significant divergence. While the operation of the Gold Standard system brought about some convergence in national interest rates among the major economies, this was not at the expense of their national monetary autonomy. In this respect national monetary policy was never simply, or even primarily, determined by global financial markets or conditions.

The operation and success of the classical Gold Standard rested on historically specific conditions (Panic, 1992; Vos, 1994, ch. 4). Given the absence, or limited nature, of democratic institutions, governments could largely ignore the domestic social and economic consequences of monetary adjustments, especially deflationary adjustments. Moreover, the willingness of investors in surplus countries to lend to deficit countries meant that as long as current account deficits were covered by long-term financial flows from surplus countries, there would be limited pressure to adjust. The countercyclical nature of international capital flows tended to prevent major crises erupting: during upswings in economic activity among the leading economies high domestic demand for investment funds reduced foreign investment and raised interest rates, but this was partially compensated by rising trade levels which increased demand for the exports of debtor countries. Downswings among the major economies meant slower growth in demand for borrowing countries' exports, but it also increased the supply of foreign investment to those countries and lowered interest rates. High levels of international migration, too, ameliorated the impact of price and output fluctuations on domestic unemployment. Moreover, many countries pursued protectionist trade policies (see ch. 3 above) and, although they may not have been used directly for the purposes of balance of payments management, they offered one mechanism for easing the domestic costs of adjustment.

4.3.3 Financial globalization during the classical Gold Standard era

International flows of finance and investment during the classical Gold Standard period were certainly *extensive*, covering all continents of the globe. A global capital market existed, organized by multinational banks, enabling capital from the richer economies to flow to those areas where there was considerable demand for investment funds. Although highly uneven, these flows had a huge impact on both investing and recipient countries and represented a key feature of world economic development during this epoch. Only British capital, admittedly the dominant source, can be said to have had a truly global reach. But this, too, remained heavily concentrated within the Empire and the Americas, while capital exports by the other major economies tended to be concentrated in Europe and imperial spheres of influence. Most countries received few foreign funds and effectively were excluded from the global financial market. Despite this the *intensity* of capital flows during this period was extraordinary: net capital flows have so far never again attained the levels of the late nineteenth century, although gross capital flows were below contemporary levels. However, these net flows relate only to a small set of major economies. Nevertheless, by comparison with earlier epochs, gross capital flows were unprecedented and for many economies financed a greater proportion of domestic investment than ever recorded before or since.

While this period witnessed a notable convergence in national interest rates, as a consequence of global financial flows, significant differentials remained. Among the leading economies interest rates were determined as much by domestic as international financial conditions such that financial authorities were able to pursue domestic objectives often irrespective of international conditions. Clearly the magnitude of financial flows brought about a considerable enmeshment of national economies but these flows were heavily concentrated among the industrial nations. Moreover, membership of the Gold Standard system was restricted for much of the period to the most advanced economies. Although without doubt the classical Gold Standard era represents the emergence of a world financial order, it was nevertheless one which remained primarily Eurocentric and which was far from global in its reach.

4.4 The Interwar Years: Global Monetary Disorder

The First World War brought the collapse of the classical Gold Standard system, and the instability of the immediate postwar period, notably the German hyperinflation of the early 1920s, prevented its early reconstruction. It was only in 1925 that Britain joined the US in returning to the Gold Standard. By 1928 the system had been reconstructed with much wider participation than previously – during 1928–31 over forty territories signed up to the Gold Standard. Thereafter, the system rapidly disintegrated as the Great Depression undermined international financial cooperation.

Not surprisingly capital flows were less intensive in the interwar years than during the classical Gold Standard period. They also tended to become more geographically concentrated. Britain continued to be the largest holder of overseas assets and a significant exporter of capital, although, as table 4.3 above shows, as a proportion of national income it was exporting around half that of the earlier period. But, as table 4.3 also reveals, as the US economy boomed its exports of capital increased. As table 4.1 shows, during this period the US became the major source of the growth in foreign investment.

In all major countries the bulk of capital was invested domestically. But even so foreign investment in Canada and the Latin American countries (which together accounted for two-thirds of the US investment stock in 1938) and Europe (which accounted for a further 20 per cent) expanded dramatically. French overseas investment held its global share until the First World War, following which it dropped sharply. In comparison 1918 witnessed the liquidation of German overseas holdings, and the emergence of significant capital exports by Belgium, Canada, Sweden and Switzerland. Japan also exported significant quantities of capital and held over $1 billion of investment in China on the eve of the Second World War. In the 1920s global capital flows and stocks of foreign investment were high. Although, in comparison with the classical Gold Standard era, there was a greater number of states importing and exporting capital, the bulk of capital flows remained increasingly concentrated among a small number of countries.

By the 1930s the economic conditions sustaining significant capital flows radically changed. Just as the success of the classical Gold Standard rested on several necessary conditions, its failure in the interwar period reflected their absence. Although the USA emerged from the war with a combined trade surplus and low domestic interest rates which ensured it became the major international creditor, it refused to take over from Britain the role of global financial hegemon. Domestic priorities rather than international obligations dominated policy. This had catastrophic consequences: the Federal Reserve's decision to put up interest rates in 1928 in an attempt to quell the speculative bull market on Wall Street triggered the Great Crash of 1929. US capital flows were procyclical – having risen in the 1920s, they fell in the 1930s with diminished expectations of foreign profitability. Whereas during the classical Gold Standard capital flows operated countercyclically, in that downturns in the world economy were partially compensated for by higher capital flows, in the 1930s debtor countries confronted domestic deflation and capital flight. Accordingly, both the intensity and extensity of capital flows declined dramatically. Moreover, structural change in the world economy, combined with widespread domestic economic and political crises, made the Gold Standard system entirely unworkable.

4.5   The Bretton Woods Era: the Reinvention of Global Finance

One paradox of the enormous post-1945 growth of global finance is the fact that it was never prefigured in the original 1944 Bretton Woods agreement which inaugurated a new world financial order. Interwar currency instability was blamed on speculators, while John Maynard Keynes, as Britain's chief negotiator at Bretton Woods, consistently and emphatically maintained that national monetary autonomy was essential to the successful management of a macroeconomic policy geared to full employment. Harry Dexter White, the USA's chief negotiator, agreed and successfully resisted Wall Street's orchestrated opposition to capital controls (Helleiner, 1994, ch. 4). The first

Article of Agreement of the International Monetary Fund (IMF), the core of the Bretton Woods system, reflected these concerns with a commitment to 'the promotion and maintenance of high levels of employment and real income, and the development of the productive resources of all members as primary objectives of economic policy'. Unlike the classical Gold Standard, the postwar international financial order – the Bretton Woods System (BWS) – was designed to ensure that domestic economic object-ives were not subordinated to global financial disciplines but, on the contrary, took precedence over them.

The BWS required that every currency had a fixed exchange rate to the dollar, with the dollar fixed in terms of gold at $35 an ounce. Unlike the Gold Standard system, private financial flows were restricted, not least by national capital controls, and largely confined to long-term investment. In practice the Bretton Woods system became a dollar system, since the USA emerged after the Second World War as the leading economy and the only major creditor nation. International transactions became over-whelmingly denominated in dollars, while sterling declined as an international cur-rency. In effect, US authorities indirectly determined the international money supply such that the rest of the world had to adjust to the extent that any such adjustment was necessary. But the system had limited extensity since it excluded all the communist countries, a significant share of the world's states and its population.

It was, however, an institutionalized system in that the IMF policed the rules of the international financial order. The IMF oversaw the operation of the system, mon-itoring countries' economic performance and providing reserve facilities to 'bail out' countries that experienced balance of payments difficulties. To prevent the disastrous competitive devaluations of the interwar period, countries facing a short-term balance of payments deficit could draw automatically on a loan equivalent to their initial mem-bership quota (fixed in relation to their IMF subscription). Beyond this, funds were only available subject to IMF conditions, which specified, in effect, necessary domestic adjustment policies. Since exchange rates were fixed, a country could only alter the value of its currency in relation to the US dollar if its balance of payments was in 'fundamental disequilibrium', a condition that was never fully defined. Devaluation in principle required the consent of the IMF, although this was occasionally flouted and in practice may have been little more than rubber-stamping (Dominguez, 1993). Revaluation was rare, while almost all developing countries devalued during the post-war period, often more than once.

Data on the intensity of international financial flows in the 1950s and 1960s are patchy at best, reflecting its low levels; apart from some FDI, capital remained firmly rooted within national borders. This is not surprising given both the existence of national capital controls and the limited infrastructure for private international capital flows. Studies of the BWS indicate a significant divergence between countries' interest rates, reflecting the impact of national capital controls (Dooley and Isard, 1980; Marston, 1993). Capital controls separated foreign exchange markets from domestic money mar-kets, enabling national monetary authorities to intervene in foreign exchange markets to support the value of their currency while insulating the domestic money supply from the effects of such intervention. Supporting the currency therefore had minimal effects on domestic economic policy such as interest rates or inflation (Darby and Lothian, 1983, chs 10–13). Capital controls, combined with the low level of cross-border flows, gave national authorities considerable autonomy at least in the short term.

The BWS embodied a compromise between the free traders, who desired open global markets, and the social democrats, who desired national prosperity and full employment. As Ruggie describes it, this 'embedded liberalism' provided for the liberalization of world trade while ensuring, through capital controls and fixed exchange rates, that governments did not have to sacrifice systems of social protection and macroeconomic policy geared to the achievement of domestic objectives, such as full employment and growth (1982). This did not mean that countries were relieved of the need to adjust domestic economic policy in response to balance of payments deficits or surpluses, but rather that adjustment could occur incrementally and in accordance with domestic economic priorities. Moreover, the low levels of private capital flows and relatively low levels of trade meant that international factors had only a limited impact on OECD economies such that they faced minimal pressures to adjust domestic economic policy in response to external conditions (Webb, 1995, chs 3–4). In this respect the BWS permitted governments significant autonomy in managing their own economies. Among developing countries the situation was quite different. Where balance of payments crises were structural rather than cyclical in nature, governments had to abide by IMF-imposed conditions.

The Bretton Woods system was highly institutionalized in so far as the IMF, and its sister agency the World Bank, acted to manage the international financial system which was, at the time, confined principally to official (government to government) capital flows and limited FDI. In this context, countries were able to pursue expansionary macroeconomic policies and retained significant autonomy in respect of national economic strategy. In comparison with the Gold Standard system it was perhaps less *extensive*, while because of capital controls it was characterized by a relatively low *intensity* of capital flows. With the rise of private international finance from the 1960s onwards, the conditions which sustained the BWS became increasingly untenable.

4.6   The Shape of Contemporary Financial Globalization

Three main changes in the 1960s and 1970s provided the basis for the phenomenal expansion of financial flows in the 1980s: the emergence of the Eurocurrency market, the collapse of the BWS and the oil price shock. Since then the combined effects of the deregulation of financial markets and technological change have encouraged a dramatic expansion in the extensity and intensity of global financial flows and networks.

The initial expansion of private international finance in the 1960s was driven by the emerging Eurocurrency market. In the 1950s Soviet authorities began depositing their dollar holdings with Western European banks rather than US banks, since they feared the US government would sequestrate them as a consequence of Cold War rivalry. European banks receiving deposits in dollars realized that instead of converting them into national currency they could lend them out. These 'Eurodollar' funds grew rapidly and expanded to include other currencies, creating a huge Eurocurrency market. Many international banks established branches in London to participate in this market, much of the Eurodollar business being conducted by overseas branches of US banks.

Eurocurrency business grew rapidly because it offered investors significant advantages over domestic banks. Since Eurocurrency banks were dealing in foreign currency they were not subject to many of the national regulations governing the operation of domestic banks, nor especially to national capital controls. Much of the initial growth in Eurocurrency funds came from multinational corporations, often US companies operating in Europe, depositing their foreign currency earnings rather than repatriating them back home where they would become subject to capital controls. As the Eurocurrency markets grew and became more liquid, they became convenient for raising large loans. A Eurobond market evolved in which borrowers issued bonds denominated in a currency other than their national currency. Banks, corporations and public authorities were able to borrow large sums at competitive rates, either through Eurocurrency loans or by issuing Eurobonds. Public corporations used Eurobonds to fund large projects and national monetary authorities borrowed, at times heavily, on the Eurocurrency markets as a ready means of raising significant amounts of foreign currency.

The rise of the Eurocurrency market in the 1960s placed increasing strain on the BWS. Moreover, speculation against the US dollar grew because of declining international confidence that its value could be sustained in the face of domestic inflation and a growing trade deficit. Pressures for decisive action increased. On 15 August 1971 President Nixon shocked world financial markets by announcing that the dollar was no longer to be freely convertible into gold, effectively signalling the end of fixed exchange rates and the demise of Bretton Woods. Despite an attempt to patch up the system with the Smithsonian agreement later that year, by 1973 the system had collapsed. In effect, the US had devalued the dollar to improve its deteriorating trade position, but, as the issuer of the primary international currency, was unable to do so without bringing about the collapse of the BWS itself. This ushered in an era of floating exchange rates, in which (in theory) the value of currencies is set by global market forces, that is, worldwide demand and supply of a particular currency.

The collapse of Bretton Woods was compounded in 1973 by the decision of the Organization of Petroleum Exporting Countries (OPEC) to quadruple the price of oil, effecting a huge transfer of funds from oil-importing to oil-exporting countries. Unable to spend all this additional revenue, leading oil exporters were left with large surpluses which they invested on the international money markets. This greatly increased the liquidity of international banks, providing them with almost $50 billion to recycle through the world economy during 1974–6, and large sums thereafter into the early 1980s. As OECD growth slowed, the banks lent increasingly to developing countries. Backed by international agencies and the monetary authorities of the major economies, they recycled much of the OPEC surplus through lending to a wider range of developing countries than ever before in the postwar period (although concentrated on certain Latin American and East Asian economies). In the process both the intensity and extensity of global financial flows were transformed.

4.6.1 The intensity and diversity of global financial flows

Consistent data on international capital markets really only commence in the 1970s. This is more than a statistical accident and directly reflects the huge expansion of these markets in this period. From negligible levels in the 1960s, private capital flows grew so that in 1997 the total net new issues of international loans and bonds amounted to $890

Table 4.4 Annual percentage growth of international capital markets, 1963–1995

	1963–72	1973–82	1983–95
Bond issues	17.6	22.9	14.1
Bond issues (constant prices)	12.4	12.2	10.1
New loans	33.6	27.6	9.2
New loans (constant prices)	27.4	16.5	5.5
Total issues and loans		25.3	12.2
Total (constant prices)		14.4	8.2
Bonds outstanding			15.7
Bonds outstanding (constant prices)			12.5
Loans outstanding		24.2	12.3
Loans outstanding (constant prices)		13.4	8.9
Total bonds and loans outstanding			13.2
Total (constant prices)			9.8
World real GDP	4.8	3.4	3.4
World export volume	9.2	4.1	6.0

Deflator: Industrial countries GDP deflator.
Sources: Calculated from OECD, 1996b; BIS, *Annual Report*, various years; IMF, *International Financial Statistics Yearbook*, various years; Bryant, 1987

billion while stocks of outstanding loans and bonds totalled $7,635 billion in March 1998 (BIS, 1998a). Table 4.4 shows how the rate of growth of capital raised through international banking and bond issues has been rapid since the 1960s, outpacing the growth of either world output or trade. Moreover, private financial flows have become more diverse since today they embrace FDI, international bank lending, international bonds, equities, new financial instruments (notably derivatives) and foreign exchange transactions. The expansion of each will be examined in turn, except for FDI, which is discussed in the next chapter.

FDI

FDI is defined as the acquisition and management of overseas productive assets. This sector grew rapidly for much of the post-1945 period and, although heavily concentrated among the major industrialized states, it has acquired an increasingly global reach. FDI is analysed in more detail in chapter 5.

International bank lending

International bank lending can be broken down into traditional lending, in which banks lend abroad in their national currency, and Eurocurrency lending, in which banks lend abroad in foreign currencies.

As figure 4.1 indicates, following the 1973 oil shock direct lending to non-OECD countries rose from below 5 per cent of the total to between a quarter and a third.

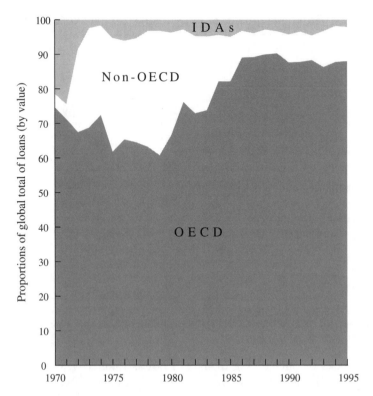

Figure 4.1 Distribution of international bank loans by borrower, 1970–1995
(*Source*: OECD, 1996b)

Table 4.5 International banking as a percentage of world output, 1964–1991

	1964	1972	1980	1985	1991
Net international bank loans	0.7	3.7	8.0	13.2	16.3
Gross size of international banking market	1.2	6.3	16.2	27.8	37.0

Source: UNCTAD, 1994, p. 128

These loans to developing and socialist economies largely dried up in the mid to late 1980s, although they show some revival in the 1990s. Since 1982 the growth of new loans to these countries has fallen below the growth of world trade, although loans are still growing faster than world output and total outstanding loans are growing faster than world trade. This slowdown in the growth of loans is partly due to the decline in loans to non-OECD countries and partly to the shift towards other forms of international finance.

International banking has been transformed from a negligible adjunct to domestic banking into an integral part of its business. As table 4.5 reveals, international banking, measured as a share of world output, has expanded dramatically since the 1960s.

Box 4.3   International bonds

An international bond is a credit instrument issued by or to overseas creditors/debtors which includes a promise to pay a specified amount of money on a fixed date and to pay interest periodically at stated intervals. Bonds are marketable securities denominated in standard units. An external bond is one issued by a borrower in a capital market or markets outside the country in which the borrower is domiciled. These bonds can be further differentiated into foreign issues and Euro or international issues. A foreign bond is one placed on behalf of a non-resident by a domestic syndicate on the market of a single country and denominated in that country's currency. Such bonds are issued by public authorities, corporations (usually multinationals) and increasingly financial institutions themselves. An international or Eurobond issue is one placed on the markets of at least two countries and is denominated in a currency which need not be that of either and is usually placed by an international syndicate of financial institutions of several countries.

International bonds

Table 4.4 above demonstrates that, as with international bank lending, issues of international bonds have grown rapidly since the 1960s. Indeed, since the early 1980s international bond issues have grown faster than international bank loans. Since that time Eurobonds have constituted the clear majority of total international bond issues (OECD, 1996b). Unlike earlier periods, only a small proportion of bonds have been issued by developing countries; although there has been some increase during the 1990s their share is still only around 10 per cent (IMF, 1995, p. 42).

International bonds constitute a growing share of world capital markets because they are a cheap and effective means of raising finance. In part this is a product of the trend towards *disintermediation*, in that finance is organized directly between savers and borrowers rather than being intermediated by a bank. This reduces operating costs and it allows deals to be tailored to clients' specific needs. While this represents a move away from traditional bank lending, banks often play a key role in arranging and underwriting these bond issues. Such business is attractive to banks because it is 'off-balance sheet' (that is, not included in banks' standard assets and liabilities) and therefore not subject to the restrictions national central banks place on banks' portfolios.

According to legend the typical holder of a Eurobond is a Belgian dentist anxious to prevent his savings from being taxed. In fact assets are mainly held by institutional investors, notably pension funds. As well as being major issuers of bonds, multinational corporations are often significant purchasers during periods of cash surplus. Some trade these assets speculatively. Bonds are issued by governments, private corporations (often MNCs) and financial institutions. The shares of each in total bond issues fluctuate but there has been a marked shift to private bond issues. Table 4.6 indicates how foreign holdings of government bonds have evolved for the key OECD states.

Table 4.6 Foreign holdings of central government debt as percentage of total, 1980–1992

	1980	1986	1992
France	–	0.8	42.6
Germany	9.1	20.2	26.3
Sweden	28.0	28.0	45.8
United Kingdom	8.9	9.8	17.4
United States	21.0	16.4	19.4

Source: IMF, 1994, pp. 66–7

International equities and the enmeshment of national stock markets

There are several ways in which it is possible to assess how far national markets for equities (shares) are being transformed by financial globalization. First, the number and total capitalization of foreign companies quoted on each national stock exchange and the number of domestic companies that have sought foreign listings can be examined. Second, we can calculate the value of domestic equities held by foreign investors and the value of foreign equities held by domestic investors (both stocks locally quoted and stocks only available on foreign exchanges can be calculated). At a global level the total number of Euro-equity issues, their value and the transnational networks that facilitate these international sales can be measured.

London has a long history of heavy dealing in foreign shares, which now account for the majority of capitalization on the London Stock Exchange. Although foreign issuing and dealing has increased on other stock markets, it constitutes a minority of stock market activity. International equity issues have grown from negligible levels in the early 1980s to over $8 billion at the start of the 1990s, and to over $40 billion annually today (IMF, 1995, 1996). These issues include Euro-equities, similar to Eurobonds, and other international issues – for instance, some privatization programmes have issued shares internationally. However, international equity issues remain low relative to national share issues.

Although international equities are significant in cross-border equity flows, a much larger source of flows arises where investors in one country buy shares on foreign stock markets; such shares may only be issued on their local stock exchanges, but foreign investors can and do purchase them. Gross cross-border equity flows have risen from over $1 trillion in the late 1980s to around $2.5 trillion in the mid-1990s (IMF, 1995, p. 189). As table 4.7 indicates, net flows have risen significantly since the mid-1980s. As with other global financial markets there is a high level of activity as investors seek to diversify their portfolios internationally; however, in the absence of large and persistent differences in rates of return between different countries, net flows of capital are much smaller than gross flows. With the demise of capital controls, and fewer restrictions on institutional investors, pension funds and insurance companies, in particular, have diversified their holdings of equities internationally (IMF, 1995, pp. 165–74). High levels of turnover on these markets reflects the fact that institutional investors are

Table 4.7 Net cross-border equity flows, 1986–1994 (US$bn)

	1986	1988	1990	1992	1994
Investor from:					
North America	3.7	4.0	12.0	46.7	55.0
USA	2.6	2.0	10.3	42.3	49.0
Japan	8.2	3.0	6.3	–3.0	13.5
Europe	21.4	14.4	4.6	8.0	46.3
UK	8.9	9.7	–0.9	–3.1	14.2
Rest of the world	8.8	11.4	–19.7	2.0	4.8
Equity from:					
North America	19.8	–3.7	–15.9	–3.9	6.3
USA	19.1	–1.4	–14.5	–4.1	1.8
Japan	–15.8	6.8	–13.3	8.9	45.5
Europe	33.6	23.0	15.9	25.5	29.1
UK	7.8	9.7	5.4	10.1	11.1
Emerging markets	3.3	3.5	13.2	21.2	39.9
Rest of the world	1.0	3.2	3.3	2.0	1.8
Total	42.0	32.9	3.2	53.7	119.6

Source: IMF, 1995, p. 190

actively trading equities across borders. A growing proportion of these flows is invested in shares issued by companies located in developing countries (see below).

Derivatives

Since the 1980s the most dramatic growth in international financial transactions has been in new financial instruments, notably derivatives. Derivatives is a generic term for instruments derived from other financial products where the basic payment is only a fraction of the total notional value of the product; derivatives essentially are futures, options or swaps (see box 4.4).

Box 4.4 Futures, options, swaps

Futures are simply an agreement to trade a quantity of a product – currency, commodity, bonds, shares, etc. – at an agreed future date for an agreed price. An option gives the holder the right to buy an agreed quantity of a product at an agreed price on an agreed date. A swap is where agents swap the payments associated with two assets – for example, two borrowers may swap payments between a fixed and a floating interest rate loan. Derivatives allow agents to hedge themselves against the risk of adverse movements in the underlying price of a product. They also offer the means to speculate heavily against movements in prices since the initial outlay is only a fraction of the notional value of the contract, enabling agents to gear up very large sums.

Table 4.8   Derivatives trading, 1986–1996

	Notional amounts outstanding of:			
	Exchange-traded instruments ($ billion)	Over-the-counter instruments ($ billion)	Turnover of instruments on exchange ($ trillion)	Millions of contracts
1986	618.3			315.0
1987	729.9			389.6
1988	1,306.0			336.2
1989	1,766.6			421.2
1990	2,290.4	3,450.3	92.8	478.3
1991	3,519.3	4,449.4	135.2	510.5
1992	4,634.4	5,345.7	181.9	635.6
1993	7,771.1	8,474.6	227.8	788.0
1994	8,862.5	11,303.2	340.4	1,142.2
1995	9,185.3	17,990.0	333.8	1,210.1
1996	9,884.6	24,292.0	321.7	

Source: BIS, *Annual Report*, various years

There are established liquid markets for futures and options in major currencies, interest rate assets, baskets of major shares and commodities. There has also been a rapid growth in over-the-counter (OTC) derivatives products sold according to the specific requirements of the buyer. The great majority of derivatives are interest rate or currency products.

The growth of derivatives trading, following the establishment of the Chicago Options Exchange in 1972, has been astronomical. Trade in international derivatives only really began in earnest in the mid-1980s but, as table 4.8 shows, the total value of contracts outstanding has risen over sevenfold to around $10 trillion, while OTC contracts have risen even faster to over twice the size of the exchange-traded market. To put this in perspective, the notional outstanding value of derivatives is higher than world GDP.

Whereas ten years ago the market was dominated by Chicago and London, other emerging markets have seen the most rapid growth in recent years. A global market for derivative products is evolving as cross-border transactions between the major national markets effectively erode the barriers between them.

International money markets

Foreign exchange markets are (in terms of magnitude) easily the largest international market of any sort, financial or otherwise. Although the huge volume of transactions and the high rate of turnover make collecting accurate data difficult, even allowing for error, the orders of magnitude tell their own story.

The annual turnover of foreign exchange has grown astronomically from an already huge $17.5 trillion in 1979 to over $300 trillion today; this is a working daily turnover

Table 4.9 Estimated annual turnover of foreign exchange, 1979–1995 (US$ trillion)

	Foreign exchange turnover	World exports	Ratio
1979	17.5	1.5	1:12
1986	75.0	2.0	1:38
1989	190.0	3.1	1:6
1992	252.0	4.7	1:54
1995	297.5	5.0	1:60

Source: BIS, *Annual Report*, various years

of over $1.4 trillion (BIS, 1998b, p. 1). Although international trade has always been a key source of demand for foreign exchange, the latter has grown from over ten times world trade flows in 1979 to over fifty times today (see table 4.9). Official foreign exchange reserves for all countries combined represent about one day's trading volume on these markets.

The majority of foreign exchange business is conducted in London, Tokyo and New York, with London retaining a dominant position. Trailing these centres, by some way, are Hong Kong, Frankfurt, Zurich and Paris. Facilitated by global communications infrastructures, instantaneous dealing continues through twenty-four hours, London taking over from Tokyo with the New York markets opening as London closes and then overlapping with Tokyo to complete the cycle. The rise in international capital market activity requires foreign exchange to effect transactions in currencies other than the agent's own; but this accounts for only a fraction of the dealings. Much is speculation and arbitrage (taking advantage of small differences in asset prices between markets). The growth of speculative activity in these markets is, in part, a result of the breakdown of the BWS.

Under a floating exchange rate system currency values are determined by day-to-day trading in foreign exchange markets, instead of being fixed to the value of the dollar or gold, as under the BWS or the classical Gold Standard respectively. In principle, exchange rates are determined by global demand for and supply of a currency, although in practice national authorities often intervene in an attempt to manage the exchange rate by keeping it within a certain target range. Floating exchange rates have also forced businesses to hedge themselves against adverse exchange rate movements. As a result floating exchange rates have increased opportunities for agents to speculate on their movements. Speculative activity grew over the 1970s and 1980s: liquidity in foreign exchange markets grew exponentially and new instruments, especially derivatives, enabled agents to take large speculative positions. The removal of capital controls by OECD countries in the 1980s and 1990s eliminated many of the official restrictions on this activity. As well as speculating on movements in floating exchange rates, speculators periodically take positions against fixed or managed exchange rates, effectively betting that governments will be forced to devalue. The ensuing massive flows of funds against a currency have produced notable devaluation crises, involving several European currencies in 1992 and 1993, the Mexican peso in 1994, several East Asian currencies in 1997, and the Russian rouble in 1998.

4.6.2   The extensity and stratification of the global financial system

Not only has the intensity of private international finance grown rapidly since the 1970s, so has its extensity. For the first time since the interwar period many developing countries and East European economies are now reincorporated into the international capital market as borrowers. But lending still remains concentrated in middle income countries in East Asia and Latin America – in 1981 over 70 per cent of the outstanding debt was owed by just ten countries (Vos, 1994, p. 140). Others, particularly the poorest developing countries, remain largely excluded from private financial markets and dependent on official aid flows (plus usually small flows of FDI). Formally, many developing countries retain extensive capital controls, although for a significant number these have been liberalized in the 1990s in response to IMF structural adjustment programmes. Moreover, in practice, elites in developing countries have frequently been able to deposit hard currency with international banks irrespective of national capital controls, as the overseas private bank accounts of deposed dictators unfortunately testifies.

But while developing countries and the transition economies (former communist states) have been incorporated into the global financial system, the nature of that incorporation varies, both among them and between them and the OECD countries. Whereas OECD countries may in some circumstances have to pay a premium on the cost of borrowing, they invariably retain access to world capital markets. By comparison countries considered by the international credit rating agencies, such as Moody's or Standard and Poor, a high risk will have limited or no access to private international finance.

Until the 1990s access to international finance for developing countries and emerging economies was limited to aid, FDI and bank loans; access to international bank loans was largely limited to a small number of East Asian economies. Moreover, for much of the postwar era they had minimal access to international bond markets by comparison with the classical Gold Standard era and the 1920s. Very few companies from developing countries issued shares internationally and few institutional investors acquired shares from developing country markets as part of their portfolios. All these key forms of international finance were thus almost completely confined to the OECD states until the early 1990s.

During the 1970s developing countries accounted for between a quarter and a third of total international bank loans, although this declined in the 1980s, remaining low until the mid-1990s. Since then domestic financial markets in developing countries have been opened up to international investors and these countries, alongside transition economies, have received significant financial inflows. Most notably, Latin America has regained access to private international capital markets so that net outflows over 1983–9 of $116 billion have switched to net inflows of $200 billion over 1990–4. Moreover, some developing countries have issued international bonds in significant quantities for the first time in the postwar period and companies in these countries have issued international equities for the first time ever.

International investors were attracted to these emerging markets by relatively high interest rates, particularly in Latin America. They were also attracted by the prospect

Table 4.10 Financial flows to developing countries, sources as percentage of total, 1960–1994

	ODA	Other official finance	FDI	Bank finance	Bond finance	Total ($bn, 1983 prices)
1960–1	55.9	18.9	18.8	6.3		34.8
1970	41.8	19.5	18.2	14.8	1.5	53.1
1975	37.3	18.5	20.0	21.1	0.7	84.6
1980	30.5	19.4	8.4	38.9	1.1	118.3
1985	44.2	13.8	7.8	18.0	6.4	99.3
1990	41.9	13.4	20.9	11.9	0.7	83.5
1994	28.1	5.2	22.6	19.8	13.5	127.0
1996	19.0	2.7	19.8	23.1	28.4	251.9

Source: OECD, *Development Co-operation*, various years

of expanding markets and aimed to diversify their holdings internationally as they took an increasingly global view of their portfolio allocation. But as table 4.10 shows, it was only in the mid-1990s that financial flows to developing countries exceeded those of 1980 in real terms. Bank finance has increased somewhat, but the most notable increase is in international bond finance. These trends are examined in more detail below.

Table 4.11 details private capital flows to developing countries and to transition economies. East Asia and Latin America continue to dominate these flows, although the transition economies have attracted an increasing share. By the late 1990s private capital flows to developing economies were higher relative to either their GDP or investment levels than during the 1970s. However, these flows declined sharply following the East Asian currency crises of 1997–8. FDI flows to the poorest economies, notably in Africa, remain less than 1 per cent of the total. But the ratio of official development aid to gross fixed investment in these countries is around two-thirds; thus, although these countries have very limited access to international finance, their economic development is critically reliant on international financial flows. By comparison the transition economies of the former communist bloc have attracted a growing share of financial flows.

As table 4.12 indicates, developing countries now account for over 10 per cent of total international bonds, although such funds are highly concentrated. Africa is largely marginalized from the bond market, with South Africa accounting for the majority of such flows. In Europe, Hungary and Turkey account for the majority of these flows and Israel accounts for the majority of flows to the Middle East.

Developing countries have also rapidly increased their presence in international equity markets: 'In 1987, about $0.50 of each $100 was invested in emerging markets, but by 1993 more than $16 out of each incremental $100 of foreign investment was invested in emerging markets' (IMF, 1995, p. 4) and these markets rose from less than 5 to over 10 per cent of total world capitalization (p. 171). The existence of significant levels of portfolio investment flows particularly to Asia, Latin America and Eastern Europe is apparent too.

Similarly, as table 4.13 reveals, developing countries account for an increasing share of international equity issues in the 1990s, although these transactions are heavily

Table 4.11 Net private capital flows to developing countries, 1977–1995 (US$ billion)

	1977–82	1983–9	1990	1991	1992	1993	1994	1995
Total	30.5	8.8	57.1	150.9	133.7	180.2	163.6	211.2
Net FDI	11.2	13.3	18.6	30.8	35.8	54.9	66.9	83.0
Net portfolio investment	−10.5	6.5	18.3	37.7	46.3	92.3	53.3	42.9
Other[a]	29.8	−11.0	20.1	82.4	51.7	33.0	43.3	85.2
Africa			2.5	3.4	2.9	7.0	12.4	11.8
Net FDI			1.4	1.6	2.6	1.2	2.2	2.1
Net portfolio investment			−0.2	−0.5	−1.0	−0.9	1.1	0.1
Other[a]			1.4	2.2	1.3	6.7	9.2	9.6
Asia	15.8	16.7	25.6	47.9	30.8	69.9	81.9	105.9
Net FDI	2.7	5.2	9.4	14.3	14.4	32.7	41.9	52.4
Net portfolio investment	0.6	1.4	−0.9	2.9	9.8	23.8	16.0	18.5
Other[a]	12.5	10.1	17.0	30.6	6.6	13.5	23.9	35.0
Latin America	26.3	−16.6	17.3	24.0	54.7	64.2	48.5	48.9
Net FDI	5.3	4.4	6.6	11.2	12.8	13.9	17.7	17.1
Net portfolio investment	1.6	−1.2	17.4	11.4	17.8	51.6	17.4	10.0
Other[a]	19.4	−19.8	−6.6	1.5	24.0	−1.2	13.4	21.8
Other developing	−11.6	8.7						
Net FDI	3.2	3.7						
Net portfolio investment	−12.7	6.3						
Other[a]	−2.1	−1.3						
Transition countries			11.6	−2.9	3.5	7.2	11.2	29.7
Net FDI				2.4	4.2	6.0	5.6	11.4
Net portfolio investment				0.8	−0.8	2.7	3.0	6.0
Other[a]			11.6	−6.1	0.2	−1.6	2.7	12.4

[a] Includes bank loans.
Sources: IMF, 1995, p. 33; 1996, p. 86

Table 4.12 International bond issues, 1989–1995 ($bn)

	1989	1990	1991	1992	1993	1994	1995
Total	252.1	226.6	297.6	333.7	500.1	462.4	501.7
Developing countries	4.7	6.3	12.8	23.8	62.8	56.8	57.9
As per cent total	1.9	2.8	4.3	7.1	12.5	12.3	11.6
Africa	0.2	0.01	0.2	0.7	0.2	2.1	1.9
Asia	1.5	1.6	3.0	5.9	22.0	29.9	25.3
Europe	2.2	1.9	2.0	4.6	9.7	3.5	6.6
Middle East				0.4	2.1	3.0	0.7
Latin America	0.8	2.8	7.2	12.6	28.8	18.2	23.4

Sources: IMF, 1995, p. 42; 1996, p. 93

Table 4.13 International equity issues, 1990–1995 ($bn)

	1990	1991	1992	1993	1994	1995
Total	8.2	15.5	22.6	34.0	49.2	44.2
Developing countries	1.3	5.4	9.3	11.9	18.1	11.2
As per cent total	15.5	35.0	40.9	35.0	36.9	25.3
Africa		0.1	0.3	0.2	0.6	0.5
Asia	1.0	1.0	4.7	5.2	12.1	8.9
Europe	0.1	0.1	0.1	0.2	0.6	0.6
Middle East		0.01	0.1	0.3	0.1	0.3
Latin America	0.01	4.1	4.1	6.0	4.7	1.0

Sources: IMF, 1995, p. 46; 1996, p. 101

concentrated. Since the 1994–5 Mexican peso crisis, flows to Latin America have declined sharply and a similar drop-off was experienced in East Asia as a consequence of the stock market and foreign exchange crises during the late 1990s.

Developing countries and the transition economies, in sum, are incorporated into the global financial system, but in a manner that is strongly hierarchical and uneven. Some countries have periodically had access to private international borrowing, but also periodically faced credit rationing. In the 1990s increased flows have linked their stock markets more closely with world markets. But the poorest countries have remained on the margins of private international finance and reliant on official aid flows. Indeed, in 1998 some ninety countries were under various forms of IMF adjustment programmes.

Deregulation of financial markets in developing countries has often led to high levels of speculative activity, largely fuelled by short-term capital inflows (Grabel, 1995). In the 1994–5 Mexican peso crisis, large capital outflows came after three years of heavy capital inflows and a boom on the Mexican stock exchange; as economic growth faltered, the exchange rate became unsustainable and was subject to a speculative attack. This crisis produced a contagion effect in that investors withdrew funds from other emerging markets, not only in Latin America but also in East Asia despite there being no direct connection with Mexico's predicament. In 1997, as growth forecasts for some East Asian economies fell, capital flight from these countries caused their currencies to collapse despite massive intervention to support them. Again, crises in one economy appeared to induce capital outflows from others. Despite attempts by the IMF (and G7) to stabilize the financial situation in East Asia, through the provision of the largest rescue package in its history, the contagion effect of the crisis swiftly engulfed many emerging economies. By late 1998 speculation had led to the devaluation of the rouble and speculative attacks on many other currencies. These developments underlined the ways in which short-term capital flows generate a high degree of volatility and systemic risk within global capital markets.

4.6.3 The infrastructure, institutionalization and organization of global finance

For decades the cost of international financial transactions has been so low as to make a minimal difference to interest rates and asset prices between countries. Advances in computing and communications technology over the past thirty years have been central to the huge volume and the *velocity* of international financial transactions. They have enabled a large volume and range of products to be offered relatively cheaply with transactions in real time, as trading occurs twenty-four hours a day across the globe. The complex risk calculations involved in dealing with the most sophisticated products, notably derivatives, are greatly aided by modern computer technology. Private banks and financial corporations too have cooperated in establishing extensive worldwide communications infrastructures to facilitate all forms of financial transactions.

Hyperglobalist accounts tend to explain the rise of private global finance as simply the triumph of markets and technology: the high volume and rapidity of transactions, combined with innovations in financial instruments, swamp national financial controls, making them redundant (Ohmae, 1990). Such a view is contradicted by the fact that banks and other financial institutions still rely on national and international regulatory authorities for their effective operation. Commercial banks require central banks to act as lender of last resort to prevent bank collapses. As the debt crises of the 1980s and the East Asian crisis of the late 1990s showed, when banks get into difficulties the most economically powerful states (mainly the US) alongside international public authorities, such as the IMF, have to step in to prevent financial collapse. Moreover, in response to various banking failures and the unprecedented volume of international financial transactions, national financial authorities have cooperated extensively over the establishment of a common framework for international banking. As a result, there is now a general international agreement on bank capital adequacy (the capital reserves banks have to keep as a cushion against losses) monitored by the Bank for International Settlements. There is also an internationalized banking supervision structure with clearly demarcated national responsibilities.

These developments, in part, have been the product of cooperation between national central banks through the Bank for International Settlements (BIS), whose membership is expanding beyond the original ten major economies (G10) to include all the key emerging economies in the world. BIS, nevertheless, is only a multilateral forum, and governments, particularly the US, have played a key role in encouraging the development of a more comprehensive international regulatory regime for finance (T. Porter, 1993, ch. 3; Kapstein, 1994b). As a result international agreements have been reached with respect to the regulation of cross-border securities trading (T. Porter, 1993, ch. 4).

The International Organization of Securities Commissions, a body made up of thirteen national financial regulatory authorities, seeks to encourage greater multilateral cooperation in the regulation of cross-border financial activities. Its attempts to establish international standards for the monitoring, surveillance and regulation of cross-border financial activities have become increasingly important, especially in respect of regulating derivatives trade and financial conglomerates. These developments reflect a general shift towards facilitating global financial activity while at the same time encouraging investor confidence that the activity in these markets observes certain minimum international regulatory standards.

Governments and international authorities have played a catalytic role in the growth of contemporary global financial markets. Some national authorities permitted, even encouraged, their growth; although many others discouraged or resisted it. As noted previously, the Eurocurrency business grew in the 1960s partly to avoid US capital controls. The British authorities were happy to see the development of this market in London, which otherwise might have faced decline given the erosion of sterling's international role. The US government acquiesced in these developments, apparently confident that they would have little impact on domestic monetary conditions or policy. Other governments, notably Japan, initially resisted the development of a Euro-yen market but liberalized in the 1980s.

Although the rise of private global finance is not simply a product of the triumph of markets and technology, but rather has been encouraged and facilitated by states, this is not to imply that governments can control these markets or reintroduce effective capital controls just as easily as they were eliminated. Liberalization among OECD countries and the establishment of common international regulatory standards represent as much a response to the unprecedented levels of international financial activity and the diminishing effectiveness of national controls as they do a direct cause of financial globalization. Regulatory authorities continue to respond to financial markets, as shown by attempts to agree common international standards for derivatives. Although governments, international agencies and central banks have created an institutional framework that has encouraged the expansion of private international finance, they no longer control the organization or intensity of global financial activity. Indeed, as Germain argues, the balance between public and private power in this domain has shifted radically in favour of the latter, to the extent that 'a significant victory has been scored for the interests of internationally mobile capital' (1997, p. 164). But the contingent nature of this 'victory' became apparent in the wake of the East Asian financial crisis of 1997 as the IMF and G7 governments began to review the regulation of global finance and discuss measures for dealing with potentially disruptive short-term flows of capital. However, proposed reforms to date fall short of a radically new 'architecture' of global financial regulation (IMF, 1998a).

4.6.4 Contemporary financial globalization: liberalization and evolving global financial markets

The intensity and extensity of contemporary cross-border financial flows are such that national financial systems are becoming increasingly enmeshed. In the Bretton Woods system capital controls constrained and regulated such flows. But financial liberalization and deregulation have contributed enormously to growing patterns of financial enmeshment. This is a trend which is likely to be reinforced further as a result of the implementation of the WTO agreement on the opening up of national financial services to global competition. Some 102 countries agreed in late 1997 to open, to varying degrees, their domestic banking, insurance and securities industries to foreign competition from 1999 and to abide by WTO rules on fair trade. Furthermore, negotiations on the liberalization of all financial services are to commence in the year 2000 (WTO, 1998).

During the 1970s and 1980s national capital controls became less effective since the existence of Euromarkets enabled such controls to be evaded, while because of the sheer scale of capital movements OECD economies became increasingly vulnerable to speculative activity (Shafer, 1995). Although capital controls continued to drive a wedge between domestic and foreign interest rates, they proved less and less effective either

Table 4.14 Countries operating controls on the capital account, 1997

Controls on:	
Capital market securities	128
Money market instruments	112
Collective investment securities	107
Derivatives and other instruments	78
Foreign direct investment	144
Real estate transactions	119
Total countries	144

Source: IMF, 1997a

in controlling the level of global financial flows or in regulating their domestic impact. Consequently, OECD governments abandoned national capital controls, thereby eliminating the formal barriers between domestic and international financial markets.

In some cases this liberalization was driven by ideological motives; in others liberalization came about since governments no longer appeared able to achieve national economic objectives or to attract international investment. But not all countries have abandoned capital controls (see table 4.14), and they remain fairly widespread within developing and transition economies. However, the definite trend is towards the liberalization of domestic capital controls (Haggard and Maxfield, 1996). This in turn has had significant implications for international monetary order, since the removal of capital controls sharply increases the difficulties of operating fixed exchange rates such that the number of countries operating floating exchange rates has expanded significantly since the 1980s from 40 per cent to over 60 per cent (Eichengreen, 1996, chs 4 and 5). The principal characteristic of the contemporary international monetary system is thus a shift from a fixed exchange rate to a flexible exchange rate system.

The growing intensity and extensity of global financial flows, combined with the trend towards the liberalization of national financial markets, the absence of national capital controls, and the move towards flexible exchange rates, suggest that a qualitative shift is underway involving deeper global financial integration. But in what sense is financial globalization associated with deepening global financial integration? Is there a single global capital market? To what extent are national interest rates now determined in the context of global financial markets?

The determination of national interest rates

Interest rates today, although converging, vary between countries (not to mention within them) and this still holds if they are expressed in terms of a common currency measure (so that an investor would receive the same return in their own currency on a foreign asset as on a domestic asset). This may be due both to imperfections in financial markets as well as to divergent economic performance among countries and world regions. Although national interest rates across the globe clearly have not been equalized, they are nevertheless subject to the disciplines of worldwide capital and monetary flows. In this sense national interest rates are determined in the context of global financial markets and conditions.

Box 4.5 Interest rate parity

Covered interest rate parity refers to a condition in which interest rates are equalized between assets denominated in different currencies through the forward exchange market guaranteeing a specified return in domestic currency. Investors buying a foreign currency asset know the maturity yield of the asset in foreign currency and can guarantee the return in their own currency by selling the yield in advance to a forward exchange dealer at the forward exchange rate. In the absence of capital controls, the forward rate should ensure that the returns on domestic currency assets are equal to the returns on foreign currency assets of equivalent risk and maturity. If returns on foreign currency assets exceed those of domestic assets, funds would flow into foreign currency assets and the forward sales of foreign currency would increase the forward demand for domestic currency, thus causing the forward rate to appreciate and/or the yield on foreign assets to fall in domestic currency terms.

Uncovered interest rate parity refers to the situation in which interest rates are equalized on assets denominated in different currencies without selling forward. If the interest rates diverge on otherwise identical assets denominated in different currencies, then equalization implies that the future movement of the exchange rate between the two currencies over the maturity of the asset will equalize returns. Thus, in effect, whether uncovered interest rate parity holds is a question of whether future exchange rate movements are assessed accurately by the markets.

Real interest rate parity exists when the real interest rate, the rate net of inflation, is equalized between countries. If uncovered interest rate parity holds and differences in national price levels are offset by exchange rate movements then real interest rates will be equalized between countries.

That the existence of a functioning global capital market should bring about an equalization of the returns to financial assets worldwide (measured in terms of a common currency) is a frequent presumption of sceptical and hyperglobalist arguments. But this presumes a model of a perfectly integrated global capital market. There have been exhaustive studies to test for interest rate convergence, focusing on covered and uncovered interest rate parity (see box 4.5). The conclusions can be summarized briefly and unequivocally: covered interest rate parity holds in the absence of capital controls, but uncovered interest rate parity does not.

Among OECD countries interest rates are converging when expressed in a common currency – differences between national rates being offset by movements in the relative exchange rate. Specifically, when currency can be sold forward, any difference between rates is exactly offset by the difference between the current and forward exchange rate for the period the asset is held, so that returns are equalized when expressed in a common currency (covered interest rate parity holds). Outside of this condition returns are not equalized, so that exchange rates do not exactly move to offset differences in interest rates (uncovered interest rate parity does not hold). This failure of exchange rates to move to offset differences in interest rates is the result both of variations over time in the premium over standard interest rates that the market demands for holding assets denominated in particular currencies, and of operational features of the foreign exchange markets (Marston, 1995; Frankel, 1993). Market operators use forecasts of exchange rates based both on analysis of economic fundamentals and on trendspotting in data series ('chartism'); typically, they take some average of the two, leading to varying forecasts, although there is also no consensus among economists over estimating equilibrium exchange rates. Since there is a range of opinions among traders, this creates the conditions for high volumes of trading and possibilities for speculation. In particular, chartism can drive the exchange rate away from its equilibrium value, the short-term focus of most traders leading to a relative concentration on such movements. Over the longer term there is evidence of interest rate parity, including evidence of convergence of real interest rates among the leading economies, implying some convergence in the costs of capital.

Testing for real interest rate parity points to the existence of a world (real) interest rate among the major economies, with small and stable risk premiums for different countries (Gagnon and Unferth, 1995; Helbling and Wescott, 1995). This further suggests that, despite the absence of interest rate equalization, long-term interest rates are determined in an evolving global capital market. As such the real global interest rate reflects the global demand for, and supply of, credit. This implies more than just a high level of interconnectedness between the world's financial centres, but their deepening financial integration (Walter, 1993).

A global capital market?

A global capital market may be said to exist if the primary financial centres in the world economy are sufficiently enmeshed that the supply of, and demand for, international credit is effectively mediated at a transcontinental level. The evidence suggests that while a fully integrated global capital market may not yet exist, the intensity and extensity of cross-border financial activity point to an evolving global capital market.

If there is an evolving global capital market, it might be expected that the returns to a standard bundle – portfolio – of assets would tend to converge. Empirical studies do point to a convergence in returns among the major capital markets; returns on emerging markets in developing countries are a different case, but they do show a tendency to converge as well (Korajczyk, 1996). Institutional investors now have large holdings overseas and trade these actively (E. Davis, 1991; Tesar and Werner, 1995). Although investors tend to display a bias towards holding domestic assets, this bias is declining (Golub, 1990; Frankel, 1994; Akdogan, 1995). In part this traditional bias may be due to national restrictions on overseas investments by major domestic institutional investors, although these have been significantly reduced in the 1990s.

Even where there is a convergence in returns across markets there are still significant incentives for investors to diversify their portfolios internationally. The high level of cross-border transactions in bonds and equities confirms this. Indeed, as long as there is even a small difference in the variability of returns between national capital markets – because, for example, they may be more or less unstable, their business cycles may not be synchronized – investors can secure gains, despite a convergence in the rates of return, by diversifying their portfolios internationally and smoothing returns over time. Thus, rather than differential movements on national capital markets being inconsistent with financial globalization, as some sceptics argue, it is precisely these differences that drive global financial flows.

Although most individual creditors, like borrowers, may not take a fully global perspective, nevertheless flows between the world's major financial centres are now sufficiently large to suggest that a global capital market is emerging. There is evidence for this in the fact that the cost of capital has tended to converge internationally (Fukao, 1993, 1995). Moreover, some of the marginal differences in these costs can be attributed to national differences in the tax treatment of investment. Bank lending rates are typically based on national interest rates: as these rates have converged internationally and increased competition has kept margins down, the rates quoted to borrowers have tended to converge. As firms are able to issue bonds, equities and other assets on international markets the costs of this form of finance have tended to converge too.

However, the sceptics typically doubt the existence of a global capital market since there still remains a very strong association between national savings and national investment rates (for instance, Hirst and Thompson, 1996b, ch. 2). If capital were truly internationally mobile, they reason, there would tend to be little or no association between national savings and national investment; rather savings would flow across the globe to wherever the returns were highest and so net capital flows would be large. Feldstein and Horioka (1980) found that national savings and investment rates remain highly correlated, while other studies show that this correlation is significantly lower between local financial markets within countries (cf. Sinn, 1992). By contrast national savings–investment correlations were lower during the classical Gold Standard period than today, while net capital flows were much greater. National savings–investment correlations were high during the interwar years, as might be expected given the collapse of the international monetary order (Obstfeld, 1995). On closer examination this evidence proves inconclusive.

The current account of a country's balance of payments is the difference between its (public and private) savings and its investment: savings and investment are equalized where the government succeeds in balancing the current account. Since economies cannot sustain current account deficits or surpluses permanently, governments seek to balance the current account, with the consequence that national savings and investment rates tend to converge (Krol, 1996; Liu and Tanner, 1996). In this respect the correlation between national savings and investment is not a conclusive test of the existence (or non-existence) of an integrated global capital market. Net capital flows by themselves are therefore not the only, or best, indicator of the existence of a global capital market. Thus the fact that, as the sceptics claim, net capital flows today may be smaller than in the Gold Standard era is not conclusive evidence that world capital markets in the 1990s are less financially integrated than in the 1890s. For the significance of unprecedented levels of gross capital flows and high capital mobility today cannot be discounted so readily.

Significant net capital movements would only be expected if there were persistent differences in rates of return between economies. Unlike the situation during the classical Gold Standard, national rates of return on similar assets do not appear to differ markedly. This fits with other empirical evidence that profit rates are similar the world over and this may partly reflect historical international capital flows (Wood, 1994, ch. 3). Armstrong et al. (1991) estimated annual profit rates for the seven major OECD countries over 1952–87. From their analysis it is possible to identify a tendency since

1971 for profit rates between these countries to converge. Furthermore, Ghosh (1995) examined variations in the current accounts of national balances of payments to test whether the major industrialized countries were using international lending and borrowing to smooth consumption over time. His results indicated that far from capital mobility being lower than expected under conditions of financial openness, for Canada, Germany, Japan and the UK (but not the USA) since 1975 it was actually higher, that is, there were excessive capital movements relative to those required to smooth consumption over time. Such evidence is consistent with the existence of high levels of speculative international financial flows that cannot be accounted for solely in terms of underlying differences in rates of return.

Clearly the operation of today's world capital market falls short of the textbook conception of a perfectly integrated global capital market: borrowers and creditors vary in their access to this market and there remains a home bias among holders of assets. Nevertheless, there is clear evidence of an evolving global capital market which, like many such markets, is characterized by imperfections and distortions. For currencies, government bonds, exchange-traded derivatives and other leading financial products, trading spans the world's major financial centres. The London, New York and Tokyo markets have become so enmeshed that they function as a twenty-four-hour single market; they account for the majority of trade in these assets and act to set benchmark world prices. But worldwide markets for equities, corporate bonds and other financial assets are evolving too as the major national markets for these assets have become significantly enmeshed and such assets are traded increasingly within all the principal world financial centres. Comparing this evolving global capital market to a perfectly integrated global capital market tends to overlook what is distinctive about contemporary developments. In such a perfectly integrated global financial market turnover might be expected to be low. By comparison the key feature of global financial markets today is the historically unprecedented volume of activity, much of it speculative, the speed with which financial transactions occur and the accompanying process of financial deepening. These features suggest that a global capital market is evolving even if it is not yet fully institutionalized.

4.7 Comparing Historical Forms of Financial Globalization

As this discussion has demonstrated, 'haute finance', as the great economic historian Karl Polanyi once termed it, has a considerable history (1944, p. 9). Early modern forms of financial globalization were limited in their extensity and intensity. The velocity and domestic economic impact of cross-border financial flows and networks too were limited significantly by poor infrastructures and localized economic systems. Moreover, the organization of finance tended to emanate from a single hegemonic financial centre, whether Amsterdam, Antwerp, or later London (Germain, 1997). By comparison the epoch of the classical Gold Standard era comes closest to the textbook case of a functioning global capital market.

At the height of the classical Gold Standard era, the intensity of capital flows attained levels which have been surpassed only in more recent times. The existence of worldwide empires and the technological advances in communications greatly expanded the reach of 'haute finance'. Few economies in this period remained insulated from the operation of a world capital market. But while the mobility of capital was largely unhindered, its domestic impact was significantly mediated by considerable levels of protectionism, imperial trading preferences, unprecedented levels of economic migration and prevailing assumptions about the limited responsibility of the state for bearing the social costs of economic adjustment. However, during the interwar period the Gold Standard system effectively collapsed. It was replaced, in the years after 1945, by the Bretton Woods system which was far from global in its membership and in which private capital flows were highly restricted as a result of national capital controls.

By comparison the contemporary pattern of financial globalization has many historically distinctive features even though many sceptics discount it as effectively a 'catching up' with past trends. Clearly there are several common features among the various historical forms of globalization described in this chapter, but these commonalities are most visible between the Gold Standard era and the contemporary epoch. But there are also significant points of divergence (see grid 4.1). For the global financial system today embraces virtually every nation-state and economy, while the magnitude of gross financial flows is unprecedented, as is the shift towards almost instantaneous, real-time, round the clock, global financial trading. Furthermore, the enormous diversity of financial products traded and the complexity of new financial instruments reflect a fundamental shift towards an autonomous global financial market in which financial activity is largely divorced from the requirements of trade, that is, the exchange of goods and services. Whereas for much of history the primary purpose of cross-border financial activity was to facilitate trade, today trade accounts for a much smaller proportion of international financial activity than perhaps in any previous era.

Levels of cross-border flows of finance today are at least comparable to those of the classical Gold Standard era. Direct comparisons are difficult because only net capital flow data exist for the classical Gold Standard period and for a limited number of countries. However, net flows are likely to be of a similar order of magnitude to gross flows since capital flows were largely one-way from the net exporters to the net recipients. As table 4.15 indicates, contemporary gross flows of FDI and portfolio investment for the major economies are for the most part significantly greater (as measured relative to GDP) than flows from the major economies during the classical Gold Standard period (see table 4.3 above). Further, they now issue from a wider range of countries. But crucially, not only are the gross flows at least as large – and probably larger – relative to the GDP of the major economies, the turnover on global financial markets, as shown in table 4.16, has attained historically unprecedented levels.

There has also been a significant transformation in the organization and forms of global financial activity in relation to that of the Gold Standard era. Whereas in the Gold Standard era the bulk of financial activity concerned bonds and portfolio investment, in the contemporary period FDI, private international bonds, derivatives, and currency trading dominate cross-border financial activity. Moreover, whereas in the Bretton Woods era the international financial system was organized primarily by, and through, governments, today the international organization of credit is dominated by a plethora of private actors (banks, financial institutions, etc.) operating according to the logic of the market (Germain, 1997). Nor is there a single hegemonic financial centre, as in the late nineteenth century, imposing a modicum of order and adherence to agreed rules, for London, New York and Tokyo are the primary centres of financial

Grid 4.1 Historical forms of financial globalization

	Pre-Industrial Revolution	Classical Gold Standard	Bretton Woods period	Contemporary period
Extensity	Medium Long-standing precious metals flows between Asia and Europe extended to the Americas in 16th century	High for currency flows as countries incorporated into trade Gold Standard arrangements confined to leading economies until 20th century	Communist countries excluded from international monetary system Virtually universal application elsewhere	Virtually universal participation in the international financial and monetary order
Intensity	Generally low, but periodically currency flows have key impact on domestic monetary conditions Limited monetization of domestic economies	Variable Very high investment flows relative to income from key investor and creditor nations International monetary conditions have increasing influence over domestic conditions	Limited by design, moderate levels of flows	High Unprecedented gross flows of capital Diversity of capital flows
Velocity	Very limited: days and weeks for transactions	Moderate to limited	Increasing: beginnings of 24-hour trading	High: instantaneous, 24-hour trading
Impact propensity	Low, with limited international transactions and monetization of economies	Financial flows often central to creditor countries' development Gold Standard arrangements initially have limited impact on participating countries, but central to Great Depression in 1930s	Low by design for industrialized countries Greater impact on credit constrained developing economies National capital controls Embedded liberalism	High: interest rates determined in the context of global markets and monetary policy heavily influenced by them; this impacts heavily on groups throughout the economy

Infrastructure	Basic communications Minimal regulation	International telegraph provides basis for global market Some international regulation	Further improvements in communications technology Extensive international regulation	Advanced communications and computer technology provides basis for very high level of transactions and private financial infrastructures Extensive international surveillance and regulation
Institutionalization	Small number of financial centres with networks of merchants and banks operating from these	Emergence of networks of multinational banks Gold Standard instituted by government agreement	International finance regulated by IMF Multinational banking re-emerges with growth of Eurocurrency business	Continued growth of multinational banking, continued importance of IMF to poorer economies Regulation through BIS and other international agreements Extensive surveillance
Stratification	Highly concentrated: international finance organized through a small number of centres Eurocentric	High: private finance organized through limited number of exchanges International transactions dominated by sterling Eurocentric	High: private finance organized through a limited number of exchanges International transactions dominated by dollar as Bretton Woods reserve currency Atlantic centric	High, but a little more diffuse than under Bretton Woods; private finance concentrated in London, New York and Tokyo, but rising business elsewhere Decentred Dollar remains the leading world currency, but increasing use of other currencies
Dominant modes of interaction	Competitive	Imperial	State dominated; cooperative	Shifting balance of power between private finance and states Collaboration and competition

Table 4.15   Gross foreign direct investment plus portfolio investment flows, 1970–1995 (percentage of GDP)

	1970–4	1975–9	1980–4	1985–9	1990–5
Canada	1.7	3.4	3.6	6.1	7.2
France		1.3	2.1	4.1	7.2
Germany	1.2	1.3	1.7	5.2	6.3
Italy	0.9	0.3	0.6	1.7	5.7
Japan		0.6	2.6	5.9	3.7
Sweden	1.0	1.2	1.7	5.0	7.0
UK	3.6	4.0	5.4	14.4	11.9
USA	1.0	1.5	1.4	2.9	3.3

Source: IMF, 1997b, p. 60

Table 4.16   Cross-border transactions in bonds and equities, 1970–1996 (percentage of GDP)

	1970	1975	1980	1985	1990	1996[a]
US	2.8	4.2	9.0	35.1	89.0	151.5
Japan		1.5	7.7	63.0	120.0	82.8
Germany	3.3	5.1	7.5	33.4	57.3	196.8
France			8.4[b]	21.4	53.6	229.2
Italy		0.9	1.1	4.0	26.6	435.4
UK				367.5	690.1	
Canada	5.7	3.3	9.6	26.7	64.4	234.8

[a] January–September.
[b] 1982.
Source: IMF, 1997b, p. 60

activity. In comparison with the Gold Standard era or even the Bretton Woods system, the surveillance and regulation of the global financial system are thus much more of a multilateral affair, institutionalized within the IMF, the BIS and the transgovernmental networks of central bankers. It is also a system in which the boundaries between international and domestic regulation have been breached such that there are considerable pressures for the harmonization or, at the very least, coordination of banking or financial rules and requirements.

Although the contemporary pattern of cross-border financial activity still remains highly uneven and hierarchical, there are significant differences in patterns of stratification compared with earlier periods. While the core of OECD states still account for the bulk of capital inflows, the industrializing world and transition economies account for a growing share which, in historical terms, is comparable with, if not greater than, the Gold Standard era. Moreover, financial conditions in those economies largely isolated from global capital flows remain significantly influenced by developments in the financial markets of New York, London and Tokyo. For exchange rates and interest rates determined in these markets often define the parameters for national macroeconomic management. As the spread of capitalism has brought with it the monetization of economies, financial globalization today has involved a process of financial deepening in that the dynamics of world financial markets reach directly into the day-to-day functioning and organization of all but a few economies. In this respect domestic interest rates and exchange rates are significantly conditioned by the operation of global financial markets. The concentration of capital flows in OECD states, though diminishing, is therefore a misleading indicator of the global reach and impact of world financial markets.

As grid 4.1 above seeks to highlight, there are similarities between the contemporary historical form of financial globalization and that of prior epochs. But in several key respects financial globalization in the late twentieth century is unique.

4.8 Global Finance and National Enmeshment

As discussed previously, the unevenness of contemporary globalization is evident in differential patterns of enmeshment in the global financial system. Even among the six SIACS which are the focus of this study there is considerable divergence with respect to their enmeshment in world financial markets.

In the postwar period the City of London retained its international financial position due in part to its central role in the Euromarket. The second major financial futures exchange after Chicago, the London International Financial Futures Exchange (LIFFE), was established in 1982. From 1945 Britain maintained a system of exchange controls until these were unilaterally abolished in 1980 as one of the first acts of the incoming Conservative government which subsequently sought greater financial liberalization within the EU. Throughout the 1990s, despite competition from other European and overseas financial centres, London has retained its centrality to the functioning of the global financial system (Germain, 1997).

After 1945 France maintained extensive capital controls as part of a state-regulated financial system, much of it publicly owned. Financial overexpansion, partly due to low interest rates, necessitated devaluation in 1958 and 1969. But floating exchange rates did not appear to offer France sufficient financial autonomy so that it sought the formation of a system of managed floating in the 'snake' and the European Monetary System (EMS) (see box 4.6). During 1981–3 the incoming Socialist government attempted a domestic reflationary policy combined with an ambitious range of social measures. This triggered major speculation against the franc which capital controls failed to combat such that the entire economic strategy had to be abandoned. In the aftermath of this reversal, shifting elite attitudes to government intervention and a desire to promote Paris as an international financial centre encouraged the authorities to liberalize the financial sector and abolish capital controls. Since the late 1980s domestic monetary policy has been focused on maintaining a high exchange rate within the European Exchange Rate Mechanism (ERM) with the aim of reducing inflation rates to German levels or below, a policy that has largely continued since the ERM crisis of 1993. Paris has a long history of international financial dealings and multinational banking associated with its former imperial links. Although bank lending has heavily predominated in the postwar period, since the financial liberalization of the 1980s there has been a large growth in the trading of other financial instruments,

Box 4.6   European monetary arrangements since 1979

The European Monetary System (EMS) was founded in 1979 to provide a fixed exchange rate system for European Community countries following abortive attempts to fix rates between them in the 1970s through the 'snake'. The Exchange Rate Mechanism (ERM) provided the formal apparatus for the participating countries, limiting fluctuations of each currency to 2.25 per cent either side of an agreed value, and providing procedures for member countries to intervene to support any currency moving towards the edge of its band. Following the EMS crisis in 1993 these bands were widened to 15 per cent. This crisis proved to be only a temporary setback for moves towards European Monetary Union (EMU) in 1999. Countries participating in EMU will form a monetary union in that they operate with a common currency, thus effectively fixing the rate of exchange between them.

including the very rapid growth of MATIF, the financial futures exchange established in 1986.

By contrast Germany faced the reverse problems in the Bretton Woods period and the 1970s. Inflows of funds put upward pressure on the mark, threatening to weaken competitiveness. Capital controls were used periodically to resist such pressure, but they were abolished in 1981. Monetary authorities traditionally have been suspicious of new financial instruments, at least until financial liberalization in the 1980s, so that the derivatives markets remain small.

In Japan capital controls were used in the postwar period to ensure that the financial sector was geared to industrial development. However, current account deficits following the 1973 oil crisis led to liberalization of short-term capital movements. Financial liberalization has been driven both by external pressure for greater foreign access to Japanese financial markets and powerful domestic interest groups lobbying for greater financial openness (Helleiner, 1994, pp. 152–6). Tokyo functions as one of the world's three major financial centres. But Japanese short-term financial markets remain underdeveloped by industrialized country standards, although by 1991 Japan had passed the US as the world's largest gross creditor. In 1998 it embarked on a further liberalization of the financial sector and abandoned remaining controls on capital flows.

Sweden operated capital controls in the postwar periods, but controls on long-term capital movements were liberalized in the 1970s, reflecting the multinationalization of Swedish industry. Controls on short-term flows were eliminated in the late 1980s following liberalization of domestic money markets. Since then there has been an active attempt to attract overseas business, as evidenced in 1989 in the opening of OM, the Swedish financial futures exchange, modelled on MATIF.

In the United States capital controls were effectively eliminated by 1974. The US has several of the largest financial markets in the world and New York is the primary focus of most global financial activity. Although the US remains the linchpin of the global financial system, and the dollar remains the leading international currency, it no longer exercises the hegemonic power it did during the Bretton Woods era. Moreover, despite the enormous financial power of the US, the globalization of financial activity has meant that it is no longer as insulated from overseas financial developments as it was at the height of the BWS.

Table 4.17 Foreign assets and liabilities as a percentage of total assets and liabilities of commercial banks for selected countries, 1960–1997

	1960	1970	1980	1990	1997
France					
Assets	–	16.0	30.0	24.9	34.6
Liabilities	–	17.0	22.0	28.6	32.7
Germany					
Assets	2.4	8.7	9.7	16.3	18.2
Liabilities	4.7	9.0	12.2	13.1	20.6
Japan					
Assets	2.6	3.7	4.2	13.9	16.4
Liabilities	3.6	3.1	7.3	19.4	11.8
Sweden					
Assets	5.8	4.9	9.6	17.7	36.4
Liabilities	2.8	3.8	15.0	45.0	41.9
United Kingdom					
Assets	6.2	46.1	64.7	45.0	51.0
Liabilities	13.9	49.7	67.5	49.3	51.6
United States					
Assets	1.4	2.2	11.0	5.6	3.8
Liabilities	3.7	5.4	9.0	6.9	8.5

Source: Calculated from IMF, *International Financial Statistics Yearbook*, various years

Patterns of national enmeshment in the global financial system among these six countries are perhaps nowhere as distinctive as in respect of the banking sector. Since 1970 international banking has expanded in parallel with the growth of global financial activity. British multinational banks had over 2,000 branches on the eve of the Second World War and were pre-eminent until their competitiveness waned in the 1970s and 1980s (Jones, 1993, ch. 10). In part, this reflects the growth of US, Japanese and German multinational banks. As banks have expanded overseas and international financial activity has grown, global finance has become more important to banking activity. Table 4.17 indicates how this has transformed the balance sheets of the commercial banking sector in each of the six OECD economies in this study. In the postwar period Britain's openness to international banking activity is strikingly borne out by the trends indicated in the table. Since the liberalization, both France and Sweden have experienced significant shifts towards the internationalization of banking. Although German and Japanese banks have tended to have a strong domestic focus and US banks serve a huge economy, even here since the 1970s foreign assets and liabilities have grown from negligible to significant proportions.

4.9 Economic Autonomy and Sovereignty in an Era of Global Finance

The explosive growth of global financial activity since the 1980s and the complexity of global financial markets have transformed the management of developed economies.

This growth provides significant opportunities for governments and corporations to tap into large and liquid capital markets and allows investors to earn the best return worldwide. However, while global financial markets play a key role in the worldwide allocation of capital, they do so in a manner that has profound implications for national sovereignty and autonomy.

Contemporary global finance is marked by both high intensity and relatively high volatility in exchange rates, interest rates and other financial asset prices. Exchange rates often diverge from values consistent with either interest rate differentials or underlying national economic fundamentals. In a perfectly integrated global financial market this should not occur; rather, theory predicts that prices should adjust quickly to shifts in underlying economic conditions. But, as noted previously, large-scale speculative activity exists. As a result, national macroeconomic policy is vulnerable to changes in global financial conditions. Speculative flows can have immediate and dramatic domestic economic consequences, as evident in the aftermath of the East Asian currency turmoil of 1997. Contemporary financial globalization has altered the costs and benefits associated with different national macroeconomic policy options, at times so radically as to make some options prohibitively expensive. These costs and benefits, moreover, vary between countries and over time in a manner that is not entirely predictable. Besides these decisional impacts, contemporary patterns of financial globalization also have significant institutional, distributional and structural consequences for SIACS.

4.9.1   Decisional impacts: macroeconomic policy

For economists the starting point for analysing the effects of global finance on national macroeconomic policy is the standard Mundell-Fleming theory. This asserts that countries cannot pursue an independent monetary policy with a fixed exchange rate in the absence of capital controls: in a perfect global capital market (uncovered interest rate parity holds so that) the domestic interest rate must equal the world interest rate. Thus national authorities must target the domestic money supply to sustain exchange rate parity. Capital controls, provided that they are effective, permit countries to establish some monetary autonomy by de-linking domestic monetary policy from world interest rates. By comparison, floating exchange rates allow countries to pursue independent monetary policies since the exchange rate moves to offset any difference between domestic and world interest rates. In principle, then, floating exchange rates allow governments considerable autonomy in the management of domestic monetary policy, provided they are prepared to accept the exchange rate consequences.

If the world was simply as described in the Mundell-Fleming theory the trade-offs between these different policies would be stark, but also clear. In practice the predicted relationships between policy and outcomes hold only weakly (Rose, 1996). Under the BWS, as noted, capital flows had only a limited impact on national economic policy in OECD countries. Since then these countries have become more open to trade, and financial flows have become far more responsive to differences in national economic conditions. In the mid to late 1970s, governments in many OECD countries believed that they could run autonomous economic policies and simply accept the exchange rate consequences. But exchange rates fluctuated heavily such that governments were not able to enjoy the policy autonomy they desired (see Webb, 1995, ch. 5).

Since then some governments, with the exception of the US, Germany and Japan, have pursued largely convergent macroeconomic policies designed to minimize disruptive financial flows (Webb, 1995, ch. 6). Of course, autonomy varies with economic credentials and size. Current account surplus countries, notably Germany and Japan, faced much less pressure to expand their economies than deficit countries faced to deflate theirs. The US was able to pursue an expansionary macroeconomic policy in the 1980s, albeit at the expense of an overvalued exchange rate, and then enlist the assistance of the other governments to help manage its adjustment over 1985–7 through the Plaza-Louvre agreement examined below.

In practice, financial globalization has increased the pressure on most OECD governments to pursue a tight domestic monetary policy, since countries perceived to be more likely to run 'inflationary' domestic monetary policies typically have a risk premium imposed on their borrowing to compensate investors for potential future inflation. In a liberalizing global capital market there are thus strong pressures on all governments to conform to a tight domestic monetary policy and to take measures to boost the credibility of domestic monetary authorities by developing an anti-inflationary track record and/or making the national central bank (constitutionally) independent from government. Thus Johnson and Siklos (1996) found that domestic monetary policies among the OECD countries largely reflect the world interest rate rather than domestic financial or economic conditions.

However, financial globalization also tends to undermine the effectiveness of traditional instruments of national monetary policy. Capital mobility, deregulation and financial innovation have transformed the capacity of governments to determine the domestic money supply and inflation levels (Shepherd, 1994, ch. 9). Financial openness, the internationalization of credit and the ability of financial agencies to switch between a range of assets makes it more difficult for governments and central banks to clearly identify, let alone control, the domestic money supply. These developments transform the capacity of governments to control effectively the money supply and interest rates, as well as the impact of both on output and inflation. National authorities still control short-term interest rates but longer term interest rates (typically the most important for investment decisions) tend to be determined in global markets over which individual governments have only indirect and often diminishing influence. Although the German Bundesbank, for instance, is famed for achieving low inflation through tight control of the domestic money supply, financial globalization has greatly complicated traditional means of achieving these policy objectives (Juselius, 1996).

One of the original motivations for financial liberalization was governments' need to tap overseas capital markets to finance domestic borrowing. In principle one of the advantages of a global capital market is that whereas government borrowing in a closed national financial market would tend to raise interest rates, borrowing on global markets may tend to put less upward pressure on interest rates. In practice markets tend to impose a risk premium on borrowing countries. Under these conditions borrowers may be confronted eventually with rising interest rates and a falling exchange rate as the markets reduce their exposure to what they perceive as 'high risk borrowers'. Thus long-term interest rates are typically higher for governments with high budget deficits and high public debts. In this respect, the increased enmeshment of capital markets, greater capital mobility and the shift to flexible exchange rates have been significant factors in transforming the effectiveness of orthodox Keynesian macroeconomic management strategies. With rapid and increased capital mobility governments may find it difficult to sustain an expansionary macroeconomic policy. For the resultant prospect of higher inflation, or higher taxes to pay for such spending, may induce either capital flight or higher interest rates to pay for government borrowing. Such developments tend to undermine or constrain expansionary macroeconomic policies (Garrett, 1996, p. 88). Financial globalization increases the incentives for governments to pursue national macroeconomic strategies which seek low and stable rates of inflation, through fiscal discipline and a tight monetary policy, since these appeal to global financial markets. Thus governments tend to adopt risk-adverse, cautious macroeconomic policies seeking to second-guess the reactions of global financial markets and to secure their approval.

4.9.2 Decisional impacts: managing exchange rates

In the Bretton Woods era of capital controls, domestic money markets were insulated from foreign exchange markets so that governments could offset foreign exchange intervention to support the value of the national currency, leaving the domestic money supply unchanged (see box 4.7). This left governments free to manage the exchange rate. With the elimination of capital controls in the 1980s it was assumed that this separation no longer held on the grounds that domestic and foreign assets were virtually perfect substitutes for each other and so foreign exchange intervention would have domestic monetary implications and vice versa. This view was challenged by the apparent success of the 1985 Plaza-Louvre accord.

The dollar had risen sharply in the early 1980s such that by the mid-1980s it was plainly overvalued (Frankel and Froot, 1990). The G5 countries (the US, UK, Germany, France and Japan) agreed coordinated intervention in the global foreign exchange market, initially to reduce the value of the dollar, then to stabilize it. These planned

---

Box 4.7 Sterilization of foreign exchange intervention

Sterilization refers to governments' attempts to offset their operations in foreign exchange markets by countervailing interventions in domestic money markets so that foreign exchange intervention has no effect on the total domestic money supply. Thus if the authorities tried to restrain an exchange rate appreciation by selling domestic currency, thus increasing the domestic money supply, they would compensate by selling bonds on domestic money markets to reduce the money supply. Most central banks routinely attempt to sterilize their interventions, but this can only be effective if domestic and foreign assets are not perfect substitutes. Selling domestic bonds increases the interest rate (a higher rate is needed to induce investors to hold more bonds) but if bonds are perfect substitutes for foreign assets then the interest rate rise will simply induce overseas funds to flow into the country to take advantage of the higher interest rates. Under a fixed exchange rate system this would expand the money supply, under floating rates it would appreciate the exchange rate by increasing demand for the currency; either way this would nullify the effect of the original intervention.

interventions were largely offset in their domestic money markets to leave each country's money supply unaffected. Of course, how far this intervention was responsible for the dollar's subsequent movement is debatable, although research indicates that it was significant (Dominguez and Frankel, 1993). Thus some degree of domestic monetary autonomy may be compatible with the management of the exchange rate given that countries' assets are not perfectly substitutable. But, in many respects, the Plaza-Louvre episode was exceptional, although it does suggest that piecemeal foreign exchange intervention can sometimes be effective within a floating exchange rate system without distorting the domestic money supply.

Floating exchange rates can lead to rapid and dramatic shifts in currency values such that governments' pursuit of stable inflation, and possibly the pursuit of low inflation too, may be jeopardized. In a desire to prevent such dramatic movements many governments have sought to manage the exchange rate by fixing its value to that of a low inflation currency (Germany for EMS members, the USA for Latin American countries), so providing an 'anti-inflationary anchor'. Before the 1990s currency crises in Europe, Mexico and Asia, it was widely asserted that this was an effective anti-inflation strategy, but these crises pose the question as to whether it is actually feasible to sustain a managed or fixed exchange rate policy with unfettered global capital mobility. Eichengreen (1994b) argues that under these conditions the only effective policy options are either free floating rates or monetary union, that is, the irrevocable fixing of exchange rates through the establishment of a common currency.

If an exchange rate is simply overvalued and unsustainable then a speculative attack is inevitable. Speculators can mobilize massive funds through derivatives markets, as George Soros did when sterling was forced out of the ERM in September 1992, but more critical are the actions of institutional investors and MNCs who tend to move out of a currency if they believe it to be under threat. If a government's commitment to a fixed exchange rate is credible such attacks will simply fail, but there are several ways in which such attacks can become effectively self-fulfilling (Obstfeld, 1996). If interest rates are forced higher to defend a specific exchange rate the domestic costs of this in terms of unemployment, higher mortgage costs, etc., may simply be too great for a government to sustain. If there is a high national debt then raising interest rates may simply be unsustainable; if the banking system is fragile then overnight interest rates in excess of 100 per cent may be necessary but also unsustainable even in the short run. In the past capital controls made exchange rates more amenable to government manipulation and management. Capital controls provided some defence against speculative attacks and some policy autonomy within a fixed exchange rate system. Since capital controls were dismantled, as in Europe as part of the Single European Market, national defences against speculative attack are very limited, hence in part the 1992 and 1993 currency crises. It is only when the anchor country in a fixed exchange rate system buys up the currencies under attack that currency parities effectively can be maintained; they will only do so, however, to the extent that it does not interfere with their own domestic monetary policy. In September 1992 the German authorities were unwilling to expand the German money supply in order to defend currencies such as sterling which they regarded as being overvalued.

Of course, claims about the effectiveness of a fixed exchange rate system under conditions of global capital mobility cannot be assessed definitively. Historically, the resurrection of the Gold Standard in the 1920s was an economic disaster, its original success (at least for core currencies) owing much to the circumstances of its operation. The BWS in effect lasted only thirteen years, from free current account convertibility in 1958 to its demise in 1971; while the EMS – a smaller system, with more frequent realignments among the major currencies – effectively lasted only fourteen years (1979–93), albeit in a much more financially integrated system. Thus definitive statements about the effectiveness and feasibility of different strategies for exchange rate management under conditions of financial globalization are likely to be overhasty. Nevertheless, it is certainly the case that contemporary patterns of financial globalization have transformed the differential costs and benefits among existing strategies for managing exchange rates, from targeting through to monetary union. Moreover, it has complicated the trade-offs between domestic economic objectives and exchange rate stability. It is also doubtful that, given the size of individual government foreign exchange reserves in relation to the potential daily turnover of foreign exchange markets, any government can manage its exchange rate without the cooperation of other governments and central banks. In this respect, financial globalization has increased the incentives for both international monetary cooperation and competition. But which is given greater emphasis at any one time will depend on conjunctural factors.

4.9.3   Institutional and distributional impacts: the welfare state

We wanted democracy, but we ended up with the bond market.
Polish graffito

Beyond the degree of autonomy states may still possess in macroeconomic policy or exchange rate management, there is a perception that financial globalization is transforming the form and functions of the modern state in the global political economy (Strange, 1996; Germain, 1997). Global financial markets are conceived as central to inducing a convergence of political and social agendas among governments of varied ideological persuasions to 'market friendly' policies: a general commitment to price stability; low public deficits and indeed expenditure, especially on social goods; low direct taxation; privatization and labour market deregulation.

These developments are argued to be particularly unfavourable to organized labour, public sector employees, welfare state beneficiaries, and other traditional interest groups of the left. In this context financial globalization shifts the balance of economic advantage further towards capital and away from labour. But global financial markets do not, as many hyperglobalists imply, simply spell the end of the welfare state. As noted above, expansionary economic policies and strong welfare programmes are not precluded by financial globalization, but rather markets impose on governments higher costs of international borrowing or falling exchange rates (Garrett, 1996). To some degree this was also the case in prior historical eras.

What is particularly distinctive about the contemporary conjuncture is that financial globalization has imposed an external financial discipline on governments that has contributed to both the emergence of a more market-friendly state and a shift in the balance of power between states and financial markets. In this respect the political agenda of SIACS reflects the constraints of global finance even though the specific impacts of financial globalization vary considerably among them.

4.9.4   Structural impacts: systemic risk and the shifting balance of financial power

Systemic risks are those potentially affecting the global financial system as a whole rather than just one state or group of financial institutions. Modern financial markets operate to allow risks to be packaged and redistributed so that institutions can hedge against specific risks such as exchange rate fluctuations; these, however, merely transform and redistribute risk, rather than eliminate or reduce it for the system as a whole. But they may also increase systemic risks. The collapse of a bank or group of banks, or loss of confidence in them, may trigger large-scale withdrawals from other banks and a more general loss of confidence which, given the enmeshment of national financial systems, can have global impacts. For example, the 1982 international debt crisis saw a combination of high real interest rates and falling world economic activity lead to suspensions of debt repayments; these become a threat not just to individual banks, but to the stability of the entire international banking system itself. In this respect systemic risk is a structural feature of the contemporary global financial system.

The magnitude and global reach of modern financial markets have increased certain systemic risks. Financial institutions may have become more exposed to default or delayed payments. Lending to developing countries in the 1990s exposes institutions to risks similar to those faced in the 1970s, but also to additional risks to the extent that these funds are linked increasingly to performance on emerging market stock exchanges and other markets. Derivatives pose new risks (Kelly, 1995). Derivatives allow agents to take large speculative positions with the potential for heavy profits, but they also involve the risk of major heavy losses, as the collapse of Barings Bank in 1995 showed. Derivatives trade may also increase risks to the extent that they lead to greater volatility in the price of the underlying asset.

Cross-border financial flows transform systemic risk in so far as financial difficulties faced by a single or several institutions in one country can have major knock-on effects on the rest of the global financial sector. This was evident in the East Asian financial crisis of 1997 as the collapse of the Thai currency rippled through foreign exchange markets, leading to precipitate falls in currency values across the region and affecting currency values in other emerging markets from Russia to Latin America. Stock markets too were affected by the rush of short-term capital flows out of these economies (see G. Thompson, 1998). In a 'wired world' high levels of enmeshment between national markets mean that disturbances in one very rapidly spill over into others. Since the bulk of international financial transactions are carried out among a small number of banks, financial difficulties facing one or more have consequences for the rest. Settlement risks arise when the parties to a transaction reside in different time zones – the first party to a transaction might deliver on their side of the contract while the counterparty might then go bankrupt and fail to deliver the offsetting currency. Liquidity risk can arise when financial institutions cannot raise the required sums to finance transactions on time. Banks regularly have $2 billion or more outstanding overnight; although short-term borrowing facilities generally allow them to cover this, a significant operational failure could present serious difficulties. This risk is particularly apparent in emerging markets where large transactions are common but payment and settlement systems are comparatively underdeveloped. Either settlement or liquidity problems for one bank can have major systemic consequences for the entire international financial order.

The existence of systemic risks produces contradictory imperatives. On the one hand, the desire on behalf of financial institutions, both public and private, to avoid a major international financial crisis produces an imperative for more extensive and more intensive international regulation of world finance. Thus, in the wake of the 1997 East Asian financial crisis, the annual IMF/World Bank summit meeting in 1998 agreed to more effective international surveillance mechanisms and greater transparency in the release of financial information in an attempt to prevent such a crisis in the future. On the other hand, it is not in the interests of any state or financial institution to abide by more stringent regulatory standards than its potential competitors. The consequence is that regulatory instruments to manage systemic risks often fall far short of those necessary to deal with them effectively. In this respect the absence of any substantive attempts, following the East Asian crisis to re-regulate, at an international level, short-term capital flows is indicative of this problem. Given the potentially volatile nature of global financial markets, and the instantaneous diffusion of financial information between the world's major financial centres, systemic risks continue to pose a permanent threat to the functioning of the entire global financial system, and no government by itself can either resolve that threat or insulate its economy from it.

The increased salience of systemic risk is also strongly associated with a structural shift in the balance of power between governments (and international agencies) and markets, or more accurately, between public and private authority in the global financial system (Germain, 1997; Pauly, 1997; Walter, 1993). Although there is a tendency to exaggerate the power of global financial markets, ignoring the centrality of state power to sustaining their effective operation especially in times of crisis, there is much compelling evidence to suggest that contemporary financial globalization is a market-driven rather than a state-driven phenomenon. Reinforced by financial liberalization the accompanying shift towards markets and private financial institutions as the 'authoritative actors' in the global financial system poses serious questions about the nature of state power and economic sovereignty. As Germain observes, 'states have allowed private monetary agents, organized through markets, to dominate the decisions of who is granted access to credit (finance) and on what terms. The international organization of credit has been transformed . . . from a quasi-public to a nearly fully private one' (1997, p. 163). In this new context the autonomy and even sovereignty of SIACS become, in certain respects, problematic.

4.10 Conclusion

Since the 1970s there has been an exponential growth in global finance such that the extensity, intensity, velocity and impact of contemporary global financial flows and networks are largely unprecedented. National financial markets and the world's key financial centres are increasingly embedded within a global financial system. Alongside these developments there has occurred a process of financial deepening, such that few economies can insulate themselves from the daily operations of world financial markets. In this respect, the volatility of global financial markets can have major domestic economic consequences, while financial conditions in one region almost instantaneously impact on national financial markets across the globe.

Compared with the era of the classical Gold Standard, or that of Bretton Woods, contemporary financial globalization has many distinctive attributes. Chief among these is the sheer magnitude, complexity and speed of financial transactions and flows. More currencies, more diverse and complex financial assets are traded more frequently, at greater speed, and in substantially greater volumes than in any previous historical epoch. The sheer magnitude of capital movements, relative to either global or national output and trade, is unique. All this relies on a highly institutionalized infrastructure such that twenty-four-hour real-time cross-border financial trading constitutes an evolving global financial market which generates significant systemic risks. Contemporary financial globalization represents a distinctive new stage in the organization and management of credit and money in the world economy; it is transforming the conditions under which the immediate and long-term prosperity of states and peoples across the globe is determined.

5

Corporate Power and Global Production Networks

Aside from global finance, perhaps the commonest image of economic globalization is that of the multinational corporation: huge corporate empires which straddle the globe with annual turnovers matching the entire GNP of many nations. In 1998 there were 53,000 MNCs worldwide with 450,000 foreign subsidiaries which had global sales of $9.5 trillion; today, transnational production 'outweighs exports as the dominant mode of servicing foreign markets' (UNCTAD, 1997, p. 1; 1998). A small number of MNCs dominate world markets for oil, minerals, foods and other agricultural products, while a hundred or so play a leading role in the globalization of manufacturing production and services. Together, the hundred largest MNCs control about 20 per cent of global foreign assets, employ 6 million workers worldwide and account for almost 30 per cent of total world sales of all MNCs (UNCTAD, 1997, p. 8). But the growth of MNCs does not tell the whole story about the globalization of production. Advances in communications technology and the infrastructural conditions which have facilitated the evolution of global financial markets and global trade have also contributed to an internationalization of production among small and medium-sized enterprises (SMEs), at least within the most advanced economies in the world. SMEs are being integrated into production and distribution networks in which the manufacturing or distribution of goods and services is globalized. Global production and distribution networks are thus no longer solely the creatures of MNCs (crucial as these corporate empires remain) but embrace cross-border linkages among SMEs (Castells, 1996; Gereffi and Korzeniewicz, 1994). This chapter explores the globalization of production and distribution networks, conceived in this wider sense, as a complement to the analysis of trade and finance.

5.1 MNCs and Global Production

The operations of MNCs are central to processes of economic globalization. They account for around two-thirds of world trade, with up to a third of world trade being intrafirm trade between branches of the same company (UNCTAD, 1995, p. 23). MNCs play a major role in the generation and international diffusion of technology, accounting for around 80 per cent of world trade in technology and the majority of private research and development (R&D). Their huge capital demands and periodic large cash surpluses have made them key players in international financial markets. They play a significant role in the globalization of trade, finance, technology and (through output and media ownership) culture, as well as in the diffusion of military technology. But MNCs are implicated most centrally in the internationalization of production and services activity: they can be conceived as stretching business across regions and continents. As Wilkins puts it:

> a multinational enterprise does *not* leave nation A for nation B. It extends over the homeland border, remaining in the headquarters country as it spreads to numerous host nations. What stretches over the political boundaries (of home and host) is the management of, the governance of, the organizational capability of, the package offered by the firm. . . . The multinational enterprise establishes, acquires and administers a network of interrelated businesses. (1994, pp. 24–5)

This chapter concentrates on the role of MNCs (although not exclusively) in globalizing the production and distribution of goods and services. MNCs provide the starting point for an analysis of historical patterns of global production and distribution, since, in various forms, they have played a role in the world economy since the medieval era.

But what is a MNC? In its widest sense a MNC is a company which produces goods or markets its services in more than one country. In its narrowest sense it refers to an enterprise which, through foreign direct investment (FDI), controls and manages subsidiaries in a number of countries outside its home base. FDI is thus one useful indicator of the growth of international production. But measures of FDI flows significantly underestimate the internationalization of production in two ways. First, FDI accounts for only approximately 25 per cent of total investment in international production – in the foreign affiliates of multinational corporations – since MNCs raise investment capital from a variety of sources (as noted in the previous chapter) to complement their FDI (UNCTAD, 1997, p. 4). Accordingly, 'the weight of international production is also considerably larger' than FDI flows indicate such that 'expressed as a ratio of world gross fixed capital formation, about one-fifth was undertaken by foreign affiliates' of MNCs (UNCTAD, 1997, p. 4). Second, as noted, global production and distribution systems do not depend solely on ownership or control but rather may simply involve cross-border production networks between firms (Borrus and Zysman, 1997). Systematic quantitative data on the latter is unavailable so that studies of specific industrial sectors, rather than measures of FDI flows, provide the only reliable clue to the magnitude and geographical scale of contemporary patterns of global production. Accordingly, in analysing the globalization of production and distribution networks this chapter makes use of quantitative data on FDI and more qualitative data on sectoral trends in the organization of production.

The globalization of production and distribution networks refers to the stretching of corporate activity and business networks across the world's major economic regions. In its most visible and institutionalized form it involves the operations of huge MNCs organizing and managing cross-border business activity through the ownership of plants, outlets or subsidiaries in different countries. On the other hand, many MNCs now outsource production to SMEs abroad ('slicing up the value chain') to achieve cheap high-quality production (see chapter 3 above). In the process global production networks or systems are created which involve not direct ownership but rather regularized contractual relationships. But equally SMEs in one country may expand abroad through franchising, or cooperative arrangements with or portfolio investment in other SMEs to form global production and distribution chains. Although big MNCs have tended to dominate global production and distribution systems this is no longer necessarily the case. Take, for instance, Caro Cuori, a small Argentinean lingerie retailer (with sales of less than 0.5 per cent of the Ford Motor company) which has outlets in Spain, Portugal, Ecuador, Canada, the US and South Africa (*Financial Times*, 10 Feb. 1998, p. 32).

Using contemporary and historical evidence this chapter seeks to construct a synoptic account of how the organization of cross-border production and distribution of goods/services has evolved since the early modern era. Broadly it is an attempt to map historically the spatio-temporal and organizational dimensions of the globalization of business activity (see the introduction). Thus it examines the extensity, intensity, velocity and impact of international business activity, as well as the significant patterns of stratification and institutionalization, the dominant modes of interaction and the infrastructural conditions which have underpinned the globalization of production in different historical epochs. Drawing on a comparison of the key historical forms of business globalization the chapter concludes by examining the distinctive features of the contemporary globalization of production. Given the role of MNCs and internationalized production in shaping, if not determining, the prosperity of nations and communities, the conclusion assesses the impacts of contemporary patterns of globalized production on the economic autonomy and sovereignty of SIACS.

5.2   International Business before the Industrial Revolution

Foreign direct investment, in the sense of investment and production dispersed across political jurisdictions, dates back at least to the medieval era, to the 'supercompanies' like the Peruzzi Company based in Florence (Hunt, 1994). This company operated throughout Europe, not only as a trading business, but also organizing the production of cloth imported from Flanders for finishing in Florence. Its internal organization entailed the dispersion of partners to key European cities and an extensive courier system. However, a branch in Tangiers notwithstanding, the Peruzzi and similar medieval companies were not transcontinental in scale, a development that only became feasible with advances in long-distance communication.

The first economically significant companies operating across continents were the great trading companies of the sixteenth to eighteenth centuries, notably the East India companies of the imperial powers (especially the Dutch and the British, see box 5.1) operating between Europe and Asia, the Hudson Bay Company operating between North America and Britain and the British Royal Africa Company. Although these companies generally operated within the single legal space of empire, and primarily organized trade rather than production, they did engage in limited production and thus were prototype MNCs. (Apart from the Hudson Bay Company, these companies were defunct by the end of the nineteenth century.)

Until recently the conventional view was that poor communication infrastructures prevented these trading companies from operating like modern MNCs, since central coordination would have been impossible. Recent research has suggested that this view is too simplistic. Carlos and Nicholas (1988) found that at their height these companies processed thousands or hundreds of thousands of annual transactions, using an extensive network of salaried managers and hierarchical structures to oversee and monitor them. Considerable effort and ingenuity went into establishing and maintaining these organizations. Although the speed of communication was slow – the trade cycle between

Box 5.1   The British East India Company

The British East India Company was incorporated by royal charter in 1600 and effectively wound up in 1858 when the British government assumed its functions. Established to defend and increase Britain's control over Indian trade, against the Dutch in particular, it developed into a joint-stock company with an effective monopoly of much Indian trade, notably in spices, agricultural raw materials, opium and textiles. Its shares, floated on the London and Amsterdam exchanges, were periodically subject to active speculation. It developed backward integration with factories and other local businesses, and thus organized production internationally. At its height the company operated with quasi-state powers, minting its own currency, exercising civil and criminal jurisdiction and maintaining its own army of thousands.

India and England, for example, took between eighteen and thirty-six months – the levels of internal coordination compared favourably with MNCs of the late nineteenth and early twentieth centuries.

By historical standards these great trading companies were extensive and organized much of the intercontinental trade of the seventeenth and eighteenth centuries. However, as noted in chapter 3, such trade was largely confined to luxury products and accounted for only a small proportion of world economic activity. Beyond this it is difficult to disentangle the impact of these companies from the wider impact of colonialism.

5.3   International Production in the Industrial Age: Multinational Business Expansion, 1850–1939

International investment grew rapidly through the nineteenth century. Although, as noted in chapter 4, the majority of this investment was portfolio, recent research indicates that FDI formed a significant share and that the internationalization of production was important in certain sectors and to certain economies (Wilkins, 1974, 1991, 1994). In the early nineteenth century overseas investment tended to be focused on raw materials and extractive industries – the primary sector. But during this period there was also significant multinational bank activity and from the 1850s some manufacturing companies established overseas operations. By the end of the nineteenth century overseas investment had also extended to agriculture, with FDI in plantations and ranches. FDI was effectively unregulated in that there were no international and few national restrictions on capital movements. Property rights were largely secured by bilateral treaties and a significant proportion of investment took place under the auspices of imperial authority.

5.3.1   FDI and international business in the classical Gold Standard era: extensity, intensity and stratification

As with foreign investment generally, FDI grew particularly rapidly during the classical Gold Standard period from the 1870s to the First World War. Dunning (1988) estimates that 35 per cent of the stock of long-term international investment on the eve of the First World War was FDI. Around 55 per cent of world FDI stocks were in the primary product sector, around 15 per cent in manufacturing and the rest in utilities and services – mainly banking and trading companies. The concentration of FDI in primary products meant that MNCs were responsible for small shares of overall manufacturing activity such that there was only a limited degree of international production.

Britain was by far the largest source of FDI, accounting for almost half the 1914 world total. The next largest source was the US, accounting for almost 20 per cent, and the remainder arose from French and German investors and some other European countries, including Sweden. Although Britain's share is comparable to its total share of all foreign investment, the US share is significantly higher. From the end of the nineteenth century particularly, US firms, in the manufacturing as well as the primary products sector, began to expand overseas production.

Although over 60 per cent of international investment went to developing areas outside Europe, much of this was heavily concentrated in a few locations, with around a dozen territories accounting for the vast majority of investment inflows. The leading recipients of foreign investment were the US, Russia and Canada, followed by major primary exporters and then Austria-Hungary (Wilkins, 1994).

MNCs in this period have some structural similarities with contemporary MNCs, but they were radically different from earlier trading companies. Initially much investment was in 'stand-alone' ventures where investors managed a concern overseas that did not form part of an international chain of production. But by the end of the nineteenth century, mining and agricultural concerns began to organize production and distribution on a more international basis. Many of the companies that later came to dominate the production and distribution of primary products, notably the major oil companies, emerged during this period.

Improvements in communications and transport increased the capacity of business to control the international production process from corporate headquarters. MNCs therefore played an important role in the emergence of global trading networks for basic commodities during the classical Gold Standard period. MNCs in the manufacturing sector, though, were much less integrated than today. Typically, foreign ventures were designed to exploit a specific advantage by producing abroad for that country's market. The degree of effective control operated by the home country parent varied a great deal. Nevertheless, although such production was small in relation to the size of host economies it could have a greater significance than its size alone indicates. Manufacturing MNCs were often among the most technologically advanced enterprises of the time, introducing new products and processes into economies and so contributing to the growth of new industries.

5.3.2   International business between the wars: extensity, intensity and stratification

The First World War disrupted flows of FDI but, since much of it was based on existing imperial links and geographical proximity, it soon revived afterwards. By 1938 the total FDI stock was around 50 per cent higher in real terms than it had been in 1914 (Dunning, 1988). Britain and the US remained the two largest sources of FDI, with around 40 per cent and 25 per cent respectively of world FDI. German FDI holdings were largely liquidated after the First World War, as was German foreign investment generally. France continued to hold around 10 per cent of the world total. This period also witnessed the emergence of FDI by Swedish, Swiss and Japanese firms. Several of today's leading Swedish and Swiss MNCs established their overseas presence in this period by exploiting their specific competitive advantages. Japan too invested abroad in several colonies, establishing significant levels of manufacturing in Korea particularly.

The extensity of FDI remained similar to that before the First World War. Over 60 per cent of FDI stocks were located in developing countries, but the largest host nations were Canada and the US. Latin American countries, the major primary producers and some European countries were also important (Wilkins, 1994). But FDI remained highly concentrated among a limited number of economies, although FDI in the primary products industries spread to a larger number of countries. The US continued to invest heavily in the Americas, but this period also witnessed the first wave of US manufacturing investment in Europe and a little in Japan.

Whereas FDI before the First World War had largely flowed freely, this changed significantly during the interwar period (Lipson, 1985). After the Bolshevik revolution in Russia foreign assets were nationalized, as was the case in Mexico too. Accordingly, given national restrictions on capital movements in the 1930s, the intensity and extensity of FDI flows were reduced.

Most international business remained concentrated in the primary products sector. The leading oil firms continued to dominate this sector while other MNCs came to control the mining and processing of a range of metals. US companies, in fruit, and British companies, in tea and sugar, invested in plantations and came to dominate trade in these commodities. FDI in manufacturing continued to grow. Typically this was driven by firms possessing a specific competitive advantage, in terms of a product or production process, and some therefore located production overseas to supply foreign markets. Trade protectionism in the 1930s sometimes encouraged the latter. Indeed, there was a significant growth in the number of cartels between the major firms in each sector, the firms using this means to divide up and control world markets for their products (Jones, 1996). During this period cartels were particularly prevalent in the primary products sector as firms attempted to manage the retrenchment of world markets.

5.3.3 The impact of international business before 1945

Like foreign investment generally during this period, FDI was limited and international production significantly constrained. FDI and MNC activity did extend across continents, but it was highly concentrated in a few countries. Many countries had minimal FDI, but for many major producers of key minerals, oil and certain agricultural goods like rubber, the intensity of MNC involvement in the national economy was often greater than at any time since (Wilkins, 1994). MNCs provided much of the investment capital for these economies, while organizing the production and export of their staple goods. These countries often attracted significant levels of portfolio investment for public expenditure on the strength of this development. The impact of MNCs on these economies was therefore large.

At the outset of this period, the role of MNCs in manufacturing production was minimal and their impact on host economies usually small, although by the 1930s MNCs had come to dominate certain industries. In some countries their impact was greater than levels of FDI stocks suggest, especially from a long-term perspective. Even before 1914 MNCs were introducing new products and processes into host counties and this accelerated in the interwar period. MNCs introduced new processed food and drink products that have since become worldwide brand names. US multinationals began to manufacture cars and other major consumer goods abroad; for example, Ford and General Motors established car plants in Europe and Japan during this period (Wilkins, 1974, ch. 4). In time these major MNCs fundamentally changed consumption patterns within host nations, and established affiliates that later acquired large shares of host markets. Through emulation and technology transfer, the growth of indigenous industries was encouraged. But production, even in these sectors, was still primarily organized on a national basis. The globalization of production remained limited in this period. Many European countries, as well as large areas of the developing world, attracted little FDI. Although, at the time, primary products were important to the world economy and MNCs played important roles in manufacturing, the great majority of production was undertaken by national and local enterprises.

5.4   The Rise of the Multinational Corporation and the Transnationalization of Production

In the postwar period MNCs have acquired a global presence. As table 5.1 indicates, for most of the postwar period stocks and flows of FDI have grown faster than world income, and sometimes trade, particularly during the 1960s and since the mid-1980s. (These figures are in current prices, that is, not adjusted for inflation, and so they cannot be compared directly between periods.) Stock measures in particular are subject to margins of error because of the difficulties with estimating their growth (see the Methodological Appendix). Even so, it is indisputable that multinationals have become major players in the world economy: apart from the 1970s and early 1980s, the turn-over of the largest 500 companies has grown faster than world output (Barnet and Müller, 1974, p. 15; Carnoy, 1993). As noted, MNCs now account for the majority of the world's exports, while sales of foreign affiliates exceed total global exports. Furthermore, as MNCs have grown there has been a significant transnationalization of production expressed in the emergence of global production and distribution networks.

Table 5.1   Annual growth rates of FDI, 1960–1993

	FDI stocks	FDI flows	Gross world product	Exports
1960–7	7.5	7.4	5.2	7.8
1967–73	11.1	14.3	10.4	18.0
1973–80	14.2	10.7	11.1	20.0
1980–5	5.3	7.3	5.6	−0.4
1986–94	15.0	19.4	8.0	10.7

Sources: Calculated from Dunning, 1993b, p. 16; UNCTAD, 1996

5.4.1   The extensity of international business operations

The initial expansion of FDI in the postwar era came from US companies: in the 1950s and 1960s at least half of all FDI flows originated from the US. American corporations invested in mining and agriculture around the globe, notably in the oil industry. As Latin American countries industrialized behind protectionist barriers, US manufacturing MNCs responded to reduced export possibilities by locating production in the region. But the major source of expansion was through overseas manufacturing in Europe and Canada.

At first, US investment was concentrated in familiar locations – it was only in the 1960s that Canada's share fell below half of total flows and Britain's share fell below half of the flows to Europe (Wilkins, 1974, p. 331). Given protectionist barriers, declining transport costs and growing consumer demand, it was often easier to supply foreign markets through overseas production than by exports. US multinationals continued to expand on the basis of their technological superiority across a range of sectors. Some European firms sustained and developed competitive advantages in particular industries after the war, and during the 1970s European and Japanese companies achieved similar levels of productivity to those of the US in some sectors. Over this period European and Japanese companies therefore began to invest abroad, European firms often expanding into neighbouring markets. Whereas European and American MNCs tended to use their most technologically advanced production techniques overseas, Japanese MNCs by contrast, during this period, largely retained their advanced production at home, while rising wages and the appreciating yen enticed them to relocate labour-intensive activity in lower wage countries.

Following a relative slowdown in FDI flows during the early 1980s, FDI boomed in the late 1980s and reached record levels in the late 1990s (UNCTAD, 1998). The Single European Market in the European Union, APEC's Osaka Declaration (proclaiming free and open trade and investment across the Asia-Pacific by 2010) and the North American Free Trade Agreement (NAFTA) encouraged the development of three major regional markets such that MNCs have been induced to locate production inside each of these 'blocs'. Initially, fears that these regional markets might become closed to the rest of the world reinforced this tendency. Japanese firms located advanced production in Europe and North America on a much larger scale than previously and European firms substantially increased their presence in North America. Much of this occurred through the purchase of existing local and national firms, so buying into established production networks directly (see table 5.2): during 1986–90 mergers and acquisitions (M&A) accounted for around 70 per cent of all inward FDI into the OECD countries and since then have accounted typically for a third to over a half of all FDI flows, but only around 20 per cent of FDI to developing countries (UNCTAD, 1994, pp. 23–4; 1996, ch. 1; 1998). Other factors too have contributed to this FDI boom.

Since the early 1990s the majority of countries have liberalized their foreign investment regulations and actively encouraged inward investment. In the period 1991–6, 95 per cent of the 599 changes in national FDI regulations across the globe were in the direction of further liberalization (UNCTAD, 1997, p. 10). This trend has been particularly important with respect to investment in services, notably financial services, where foreign companies had previously faced various national restrictions. Although the

Table 5.2 Regional shares of cross-border M&As, 1990 and 1995 (percentages)

	IN–OUT		OUT–IN	
	1990	1995	1990	1995
World	*100.0*	*100.0*	*100.0*	*100.0*
Industrialized countries	95.4	89.4	83.1	70.3
Europe	61.0	45.4	41.1	31.7
European Union	57.0	41.9	37.6	30.9
Belgium	0.4	3.2	0.7	2.2
France	14.0	5.7	3.9	5.6
Germany	10.0	9.2	5.0	2.7
Netherlands	2.6	4.9	1.3	1.1
UK	16.0	10.6	15.7	15.3
Switzerland	3.1	2.5	2.7	0.4
US	13.6	27.8	34.0	26.2
Japan	15.7	6.9	0.1	0.7
Developing countries	4.7	10.5	11.3	27.7
Latin America	0.2	1.1	5.3	4.6
Asia	4.4	8.8	5.9	12.8
South East Asia	3.0	8.2	5.7	12.5
Hong Kong	0.7	1.7	1.2	0.4
Singapore	0.2	1.1	0.4	0.3

Based on value. 'In–out' means M&As of foreign companies by companies of home countries. 'Out–in' means M&As of companies of home countries by foreign companies. 'Developing countries' do not include the former Soviet Union or Eastern Europe etc., so totals of shares of industrialized countries and developing countries do not match figures given for world (100 per cent).
Source: Prepared by JETRO from UNCTAD, *World Investment Report 1996* (http://www.jetro/go/jp)

majority of FDI flows in this period were between OECD countries, financial liberalization within other countries and improved investment opportunities induced significant flows to East Asia and Latin America; some of this was attracted by privatization programmes, which accounted for around 5–10 per cent of FDI flows to developing countries during 1989–94, and the majority of FDI flows into the emerging market economies of Eastern Europe (UNCTAD, 1996, p. 5). For the first time since 1945 Eastern Europe has witnessed large FDI inflows. A number of high-profile joint ventures have emerged, notably Volkswagen's dramatic revamping of Skoda. By the 1990s, with the extension of FDI to the transition economies, FDI had acquired a global reach, with MNCs operating in practically all economies. This picture is reinforced by the pattern of bilateral investment treaties designed to promote FDI. In 1997 there were 1,513 such treaties covering over 162 countries, a significant increase on 1992 (UNCTAD, 1997, p. 11; 1998).

In the late 1990s few economies were outside the reach of MNC activity and global production networks. As table 5.3 indicates, all regions of the globe, to a greater or lesser extent, are both the home of and host to MNCs or their foreign affiliates. But what is striking is the scale of MNC activity within, and from, the developing countries. This is indicative of the trend since 1989 of the growing attractiveness of developing

Table 5.3 Number of parent corporations and foreign affiliates, by area and country, latest available year (number)

Area/economy	Parent corporations based in country	Foreign affiliates located in economy[a]
Developed countries	36,380	93,628
Western Europe	26,161	61,902
European Union	22,111	54,862
Japan	3,967[b]	3,405[c]
United States	3,470[d]	18,608[e]
Developing countries	7,932	129,771
Africa	30	134
Latin America and the Caribbean	1,099	24,267
South, East and South East Asia	6,242	99,522
West Asia	449	1,948
Central and Eastern Europe	196	53,260
World 1997	44,508	276,659
World 1998	53,000	450,000

The data can vary significantly from preceding years, as data become available for countries not covered before, as definitions change or as older data are updated.
[a] Represents the number of foreign affiliates in the economy shown, as defined by it.
[b] The number of parent companies not including finance, insurance and real estate industries in March 1995 (3,695) plus the number of parent companies in finance, insurance and real estate industries in December 1992 (272).
[c] The number of foreign affiliates not including finance, insurance and real estate industries in March 1995 (3,121) plus the number of foreign affiliates, insurance and real estate industries in November 1995 (284).
[d] Represents a total of 2,658 non-bank parent companies in 1994 and 89 bank parent companies in 1989 with at least one foreign affiliate whose asset, sales or net income exceeded $3 million, and 723 non-bank and bank parent companies in 1989 whose affiliate(s) had assets, sales and net income under $3 million.
[e] Represents a total of 12,523 bank and non-bank affiliates in 1994 whose assets, sales or net income exceeded $1 million, and 5,551 bank and non-bank affiliates in 1992 with assets, sales and net income under $1 million, and 534 United States affiliates that are depository institutions. Each affiliate represents a fully consolidated United States business enterprise, which may consist of a number of individual companies.
Source: UNCTAD, 1997, 1998

countries to Western MNCs, but also their growing participation in global production networks as home to indigenous MNCs and the source of significant outward flows of FDI (UNCTAD, 1997, pp. 1–6; Dicken, 1998). In the late 1980s developing countries were home to some 3,800 indigenous MNCs; by the mid-1990s, as table 5.3 indicates, this had more than doubled. This is an indication of the expanding reach of global production and distribution systems.

5.4.2 The intensity of FDI and multinational production

Just as the reach of MNCs has grown, so has the intensity of their activities. Although there are comprehensive FDI data, there are less systematic data available on the total activity of MNCs and their overseas production. But the importance of MNCs in the world economy has undoubtedly grown in the postwar period, as the following analysis suggests.

Table 5.4 Overseas affiliates' production as percentage of GDP

	World GDP	World private GDP	World manufacturing output	World services output	Developing country GDP	Developing country private GDP
1970	4.5					
1977	5.4		11.5	2.3		
1982	5.8	8.1	12.7	2.5	4.4	5.7
1988	6.3	8.8	15.6	3.1		
1990	6.4	9.3	16.5	3.4	3.9	4.9
1992	6.2	9.0	17.6	3.7	4.3	5.4
1995	7.5	10.9			6.3	8.0

Sources: Estimated from World Bank, 1997; World Bank, *World Development Report*, various years

One measure of the overseas activity of MNCs is the ratio of FDI flows to total capital formation (that is, new productive investment). At the global level FDI flows have doubled from around 2 per cent of world capital formation in the 1980s to around 4 per cent in the first half of the 1990s (UNCTAD, 1996, p. 16). Although this is in line with the growing importance of overseas production, it is misleading. For MNCs do not finance their overseas operations only through FDI – overseas affiliates can and do finance their expansion through retained profits and borrowing on domestic/world capital markets. As noted, only 25 per cent of total investment in international production is financed through FDI (UNCTAD, 1997, p. 4). Further, since a significant proportion of FDI occurs through mergers and acquisitions, not new investment, it is difficult to assess precisely how much of the actual increase in world capital stock is financed by FDI.

A further measure of the intensity of multinationals' overseas activity can be gauged by comparing sales of overseas affiliates to world economic activity. Sales of foreign affiliates have grown faster than world exports: in the 1970s and 1980s they had achieved levels comparable with world export levels but in the late 1990s they were around 30 per cent higher (UNCTAD, 1994, p. 130; 1997, p. 4). Foreign affiliates' sales as a percentage of world GDP has risen from 10–15 per cent in the 1970s to around 25 per cent today.

Direct measures of overseas production are lower since production reflects the value added to inputs, some of which are imported. Figures here are 'guestimates'; few national statistical agencies systematically collect data on MNC activity so that global data are constructed from various national estimates. These estimates are based on limited data and hence are tentative. As table 5.4 shows, overseas affiliates' share of world GDP has risen from below 5 per cent in 1970 to around 7.5 per cent today. This amounts to at least 10 per cent of private world GDP. Overseas production has risen most clearly in manufacturing where it was around 10 per cent in the 1970s but has risen to almost 20 per cent today; shares of services output are much lower but they too have been rising. Foreign affiliates' shares of developing countries' GDP and manufacturing have risen too, although they remain a little lower than the world shares.

Since the 1970s overseas production by MNCs has increasingly become part of international chains of production so that international trade within the same MNC has

Table 5.5 Stocks of outward FDI by major investing economies, 1960–1994 (US$bn, percentages in brackets)

	1960	1975	1980	1985	1994
USA	31.9	124.2	220.2	251.0	610.1
	(47.1)	(44.0)	(42.9)	(36.6)	(25.3)
France	4.1	10.6	23.6	37.1	183.3
	(6.1)	(3.8)	(4.6)	(5.4)	(7.6)
Germany	0.8	18.4	43.1	59.9	199.7
	(1.2)	(6.5)	(8.4)	(8.7)	(8.3)
Netherlands	7.0	19.9	42.1	47.8	146.2
	(10.3)	(7.1)	(8.2)	(7.0)	(6.1)
Sweden	0.4	4.7	5.6	12.4	51.2
	(0.6)	(1.7)	(1.1)	(1.8)	(2.1)
Switzerland	2.3	22.4	21.5	21.4	99.6
	(3.4)	(8.0)	(4.2)	(3.1)	(4.1)
UK	12.4	37.0	80.4	100.3	281.2
	(18.3)	(13.1)	(15.7)	(14.6)	(11.7)
Japan	0.5	15.9	18.8	44.3	284.3
	(0.7)	(5.7)	(3.7)	(6.5)	(11.8)
Developed economies	67.0	275.4	507.5	664.2	2,243.8
	(99.0)	(97.7)	(98.8)	(96.9)	(93.0)
World total	67.7	282.0	513.7	685.5	2,412.2

Sources: UNCTC, 1988; UNCTAD, 1996

grown rapidly. This intrafirm trade presents numerous measurement and data collection problems; these turn partly on the criteria for deciding what kind of commercial relationship between the buyer and seller constitutes being within the same firm, particularly as the last twenty years have witnessed the emergence of a variety of institutional arrangements beyond simply wholly owned subsidiaries. Official agencies often do not systematically collect data on intrafirm trade. Overall, though, the estimated figures are broadly consistent: Bonturi and Fukasaku (1993) found that for several OECD countries between a quarter and a third of their trade is now intrafirm. UNCTAD (1995, p. 23) and OECD (1993c) both estimated that intrafirm trade accounted for around a third of world trade.

Finally, other measures of the internationalization of production, such as the number of cross-border interfirm agreements, reinforce this identifiable trend towards significant levels of global production. In 1990 there were 1,700 such interfirm agreements, but by 1995 there were some 4,600 (UNCTAD, 1997, pp. 5–6).

5.4.3 FDI: patterns of stratification

Although the extensity and intensity of FDI and multinational production have grown in the postwar period, there are distinct and uneven patterns to both. The great majority of FDI continues to originate from a small number of OECD states. As table 5.5

shows, throughout the postwar period MNCs from just eight countries – the G5 economies plus the Netherlands, Sweden and Switzerland – accounted for over three-quarters of world FDI stocks. Note that stocks are measured by historic values; this understates their current value, which is probably around 50–70 per cent higher than the recorded values (Graham, 1996, p. 11).

During the contemporary period there have been some important distributional shifts. The USA clearly remains the largest overseas investor and its foreign FDI stock has continued to grow in absolute terms. But its share of global FDI has fallen, from around 50 per cent in 1960, to around 25 per cent today. Similarly the shares of Britain and the Netherlands, two major traditional investors, have fallen over this period even though their FDI stocks have risen absolutely. Conversely Japanese and German firms have sharply increased their share of world FDI stocks from negligible levels in the 1960s to substantial shares today, with Japanese firms now having the second largest holdings of FDI. Latterly, France and Sweden have also increased their relative shares. So too has FDI from developing countries, which reached record levels in 1996 (UNCTAD, 1997, p. 13). In parallel, whereas in the 1950s and 1960s almost all of the world's largest firms were based in OECD states, a few but growing number of MNCs based in developing countries have also achieved global prominence (Bergesen and Fernandez, 1995; Dicken, 1998). Indeed, in the late 1990s, the South Korean conglomerate Daewoo and the Venezuelan company Petroleas de Venezuela SA entered the list of the world's one hundred largest MNCs (UNCTAD, 1997, p. 8).

Nevertheless, the vast majority of MNCs and FDI flows originate within, and move among, OECD countries. However, it is worth noting that the concentration of FDI flows (as opposed to stocks) among OECD states has been falling such that 'there has been a steady decline in their share of global [FDI] inflows since 1989' (UNCTAD, 1997, p. 13). FDI outflows from developing countries are growing although they account for less than 10 per cent of global FDI stocks.[1] This picture is reinforced by the geography of cross-border mergers and acquisitions (see table 5.2 above). Such activity is becoming less concentrated among OECD states and more widely diffused. These are important developments which distinguish the contemporary era from earlier historical phases of cross-border FDI activity.

Throughout the postwar period FDI flows to developing countries have continued to grow, as have stocks. The extensity of FDI is such that virtually all countries in the world have some FDI stocks, although the levels vary widely. However, for most of the postwar period FDI among OECD economies has grown faster than that to developing countries so that FDI stocks (as opposed to flows) remain significantly concentrated in the former. As table 5.6 shows, by 1960 two-thirds of FDI stocks were located in developed countries, roughly the reverse of the prewar picture. Since then the developed countries' share has grown to around three-quarters.

Table 5.7 indicates the distribution of inward FDI stocks in more detail. Britain retains its importance, but the relative position of Canada has fallen sharply. Western Europe has regained its position as host to over 40 per cent of FDI stocks, with recent surges of inward FDI. Whereas for much of the postwar period the US was a heavy net outward investor, since 1980 it has become a major site for inward FDI.

---

[1] The distinction between FDI stocks and flows is significant since the former measures historically accumulated FDI, while the latter measures inflows or outflows of FDI over time.

Table 5.6 Distribution of inward FDI stocks between developed and developing countries, 1960–1994 (percentages)

	Developed economies	Developing economies
1960	67.3	32.3
1973	72.9	27.1
1980	77.5	22.5
1985	73.5	26.4
1994	73.8	25.3

Sources: Dunning, 1988; UNCTAD, 1996

Table 5.7 Stocks of inward FDI by host economies, 1960–1994 (US$bn, percentages in brackets)

	1960	1973	1980	1985	1994
USA	7.6	17.3	83.0	184.6	504.4
	(13.9)	(10.4)	(17.2)	(25.1)	(21.5)
Canada	12.9	27.6	54.2	64.7	105.6
	(23.7)	(16.8)	(11.2)	(8.8)	(4.5)
Western Europe	12.5	60.8	200.3	244.8	972.0
	(22.9)	(36.5)	(41.6)	(33.3)	(41.5)
France			22.6	33.4	142.3
			(4.7)	(4.5)	(6.1)
Germany			36.6	36.9	125.0
			(7.6)	(5.0)	(5.3)
Sweden			3.6	5.1	19.1
			(0.7)	(0.7)	(0.8)
UK	5.0	14.8	63.0	64.0	214.2
	(9.2)	(8.9)	(13.1)	(8.7)	(9.1)
Japan	0.1	1.3	3.3	4.7	17.8
	(0.2)	(0.8)	(0.7)	(0.6)	(0.8)
Africa	3.0	4.8	20.8	27.0	55.0
	(5.5)	(2.9)	(4.3)	(3.7)	(2.3)
Latin America	8.5	20.9	48.0	76.3	199.2
	(15.6)	(12.5)	(10.0)	(10.4)	(8.5)
Developing Asia	4.1	8.0	38.0	91.8	334.8
	(7.5)	(4.8)	(7.9)	(12.5)	(14.3)
Central and Eastern Europe			0.1	0.2	19.7
					(0.8)
World total	54.5	166.7	481.9	734.9	2,342.2

Sources: Dunning, 1988; UNCTAD, 1996

Although inward FDI is virtually ubiquitous among developing countries, it is highly uneven, with the poorest economies home to less than 1 per cent of the world's inward FDI stocks. Since the early 1970s the share of the top ten developing country recipients of FDI has risen from less than half to around two-thirds of FDI stocks in developing

Table 5.8 Regional intensity of outward investment stock, 1990

	North America	Latin America	Europe	Africa	South Asia	East Asia
North America	2.03	1.12	0.84	0.49	0.32	0.80
USA	1.99	1.15	0.88	0.53	0.32	0.84
Europe	0.97	0.53	1.30	1.13	1.77	0.55
France	1.00	0.23	1.56	1.33	0.00	0.14
Germany	0.82	0.52	1.55	1.00	0.46	0.38
Sweden	0.61	0.31	1.90	0.00	0.00	0.00
UK	1.32	0.56	0.79	2.11	0.72	1.01
East Asia	1.28	1.09	0.50	1.11	0.28	1.95
Japan	1.34	1.13	0.46	1.20	0.31	1.94

Figures refer to the share of the host region in outward investment stock of a given country divided by the share of the host country in worldwide FDI stock excluding FDI stock in the investor country. The higher the figure the greater the regional concentration of FDI.
Source: UNCTAD, 1993, p. 169

countries (calculated from UNCTC, 1983 and UNCTAD, 1996). Africa has become more marginalized with the decline of FDI in primary production although there are indications that this is changing (UNCTAD, 1997). Latin America has declined in relative terms, but remains an important location. The most dramatic rise has been in East Asia, although this is unlikely to be sustained in the aftermath of the regional economic crisis. China, in particular, has received large inflows of FDI since MNCs perceive huge growth potential as it undergoes economic transformation. In 1994, China accounted for around 15 per cent of total inward FDI stocks in developing countries and over a third of the total inward FDI flows to developing countries (UNCTAD, 1996).

The concentration of FDI among OECD states has led many sceptics to claim that FDI is characterized by a distinctive regional bias, namely that it is organized around the 'triad' of Europe (the EU), NAFTA and APEC (see Hirst and Thompson, 1996b, ch. 4; Ruigrok and Tulder, 1995, pp. 148–51; cf. UNCTC, 1991). There are two issues here:

- First, although there may be a regional clustering of FDI stocks, there can be no disputing that the data demonstrates significant interregional flows of FDI. In the terms of this study, such FDI flows are clearly a global phenomenon. The fact that FDI is concentrated among OECD countries reflects its stratification rather than its regionalization: that is, it is uneven and organized hierarchically.
- Second, even given this pattern of stratification, there do not appear to be strong patterns of regional concentration of FDI flows. Estimates comparing trade and FDI flows for 1985 and 1990 found even less regional concentration in FDI flows than in trade (De Jong and Vos, 1995).

Figures in table 5.8 shows the intensity of regions' outward investment stock holdings. As this is a measure of stock, not flow, it is not directly comparable with trade figures, but it does show that although investors display some bias towards their 'home region', this is not high and is consistent with significant levels of interregional

Table 5.9 Share of foreign enterprises in manufacturing production, 1970–1991 (percentages)

	1970	1980	1991
United States	3.1	3.9	14.8[a]
Canada	–	50.6	49.0[b]
Japan	2.3	4.6	2.8[c]
France	–	26.6	26.9
Germany	14.0	15.7	13.8[a]
United Kingdom	12.1	19.3[d]	25.5
Sweden	5.2	7.9	18.0[a]

[a] 1992.
[b] 1989.
[c] 1990.
[d] 1981.
Sources: Clegg, 1987, p. 67; OECD, 1996a, p. 36

FDI. Again, levels of regional bias are lower than for trade (UNCTAD, 1993, p. 170). Indeed, the strongest regional biases for FDI are outside the 'triad'.

5.4.4   Multinational production: patterns of stratification

Since national statistical agencies do not systematically collect data on MNCs or international production, any statistical evidence is patchy and confined largely to manufacturing. Here patterns of MNC activity for each of the six SIACS in this study will be examined alongside those for developing and transition economies.

As table 5.9 reveals, foreign affiliates account for significant shares of manufacturing output among the case study economies in this study, except for Japan. The USA's shift from being overwhelmingly a net exporter of FDI to its current position as the largest host country to FDI (as well as an exporter) is reflected in the increased share of foreign affiliates in its domestic manufacturing: by the mid-1990s the share was around 20 per cent (Ham and Mowery, 1997). Until the 1970s US industry had a clear technological lead across most sectors; as this was eroded it became profitable for overseas firms to locate in the US. The share of US multinationals in US private output (excluding banking) fell from around a third to a quarter during 1977–93, but this masks important sectoral differences, with US MNCs continuing to dominate domestic manufacturing (Lipsey et al., 1995). This fall is probably more because of the rise of the services sector, which traditionally has lower levels of MNC penetration, than because US MNCs lost domestic market share to foreign affiliates.

Through the postwar period Britain was both a major exporter of FDI and a major host country, reflecting its broadly liberal policy towards FDI. Although initially British MNCs' investments were concentrated in the Commonwealth, since the 1970s, in particular, investment has become concentrated in OECD countries (Hood and Young, 1997). British MNCs possess particular advantages in consumer goods, chemicals and engineering products and so have established global networks of production in some parts of these sectors. On the other hand, inward FDI into Britain has been heavy; typically, foreign concerns have had higher productivity levels than domestic firms and in some industries, notably cars, inward investment has been central to their transformation. As a consequence, foreign affiliates' share of British manufacturing had risen to around a quarter by the early 1990s such that foreign companies dominate the automotive and computer industries especially. Besides serving the British market, US and more recently Japanese MNCs have located production in Britain as a convenient bridgehead into the European market. However, particularly since the liberalization of domestic financial services markets in the mid-1980s, Britain has attracted heavy inward FDI in financial services and a number of City firms have been taken over by foreign companies. Thus, although the City of London has retained its advantage as the premier financial centre in its time zone, British financial firms have lost competitiveness and lost ground to foreign MNCs operating from London.

For much of the postwar period France operated an industrial policy of encouraging national champions in a range of industries. A number of large MNCs emerged, operating in both OECD and developing countries; by 1992 the 300 largest French MNCs had over half of their sales and over a quarter of their assets overseas (Michalet, 1997). Although, as part of its industrial policy, the French government operated restrictions on inward FDI, some FDI was still permitted and even encouraged in certain sectors. In the mid-1980s France liberalized its FDI regime, abandoned much of the earlier industrial policy and actively encouraged non-EU MNCs to locate in France to give access to the European market. With rising inward FDI, foreign affiliates' share of French manufacturing has risen to over a quarter.

Although Germany has operated a broadly liberal policy towards FDI, inward FDI is low while outward FDI stocks are almost twice as large. The industrial strength of German firms and high wage levels have discouraged inward FDI so that foreign affiliates' share of domestic manufacturing remains low. By contrast, German MNCs have established extensive production overseas and have been leading investors in Eastern Europe in the 1990s.

The major manufacturing firms in Sweden are all MNCs, often of long standing. Swedish MNCs have invested mainly in other OECD countries. Policy towards outward FDI was liberalized in the 1970s, but policy towards inward FDI was liberalized only in the 1980s. Inward FDI and foreign affiliates' share of Swedish manufacturing have both risen.

Japan has very low shares of inward FDI and foreign production in the manufacturing sector. By comparison, Japanese MNCs have exploited their competitive advantages in cars and electronics through overseas production so that Japan has become a major source of FDI. Japanese firms initially grew by producing for the domestic market and exports; it was only in the 1970s that they relocated production abroad. Until liberalization in the 1980s inward FDI to Japan was heavily restricted; even after liberalization, the consequence of both internal and external pressure, inward FDI has remained low. The nature of share ownership can make it difficult for foreign firms to acquire Japanese companies and foreign firms have often found it difficult to penetrate the closed networks of producers and distributors in the Japanese economy. Although figures are subject to a considerable margin of error, they indicate that home MNCs account for around half of Japanese manufacturing value added, emphasizing their continued dominance of home production (Lipsey et al., 1995).

Table 5.10   Inward FDI in transition (former planned) economies, 1993

	Net FDI inflow (US$m)	As percentage of GNP	As percentage of gross domestic investment
Bulgaria	55	0.5	2.7
China	25,800	4.5	10.9
Czech Republic	950	3.4	20.0
Estonia	160	3.2	12.5
Hungary	2,349	6.9	34.4
Kazakhstan	150	0.6	1.8
Latvia	20	0.4	3.5
Lithuania	12	0.2	1.4
Moldova	14	0.3	4.3
Poland	1,715	2.0	12.4
Russian Federation	700	0.2	0.8
Slovenia	112	0.9	4.5
Ukraine	200	0.2	2.2
Uzbekistan	45	0.2	0.7
Vietnam	300	2.5	11.8

Source: Calculated from World Bank, 1995

Beyond these six SIACS, developing countries and transition economies have become increasingly significant sites for internationalized production. This is evident in, among other things, the number of foreign affiliates of MNCs located in developing countries (see table 5.3 above). It also reflects what was referred to in chapter 3 as the new global division of labour. But patterns of MNC involvement vary widely. Until quite recently foreign MNCs accounted for a negligible proportion of national output in a significant number of developing economies, including India. Among other Asian economies, only around 10 per cent of Korean and 20 per cent of Taiwanese manufacturing output is accounted for by foreign MNCs, a reflection in part of restrictions on inward FDI (see Lipsey et al., 1995). The shares for Hong Kong, Indonesia and Thailand are also similar. By comparison, in Malaysia foreign MNCs account for over 40 per cent of value added in manufacturing; in Singapore the proportion is around 70 per cent (see Lipsey et al., 1995).

Elsewhere there are also significant variations. The Chinese economy is in the process of a major transformation: whereas in the early 1980s foreign firms had virtually no domestic presence they now account for around 10 per cent of manufacturing value added, a share that is rising rapidly, and 19–29 per cent of the output of all private enterprises (Ramstetter, 1998); in the Guangdong province alone foreign MNC production probably amounts to at least a third of total output. For major Latin American economies the share of domestic manufacturing accounted for by foreign MNCs is probably around 30 per cent. Few estimates are available for Africa, but although MNCs may be important in particular industries, overall their share of output is probably low.

Although the transition economies account for a small (but growing) proportion of FDI stocks and flows, they have been incorporated rapidly into MNC production networks. As table 5.10 shows, FDI flows now make a significant contribution to investment

Table 5.11 Distribution of FDI stocks between primary, secondary and tertiary sectors, 1970–1994 (percentages)

	1970	1975	1980	1985	1990	1994
Developed country outward investment						
Primary	22.7	25.3	18.5	18.5	11.2	8.7
Secondary	45.2	45.0	43.8	38.7	38.7	37.4
Tertiary	31.4	27.7	37.7	42.8	50.1	53.6
Developed country inward investment						
Primary	16.2	12.1	6.7	9.2	9.1	–
Secondary	60.2	56.5	55.2	46.2	42.5	–
Tertiary	23.7	31.4	38.1	44.5	48.4	–
Developing country inward investment						
Primary	–	20.6	22.7	24.0	21.9	–
Secondary	–	55.9	43.6	49.6	48.6	–
Tertiary	–	23.5	22.7	26.4	29.5	–

Secondary refers to manufacturing generally; tertiary refers to services.
Sources: UNCTAD, 1993, p. 62; 1994 from OECD, 1996c, estimated from data for USA, Canada, France, Germany, Netherlands, Sweden, Switzerland, UK and Japan

in these countries; the figures for China and Vietnam in particular are probably significant underestimates. Indeed, these figures are noticeably higher than for most developing economies. In less than a decade European MNCs, especially in the automobile industry, have incorporated Eastern European economies into their production networks.

As noted previously, there are also significant (and increasing) levels of FDI outflows from developing countries and a significant number of parent MNCs based in these economies. Between 1993 and 1995 the foreign assets of the fifty largest MNCs based in developing countries increased by some 280 per cent compared to 30 per cent for the world's top hundred (almost exclusively OECD) MNCs (UNCTAD, 1997, p. 8). Patterns of global production are thus becoming more complex in respect of the geography of ownership and control.

These shifting patterns of stratification of international production reflect not only a more complex global division of labour but are also closely related to changing sectoral patterns of global production. Immediately after the Second World War the majority of FDI was concentrated in the primary product sector (Jones, 1996, p. 61). But, as table 5.11 shows, FDI in primary products has since tended to decline. As well as reflecting the general decline of primary production in the world economy, during the Cold War many developing countries nationalized raw material production. MNCs in these industries typically responded by concentrating on the refining and distribution of raw materials, although a number of large MNCs continue to dominate extractive or agricultural, as well as processing and distribution, operations.

By comparison, today MNCs account for the majority of the world's manufacturing exports. Given increased international sourcing from both affiliates and subcontractors, trade in intermediate products (unfinished goods) has risen as MNCs stretch the production process transnationally (see OECD, 1994a, ch. 5). MNCs are thereby creating a new global division of labour, through intrafirm trade, as production is organized worldwide to take advantage of lower production costs or particular national competitive conditions. In this regard MNCs have become increasingly significant to the manufactures export sectors of a number of NIEs (Blomström, 1990). Overseas affiliates of MNCs now account for 25 per cent or more of total exports from the G5 countries (the US, UK, Germany, France and Japan) (Julius, 1990). Moreover, even where exports are produced by SMEs, distribution and marketing arrangements with MNCs are often crucial in securing access to world markets (Perraton, 1998).

Although a significant proportion of FDI is concentrated in manufacturing, FDI in services has expanded enormously and now accounts for a growing proportion of international business activity and of FDI stocks. Most of this activity remains concentrated in the traditional areas of banking and trade, but it has grown recently in other sectors, including other financial and business services, data processing and tourism (Daniels, 1993; Dunning, 1993a, ch. 10). In part this is a product of the way MNCs have established an infrastructure for international trade in services. As MNCs operate abroad they require the provision of services at a standard equivalent to that in their 'home' country. This has encouraged the global expansion of accountancy, legal and corporate financial services. The enormous growth of international business activity in the services sector is also paralleled by a more limited expansion of international business activity in retailing and distribution. In all these respects the shifting sectoral balance of such activity distinguishes the contemporary era from earlier epochs.

5.4.5 The infrastructure and institutionalization of business globalization

Although international coordination of production had been made feasible by the telegraph and the telephone before the war, it remained limited. Over the last thirty years, communications technology has vastly improved and become significantly cheaper. Alongside this there have also been major advances in transport infrastructures such as shipping and containerization. The information and transport revolutions, together with innovations in management strategies, have transformed the ability of firms to organize production transnationally. MNCs have been at the forefront of those corporations exploiting new global infrastructures to organize international production within the firm itself.

Since the 1980s the information technology revolution, among other factors, has encouraged a plurality of modes of organizing international production beyond simply either the internal hierarchy of the traditional MNC, in which the home headquarters simply controls foreign subsidiaries, or arms-length competition between firms. Three main developments, not necessarily in order of importance, reflect this shift towards the growing significance of networks of international production. First, within many MNCs the management of transnational networks of production has shifted away from centralized control to less hierarchical forms of management granting affiliates greater autonomy and encouraging channels of two-way communication. The complexity of managing international chains of production, especially where affiliates adapt new technology and/or need to respond to changing market conditions, can make this a more effective international management strategy than a strict hierarchy (Ernst, 1997; Borrus and Zysman, 1997). Secondly, MNCs increasingly contract out business to SMEs; these may have lower costs and be more flexible, thus allowing MNCs to pass on the costs of adjustment to changing market conditions. Given MNCs' knowledge of global markets, their competitive advantage as processors of market information and organizers of markets may have increased relative to their advantage as organizers of production (see Casson, 1995). Thirdly, in a development dubbed 'alliance capitalism' by Dunning (1997), firms in the same industry are increasingly cooperating in a range of ventures. Joint ventures and a range of non-equity arrangements between firms in different countries have been common in the postwar period, but, as noted earlier, the number concluded annually has jumped in recent years from 1,760 in 1990 to 4,600 in 1995 (UNCTAD, 1997, p. 12). These include subcontracting relationships and franchising, as well as cooperative ventures to develop particular products and enter specific markets. These figures exclude strategic alliances (that is major cooperative ventures between firms in different countries to undertake R&D and thus develop technology together). The number of such alliances concluded annually rose from 280 in 1991 to 430 in 1993, although the rate of increase has since slowed (UNCTAD, 1997, p. 14). During the 1980s over 4,000 of these alliances were formed, predominately in the most technologically dynamic industries, with over half in biotechnology and information technology (OECD, 1996a, p. 45). Many of these alliances are not simply cross-border but intercontinental and therefore have a genuinely global dimension. For example, during the 1980s US MNCs concluded almost 600 strategic alliances with Japanese companies and over 900 with European companies (Ham and Mowery, 1997). The significance of strategic alliances is twofold. First, firms no longer simply confront each other as competitors but increasingly collaborate in order to develop their respective competitive advantages jointly. Secondly, firms can no longer simply rely on their own, or their home country's, technology base to generate competitive advantage and increasingly have to operate globally to achieve it.

But it is not simply large MNCs which have exploited the information and transport revolutions, for locally based SMEs have done so too, with the aim of securing larger markets for their products or minimizing production costs. As Castells notes:

> the strategic aim of firms, large and small, is to sell wherever they can throughout the world, either directly or via their linkage with networks that operate in the world market. And there are indeed, to a large extent, thanks to new communication and transportation technologies, channels and opportunities to sell everywhere. (1996, p. 95)

Some SMEs are incorporated into either producer-driven global networks, in which large MNCs centrally organize production by subcontracting components manufacture across the globe (as in automobiles), or buyer-driven global networks (as with Nike, Benetton), in which

> large retailers, brand-named merchandisers and trading companies, play the pivotal role in setting up decentralized production networks in a variety of exporting countries, typically located in the Third World [where] production is generally carried out by independent Third World factories that make finished goods (rather than components or parts) under original . . . specifications . . . supplied by the buyers and branded companies that design the goods. (Gereffi, 1994, p. 97)

But while those SMEs locked into global production networks have no direct control over them, new modes of communication have encouraged cross-border networking between SMEs themselves through the establishment of cooperative ventures in several sectors and the creation of market niches (Castells, 1996, p. 160; O'Doherty, 1995). These developments have contributed to the emergence of a 'global manufacturing system in which production capacity is dispersed to an unprecedented number of developing as well as industrialized countries' (Gereffi, 1994, p. 25). Whether this represents a new mode of capitalist production, as Castells and Gray among others argue, is a matter of intense debate (Lash and Urry, 1994; Castells, 1996; Gray, 1998). It is, however, undeniable that infrastructural conditions have facilitated a globalization of the business enterprise beyond the confines of the giant MNC.

Unlike in trade or finance, a coherent international regime governing MNCs and international production has not emerged in the postwar period. Attempts by developing countries within the UN to draw up codes of conduct for MNCs foundered in the 1970s as a consequence of opposition from OECD states. Consequently restrictions on FDI remain and foreign firms are often subject to different rules from domestic ones. Countries operate restrictions on foreign firms' access to key areas of their economies, by barring them altogether or by placing limits on levels of foreign ownership. New FDI may be subject to review and only permitted on the say-so of national authorities. Countries may differ in the rules governing foreign acquisitions of domestic firms, especially with hostile takeovers. They may impose operational requirements on foreign firms, such as requiring them to use a certain proportion of locally produced inputs, employ a certain number of locally recruited employees or reach certain export targets. Tax systems may effectively discriminate against foreign firms, or favour some where incentives are used to attract inward FDI.

As noted, Britain, Germany and the USA operated broadly liberal policies towards FDI in the postwar period in comparison with the more restrictive policies of other OECD states. But since the 1980s, domestic FDI regimes have been liberalized more widely (Safarian, 1993). OECD countries have generally abandoned earlier regimes for screening inward FDI and developing countries have removed many of the earlier restrictions. Domestic pressure for liberalization has been reinforced by pressure from multilateral and regional institutions (the EU Single European Market programme, NAFTA, APEC and the OECD continue to press for liberalization). Moreover, governments have shifted towards the view that they cannot afford to forgo the benefits of inward FDI.

Among developing countries policy towards FDI and MNCs has altered considerably during the postwar period. Earlier on, while some actively welcomed inward FDI, others placed a variety of restrictions on MNCs. Besides limiting FDI in certain areas, developing countries often imposed operational requirements on MNCs. Moreover, there were a number of significant nationalizations and expropriations in developing countries in the 1950s and 1960s, largely in the primary sector industries. But nationalizations and expropriations have declined to negligible levels since the growing significance of manufacturing FDI means that nationalization would deprive an economy of vital inflows of new technology.

Although there are no systematic measures of the degree of openness to FDI, the quantitative and qualitative evidence points to a clear trend towards the liberalization of domestic foreign investment controls during the 1980s but especially the 1990s

(UNCTAD, 1996, ch. 5; Safarian, 1993, ch. 12). Among developing countries and emerging market economies liberalization has been incremental but still substantial, with over a hundred countries making their FDI regime more open in the period 1991–5. In the absence of a global regime for FDI, bilateral investment agreements, as noted, have become a key mechanism for facilitating international production by clarifying tax rules and regulations. In 1996 alone, 182 such treaties were concluded – in excess of three a week – bringing the total number of such treaties to 1,513 in 1998 (UNCTAD, 1997, p. 11; 1998). The pattern of these treaties has changed too, as more developing countries seek to host FDI. OECD states now account for 62 per cent of such treaties compared with 83 per cent in 1989. Moreover, in 1996 a third of all such treaties were concluded solely among developing countries (UNCTAD, 1997, p. 11). In part such developments reflect the way developing countries have been under pressure from the World Bank and other multilateral agencies to liberalize FDI controls.

The institutional push for liberalization of FDI has come from the major OECD governments, from the OECD itself and from within regional arrangements such as NAFTA, EU and APEC. Membership of the OECD requires governments to abide by explicit codes and standards with respect to foreign investment which involve according 'national treatment to international investors' and enacting 'transparent, liberal and stable foreign investment rules' (OECD, 1998, p. 1). With the enactment of NAFTA, the USA's liberal FDI rules have been generalized to Canada and Mexico. APEC too is developing a common set of liberal FDI rules. Among European countries the picture still varies; EU legislation ensures free capital movements among member countries and places some limits on the use of subsidies and other incentives to FDI, while with the decline in active industrial policies, restrictive measures towards inward FDI beyond subsidies and similar incentives have been all but been abandoned.

Among developing countries there has been a marked shift towards liberal FDI regimes. With the exception of Brazil, most Latin American economies have inaugurated liberal policies, with limited screening of investment projects and limited restrictions on multinational operations. In the aftermath of the 1997 crisis virtually all East Asian countries have pursued liberal policies towards inward FDI. China, in particular, has shifted from virtually complete control to a more open regime. The position varies widely among African countries, but many have removed restrictions and requirements on MNCs during the 1990s. Among transition economies, particularly the more advanced, many restrictions on FDI have been reduced or eliminated, although in some cases there remains a strong preference for joint ventures with domestic firms rather than wholly owned foreign subsidiaries.

Although there is no formal multilateral regime for FDI, elements of a global regime are emerging. Negotiations on a Multilateral Agreement on Investment, eliminating virtually all national controls on FDI, were postponed indefinitely in late 1998. Nevertheless, the OECD continues to press for greater transparency and international harmonization of FDI regulations. The liberalization of controls on MNC activity is also pursued through the WTO. In the late 1990s it was responsible for implementing the GATS (General Agreement on Trade and Services) agreement which seeks to partially liberalize services trade, thus enhancing the position of MNCs in the services industry. The WTO agreement on trade in intellectual property rights (TRIPS) enhanced multinationals' rights over global exploitation of patents, trademarks and similar sources of competitive advantage. The agreement limiting trade-related investment measures

(TRIMS) restricts the ability of governments to impose performance requirements on MNCs. In addition, landmark agreements liberalizing trade in financial services and tele-communications have been agreed and these will have significant consequences for MNC activities and investment in these sectors (see chapters 4 and 1 above respectively).

Beyond these multilateral measures there is also increasing pressure for coopera-tion, coordination, and even harmonization of national rules for business competition and antitrust policy. Given the intensity of MNC activity and the existence of global production networks, any domestic measures which potentially restrict business com-petition are subject to global scrutiny, either within multilateral agencies, such as the OECD or WTO, or regional bodies like the EU or NAFTA. One consequence of this is that national competition policy is increasingly subject to external surveillance. It is now commonplace for American or European competition authorities to intervene, either diplomatically or legally, in what might before have been regarded as purely domestic issues concerning major business mergers or acquisitions which could poten-tially undermine the competitive position of their own industries or corporations. In the celebrated case of the Boeing-McDonnell Douglas merger in 1996–7, US competi-tion authorities sought the tacit approval of the EU Commission (which sanctioned the merger with some provisos) in order to prevent any retaliatory action in the form of restrictions on the new company's business activities in the EU. Such high-profile cases have encouraged moves towards a global regime for business competition and, at the very least, more intensive international surveillance of 'domestic' business practices and competition rules.

These developments imply a major shift towards equal treatment of both foreign and domestic firms. Sometimes the latter are placed at a disadvantage as governments actively try to attract inward FDI. Many developing countries have established free trade zones in which normal domestic regulatory requirements do not apply; as more countries have liberalized there has been a shift to offering tax holidays and other inducements. OECD countries, at both the national and subnational levels, also offer a range of preferential tax arrangements, outright subsidies and similar inducements to attract new inward FDI. As a consequence, the pressures for ensuring a level 'global playing field' have forced governments to take a greater interest in the domestic regu-lations and policies of competitors, in all areas from taxation to health standards, which potentially may put their businesses at a competitive disadvantage in the global market-place. In the process, domestic policies which impact on business in one country acquire an international dimension, whether intentional or not.

5.5 MNCs and Global Production Networks

Firms engage in international production because they possess a specific competitive advantage that is best exploited in this way. The advantage may be a patented product or technique, but may also include management techniques and intangible assets in the skills and expertise of the firm or its personnel. But even so, firms do not have to produce abroad even with such advantages: foreign markets can be served by exports or by licensing the technology to overseas producers; or the production process can be subcontracted to independent companies, possibly licensed to use the firm's techno-logy. However, the development of global production networks necessarily involves the strategic organization of transnational transactions within the firm or among groups of firms rather than through the market mechanism. Although economic globalization is often understood simply as the spread of global markets, the growth of MNCs and global production networks represents something rather different: the growing transnational organization of production and distribution within and among firms instead of through markets. International markets are not, therefore, perfect: if they were, MNCs and global production networks would not exist. As a consequence the costs of doing business for MNCs are significantly lower if they organize economic activity within the firm, or through networks of firms, rather than through market relationships.

Restrictions on international trade, as well as transport costs, induce firms to locate and produce overseas instead of exporting to foreign markets. MNCs may organize production internationally to take advantage of lower cost conditions abroad for particular stages of the production process. But the strategic advantages of organizing international production within the firm, rather than sourcing from independent producers, arise from two factors: first, it helps to prevent the diffusion of any corporate technological advantage to potential competitors; and, second, to the extent that an MNC's competitive advantage rests not simply on codified knowledge but also on a range of tacit knowledge and expertise within the firm, the optimal means of exploiting this is through intrafirm overseas production rather than licensed production or subcontracting abroad.

5.5.1   Global competition and the globalization of business organization

MNCs have grown in the postwar period because they have exploited their competitive advantages internationally. In some cases these competitive advantages derive from economies of scale and scope, superior management techniques and/or worldwide sales networks. But the key source of competitive advantage for MNCs in the postwar period has been technological innovation (Cantwell, 1989; Clegg, 1987). MNCs tend to be among the most innovative companies and are heavily represented in the most technologically dynamic industries. They are responsible for the majority of private R&D expenditure. Moreover, technological innovation has aided the process of 'slicing up the value chain' (see chapter 3) whereby a single production process can be parcelled out and distributed around the globe. The expansion of MNCs thus reflects both their capacity to innovate and their capacity to exploit this internationally.

However, while MNCs dominate the global production and distribution of many goods and services, their technological and organizational advantages have not made them impregnable to competition. In a range of sectors, from electronics to garments, some SMEs have a capacity for continual innovation and flexibility which creates an environment of 'hypercompetition' in which established MNCs are placed on the defensive (D'Aveni, 1998). Competitive advantages thus no longer reside simply in products and technologies but also depend on the speed with which innovation takes place and new products (styles, etc.) can be produced and distributed (see Borrus and Zysman, 1997). This speeding up of global competition has been enhanced greatly by the 'informatics' revolution (Castells, 1996; D'Aveni, 1998). Such factors have encouraged the growth of producer- and buyer-driven cross-border networks of production and distribution which allow 'small and medium businesses to link up with major corporations, forming networks that are able to innovate and adapt relentlessly' (Castells 1996, p. 165).

The globalization of business thus depends on the innovatory capacity of firms and their ability to organize efficiently cross-border production and distribution networks with the aid of advances in both communications technology and management techniques. If, as in the past, multinational production were undertaken simply to circumvent trade barriers, it might be expected that its expansion would have slowed, or even reversed, because trade restrictions and transport costs have fallen dramatically. Instead, it has continued to expand, suggesting that trade barriers alone no longer explain the growth of transnational production; rather, what is more crucial is the capacity of firms for technological and product innovation.

As technological innovation becomes more critical to MNCs' competitive advantages, there are increased incentives to organize production and distribution within the firm or geographically dispersed networks of firms orchestrated by MNCs. Dunning (1993a, ch. 12) argues that this is creating a novel situation in that intrafirm transactions are becoming more significant relative to market transactions. Herein lies a curious paradox, for just as economic globalization has contributed to the evolution of global markets, business globalization has encouraged the substitution of market transactions by intra- (and inter-) firm networks. If this is the case it might be expected that the share of intrafirm trade in world trade would rise as transactions within MNCs rise. As noted above, although intrafirm trade is high, it appears to have remained stable as a proportion of total trade over the past decade. But since trade has risen relative to world income this would tend to imply that intrafirm trade has risen relative to world output.

Although individual MNCs vary in their capacity to organize intrafirm production and trade, MNCs collectively supply markets throughout the world and produce from sites across the globe. Even though individual MNCs do not supply every single national market or source from every country, collectively their activities have generated a structural shift towards greater global competition because of the expansion of global production systems.

Sceptics tend to doubt there has been such a shift. They note that even the largest MNCs often have the majority of their production, sales, assets, profits and R&D facilities in their home country (see Hirst and Thompson, 1996b, ch. 4), and conclude that 'global corporations are national firms with international operations' (Hu, 1992). Other authors, notably Porter (1990), accept that MNCs now compete globally but argue that they remain rooted in their home country economic systems and cultures; in this view, they derive their competitive advantage principally from this national base and operate global strategies to meet the competition. Stopford and Strange (1991), among others, argue that while this view captures important aspects of multinationals' postwar growth, a national base is becoming insufficient to maintain a corporate competitive advantage. Over time companies abroad have acquired their own technological advantages. Other sources of competitive advantage, such as superior management techniques, also diffuse over time. Various authors – including Dicken (1998), Dunning (1993a) and Howells and Wood (1993) – argue that MNCs now no longer simply derive their competitive advantage from their home base, but are increasingly tapping into sources of competitive advantage worldwide and, as a consequence, organizing their production on a global basis. Their ability to produce in a range of countries and to realize competitive advantages generated in different locations gives them a global vision and a global competitive advantage. In the hyperglobalization view of authors such as Julius (1990), Ohmae (1990) and Reich (1991), MNCs are 'footloose', readily moving between countries, shifting production and tapping into sources of national competitive advantage to maximize their profits, often at the expense of an immobile workforce.

Two central questions flow from these conflicting views. First, do any of these views adequately explain the present pattern of international production? Second, are MNCs still best understood as national companies with overseas operations in which their competitive advantage is derived solely or primarily from their home base? Below we examine the operation of MNCs in four key industrial sectors, delivering a set of answers to these questions that is more complex than any of these approaches suggest.

5.5.2   Global production networks: sectoral comparisons

Some insight into these questions can be provided by a comparison of the differences between, and the nature of, the organization of global production in key industrial sectors. This section offers such an examination of four industries: automobiles, electronics, chemicals and textiles. Together these sectors account for around half of the industrial FDI stocks of the major investing economies, that is, France, Germany, Japan, Netherlands, UK and US (OECD, 1996c). International sourcing, distribution and overseas sales are strategically important in all these sectors, while FDI flows contribute significantly to capital formation in all these industries. Textiles and clothing account for only about 2 per cent of world FDI stocks, but this is one of the most geographically dispersed industries, and one in which global networks of production and distribution are central. By comparison the chemicals industry accounts for over 20 per cent of industrial FDI stocks, while the electrical equipment and motor vehicle industries each account for over 10 per cent.

The car industry

The car industry was arguably the lead industry during the postwar economic boom. US producers, such as Ford and General Motors, had established operations, but the postwar period witnessed their unprecedented international expansion, into Europe particularly. Protection of national markets and transport costs made FDI the obvious tool for serving these markets as US firms replicated mass production assembly lines in Europe and elsewhere. Although the big firms succeeded in gaining significant market shares, within protected European markets national competitors emerged, often championed by their governments.

In the 1970s Japanese producers made competitive inroads into both the US and European markets. Their competitive advantage derived from innovative management techniques known broadly as 'lean production'. These techniques reduced costs and raised quality, while also reducing the lead time for introducing new models. Initially,

Japanese producers competed through exports: they achieved flexibility in part through close subcontracting relations with components firms and this encouraged a strategy of geographically concentrated production located near to supplying firms. During the 1980s import restrictions in the US and Europe induced Japanese car producers to internationalize and locate production in these markets. Japanese MNCs initially used high levels of imported inputs but gradually developed greater linkages with suppliers in host countries. Increased subcontracting to component suppliers also reflected moves by Japanese components producers into the European market. US and European producers responded to Japanese competition by adopting many of their management techniques and engaged in considerable corporate restructuring.

Internationalized production and falling barriers to trade have induced global competition in the car industry (OECD, 1996a, ch. 4). Among the leading car producers at least 40 per cent of their production is sold abroad either through exports or foreign affiliates' production. International sourcing accounts for between a quarter and a third of all component manufacture and intrafirm trade accounts for the majority of trade in this sector. US firms have developed the most geographically extensive networks of production as a cost-reducing strategy, so that the production process in Europe, for example, is now stretched across several countries. However, the dream of a world car, with one model being sold worldwide and production organized globally, remains unrealized – although Ford has come close with its Mondeo range. By comparison European firms have less geographically extensive networks, but they have increased their overseas presence through reorganizing production processes across Europe, including Eastern Europe. There has been considerable cross-border consolidation within the industry, notably in Britain, as foreign MNCs have taken over domestic producers. European firms have also expanded their global reach through joint ventures and other collaborative arrangements with East Asian producers. Although Japanese corporations traditionally have organized sourcing of parts as geographically close to their assembly plants as possible, cost pressures have forced them to source internationally from affiliates and subcontractors abroad: Japanese firms now operate networks of production linking Europe and South East Asia (UNCTAD, 1996, pp. 100–2).

The electronics industry

Electronics was one of the first industries in which stages of the production process were diffused to developing countries. Not only is the production process spread internationally, but there are also high levels of intercontinental trade and firms compete in markets worldwide. In the computer and allied industries particularly, high levels of competition in respect of prices and product innovation produce hypercompetition. This, in turn, induces firms to sustain competitive strategies, but also cross-border collaborative arrangements with other firms (Ernst, 1997; Borrus and Zysman, 1997).

There are important common features between the computer industry and that part of the electronics industry focused on consumer products such as televisions, VCRs, etc.; there are also some key differences. Most East Asian and North American computer exports are to other regions and probably most trade in computers is intrafirm (OECD, 1996a, ch. 3). The industry is dominated by US and Japanese firms, with

European firms holding much smaller shares. Initially, US firms invested in Europe but from the 1960s East Asia and Latin America became more important as the labour-intensive parts of the manufacturing process were relocated to these regions; although the computer industry was among the most technologically advanced, stages of the assembly process could be parcelled out to production facilities abroad. In the 1970s Japanese producers achieved notable competitive success and came to dominate sectors of the industry; as with the car industry, their innovative management techniques were crucial. Until the mid-1980s Japanese firms were much more domestically oriented than US firms: they retained a greater share of production domestically and sourced more from domestic firms as they derived a competitive advantage from producing at home. In response to Japanese competition, US firms not only increased their attempts to reduce costs through overseas production, but also intensified their involvement with Asian suppliers. By contrast, European producers performed poorly in the face of this competition, despite government support.

In the 1980s Japanese electronics giants substantially increased their overseas investment, with market-seeking FDI in Europe and North America and more extensive production in East Asia in the wake of the yen appreciation and rising labour costs at home. As a consequence a hierarchy of production organization has developed across Asia. The most labour-intensive production processes have migrated from the leading economies, notably Korea, to less advanced economies, including China. Korea has become a significant producer of finished electronic products in its own right and poses a competitive challenge to existing producers. Production networks have spread wider among East Asian countries and MNCs in Europe, while the US has deepened its networks with suppliers in this region. For firms in this industry, managing complex supply chains is a key source of competitive advantage.

Ernst (1997) argues that the industry is shifting from 'partial' to 'systemic' globalization. Firms confront intense competitive pressure in relation to prices and product development and this has led to the reorganization of their operations both geographically and functionally. As noted above, coordination of the production process is central to a company's competitiveness in this industry. Parts of the production process have very high economies of scale, so that in PC production in particular, firms have attempted to rationalize their operations by concentrating on these activities (together with R&D), while outsourcing other stages of the production process to low-cost producers. However, rather than simply shifting production completely outside the firm, MNCs have developed deep and extensive relationships with supplying firms – producer-driven production networks – even to the extent of blurring ownership distinctions between the firm and its suppliers. Moreover, product development requires not only central R&D but also continuous innovation and improvement throughout the firm. It is through intensive two-way relationships between producers, within these producer-driven networks, that companies are able to sustain continuous product improvements (see Borrus and Zysman, 1997). Shifting from hierarchical organizational structures towards networks among branches of an MNC, and/or between it and its suppliers and customers, provides greater flexibility in production and makes continuous product innovation much more feasible as well as more economical. Production networks such as these represent a new mode of corporate organization: the network enterprise (Castells, 1996, p. 168).

The competitive pressures facing MNCs to achieve several objectives – low prices, product development and rapid diffusion to the marketplace – impose conflicting demands on them. One result of this is a high level of strategic alliances and other forms of collaborative arrangements between firms, with about half of these being between companies located on different continents (OECD, 1996a, ch. 3). In this sector MNCs increasingly cannot rely solely on their home base to generate competitive advantage, but also need to draw on overseas networks, collaboration with overseas firms and overseas R&D investment most especially for new product development. Although internationalization of R&D in the computer industry is a recent phenomenon it is becoming more significant within and between the world's major economic regions (Archibugi and Michie, 1997a).

By comparison consumer electronics firms are more geographically concentrated, although the industry has witnessed a considerable transnationalization of production (OECD, 1996a, ch. 5). Calculating intrafirm trade is difficult in this sector but it does not appear to be high, only around 10 per cent for US firms. This may be because US firms have made greater use of subcontracting whereas European and Japanese MNCs focus production in overseas affiliates and consequently have higher intrafirm trade (see Borrus and Zysman, 1997). Standardization of production and rising skill levels in some developing countries have led to over half the world's television production being located outside the OECD. The industry is characterized by high scale economies in assembly so that assembly is geographically concentrated but with geographically dispersed sourcing of component parts from low cost producers. Japanese and, latterly, Korean producers have established production networks in East Asia, with assembly in OECD countries and component production, by affiliates or subcontractors, in lower wage economies. Japanese firms have also located production in Europe and the USA to ensure market access. Asian and European producers have shifted towards global strategies for production, distribution and R&D. US producers have lost ground heavily, such that the majority have been taken over by Asian and European companies so today most production in the US is undertaken by foreign firms; technological innovation within the US, though, remains important so that major producers have R&D establishments located there. European producers have fared better, but even in Europe imports and foreign affiliates together account for the majority of sales of consumer electronics.

The chemical and pharmaceutical industries

International production in the chemical industry dates from before the First World War. During the interwar period the chemicals industry was cartelized, but since the Second World War it has experienced intense global competition. The industry is divided into industrial (around a half of the total), agricultural and pharmaceutical products (around a third); petrochemicals products make up much of the first two categories. The industry has grown over the postwar period and now accounts for over 10 per cent of manufacturing; three-quarters or more of chemicals production and sales are in the OECD countries. Petrochemicals industries are characterized by high economies of scale and relatively standardized technology; some pharmaceuticals production also has high economies of scale, but innovative pharmaceuticals production is mostly characterized by high levels of R&D expenditure.

US petrochemicals firms rapidly established multinational operations after the war and the largest pursued global strategies of distribution, organizing their production accordingly. ICI had already acquired a strong international presence, largely based on trading within the British Empire; other European firms initially developed domestic production and expanded internationally while retaining an important home base. With high scale economies in petrochemicals, firms concentrated production in a few locations and served markets by exporting. Even with relatively standardized technology MNCs generally preferred to concentrate production geographically, rather than licensing it, in order to preserve technological advantages. Since the major markets are located in OECD economies and wages are a relatively small proportion of total costs there has been little economic incentive to shift production to developing countries as in other industries. By the 1980s increased competition, together with declining markets and rising costs, led to falling rates of return; these provoked a significant rationalization of the industry so that it is becoming more highly concentrated (Chapman, 1991, ch. 10).

In comparison, multinational production is much more common in the pharmaceutical industry, in large measure because of segmentation between markets arising from heavy demand from localized health services, which is best met locally. Accordingly, production is highly internationalized; overseas affiliates account for up to half of all pharmaceuticals sales and the majority of production in OECD states (OECD, 1996a, p. 49; Ballance et al., 1992, ch. 3). But pharmaceutical products require enormous research and development expenditures. This is heavily concentrated geographically, with over half of total expenditure located in the G5 countries plus Switzerland. For much of the postwar period pharmaceuticals reflects the logic of companies generating globally competitive products from their national base. Increasingly, however, this is proving to be insufficient. Although the majority of MNCs' R&D is in their home country, both European and US pharmaceutical MNCs have established significant overseas research facilities; Japanese MNCs tend to concentrate R&D at home but they are increasingly forming commercial arrangements with foreign firms for technology and product generation (OECD, 1996a, ch. 2). Since the 1980s there have been several major cross-border mergers and acquisitions by pharmaceutical firms. Cross-border strategic alliances are also particularly high in the chemicals and biotechnology sectors (UNCTAD, 1994, p. 139). The high costs of new product development are creating a more highly concentrated industry but one in which production is organized globally.

The textiles and clothing industries

The textiles and clothing industries are among the most widespread across the globe. Since production technology is relatively easy to acquire and operate, given low scale economies, these industries are often important in developing countries' manufactured exports. FDI is relatively insignificant in these sectors even though large firms, through buyer-driven business networks, often dominate the distribution of finished goods (Dicken, 1998, ch. 9; OECD, 1996a, ch. 8). Wages form a high proportion of total costs,

Box 5.2 The Benetton model

Originally a small family-owned knitwear company, Benetton has expanded since the 1980s into a significant multinational business enterprise with 5,000 franchised stores in all the world's major markets. Controlled directly from its central HQ in the Veneto region of Italy, the company utilizes advanced communications systems to monitor and manage its global distribution network. Similarly products are manufactured by small independent firms in Europe and elsewhere, organized as a transnational production network directed from Benetton's HQ. The company represents a curious combination of hierarchical control through horizontal networks of distribution and production.

Source: Extract from Castells, 1996, p. 162

but demand conditions can vary rapidly with changes in fashion. Textile and clothing firms in developed countries have responded to this by subcontracting stages of the production process to independent firms, often in developing regions (see box 5.2). Initially these producers were in nearby countries: North Africa and Mediterranean countries for European firms, the Caribbean and Latin America for US firms and East Asia for Japanese firms. Subsequently, sourcing has become much more dispersed so that firms source across continents: East Asia, including China, has become a key global supplier (Taplin, 1994; Korzeniewicz, 1994).

Global sourcing not only provides SMEs or MNCs within OECD states with access to low cost producers but also ensures flexibility of supply. These buyer-driven business networks enable MNCs or SMEs to pass on the risks of changing market conditions to their subcontractors. Although only a significant minority of production in this sector is controlled by MNCs, many still play a key role in supplying expertise and organizing marketing and distribution networks.

5.5.3 The globalization of business: organizational forms

Since the 1980s, as the above discussion indicates, the global organization of production and distribution within key industrial sectors has intensified. MNCs have been central to this development. US firms typically have the most extensive and long-standing overseas operations, although this also applies to some European producers. Many European firms have developed their multinational production from their home base, and this is true of virtually all Japanese producers. Expansion overseas to avoid actual or potential protection has been a key factor in inducing reluctant Japanese and other companies to produce overseas. But MNCs have not simply expanded overseas to ensure market access: they have done so to rationalize the corporate production process through transnationalization.

This highlights a central point. MNCs have moved towards establishing transnational business networks incorporating their affiliates, subcontractors, customers and other firms in the industry (Howells and Wood, 1993; UNCTAD, 1994, ch. 3). But these producer- and buyer-driven networks imply some dispersion of power and decision-making such that the classic representation of the MNC (and multinational production) as a vertically integrated, hierarchical structure no longer reflects the tremendous diversity of existing organizational forms (Ruigrok and Tulder, 1995; Borrus and Zysman, 1997). Ruigrok and Tulder provide a useful typology for categorizing the organizational forms of global production and distribution networks (1995, ch. 8). Adapting their typology, it is possible to identify two organizational forms which represent opposite ends of a spectrum: dispersed production with high central control and dispersed production with low central control. In practice MNCs (and global production networks) often fall somewhere between these extremes.

Geographically dispersed production under low central control refers to transnational production systems in which the production units have considerable autonomy. Historically this involved stand-alone production, that is, firms established overseas plants to service local markets but without these operations being integrated into transnational production systems. This is not simply a device to reach protected markets since where demand conditions vary significantly between countries it can be an effective strategy for supplying foreign markets. Services, in particular, are often delivered locally. Rather than maintaining strong central control some MNCs are moving to more diffuse systems of corporate management. For overseas operations to function effectively it may be necessary to allow them greater autonomy rather than impose centralized control; this particularly applies to the R&D divisions, but can apply more widely. Furthermore, in many sectors MNCs have moved away from direct ownership and control and towards greater use of subcontracting relationships with (formally) independent supplier firms.

Geographically dispersed production under strong central control entails organizing the production process on a global scale as a centrally coordinated strategy. This accords with popular perceptions of large MNCs controlling worldwide networks of production but it no longer necessarily occurs through direct ownership of foreign subsidiaries. This organizational form is to some extent common in mineral extraction and agriculture. Some manufacturing assembly is organized with the strict hierarchy of the production line operating at the transnational level. It may also be reflected in the services sector as well as manufacturing: for example, US firms use data inputting offices in Central America and the Caribbean, and European firms do likewise as far afield as South Asia. It also covers cases where MNCs produce a good or service locally but retain central control over production and quality; for many internationally recognized goods or services the trademark (such as Benetton) is intended as a guarantee of consistent quality the world over.

Alongside these distinct organizational forms it is possible also to identify corporate strategies of global switching and global focusing (Howells and Wood, 1993, ch. 10). Global switching refers to the capacity of MNCs to switch production between sites internationally in response to changing market conditions. Global focusing, by contrast, refers to the corporate strategy of concentrating production in a small number of sites perceived to have the strongest long-term advantage. Since the 1980s many MNCs with significant numbers of subcontractors have sought to rationalize by developing deeper relations with a smaller number; by contrast firms with a limited number of subcontracting relationships have tended to expand them. Both strategies are essentially ideal types, but they focus attention on the strategic choices facing firms in responding to the challenges and opportunities of global competition.

5.5.4 'Footloose' MNCs and global production

Whatever their organizational form, geography still matters: MNCs cannot simply locate anywhere or everywhere. In most sectors access to major markets is both an important constraint on location and a major incentive for multinational production; in this respect the globalization of production and distribution has its limits. Production cannot be simply shifted or reorganized at will. The skills and infrastructure base of national economies still constrain the capacity of firms to switch production. Nevertheless, business has become more mobile over time.

For MNCs, subcontracting rather than production through wholly owned subsidiaries can provide the most economically efficient mechanism for diversifying and adjusting global production since it entails the least loss of sunk costs. It is therefore not surprising that the most rapid geographical dispersion of industry to low cost producers has been achieved through subcontracting in the textile and clothing industries operating with standardized technology. Nevertheless, as the earlier discussion has highlighted, significant segments of the production process in many sectors have been dispersed beyond OECD countries, initially to NIEs and subsequently to less advanced economies. Further, although OECD countries remain the focus for the majority of FDI, MNCs are shifting their investments between them in response to changing economic conditions.

However, if the globalization of production is assumed to be synonymous with capital mobility ('footloose' capital), then clearly it is relative not absolute: firms have to produce somewhere and the advantages of familiarity, agglomeration and economies of scale necessarily generate a certain geographical concentration. Production is rarely shifted solely in response to changing costs, some of which can be hedged against. Moreover, while the capacity of MNCs and SMEs to shift production abroad has increased over time, such mobility is constrained. Nevertheless, it has become a significant bargaining chip in negotiations with governments (national or local) concerning new investment. In this sense the perception of more mobile production may be more important than the actual behaviour of business.

One significant constraint on mobility, sceptics often argue, is the reliance of many businesses on the competitive advantages generated in their home country. Although this is a view which has much validity, such advantages can nevertheless be exploited globally by MNCs and so diffused abroad. Cantwell (1997) notes that the introduction and global diffusion of technological innovations have speeded up with greater global competition and more internationalized production. Although corporate R&D bases have historically been heavily concentrated in MNC home countries, national innovation systems increasingly appear insufficient by themselves to generate competitive advantage (Cantwell, 1997; Mowery and Oxley, 1997). International networks of technological innovation are thus becoming more significant. More and more, MNCs are attempting to tap into overseas innovation clusters, both through direct investment and cooperation or collaboration with overseas MNCs and firms. Innovatory capacity is now a significant determinant of inward FDI into developed countries (Narula, 1996, ch. 4). Consequently MNCs are not just diversifying production but also their R&D operations to sustain innovation and a competitive edge. This diversification of R&D still tends to be highly geographically concentrated within OECD states (Archibugi and Michie, 1997a). Nevertheless many MNCs are less reliant on their home base than was previously the case.

The constraints on the geographical mobility of industrial capital are perhaps more apparent in the regionalization of production, distribution and FDI. But though there is some regional clustering of production networks and FDI within the world economy, this is complementary, rather than contrary, to the globalization of business and production. For, as noted previously, FDI flows between the triad of NAFTA, the EU and Asia-Pacific represent a significant globalization of business activity. This expansion of transregional production and distribution networks reinforces the interlocking nature of business activity within, and across, these three key economic regions. In this respect the regionalization and globalization of production can be judged mutually reinforcing tendencies. This was demonstrated signally in the East Asian economic crisis of the late 1990s in so far as the interlocking nature of production and distribution networks in a number of sectors meant that manufacturing firms and businesses throughout Europe and America had to adjust production to accommodate rapidly changing economic circumstances in the region. Such crises demonstrate that even though the mobility of industrial capital is constrained (relative to finance capital) the capacity of MNCs to adjust and reorganize production in an era of more flexible production systems is considerable and has significant repercussions for national economic management.

5.6 Historical Forms of Business Globalization

It is sometimes claimed that FDI has only just attained levels comparable with the classical Gold Standard era (cf Dunning, 1988; UNCTAD, 1994, p. 30). Although this may be the case for a small number of OECD and developing economies, it is a somewhat misleading claim for four reasons (see Wilkins, 1994):

- First, as noted previously, contemporary estimates of FDI stock probably understate their real value.
- Second, at the turn of the century, the capacity of business to organize production internationally was limited, such that most transnational business activity was in primary products, merchandise trade and finance rather than production.
- Third, production and management technologies were not widely diffused in this earlier period since the economics of empire sustained a clear international division of labour between North and South.
- Fourth, measures of FDI by themselves provide only limited evidence of the magnitude of international production. As noted, FDI represents only a fraction of total investment in overseas production (25 per cent in 1996 according to UNCTAD estimates) while it also fails to capture the growth of new organizational forms of global production and distribution (such as subcontracting and strategic alliances) not involving ownership of subsidiaries overseas.

By comparison with earlier epochs of business globalization the contemporary phase (see grid 5.1) is both more extensive and more intensive as measured in terms of FDI, numbers and size of MNCs, subsidiaries, etc. As Gopinath notes, today 'production capacity is dispersed among an unprecedented number of developing and industrialized countries' (1997, p. 1). Although before 1914 there were significant FDI flows relative to national economic activity, these are comparable, if not higher, today. While investment is concentrated in developed OECD states, the 1990s have nevertheless witnessed a major wave of investment into hitherto closed economies, such as China and Eastern Europe, and many developing countries have become more open to and attractive locations for FDI (UNCTAD, 1997). Given the emergence of worldwide production and distribution networks, the impact of business globalization also reaches into critical areas of the industrial base of most economies. For MNCs and the production networks they control tend to operate in the most technically advanced sectors of economies, sectors vital to wealth creation and national economic security.

Significant amounts of both inward and outward investment flows among OECD economies are now in the services sector. The shift of FDI towards services is a further distinctive feature of the contemporary epoch. By comparison, in the classical Gold Standard era, international business tended to be concentrated in the primary sector. Although still highly concentrated in OECD economies the spatial pattern of FDI and global production is changing as transition and developing economies become significant sites of MNC production and foreign investment. Moreover, some NIEs are becoming significant sources of outflows of FDI, and the growth of MNCs domiciled in these countries is an important new development. In these respects the stratification of global production is quite different from that of the classical Gold Standard era.

The global diffusion and speeding up of international business competition represent a further shift in comparison with earlier periods. The existence of global, almost real-time communications infrastructures fundamentally transforms the capacity of firms to organize their operations globally; their capacity to adapt organizational forms and production levels to rapidly changing competitive conditions; and the speed at which goods and services flow within production and distribution networks. In this respect transnational business and production have acquired a diversity of organizational forms of which the classic highly centralized, vertically integrated corporation is but one. Overseas production also appears to be becoming more significant for MNCs. According to UNCTAD the largest MNCs are becoming more transnational than perhaps was the case even in the more recent past (UNCTAD, 1997, p. 8).

Dunning estimates that in 1982 overseas production accounted for 30 per cent of the total output of the world's 500 leading industrial companies (1993b, p. 37) and this figure has since risen. Overseas sales of the largest 350 companies rose from 30 to 40 per cent of their total sales during the 1970s, while in 1980 around a third of their total assets was located overseas (UNCTC, 1983, p. 48). Among the leading 100 (non-financial) MNCs (measured by foreign assets) overseas sales amounted in 1994 to 55.3 per cent of their total sales. These same companies also accounted for a third of world FDI stocks. Moreover, of those 100 MNCs for which data are available, 49.5 per cent of assets and 46.9 per cent of total employment are located overseas (calculated from UNCTAD, 1996, pp. 30–2). For the major MNCs, based in OECD states or elsewhere, overseas activity is no longer (if it ever was) marginal to corporate operations, as the sceptics often suggest, but rather is increasingly central.

Grid 5.1 Historical forms of global production

	1600–1800	1870–1939	1950–1973	1973 on
Extensity	Trading companies active in Asia, Africa and North America Commodity chains	Emerging MNCs operating in Europe, North America and the major primary exporters Commodity chains	MNCs active in the industrialized economies and increasingly in developing ones, but excluded from communist countries	MNCs active in almost all countries in the world as emerging market economies are incorporated in the 1990s Growth of regional and global production/distribution networks
Intensity	Trading companies important in luxury products, but these form a small proportion of the economies	MNCs important for investment in and development of certain primary producer nations, and in certain manufacturing industries	Rising intensity in manufacturing particularly; MNCs come to dominate a range of industries	High: MNCs dominate world trade and account for around a quarter of world output International production exceeds world exports
Velocity	Low	Relatively high: speeding up of production	Moderate	High: speeding up of production processes and global competition
Impact propensity	Although important for certain products, generally small	Important for certain primary commodities In some manufacturing industries MNCs introduce new products and processes	High in creating global competition for many primary and manufactured products and spreading technology worldwide	Impact rises further: continued trends from pre-1973 period; increased ability to shift production worldwide, although this still falls short of perfect mobility
Infrastructure	Basic communications through transport systems	International telegraph provides improved communications Stand-alone production	Innovations and improvements in telecommunications aid central coordination Virtually integrated organizations	Improvements in existing technology and major innovations – fax, e-mail, etc. – allow a large volume of instant communications and more diverse forms of organizing international production

Institutionalization	Trading companies often operate under auspices of empire and exercise power of their own	Largely open regime for international business before WW1 Some restrictions imposed later, particularly in the 1930s	Broadly open regime, but with important exceptions Countries vary in controls and restrictions on foreign investment flows and MNC activities Nationalization in some developing countries	Trend towards very open regime with liberalization of controls on MNCs and foreign investment flows Moves to harmonize conditions so that foreign business faces similar regulations worldwide
Stratification Hierarchy	Strong: trading companies mostly operate from imperial powers and in imperial territories	Strong, with main companies operating from major economies especially UK and the USA Major investments in primary producers and other major economies	Manufacturing MNCs initially dominated by US companies Established companies from other countries continue operations and others emerge	MNCs and FDI flow still emanate from richest economies, but from a wider range Important number of European and Japanese companies and growth of MNCs based in developing economies Diffusion of production and growth of Asian, Eastern MNCs
Unevenness	High: investment confined to certain key areas	High: whereas investment high in primary producers, very low outside these and the major economies North–South division of labour	Significant investments throughout the non-socialist world, but increased concentration of international business and investment in industrialized economies Investment generally small in low income economies	Investment still concentrated in the industrialized economies Increasing flows to/from developing countries, but these are concentrated on a small number of industrializing and transition economies New global division of labour

Moreover, competitive conditions and global infrastructures have encouraged a transnationalization of production and distribution among small and medium-sized companies, such that international business activity is no longer the sole preserve of huge corporate empires, although these undoubtedly remain dominant. In this respect the contemporary globalization of production is not exclusively a story about the rise of the MNC or the growth of FDI, as many sceptics and hyperglobalizers often imply, but is cast much wider to embrace the globalization of business networks. Nevertheless, the global corporate empires of today (Ford, GM, Hoescht, BP, etc.) have acquired greater power and influence then perhaps at any other time (Korten, 1995; Strange, 1996).

While there has been a significant expansion of transnational production in the last three decades it has also become more institutionalized, as strategic alliances, subcontracting, joint ventures and other forms of contractual arrangements regularize interfirm networks and arrangements (UNCTAD, 1997). Such arrangements have been facilitated by the liberalization of controls on FDI and capital movements and of other restrictive measures. In some respects this is a return to the more open investment climate of the turn of the century, although freed from the constraints of imperial priorities and policies. This is reflected in changing patterns of stratification as more FDI flows to NIEs and developing countries, the organization of global production encourages a new global division of labour, and the transnationalization of business within developing countries becomes a more visible feature of the global political economy (Strange, 1996; UNCTAD, 1997).

Despite some obvious continuities with the past, such as the lasting impact of imperial ties on European FDI and MNCs, the contemporary globalization of business and production has transformed 'what goods and services are produced, how, where and by whom' (Strange, 1996, p. 44). Of course, multinational production still accounts for only a minority of total world production. Nevertheless, its growing significance has profound implications for the economic autonomy and sovereignty of nation-states, although its specific impact is conditioned by patterns of national enmeshment in global production networks.

5.7 Contemporary Patterns of National Enmeshment in Global Production Networks

Earlier sections have noted the differential enmeshment in global production networks of the six OECD economies that are the focus of this study. Here, by way of a summary, a brief comparison of outward and inward stocks of FDI in relation to GDP provides a crude measure of the differential importance of FDI to these six economies. How significant foreign MNCs are in domestic production, and overseas FDI is for the domestic economy, have been reviewed in section 5.4.4.

Tables 5.12 and 5.13 detail outward and inward stocks of FDI for the six case study economies. Although outward stocks for France and the UK were considerably higher relative to GDP in the classical Gold Standard era than today, for the other four countries they are now significantly higher or roughly equivalent. This shift is not surprising given the global dominance of European economies in the pre-1914 era.

Table 5.12 Outward FDI stocks as percentage of home country GDP, 1914–1994

	1914	1960	1973	1980	1985	1994
France	18.3	6.8	3.5	3.6	7.1	11.8
Germany	10.7	1.1	3.5	8.0	8.1	9.9
Japan	7.8	1.2	2.5	1.8	6.2	9.9
Sweden	–	2.9	5.8	4.5	11.6[a]	28.9
UK	53.2	14.9	14.8	15.0	19.3[b]	26.4
USA	6.8	6.3	7.7	8.5	5.5	9.0

[a] 1986.
[b] 1987.
Sources: OECD, 1996c; Dunning, 1988; IMF, *International Financial Statistics Yearbook*, various years

Table 5.13 Inward FDI stocks as percentage of host country GDP, 1914–1994

	1914	1960	1973	1980	1986	1994
France			1.5[a]	3.5	6.4[b]	9.0
Germany				4.6	5.0	7.4
Japan	1.4	0.2	0.9	0.3	0.5	0.7
Sweden				2.9	4.3[c]	11.4
UK	1.6	6.9	8.2	11.8	13.1[d]	18.2
USA	3.7	1.5	1.3	3.2	4.4	7.2

[a] 1975.
[b] 1985.
[c] 1986.
[d] 1987.
Sources: OECD, 1996c; Dunning, 1988; UNCTC, 1988; UN-TCMD, 1992; IMF, *International Financial Statistics Yearbook*, various years

However, for all six countries the postwar trend has been for outward FDI stocks to grow relative to the home economies (see table 5.12). By comparison inward stocks of FDI (see table 5.13) are now higher relative to domestic economies than in the pre-1914 era, except in the case of Japan.

Over the postwar period the UK consistently had significant levels of inward investment, reflecting in part its relatively liberal policies towards FDI (see table 5.13). The USA too had relatively high inward FDI in the late 1980s. The historic trend towards higher levels of outward FDI than inward FDI is evident in the cases of Sweden, the UK, France, Japan and Germany. By comparison, since the late 1980s, the USA has had an approximate equality between inward and outward stocks of FDI despite having much higher levels of outward investment for much of the postwar period. In the latter part of the 1980s inward and outward stocks approached equality on a historic cost basis, although in current value terms the US remained a net outward investor. Following the surge of US outward investment in the 1990s it is now a net outward investor even on a historic cost basis.

5.8   The Globalization of Business: Domestic Impacts

The globalization of business and production makes national economies and the fortunes of communities within them increasingly interconnected. In orthodox economics, FDI in principle can have a positive or negative impact on national welfare, but many hyperglobalizers argue that global competition and production increase the efficiency of the world economy since MNCs encourage an international division of labour such that countries become more specialized in producing goods in which they have a comparative advantage. Competition reduces monopoly profits and increases the pressure for innovation. MNCs are thus argued to improve national economic performance since these firms tend to have higher productivity than domestic firms and operate to diffuse new technology and raise the skill levels of the national workforce (UN-TCMD, 1992; OECD, 1994a).

More critical interpretations argue that the globalization of business involves a growing divergence between corporate priorities and those of national governments and their citizens. For much of the postwar period this critique was common in many countries, especially developing countries. In developing countries MNC activity was often regarded as distorting development priorities, restricting the growth of a domestic economic base and producing excess profits which were repatriated out of the country. A similar critique has emerged in core investing countries, including the USA, claiming that MNCs are transferring abroad jobs and technology, and hence the basis for national prosperity. Moreover, the ability of corporations to organize production globally is perceived as giving them enormous structural power relative to national governments and labour.

Those sceptical of the globalization thesis take a more traditional view in conceiving MNCs as essentially national companies with international operations and therefore still amenable to national direction. These contrasting views set the context for examining the decisional, institutional, distributional and structural impacts of the globalization of production for the sovereignty and autonomy of SIACS.

5.8.1   Decisional impacts: global business and the conduct of national economic policy

Global production networks may compromise the effectiveness of government economic policy in several ways but most especially by altering the cost and benefits of economic policy choices and policy instruments. The operations of MNCs impact on the effectiveness of the traditional tools of macroeconomic management. Cowling and Sugden (1996) argue that the relationship between demand management, capacity utilization and unemployment among developed countries has changed. Demand management policies have less impact on unemployment and output than in the early postwar period in part because rising revenues in one country may be siphoned off to finance investment elsewhere by MNCs. Moreover, MNCs can borrow abroad when domestic interest rates are high, and conversely take advantage of low domestic interest rates to borrow to fund projects overseas. This clearly compromises the effectiveness of national monetary policy. As significant global financial actors, MNCs also play an important role in exchange rate markets. As noted in chapter 4, although speculators may initiate an attack on a currency, it is when MNCs (and institutional investors) shift out of that currency, even as a precautionary measure, that pressure on the exchange rate can become irreversible. Of course the apparent erosion in the effectiveness of national macroeconomic policy instruments since the 1970s, as noted in previous chapters, is a complex phenomenon, partly reflecting other aspects of economic globalization and domestic factors.

Although the perceived capacity of MNCs to shift production might be expected to reduce countries' ability to tax capital, reduce their tax base and increasingly move the burden of taxation on to less mobile factors such as labour, this is not necessarily the case. There are two key aspects to this issue: the pressure on governments to reduce taxes on capital to retain and/or attract multinational business, and multinationals' ability to minimize tax liabilities through transfer pricing. (Transfer pricing involves the under- or overcharging by MNCs through internal transactions so as to artificially boost profits in low tax countries and reduce them in high tax ones.) Cassou (1997) found that corporation and income tax rates do affect outward FDI flows; other studies have been less conclusive. This is not surprising as tax is only one cost facing MNCs. Nevertheless, corporate tax rates among developed countries have tended both to fall and to converge over the past two decades (OECD, 1991d; Tanzi, 1995, ch. 7). How far this is due to the globalization of production, and how significant it is for national tax revenues, is less clear. The evidence is more conclusive with respect to tax incentives and concessions for inward FDI since most states compete for FDI on the basis of such incentives. In this respect, global competition to attract FDI has now come to embrace tax measures. But tax competition between nations – and regions within them – is likely to be self-defeating, leading to rising incentives being offered while their effectiveness diminishes. Nevertheless, countries and regions continue to be drawn into a 'beauty contest' by competing on tax incentives. But low tax countries have tended to resist growing international attempts to harmonize corporate tax rates.

The macroeconomic significance of transfer pricing remains unclear; since much of it is illegal, obtaining reliable figures is obviously difficult (Plasschaert, 1994). There are clear incentives for MNCs to exploit transfer pricing mechanisms, and high levels of intrafirm trade provide substantial opportunities for doing so. However, companies are limited by fear of action by national tax authorities, which have monitored the practice (at least since the 1970s) and regularly exchange information. Further, transfer pricing may conflict with internal accounting and control systems. Such evidence as there is indicates that transfer pricing is practised on a significant scale, but it is of secondary importance to profits and government tax revenues. Rousslang (1997) estimates that transfer pricing results in a tax saving of around $8 billion for MNCs, but this is only around 4 per cent of worldwide taxable income of manufacturing MNCs.

It is in the area of industrial policy, particularly for continental European countries, that the impact of international production is perhaps most acute. Attempts by governments, as in France, to pursue a coherent industrial policy have been sharply modified by the rise of MNCs and global production networks. The ability to transfer production abroad undermines an industrial strategy which relies on the creation of 'national champions'. More effective industrial strategies require the creation of Europe-wide companies, as in the case of Airbus, to compete with the US and Japanese MNCs. This does not mean that national industrial and technology policies are redundant.

Notwithstanding the internationalization of small and medium-sized enterprises, industrial policy can operate to encourage the latter, particularly given their capacity to generate employment opportunities domestically. In this context the globalization of production influences the costs and benefits of different policy options within the overall ambit of national industrial strategy.

5.8.2   Institutional impacts: global competition

MNCs are central to globalizing competition. Trade, as noted in chapter 3, plays a key role, but multinational production is just as important. Transnational production, as noted earlier, has interposed global competition within domestic markets so that many firms are forced to produce at the world productivity frontier or go out of business (Cantwell, 1989; Baily and Gersbach, 1995). Corporate and national agendas, and the longer term strategic choices faced by many domestic firms, are thus influenced considerably by the impact of global competition.

Initially, global competition meant American MNCs reaching ever deeper and wider into foreign markets. Since the 1970s European and Japanese firms have achieved similar productivity levels to US firms resulting in direct competition between them. This has been reflected in FDI flows as many MNCs established or consolidated their operations in major world markets. As noted, American MNCs have lost significant market shares to their competitors since the 1970s. One key indicator of the degree of global competition is that the rates of return for MNCs in high-tech industries are neither high in relation to domestic firms in the same sector nor high in relation to firms in other industries (Kapler, 1997; cf. Graham, 1996). Where MNCs could once rely on their competitive advantages to earn above-average profits the intensity of contemporary global competition makes sustaining such profits increasingly difficult.

While the level of global competition varies between sectors, and between countries, the growth of transnational production has made it more intense and enhanced its geographical reach. Political and business rhetoric in the majority of OECD countries, in consequence, has become imbued with an ideology of global competition which conditions the institutional agendas of firms, unions and government (Hoogvelt, 1997; Thompson, 1998).

5.8.3   Distributional impacts:
labour and global production

MNCs are often perceived as harmful to labour. Their ability to organize production transnationally, it is argued, increases corporate power relative to the power of labour, putting downward pressure on wages and working conditions. Beyond this MNCs are able to transfer technology abroad so that skilled jobs are lost to low wage countries and thus workers in advanced economies appropriate less of the material gain from technological innovation (Sachs and Shatz, 1994).

However, evidence from both OECD and developing countries indicates that MNCs pay above-average wages, although once other factors are controlled for it is not clear that this is significant (OECD, 1994a; UN-TCMD, 1992). MNCs are often criticized for providing poor pay and conditions in some industries, notably clothing and footwear. In some, but by no means all, cases, pay and conditions are comparable with domestic firms. Generally the cases where the worst pay and conditions have been reported are not among subsidiaries of MNCs but among domestic firms in developing countries producing under contract to MNCs (Barnet and Cavanagh, 1994, pp. 310–38).

Shifting production to reap the benefits of low wages is particularly evident in industries such as clothing, footwear and sports goods; in the postwar period MNCs have not only shifted production in these sectors from OECD countries to developing economies, but have also successively moved it further down the wage scale from middle to low income countries. Latterly this pressure has become more widespread. West European MNCs have laid off workers in their home countries while expanding employment and operations in lower wage countries; for example, during the 1990s the Swiss-Swedish manufacturers ABB shed 59,000 jobs in Western Europe and North America while creating 56,000 elsewhere, mainly in Asia and Eastern Europe (*Financial Times*, 24 Oct. 1997, p. 18). More generally, Hatzius found that FDI flows into and from Britain and Germany, and from Sweden, have become more sensitive to labour costs (1997a; 1997b), implying that multinationals now find it easier to organize production abroad in response to these costs. Labour costs include not just wages but also employment costs, including employers' social security contributions. In the countries affected, downward pressure on the latter implies either declining social provision or the transfer of more of the burden to labour either through higher employee contributions or greater private provision.

Of course, as discussed, MNCs cannot necessarily shift production abroad at will. Lawrence (1994) compared US multinationals' operations in 1979 and a decade later, finding that although wages in developing countries were 28.5 per cent of average wages for the same operations in OECD countries, labour productivity was only 40.3 per cent of that in OECD countries. Differential productivity levels obviously limit the possibilities for shifting operations to low wage countries. Among US MNCs Lawrence found that relocation to developing countries and outsourcing did not explain much of the fall in manufacturing employment in the USA. But Sachs and Schatz question this finding (1994).

In addition, as observed earlier, MNCs tend to be at the forefront of technological innovation and require access to technology and skilled personnel, as well as core markets. Of course, if the production technology can be developed in such a way that it is operable by low paid workers in developing countries, MNCs are best placed to relocate production to such countries. In this respect the globalization of production may contribute to widening wage differentials between skilled and unskilled workers within and between countries.

If MNCs could shift production costlessly this would imply that wages were determined globally. Since shifting production abroad incurs some costs this would not be expected to hold absolutely, but as the costs of relocation fall then we would expect wages to be increasingly determined by global competitive forces. Analogous with the experience of trade (see chapter 3) a global convergence in wages might be expected, although not the complete annihilation of wage differentials. But labour movements in countries such as Sweden, with a high level of internationalized production, have been able to extract significant concessions from capital. Wage levels are thus unlikely to converge globally. Nevertheless, the balance of power between labour and multinational capital, under conditions of globalization, is undoubtedly shifting in favour of the latter (Kurzer, 1993).

5.8.4   Structural impacts: FDI, MNCs and national economic performance

As MNCs are central to OECD economies and domestic technological innovation, they unquestionably play a critical role in their growth (see Cantwell, 1989). Overwhelmingly studies have focused on the impact of FDI on recipient countries. As noted, inward FDI plays a key role in forcing many domestic firms to produce at the world productivity frontier and stimulates domestic innovation, factors which tend to raise productivity growth. The OECD (1994a) found evidence that foreign affiliates in OECD countries tend to have higher productivity than domestic firms and have positive effects on growth and national economic performance. Inward FDI can have a significant effect on growth through raising the rate of technical progress, the rate at which countries catch up to world productivity and the effects on the rest of the economy. Nevertheless the evidence is inconclusive.

Surveying studies of overseas affiliates in developing countries, Caves concludes that they 'seem to enjoy no intrinsic productivity advantage independent of the transaction-cost advantages that make them MNEs in the first place' (1996, p. 227). Past studies have indicated a range of effects of FDI on growth, some negative. Blomström et al. (1992) found that FDI was a significant positive factor in growth for middle income countries but not for low income countries. Both quantitative and qualitative evidence indicates that pre-existing economic institutions and infrastructures are central to capturing spillover benefits from inward FDI but that such benefits are often small (Chan, 1995; de Mello, 1997). This suggests that FDI generally only plays a significantly positive role in those countries that have already achieved a prior level of development and have the infrastructure and the skills base to sustain growth.

Furthermore, some sceptics argue that national economic performance is directly related to the competitive performance of home-based MNCs in world markets (and vice versa). Where these perform well so will the national economy as the benefits accrue domestically. At the other extreme, hyperglobalizers assume that because MNCs can relocate production easily this suggests no necessary connection between national economic performance and that of home-based MNCs. Reich (1991), for instance, argues that the performance of home-based MNCs and national economic performance are no longer, under conditions of economic globalization, directly correlated.

There is a range of evidence that bears on this issue. Cantwell found that the association between countries' trade performance and the performance of home-based MNCs varied (1989, chs 5–6). In 1974 there was limited association between the performance of US and British firms in particular industries and that of their economies, but a much stronger association in France, Germany, Italy and Japan. By 1982 the association had become even weaker for the US and Britain and had also weakened for France. Overall, performance of domestic MNCs does not necessarily have a direct impact on national trade performance. Other studies also have found important differences between the performance of MNCs and that of their home country. In the cases of the USA and

Sweden, over the past twenty years national shares of world manufacturing exports have fallen significantly, while exports by foreign affiliates of US and Swedish MNCs have risen and then stabilized (Blomström and Lipsey, 1989, 1993; Kravis and Lipsey, 1992). It is particularly notable that while the US has experienced falls in its share of high technology exports, this has not been the case more generally with US MNCs. In other words, US and Swedish companies have maintained and strengthened their world competitive position in part by producing for export abroad. The picture for Japan is less clear, but even so Japan's share of world exports fell in the late 1980s, while Japanese multinationals' share of world exports has continued to rise.

Although systematic evidence is lacking, research suggests that over time the globalization of production involves a progressive decoupling of national economic performance from that of home-based MNCs. Further, this process appears to be pronounced for high technology industries, where the profits from innovation might be expected to be highest. The broader implications of this are significant. For while, as noted previously, governments have sought to support home-based MNCs and create a favourable investment climate for FDI, this does not necessarily enhance national economic performance. Yet, among OECD states in particular, the magnitude and economic significance of FDI and MNCs in relation to national economic activity are such that the needs of multinational capital cannot be ignored. Gearing national economic policy to these needs can have significant consequences, not all of which are positive, for the structure and performance of national economies.

5.8.5 Structural impacts: corporate power versus state power?

For the hyperglobalizers, such as Ohmae, the growth of MNCs and global production networks defines a borderless economy in which the power of governments to manage the national economy is being eroded (Ohmae, 1990). By contrast the sceptics, such as Hirst and Thompson among others, argue that neither the activities of MNCs nor the internationalization of production define a more integrated global economy in that international business remains 'heavily "nationally embedded"' such that 'it is not beyond the powers of national government to regulate these companies' (Hirst and Thompson, 1996b, p. 98). However, both these contrary positions tend to misrepresent the nature of the transformation of production underway and its relationship to state power. For on the one hand the hyperglobalizers posit a simple zero-sum view of power – corporate power versus state power – while the sceptics imply that the existence of gigantic corporate empires and regional/global production networks does not fundamentally alter the capacity of individual governments to regulate the 'national economy'.

What both these arguments tend to overlook is not only the complex interrelationships between corporate and state power but also the ways in which the globalization of production enhances the structural power of corporate capital. This is not to argue that MNCs programme the decisions of governments or that MNCs are making states redundant. Rather the point is that as the globalization of production transforms the conditions under which wealth is created and distributed, it simultaneously transforms the context in which, and instruments through which, state power and authority are exercised. In this respect the globalization of production invites an uneasy balance of power between SIACS and MNCs in which the role and functions of national government are having to adjust to a new world production order.

5.9   Conclusion

Today, the globalization of production is organized in large measure by MNCs. Their pre-eminence in world output, trade, investment and technology transfer is unprecedented. Even when MNCs have a clear national base, their interest is in global profitability above all. MNCs have grown from national firms to global concerns using international investment to exploit their competitive advantages. Increasingly, however, they are using joint ventures and strategic alliances to develop and exploit those advantages or to share the costs of technological innovation. But the growing globalization of production is not limited to MNC activity, for over the last three decades there has been a significant growth in producer-driven and buyer-driven global production and distribution networks. The globalization of business is thus no longer confined to the MNC but also embraces SMEs.

MNCs, however, are the linchpins of the contemporary world economy. Around 53,000 MNCs account for at least 20 per cent (some estimate 30 per cent) of world output and on some estimates up to 70 per cent of world trade (Dunning, 1993b, p. 14; Strange, 1996, p. 47; Perraton et al., 1997; UNCTAD, 1998). Despite regional concentrations of production, transnational business networks span the three core regions of the world economy, linking the fortunes of disparate communities and nations in complex webs of interconnectedness. Contrary to the sceptics, MNCs are not simply 'national firms with international operations', nor are they, as the hyperglobalizers argue, 'footloose corporations' which wander the globe in search of maximum profits (Hu, 1992; Reich, 1991). Rather MNCs play a much more central role in the operation of the world economy than in the past and they figure prominently in organizing extensive and intensive transnational networks of coordinated production and distribution that are historically unique. MNCs and global production networks are critical to the organization, location and distribution of productive power in the contemporary world economy. This is reflected too in shifting patterns of global migration – people on the move – discussed in the next chapter.

6
People on the Move

One form of globalization is more ubiquitous than any other – human migration. At its simplest, migration refers to the movement of people and their temporary or permanent geographical relocation. People have always been on the move and they have moved great distances. There are many impulses behind these movements: victorious armies and empires have swept across and implanted themselves into new territories; the defeated and dispossessed have fled to defensible land and safer havens; the enslaved have been torn from their homes and relocated in the lands of the enslaver; the unemployed and underemployed have searched for work; the persecuted have sought asylum; and the curious and adventurous have always been travelling, drifting and exploring. This chapter examines historical forms of global migration through the conceptual lens outlined in the introduction. The key concepts that can be brought to bear on patterns of migration concern: their *extensity*; their *intensity*; their *velocity*; their *impact* on host and home, states and societies – impacts which display a considerable *unevenness* and arise, in part, from *hierarchies* of power among different migrant and host groups. In addition, it is important to consider the *infrastructures* of transportation and communication and the *institutions* that sustain global labour markets and migratory flows.

William McNeill has argued that two distinctions, one geographical, one social, characterize most forms of migration in human history: central and peripheral migrations; elite and mass migrations (1978). Most often, elite migrations have been military-led conquests on the periphery of states and empires, followed by the settlement of border regions and marches by an aristocracy and their subalterns. This may be accompanied by elite migrations of missionaries, merchants and bureaucrats as well as mass migrations of settling nomads and peasant agrarians moving on to new, less populated lands. McNeill distinguishes such migrations to the periphery from flows to the centre: elites migrate to the centres of political power and economic activity in cities and royal courts, while the rural poor and the skilled head for the city in search of work. McNeill's model is well suited to the greater part of human history in which centre and periphery, urban and rural provide a more accurate representation of political space than one demarcated by fixed political borders. Indeed, it could be argued that it was outward migrations that helped define and extend the outer limits of political control of a state or empire rather than the crossing of immutable political boundaries. To chart the geographical form of migrations prior to the advent of nation-states is to simultaneously chart the changing character and location of state boundaries and frontiers.

6.1 Globalization and Migration

Globalization, in this chapter, refers to movements of peoples across regions and between continents, be they labour migrations, diasporas or processes of conquest and colonization. In addition, we shall use the globalization of migration to refer to transoceanic or transcontinental movements which preceded the formation of nation-states: for example, the flows of enslaved Africans to the Americas from the sixteenth to the nineteenth century, prior to the existence of any recognizable African nation-states. Of course, not all cross-border migrations have been global in their extent. The exodus of ethnic Germans from Eastern Europe and the Soviet Union in the immedi-ate post-Second World War era, or the flows from Iberia and Italy to Northern Europe in the 1950s, would count as a form of *regionalization* or regional migration, given the contiguity and clustering of the states and societies enmeshed in these flows.

If the geographical extensity of patterns of migration is variable then so too is the intensity of the flows established. By examining the size of migrations relative to home and host populations, an indication of intensity can be given. It also matters, as noted above, whether migrations are an elite or mass phenomenon. Such qualitative factors are important in weighing evidence of intensity. We have, therefore, tried to provide relative and qualitative measures of migration.

The rapidity or velocity of migration can be assessed in two ways. First, we can consider the movement of people across regions in given time periods, assessing the length of time a mass migration takes from its inception to its conclusion. Second, we can consider velocity in individual terms – the amount of time it takes a migrant to get from his or her original locale to a new host country. Clearly, changes in transportation technology have made a major difference in this respect.

What areas of social life do migration patterns, global or otherwise, intertwine with and transform? Much of the literature on migration focuses on the movement of labour. Yet what we are describing, first and foremost, is the movement of peoples not labour; even if, more often than not, their labour has been the key to their movements. The movement of commodified wage labourers responding primarily to the push and pull of market forces, of supply and demand, is only one facet, albeit an important one, of the mass movement of human beings around the planet. Migrations also intersect with, and are constitutive of, networks of political, military and cultural power (see chapters 1, 2 and 7). A casual glance at the origins of migrations suggests as much. Patterns of military globalization, of conquest and colonization, generate new streams of colonizers from victorious to defeated societies or of refugees from war zones to places of asylum. Accordingly, the impact of global and regional patterns of migration on host and home societies is, as we might expect, often multifaceted. Given that patterns of migration entwine with and transform patterns of economic, cultural and political interaction, we can expect impacts in all these domains.

Most obviously, migration has affected patterns of work and employment. However, we would be hard pressed to capture all the economic effects of migrations through issues of employment and work alone. For example, the large-scale migration of Hong Kong Chinese families and their capital to western Canada in the 1980s and early 1990s has not had its primary economic impact in the labour market. The transformation of business ownership, the housing markets and international trade patterns in contemporary British Columbia and Vancouver testifies to this. Similarly, the main impact on the Algerian economy of Algerian migration to France has probably not been a reduction in the level of domestic unemployment. This has been dwarfed by the impact of remitted hard currency on the balance of payments and the undermining of the official exchange rate through informal black market currency movements.

In addition, people move with their cultures. For the establishment of settlements and migrant communities creates a range of new social relationships between home and emigrant community, home and host societies that previously did not exist. The establishment of immigrant communities with or without extensive connections to their original residence creates and transforms patterns of cultural power and social identification. The presence of an immigrant community inevitably generates a point of comparison and contrast with indigenous cultures. The movement of people brings the movement of new ideas, religions, beliefs, etc., in its wake.

The movement of people, of course, does not occur in a vacuum but must be organized and coordinated across time and space. Migration requires infrastructures and institutions of transport, communication and regulation. The infrastructures of transport and communication affect the costs, risks, speed and scope of potential migrations. The existence of cheaper transportation and telecommunications affects the extent to which immigrant communities can maintain contact with their home societies. But beyond these kinds of infrastructure, migrations have been formally and informally coordinated and regulated. Even the flight of the dispossessed and the defeated will be informally coordinated by refugees or subject to intervention by host countries or international agencies. Contemporary migrants travel in a world in which international law has begun to impact on domestic legislation and international organizations monitor and intervene in migratory processes (see section 1.3.3 above). The extent to which both infrastructures and regulation have attained interregional or transcontinental levels will affect and shape the globalization of migration itself.

The stratification of global and regional migration can be analysed, in the first instance, in terms of the unevenness of origins and destinations. The unequal distribution of access for different groups in different places and the relative power of migratory flows and state agencies seeking to control and shape them can be thought of in terms of hierarchies of power. McNeill's distinction between elite and mass migration points not only to the different social composition of migrations but also to the differential capacities of different social groups to amass the resources for migration and successfully enter other societies and territories. This hierarchy of power among migrants is mirrored by the hierarchy of state power in which different states have differential capacities to control population movements, maintain the integrity of their borders and shape the structure of international migratory regimes.

These concepts provide a vocabulary for describing and comparing the major historical forms of global and regional migration. However, the quality of historical data available on migration varies from epoch to epoch and from state to state. The limits of state power in the premodern and early modern era are indicated by the minimal census data available on either the ethnic composition of states or levels of migration. In an era when so few people were citizens, why would states bother to count their numbers or origins? Calculations of the size of premodern and early modern migrations must often be established from fragmentary and indirect measures; mainly from partial economic and shipping data. By comparison, the integrity of territorial borders and the distinction between citizens and foreigners is constitutive of the modern nation-state. Territorial definition and national identity are at the core of any nation-state's existence and this is reflected in a more systematic collection of migration data, although due caution is required before making any generalizations (Wagner et al., 1991; Ritz, 1989; Zlotnik, 1989).

With these caveats in mind, section 6.2 sketches the scope and form of human migrations up to the end of the Second World War. We start by exploring premodern migrations which provide a context for understanding later developments. We then focus on the global expansion of European empires, and the global economic interactions they created. These empires, we argue, formed the basis of an era of global migration that was systematically different from earlier periods. That said, the era of global migrations between 1500 and 1945 was not uniform. We distinguish an early modern phase of geographically extensive but socially less intensive migration up until the end of the eighteenth century from a phase of intense global mass migration in the nineteenth century and early twentieth century. This modern period also saw new and distinct patterns of regional migration related to differential patterns of industrialization. The period closes with the great global wars of the twentieth century, and the accompanying economic dislocation, which effectively terminated global labour migrations but unleashed a wave of forced movements, particularly in Europe.

In section 6.3, we examine contemporary patterns of global migration. We argue that by the 1990s global (and regional) migrations were approaching the geographical scale and intensity of earlier eras of migrations, but can be distinguished from their predecessors in terms of their distinctive geography, social composition and infrastructure. In section 6.4 we summarize the accumulated evidence, comparing and contrasting different historical forms of global migration and, in section 6.5, we examine differences in national enmeshment in these forms among the six SIACS which are the focus of this study. Following this, we explore the demographic, economic and political impacts of migration on nation-states, before finally assessing the implications of these flows and patterns for the autonomy and sovereignty of SIACS.

6.2 Historical Forms of Global Migration

The large-scale movement of people and peoples has an enormously long history (Fagan, 1990; Emmer, 1993). Since the emergence of the first rudimentary states over six thousand years ago human migrations have crossed political boundaries as well as extending and reshaping them. Mobile nomads have crossed continents and carved out new empires. Some older polities have acquired an internal dynamism that allowed them to push outwards from the centre. Religion and economics have propelled missionaries and merchants across continents. Elements of these processes have been sketched in chapters 1 and 2 on the changing geography of states and warfare. Here we outline some of the main lines of global migratory history since the emergence of settled agrarian civilizations.

6.2.1 Premodern global migrations: extensity and intensity

The most important early large-scale migrations occurred in Asia. At their hub lay Chinese civilization with its fluctuating peripheries around a river valley core (Lee, 1978; Diamond, 1997). Periods of imperial expansion were accompanied by elite and mass migrations to previously peripheral areas in the north, south and west which reached their heights in the third century BC and the fourth and fifteenth centuries AD. Migrations were often sponsored and regulated by various Chinese states, implemented and organized by the army and accompanied by parallel, privately orchestrated migrations of a substantial size. In the twenty-five years before 200 BC, it is estimated that almost 2 million migrants moved under the auspices of the Han state. These immense migrations are comparable in size to the great migrations of the eighteenth and nineteenth century, though their geography is regional rather than global. Moving in the opposite direction nomad armies north of the Great Wall periodically amassed sufficient strength and organization to penetrate deep into China itself, as well as across the Asian land mass and as far as Europe and the Middle East. The Mongol empires that existed from the twelfth to the fourteenth century brought successive waves of warrior conquest and migrations, first to China where they formed the ruling dynasty, and subsequently further to the west. Indian civilization had been transformed by the military migrations of Aryans over a millennium before the birth of Christ, and the Islamic Moguls initiated extensive change again. However, no major outward military thrusts and accompanying migration were to emanate again from these lands prior to the nineteenth century. Finally, it can be noted that while all these early migratory movements occurred across already settled territories, simultaneously Polynesian islanders began processes of long-distance sea migration and island hopping, reaching unpopulated New Zealand at the turn of the first millennium and Hawaii and Easter Island a few hundred years later.

In the Middle East the rise of Islam, and the decisive moral and military edge it generated among nomadic Arab tribes, provided the greatest boost to outward migrations. Processes of nomadic conquest and settlement that transformed the human composition of the region were led by Arabs and then the Egyptians in the early centuries of Islam. These major movements were followed by smaller but important migrations southward into East Africa, westward from the Sudan into what is now Nigeria and by the rise of Turkish tribes in central Asia that eventually conquered Byzantium and formed the Ottoman Empire. Islam's retreat from Iberia was balanced by expansion into the Balkans and across the Indian Ocean into the Malaysian peninsula and the Indonesian archipelago.

In Africa the desertification of the Sahara region between 3000 and 1000 BC separated sub-Saharan African migrations from North Africa and saw a steady flow of migrant peoples southwards from the Savannah to the West African forests. The Bantu-speaking peoples, who had settled in what is now Cameroon and Nigeria, began a complex process of migration, conquest and diffusion. As agriculturalists they acquired a demographic and military edge over Africa's hunter-gatherers. With the acquisition of iron technologies in the fifth century BC, the pace of Bantu expansion rose, allowing them to reach the Indian Ocean by 100 BC and Northern Natal around AD 250 (Curtin, 1997). Swahilis from Persia and the Gulf established a complex network of migrant communities, ports and trading stations along the East African coast from the twelfth to the fifteenth century. The Islamic Hausa people migrated from Western Sudan to what is now Northern Nigeria between 1300 and 1800, establishing new states and sultanates in the region. In the Americas the Aztecs, Incas and Maya in Mexico, Central America and the Andes, respectively, expanded periodically through conquest and migration right up until the arrival of the Spanish (Fernández-Armesto, 1995).

The civilizations of classical European antiquity saw the large-scale movement of Greek and Roman armies and settlers, the establishment of far-flung Phoenician colonies and a thriving trade in slaves across the Mediterranean basin, penetrating along its supply routes through North Africa, Mesopotamia and the Levant. Further north Celtic and German tribes from the Eurasian steppes spread across Europe north of the Alps. Patterns of European settlement were transformed by the 'barbarian' invasions and the collapse of the Western Roman Empire in the fifth century AD. Even then the barbarian kingdoms and their medieval successors ebbed and flowed with population movements for centuries: invasions from the steppes by nomadic Slav armies late in the first millennium AD fanned out into the Balkans, central Europe and central Russia; Islam advanced into Iberia in the eighth century; the Latin crusaders established settler states in the Levant; Scandinavians invaded and then settled in Normandy, England, Scotland, Iceland and Greenland; the medieval conquest, colonization and conversion of the Balkan and Baltic regions as well as northern Finland was undertaken by migrant Germanic military orders and peasants. Finally, the Jewish diaspora from the Levant spread across Iberia, Italy, France, England and Germany from the fall of the Western Roman Empire until the tenth century, after which successive expulsions from England (1209), France (1306), Spain (1492) and Portugal (1496) shifted the centre of gravity of Jewish settlement to the East, above all to Poland, Lithuania and the Ukraine.

Throughout the medieval period skilled labourers and artisans in the mining, metallurgical and textile industries gravitated to centres of production across the European continent (Bartlett, 1994). Ruling elites and military orders moved even more fluidly, by virtue of military conquest and dynastic alliances cemented by marriage: the Hohenzollerns transported themselves from the Italian peninsula to the Baltic; Norman aristocratic houses moved from Scandinavia through France to England and Sicily; the Habsburgs spun a web of marriage and kinship across the continent. Religious minorities were expelled on a grand scale during the wars of religion in the sixteenth and seventeenth centuries, including, most notably, 500,000 Huguenots from France.

6.2.2   Early modern migrations: regional and global

From the seventeenth century onwards, the dynamics of imperial conflict in eastern, southern and central Europe, between Austria, Prussia, Russia and the Ottoman Empire saw major displacements of ethnic groups across ever-changing boundaries. Mercantalist-orientated states and empires drew on flows of skilled labour – for example, the Dutch moving to Germany and England to conduct land drainage schemes; Peter the Great bringing artisans and gunsmiths to imperial Russia (Lucassen, 1987). Further, the massive movement of Russian peoples eastwards from the eighteenth century began a movement that culminated in the colonization of the Siberian hinterland of the Tsarist empire.

Most of these migrations, given our earlier definition of globalization, were regional rather than global in extent (though Islam's African, European and South East Asian outposts do indicate processes of global migration). They tended to involve the reshaping of political boundaries and space, although there was some movement of peoples across boundaries. However, a case can be made that levels of migration significantly increased from the late sixteenth century onwards as a result of Europe's changing economic and military dynamics (see chapters 1, 2, 3 and 4). The early years of European expansion were not marked by an easy or effortless dominance but by the precariousness of Europe's technological and military edge and the minuscule level of actual migration that followed the conquest of the New World (Fernández-Armesto, 1995). The transoceanic extent of the European invasion may have geographically exceeded most earlier processes of conquest and migration, but its intensity and durability initially remained low. However, three patterns of global migration and movement emanating from, or controlled by, European powers heralded an era of migration that came to exceed its historical predecessors both in extent and intensity (see map 6.1 below). These migrations were the completion of the European conquest and population of the Americas and Oceania; the transatlantic slave trade that fuelled the economic development of the colonies; and the mass movement of Asian labour that replaced the labour flows extinguished by the termination of slaving.

6.2.3   The emergence of mass migration: from early modern to modern migratory patterns

While the dynamic of European migrations has displayed a multifaceted profile and a complex and fragmented geography we can capture many of the main elements of that process in what Alfred Crosby has described as the *biological expansion of Europe*: the movement of European peoples, flora, fauna and microbes to parts of the world that had been ecologically and socially separate from Europe for millennia – the Americas and Oceania (Crosby, 1983). It was the events of 1492 that began the transatlantic deluge, although the outward expansion of Europe had its roots some three or four hundred years earlier and had only been halted by economic and demographic collapse in the fourteenth century and the technological limits of European open sea navigation. What distinguished the American and Oceanic encounters is that Europeans faced so little military resistance or threats from the indigenous ecosystems. European expansion on a similar scale into the populated heartlands of Asia and Africa was checked for nearly three hundred years by a combination of the pre-existing density of population, the relative resilience of states and the hostility of the micro-organismal and macro-ecological environment. It is no surprise that the only significant and durable European migrations to Africa before the middle of the nineteenth century were located in the extreme north and south (Algeria, South Africa, Zimbabwe) and that, likewise, no enduring European settlement of the Asian land mass was achieved beyond the toeholds of colonial trading posts and emaciated bureaucracies. (On the very small size of Dutch emigrant communities in the Dutch East Indies, see Lucassen, 1995;

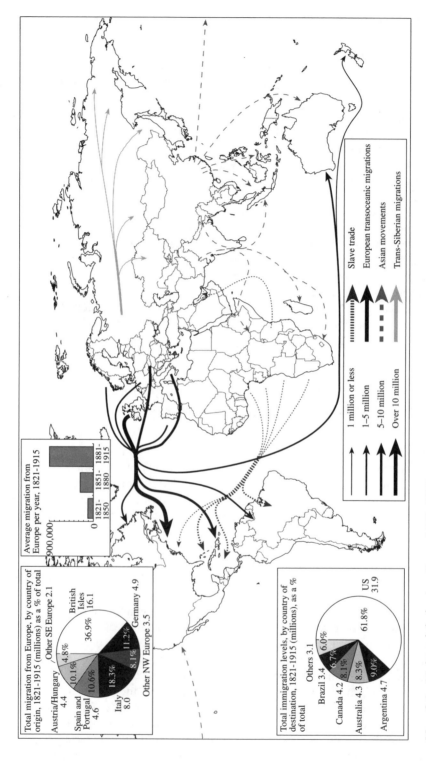

Map 6.1 Major global migrations, 1600–1915 (*Source:* Adapted from Kenwood and Lougheed, 1989)

and in the Cape, Curtin, 1997.) We focus below on the extensity and intensity of human movements that followed in the wake of European conquest and colonization.

For much of the sixteenth, seventeenth and eighteenth centuries European emigration to the Americas and eventually to Oceania proceeded at a slow pace (Bailyn, 1986; Kenwood and Lougheed, 1989; Baines, 1991). In the first century and a half of Spanish domination, less than half a million made the passage across the Atlantic, while a mere 70,000 Portuguese had settled in Brazil (on Spanish emigration, see the claims of Mörner, 1976; and the scepticism of Altman, 1995). Populations of European descent in the Caribbean were also tiny. On the eve of the American Revolution the colonial population, in much the most populous European outpost, was no more than 2–3 million. No permanent European settlement had been established by this point in Oceania. The costs and risks of transatlantic migration and the precarious quality of the colonies themselves, and of the economies established across the ocean, saw to that. The majority of European migrants to North America were of British descent, yet total migration from Britain and Ireland to the North American colonies was a mere million by 1776, alongside smaller numbers of Germans, Dutch and Scandinavians. Some French emigration had occurred both to the USA and to Quebec further north. However, with defeat in the Seven Years' War, the loss of American colonies and the cataclysm of the French Revolution, French transatlantic migration dwindled. The establishment of trading posts and coastal forts by the Dutch, Portuguese and Spanish in Africa and the Pacific in the seventeenth and eighteenth centuries had precipitated no more than a trickle of European migrants.

In the early nineteenth century the pace and scale of migration quickened. Cheaper, more regular, reliable transport was one reason for this. The cost of steerage from Europe to New York fell from around $40 in 1870 to $20 at the turn of the century (Zolberg, 1997). But the key reason for this torrent of migration was economic. On the one hand, there was a very large surplus of agrarian workers emerging in an industrializing Europe, and, on the other, there was the simultaneous and explosive industrialization of the land-rich but labour-scarce USA and other European-founded states and colonies. The great mass of transatlantic international migrations took place between the end of the Napoleonic Wars and the First World War. Total estimates vary from a high of 50 million between 1850 and 1914, to a lower estimate of approximately 46 million international migrants between 1821 and 1915; 44 million were from Europe and around 2 million from Asia. The vast majority headed for the Americas, and of those the majority headed for the USA. The bulk of the European movements actually occurred after 1880. Prior to 1880 11–12 million Europeans migrated, while 32 million left between 1880 and 1915 (Kenwood and Lougheed, 1989). That shift reflected a geographical change, with the majority of pre-1880 migrants coming from northern and western Europe, the majority after that from southern and eastern Europe, especially Italy. The British Isles provided over a third of all migrants in this period, and its proportion remained at a substantial level for some time to come. By comparison, German emigration declined after 1880.

Broadly speaking the British and Irish went to the USA, the white imperial dominions and the Caribbean; the Germans to the USA and in small numbers to Argentina and Brazil; the Italians to the USA and Latin America and the Iberians predominantly to Latin America. Southern and eastern Europeans flowed overwhelmingly to the USA. The active export of Europe's rural poor was facilitated in a number of ways.

Restrictions on emigration were lifted in Britain, Sweden and Germany in the mid-nineteenth century, though the French state pursued more restrictive exit policies. State bodies, trade unions, philanthropic organizations and colonization societies all made financial assistance available. In the UK, the Colonial Land and Emigration Department, established in 1840, sold lands in Australia and used the funds to facilitate emigration. Local rates were also made available for pauper emigration. Similar models were followed in Germany, especially after the 1848 uprisings. After the 1850s financial assistance came predominantly from colonial administrations and interests, especially in Australia and Latin America, which struggled to compete with the pull of North America. Remittances from emigrants also proved a significant factor in aiding the further emigration of relatives (Kenwood and Lougheed, 1989). In these respects, patterns of migration came to be institutionalized.

While war and economic crisis were the key factors in ending these unprecedented transatlantic flows, political attempts to control them were already underway in the USA. Well before the First World War, racist sentiment and organized labour had conspired to limit and control migration from Asia to the USA. With the active support of many state governments, coercive controls over Asian migrants were established and calls for the termination of Asian migration grew louder, culminating in the 1920s with Supreme Court decisions that excluded Chinese, Japanese and Indian migrants from naturalization and the acquisition of US citizenship (Zolberg, 1997). After the First World War the shape of transatlantic migration was transformed as well. The USA began to limit European immigration drastically and draw on both illegal Mexican cross-border labour and the vast reservoirs of African-American and white rural labour in the south to supply the expanding industries of the north and east. In the two years before the First World War over 3.3 million people emigrated to the USA. By the mid-1920s this had dropped to around 300,000 a year and by the 1930s to less than 100,000 a year. The size of annual migrations as a percentage of total population dropped from 1.23 per cent in 1914 to less than 0.05 per cent for the years 1932–45 (figures calculated from Mitchell, 1983). A relatively higher proportion of European emigrants therefore headed for Latin America and Oceania, though the shift in absolute terms was small. Nonetheless, the 1920 census marked the demographic high point of white dominance in the USA.

6.2.4 The slave trade

The European conquest and population of the Americas was intimately tied to the other great mass movement in the seventeenth and eighteenth centuries, the slave trade, the forcible movement of people overwhelmingly from sub-Saharan Africa across the Atlantic to the Americas and the Caribbean (Curtin, 1969; Fox-Genovese and Genovese, 1983; Blackburn, 1988, 1997). The demographic destruction of the Americas and the Caribbean created vast unpopulated empires in which land was plentiful and labour scarce. Despite the use of indentured European labour and the promise of economic opportunities, few Europeans were prepared to make the crossing in the seventeenth and eighteenth centuries. Creating a labour force for the New World would initially require extensive coercion. The Atlantic slave trade persisted for over four hundred years, from the mid-fifteenth century to the mid-nineteenth century. It built on, and intersected with, an extensive slave trade in the Indian Ocean basin tying East Africa to the Middle East, the Ottoman Empire and European colonies in the Indian Ocean. As ever, data is sketchy, but estimates suggest that between 1500 and 1900 around 4.3 million people were taken from north east, east and central Africa to the Middle East and the Arabian peninsula (Clarence-Smith, 1989).

The European enslavement of Africans can be dated back to at least the 1450s when Portuguese sailors travelling the coast of Africa began supplying an emerging European market for house slaves. But it was the establishment of American and Caribbean colonies and plantation economies that provided the decisive economic push in the expansion of the slave trade. By the beginning of the eighteenth century the Portuguese were overtaken by the British, and squeezed by the French and Dutch, as the triangular relationship between Europe, Africa and the Americas was developed into a routine circuit of commodity exchange of manufactured goods, labour and agricultural produce. The number of Africans transported across the Atlantic is hotly disputed, and estimates have ranged between 5 and 20 million. Contemporary historical debate has settled on a figure of around 9–12 million people transported between 1445 and 1870 (see especially Curtin, 1969; and for that author's most recent estimates, used here, Curtin, 1997). Roughly 325,000 slaves (3 per cent of total shipments) were transported in the sixteenth century, rising to 1.9 million (16 per cent) in the seventeenth and 6.7 million (58 per cent) in the eighteenth before declining in the nineteenth to 2.6 million (23 per cent).

Slave raids by both Europeans and Africans were conducted from the sixteenth century all along the sub-Saharan West African coast and they penetrated into the hinterlands: the extent of depopulation and social dislocation was immense, while the character of the ethnic, economic and cultural life of the southern USA, the Caribbean and the Iberian possessions of Latin America was transformed. The majority of slaves were destined for Brazil and the Caribbean. Over 4 million were shipped to Brazil over three centuries. From fewer than 300,000 slaves in the Caribbean in the early eighteenth century there were almost a million in French and British possessions a hundred years later. In 1835 around 20,000 whites and 300,000 black slaves were living in Jamaica, a ratio that was characteristic of European colonies in the Caribbean. In 1860, 34 per cent of the population of the southern US states were slaves: 3.8 million out of 11 million people in total (Kenwood and Lougheed, 1989). This demographic balance was not the result of substantially higher forced migration to the US; indeed less than 10 per cent of the slave trade was destined for the US. Rather, American slave owners devoted themselves more ruthlessly and systematically to the propagation of an indigenous slave population. It is clearly difficult to overestimate the enduring moral, political, cultural and economic consequences of this and the wider treatment of slaves.

6.2.5   Asian diasporas: indentured and contract labour

With the abolition and eventual decline of the slave trade in the mid-nineteenth century, the mass migration of Asian labourers – or the coolie system, as it was known – began to develop. This allowed colonial economies to replace slave labour and, in the case of Australia, acquire a source of ultra-cheap labour at the very moment that the use of convict labour from Britain was in decline (Tinker, 1974; Potts, 1990; C. Clarke et al., 1990). Coolie labour was generally based on short-term contracts bound by penal sanctions, linked to debts incurred in transit and invariably barbaric in its working conditions and levels of pay. Accurate estimates of the movement of Asian labour are difficult to come by. The seasonal and often illegal nature of the migrations further complicates an already fragmented picture, but it is clear that the late nineteenth and early twentieth century saw the large-scale movement of workers from India, China, Japan and Java to the USA, and to British, French, German and Dutch colonies in Asia, Africa and the Caribbean. This was truly a global migration.

Probably the most statistically significant migration in the nineteenth century was the movement of Indian workers. This migration comprised indentured labourers travelling to British and other colonies, shorter term contract labourers, clerical and administrative staff for far-flung British imperial outposts, and more independent elite migrations in pursuit of commercial opportunities. A middling estimate of the numbers involved suggests that between 1834 and 1937, 30.2 million people left India and 24.1 million returned, giving a net migration figure of around 6 million (Tinker, 1974; Potts, 1990). Segal suggests a lower figure for net migrations over the period 1815–1914 of around 3 million (Segal, 1993). The geographical scope of these migrations was immense. Within the Pacific region, Indians went to Burma, Malaysia, Singapore, Australia and Fiji, 4.5 million arriving in Malaysia alone. Over 500,000 Indian workers migrated to British Caribbean possessions between 1838 and 1918, and over 300,000 went to French Mauritius between 1834 and 1867 (Vertovec, 1995). Indians also migrated to Tanzania, Kenya, Malawi, Zambia, South Africa and Uganda (Thiara, 1995).

Comparable to these migrations were the enormous waves of Chinese migration – temporary, seasonal and permanent – across South East Asia and to the USA (and, to a lesser extent, Europe). In the USA they formed the backbone of the workforce that built America's railroads and dug the earth in the California gold rushes (Hui, 1995). Chinese workers could also be found on Dutch plantations in Sumatra, and in the cities of the Transvaal. Given the diversity and illegality of the coolie trade, data are inevitably fragmentary and there is considerable disagreement over total levels of migration. It has been suggested that, at its height, annual movements in South East Asia involved 750,000 people a year. Over the forty years between 1848 and 1888 Wang has estimated that around 2.35 million migrants left China (S. Wang, 1978). Segal has offered an estimate of 12 million migrants between 1815 and 1914 (A. Segal, 1993). This (lucrative) trade was run by Chinese business operating in the south of the country.

Japanese migration, some of which involved indentured labour, began in the 1860s when the Meiji Restoration ended centuries of self-imposed Japanese isolation from the rest of the world. In the 1870s there was a trickle of emigration from Japan to Hawaii and other South Pacific Islands. At the turn of the century domestic economic recession boosted emigration, and people began to flow towards the west coast of North America, both in Canada and California. After the First World War, US immigration restrictions diverted these mounting flows towards South America where substantial Japanese communities were established in Peru, Argentina and, above all, Brazil: 188,000 Japanese migrants left for Brazil between 1908 and 1941 (Shimo, 1995). Official estimates put the total level of migration over the period 1900–42 at around 620,000 (Ministry of Foreign Affairs, 1971). Immigration to Japan was much smaller than this. Official figures show that in 1910 there were only 15,000 foreigners resident in Japan, a figure that only grew to 54,000 by 1930. This constituted less than 0.1 per cent of the population. During the Second World War this figure rose dramatically as the increasingly repressive Japanese occupation of Korea brought many Koreans to Japan as labourers. By 1943 there were around 560,000 Koreans in Japan.

Finally, substantial numbers of Micronesians and Melanesians were forced into indentured labour. Over 250,000 Pacific islanders were recruited as indentured labourers for Australia, Peru, Fiji and Hawaii between 1840 and 1915 (Potts, 1990). The system of indentured labour was slowly abolished in the early twentieth century, but in the Dutch East Indies it persisted up to 1941.

6.2.6 Regional migrations and early industrialization

As we have already made clear, cross-border migration of labour in Europe has a long history. Moreover, these movements of labour were overlain by the dynamics of empire and nation-building and the transatlantic migration process. Nonetheless, there is ample evidence to suggest that the industrialization of Europe in the late nineteenth century, the widening difference in performance of national economies and the construction of cross-continental railroads led to a new and intensified wave of *regional* migration.

Broadly speaking, we can divide the European continent into labour-importing countries and labour-exporting countries, though over time there was a blurring of the two categories. Sweden, for example, shifted from an exporter to a net importer of labour after the First World War. Germany and Britain, despite importing labour, continued to send migrants overseas in the late nineteenth and early twentieth centuries. The main recipients of migrants were Britain, France, Germany and Switzerland. The main exporters were Poland, Ireland and Italy. Spain and Portugal were hardly involved in these migrations but experienced steady outward flows to their ex-imperial Latin American possessions.

The most important destination country for European emigration was France, which had low levels of transatlantic emigration throughout the nineteenth century, relatively small migrations to colonial possessions and a rather slow pace of urbanization relative to other European states (Cross, 1983; Hollifield, 1992). It has been argued that 'the rural exoduses that provided labour for English and German migration did not begin in earnest in France until the twentieth century. Thus French capitalism was forced to invent a working-class, in view of the unwillingness of rural workers to leave their farms, by importing labour from abroad' (Hollifield, 1992, p. 47). In coal and steel, foreigners formed the backbone of the workforce but they could also be found in agriculture, services and transportation. Alongside relatively small internal migrations, workers flooded into France from Belgium, Italy, Iberia, Germany and the Austro-Hungarian Empire as well as from Holland, Russia and Poland. Foreigners formed 1.1 per cent of the population in 1850, climbing to 3 per cent on the eve of the First World War and attained a high of 6.6 per cent in the mid-1930s: a figure not exceeded until the 1970s. In absolute terms this entailed an increase from 380,000 foreigners in France in 1851 to 1.16 million in 1911 (figures calculated from Mitchell, 1992).

Germany, by contrast, did not permit the levels of permanent migration and residence that the French allowed (Homze, 1967; Herbert, 1990). Immigration to Germany is unrecorded prior to 1900, and in the first decade of the century records show a mere

49,000 migrants, a figure climbing to 841,000 in the 1920s before collapsing again to 413,000 in the 1930s. These are almost certainly underestimates as seasonal workers from Poland were allowed into Prussia from 1880. They filled the vacuum left by German emigration to the cities and provided sufficiently inexpensive labour to maintain the precarious profitability of Junker estates. In 1871 around 0.5 per cent of the population was of foreign origin, but this had climbed to 1.9 per cent by 1910 – almost a quadrupling (calculated from figures in Mitchell, 1992). This marked the high point of voluntary emigration to Germany and the level of official foreigners declined until the mid-1950s. Those unfortunate enough to be in Germany at the outbreak of war in 1914 were forced to stay for the duration: a pattern of forced foreign labour replicated by the Nazis, with many more people involved, from 1939 to 1945 (Herbert, 1990). The low level of immigration to Germany contrasts with the higher levels of emigration. In the 1870s over 700,000 Germans emigrated, mainly to North America. This figure almost doubled in the 1880s before declining again to a mere 91,000 between 1910 and 1919 (calculated from figures in Mitchell, 1992; see also Nugent, 1995).

Britain continued to be a key source of transatlantic migration throughout the period of industrialization, but also began to receive significant inflows of workers as well (Foot, 1965; Garrard, 1971). The desperate situation of Ireland had generated a steady stream of migrants across the Irish Sea, replacing the gaps left in the labour market by Welsh and Scottish flows to the USA. From the late nineteenth century these flows were supplemented by the arrival of Eastern European and Russian Jews, Italians and Lithuanians. Emigration from the UK totalled over 2.2 million in the 1870s and the same again in the following decade. It fell off in the 1890s to only 1.7 million before rising in the first two decades of the twentieth century to 2.8 and 2.3 million a decade. Emigration began to slow in the early 1920s, with total emigration for the decade a mere 1.5 million before the US shut its doors; in the 1930s emigration fell to only 242,000. At its peak emigration was running at a level of 0.8–1.0 per cent of the total population annually. Immigration into Britain, by contrast, never exceeded 0.5 per cent of the population, even at its height in the years before the First World War. Nonetheless, total immigration to the UK in the decade 1910–19 was over 1.3 million, more than double the levels of the 1870s and three times the levels of the 1930s (calculated from figures in Mitchell, 1992).

Sweden witnessed considerable levels of emigration during this period despite its own very rapid and successful industrialization after 1880 (figures from Norman and Runbolm, 1976; Mitchell, 1992; Gjerde, 1995). In the 1870s over 270,000 Swedes left for other countries (reaching levels as high as 1.2 per cent of the population emigrating annually). In subsequent decades the pressure continued with 363,000 emigrating in the 1880s and 233,000 in the 1890s. However, by the 1920s annual emigration had fallen to only 68,000, while in the 1930s it fell as low as 25,000 a year. Immigration to Sweden during this period was considerably less: 65,000 in the 1880s, 83,000 in the 1900s. However, immigration levels stayed fairly constant so that by the 1930s immigration actually exceeded emigration three times over.

6.2.7   Migration in an era of global war

For most of the long nineteenth century (1760–1914) economic forces were the primary movers of migratory flows. The early push of religious persecution and the pull

of distant and exotic wealth in the seventeenth century gave way to the blunter realities of differential economic development, and opportunities in the Americas for
many Europeans. For African slaves and Asian labourers, the economic squeeze was
supplemented by military and legal coercion. While the slave trade had been halted
in the nineteenth century the scope and scale of European and Asian migrations continued to escalate into the early twentieth century. These great waves of migration
were brought to an almost complete halt by the First World War. When the smoke
cleared in 1918 the situation was transformed; the demand for European, Asian and
African labour in the colonies was in decline; a nationalist and exclusionary politics
was on the rise in many states, and the restrictive immigration policies that flowed from
this further slowed the pace of these older global migrations. Economic dislocation
in Europe after the First World War, combined with the global economic downturn of
the 1930s, ensured that levels of global migration remained very low throughout the
interwar period (Zolberg, 1997).

In Europe significant population movements continued, driven by warfare and ethnic
conflict. Poles headed from old Russian and Austrian Poland to the newly independent
Polish state. Germans simultaneously decamped from western Poland and headed
for the Weimar Republic. Russians fled the revolution, around 1.1 million leaving for
Europe before 1922. Prior to the war Armenians had begun to flee Turkish persecution, which continued into the early 1920s and saw around half a million Armenians
migrate. In the wake of the Greco-Turkish war of the early 1920s, 1.2 million Greeks
left Turkey for Greece (Kulischer, 1948).

The First World War was fought predominantly between empires, and while nationalist conflicts and ethnic differences drove some migrations, they pale into insignific-
ance against the impact of the Second World War and the uneasy peace of the early
postwar era. During this war, huge numbers of people fled the advancing German
armies while the Germans forced millions into concentration camps, mainly in Poland.
With the conclusion of the war around 6 million ethnic Germans in Poland left for
Germany and around 4 million left the Soviet zone of occupation for the West. Once
again, as the Polish state's borders shifted westward, 3 million Poles left eastern old
Poland (ceded to the Soviet Union) for the new Poland. And over 2.5 million ethnic
Germans left Czechoslovakia for Austria and Germany.

In the immediate aftermath of the war significant forced migrations continued. Around
700,000 Palestinians were ejected from the newly formed state of Israel (B. Morris,
1987; Adelman, 1995); 15 million refugees were exchanged between India and Pakistan
during and after partition; and in the early 1950s around 5 million Koreans fled from
the north to the south (Zolberg, 1997). However, as we shall see, the power of economic forces to shape migration recovered its strength in the postwar era in Europe and
the West in general, while state-building and war have become increasingly important
generators of migratory flows in the developing world.

6.3 Contemporary Patterns of Migration

While the relative geographical extensity and intensity of pre-1914 and post-1945
migrations are closely balanced, there can be no doubt that the postwar era has seen
a massive expansion in migratory flows relative to the interwar period. There is now
almost no state or part of the world that is not importing or exporting labour (see

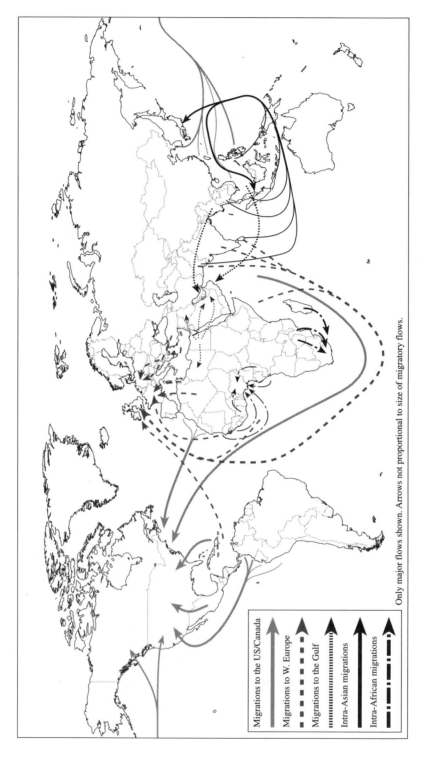

Only major flows shown. Arrows not proportional to size of migratory flows.

Migrations to the US/Canada
Migrations to W. Europe
Migrations to the Gulf
Intra-Asian migrations
Intra-African migrations

Map 6.2 Major global migrations, 1945–1995

map 6.2). With the collapse of European and Soviet communism a swathe of new areas, previously sealed off, have become caught up in migratory flows. These flows are not exclusively towards the OECD states, though a significant component of them is. There are also major patterns of migration within South East Asia, the Middle East and North Africa, sub-Saharan Africa and Latin America. All these areas have become locked into both *global* and *regional* patterns of migration. In this overview we try to distinguish between the two, while describing their interrelationship.

6.3.1 The globalization and regionalization of migration

The contemporary era of migration begins with the end of the Second World War, which induced massive population displacements (see section 6.2.7 above). Charting the overlapping geographies and time-scales of the postwar migrations that followed is complex. In terms of intensity and geographical extensity, the most significant flows have been the economic migrations to OECD countries, in Western Europe, Oceania and North America. However, these migrations were not all of a piece.

In Western Europe, early postwar migration was often regional in its scope. European countries then became enmeshed in more extensive migrations. In the 1950s and 1960s, Belgium, France, Germany and Switzerland began active programmes of overseas labour recruitment, drawing first on the Southern European periphery before extending their reach to Turkey and North Africa. Sweden drew on its own Finnish northern periphery. Most of these migrants came as part of semistructured, semi-official guest-worker programmes and their migrations were intended to be temporary rather than permanent. Overlapping with these movements ex-colonial states furnished large global flows to France, Britain and the Netherlands. Given the colonial connection these movements were more permanent, and combined returning colonial administrators and settlers as well as indigenous colonial peoples.

In the mid-1960s emigration to Australia and North America began to take off; initially migrants came from Europe but these flows soon gave way to Latin American, Asian-Pacific and Caribbean movements. In this regard, while the global element of migrations to the USA and Australia has always been large, the regional component of migration flows has intensified as European flows have diminished and Mexican flows to the USA and Asian-Pacific flows to Australia have picked up.

The global economic downturn of the mid-1970s slowed Western European immigration as guest-worker programmes were terminated and immigration regulations tightened, though family reunions continued to maintain a significant level of immigration. Transatlantic flows were finally reversed as, for example, emigrants from Argentina and Brazil headed for Spain, Italy and Portugal. The Mediterranean states became labour importers as well as exporters and experienced their first wave of illegal immigration from North Africa and, in the Italian case, from the impoverished postcommunist Balkans. The 1980s saw an almost universal tightening of immigration and citizenship laws in Western Europe. In North America and Australia, by contrast, immigration escalated and showed an even more determined shift from people of European origin to people of Asian and Latin American origins. We consider these flows in more detail below.

6.3.2   The stratification of migratory flows

As opportunities to migrate to Western Europe declined in the 1970s, and the process of differential economic development became sharper in the developing world, new global and regional migratory patterns emerged. Among the most global of these were the migrations to the Middle East, where the 1974 oil price rises generated a phenomenal demand for labour in the oil-rich but sparsely populated states of the region (Seecombe and Lawless, 1986). Even so, intraregional flows cut across global flows. Large numbers of Egyptians and Tunisians migrated to oil-rich Libya from the mid-1960s onwards, though their status remained precarious and their numbers subject to the political whims of the regime. Palestinians formed an equally important component of the regional diasporas: already displaced by the formation of the state of Israel in 1948, the occupation of the West Bank in 1967 displaced them further. Migration involved movements to Israel itself on a day-by-day basis for work, as well as more permanent settlement in Jordan and contract labour in the Gulf states. A decade later the Lebanese civil war generated a similar diasporic exodus. The main labour-importing states in the region have been Kuwait, Saudi Arabia, Qatar, Oman, Bahrain and the United Arab Emirates, as well as Iran and Iraq to the north. The main exporters have been Egypt, Yemen, Jordan, Lebanon and Sudan. The estimate for all migrants among these states prior to the Gulf War is around 2–3 million (A. Segal, 1993, based on Martin, 1991). In the early 1980s the declining revenues from oil, and fear over immigrants' political allegiances (for instance, to anti-government Islamicist organizations) led to a downturn of these regional flows and to increasingly global labour recruitment from East Asia and South Asia. These new migrants were assumed by the region's rulers to be more pliant. Indians, Bangladeshis and Pakistanis, including many highly skilled workers, began to move west, while women working as domestic servants and in service industries began to arrive from Sri Lanka and the Philippines. In Kuwait, Qatar and the United Arab Emirates foreigners actually outnumber natives.

Patterns of migration within Asia show a similar combination of global and regional flows (Fawcett and Cariño, 1987; Skeldon, 1992; Fong, 1993). Prior to the 1970s, levels of migration, other than those to OECD countries, were low. In the 1970s migratory flows accelerated but shifted from European destinations to North America, Australia and, as noted above, to the Gulf states. In 1965 a mere 17,000 Asians emigrated to the USA; in the mid-1980s annual migration was around 250,000, constituting nearly 45 per cent of all legal migration to the US. By the late 1980s and early 1990s the numbers of Asians resident in the USA had climbed to 6.9 million, alongside 717,000 in Australia (4 per cent of the population) (US Department of Commerce, *Statistical Abstract*, various years). New Zealand alone of the Anglo-Saxon states in the region did not receive substantial Asian inflows, though it did receive a steady flow of Pacific Islanders.

Within Asia the main labour importers since the mid-1970s have been Japan, Singapore, Taiwan and Brunei. Immigration was driven by their rapid economic development and tight domestic labour markets. In 1991 migrants made up 11 per cent of the Singaporean labour force. The main exporters of labour have been China, the Philippines, India, Bangladesh, Pakistan, Indonesia and Sri Lanka. South Korea, Malaysia, Thailand and Hong Kong have exported and imported labour in roughly equal amounts. Alongside these economically driven flows Asia has also experienced very substantial refugee flows. In the early 1990s around half of the world's 15–20 million refugees were located in Asia, displaced by the Indo-Chinese wars, the regional revolutions and civil wars of the 1960s and 1970s, and the Soviet invasion of Afghanistan in 1979. By 1989 3.6 million Afghans had fled to Pakistan and over 2 million to Iran (Zolberg, 1997).

Sub-Saharan Africa has generated significant global flows of migrants in the post-war era, mainly to ex-colonial states: Nigerian, Tanzanian and Ugandan Asians have migrated to the UK; Central and West Africans to France; Zairians to Belgium (Curtin, 1978; Castles and Miller, 1993). However, the OECD has argued that these movements are dwarfed by regional migrations within Africa (OECD, 1993a). Regional labour migrations have flowed primarily to Nigeria, South Africa, Gabon and the Ivory Coast. The main countries of emigration have been Zaire, Angola, Mozambique, Cameroon and Botswana as well as all of the North African nations, though rarely have their emigrants crossed the Sahara. The scale of migrations of West Africans to oil-rich Nigeria is most sharply revealed by the level of expulsions that occurred after the economic downturn of the early 1980s. South Africa has provided the other major pole of migration, where a long-established tradition of labour importation to the goldfields of the Transvaal continues to operate. Migrants have come from Botswana, Lesotho, Malawi and Mozambique for over a century. Since the 1960s these migrations have declined as indigenous trade unions have strengthened their hold on the labour market. Foreign workers in the mining industry have declined from over 600,000 in 1960 to fewer than 400,000 in the late 1980s and numbers continue to fall. However, such is the economic disparity between South Africa and its northern neighbours that unorganized and illegal migration continues, disappearing into the vast, unpoliced townships of urban South Africa.

The scale of war and refugee movements particularly mark African patterns of migration (K. Wilson, 1995; Zegeye, 1995). Torn by wars of state formation and ethnic conflict in southern Africa and the Horn of Africa particularly, Africa's refugee population climbed from 300,000 in 1960 to over 1 million in 1970 and 3.5 million in 1981. UNHCR figures for 1990 refer to only 2 million international refugees in the continent, but this radically underestimates the numbers of displaced persons in Sudan – probably over 3 million (Curtin, 1997). With the cataclysmic events in Rwanda and Burundi in 1994–6 and the Sudanese civil war, the total refugee population of the continent probably now exceeds 7 million (see Curtin, 1997, for a discussion of this figure).

Latin America, as already noted, has shifted from being a continent of immigration to one of emigration (Balan, 1988; Castles and Miller, 1993). Between 1800 and 1970 around 21 million immigrants arrived in Latin America, overwhelmingly from Southern Europe and destined for Brazil and the southern cone states – Chile, Paraguay, Uruguay, Argentina. In the immediate postwar years the last significant groups of European migrants arrived, including half a million Italians to Argentina between 1945 and 1957 and another 300,000 to Venezuela in the 1950s. Since then the pattern of Latin American migration has been threefold. First, there has been a steady increase in the levels of northwards emigration, legal and illegal, and principally to the USA (especially from Mexico and Central America). Second, there has been a much smaller flow of migrants to Southern Europe. Third, a growing array of regional migrations has occurred. Seasonal, agricultural migrations have been initiated between Colombia and Venezuela as well as between Bolivia, Chile, Paraguay and Argentina. Many of these are illegal migrations drawing on the Caribbean.

Finally, we turn to Eastern Europe, which up until 1989 was effectively cordoned off from regional and global migratory flows. With the collapse of communist states and their highly restrictive emigration policies, patterns of European migration at least have been transformed. The 1990s have witnessed over 2 million Soviet Jews emigrate to Israel. To the immediate east of Western Europe, Hungary, the Czech and Slovak republics and Poland have generated very little long-term migration. However, these states have increasingly become buffer zones, where migratory flows (that have begun further south and east, in the states of the ex-Soviet Union and in the Balkans) pause before attempting to travel further westwards. In 1991, Poland had an estimated 700,000 foreign workers, many seeking to continue their journey west. Further south the civil war in the former Yugoslavia has generated the largest numbers of displaced persons in Europe since the Second World War.

Alongside these global and regional flows of migrant labour a whole range of other flows of travellers and temporary migrants have developed in the years since 1945. The postwar era has seen an explosion in international tourism, increasing levels of business travel and expanding student exchange programmes (see chapter 7). In the last twenty years there have also been, as noted previously, increasing volumes of both refugees and asylum seekers (Zolberg et al., 1989; Widgren, 1993). The distinctions between these categories are ever more blurred, both in reality and in the murky world of national and international migration statistics. These movements of people occur between OECD and developing states and within the developing world itself. Their roots are complex. Some movements are the result of wars between states, but these make up only part of the refugee exodus. As Zolberg has argued, they are predominantly 'the by-product of two major historical processes – the formation of new states and confrontation over the social order in both old and new states' (Zolberg et al., 1989). In addition, this dynamic was overlain by the Cold War and superpower rivalry to produce a complex pattern of refugee movements. In the postwar era, refugees fled from communist revolutions in China (1949), from Eastern to Western Europe immediately after the war as well as after the uprisings in Hungary (1956) and Czechoslovakia (1968). The wars in Korea (1950–3) and Indo-China (1946–75) both produced a flood of refugees, while many Cubans steadily made the passage to the USA. UNHCR estimates suggest that the numbers of refugees in the developing world rose sharply as the process of decolonization and new state formation took off, from around 2 million in the 1950s to current levels of around 25–30 million. Of this total around 14–15 million are displaced persons within their own state (UNHCR, 1993; 1994, p. 3).

During the Cold War governments in the West viewed flight from the East as something to be encouraged. Liberal and open asylum regulations were part of the West's claim to moral and political superiority over the East. However, in the 1970s and 1980s the tumult of state building and state collapse in the South brought unanticipated numbers of asylum seekers to both Europe and North America. In 1973 the total number of asylum applications in the OECD was 25,000. In 1990 it had reached an annual level of almost 550,000. The cumulative total from 1983 to 1990 is 2.2 million people. Coupled with the tightening of immigration laws in the West over the same period, current trends suggest that at some point in the near future the number of asylum seekers will exceed the number of voluntary migrants presenting themselves at the borders of OECD countries.

6.3.3 Trends and patterns in contemporary migration: diversity and complexity

The contemporary era is witnessing a very complex pattern of overlapping and inter-acting global and regional migratory flows of both an economic and non-economic nature. At the centre of these global flows have been economically driven migrations to OECD countries initially at a regional level, from poorer to richer Western states, and then at a global level from the developing world. In the 1950s the flows were predominantly to Western Europe, but they subsequently shifted to North America and Australia. In addition, global migrations have focused on the Middle East. The other large migratory flows have been regional and have developed apace from the 1960s within South East Asia, western and southern Africa, Latin America and within the Middle East.

Clearly, much contemporary migration is driven by the operation of increasingly transboundary labour markets created by both informal and ad hoc as well as formal and institutionalized arrangements. But from the late 1960s economic migrations were traversed by a rising tide of war-driven migrations, refugee movements and asylum seeking. While Western Europe and the USA have been touched by these global migrations, the vast majority have been regionally concentrated in areas of conflict in Asia and Africa. In addition, basic economic forces driving migrations have themselves frequently been overlain by political factors shaping the migration process. A variety of imperial connections and obligations have boosted the level of immigration into France, Britain and the Netherlands, determined its geographical composition and changed the terms on which immigrants enter these countries. Under constitutional obligation, the Federal Republic of Germany received a steady flow of Germans from the German Democratic Republic and East Central Europe. The same principles of citizenship that exclude the former from the immigration figures have massively inflated the numbers of those defined as temporary workers and dependants – even those who are second-generation, German-born (see section 6.5 for a discussion of this). Sweden, because of its special cultural and political relationships with the rest of Scandinavia, has received large numbers of other Scandinavians as part of an open regional labour market considerably more liberal than anything the European Community established prior to the Single European Market. In addition, Swedish foreign policy in this era, with its stress on internationalism and human rights, generated the domestic consensus required to allow significant numbers of political refugees into the country – which explains Sweden's significant Chilean and Kurdish populations. Even Japanese patterns show political factors at work as the vast majority of the immigrant population have been Koreans who relocated to Japan during the occupation of their country. As such, distinct national levels of migration have been accompanied by distinct geographical patterns of inward migration.

The historical pattern of migration for most European countries has been fourfold. First, there was a low starting point after the Second World War, temporarily raised by the shifting movements of the many displaced peoples generated by the war itself. Second, there was increasing growth in migration rates in the 1950s, accelerating in the 1960s and peaking somewhere in the early 1970s. The impact of the oil shocks on economic performance, the fall in the demand for labour and the consequently bitter politics of immigration are clearly evident in the statistics. Third, after the mid-1970s, migration continued, if at slightly lower levels and driven more by family reunions than the push and pull of global economic factors. Fourth, in the 1980s, varying between countries, the rate of migration began to accelerate again. This intensified in the early 1990s as the economic booms in Western Europe, the post-1989 turbulence in East Central Europe and the former Yugoslavia and the creation of the Single European Market pushed levels of immigration back up again.

The USA attempted to keep a lid on immigration levels after the war using large reserves of African-American and rural labour as well the export of capital to absorb the consequences of full employment. The transformation of immigration legislation in the mid-1960s, abolishing regional quotas and allowing for extensive family reunion, did not result in an immediate upsurge in migration but, from the early 1970s onwards, the USA has seen a sustained wave of immigration that dwarfs even the high levels of German and French immigration. The sources of migration to the USA have shifted from Europe to the Asia-Pacific and Central and South America. Significant numbers of Canadian and Mexican migrants have given these new flows a regional dimension as well. Japan, by contrast, saw very little migration into and out of the country for most of the postwar era. It has retained a small foreign population, though by the late 1980s this too was beginning to grow, mainly from illegal rather than legal sources.

Shifting historical patterns of migration have also been accompanied by changes in the make-up of the immigrant population and their employment opportunities. In the 1950s and 1960s most immigrants were destined for menial jobs in the public services and dirty jobs in the manufacturing sector. However, OECD employment in both of these economic sectors has either stagnated or shrunk in the 1980s and 1990s (see chapter 3). In effect, migration, like the economies of the West, has assumed elements of a postindustrial form. First, increasing numbers of migrants have gone into private service industries and domestic services, with a corresponding rise in the numbers, and employment, of female migrants (King, 1995). Second, alongside these flows there has been a steady movement of highly skilled, highly trained professionals, that is, elite migration. As multinational corporations have expanded their international operations (see chapter 5) and national immigration agencies have targeted highly skilled workers, these flows have climbed. They include movements within the West as well as a significant 'brain drain' from the developing world to the West (Salt and Findlay, 1989; Salt and Ford, 1993). In the first few decades of the postwar era, the UN has calculated that international migration of highly skilled labour was around 300–400,000 people. The major sources of this burst of elite migration were India, China, Sri Lanka and Ghana. The USA absorbed 120,000 of these migrants and the UK and Canada over 80,000 each (A. Segal, 1993). Since the 1970s, the Gulf states have become key importers of highly skilled labour, but flows to the West continue apace with the addition of people from the Philippines, Pakistan, Argentina and Brazil.

6.4 Historical Forms of Global Migration: a Comparison

We can return now to some of the questions and issues with which we began this chapter (section 6.1), and attempt an overall comparison of global migration in the key historical epochs discussed so far. The very earliest long-range migrations occurred in a context in which states either did not exist or were minuscule and where the writ of political authority was significantly limited in scope. Economic pressures, ideological forces and inquisitiveness drove the first global migrations. With the establishment of settled centres of power, migrations tended to accompany the outward thrust of military might, occasionally preceded but more often accompanied by or followed by missionaries, traders and agrarians. The expansion of the Roman Empire and the Chinese Empire are examples of this. The expansion of the Islamic world demonstrates the importance of nomad military migrations that created new imperial centres from a nomadic starting point – the Aryans in India, the Mongols across Asia and the Barbarian invasions of Europe fit this pattern.

Viewed in this perspective the migrations that initially accompanied the outward push of European empire-building from the fifteenth century onwards are closer to the Chinese or Roman pattern of settled states expanding outwards. However, established imperial outposts and emigrant communities were separated from the metropolis by vast transoceanic distances and in that regard are closer to the network of Islamic states which spread out across the Middle East and around the Indian Ocean. But, unlike Rome, China or Islam, European empires in Oceania and the Americas encountered civilizations that they were able, quite literally, to obliterate, demographically and politically. This created the possibility of permanent mass migrations that exceeded earlier forms of imperial expansion. While military and cultural power remain significant factors in explaining these migrations, economic power attained a greater significance than in earlier epochs. Indeed, the demand for labour generated by this early imperial expansion was so great that the slave trade which accompanied it was not only larger than the earlier Roman or Arabic slave trades, but directed to the colonies rather than back to the metropolis.

As the European empires have been dismantled by the formation of nation-states in the Americas and then through revolution and decolonization in Africa, the Middle East and Asia, migrations accompanying conquest and imperial expansion have shrunk. The abolition of the slave trade further diminished the importance of military power in organizing migration. The Asian migrations of the nineteenth and early twentieth century continued to feed the labour markets of imperial European outposts and its successor nation-states. However, the major transatlantic migrations from Europe to the Americas in the nineteenth and early twentieth century are more characteristic of contemporary migrations – in which citizens of one nation-state emigrate to another nation-state caught in the push and pull of differential economic development and opportunity. While war and conflict continue to generate refugee and asylum flows, the overwhelming majority of contemporary global migrations are economically driven, leaving political borders untouched. We return to the implications of these shifts for states' capacity to control their borders and population later.

6.4.1   Historical forms: spatio-temporal comparisons

The migrations of the pre-Neolithic era in which homo sapiens reached every corner of the globe were as globally extensive as any subsequent pattern of migration; however, the numbers involved were minuscule, even when the very small global population

Grid 6.1 Key historical flows of global migration

	Premodern Pre-1500	Early modern Approx. 1500–1760	Modern Approx. 1760–1945	Contemporary Approx. 1945 on
Key migratory flows	Hunter-gatherers expand into previously unpopulated areas – latterly from North East Asia into the Americas and from East Asia through the Pacific Island chains Within Eurasia-Africa, most migrations driven by agrarian empire building, mass movements in their wake either displacing or incorporating hunter-gatherers and weaker agrarian societies Large-scale migrations of this form include the Roman and Greek empires, formation of Chinese civilization, southward drift of Bantu-speaking peoples in Africa Some key large-scale migrations led by nomadic herding peoples pursuing new grazing lands and/or imperial adventures, including barbarian invasions of Europe (5th century); expansion of Arabic nomadic warriors; Mongol empires 12th century onwards Jewish Diaspora from Middle East across North Africa, Western Asia and Europe	Settlers/colonists from Northern and Western Europe to colonies in North America, Latin America, Caribbean Very small European migrations to East Asia, Southern Africa Slave trade from sub-Saharan Africa to the Americas and the Caribbean Slave trade from sub-Saharan Africa to North Africa and the Middle East By comparison, small-scale migrations within Europe	Up to 1914, huge economic migration from Europe to the Americas and the newly colonized areas of Oceania Parallel overland migrations by Russian colonists into Central Asia and Siberia Transatlantic and Indian Ocean slave trades peak before termination in the mid to late nineteenth century Up to 1914, complex mixture of Asian (Chinese, Indian, Japanese, Pacific Islander) migrations mainly tied/contract labour: within Asia; to European colonies in Africa, the Caribbean and the Pacific; and to North America and some parts of Latin America Differing levels of industrialization in Europe and Southern Africa drive regional labour migration	End of WWII and accompanying political settlements bring wave of intense regional migrations, expulsions, etc. (Germany, Poland, Israel and Palestine, India-Pakistan, Korea) Core migratory flows in this period are economic migrants to OECD states After 1973 global and regional flows to the Middle East from North Africa, Southern Asia, South East Asia Highly skilled economic migrants on the rise, both staffing MNCs and considerable 'brain drain' from South to North Post-colonial state formation and civil wars lead to increasing numbers of international asylum seekers, international refugees, regionally displaced persons Increasing numbers of tourists, travellers, international educational exchange

Grid 6.2 Historical forms of global migration

	Premodern Pre-1500	Early modern Approx. 1500–1760	Modern Approx. 1760–1945	Contemporary Approx. 1945 on
Extensity	Early population of the earth very extensive. Last uninhabited lands reached after the turn of the first millennium Subsequent migrations tend to be regional or local with the exception of great nomadic imperial adventures – Islamic Arabs, nomadic Mongols, etc.	Transatlantic settlers and slaving constitute new global flows	Main migrations now truly global in extent – European expansion and Asian diasporas incomparably global Regional migrations within Europe and Southern Africa and from European Russia to Siberia After WWI – reach of global flows contracts, post-WWI settlement and new nation-state formation create short-term, localized flows	Core economic migrations very extensive – global patterns of migrations to Europe, Australasia, North America, Middle East Large regional migrations, within Africa, East Asia, Latin America Diversity of flows
Intensity	Generally low Waves of imperial and military adventures produce occasional and intense bursts of permanent settler activity	Medium – slave trades and European colonization rising in intensity in 18th century	Up to 1914 very intense, especially in final years of 19th century. European emigration massively increases; slave trade dwindles; Asian migrations soar Dramatic fall after WWI though spurts of military-induced migrations and expulsions	Medium but rising throughout the period

continued

Grid 6.2 *continued*

	Premodern Pre-1500	Early modern Approx. 1500–1760	Modern Approx. 1760–1945	Contemporary Approx. 1945 on
Velocity	Velocity of individual travel/migration low However, empire building and nomadic movements show almost unprecedented speed of collective movement and migration	Velocity of individual travel/migration low Large-scale movements of entire nomadic societies terminated by growing relative strength of all sedentary/agrarian societies	Velocity of individual travel/migration medium and increasing	Velocity of individual and group travel/migration very high
Impact propensity	Migrations intimately bound up with the formation and dissolution of empires and civilizations Migrations create societies and borders rather than crossing them In general hunter-gatherers eradicated or incorporated by expanding agrarian societies	Main migrations to the New World constitutive of world historic shift; demographically, culturally, ecologically, politically	Transatlantic migrations serve as economic and political escape valve for industrializing Europe Migration serves as the human basis for the rise of the US state and economy	Europe at high point of ethnic homogeneity begins to acquire sizeable non-European minorities Europe averts some of the problems of full employment and ageing societies Impact on welfare expenditure and income broadly neutral US becomes more plural and more diverse All states faced by prospect of political and cultural redefinition of the meaning of national identity and citizenship
Infrastructure	Migration overwhelmingly by land – dependent on	Transoceanic shipping systems across the	Shipping systems mechanized and	Air travel transforms prospects for

	existing roads and routes Some maritime migrations across enclosed seas (the Mediterranean) or by island hopping (Pacific islands); transoceanic shipping and merchant migrations possible in the Indian Ocean	Atlantic, the core infrastructure of the era's global migrations	regularized; railways aid land movements	economic migrants
Institutionalization	Organization either informal in hunter-gatherer societies or via elites, state builders and military organizations in agrarian/nomadic societies	Increasing organization of migration processes as colonial enterprise Development of early transatlantic chain migration Systematic economic organization of slave trades	Institutionalization increases as states acquire capacity to implement immigration policies in the late nineteenth century Commercial, public and voluntary institutions for recruiting labour and aiding passage established in Europe, North America, Asia and European colonies	High institutionalization of transport systems, border control, labour markets However, this accompanied by increasing illegal migrations International refugee regimes and asylum agreements regulate war-induced migrations Increased surveillance of migration
Stratification	Hierarchies in this era between civilizations/societies as agrarian societies dominate hunter-gatherers and nomadic societies gain occasional power over sedentary societies	Slave labour, contract and indentured labour create clear hierarchies of power between organizers of migrations and migrants – both voluntary and involuntary	Slave labour, contract and indentured labour create clear hierarchies of power between organizers of migrations and migrants – both voluntary and involuntary	Among migrants a hierarchy of ease of movement exists: high-skill migrants have more options than low-skill migrants, refugees and asylum seekers have still fewer State power over individual migrants rising, states' power over collective mass flows may be diminishing

of the time is taken into account. From the emergence of settled agriculture to the early modern era, it is probably true to say that migrations were less geographically extensive than the very earliest flows but more substantial in numbers. As we have seen, this long era saw important migrations within the fluctuating boundaries of imperial systems and shifts of nomadic tribal peoples from steppe lands to settled agricultural plains, in turn displacing already established societies to more peripheral locations. The waves of Eurasian nomads who crossed into Europe are the clearest example of this, though similar movements occurred within Africa and on the Indian subcontinent. This era also saw the first major migratory diaspora – that of the Jews across the Levant, North Africa and Europe. However, while no continent or region was completely and unequivocally isolated from others, the degree of transoceanic interchange was very low. The Vikings' attempted colonization of North America, for example, fizzled out in the tenth or eleventh century; they survived another two centuries in Greenland before being confined to their mid-Atlantic Icelandic redoubt. Perhaps the only truly global pattern of migrations combining military conquest, imperial expansion, missionaries and merchants were those associated with the expansion of the Islamic world. Predominantly elite in their social make up and small in their absolute scale, Islamic migrations were extensive in their reach, from Iberia and Morocco in the west, sub-Saharan Africa in the south, to Persia, northern India, and eventually to the Indonesian archipelago in the east. Thus most of the premodern era is characterized by *regional* migrations and associated displacements.

The migrations which accompanied, and which are in some sense constitutive of, modernity heralded a new wave of truly global movements of peoples. European expansion saw flows from all over Europe to North and South America, the Caribbean, parts of northern and southern Africa and Oceania. The slave trades were constituted by forced migratory flows from across Africa (though regionally concentrated) to North and South America and the Caribbean. The great nineteenth-century flows of Asian peoples channelled migrations from India, China and South East Asia along the conduits of European empire and American industrialization to the Caribbean, Africa, the United States and Canada and extensively within Asia.

How do contemporary patterns of migration compare in terms of their geographical extensity? The key feature of the contemporary era is economic migration to OECD countries. In Western Europe these began, primarily, as intraregional migrations from Southern Europe to Northern and Western Europe. However, these movements were soon surpassed by migrations from ex-colonial possessions and states beyond Europe. For the first time significant incoming migratory flows were established between Western Europe and the Caribbean, the Middle East, North Africa, Latin America and South Asia. Similarly, in North America and Australia, where these migratory flows began later, the already global flows from Europe to the New World of the nineteenth and early twentieth centuries were accompanied and eventually superseded by flows from Latin America, the Caribbean and Pacific-Asia to North America and from Pacific-Asia to Australia. Moreover, all these OECD nations continued to experience intra-OECD migrations of skilled personnel staffing the nodes of an increasingly global economy. In the last twenty years these flows have been accompanied, at a global level, by the movements of people from South Asia to the Gulf and Middle East.

Another dimension to the extensity of contemporary migratory flows is the many regional systems of migration that have emerged alongside these global flows. As we discussed earlier (section 6.3), regional migration has continued within North America and Western Europe but it has also taken off in Latin America, within Africa and across South and South East Asia. With the fall of European and Soviet communism and the end of their restrictive travel regimes a further swathe of the world's states has been opened up to international migration. There are few states that do not experience the movements of migrants inwards or outwards in one form or another – though not all of those movements are global. Overall, contemporary migratory flows are probably more geographically extensive and more global than those of the premodern era and at least as extensive as those of the eighteenth and nineteenth centuries. This, of course, tells us nothing about their relative intensity.

Accurate data for the intensity of migratory flows over long time periods are difficult to accumulate. The debate among historians suggests figures for the European migrations of the nineteenth to early twentieth centuries of around 45 million people. The estimates of the size of the slave trade are, given the unspeakable mortality rate on slaving ships, variable depending on whether we are counting Africans leaving Africa or arriving in the Americas. A mid-range figure of around 9–12 million from the early sixteenth century to the mid-nineteenth is probably the correct order of magnitude. The magnitude of the Asian diasporas of the nineteenth century also vary depending on whether we are counting permanent or return migrations. The historical consensus points to a figure of around 35 million people, returners and permanent migrants, over a hundred-year period, 1820–1920. However, the number of permanent migrants is much lower, perhaps around 12 million.

In terms of chronology the magnitude of total global migrations grew over the early modern and modern periods. Early European migrations to the Americas were small, as were those to Latin America and the Caribbean. The slave trade of the eighteenth and nineteenth centuries was certainly larger in terms of sheer numbers than the flows of the two prior centuries. However, the peak years for global migration during the modern period must be the late nineteenth and early twentieth centuries. In the forty years from 1880 around 30 million Europeans emigrated to the Americas and Australia, while the bulk of the Asian migrations took place at this time as well. The annual depopulation rates for European nations, which provided most of the transatlantic migrants, were larger than those for Africa during the peak of the slave trade.

It is clear that the interwar years marked a radical reversal in the scale of global migrations. Transatlantic and Asian migrations almost ceased, while intra-European migrations declined rapidly. The more difficult comparison is with the contemporary era. Again, calculating gross migratory flows is hampered by the prevalence of return and short-term migration and large numbers of illegal migrants. Moreover, any comparison of these two great eras of migration needs to take into account the vastly larger populations of the late twentieth century. What follows is not in any way a definitive quantitative comparison but one that seeks to establish crude orders of relative magnitude. The three main countries of immigration in the postwar period have been the USA, Germany and France. Official data suggest that between 1945 and 1990 over 18 million people emigrated to the USA (US Department of Commerce, *Statistical Abstract*, various years). However, this time-span does not include the substantial migrations of the 1990–5 period during which around 1 million legal migrants have entered the USA every year. Adding these would give a figure of around 25 million people in fifty years. This is still less than the 30 million who emigrated to the USA from 1880 to 1920. However, there have also been very substantial illegal immigrations into the USA across the Mexico border from the mid-1960s onwards. Again, there are very considerable numbers of return migrations to consider here. A figure of around 1–1.5 million a year has been suggested for illegal immigrants to the US in the 1980s and 1990s, although this may be too high (Bustamente, 1989). Halving this estimate would boost the total postwar level of immigration to over 35 million people. However, the US population in 1990 stood at 248 million, while in 1900 it was only 75 million and in 1880 only 50 million. Thus we can reasonably conclude that contemporary migrations to the USA, while of similar absolute intensity, are of lesser relative intensity than those experienced at the end of the nineteenth century.

That said, the US migrations of that period were by some way the major migrations to Western societies. In the postwar era, they have been accompanied by very large migrations to European nations (for a similar comparison, with similar conclusions, see Morawska and Spohn, 1997). In the case of Germany, total gross migration for the period 1950–88 totalled 24.5 million, while those to France totalled 21.9 million. The UK, the Low Countries, Switzerland and Scandinavia add around another 25 million migrants over the same period. (Estimates calculated from SOPEMI, 1991 and earlier years; and Mitchell, 1975; 1992.) If one adds Australia and Canada, both of which have experienced large migratory flows, then the non-US total for the period 1945–90 is around 80 million. This gives an estimated total well over 100 million for postwar migrations to OECD countries, with the majority of those movements taking place in the thirty years between 1965 and 1995 – more than triple the great transatlantic migrations of the 1880s to 1920. European populations have increased more slowly than the population of the US and thus the European component of migration is probably as intense as the American experience at the turn of the century – although this is diluted by the much larger numbers of return migrations concealed in the gross figures.

In the end, it is a close call. The transatlantic surge of 1880–1920 was certainly more intense than the early colonial emigrations, the slave trade or the Asian migrations of the nineteenth century. It was probably more intense than the global flows of the postwar era – but only just. The comparison between nineteenth-century Asian migrations and contemporary ones is more clear-cut. The former were greater. However, intra-Asian migratory flows are only just beginning to mount as differential rates of economic development generate the preconditions for large movements of labour. If these migrations continue to expand and American migrations continue – and there is no sign of them abating – then the contemporary pattern of migration may supersede its predecessors in terms of intensity as well as extensity. Such trends would clearly be aided by the greater speed of individual and collective travel today. The development of modern communication and transport infrastructures has obviously increased the velocity of the movement of people, although how far this will lead to substantial changes in the gross and net flows of migration is uncertain at this time (see 'velocity' in grid 6.2; and cf. chapter 7 on international travel and tourism).

A systematic comparison of the impact of global migration is in some respects impossible. The early peopling of the remote corners of the world, the transatlantic migrations and European conquests and settlements were unique historical events that are totally unrepeatable and whose world historical impact is unassailable. A similar argument can be made for the slave trade, though the limited permanent settlement of Asian migration in the nineteenth century has left a slighter historical trail. Clearly, the effects of all these global and regional migrations have been immense. To gauge the impact of contemporary forms of migration we need to examine impact in relation to societies and economies that are radically different from the host countries of former times. This makes simple statistical comparisons almost irrelevant. But several important points can be noted.

The most obvious impact of migration is demographic, altering the composition and size of the population of both the source country and the recipient country. For modern welfare states such shifts have far-reaching implications – quite different than those in earlier epochs – for the level and provision of welfare services, housing and education as well as the operation of the economy itself. Conventional xenophobic wisdom has argued that the consequences of this are uniformly negative for host welfare states. Immigrants crowd out the indigenous poor and working class from the bottom end of the job market, overburden already dilapidated welfare systems and generally constitute an overall drain on the public finances. However the evidence, such as it is, does not support this position. In most of the West, indigenous population growth has slowed to almost nothing and in some cases actually gone into decline. This has been accompanied by a major shift in the age structure of populations. As life expectancy has increased and the birth-rate has fallen the populations of many countries are undergoing a significant ageing. The impact of this on the total demand for and cost of welfare services and pensions is gathering pace. However, the impact of ageing on the labour force and labour market is made all the sharper by higher levels of early retirement, deliberate withdrawal from the labour market and an increasing amount of time spent by the young in full-time education and structural unemployment. Thus the dependency ratio of those in work to those not in work or outside the labour force has begun to creep upwards, placing fiscal pressure on welfare states (see Swan et al., 1991).

Immigration is currently making a significant contribution to population growth and thus alleviating some of the ageing problems in OECD countries (OECD, 1993a). Net immigration is the most important absolute and relative contributor to population growth in Austria, Germany, Italy, Luxemburg, Sweden and Switzerland. Migration matches the contribution of indigenous population growth in the USA, Canada, Australia, Greece, Norway and the Netherlands. Finally, migration is a small contributor to demographic change in France, the UK, Belgium, Portugal and Spain. Moreover, in the few systematic studies of the contribution of immigrants to welfare through taxes paid set against the benefits received, no conclusive evidence exists to suggest that benefits received outweigh contributions (Borjas and Trejo, 1993; see also the overview of research in Tapinos and de Rugy, 1993). Indeed, in Western Europe and Canada the impact of immigrants on the welfare state may actually be positive (Simon, 1984, 1989; Akbari, 1989).

By comparison, the economic impact of historical patterns of migration on the labour market and the broader economy is more difficult to establish (for an overview see Tapinos and de Rugy, 1993). The estimation of the impact of migration on wage rates and overall economic performance in host economies is fraught with problems of definition, data gathering, model building, etc. The quantitative work that has been done can be considered at best equivocal (we will return to this issue, in section 6.6, with reference to qualitative research). On the other hand, for migration 'source' countries there has been an obvious economic benefit in the reduction of domestic unemployment (Ghosh, 1996). Studies of South Korea, Pakistan and Sri Lanka all point to the considerable impact of contemporary migration in reducing unemployment (ILO/UNDP, 1988). However, migration may well draw on people who did not participate in the domestic labour force, and in that respect leave high levels of unemployment undiminished. Contemporary migration, in comparison with previous epochs, also tends to cream off some of the most skilled and educated parts of the workforce, impoverishing the domestic economy. The UNDP reports that India, China, South Korea and the Philippines alone lost 145,000 scientifically trained workers to the USA between 1972 and 1985. But, as in the nineteenth century, the main economic benefit of contemporary migration is the reverse flow of remittances from workers to their home country. In 1990 developing countries received a gross flow of $46 billion linked to migrants and net income of $37 billion (UNDP, 1994). Given that a very considerable volume of these flows does not pass through official channels, total remittances are likely to be much higher and, thereby, exceed official development aid flows to these states (see Atalik and Beeley, 1993).

6.4.2 Historical forms: organizational comparisons

In terms of transportation, it is reasonably clear that air travel has superseded the oceangoing ship as the main means of global migration today. Some regional migrations continue to cross land borders – particularly the passage of people from Mexico to the USA. However, shifts in types of transportation have not altered, indeed they may have enhanced, the concentrations of migration flows through key points – airports, certain cities, etc. As a consequence, migratory flows to the West now encounter a more formidable and institutionalized set of border and entry controls than was ever possible on long, unpoliced land borders in an era when citizenship documents were rare and thinly spread.

The slave trade and the movements of Asian labour were organized 'from above' by an alliance of colonial planters and administrations and, in the case of Chinese and Indian migrations to North America, by railroad companies. In the nineteenth century colonial ministries in Europe and colonial authorities abroad combined with philanthropic societies and charities to steer the movement of European emigrants to the 'New World'. In the postwar era in Europe, the state has continued to be central to organizing and regulating migrant flows, but it is not colonial offices but employment ministries that have been key to this. Alongside these agencies, depending on the character of policy-making in a given country, representatives of capital and labour have also been involved, particularly from those specific industries where labour shortages have been sharpest. Placement agencies and recruitment firms have sprung up in sending states, indigenously organizing the flow of labour, legal and illegal, to receiving states. Once again, these organizations have combined with more spontaneous pressures for migration, and with the process set in train, have had to channel and organize family reunions as well as fresh immigration.

At an international level the degree of regulation of the migratory process remains nugatory. Although the treatment of refugees and asylum seekers has been increasingly regulated by international treaty and agreement, no codified international regime or body of law has emerged to regulate the movement of labour that bears any comparison with those regulating trade and capital movements. The International Labour

Organization (ILO) since its inception in the early twentieth century has sought to establish basic rules regarding the treatment of labour (and is now advocating a declaration on fundamental rights in this regard). But only in the European Union has any stringent international legal framework for labour been established, although even this depends on national enforcement. At the national level stronger policing of borders and more stringent regulation of migration have sought to restrict the international mobility of peoples. At the same time, migrants confront more restricted rules for acquiring citizenship rights (see Hollifield, 1992).

These developments reflect a distinct shift in the patterns of stratification between nineteenth-century and late twentieth-century migrations. Whereas in the nineteenth century the direction of migratory flows was generally north to south, today it is primarily south to north, and east to west. This has had significant consequences for European states, in particular, as new levels of immigration have brought new patterns of social stratification. This is starkest in the cases of Sweden and Germany. In both states, the percentage of foreigners in the population in the late nineteenth century was very low: 0.1 per cent in Sweden and 0.5 per cent in Germany. Both figures grew in the following thirty to forty years, peaking at 0.4 per cent in Sweden in 1920 and 1.9 per cent in Germany in 1910. The interwar years saw decline, before the rapid and explosive growth of the postwar era. Between 1960 and 1990 the percentage of foreigners in the population grew from 2.5 to 5.6 per cent in Sweden and from 1.2 to 8.2 per cent in Germany. At the same time, both have acquired a significant number of non-European and black migrants for the first time (historic data calculated from Mitchell, 1975; 1992; recent data taken from SOPEMI, 1991 and earlier years; 1992).

Britain shows a similar trajectory, complicated by the level of naturalizations achieved by people coming into the UK. The 1990 data suggest a foreign population of around 3.3 per cent of the total, but this conceals very visible and very significant ethnic communities with British citizenship. Britain, like Germany and Sweden, is a multiethnic if not multicultural state in a way it never was in the nineteenth century. France is slightly anomalous given the very high levels of inward migration and low transatlantic migration experienced in the nineteenth century. The foreign population in France made up 2.1 per cent of the population in 1870, climbing to 6.6 per cent in the 1930s before declining again to a postwar low in the 1950s. Migration recently has massively expanded that percentage so that foreigners constituted 6.4 per cent of the population in 1990 (historic data calculated from Mitchell, 1975; 1992; recent data from SOPEMI).

Data for Japan are difficult to calculate but we can safely argue that contemporary levels of immigration are historically unprecedented. The USA, as we might expect from our discussion of intensity, has been a multiethnic state since its inception and foreigners constituted an exceptionally large 13.9 per cent of the population in 1870, rising to a peak of over 14 per cent in 1910. The collapse of interwar immigration combined with rapid indigenous population growth saw the figure fall to around 6 per cent in the postwar era. However, the recent immigrations have begun to push that figure back up to above 8 per cent, and with illegal immigration it may well be over 10 per cent. Immigration in the first half of the 1990s was running at a historically unparalleled rate (measured as immigrants per 10,000 of the population) and there is no sign of a radical downturn (historic data calculated from Mitchell, 1983 and US Department of Commerce, 1972; recent data from SOPEMI). Moreover, the US may be approaching a level of ethnic diversity greater than in the nineteenth century – a diversity that is not simply intra-European and African but increasingly Hispanic and Asian as well.

However, these trends alone do not disclose the considerable differences in the cultural experience and social connections of migrant groups. A useful distinction made by Castles and Miller is between the formation of ethnic minorities and that of ethnic communities (1993). In the case of the former, ethnic groups are not only segregated in the labour market and in residential ghettos but experience significant social, cultural and political exclusion. They will tend to exist as marginalized groups on the fringes of a defensive and indigenous society that denies immigrant communities full or even partial citizenship and does not accord them a significant or rightful place in a broader multicultural nation. Ethnic communities, by contrast, exist where 'immigrants and their descendants are seen as an integral part of a multicultural society which is willing to reshape its cultural identity' (Castles and Miller, 1993, p. 195). In fact, as the authors argue, no nation has groups which fit either category completely, nor do these ideal types capture the different experiences of different ethnic groups in the same nation. But nearly all countries lie somewhere between the two poles. They hold that Australia tends towards the model of ethnic communities, while Germany is closer to the model of ethnic minorities. We return to some of the complex cultural consequences of migration in chapter 7 on cultural globalization. Here we focus on the impact of migration on conceptions of national identity and citizenship.

Castles and Miller outline four models of citizenship in Western countries which serve as proxies both for attitudes to citizenship and national identity and for clusters of public policies that emerge from that cultural context: immigration policies, naturalization policies and educational and cultural policies. Those four models/strategies are: illusory; exclusionary; republican-imperial; and multicultural. Illusory attitudes to immigrants are not so much a citizenship model as the deliberate disregard of immigrant communities. In both Japan and Italy state authorities and politicians have turned a blind eye to substantial illegal immigration. This does not mean of course that the civic status of migrants is side-stepped; rather, it is a non-decision that ensures a high degree of marginalization and exclusion, and a cloak of political silence under which a more local racism can be practised. The exclusionary model is broadly a model of ethnic nationalism in which kin, ethnic and linguistic status provide the basis of citizenship. In Switzerland, Germany and Belgium, where this model has tended to prevail, migrants have arrived primarily through highly regulated guest-worker programmes. The legal status of immigrants is acknowledged but is subordinate to that of citizens of the host nation. Possibilities for naturalization and the assumption of citizenship have been highly circumscribed and official and informal cultural contacts between immigrants and the host community are inequitable and distant.

The imperial-republican model is more variegated than any other for it combines a complex and unresolved amalgam of models of citizenship. The model ties civic status ultimately to residence (rather than race) and allows the transition from immigrant to citizen more easily than the exclusionary model. This particularly applies to second-generation migrants born in the host country and to citizens of ex-colonial states who come to the metropolis on more favourable, if still ambiguous, terms than guest-workers. National identity is less exclusionary, inevitably acknowledging the mutual inter-action of metropolitan and colonial culture and society – but remains one in which the metropolitan culture is dominant. This model is exemplified in Britain and France and to an extent in the Netherlands.

Finally, the multicultural model of citizenship is one in which immigration is usually permanent and the transition to citizenship assured. In its ideal form it envisages a civic nationalism in which identities are plural or hyphenated and in which earlier immigrant cultures are redefined in the light of new waves of immigration. This is, of course, a very idealized model, and Castles and Miller acknowledge the severe asymmetries of power and legitimacy displayed, for instance, in the USA between the dominant white culture and the plurality of Hispanic, Black and Asian cultures and groups. They argue that Canada, Australia and Sweden come closest to this model/strategy of citizenship.

While the storm of nationalist politics and the tumult of identity, citizenship and legitimacy have raged much more intensely in the developing world (and in the ex-Soviet states), all of our six case study countries have and continue to be concerned by these issues. Economic uncertainty in the postwar years combined with an incapacity to come to terms culturally with the presence of large numbers of non-Europeans have meant that the strategies of citizenship and national identity pursued in Europe and America have all come under attack (Lithman, 1987; Solomos and Wrench, 1993). Looking at one end of the spectrum, Sweden demonstrates that even the seemingly most entrenched multiculturalism has been prey to these forces. In Sweden, official multiculturalism has been expressed though generous naturalization provisions and asylum and welfare policies for immigrants. Second-language schooling and generous social security arrangements have stemmed from the inclusive universalism of Swedish social democracy. Having made its political fortunes as the vector of a cross-class universalism enshrined in the Swedish welfare state, social democracy with its ideology of egalitarianism was unlikely to tolerate exclusion on the grounds of ethnicity. However, the financial and ideological pillars of an inclusive social democratic welfare state have become shaky, and in turn the treatment of immigrants and the nature of Swedish national identity have come into question. With the mounting presence of immigrant communities and precipitous economic and political uncertainty, the early 1990s saw the emergence of explicitly racist nationalist groups and a more diffuse xenophobic populism.

If Sweden has seen the rise of racist nationalism in recent years it is no surprise that those states with a less inclusive model of citizenship have experienced a similar political fate (Harris, 1990). Germany and France began the process of postwar immigration with more exclusionary notions of national identity and these have helped feed a more sustained and powerful far right politics, principally Die Republikaner in Germany and the Front National in France. Similar movements combining protest politics, disaffected elements of the working class and elements of the middle classes have emerged in Belgium, Austria and the Netherlands, while many of these sentiments were subsumed within the Legga Lombarda in Italy. In Britain, the electoral fortunes and organizational capacity of the far right has been somewhat truncated by the hurdles of the electoral system and the occupation of much of this political territory by right-wing sectors of the Conservative Party.

America stands somewhat astride of these trends. Ethnicity and national identity have been a contested terrain since the inception of the USA. Moreover, the rejection of the older assimilationist melting-pot model of American identity was initiated not by new waves of immigration but by the explosive protests of the civil rights movement in the 1960s. This indigenous conflict has fuelled subsequent debates about American identity and about the contrasting republican-assimilationist and multicultural models. Though the roots of these conflicts are different from those of the European debate, there are similarities in the response. America has seen a revival of white supremacism, an increasingly strident attitude towards illegal immigrants and reassertion of the supremacy of the WASP culture challenged by the upheavals of the 1960s. The success of the Californian 1997 referendum on reducing state benefits and services for undocumented aliens indicates a new acceptance of a very draconian and exclusionary model of citizenship.

6.5 Migration and National Enmeshment

It is clear from the global picture of postwar migrations that, compared to the prewar situation, nearly all our six case study countries have become labour importing rather than labour exporting. While emigration has continued from all six it is, with the exception of the UK, at lower levels than those experienced in the nineteenth and early twentieth century. Immigration in various forms has been the dominant contemporary pattern of enmeshment in migratory flows for these countries.

At the end of the Second World War the USA had in place a variety of restrictive immigration laws passed in the interwar years as well as more restrictive wartime measures. These were relaxed somewhat in the late 1940s to accommodate some 200,000 displaced persons and refugees who settled in the USA. Further restrictive legislation was passed in the 1950s, seeking both to limit the overall total of immigration and restrict it as far as possible to Northern Europeans by the imposition of country-specific and hemispheric quotas (Riemers, 1985; Portes and Bach, 1985; Borjas, 1990). The bulk of official immigration into the US during this period was from Europe and totalled a mere 1.2 million people from 1946 to 1955. Amendments to the 1950s legislation in the 1960s and 1970s increased the official immigration quotas to a total of around 300,000 persons a year: still small by pre-1914 standards.

However, the story of postwar US immigration demonstrates the ultimate failure of this legislation, both in terms of the actual volume of immigration and the skewed quota system, designed to keep Eastern and Southern Europeans, Latin Americans and Asians out. Not only did immigration flows continue unabated, they massively accelerated in the 1970s and 1980s, and their geographical origins fundamentally switched from the historic transatlantic passage to northward flows from Latin America and the Caribbean and transpacific flows from Asia. In the 1980s the rate of immigration – permanent and temporary, legal and illegal – exploded in the US. It is difficult to overestimate the importance of illegal immigration in the US case. US agencies deported around a million persons a year in the 1980s, predominantly Mexican, for inadequate documentation. Some estimates suggest that for every person caught at least four to five slip through the net. This implies an annual flow of something in the region of 4–5 million people, of whom many have effectively assumed permanent residence (Johnson and Williams, 1981; Bustamente, 1989). More restrained estimates suggest that permanent illegals add 200,000 to the US population each year (Papademetriou, 1991). Permanent legal settlement tells a similar story, growing from around 500,000 persons a year in 1980 to over 1.5 million in 1990. Of that number only 112,000 were European compared to 679,000 Mexicans and 338,000 Asians. As a consequence of this surge, the official number of foreign residents, which fell from 6.8 per cent of the population in 1950 to 4.7 per cent in 1970, had grown to over 8 per cent in 1990 and continued to grow throughout the decade (older data calculated from Mitchell, 1983; more recent data from SOPEMI). Taking illegal immigration into account it is quite possible that the figure now exceeds well over 10 per cent of the population and is thus approaching the levels experienced at the turn of the century.

France has continued to experience considerable immigration (SOPEMI, 1991 and earlier years; 1992; Freeman, 1979; Hollifield, 1992). From an initially low level of immigration in the early 1950s, annual immigrant flows constituted over 2 per cent of the labour force in the early 1960s. This rate climbed steadily through the 1970s to 7.7 per cent in 1985, after which it has remained at a high level (older data calculated from Mitchell, 1975; 1992; more recent data from SOPEMI). Moreover, the inclusion of pre-independence Algeria in metropolitan France disguises the level of migration from North Africa to France prior to Algerian independence. Early waves of temporary labour came from Italy but were soon replaced by flows from Iberia, and then Turkey, North Africa and French West Africa. The growing wealth of Southern Europe, and the process of French decolonization, underlay that change. In 1975, Italians, Portuguese and Spanish immigrants made up 50 per cent of the foreign population in France and North Africans 33 per cent. By 1992 the respective figures were 31 per cent and 39 per cent, while the numbers from Eastern and Central Europe, as well as migrants from ex-French African colonies, had grown substantially. By 1982 the number of foreigners in France constituted 6.8 per cent of the French population (SOPEMI). Although there are some demographic differences between host and immigrant populations these have narrowed and thus the size of the foreign population as a percentage of the total population is a reasonable guide to the make-up of the labour force. Throughout the 1980s this fluctuated around 6–7 per cent although it was much higher in certain industries and much lower in others. For example, in the auto industry foreigners made up over 18 per cent of the workforce at the end of the 1970s (Hollifield, 1992).

Official German data show almost no immigration in the late 1940s. After this there is a steady flow of around half a million immigrants each year in the early 1950s, rising to over 800,000 a year in 1965 and peaking again at over a million in the late 1960s and early 1970s (Castles and Kosack, 1985; Hollifield, 1992). This growth slowed down in the late 1970s and early 1980s before gathering pace again through the late 1980s and 1990s. German data are complicated by the different ways in which the migration of ethnic Germans from East Central Europe and those fleeing the GDR have been classified by comparison to the migration of temporary workers. German immigration data does not include the latter. This serves to underestimate the level of immigration to the Federal Republic relative to other European nations. By contrast, the very restricted terms on which non-ethnic Germans have entered the country, and the failure (until 1998) to award German citizenship to second-generation immigrants, especially the very large number of second-generation Turkish-Germans, inflates migration and size of foreign population data in Germany relative to other European nations.

The initial wave of temporary workers in the 1950s were Italians with a certain number of other Southern Europeans. The sealing of the Berlin Wall in 1961 rapidly accelerated an already clear trend of inward migration of temporary workers as the influx from the East became a trickle. By the 1960s these flows were being replaced by workers from Yugoslavia and above all other places from Turkey. Rates of immigration relative to population peaked in the early 1970s, dropping from around 4 per cent of the population to a low of 1.7 per cent in 1975, after which rates hovered around 2 per cent per annum. By the late 1980s these rates had begun to climb sharply again. By 1980, the Federal Republic had a size of foreign population exceeding, in absolute terms, that of any other European country: 4.45 million people, of whom about a third were of Turkish origin and a further third from Yugoslavia and Italy (older data calculated from Mitchell, 1975; 1992; more recent data from SOPEMI). By 1990 the number of foreigners had reached 5.24 million, with the bulk of new entrants from Poland and Turkey and a reduction in the numbers of Southern Europeans. This increase was matched in proportional terms as the percentage of foreigners in the population climbed from 7.2 per cent in 1980 to 8.2 per cent in 1990 – a figure exceeded in Europe only by Belgium (9.1 per cent) and Switzerland (16.3 per cent) (SOPEMI, 1992).

Sweden experienced large inflows of foreign workers from the 1950s onwards, significantly boosted by the creation of a common Nordic labour market encompassing Sweden, Denmark, Norway, Finland and Iceland (Lithman, 1987). From the early 1960s flows of immigration were running at 0.35 per cent of the population per annum – significantly less than our other European countries – and rose sharply throughout the 1960s before peaking in 1971. A steady but lower rate of immigration was maintained for the following decade and a half before accelerating again in the late 1980s. The importance of the open Nordic labour market can be seen by examining the composition of Sweden's foreign population in 1980. Other Scandinavians made up 57 per cent of foreigners, with Finns making up an overwhelming 44 per cent of the foreign population. The others were mainly Yugoslavians, Turks and post-Allende Chileans. However, by 1990 Scandinavians made up only 38 per cent of the foreign population as the numbers of Turks, Iranians, Poles and Greeks grew. In relative terms Swedish immigration was slightly less than that experienced by France and Germany: foreigners comprised around 5.1 per cent of the population and the workforce by 1980 and 5.6 per cent by the end of the decade (older data calculated from Mitchell, 1975; 1992; more recent data from SOPEMI).

Britain has also experienced significant flows of immigration in the postwar era, starting earlier and finishing earlier than most of Western Europe (Gilroy, 1987; Solomos, 1993). This has in part been driven by the bringing in of foreign labour and by the complex politics of citizenship that decolonization created. Interestingly, the UK is the only one of the six case study countries to present a rate of annual emigration often greater than that of immigration. Immigration remained at a low level throughout the 1950s but began to climb significantly in the 1960s and remained at around 200,000 people a year for the next two decades, though levels declined somewhat in the mid-1970s. By the mid-1980s the size of the foreign population in the UK had reached 2.8 per cent of the total population and grew to 3.3 per cent in 1990 (older data calculated from Mitchell, 1975; 1992; more recent data from SOPEMI). However, these figures disguise the overall level of immigration and the increasing ethnic heterogeneity of the UK population. For example, the data on the foreign population suggest that in 1985 there were 138,000 Indians, 49,000 Pakistanis and 135,000 people from the Caribbean in the UK (SOPEMI, 1991 and earlier years; 1992). However, data on the ethnic composition of the UK for the same year give considerably higher figures, reflecting a high rate of naturalization.

Finally, Japan experienced relatively low levels of immigration and emigration right up until the 1980s (data from SOPEMI; Fong, 1993). The early postwar years of economic reconstruction did witness some outward flows of migrants but with the surge of economic growth that began in the 1950s these ceased. Indeed, a reversal soon occurred as many people of Japanese ethnic origin living in South and North America began to return home. The Korean population, expanded by forced movements during the Second World War, remained in Japan and numbered around half a million people – less than 0.5 per cent of the total population. In the 1980s the level of emigration, especially temporary emigration, has increased as skilled Japanese labour has followed the export of Japanese capital to Europe, the USA and South East Asia. This has been matched by a growing flow of unskilled labour, mainly illegal, and overwhelmingly short term, to Japan. By the late 1980s thousands of people from Pakistan, India, the Philippines and Indonesia were making their way to Japan in order to fill the host of poorly paid service jobs. The numbers of illegal immigrants refused entry annually increased fivefold, while annual expulsions of illegal immigrants tripled from 1986 to 1991, standing at an annual level of 35,000 a year (OECD, 1993a).

Overlapping with these trends in economic migration, different countries have had different experiences of flows of refugees and asylum seekers. Overall Europe has taken around four-fifths of all OECD asylum applicants and North America the rest. Japan has received hardly any asylum seekers at all. Within North America the US has taken the lion's share of applicants and seen numbers rise from 20,000 in 1983 to a 1989 peak of 100,000. Refugee and asylum policy has been closely tied to foreign policy, with almost anyone from a communist state during the Cold War being accepted. In the postwar era up to 1989, the US accepted 473,000 people from Cuba and 411,000 from Vietnam. The exodus of Haitians and Cubans produced record levels of asylum applications to the US in 1994. Within Europe it is Germany, with the strongest economy and most liberal asylum laws, that has received the greatest numbers of asylum seekers. In 1981 Germany accounted for 65 per cent of all asylum seekers in Europe, falling to 47 per cent in 1991. However, the absolute increase is enormous, from 107,800 in 1980 to over 750,000 in 1991. In the four years 1988–91 Germany received asylum applications from over 670,000 people. France, Sweden and the UK have experienced the same rising trend; between 1980 and 1991, applications rose in France from 18,000 to over 50,000, in Sweden from 6,000 to 41,000 and in the UK from 9,000 to 57,700. In proportionate terms both France and Sweden have taken in around 10 per cent of asylum seekers each (Sweden has less than a fifth of the population of France) and the UK a little less.

6.6 Globalization, Migration and the Nation-State

What are the implications of contemporary global and regional migrations for the autonomy and sovereignty of nation-states? A number of tentative arguments can be made with respect to the decisional, institutional, distributional and structural consequences of contemporary patterns of global migration for SIACS in particular. First, the flow of illegal and undocumented migrants, economic and non-economic, demonstrates the limited capacity of many nation-states to secure independently their own borders. Second, those states that have extended surveillance of their borders have been unable to stem the flow of illegal migrants. Third, the growth of international attempts to control or coordinate national policies with respect to migrations demonstrates a recognition of the changing nature of state autonomy and sovereignty and the necessity to increase transborder cooperation in this domain. Fourth, in the realm of economic and cultural policy, migration has transformed the domestic political milieu within which SIACS must operate: the collective strength and pattern of alliances of political actors has changed; and migration has reshaped political interests and perceptions of these interests. Finally, migration has altered the kinds of policy options available to states and the balance of costs and benefits that those policies bear. We explore each of these claims below.

6.6.1 Decisional impacts: border controls versus surveillance

The capacity of SIACS to seal their borders has never been perfect. Prior to the last two centuries, states had been demarcated by the amorphous and permeable grey areas of frontiers, marches and peripheries in which sovereignty gradually dissolved rather than being abruptly truncated (see chapter 1). States have always tried to control the movement of peoples through these regions and have been concerned with patterns of peripheral settlement and population movement. European states have a long and dishonourable record of forced expulsions – the Jews and the Huguenots, for example. However, it is anachronistic to compare these states' policies with contemporary forms of border control. For states, as chapter 1 shows, have only recently acquired borders in their contemporary form – as fixed, intentionally determined boundaries demarcating the precise territorial writ of a given state's sovereignty. It is only with the emergence of nation-states and their borders that the bureaucratization and documentation of citizenship – passports, visas, etc. – have become widespread and states have acquired the bureaucratic means to try and control inward migration flows.

Contemporary forms of border control were pioneered in the USA in the late nineteenth century. The concentration of immigrants in oceangoing ships in a few key harbours on the east and west coasts of the USA meant that a greater concentration of state resources could be brought to bear on migratory flows than is possible over long land borders. While the development of reception centres, passport control and immigration criteria were developed in this era, they initially served a very open immigration policy. It was only with the tightening of US immigration policy in the interwar years that this apparatus was put to the test. The precipitous drop in emigration to the US suggests that these administrative and coercive innovations – which have been progressively adopted by all nation-states – increased the power of states relative to migratory flows. In the postwar era these bureaucratic systems have had to cope with greatly increased migratory flows and a greater diversity of international travellers. Permanent migrants arrive with contract workers. There has been a phenomenal increase in international tourism, asylum seekers, students, family reunions, etc. Increasing numbers and the increasing complexity of these bureaucratic categories have strained the capacities of border control agencies. Tourists can overstay and students can disappear into the population after their course ends (Zolberg, 1993). In liberal democratic states, checks on the intrusiveness of immigration controls have made these loopholes wider.

While international air traffic has kept migratory flows fairly concentrated, illegal and legal migration is still occurring across land borders, which are as prohibitively expensive and geographically difficult to control as ever. The USA, in particular, cannot meaningfully patrol its long Mexican border. The problem is considerable for Germany and France as well by virtue of their long land borders: unlike the situation with the US–Mexico border, these fall partly within the European Union and are in effect open borders. However, as migration to the island states of Japan and the UK demonstrates, physical barriers are becoming less and less relevant to border control. Levels of illegal migration appear to be climbing in the West. Both Japanese and American agencies report return rates of about 20 per cent. Despite these efforts, the ILO estimates that there were 650,000 illegal immigrants in Germany in 1991 and 600,000 in Italy, and perhaps 2.6 million in Western Europe as a whole (Böhning, 1991). There are probably more illegals in southern California alone than this.

All Western European countries tightened up their immigration legislation and enhanced policing powers in the 1970s and 1980s. These measures included strict sanctions on airline carriers; tighter visa requirements; denying access and the due process of law to asylum seekers; and the active penalization of undocumented aliens. Yet none has been able to reverse the broad tide of rising migratory flows from illegal cross-border entry, though they may have contained its growth.

Given this shift, states have turned to a variety of forms of internal surveillance and control of the composition of their populations. In most SIACS there are legal, constitutional and political obstacles to giving the police major powers to stop and check identities on suspicion. Where those powers have been allocated they have often resulted in abuse of civil liberties or regular and systematic discrimination against visible minorities. As a consequence, liberal democracies have tried to control illegal migration by controlling access to the labour market. This includes an increasing tendency to penalize employers using illegal labour. However, even in the US where this has been a fairly draconian policy, it seems to make only a marginal difference. Once again, this reflects the limits of state institutions and the resources and technologies available to them and the failure of those same agencies to enlist the support and cooperation of social actors who might aid them (Castles and Miller, 1993).

Three important aspects of state sovereignty and autonomy are illuminated by the discussion of border control and surveillance. First, the balance of collective power between states and migrants – particularly those who seek to evade border controls – has shifted over time. The powers of SIACS have been increased by the establishment of immigration agencies, the documentation of citizenship and the funnelling of migrants through harbours and airports. But the capacity of migrants to evade the grasp of the state has also risen as overall numbers of travellers have increased, and as the increase in tourism and student exchanges has opened more loopholes in immigration agency practice. Second, SIACS' capacity to implement policy is not always, indeed is rarely, dependent on the state's absolute autonomy from and power over social actors – such as employers using illegal labour. Rather, SIACS can only successfully implement their public policy objectives when they have secured a reasonable degree of cooperation from social actors. In the case of illegal migration, they have often failed to do so. Third, immigration policies cannot be seen in isolation from other policies affecting the labour market. Some states have intervened in the domestic labour market with the consequence that the employment of foreign and undocumented labour has become more attractive. In the US particularly, the erosion of organized labour has made such recruitment easier, while in France and Germany the high social security costs of employing registered and legal workers have encouraged the use of foreign workers as a way of evading contributions.

6.6.2 Institutional impacts: international cooperation and policing cross-border migration

SIACS wishing to regulate these contemporary migratory flows have been forced to engage in forms of international cooperation to stem the flows at source, either through development and economic aid, or through international policing efforts. The development model, controlling push factors in the migration process, has mainly been conducted at the level of rhetoric or within organizations that are comparatively powerless, like the European Parliament. While Japan has explicitly engaged in training and investment projects in South East Asia with the aim of limiting flows, there is little to suggest a broader shift in Japan's or anyone else's aid and development policies: rather, there is a gradual shrinkage of budgets. Collective attempts at refugee and migration regulation have been equally limited so far. The EU has made some progress on this through the Dublin and Schengen agreements. Nonetheless, it is worth noting that attempts by national governments to control migration collectively have come into sharp conflict with pre-existing international laws, conventions and obligations. Both the French and German constitutional courts have successfully challenged elements of the Dublin and Schengen agreements; the former where banishment orders and controls on asylum seekers contravened the Geneva Convention on refugees; the latter where the inclusion of Greece as a 'safe third country' for asylum seekers did not accord with the German judiciary's estimation of Greece's human rights record.

6.6.3 Distributional impacts: differential patterns of employment and prosperity

Studies of the impact of immigration on overall wage rates in a host economy, and the differential impact of immigration on the wage rates of different class and ethnic groupings in national labour markets, suggest marginal but arguably constructive impacts (see the survey in Ichino, 1993). As immigrants fill the bottom rungs of the labour market, the native workforce moves into higher paid employment. This is certainly the view of research done in Europe in the 1960s and early 1970s and for contemporary Canada, Australia and the US (Borjas, 1987, 1990, 1993).

A more detailed picture of the economic consequences of migration for host economies can be gleaned from qualitative considerations. The impact of migration is clearly dependent on the precise character of the immigration in the first place. Migrants cannot be considered as a homogeneous mass when their economic impact is assessed. Conversely, there will be widely differing consequences for different groups in the host economy. There is considerable polarization among immigrants in host labour markets. In many OECD countries a significant percentage of foreign workers are highly skilled professionals, often from other Western countries. At the other end of the scale immigrant workers take some of the most insecure, poorly paid and lightly regulated jobs.

In the last two decades both of these niches have expanded in OECD economies. The dismantling of labour market regulations and the emergence of smaller companies and informal economic activity have created jobs that only impoverished immigrants will actually take on. The growth in income of the wealthiest segments of US society in particular has generated a significant demand for domestic labour. Simultaneously, the expansion of high-tech and service industries has created jobs in professional, managerial and technical occupations often encountering national skill shortages. Immigrant communities have also been significant in creating jobs and businesses themselves (Light and Bonacich, 1988; Waldinger et al., 1990). In Britain, Asian entrepreneurs have revitalized the retail, catering, textile and clothing industries. They have their counterparts among Turks in Germany, Algerians in France, and Koreans and Chinese in the USA.

On balance the impact of migrants on OECD economies has probably been positive across distinctive periods. Arguing counterfactually it is clear that in the absence of large-scale migrations European economies would have run into very significant labour market problems in the 1950s and 1960s. The extraordinary period of sustained economic growth, full employment and reasonably low inflation was achieved in part because the inflationary consequences of tight labour markets were damped by a steady stream of low paid migrants into the bottom end of the labour market (Kindleberger, 1967). While this may, particularly after 1973, have increased the pressure on unskilled men in the domestic labour market, they were in for challenging times whatever. Moreover, it is not they but immigrant communities who have borne the heaviest brunt of the restructuring of OECD economies in the 1980s. Ethnic minority unemployment rates exceed those of native Europeans everywhere. Similarly, the enduring competitiveness of Californian agriculture and much American manufacturing cannot be divorced from the fact that the USA is the only advanced economy with such a readily accessible supply of very cheap, unregulated or illegal labour. It has also proved the most attractive destination for skilled professionals from across the globe, which is likely to account for some part of its competitive edge in service and high-tech industries. The Japanese economy, so far, seems more untouched by these economic changes, though this is clearly the flip-side of Japan's massive wave of overseas foreign investment. Japanese capital has chased cheap labour rather than the other way around (see chapter 5).

6.6.4 Structural impacts: national identity and national citizenship

People do more than work. The structural impact of economically driven migrations inevitably spills over into social, cultural and political domains. European countries now have significant black populations for the first time. The USA has of course had a black, Hispanic and Asian population for a long time, but here too the numbers are rapidly rising. Mostly among the poor there is also a common pattern of residential location (though enclaves of well-off immigrant communities do emerge in host countries). Immigrant communities have clustered in large cities and within those cities have formed concentrated ethnic neighbourhoods. In Britain, Afro-Caribbean and Asian communities have concentrated in London, Birmingham, Bradford, Liverpool, Bristol and Leeds. Asian immigrants to the USA are concentrated in the big cities of the West Coast, Hispanics in southern California and Texas. Over half of the immigrant communities of the Netherlands are concentrated in the four biggest cities. This in turn is the result of state housing policy, the geography of labour markets and the active creation of urban neighbourhoods by immigrant communities themselves (White, 1984; Glebe and O'Loughlin, 1987).

The question of national identity in progressively multicultural societies has been increasingly forced on to the political agenda by the contemporary globalization and regionalization of migration. SIACS seeking to pursue an exclusionary model of citizenship and identity may find themselves increasingly with substantial minorities geographically concentrated in their midst and, more likely than not, with a rising tide of discontent and conflict. They are unlikely, on balance, to have provided themselves with any greater room for manoeuvre in doing so. They will simply have exchanged one set of political and cultural problems for another. Those states that try and pursue a multicultural model of identity and citizenship may avoid the worst excesses of the exclusionary course. However, such a strategy illuminates a further domestic, rather than external, constraint on the autonomy of SIACS. For SIACS are, in general, poor catalysts for cultural change, and especially in liberal democratic societies where they are deprived of any kind of monopoly over education and cultural outputs. SIACS wishing to implement a genuine multiculturalism will have to take their cue, and draw support, from a more enlightened and multicultural civil society. But the resources for this often seem perilously small and in need of repair.

6.7 Conclusion

Contemporary patterns of migration are more geographically extensive than the great global migrations of the modern era, but on balance are slightly less intensive. There have been considerable shifts in the technological and social infrastructure of migrations across these eras. In terms of enmeshment, Western European states have acquired their most multiethnic character to date, developing significant non-European immigrant communities. Japan has acquired significant foreign communities for the first time, while America is returning to levels of foreign population not experienced since the height of immigration in the years before the First World War. The autonomy of nation-states is being redefined by the impact of past legal migrations and the continuing impact of illegal migration. SIACS' capacity to patrol their borders and police their population is no longer adequate when measured against the tasks required. International cooperation has not as yet made the achievement of these tasks much more feasible. Moreover, notions of citizenship and national identity are being renegotiated in response to contemporary patterns of global migration and cultural globalization. But in many cases the trajectory of these negotiations is far from clear.

7

Globalization, Culture and the Fate of Nations

Few expressions of globalization are so visible, widespread and pervasive as the worldwide proliferation of internationally traded consumer brands, the global ascendancy of popular cultural icons and artefacts, and the simultaneous communication of events by satellite broadcasts to hundreds of millions of people at a time on all continents. The most public symbols of globalization consist of Coca-Cola, Madonna and the news on CNN. Whatever the causal and practical significance of these phenomena, there can be little doubt that one of the most directly perceived and experienced forms of globalization is the cultural form. Despite the complexity of cultural interactions between societies over the last three thousand years, the intensifying movement of images and symbols and the extraordinary stretch of modes of thought and modes of communication are unique and unparalleled features of the late twentieth century and the new millennium. There is no historical equivalent of the global reach and volume of cultural traffic through contemporary telecommunication, broadcasting and transport infrastructures.

7.1 Analysing Cultural Globalization

Contemporary debates have thrown up three broad categories of argument about the nature and impact of cultural globalization (see the introduction). *Hyperglobalizers* of various kinds describe or predict the homogenization of the world under the auspices of American popular culture or Western consumerism in general. As with other forms of globalization, hyperglobalizers are matched by *sceptics* who point to the thinness and ersatz quality of global cultures by comparison with national cultures and to the persistent, indeed increasing, importance of cultural differences and conflicts along the geopolitical faultlines of the world's major civilizations. Those taking a *transformationalist* position describe the intermingling of cultures and peoples as generating cultural hybrids and new global cultural networks. We will return to aspects of these debates later, but it is clear that these accounts are predominantly about the *impact* of *contemporary* cultural globalization on national communities. This raises three problems. First, there is a tendency for the advocates of such positions either to exaggerate or to underplay the breadth and depth of contemporary forms of cultural globalization. In the absence of a systematic framework for describing cultural flows across and between societies, rather than just investigating their impact, no proper assessment of cultural globalization can be made. Second, few accounts offer a satisfactory conceptual purchase on historical questions. Most assume a world in which global flows of culture are to be contrasted with flows and institutions at the national level. While this is of central relevance to contemporary debates, it is of little use in tackling the world before nation-states and national cultures. Third, the accounts fail to differentiate adequately between impact *qua* changes to a nation's cultural identity and values, and impact *qua* the transformation of the context and processes of national cultural formation. As we will show, this distinction is of fundamental importance. In this chapter we seek both to engage with the dominant debates about contemporary cultural globalization and, utilizing the framework established in the introduction, to develop an account of cultural globalization that is sensitive to its changing historical forms.

Our argument, to anticipate, is fivefold. First, that the existence of transregional, transcivilizational and transcontinental cultural flows and institutions – cultural globalization – has deep historical roots. Indeed, it could be argued that the historical high point of cultural globalization, in terms of its capacity to shape societies and identities, lies much earlier than the modern era in the form of world religions and imperial elite cultures. Second, we argue that from around the late eighteenth century onwards, the centrality of these older forms of cultural globalization was displaced, on the one hand, by the emergence of nation-states, national cultures and national cultural institutions, and, on the other, by the development and diffusion of new secular Western ideologies and modes of thinking: pre-eminently those of liberalism, socialism and science. Third, despite the cosmopolitan and internationalist claims of aspects of these ideologies and modes of thinking, and the development of new technologies of cultural transmission from the latter half of the nineteenth century (telegraphy, flight, cinema, etc.), the balance of effective cultural power for most of the last two hundred years has lain with nation-states and national cultures. Fourth, in the contemporary era a series of technological and institutional transformations have once again altered that balance. New technologies of telecommunications and the emergence of international media corporations, among other factors, have generated global cultural flows whose stretch, intensity, diversity and rapid diffusion exceed that of earlier eras. Accordingly, the centrality of national cultures, national identities and their institutions is challenged. Fifth, this challenge comes, in part, from the products and meanings of popular cultures and the diffuse and ambiguous cultural field of consumerism and materialism. As a consequence, it is a complex and exceedingly difficult task to interpret accurately the impact of this new form of cultural globalization on political identities, national solidarity, cultural values, etc. We find that the dominant debates are at best partial when they explore the impact of contemporary cultural globalization, and that a considered weighing of the evidence at this time – while pointing to the potential fragility and mutability of national cultures and identities – remains highly indeterminate. Cultural globalization is transforming the *context* in which and the *means* through which national cultures are produced and reproduced, but its particular impact on the nature and efficacy of national cultures – on the hold and influence of their messages, values and content – is, as yet, harder to decipher.

7.1.1   Concepts

The concepts of culture and communications are not without their ambiguities. The idea of culture, in particular, has a long and complex history in the discourses of Western aesthetics, social and political theory and sociology. We can probably hold that culture refers to the social construction, articulation and reception of meaning. We are using culture in its fullest, if sometimes ambiguous sense: culture as a lived and creative experience for individuals as well as a body of artefacts, texts and objects; it embraces the specialized and professionalized discourses of the arts, the commodified output of the culture industries, the spontaneous and unorganized cultural expressions of everyday life, and, of course, the complex interactions between all of these. Communication, in this context, refers to the ways in which these artefacts, beliefs and messages are moved through time and space. This in turn can be broken down into a number of discrete processes. For messages and meanings must be recorded, preserved and reproduced. In turn, they must be physically transmitted or moved to another place and another time. Communication therefore requires media of storage and transmission, institutions that make that storage and transmission possible, and media of reception (J. B. Thompson, 1990).

Spatio-temporal dimensions of cultural globalization

For the purposes of this chapter, the most apposite of the concepts developed in the introduction to this book is the idea of globalization as the movement of objects, signs and people across regions and intercontinental space. The globalization of culture entails the movement of all three. Obviously enough, people have proved to be the most important and most influential agents of cultural transmission. Indeed, until the advent of telecommunications in the nineteenth century (and perhaps the pigeon post of the eighteenth century) all communication (or lack of it) has been tied to modes of transportation; for no person, book, sign or message could move independently of people and the horses, ships and carts that transported them. However, the globalization of culture has also involved the movement of objects. For while individual agents have been important carriers of cultural practices, they themselves have been limited to communication by presence. Alongside people, cultural forms and ideas have been spatially diffused through books, written records and cultural artefacts of all kinds, from the mundane to the erudite. Finally, with the emergence of telecommunications, the artefactual nature of cultural transmission has diminished as disembodied signs – in the form of electrical impulses – circulate, almost instantaneously, through space and time. We can map the globalization of culture in terms of the geographical *extensity* of these movements and the *intensity* or volume of such movements relative to the national and local. Cultural globalization can also be charted in terms of the speed – the *velocity* or rapidity – at which images or ideas can be communicated from one place to another.

As in other cases of globalization, an exclusive focus on flows fails to register the importance of the enduring relationships established by such flows and the experience of participants at either end of the flows. In the case of cultural flows, this refers to the producers and receivers/consumers of culture and the transmission of cultural phenomena between them. Obviously some flows, movements or objects are entirely transitory and leave no indelible social mark. A single traveller from one isolated community to another is unlikely to establish or create a permanent cultural transformation in either place or create an enduring network of interaction and reciprocal cultural influences. However, where such relationships are established we can view the globalization of culture as the stretching and deepening of cultural relationships and practices. This is perhaps the idea at the core of Michael Mann's concept of transcendent cultural power in which the movement of people and texts helps establish a pattern of shared cultural belief over an extensive area and, thus, patterns of reciprocal interaction between separate places in which cultural ideas in one place influence those in another (Mann, 1986). Of course, the degree of interaction and cultural similarity will vary. Thus, alongside stretching, we can also talk of the deepening of cultural relationships where changes, debates and innovations in one place are more likely to be transferred to (or rejected in) another. This bringing together of places and people separated in time and space can also be viewed as a form of time-space compression. However, the *impact* of the globalization of culture is difficult to calibrate. Diverse types of encounter are possible – including homogenization, contestation, hybridization and indifference – and need to be weighed in relation to shifting contexts and conditions.

The organizational dimensions of cultural globalization

It is unhelpful to focus exclusively on the conscious active agency of individuals and the local direct impact of artefacts and objects in describing the globalization of culture. For to do so is to conceive cultural globalization as dominated by proselytism and evangelicalism. Of course, cultural practices can be and are actively imposed in places distant from their original site of production. Empires, in particular, stand as an important example of the extensive reach of new cultural ideas that are backed in their impact by the possibility of coercive force and the reality of political subordination. But the historical record suggests that the process of the globalization of culture is more complex and varied in its forms and in the relationships between producers and receivers. Thus an important facet of this process is captured by reference to the notion of *modes of interaction*, that is, the dominant ways in which cultural globalization operates from imposition, through emulation to diffusion. The movement and adoption of cultural practices can occur by active importation and reproduction. Alternatively, less consciously organized processes of cultural diffusion exist where cultural practices are slowly digested by other cultures through repeated contact and local adaptations.

The idea of empire connects us with a further element of the globalization of culture: the establishment of the *infrastructures* of cultural production, transmission and reception, and the extent to which cultural flows and processes are *institutionalized*, that is, regularized and embedded, across time and space. As with any form of power, cultural power cannot be mobilized and deployed in the absence of organizations that create, transmit, reproduce and receive cultural messages or practices. These include modes of transportation as well as modes of communication. However, both of these imply more than technologies, central as these are. For technologies must be deployed and operated by social organizations. Oceanic shipping requires shipbuilders, mapmakers and shipping companies. Cultural imperialism requires the creation of colonial educational establishments and the training of teachers. All these kinds of interaction also require some kind of minimal shared linguistic competencies – the spread of language use, bi- and multilingualism, translation facilities, etc. – which constitute, alongside technologies and organizations, a key element of cultural infrastructures. We can talk, therefore, of the globalization of culture when and where there emerge infrastructures and institutions of cultural transmission, reproduction and reception on a global – transregional or transcontinental – scale. Thus, for example, in terms of television this might include the development of an international market in television programming, the creation of transnational television production and distribution companies, the global diffusion of television sets to many publics across the world, the establishment of transnational systems of satellite broadcasting, and the emergence of relevant regulatory regimes.

As ever, all these modes of cultural globalization – the stretching and deepening of relationships, the movements of signs, objects and people, cultural diffusion and emulation and the establishment of infrastructures and institutions – can involve distinctive patterns of *stratification*, that is, hierarchy and unevenness. It is obvious enough in the case of telecommunications that access to global telecommunications links is incredibly asymmetrical or uneven between and within societies. It is clear enough in the case of television programming that only a very few countries and companies produce for export. And it is clear that most of us, most of the time, are receivers and consumers of 'popular culture' rather than transmitters and producers (although the Internet is beginning to erode this distinction).

We believe that this conceptual armoury provides a flexible set of instruments for exploring the origins and consequences of cultural globalization; it avoids a narrow focus on the impact of cultural globalization and allows the exploration of the transformations and developments that make such impacts possible in the first place. Further, we can use this framework to track historical forms of cultural globalization, seeing how the very national cultures that seem so entrenched today have been forged, invented and reinvented over a long period, and that today's cultural flows have distinguished historical predecessors. It is to these predecessors that we now turn.

The rest of the chapter is organized into a number of sections. In section 7.2 we examine some of the main historical forms of cultural globalization that predate the twentieth century, forms whose causal significance is probably more important than the global spread of corporate symbols and pop culture: the great world religions, extensive empires, modern nationalism and transnational secular ideologies. In section 7.3 we examine some of the evidence, both quantitative and qualitative, that is available concerning the globalization of culture and communications in the contemporary era. We focus on six key areas: telecommunications and language; media industry multinationals; radio and the music industry; cinema; television; and tourism. This is followed, in section 7.4, by a comparison of the key historical forms of cultural globalization, focusing on whether there are distinctive new features in today's global cultural constellation. Finally, in section 7.5, we summarize our findings and reflect on the strengths and weaknesses of the idea of cultural globalization with particular reference to its impact on national cultures, national identity and the politics of SIACS.

7.2 Cultural Globalization in Historical Perspective

It is incontestable that the globalization of culture has an enormously long history. As shown by our accounts of the global diffusion of trade (chapter 3) and global migrations (chapter 6), people, objects and ideas have been circulating around the planet for a considerable period. We cannot offer a comprehensive picture of this here. However, to establish what is distinctive about the contemporary globalization of culture, we will examine the early forms of technological and social innovation that facilitated the spatial transformation of cultural practices. In each case, we examine the extensity, intensity, velocity, impact and supporting organizational form of these developments. On the basis of this analysis, we can put more recent claims about the globalization of culture into proper historical perspective.

7.2.1 World religions

Paradoxically, none of the conventional list of world religions – Christianity, Islam, Confucianism, Hinduism, Judaism and Buddhism – is present in significant numbers in every continent or region, though Christianity and Judaism have spread their adherents to most corners of the globe. Hinduism, Buddhism and Confucianism are all more tightly concentrated in their regional strongholds – South Asia, East Asia and China. Islam occupies a middling position, strong in the Middle East and North Africa with significant numbers in the rest of Africa and East Asia. All, of course, have their small and not so small migratory or diaspora communities in the most unexpected of places: over a million Japanese Shintoists in Brazil; 4 million Turkish-German Muslims in the heart of Christian Europe; the Goan Catholic enclave on the west coast of India. The definition of a world religion is, in a sense, post hoc. For the faiths that are usually dubbed 'global' have only been described as such once the spatial extent of the faithful has already greatly exceeded its place of origin and creation. As Mann puts it, 'they became significant because of one shared characteristic: a translocal sense of personal and social identity that permitted extensive and intensive mobilization on a scale sufficient to enter the historical record' (1986, p. 363).

Thus it is their geographical extensity, albeit often a regionally focused one, and their social impact that truly mark out the world religions from the many faiths that did and do exist. They are systems of belief and ritual that have had the capacity at crucial historical moments to reach out from their place of origin and embrace, convert and conquer other cultures and other religions. Most clearly in the cases of Islam and Christianity, the mobilizing capacity of religion was coupled with the capacity to extend military power and cultural influence. Neither Chinese nor Indian civilization ever embarked on such bouts of conquest and thus their indigenous faiths remained within their own loosely defined borders, but it is worth remembering just how large those territories were themselves.

Applying our conceptual model of globalization to the world religions, we can argue that they have assumed an extraordinary extensity. Although the foundation of world religions stretches back over a number of millennia, we can compress their initial impact to around a thousand-year period between 300 BCE and 700 CE. Buddhism and Hinduism assumed something like their contemporary form in the three centuries before Jesus's birth, while Islam had reached its core regions by about 700 CE. Over this thousand-year period the main agencies of religious expansion were organized clerical hierarchies. Sometimes they operated in alliance with dominant states and political and economic elites, at other times interstitially within and across the frameworks set by states. The capacity of these religions to spread and to penetrate into the organization and beliefs of everyday life was facilitated by both theological and technological innovation. Buddhism and Hinduism, while remaining confined to South and East Asia, generated theological frameworks of sufficient complexity and adaptability that they could embrace and attract adherents across cultures and linguistic groups

(Weber, 1951, 1958). The innovation of monotheism, although a Jewish creation, was multiplied in its potential reach and power by Christianity and Islam, both of which joined a singular moral code to a vision of salvation potentially open to all. Islam achieved a presence in diverse regions as early as the eighth century, a presence it has retained, although it remains thinly spread in many places (Gellner, 1981). Christianity would have to wait until the military and colonial expansion of Europe in the sixteenth and seventeenth centuries to acquire a global presence. The invention of writing allowed for the diffusion of a set of core texts which provided the infrastructure for establishing shared and stabilized beliefs and doctrines across large areas (Giddens, 1985; Goody, 1986). The development of writing and the movement of texts, as well as interpreters, made possible the development of cross-cultural networks of shared belief and behaviour with a systematization and routinization that was not possible in a preliterate world. It is this, combined with the development of institutionalized and regularized clerical hierarchies – the key cultural infrastructure of world religions – that made possible the stretching and deepening of cultural relations between otherwise separate and different societies. That said, these processes of cultural globalization occurred slowly, taking decades to initiate and centuries to embed themselves.

Of course, world religions also display cultural hierarchy and unevenness in their spread. The religion of clerics and elites has rarely been identical to that of the mass of the population nor has the community of the faithful been particularly democratic in its regulation of belief and practice. Similarly, given the immense differences between adherents of these faiths across different societies it is little surprise that all show large geographical variations and complex mixtures with pre-existing cultures and religions. In terms of their impact, there is little doubt that the world religions are among humanity's most significant cultural innovations. World religions have furnished religious and political elites with immense power and resources, be it in their capacity to mobilize armies and peoples, in their development of transcultural senses of identity and allegiance or in their provision of the entrenched theological and legal infrastructure of societies. In these respects, world religions unquestionably constitute one of the most powerful and significant forms of the globalization of culture in the premodern era, indeed of all time.

7.2.2   Empires

Alongside, and indeed often intimately intertwined with, the progress of the sacred realm on earth has followed the expansion of the secular realm of politics and military force, though in many ways the distinction is one that can only be drawn from the vantage point of a secularized later twentieth century. Empires have often been characterized by the attempt to impose centralized political authority over a loosely defined territory that is populated by a multiplicity of different social and ethnic groups. In this respect, empires and the process of empire building can be conceived as a form of political globalization stretching and deepening relationships of authority and control (see the discussion of this issue in chapter 1). Here our central concern is the role of cultural power in creating and maintaining political empires.

All empires inevitably face a series of interrelated structural problems or contradictions, particularly those that do not rely solely or predominantly on the repeated imposition of coercive force to obtain cooperation or subservience from their provinces (Eisenstadt, 1963; Mann, 1986). The essential problem is one of centralization and decentralization. For while empires are ruled from the centre, their capacity to enforce rule is often limited. Constantly imposing orders from the centre requires time, resources and effective infrastructures. Therefore empires need, as far as possible, to delegate power to the periphery. But in doing so, they threaten their own integrity. One way of partially circumventing this dilemma is cultural: an empire can try and create a universal ruling class bound by ties of kinship, belief and religion so that the essential political division in the imperium becomes vertical – between classes – rather than horizontal – between centre and periphery. Thus successful empires have inevitably been ones in which the extensive reach of military and political power has been reinforced by the reach of cultural power. Often cultural expansion arose interstitially, and unintentionally, between subaltern rather than ruling classes. The early expansion of Christianity within the Roman Empire is a good example of this. By contrast, cultural diffusion, emulation, stretching and deepening and the creation of cultural infrastructures can be part of an intentional strategy of rule.

There is hardly space here to review the role of empires in the globalization of culture in anything but the most perfunctory manner, so we will concentrate on two empires, one premodern, one early modern: the Roman and the British. Below we sketch some of the main forms taken by cultural globalization under these differing imperial auspices, before turning to the unique cultural innovations of the modern era.

The Roman Empire

What distinguished the Roman Empire from its predecessors in the Mediterranean and Near East, although not necessarily from Han China in the Far East, was its capacity to deploy political power consistently from the centre over a regularized territorial empire. In contrast to earlier imperial rule, say in Persia or classical Greece, the Roman Empire was held together by more than the roving use of military coercion and irregular tax and tribute taking. Authoritative, binding regulation, influence and strategy were all conducted, at a greater or lesser intensity, over a huge area for the best part of five centuries. This decisive shift in power wielded by the Roman imperial state was made possible by a series of innovations. Most important, probably, was the enhanced logistical capabilities of the Roman legions and their capacity for complex civil engineering, roadbuilding and organization. But alongside this phenomenal increase in the extensive reach of military power was a series of cultural innovations that allowed the Romans to generate and reproduce a transimperial ruling class bound by ties of more than just kinship: political community, immanent class solidarity and shared cultural rituals, beliefs and aesthetics (Millar et al., 1967; Mann, 1986). Few premodern empires before this could match the stretching of cultural relationships this entailed. None could match its deepening.

The key to this deepening was that after military conquest Rome left much of the local elite in position, incorporating them culturally and politically into the Roman state and the ruling class – though the dividing line between the two were, prior to the formation of an imperial civil service, rather blurred. Literacy was the key to this achievement. Through specialized and organized instruction, literacy was almost universal among the Roman ruling class, men and women. Latin in the western half of the empire and Latin and Greek in the east formed the shared official languages of politics and culture. Theatres and amphitheatres were deliberately built in the provinces and drama and poetry spread throughout the Empire. Finally, local religious cults were loosely grafted into the Roman Pantheon. Evidence of the success and integrity of the Roman ruling class is the geographical diffusion of the imperial succession. While infrastructurally the imperial seat remained in Rome until 330 AD, the ruling families passed from Rome itself through the Mediterranean and North Africa and eventually into the Balkans and Danubian regions.

The British Empire

At its height the British Empire was the most global of any formal empire. Although colonial policy was variable and often rather haphazard, it is clear that in many of the dominions and colonies there was a strong cultural or ideological dimension to both the execution of British dominance and the maintenance of complex links between centre and periphery, metropolis and province. This took a multiplicity of forms, but two of the most important were the conduct of imperial educational policy and the establishment of an imperial communications infrastructure, both of which offer clear examples of the globalization of culture and communications. In the educational field, British, or rather English, ideas and cultural practices were diffused through the institutional structure of early colonial educational systems and in their content. Across the world, the English models of public school and grammar school education were replicated for the children of local elites, while textbooks and curriculum were invariably English in origin and subject matter. Above all, the main language of education and instruction was English. Particularly effective in socializing colonial elites were the small but significant movements of students to Oxford and Cambridge, where they received a suitable education for service in colonial administration or, later, for post-independence government.

While Rome built roads to provide the essential sinews of long-distance rule, British efforts were directed somewhat differently. The role of the British Empire in stimulating and using early telecommunications systems is instructive (Headrick, 1988). The telegraph system was first invented, demonstrated and patented in 1837. Seven years later in 1844, the first long-distance communication was successfully conducted in the USA between Washington and Baltimore. From the very inception of the technology, people had tried to develop submarine cables. This required the creation of a suitable insulating coat for the cables and methods of laying the cables on the seabed. Gutta-percha, a form of tropical latex, provided the former, while the latter was solved by a Prussian artillery officer, Werner von Siemens. In 1853 a cable was laid between Britain and Ireland and the first transatlantic cable was laid in 1858. However, technical problems and poor insulation cut transmissions short after a few months. It required further technical refinement before the first successful and permanent cable was laid across the Atlantic in 1868. The British government had been closely involved with cable technology from the beginning but was pressed into a deeper involvement by the 1857 Indian rebellion and the need for effective and speedy communication with the imperial periphery (see section 1.1.4 above). Early submarine efforts in the late 1850s foundered on inadequate technology, while the land-line through the Ottoman Empire was considered strategically unacceptable. In 1870 the first successful British-Indian submarine telegraph system began to operate.

After this, cable-laying continued apace, led by the Eastern Telegraph Company which received considerable indirect support from the British government in pursuit of colonial objectives: ocean-bed surveys, large volumes of official traffic, landing rights and diplomatic support. After 1878 the British government extended substantial subsidies for commercially limited, but also strategically important, lines; for example, a £1.75 million subsidy for the Australia–South Africa cable in the 1890s. By 1887 there were 214,000 kilometres of undersea cable, 70 per cent of them British. British dominance declined a little in the following decades as other empires built their own telegraph networks, but in 1908, 56 per cent of the 473,000 kilometres of cable were still British (Headrick, 1988). However, it is worth noting that despite notionally bringing centre and periphery closer together it is not at all clear, as indicated in chapter 1, that the cable system allowed any more effective direct exercise of political power from the centre, though it certainly extended the infrastructure of communication for both military (see chapter 2) and civil interests.

7.2.3 Modern national cultures and transnational secular ideologies

The global imperialism of Western states from the sixteenth to the twentieth century provided some of the essential infrastructures for the imposition and diffusion of Western ideas, values and cultural institutions and practices across the world. However, the key content of that imposition was generated within the West's own heartlands: modern national cultures, nationalism and transnational secular ideologies and discourses.

National cultures

We have already discussed the origins and character of the European nation-state in chapter 1. The development of the ideas and narratives of the nation and national cultures was an essential element of that process. Simultaneously, the emergence of this new form of territorially bounded and demarcated state helped encourage and solidify the cultural projects of nationalists. Exploring this highly contested area requires, at the very least, some definitions. As chapter 1 argues (see pp. 45–9), the nation is a cross-class community, whose shared sense of identity, solidarity and interest is rooted in an ethnic identity and common historical experience (real, imagined or interpreted) and whose central political project is the possession of a distinctive state in a bounded territory. Nationalism, in this perspective, can be seen as both a psychological and a cultural affiliation creating a connection with the community of the nation, and a political and cultural project which seeks to achieve self-determination and to create and shape states. National cultures are the complex bodies of real and imagined practice, belief, ritual and attitude that have emerged out of these projects (see Mann, 1993).

In the sense proposed here, no fully fledged nation – as a social and cultural entity – can be found very much earlier than the late eighteenth century. Of course, cross-class communities have existed prior to the emergence of nations, and ethnic identity was a powerful unifying force in many societies prior to this. However, the historical record suggests that even where a proto-sense of the nation existed prior to the eighteenth century – for example in France, Sweden or England – it was always but one identity or point of allegiance. It necessarily competed with larger transnational identities and more particularistic, local and regional identities. Moreover, the actual degree of cultural interaction and social interconnection achieved across class lines in large areas was minimal. Nations emerged as distinctive collective social actors only when proto-nations were transformed by the economic, social and political changes of the long nineteenth century.

An extensive literature exists on the social preconditions of the emergence of modern nations and nationalism (cf, Smith, 1971; B. Anderson, 1983; Giddens, 1985; Hobsbawm, 1990; Mann, 1993). Among the most important factors were increasing levels of literacy across class lines that facilitated intraclass communication and the diffusion of national histories, myths and rituals, and the increasing power and importance of states, for as states became more enmeshed with societies (primarily through taxation and conscription) the importance of possessing one's own state correspondingly increased. The relationship between emergent nations and states varied. In the cases of England, France and Spain, the emergent nation effectively supported the existing state machinery, which in turn ensured that competing national identities were overwhelmed or pushed to the periphery (the Welsh, Bretons, Catalans). In the case of Germany, the nation was larger than any of the fragmentary German states and thus nationalists became a force in the creation of a newer, larger state. In the case of Austria-Hungary, nations emerged within a transnational imperial state and sought to dismember the latter. Given these very varied contexts, emergent national cultures and nationalisms came in many forms – ethnic and civic, rational, constitutional and romantic, core and peripheral. It is not our purpose to investigate these differences here. Rather, the question we wish to pursue is how the rise of nations, nationalism and national cultures intersects with the narrative of cultural globalization we have elaborated.

Prior to the emergence of nations and nation-states, most cultural communication and interaction occurred either between elites across many different societies or at very local and restricted levels. With the advent of nations and nation-states, the spatial and social reach of many cultural networks and cultural institutions changed. Forging the nation required cross-class communication rather than intra-elite communication. It also involved, where necessary, controlling the kinds of cultural messages and symbols available to the public. The core of this project has been the creation, partially rooted in enduring cultural and social features of societies, partially invented and often only partially successful, of a national culture. Once again, the literature on this topic is extensive (for example, Hobsbawm and Ranger, 1983; Colley, 1992). For our purposes, what is important to note is that these new cultural identities were centrally concerned with consolidating the relationships between national identity, national self-determination and the territorial boundaries and control of states, though this is not to suggest that the cultural identities and the borders of nation-states necessarily coincided (for they often did not). Czech nationalism emerged within the borders of the Austro-Hungarian Empire and sought to create a distinct and smaller state within those boundaries. The same could be said for the less successful Catalonian nationalism. German national identity and culture was created right across the borders of the many fragmented German statelets and duchies of the eighteenth and nineteenth centuries. Even with the formation of a united German nation-state in the late nineteenth century it was far from clear that the new state was the sole repository of the German people, or German culture.

While the formation of national identities and national cultures was a task undertaken by many diverse social actors and institutions, state organizations and state officials have invariably been deeply enmeshed in the project. The central contribution of these actors has often been the creation of new cultural infrastructures corresponding in territorial reach with the borders of the state and providing the channels for the diffusion of newly imagined national cultures and identities – and where necessary for the control, suppression or eradication of competing identities and peripheral nationalisms. Almost every national government and state has pursued some systematization of a national or official language and often sought to control, limit or ban the use of other languages in the public sphere. Most such authorities have created or attempted to create a national schooling system and have shown particular interest in controlling the curriculum. In addition, many states over the last century have acquired, or attempted to acquire, control over the national press, created a uniform national postal service, constructed national telegraphy and telephone systems and, as television and radio technologies have become available, established control over national broadcasting systems. And all states have used their standing armies as symbols and a means of socialization into nationhood. These organizations and cultural practices were consciously used to construct national histories, define national identities and inculcate national allegiances. While earlier epochs saw cultural institutions that either stretched across many societies (world religions) or were highly localized in their form and allegiance, the emergence of nation-states led to the creation of cultural flows, institutions and identities at a scale between these, and to the development of cultural infrastructures permitting much more effective cross-class and uniform cultural messages and practices to be spread.

In Europe the rise of nations and nationalism led to the organization of cultural life along national and territorial lines, and helped consolidate older states often at the price of peripheral nations and ethnic groups. It contributed to the creation of new nation-states and the collapse and fragmentation of older multinational empires. Paradoxically, it was partially through the tendrils of European empire that the idea of nations, national culture and nationalism spread to Asia, Africa and the Middle East. The potency of this new mode of social organization was not lost on the rest of the world and contributed to the intensity and power of anticolonial movements in the twentieth century. However, while Europe's moment of cultural hegemony diffused the cultural instrument of its own later destruction – national self-determination – it also saw the diffusion of new transnational cultural practices.

Transnational secular ideologies

As we have already seen, the spread of complex modes of thought over vast distances with considerable social consequences is no monopoly of the modern era. However, what does distinguish European modernity, especially from the late eighteenth century, is the emergence of ideologies and modes of thought that are unflinchingly secular in their orientation and simultaneously claim a universal applicability. The ambiguous fruits of the European Enlightenment include the emergence of modern science and modern moral political philosophies and programmes. In retrospect, it is clear that these notionally universal discourses retained historical and geographical particularisms. Nonetheless, the arguments and claims of liberalism, socialism and science have consistently found receptive audiences well beyond their North American and European heartlands.

Socialism, and particularly its Marxist variant, has its roots in the experience of European nineteenth-century capitalist industrialization and urbanization – forged from both philosophical reflection and practical struggle. Yet the ideas and language of socialism swiftly spread to more backward regions of the world economy and ultimately to societies almost untouched by those changes. That is not to suggest that those ideas did not undergo a profound transformation in their passage east and south. Nonetheless, it is incontrovertible that ideas and arguments initially forged in the cauldron of early European industrialization swiftly found their way to Russia, China, Japan, the Caribbean and Latin America. It is equally incontrovertible that in their many local variations, socialism and Marxism have proved a central factor in the organization and outcome of political struggle and political rule.

The international travels of socialism and Marxism have received a great deal of attention – not surprisingly, given the conscious use of these ideas by vanguard parties domestically and as an instrument of Soviet foreign policy internationally. Less attention has perhaps been paid to the parallel diffusion of scientific and liberal discourses from the West to the rest of the world over the last two centuries. In part, this relative lack of attention may stem from the fact that these discourses have been diffused in conjunction with a whole set of institutional organizations and practices, while socialism to a great extent has been diffused as an ideological force in its own right. Western science, for example, reached many parts of the world as part and parcel of the diffusion of new technologies and industries, of medical techniques and practices and of agricultural innovations. As a result, the spread of a Western scientific worldview, though global in its extent, has been slow to percolate beyond the elite stratum of scientists, technologists and educationalists intimately involved in its disciplines. Although elite theological and public cultures in the West and beyond have been forced to grapple with the discrepancies and conflicts created by scientific and religious worldviews, for most of the twentieth century much of daily life has continued to be organized around principles and models of the world that have a longer antiquity (Hobsbawm, 1994, ch. 8).

The global spread of Western liberalism falls between the proselytizing of international socialism and the structural diffusion of Western science. On the one hand, Western liberalism has spread a distinctive set of ideological positions and political values: civil and political rights, limited government, self-determination, etc. The adaptation of liberal doctrines by Indian elites during the second half of the nineteenth century is perhaps the best known example of this (see Spear, 1990). The increased participation by Indians in top administrative posts and their increased contact with liberal political notions – through elite Indian higher education, involvement with British officials and governmental offices – contributed to the development of Indian nationalism. On the other hand, the steady diffusion of capitalist market relations brought the basic elements of neoclassical economics to a wider audience long before its doctrines were formally presented or widely taught. The capitalist marketplace itself inescapably engendered a particular set of orientations and practices.

7.2.4 Premodern and modern forms of cultural globalization: a comparison

Drawing up a balance sheet from such disparate materials is complex and fraught with problems of overgeneralization. Tentatively, we can sketch the trajectory of cultural globalization prior to the contemporary epoch. Cultural diffusion and emulation has been a chronic feature of human history since the beginning of settled civilization. This is exemplified by human migrations and military globalization (see chapters 6 and 2). Trade provided a key conduit for these diffuse movements of ideas and artefacts across great distances (see chapter 3). But prior to the modern era, world religions and empires provided the main cultural-institutional complexes through which long-range communications and cultural interaction could take place, and more settled or embedded stretched relationships of cultural interaction could be established.

Alongside world religions, we have noted how cultural practices were diffused and imposed as part of the 'multicultural' strategies of empires. Given the logistical limits of imposing rule by military force alone, imperial capitals sought to build enduring alliances among elites across ethnic and geographical divisions. Even where the strategy eventually failed in terms of empire building, it could leave a distinct cultural legacy. For example, the short-lived Macedonian empire of Alexander the Great was instrumental in the diffusion of the Greek language and Hellenistic science, philosophy and literature across the Near East. The Roman Empire provided the institutional context in which first Hellenic culture and then Christianity could percolate into North Africa and Western and Northern Europe. The empire of Han China provided a similar framework for the diffusion of Chinese script, literature, ritual practice, science and technology. Two notes of caution must be added to this synoptic account of imperial cultural politics. While, of course, cultures spoke to cultures and religions spoke to religions, they did not always generate fruitful encounters. The regional quality of the world religions reflects faultlines and divisions among themselves and the empires with which they were entwined. In addition, for the most part, for most people, these grand cultural interactions were only glimpsed – identities, practices and beliefs were overwhelmingly local. Very few cultural forms stood between the village and great empires.

After the fall of Rome and Han China and the initial wave of Islamic expansion, empires continued to rise and fall, facilitating some and preventing other patterns of cultural diffusion. However, there is little in the historical record to match Islam's major military and cultural expansions until the imperial adventures of the West began in the fifteenth and sixteenth centuries. The great empire builders of the era between these dates were the nomadic warriors of the Eurasian steppes. But they failed to match their military prowess with cultural innovation. Their movements and conquests resulted in the retrenchment of older cultural patterns rather than their transformation. Even the imperial successes of the West from the sixteenth century onwards rested heavily on a military, demographic and epidemiological edge over the peoples of the Americas. It can be argued that force and the common cold were more decisive than theology in demonstrating the power of the God of Christianity. The frail imperial and colonial structures that conquered the southern half of the Americas prior to Europe's industrial and political revolutions proved initially incapable of cultural expansion in the densely settled and epidemiologically impervious societies of Africa and Asia.

While European empires would eventually become more successful instruments of cultural power outside Europe, that awaited the emergence of nationalism and nation-states in Europe and the Americas from the eighteenth century onwards. Within this zone, the complex patterns of transnational and even transcontinental elite cultural flows, and the distinct domain of popular local particularisms, were gradually reshaped. States sought unified nations to rule and nationalists sought self-determination through states. As a consequence, albeit as an uneven and contested process, more and more cultural institutions and cultural flows came to be located within the borders of emerging nation-states. Language, schooling, transport and communication systems, liturgical practice and identity all came to be defined increasingly in terms of the territorially bounded nation. External or alien cultural influences were suppressed or treated with suspicion and hostility. Cosmopolitanism and internationalism maintained an audience in the West. Transnational cultural practices and institutions continued to exist. Indeed, from within the heart of the European nation-state system, there emerged powerful secular ideologies and discourses – liberalism, Marxism and modern science – whose Enlightenment rationalism, rightly or wrongly, suggested their universal appeal and applicability. Yet, on balance, it was nationalism that became the more powerful cultural force, at least in part because it was systematically backed, funded and deployed by modern states. On this reading, the high point of cultural globalization lies in the past, while the most powerful and significant cultural flows and cultural relationships have developed within the boundaries of modern nation-states. But, in the era of the Internet and CNN, is this reading still convincing?

7.3 The Shape of Contemporary Cultural Globalization

Contemporary cultural globalization is associated with several developments: new global infrastructures of an unprecedented scale, generating an enormous capacity for cross-border penetration and a decline in their cost of use; an increase in the intensity, volume and speed of cultural exchange and communication of all kinds; the rise of Western popular culture and interbusiness communication as the primary content of global cultural interaction; the dominance of culture industry multinationals in the creation and ownership of infrastructures and organizations for the production and distribution of cultural goods; and a shift in the geography of global cultural interaction departing in some significant ways from the geography of the pre-Second World War global order. In this section we review some of the empirical evidence about these developments, leaving discussion of their political and social impact until section 7.5.

The development of global cultural infrastructures and the emergence of a culture industry managed by MNCs are dealt with in sections 7.3.1. and 7.3.2. In sections 7.3.3, 7.3.4 and 7.3.5 we examine, in particular, the development of key mass media sectors: the global spread of radio and recorded music, and of cinema and television. These

sections include material on new technologies and infrastructures of communications as well as on the role of MNCs, but point as well to the centrality of Western
popular culture, changing cultural geographies and the increasing intensity and velocity
of cultural exchange. In section 7.3.6 we look at one final contributor to the changing
cultural landscape – the mass tourism industry.

7.3.1   Global infrastructures:
telecommunications and language

The postwar world has no monopoly on the exploitation of telecommunications. However, there are clear grounds for arguing that this period has seen both a quantitative
and a qualitative transformation in the scope and intensity of telecommunication flows
and their broader social consequences. These transformations have stemmed, first and
foremost, from a series of technological innovations that both built on and superseded
the communication technologies of the late nineteenth and early twentieth centuries.
The postwar era began with the same basic telephonic technology as the early part of
the century. This consisted of analogue signals travelling down wire or cable using
cumbersome, mechanical crossbar switching. Since then an almost continuous wave of
technological change has transformed the capacity, cost, speed and complexity of telecommunications systems. First, analogue signals have been replaced by digital systems
which have allowed the intermeshing of computers, telecommunications systems and
all forms of media (sound, visual, etc.). Cables and wires can now carry an enormous
range of information compressed into digital format alongside the usual voice and
simple text messages of earlier eras. Second, switching systems have been completely
reorganized with the introduction of electronic circuit switching and internationally
coordinated and standardized numbering systems. Third, while cable and wire technology has enormously improved in efficiency, it has in some cases been superseded by
the advent of new mechanisms of transmission. Fibre-optic cable has massively expanded
the number of channels that a cable can carry, while reducing their cost. Microwave
and satellite systems have dispensed with the need for cabling altogether. These various
technologies have effectively transformed and indeed globalized the infrastructure of
telecommunications.

The first new systems of communication established in the postwar era were telex
systems, which allowed two-way interchange of text as opposed to the single direction
telegraphy of the prewar era. This provided much of the international communications system in the 1950s and 1960s. However, in 1956 the first dedicated transatlantic
telephone cable was laid and began the steady replacement of telegraph and telex by
telephone for most types of international communications (although the telephone
– using radio technologies – had been in transatlantic operation since 1927). In 1957
the first dedicated transpacific cable was completed. Both cables initially provided
for fewer than a hundred voice paths. Over the next two and a half decades the cost
of laying cable declined rapidly and demand steadily grew. By 1983 there were over
18,000 transatlantic voice paths, some 3,600 transpacific paths and almost 200 sea
cables in operation around the globe (Hepworth, 1989; Staple, 1991). Cable technology
has been steadily superseded by both fibre-optic cables, which can carry an enormously

Table 7.1 Growth of voice paths on key global telecommunications routes, 1986–1996

	Transatlantic voice paths		Transpacific voice paths	
	Cable	Satellite	Cable	Satellite
1986	22,000	78,000	2,000	39,000
1990	145,000	283,000	37,800	39,000
1996	1,264,000	710,800	864,600	234,000

Source: Staple, 1996

greater load, and by satellite technologies which obviate the need for any cabling. By 1997 a single transoceanic cable could carry over 600,000 voice paths by itself. Not surprisingly the unit cost of creating a transoceanic voice path had plummeted from around $500,000 a path in the 1950s to around $1,000 a path in the mid-1990s (Staple, 1996).

The first experimental communications satellite was launched by the USA in 1962. This was followed by the inauguration of INTELSAT (International Telecommunications Satellite Organization) which expanded access to satellite communications and made a share in the existing telephone and television channels available to most nations (see section 1.2.3). In 1965 the Americans launched the first fully functioning communications satellite. The USA, not surprisingly given the scale of its space programme, dominated the production and use of satellite technology for most of the following period. Today only about 20 per cent of all current satellites are US launched and owned, although they carry over one-third of the total transponders (each satellite carries more than one channel for communication). Another third of the 200 satellites in operation in 1991 were operated by INTELSAT and shared by many nations. The only other independent launch programme of significance came from the former Soviet Union with around 15 per cent of satellites, but Europe, and some countries such as India and Brazil, are developing their own programmes. Not surprisingly, satellites began to displace maritime cables for international communications in the 1970s (Brunn and Leinbach, 1991; Staple, 1991). However, in the 1980s and 1990s the new fibre-optic cables challenged satellite technology on the most communication-intensive routes in the world. The first transatlantic fibre-optic cable was completed in 1988 and there are now additional cables across the ocean (see table 7.1).

In terms of the numbers of channels and their geographical reach, there has undoubtedly been a globalization of the telecommunications infrastructure in the postwar era. Obviously enough, that infrastructure is not evenly placed around the globe. The vast majority of international cables, both old and new, lie across the North Atlantic, North Pacific and the Mediterranean. The number of lines between Latin America and Africa across the South Atlantic, for example, is much smaller. Similarly, ownership and use of satellite technology is very heavily skewed towards the West and the states of the ex-Soviet Union. Nonetheless, in the postwar era more and more states have at least been able to lock into these networks and have established small national telecommunication systems with international links; all of which has ensured that for anyone linked into the system the concept of time-space compression is a lived reality.

Table 7.2 Global unevenness of telecommunications infrastructure and use, 1995

	Population (millions)	Main lines per 100 people	Cellular phones ('000s)	Fax machines ('000s)	PCs ('000s)	Outgoing mMiTT	Incoming mMiTT
China	1,201.0	3.0	3,629	270	2,600	533	551
France	58.1	56.0	1,379	1,200	9,300	2,804	2,959
Germany	81.9	49.0	3,500	1,447	13,500	5,244	3,881
India	929.3	1.3	135	50	1,000	341	806
Japan	125.1	49.0	10,204	6,000	19,000	1,638	1,140
Sweden	8.8	68.0	2,025	n.a.	1,700	900	n.a.
UK	58.5	n.a.	5,737	n.a.	10,900	4,016	4,021
USA	263.1	63.0	33,786	14,052	86,300	15,623	7,010

mMiTT = millions of minutes of telephone traffic.
Source: Adapted from Staple, 1996

What else can so dramatically indicate the eradication of space than the ability to conduct a conversation across the oceans (with almost instant connection) or to receive visual images through satellite technology from anywhere on the planet. Moreover, with the establishment of global mobile telephone networks, such as Iridium, a further telephonic revolution is beginning.

In terms of overall flows, the volume of international telephone calls climbed from 12.7 billion call minutes in 1982 to a staggering 42.7 billion call minutes in 1992 and 67.5 billion in 1996. The subsequent annual rate of growth has been around 18–20 per cent (Staple, 1991, 1996; ITU, 1994a). Over the same period the volume of telex and telegraphy traffic fell by 10 per cent a year. Within the gross total of international telephone traffic, over 50 per cent of calls originated in just five countries: the USA, which accounts for one-quarter of all international calls by itself, alongside Germany, France, the UK and Switzerland. Of all international telephone traffic 80 per cent originates from just twenty countries, all of which are OECD members bar China-Hong Kong, Singapore and Saudi Arabia. Not surprisingly, the vast majority of this telephone traffic remains within the richest regions of the world, with the traffic between North America, Japan and Europe accounting for 75 per cent of international calls. The unevenness of international telephone usage (see table 7.2) can be expressed in terms of the minutes of international telephone traffic per capita per annum. The OECD has an average level of use of 36.6 minutes per person per year. The world average is 7.8 and in sub-Saharan Africa the average is just 1 minute per person, per year (ITU, 1994a).

The growth of international telephone traffic has many sources: decreasing costs, increasing international business connections, rising numbers of migrants and tourists calling home. However, perhaps the most significant source of future growth will come from the integration of telecommunications, computing and media technologies. It is this fusion that forms the basis of the Internet and ISDN traffic. The Internet (or World Wide Web), which uses telephone lines to connect computers all over the world, grew from its small military beginnings in the 1970s and 1980s. Subsequently, the figures for connections and users have grown exponentially as computer use diffuses more widely and the hardware for net-surfing becomes cheaper and more accessible. In the early 1990s something in the region of 100,000 computers were connected, by 1996 there were already over 12.8 million Internet hosts, and by the year 2000 there are likely to be well over 100 million users worldwide. As with other forms of telecommunications, the rate of diffusion varies enormously within the OECD as well as between developed and developing countries. In 1997 the numbers of Internet hosts per 1,000 inhabitants ranged from 55.5 in Finland and 38.4 in the US to as little as 0.2 and 0.3 in Turkey and Mexico respectively (OECD, 1997). Beyond the OECD not only does the level of connection to the net fall but some areas of the world – particularly parts of sub-Saharan Africa – remain unconnected.

However, none of this telecommunications infrastructure could really facilitate regularized global communications if it were not accompanied by a further form of collective infrastructure – shared languages and linguistic competencies. While human beings can communicate with each other in many ways and many media other than written and spoken language – visual art, dance, music – it is the existence of shared languages or language capacities that is the key infrastructure of intercultural communication and interaction. We can apply the idea of globalization to language in a number of ways. The first and most obvious is the diffusion of any one individual language across the globe. The second sense in which language or language capacities have been globalized is through the diffusion of bilingualism or multilingualism, easing the transmission of cultural products and ideas. Although there are over 5,000 languages in the contemporary world and many more dialects and regional variations, only 1,000 of these have ever been written down and it is in the written form that language most effectively travels through time and space. De Swann has described and analysed this linguistic complexity in terms of an evolving global language system in which ten to twelve languages now account for the first language of over 60 per cent of the world's population (De Swann, 1991). Thus contemporary patterns of language use reflect the accumulated consequences of many centuries of migration and linguistic transformation.

Of those core languages, three are used almost exclusively by native speakers in a pretty much contiguous territorial area: Japanese, German and Bengali. The expansion of German and Japanese as second languages was sharply curtailed by the Second World War, the subsequent dismemberment of the German and Japanese empires and the cultural odium in which Germany and Japan were then held – which effectively debarred these languages from assuming anything more than a very limited role as second languages. This, of course, contrasts sharply with the spread of German in the late nineteenth and early twentieth centuries through Central and Eastern Europe and the Scandinavian countries. Each of the other major languages of the world currently serves in some way or another as a lingua franca which makes it a pivotal element of both the past and present globalization of language and culture. In one set are languages that extend their reach across both native speakers and those that use the language as a second tongue over a contiguous area: they include Arabic, Malay and Hindi, Russian and Chinese. The main phases of expansion of these languages occurred some time ago – although in the case of Russian the consolidation of the Soviet Union after the Second World War introduced it as a second language into outlying areas of its empire: the Baltic states and Central Asia, for example.

Table 7.3   Book translations, averages, 1983–1985

	Total translations	Percentage of books translated from					
		English	French	German	Italian	Spanish	Scandinavian
France	3,979	65.0	3.3	10.0	5.4	2.6	1.3
Germany	6,676	60.7	11.9	3.4	3.2	1.9	3.9
Japan	2,696	78.3	7.9	7.5	1.2	0.7	0.5
Netherlands	4,286	56.8	18.0	15.1	1.3	1.1	2.4
Spain	7,711	50.1	20.0	10.6	6.3	0	1.9
Sweden	1,937	65.5	5.5	6.5	0.7	1.3	12.5
UK	1,139	4.0	23.2	25.7	6.8	3.1	6.2
USA	606	0.3	21.8	23.8	5.2	6.1	4.5

Source: Therborn, 1995

In another set are languages that are more globalized in their usage, in that native speakers are stretched much more widely around the world in non-contiguous territorial areas. These are the languages, of course, of European empire: English, French, Spanish and Portuguese. All these languages serve as regional lingua francas providing the medium of mutual intelligibility in particular areas of the world and between particular countries. But it is English that stands at the very centre of the global language system. It has become the lingua franca par excellence and continues to entrench that dominance in a self-reinforcing process (Crystal, 1997). It has become the central language of international communication in business, politics, administration, science and academia as well as being the dominant language of globalized advertising and popular culture. The main language of computing is English – providing the written language for Windows and Internet protocols. Estimates suggest that 80 per cent of all the electronically coded information stored in the world is in English (Economist, 1996). English is also the language used for international safety procedures such as air traffic control. One aspect of the dominance of English can be seen from book translation figures in table 7.3 clearly showing that it is books originally written in English that are overwhelmingly the object of translation into other languages. In a sense, this dominance is hardly surprising. As the fortunes of the other languages show, language use is closely connected to the rhythms of power. English has been the native language of the two modern hegemonic powers, Britain and the USA. Moreover, that power has been exercised in all domains of human life – the economic, political and military, of course, but in the cultural domain as well.

7.3.2   Cultural MNCs, global cultural markets

As we argued in chapter 5, the modern era has no monopoly on large multinational corporations and the telecommunications and culture industries have from their inception had an international dimension. From the late nineteenth century, early telecommunications corporations benefited from international and imperial possessions, while international news agencies spread their bureaus around the world and publishing houses dispersed their catalogues widely. Nonetheless, in the postwar era every sector of the communications and cultural industries has seen the rise of larger and larger corporations, which have become increasingly multinational in terms of their sales, products and organization. In this section we do not offer a comprehensive picture of the sector but sketch some of its main features and leading operators.

Until the 1970s, large telecommunications corporations and media-entertainment conglomerates could be found in many countries, but they were for the most part national corporations servicing domestic markets and they were engaged in quite separate sectors. Telecommunications companies and television broadcasters in most countries had been owned or part owned by the state, and private sector firms had to operate in a highly regulated sector. Given the limited reach of many of the world's languages, newsprint and publishing firms, while often large, were also generally restricted to national markets. Governments sought to regulate cross-media ownership. Since the 1970s, the national and global regulation of telecommunications and media industries has been transformed, some domestic markets have become ultracompetitive and/or saturated, and the distinct technologies on which different media sectors used to depend have become increasingly fused together. This has resulted in five main trends in corporate organization and activity: the increasing concentration of ownership; a shift from public to private ownership; the increasingly transnational structure of the corporations that survive through the establishment of subsidiaries or, more likely, the purchase of local firms, titles, etc.; general corporate diversification across different types of media products; and an increasing number of mergers of cultural producers, telecommunications corporations and computer hardware and software firms.

Deregulation and liberalization of the business environment (see chapters 4 and 5) have had a major impact on the communications sector. Telecommunication corporations have been privatized all over the world, foreign competitors have entered previously closed markets and there has been a wave of multinational alliances. At the same time, barriers to cross-media ownership have come down, and foreign firms have been allowed to purchase domestic corporations. The landmark WTO agreement on the global liberalization of telecommunication industries (WTO, 1997) has reinforced these trends. The simultaneous deregulation of telecommunications and media industries has been accompanied by an increasingly complex web of interlocking alliances and co-funded projects. The digitization of information, including music, visual imagery and text, has seen extensive potential synergies emerge between telecommunications companies, computer hardware and software firms, media corporations and broadcasters. In all these sectors, both internationally and domestically, mergers have built larger and multifaceted corporations. Nonetheless, the companies that can actually create the products to be distributed through the new telecommunications, broadcasting and computing infrastructures are the ones that remain at the heart of the process. It is in this context that a truly global set of media-entertainment-information corporations has come into being. They have not entirely displaced domestic competitors, nor have they eradicated foreign corporations in their home states. However, there can be little doubt that above the plethora of local and national culture industries, a group of around 20–30 very large MNCs dominate global markets for entertainment, news, television, etc., and they have acquired a very significant cultural and economic presence on nearly every continent.

Table 7.4 First-tier media conglomerates, business involvement by sector, 1997

	Media turnover (US$bn)	Film and video production	Film and video distribution	TV production	Terrestrial TV	Cable TV	Satellite TV	Digital TV	Recorded music	Radio	Newspapers and magazines	Book publishing	Online publishing
Time-Warner	25	✓	✓	✓	✓	✓	✓	✓	✓	✗	✓	✓	✓
Disney	24	✓	✓	✓	✓	✓	✓	✗	✓	✓	✓	✓	✓
Bertelsmann	15	n/s	n/s	n/s	✓	✓	✗	✓	✓	✓	✓	✓	✓
Viacom	13	✓	✓	✓	✓	✓	✓	✗	✓	✗	✗	✓	✓
News Corporation	10	✓	✓	✓	jv	jv	✓	✓	✗	✗	✓	✓	✗
Sony	9	✓	✓	✓	✗	jv	jv	✓	✓	✗	✗	✗	✗
Universal	7	✓	✓	✓	✗	jv	jv	✗	✓	✗	✗	✓	✗
TCI	7	✗	✗	✗	✗	✓	✓	✓	✗	✗	✗	✗	✓
Phillips													
Polygram	6	✓	✗	✓	✗	✗	✗	✗	✓	✗	✗	✗	✗
NBC	5	✗	✗	✓	✓	✓	✓	✓	✗	✓	✗	✗	✓

n/s = no significant involvement.
jv = joint venture involvement only.
Source: Information adapted from Herman and McChesney, 1997

All of these corporations have their home base in OECD countries and the majority of them in the USA. Taking a wide swathe of corporations, UNESCO reported in 1989 that of the 81 largest communication corporations (by turnover), 39 were from the USA, 28 from Western Europe, 8 from Japan, 5 from Canada and 1 from Australia (UNESCO, 1989). On the basis of the top twenty corporations (by turnover) in 1992, the picture is very similar (Hamelink, 1995). Of those twenty firms the largest number came from the USA: these included Time-Warner, Walt Disney, Capital Cities-ABC, CBS, McGraw Hill and Viacom. The Japanese presence in the sector derives not from the expansion of indigenous culture industries but from the media and electronic hardware industries. Both Sony and Matsushita bought their way into the global culture industries by their purchase of American firms; Columbia in the case of Sony and MCA (Music Corporation of America) in the case of Matsushita. News International is notionally an Australia-based firm owned by Rupert Murdoch, a notional Australian. The expansion of the Murdoch empire was certainly based on extensive interests in Australia and then in Britain, but it was the purchase of the American film studio, 20th Century Fox, that allowed News International into the American market and made it a global player. Within Europe only four states have generated media MNCs of any considerable economic weight and international scope. Based in the UK, Thorn-EMI, Rank, BBC, Pearson and Reuters have all acquired a global presence. Continental European countries have produced larger and more concentrated firms; Bertelsmann based in Germany; Matra-Hachette and Havas from France; and Elsevier and Polygram from the Netherlands. Bertelsmann and Hachette, in particular, have expanded globally by using revenues from European markets to buy into the American market, Bertelsmann purchasing RCA records, Doubleday Books and Random House, Hachette acquiring the large Diamandis publishing group. Given its domination of Italian television the Berlusconi Group is of equivalent economic size to these groups, but it has yet to acquire a significant global presence. However, it has spread its interests across Western Europe. All of the largest communication corporations have different portfolios of businesses and media interests, combining newspapers and news gathering, magazine and book publishing, television broadcasting and production, film production and distribution, video sales and rentals, and recorded music (see tables 7.4 and 7.5).

The domination of markets by these corporations varies according to sector. In news gathering the field is dominated by three news agencies, UPI (United Press International), AP (Associated Press) and Reuters, while visual news gathering outside of the main networks is controlled by two corporations, Reuters and WTN (World Television News). Internationally available television news is divided among CNN, News International and, most recently, the BBC. Global recorded music sales are concentrated in six companies: Thorn-EMI, Polygram, Warner and Sony held 73 per cent of the global market in 1991, while Bertelsmann and Matsushita account for much of the rest (Herman and McChesney, 1997). The domination of global TV and film markets is addressed in sections 7.3.4 and 7.3.5, where the extent of US leadership is made clear. TV programmes and films, though often made by independents and medium-sized companies, are invariably financed and distributed by the major TV networks and film studios. We return to the impact of these corporations on national cultures and national governments in section 7.5. First, we turn to the specifics of globalization in three particular cultural markets: music, cinema and television.

Table 7.5 Major media corporations, key joint ventures, mid-1990s

	First-tier media firm partners	Second-tier media firm partners	Telecommunications and information firm partners
Time-Warner	Viacom, TCI, Sony, NBC, Bertelsmann, News Corporation	Kirch, EMI, Kinnevik, Cox, Hachette, United News and Media, PBL, Comcast	US West, Bell South, Ameritech, Oracle
Disney	Bertelsmann, NBC, TCI	Kirch, Hearst, CLT, Dreamworks, Canal Plus, TFI, Cox, Comcast	Ameritech, SBC, GTE, Bell South, America Online, US West
Bertelsmann	Time-Warner, Sony, Universal, Polygram, News Corporation	Kirch, Canal Plus, United News and Media, Havas, CLT, EMI, Pearson, BBC	America Online
Viacom	Time-Warner, Universal, Polygram, News Corporation, Sony	Kirch, Pearson, Chris-Craft	Nynex, Sprint
News Corporation	Time-Warner, Viacom, TCI, Polygram, Sony, Bertelsmann	EMI, Canal Plus, Softbank, Granada, Globo Televisia, MGM, BBC, Carlton	
Universal	NBC, Bertelsmann, Viacom	Kirch, CLT	
NBC	Time-Warner, Disney	Canal Plus	Microsoft, National Geographic
TCI	All major media corporations	Kirch, Canal Plus, United News and Media, Havas, CLT, EMI, Pearson, BBC	America Online

Sources: Information from Herman and McChesney, 1997; Internet Infoseek, the Business Channel

7.3.3 Radio and the music industry

Of all of the electronic media of modern mass communication, radio has been the most easily globalized. Its origins lie in the early twentieth century and it was originally promoted as an alternative to telegraphy, obviating the need for expensive submarine cables or cross-continental lines, both of which were exposed to foreign powers and attack. Both the French and British governments had begun the construction of imperial communication networks based on radio before the First World War. With the creation of short-wave frequencies the radio became technologically simpler: broadcasting networks were cheaper to set up and the prices of receiving devices plummeted. As a consequence of both of these factors, radio experienced transnationalization of its broadcasting scope and global diffusion in its use and ownership long before other

Table 7.6 Ownership of radio receivers, 1950–1986

	Number of receivers (millions)				Receivers per 1,000 people			
	1950	1965	1975	1986	1950	1965	1975	1986
World	182.0	573.0	1,032.0	1,176.0	77.0	170.0	255.0	362.0
Africa	1.5	10.0	20.0	94.0	7.7	32.0	69.0	164.0
Asia	11.5	53.0	138.0	468.0	9.1	28.0	60.0	164.0
Europe	64.0	222.0	348.0	523.0	109.0	272.0	478.0	676.0
North America	97.5	251.0	424.0	532.0	453.0	1,173.0	1,797.0	1,992.0
Latin America	6.5	34.0	81.0	134.0	62.0	137.0	251.0	327.0
Oceania	2.5	3.0	13.0	25.0	167.0	171.0	619.0	1,000.0
Developed countries		498.0	841.0	1,182.0		486.0	762.0	968.0
Developing countries		75.0	191.0	594.0		32.0	66.0	160.0

Source: Information adapted from UNESCO, 1950, 1988

electronic media. While radio continued to function as part of imperial and military chains of command after the First World War, the interwar years saw the establishment of national and local radio stations in Europe and North America, broadcasting a mixture of music, news and sporting commentaries. There are some examples from before the Second World War of the use of radio across national boundaries – though predominantly for propaganda and political purposes – but during the war the various government-run radio stations took this to new heights: Germans broadcast to the UK, the BBC broadcast to occupied Europe and Ezra Pound lent his poetic, if not political, wisdom to Mussolini, broadcasting to the Allied Forces. In the postwar era, the Cold War was a significant stimulant to the expansion of transboundary broadcasting. Radio Free Europe and Voice of America, as well as transboundary German stations, were all responses to the division of Europe and the ideological warfare it brought in its wake.

Alongside these more explicit transnational functions of radio broadcasting, the medium has also been a significant agent of cultural diffusion. Above all, it has been the medium for broadcasting and popularizing Anglo-American popular music. Rock 'n' roll and its various descendants found their way to Europe via the radio as much as the concert hall and the record shop. In an interesting contrast within the West, the radio has also been an important instrument of localism and the maintenance and re-creation of local identities with special ethnic stations, pirate radio and the importation of new, foreign musical styles and genres. Most pirate stations have been nationally based, but the limited access national governments made available on radio frequencies in the 1960s led to the formation of transnational pirate broadcasters. When offshore transmissions began in an effort to circumvent strictly national regulation of radio in the UK in the sixties, the government initially responded with a very heavy hand.

In some ways the musical form is one that lends itself to globalization more effectively than any other. This is because it is one of the few popular modes of cultural expression and communication that is not dependent on written or spoken language for its primary impact. Therefore, in highly literate societies, it is a form that can transcend the limitations and particularities of language difference without recourse to the expense and complexity of translation. This is not to suggest that there are not some very sharp difficulties in the cultural translation of music, meeting distinctive and particular local and national traditions of music production and reception. But the relative ease of cultural diffusion in this sphere has been reflected in the spread of many genres and major artists all over the world; there can be few more global products, images and messages than those associated with Madonna, Michael Jackson and the Spice Girls. Of course, the production, distribution and reception of these products has been highly skewed, but before we can examine the variable geography of musical globalization we need to consider what type of music and what type of industry we are dealing with.

The modern popular music industry has no real historical antecedents. In the absence of methods of sound storage and reproduction, music remained a highly localized phenomenon consumed at the site of production. Musical styles, methods and instruments did not remain stationary prior to such technologies; the theory and practice of classical orchestral music spread across the elites of Europe from the seventeenth century onwards; and the styles and music that derived from and contributed to religious worship and culture could spread through their own ecclesiastic networks (Joyce, 1993). Patterns of migration and movement served to diffuse musical styles and skills away from their point of origin and allowed encounters and fusions between otherwise separated musical traditions. The movement of African musical traditions to the Americas through the slave trade is probably the most important example of this. However, the small circuits of music publication, commercialized orchestras, public performances and patronage-based music production were all that preceded the creation of technologies on which musical sounds could be stored, transported and reproduced: the phonograph or record player, the various types of electromagnetic cassette and, most recently, the compact disc. In addition, the music industry has been built on the spread of increasing modes of transmission of music, through personal stereo systems, dedicated pop radio, television, music videos and video channels. On the basis of such developments, an institutional complex arose of companies and recording artists, pressing records and marketing products, which has grown progressively in size and complexity over the last eighty years.

Technology aside, the growth of the music industry has also been borne on the back of significant social and demographic shifts in the core societies and markets of the West. For in financial terms the core of the international music industry has been popular contemporary music rather than classical or religious music – in short, rock and pop – and it has overwhelmingly been American (and to an extent British) in its production, organization and content. These developments have come from and, in turn, contributed to the emergence of distinctive youth cultures and subcultures, created by the economic and social transformations of the postwar West – growing affluence, changes in education, changes in the labour market, and the erosion of tradition and traditional community. Accordingly, the transnationalization of the music industry has simultaneously been the story of the diffusion and export of American-style popular music, artists and genres and a range of associated aspects of the cultures and subcultures from which it grew.

The globalization of the music industry has thus taken a number of forms. First, it has involved the creation of transnational corporations producing and marketing records.

Second, it has involved the import and export of musical products and the penetration of national markets by foreign artists and music. Third, it has in part been based on a broader transfer of styles and images that are largely rooted in American youth culture and black cultures that have provided the ultimate source of the industry's cultural output – even if they have been diluted and repackaged in the process (Negus, 1993). The UK exemplifies these trends. Nearly 20 per cent of its output is exported, and the country has run a healthy balance of payments surplus on the back of this. However, UK companies control only a small fraction of their market. Foreign corporations control around two-thirds of UK sales, but often with British artists on their books. Thus economic and cultural flows are both intertwined and sometimes oppose each other.

Where other Western countries differ from the US and UK is in the relative paucity of domestically generated popular music. All of them import a significant proportion of their recorded music from the US, reproducing the pattern of dominance established in the 1950s and 1960s (see IFPI, 1994). This is also reflected in the decline of the domestic record industries in these countries (Hung and Morencos, 1990). In all of them, Britain is the only other significant pole of popular music. Nonetheless, other nations have had faltering successes, locally and more globally. France has maintained a relatively strong domestic industry and market for its own particular brand of crooning and pop, although it has proved less popular outside the Francophone countries. Sweden has generated the disco equivalent of Volvo, in the shape of Abba. More recently, the Swedes' capacity to learn and use English with remarkable fluency has opened up overseas markets to domestic artists working in English (Malmans, 1982; Burnett, 1992). Germany has yet to achieve commercial success in diverse foreign markets, though in some genres – techno, garage and house music – the Germans have been successful (Zeppenfeld, 1979).

Outside the West there is an enormous range of local musical traditions and styles. However, it is only under the auspices of the global music industry that these musical forms and artists have begun to receive a significant hearing outside their homelands under the banner of what is now called, by the marketing departments of leading corporations, 'world music'. But world music currently takes only a very small share of Western markets (Robinson et al., 1991).

7.3.4 Cinema

The actual numbers of films produced and the total hours of screen time created by the global film industry are relatively small by comparison to the global volume of television produced or the numbers of hours of radio broadcast, or indeed the sheer volume of books published and newsprint created. Yet the cinema industry occupies a special place, aesthetically, culturally and politically, in the contemporary world. Films are in some senses the premium products of the audio-visual industries; not only do they possess both their own distinct circuits of distribution through cinemas etc., but they also form the product core of the video sale and rental business. They provide premium programming for nearly all television stations and have channels on cable and satellite television purely devoted to their broadcast. Finally, from our perspective, film and cinema make up both the oldest of the culture industries *qua* culture industry and the industry which was globalized earliest in terms of organization and genre. Outside the West, television is still in its relative infancy, but cinema, which has always been collectively consumed and does not require the purchase of an individual means of reception, has been experienced for most of the twentieth century. Thus, while television as a medium is consumed more intensively and voraciously than cinema, it is fitting to begin our discussion of the globalization of the audio-visual industries with film and cinema.

What makes a film a national product? Does the latter mean it must be a homogeneous product, written, directed and filmed by nationals in a national setting? If so, then hardly any film could qualify as truly national. Few industries support a more multinational and itinerant workforce than the film industry. It would be exceptionally time-consuming and complex to collect meaningful data on such a topic. Sharper definitions and better quality data are available on the financial side of film production because national governments and ministries of culture, in particular, have been concerned with the economic consequences of international shifts in film production and finance. They have therefore collected information on these matters. Interestingly, even a cursory glance at the assembled data suggests that the degree of detail of national statistics on the subject is directly related to how worried national governments are over the globalization of their film industry, the shrinkage of domestic production and the perceived economic and cultural threat that this poses. Thus French, Italian and Spanish data are altogether more comprehensive than data collected by the UK government, which effectively abandoned intervention in the national film industry during the 1980s and early 1990s, and by the US government, which has neither the need nor the inclination to intervene at any great length.

Alongside data on the national and international production and finance of films, we can look at the overall data on the import and export of films across national borders. However, the fact that films are consumed as semi-public goods means that the data on flows of films do not necessarily correspond accurately with the ways in which they are received and the numbers of people who watch them. It is certainly the case in America that foreign films constitute a much larger percentage of total releases than they do of total audience or box office receipts. Therefore a second set of data, on audience shares and box office receipts, reflects more accurately the enmeshment of national film audiences and distribution circuits (Wildman and Siwek, 1988).

If globalization is taken to mean simply the diffusion of film-making capacities and organizations around the world, then it is fair to say that there has been a straightforward globalization of the film industry. According to statistical surveys undertaken by UNESCO, a significant number of nations both inside and outside the West have the capacity to produce feature films. However, it is also clear that only a very few nations actually produce large numbers of films. In the 1980s, for example, only the USA, Japan, South Korea, Hong Kong and India were producing more than 150 feature films a year and only another twenty or so nations, mainly Western, were producing more than fifty films a year. The main second rank producers were the USSR, France, Italy, Spain, Germany and the UK. The majority of nations, although they had the capacity to produce films, were actually releasing fewer than twenty films a year.

One of the main manifestations of globalization in the film industry has been co-production, where the development of a film is funded by money from organizations in more than one nation. The forms this takes are many and varied, including 50:50 deals between two equal partners, variants of minority and majority stakeholding, multiple

Table 7.7 Distribution of sales of films by major exporting countries, early 1980s

	Number of countries distributed in	Number of other countries where its sales are main source of films	Number of other countries where its sales are in top 3 sources	Number of other countries where its sales account for at least 5% of imported films
USA	79	56	77	79
France	68	5	36	40
Italy	71	2	39	52
India	42	6	39	52
USSR	55	10	17	28
UK	69	1	19	33
FRG	56	0	8	15
Japan	46	0	5	7
Hong Kong	4	19	28	53

Source: Wildman and Siwek, 1988, p. 16; data originally from UNESCO, *Statistical Yearbook*, 1984

stakeholders, etc. The US film industry has not relied on co-productions as a source of finance or potential distribution networks given the internal strength of the indigenous film industry, the large size of its domestic market and its well-organized international distribution networks. The same can be said for the Indian and Hong Kong industries, which have been relatively self-sufficient. However, in Europe co-productions have at certain times been an important source of finance. In France co-productions accounted for only 15 per cent of film finance projects in 1950, but this climbed steadily over the next fifteen years to reach around 70 per cent of film projects in the mid-1960s. After this, the level declined and by the late 1970s had returned to its initial postwar levels, before undergoing something of a revival in the late 1980s. By the mid 1990s the level of co-productions in Western Europe had reached 50 per cent of all movies. Smaller European film industries like the Portuguese and Belgian are almost totally reliant on international co-production finance (Gyory and Glas, 1994; Screen Digest, 1996, 1997b).

As one might expect, the basic prerequisite for significant film exports is a strong domestic level of production, and thus there is a close correlation between levels of overall film production, film exports and relatively lower levels of imports. In the 1980s the major film exporters in the world were the USA, India, France, Italy, the USSR (though the current state of the Russian film industry is distinctly less promising, since it is no longer heavily subsidized), the UK, Germany, Japan and Hong Kong. It is unquestionably the USA which dominates world trade in films: the US industry distributes its films in more countries than any competitor, it is the largest exporter to more markets than any other and, since the demise of the Soviet Union, it is the main exporter to all of the nations that previously received the fruits of the Soviet film industry. Beyond the US the most important exporters are France, Italy and India. Regional and colonial connections are important in this respect. French films are naturally more popular in French-speaking countries and in the former colonies of North Africa, while India is a major supplier in South East Asia and Africa.

While sources of finance and the import and export of films are important indicators of the cultural and financial health of domestic cinema industries, another useful test for assessing the diffusion of foreign cultural products is to examine the level of domestic and foreign films released in any given year in cinemas. The data here suggest that the USA, with the exception of its small arts house circuits, has remained pretty impervious to the charms of foreign films. However, in Europe, despite some periods of national cinematic renaissance, the trend has generally been towards an increasing number of foreign releases – overwhelmingly American. The UK, not surprisingly given the shared language and the weakness of domestic production, has been the most reliant on US imports. In 1950 foreign films made up 78 per cent of all releases. As the domestic industry recovered from wartime limitations and contractions, this level fell to around 70 per cent in the early 1960s, but has climbed steadily since to the point where foreign films made up almost 90 per cent of releases in the late 1980s and early 1990s. There are exceptions to this trend. In France the level of foreign releases actually fell in the 1980s to around 65 per cent (Gyory and Glas, 1994).

Box office receipts tell a similar story of import penetration in European countries and in Japan as well, while the US market remains domestically dominated. Indeed, with the exception of a few years of recovery in continental Europe in the late 1960s and early 1970s, US films have taken an increasing share of domestic receipts, sharply growing in the 1980s. In Italy, for example, foreign film receipts declined from a post-war high of 78 per cent to less than 40 per cent in 1971 but had exceeded 80 per cent of all receipts by 1990. In France, despite increasing numbers of domestic releases, foreign films swept the market in the late 1970s and 1980s, taking over 60 per cent of receipts by 1990, compared to only 40 per cent in the early 1970s. In the UK and Sweden the domination of American films is even greater at the box office. In Sweden in 1990 domestic receipts fell below 10 per cent, which is where they also hovered in the early 1990s in Britain. Across the EU as a whole the share of US receipts at the box office rose from 60.2 per cent in 1984 to 71.7 in 1991. However, since the early 1990s there has been something of a comeback for domestic and other European films at the box office. The EU average for the share of US films in box office receipts dropped to 63 per cent in 1996, falling as low as 53 per cent in France and down to 81 per cent in the UK. Finally, it should be noted, Japan, which has had a relatively healthy domestic industry and appeared to be a relatively difficult market for US films to penetrate, has succumbed to US movies as well. Foreign receipts at the Japanese box office – predominately American – have risen from 45 per cent of the total in 1980 to almost 60 per cent in 1990, a figure that has continued to creep upwards in the late 1990s (Gyory and Glas, 1994; Screen Digest, 1996, 1997c).

7.3.5 Television

It is important to note that the cinema has become a declining sector for revenues in the film industry as more and more money is made through television sales and video rentals. Here data has been collected even less systematically and, for obvious reasons, less accurately. However, what data there are suggest that the US is maintaining and strengthening its economic dominance in these new sectors (IFPI, *Video Statistics*, various years).

While the global presence of the film industry is long established, the globalization of the television industry has been a more recent phenomenon. In part this is because the technology is newer, but perhaps more significant in explaining its rate of global diffusion has been the character of the technology itself and the much greater involvement of national governments with the medium: as owners, producers, financiers, regulators and censors. Both arguments require some historical explication. Although the technology for the production and broadcast of television developed before the Second World War and broadcasting began in the US and UK in the 1930s, it was only in the late 1950s and early 1960s that television ownership started to become relatively widespread in the West. As late as 1954 there were only 125,000 TV sets in France and fewer than 90,000 in West Germany, a density of ownership that was less than 3 sets per 1,000 people (UNESCO, 1963).

Television requires a higher level of individual capital investment from households than cinema. It was a technology of relative affluence and in the lean decade after the Second World War it was unlikely to flourish in economies where domestic consumption was much less important than investment and production. In these conditions the cinema continued to attract significant mass audiences for domestic and imported movies. Television remained a secondary medium and almost entirely domestically generated. As economic growth accelerated in the 1960s across the West, and more of that growth filtered through to domestic consumption, TV ownership rose rapidly and the relative cost of TV sets fell. The subsequent global spread of television ownership, the basic precondition of the development of trade in TV programmes and the spread of TV genres, has followed a similar trajectory. It is only in the 1980s and 1990s that sufficient domestic markets have emerged outside the West for a genuinely global television market to develop.

Despite the individualization of consumption and the predominately domestic use of television compared to the cinema, television initially possessed a peculiar public quality. In a given territorial area there could only be so many frequencies on which terrestrial television could be broadcast, and therefore some kind of government intervention and regulation was inevitable from the outset. Given the simultaneous transmission of broadcasts direct into private homes, governments, both democratic and otherwise, took a close interest in the content and financing of television from an early stage. Except in the USA, all early television broadcasters were owned or part-owned by the public sector; they were generally financed by a mixture of state revenues, publicly organized licence fees and some advertising. Thus, despite the potential for transnational broadcasting, the organization and orientation of early television stations were relentlessly national. Of course, the spillover of terrestrial frequencies across national boundaries did occur, especially in the densely packed airspace of Europe – and in the case of West–East spillover, this was of considerable political importance. But international broadcasting of this kind was essentially limited and an accidental byproduct of the technology.

In the last twenty years, a series of technological and political changes have transformed the televisual landscape and have contributed to the globalization of television as a medium and as an industry. First and foremost, the number of countries with broadcasting systems and the number of televisions available on which to watch their output have steadily risen. From its Western core, television has spread in the postwar years across Eastern Europe and the Soviet Union, into Latin America, Asia and Africa. Second, first within the West, but later in other areas as well, the number of terrestrial channels has steadily climbed. In part, this has been because governments

Table 7.8 Ownership of television sets, 1959–1992

	Total number of TV sets (millions)					TV sets per 1,000 people				
	1959	1969	1980	1988	1992	1959	1969	1980	1988	1992
Total	87.0	251.0	558.0	756.0	873.0	39.0	89.0	125.0	148.0	160.0
Africa	0.04	1.1	8.0	17.0	26.0	0.2	3.2	17.0	28.0	38.0
Asia			98.0	160.0	235.0			38.0	53.0	73.0
East Asia	3.5	23.0				25.0	138.0			
South Asia	0.1	2.5				0.1	2.3			
North America	56.2	89.0	166.0	214.0	226.0	287.0	397.0	661.0	790.0	800.0
Latin America	2.7	15.0	36.0	64.0	76.0	13.0	54.0	99.0	149.0	166.0
Europe	20.3	86.5	243.0	289.0	300.0	48.0	188.0	324.0	372.0	381.0
Oceania	0.7	3.3	7.0	11.0	11.0	43.0	175.0	296.0	411.0	375.0
Developed countries			478.0	585.0	616.0			416.0	485.0	498.0
Developing countries			80.0	171.0	257.0			24.0	44.0	61.0

Source: UNESCO, Statistical Yearbook, 1970, 1988, 1994

have been prepared to enlarge the funding base for television companies, for there is clearly a limit to the numbers of channels and programmes that can be funded by subsidy/licence fee alone. By allowing advertising revenue and sponsorship into the television funding mix – be it through public corporations taking advertising or wholly private stations – the potential output and funding base of national TV has risen. However, the expansion of output has rarely, if ever, been matched by a corresponding increase in the capacity of national audio-visual industries to supply all of the potential broadcast slots. Thus the expansion of television output across and within countries has fuelled the demand for television imports.

Third, these shifts have been accelerated in recent years by technological and regulatory changes. The most important technological shifts have been the advent of satellite and cable television. When cable and satellite are included, the number of channels in Europe, for example, increased in the five years from 1988 to 1993 from 104 to 165 and within the EU from 77 to 129 (IDATE, 1993, p. 39). In 1997, the total number of channels broadcasting in Europe had risen to over 250 (Screen Digest, 1997a). Both of these technologies allow television corporations to circumvent the regulatory capacity of nation-states to some degree, and to break free from the national limits of terrestrial broadcasting structures. These technologies effectively break the natural monopoly of limited suitable electromagnetic frequencies imposed on terrestrial television. Furthermore, because satellites can broadcast to a number of different national territories, but are doing so from space, the jurisdiction of the receiving countries does not necessarily cover them. The take-up of such satellite services has been greatly enlarged by their interaction with cable networks. In these combined situations a few receivers are linked to a broader cable network, thereby circumventing the need for many subscribers to invest in the expensive reception hardware. Not surprisingly, given start-up costs, the take-up of these services is currently much lower than of terrestrial television and uneven across countries, regions and social groups, but the trend is unquestionably upward. Market penetration of cable television has risen in Western Europe, for example, from 17 per cent in 1990 to over 25 per cent in 1995 and for satellite from 2 per cent to 12.6 per cent over the same period (Screen Digest, 1997a).

Fourth, technological and economic changes have been accompanied by waves of political and legal deregulation in almost every Western and many developing states. This has taken a number of forms but it has usually included the commercialization or privatization of existing terrestrial channels; the establishment of loose regulatory frameworks for the provision of satellite and cable services; the abandonment of regulations which sharply restrict television company ownership to home nationals; and the end of regulations which attempt to prevent excessive cross-ownership of media companies. This combination of technological change and deregulation has fuelled the global market for programming and made possible the cross-border ownership of television stations and the global dissemination of some television channels. It has also stimulated some genuine cross-border production and co-financing alongside national production of programmes for global markets. We look briefly at the research on imported TV output.

Considerable effort has been given to measuring the volume of television output domestically produced and the volume imported. The methods for conducting such surveys vary considerably and results depend on a number of factors: for how long a sample of television output is taken; at what time of the year; whether the researchers focus on peak-time viewing or the whole schedule; which channels are examined. There can be considerable differences in levels of foreign inputs between different channels in the same country. News, weather and sport – almost always domestically generated – are included in some samples but not in others. Nonetheless, some considerable progress has been made in making the many research projects in this area comparable (Nordenstreng and Varis, 1974; Varis, 1986; Sepstrup, 1991).

A number of points can be gleaned from this research. First, the USA stands out as an exception. The USA alone has maintained an extremely low level of foreign imported programming in its domestic output. In 1973 the level of imports on the major networks was a mere 1 per cent of total output and this climbed to only 2 per cent a decade later. Second, the dominance of the US product at home is reflected in the phenomenal export success of the US television industry. America's huge export earnings from its audio-visual industries have been traditionally based on the strength of the film sector, exporting for both cinema distribution and television showings. However, an increasing volume of made-for-television programmes have been exported over the last twenty years. In the early 1970s the USA was exporting something in the region of 150,000 hours of programmes a year. This made it the biggest exporter of television programmes by some considerable way – with more than triple the combined exports of the next three biggest exporters. That dominance is reflected geographically in that the USA was, and is, the single biggest exporter to every region of the world and almost every single country; this includes the major markets of Western Europe and Latin America as well as the developing or smaller markets of the Middle East, Asia and Africa. In the case of Latin America, despite the competitive advantage one might expect for Spanish television, the USA supplies at least 75 per cent of imported programming. The figure for Western Europe was around 45 per cent in the 1980s. It has proved exceptionally difficult to put an accurate figure on the total financial income of these sales, but the Motion Picture Association of America has estimated that income from foreign programme syndication for all US companies rose from $66 million in 1963 to $485 million in 1983 (Renard and Litman, 1985). It now stands considerably higher than this.

Third, one group of OECD nations – France, Germany and the UK – displays a considerably larger use of imported programming than the USA, but its use is somewhat less than many smaller Western nations. As we might expect, this group of countries also possesses a relatively strong domestic television industry, with some considerable export success. Imported programming in Germany accounted for 26.5 per cent of output in 1973 and 27 per cent in 1986. In France the figures for the same years were 9 per cent and 16 per cent and for the UK the figures were 13 per cent and 27 per cent. Both Japan and Italy were importing around 10 per cent of output in the early 1970s, a figure comparable to those mentioned above, but more recent data are not available. Anecdotal evidence and balance of payments statistics suggest that the level of imports has increased to at least a similar rate to that of France, Germany and the UK.

Fourth, after the USA, France, Germany and the UK are the major exporters of TV programmes – indeed there are few others of the same order of magnitude – though Brazil, Mexico, Egypt, Hong Kong, Spain and Australia are increasing their exports (Wildman and Siwek, 1988; Sinclair et al., 1996). Of the three European nations, the UK has been the main exporter to the rest of Western Europe (especially the smaller countries) as well as to the US. France and Germany have conducted a smaller level of trade but only with linguistically similar countries. Interestingly, there has been relatively little trade between the three exporting nations (in strong contrast to trade in general, see chapter 3).

Sweden, by contrast to the countries discussed, has a relatively underdeveloped TV industry, high and increasing levels of programme imports and very low levels of programme exports. In this regard it reflects the predicament of most small countries. In 1973 imports already constituted 33 per cent of domestic output and they climbed to 37 per cent in 1988. However, it is important to note that high levels of import penetration are not an established part of all small countries, a number of which continue to develop their own TV industries, while others are constrained in their purchases by foreign exchange limits (see Wildman and Siwek, 1988).

7.3.6   Tourism

Tourism is simultaneously one of the most obvious forms of the globalization of culture and one of the most difficult to evaluate. Few phenomena bear sharper testament to the time-space compression of societies than the diminishing costs and increasing ease of international travel for the purposes of leisure, and, consequently, the increasing numbers of people from nearly all Western social classes who can escape their routine environments and experiences. Other forms of international cultural exchange, in the West at any rate, are widespread. But what other activity exposes so many people, from so many social strata, to such a wide, immediate and tangible experience of other cultures, locations and frames of reference? By the same token what other activity locks so completely specific locales – locales for tourists, that is – into wider international cultural patterns (Urry, 1990)?

Yet these predominately cultural interpretations must, even on a cursory examination, be qualified. First and foremost, tourism must be viewed from an economic as well as a cultural perspective. While independent travelling is relatively widespread, no international tourist can escape from using the many companies, large and small, domestic and international, that organize and coordinate travel and tourism. Second, economic criteria shape the pattern of who can travel, where they go, how often they go and what they do on arrival. By the same token, economic factors shape the experience of tourist destinations, the structure of investment, the nature of the job market and the overall enmeshment of a country in the international economy – for, of course, tourism can be and often is enormously significant as an employer and an earner of foreign currency. Tourism also influences infrastructure provision and can be a significant site of foreign direct investment. Third, not all tourism is international. Indeed, the roots of tourism as a relatively widespread mass phenomenon in the West do not lie in international travel but with domestic travel. Finally, the pressure of economic forces, in part, shapes and characterizes the nature of the tourist's cultural experience. For it is obvious that the very presence of tourists, especially in any large numbers and carrying significant economic consequences, transforms the cultural and economic character of the locales they visit.

While governments and promotional organizations collect data on tourism, the main agencies responsible are customs and immigration agencies measuring and controlling cross-border flows. While the OECD has done some work in making information comparable, there remain limits to the international data (OECD, 1986). In particular, short-stay and long-stay visitors are classified differently in different countries. Similarly, different countries collect data on business visitors and other tourists differently. In any case, what data are available are only one measure of human flows and economic transactions, because the broader socio-cultural consequences of travel for both visitors and hosts need to be taken into account.

Although international tourism as an organized business can be traced back well over a century and international travel considerably further, relatively reliable data on international tourist flows were not collected before 1950. At this time, the approximate number of international tourists stood at 25.3 million and total tourist expenditure at just over $2 billion. The following decades tell a story of continuing and accelerating growth. By 1960 the number of international tourists had grown to 69.3 million and their expenditure had climbed to $6.9 billion; by 1970 these figures stood at 159.7 million and $17.9 billion; by 1980 they had risen to 284.8 million and $102.4 billion and by 1990 to 454.8 million and $255 billion. Despite the economic slowdown in the OECD countries in the early 1990s, annual tourist numbers had climbed above half a billion a year by 1995 and those 561 million tourists spent over $380 billion in that year. In terms of sheer numbers of people the figures are unprecedented, and while the growth rate has slowed from the explosive increase of the early postwar years, the overall rate of expenditure growth is actually increasing. Moreover, on current trends, the World Tourist Organization has estimated that the global tourist total will be just under a billion by 2010 (World Tourist Organization, 1991, 1997).

However, as we might expect, neither the origins of international tourists nor their final destinations, and thus the distribution of international tourist expenditures and

Grid 7.1 Key historical agents and contexts of cultural globalization

	Premodern Pre-1500	Early modern Approx. 1500–1850	Modern Approx. 1850–1945	Contemporary 1945 on
Main agents of cultural globalization	Cultural diffusion and emulation – established through migration, war and trade	Cultural diffusion and emulation – established through migration, war and trade	European global empires	Large public and private media, tourism, transport and communications corporations
	World religions	World religions	Transnational secular ideologies, i.e. socialism, nationalism and liberalism	
	Multicultural empires	Multicultural empires	Transnational secular discourses, i.e. Western science	Transnational secular ideologies and discourses, global expert networks
	Pursuit of salvation and political power key motivations	Pursuit of salvation and political power remain key motivations	Pursuit of salvation and political and economic power key motivations	Pursuit of profit/entertainment key motivations
Other key cultural networks	Most cultural networks and flows very localized	Most cultural networks and flows very localized	Formation then entrenchment of European, Latin and North American nation-states and nationalism	Nation-states and nationalism achieve almost global coverage

receipts, are evenly divided across the globe. The vast majority of those movements in the last thirty years have occurred within and between North America and Western Europe. It is only in recent years that the Japanese and Australians have significantly increased their shares of international travel (OECD, 1986). More recent figures suggest that this unevenness persists. In 1994 only 2.5 per cent of international tourists came from Africa, 1.2 per cent from the Middle East and 0.6 per cent from South Asia. Europe provided 53 per cent of international tourists, and the rest were fairly evenly divided between the Americas (mainly North America and Mexico) and Asia (mainly Japan, Taiwan and Australia). In terms of spending by tourists, the figures show a similar concentration with over 60 per cent of all tourist expenditures coming from ten countries (the G7 plus Austria, Belgium and the Netherlands) (World Tourist Organization, 1997).

7.4 Historical Forms of Cultural Globalization: In Sum

While it is important to acknowledge both the scale of premodern forms of cultural globalization and the subsequent dominance of national circuits of culture (discussed in section 7.2), there has been a quantitative and qualitative shift in cultural globalization in recent times. This is *not* to endorse any existing account of cultural globalization – hyperglobalizers, transformationalists, etc. Rather, as the above evidence suggests, it is to note that the late twentieth century has seen a series of decisive shifts in the geographical scale, immediacy and speed of cultural interaction and communications – and the emergence not only of historically unique technologies but the institutionalization of diverse forms of cultural production and interaction, many of which increasingly cut across the territorial boundaries and social spaces of national cultures and nation-states. The key elements of these shifts are set out below, and in grids 7.1 and 7.2.

First, the early twentieth century witnessed a wave of new technological innovations in communications, and transportation, and their transformation, along with older technologies, into functioning global infrastructures. These shifts have opened up a massive series of communication channels that cross national borders with ease, increase the range and type of communications to which any region or locale has access, and radically diminish the costs of transmission and transport. The growth of infrastructures of communication did not, however, simply increase worldwide communication at the expense of the national, for it facilitated an increase both in national communication patterns and in transnational cultural flows. In the late twentieth century a further wave of innovations has emerged whose speed and range dwarf earlier technologies: digitization of information and images, satellite broadcasting and telephony systems, new cable and fibre-optic technologies and the integration of computer and telecommunications networks whose ultimate expression are the global networks of the World Wide Web. Alongside these technological infrastructures a number of international agencies and organizations have sought some global regulation of cultural flows. These include those explicitly concerned with global communications and cultures such as UNESCO, the global regulators of technological infrastructures such as the ITU or INTELSAT (see section 1.2.3) and the World Trade Organization, which has become enmeshed in the issue of cultural protectionism where this impacts on the liberalization

Grid 7.2 Historical forms of cultural globalization

	Premodern Pre-1500	Early modern Approx. 1500–1850	Modern Approx. 1850–1945	Contemporary 1945 on
Extensity	All world religions and empires remain regional though stretching across many societies and cultures	Christianity expands to Americas on the back of demographic and military victory	Western global empires develop, creating thin inter-elite cultural connections. This provides part of the infrastructure for the diffusion of transnational secular ideologies and discourses to Asia, Africa, Latin America	Infrastructures of telecommunications, linguistic interaction and transport more extensive than ever before
	Hinduism restricted to Indian subcontinent; Buddhism restricted to South and East Asia; Christianity restricted to Europe and Near East; Islam most global in the early phase of world religions, from South Asia to North and East Africa	Capacity of Western culture to penetrate and influence outside of the New World very limited	Western global empires develop early infrastructures of transcontinental and interregional telegraphic communications	Use of English as a global language unparalleled
			Western global empires embed European languages as key global lingua francas	Scale of corporate ownership, operations and reach of global markets in cultural products very extensive though highly uneven
	Most successful enduring multicultural empires also regional: Roman Empire, Han China		Emergence of early international media corporations – news agencies	Global diffusion of new means of cultural reception and transmission (TV, radio, etc.)
	Nomadic Mongol empires bigger but culturally weak		Increasingly cultural institutions and flows organized at the level of emerging nation-states in West	Movement of popular cultural artefacts largely within West but also from North to the South
				A small but growing trend sees return of popular and literary cultural forms from South to North

Intensity	Low	Low	Increasing at a global level compared to premodern era, but in relative terms becoming less important in West given rise of national cultures, institutions, circuits of communication and transport	Sheer volume of regularized movement and communications unparalleled within states and across regions Digitization of all media
Velocity	Negligible	Low	Increasing as modes of transport become faster and more reliable and early telecommunications makes simple text/voice instantaneous communication possible	Instantaneous communication possibilities, transport speeds incomparably faster and cheaper than ever before
Impact propensity	Initial arrival of world religions and empires transforms cultural life of converts, often bringing literacy along with profound shifts in worldviews Long-distance cultural flows and relationships within Eurasia provide key instruments of imperial cohesion, and possibility of diffuse peace and shared cross-community identities	Initial European expansion more powerful in extending military/environmental reach of Europe than cultural reach Christianity established in Americas but only tiny outposts in Africa and Asia. Minimal impact on entrenched civilizations – Islamic, Indian, Chinese, etc.	Colonial communication infrastructures increase surveillance of colonies by metropolis Nationalism achieves powerful if variable cultural influence on elite and mass audiences in Western nations Nationalism has some impact on colonial elite cultures, less on popular cultures	Transformation of possibilities and costs of global cultural, economic and political interaction; aids establishment, operation of MNCs, INGOs, etc. Increasing foreign component to national systems of ownership and control of media corporations, cultural product markets

continued

	Premodern Pre-1500	Early modern Approx. 1500–1850	Modern Approx. 1850–1945	Contemporary 1945 on
Impact propensity *contd*	Diffusion of new ideas, technologies across major civilizations within Eurasia and parts of Africa has important cumulative effects, e.g. diffusion of printing	Impact of encountering other cultures probably greater on European culture initially than vice versa	Other transnational ideologies and discourses predominantly impact at elite level. Marxism, through intellectuals and mass political movements, has major impact in Soviet Union, China, etc. Spread of science transforms context and status of many beliefs and practices outside of West Rise of nations and nation-states has important impacts on organization and spatial extent of systems of communications, transport, education, cultural institutions of all sorts (national press, national media, etc.)	Increasing difficulties presented for totalitarian/authoritarian cultural projects and control of information Increasing difficulties presented for state-led nationalist cultural projects in the culture industries Localized but intense economic and cultural consequences from mass tourism Transformation in the cultural context of national identity formation
Infrastructures	Reliable non-oceanic shipping Writing Imperial frameworks for safe and regular land/sea passage over long distances	Reliable oceanic shipping Mechanized printing Imperial frameworks for safe and regular land/sea passage over long distances	Railways Telegraphy Steam-powered/mechanized shipping Imperial systems of control	Telecommunications, cable, satellite, computing, Internet Radio, television Jet airliners

Institutionalization	No formal institutions exist for regulating or mediating intercivilizational encounters	No formal institutions exist for regulating or mediating intercivilizational encounters	Early international public unions begin to regulate cultural interactions – introducing standard time, early international copyright law, regulation of international telegraphy and postal services	International cultural interactions and infrastructures increasingly regulated – in part by corporate and trade law. Political organizations – like UNESCO – have weak regulatory capacity
Stratification	Cultural flows dominated by imperial and theocratic bureaucracies and ruling classes Scientific, literary, philosophical cultures and ideas have an elite and narrow audience, i.e. Hellenization of Near East after Alexander; spread of Islamic mathematics to medieval Europe	World religions enjoy mass audience – though often reliant on prior military conquest	Fundamental inequalities between metropoles and colonies in terms of control over cultural institutions, flows and messages grounded in fundamental military, political inequalities and domination Elite audience for transnational discourses and ideologies Predominantly elite audience in colonies for imperial communications Mass audience for nationalism – though invariably elite dominated	Mass audience for popular culture, highly uneven within societies especially by generation Mass consumption of tourism, mainly restricted to wealthy societies and wealthy social classes Maintenance of elite intellectual, cultural power networks Dominance of Western cultural flows but increasing diversity of flows

of trade. This regulation has not hindered communication; in fact, communication continues to increase at all levels – national, regional and global.

Second, contemporary cultural globalization differs from past forms in that a far greater intensity of images and practices is moving with a far greater extensity and at a far greater velocity than in earlier eras. At both a domestic and an international level, economies and cultures are becoming more information dense. The role of symbolic manipulation and control of applied and strategic knowledge has sharply increased, and not only in the West (Bell, 1973; Reich, 1991; Lash and Urry, 1994). The saturation of television, radio and telephone ownership in the West, their marked increase in the South and the emergence of new domestic technologies of communication have expanded the volume of signs and signification that people are exposed to. This domestic rise in information density is coupled with the increasing appearance of foreign signs, symbols and artefacts within national economies and cultures (Deibert, 1997). Radio broadcasts, commercial advertising, film exports, television schedules, book and magazine sales all show increasing rates of transnationalization of references and products. While the extensity and intensity of cultural diffusion and exchange have risen, so to has the speed at which these processes can occur. Increasingly communication has become instantaneous. In the field of news reporting, this speed-up is particularly marked as satellite broadcasting makes live pictures from across the world a feasible proposition for all major newscasters. This kind of real-time cultural link – be it through widely diffused telephone use, live broadcasting or video-conferencing – introduces a speed and immediacy to elements of contemporary cultural globalization in a way that is historically distinct. There remain, of course, significant differences in information velocity and density and in the foreign/domestic, global/local ratios in different places at different times.

Third, it is very important to note that these systems are intensively used for business and commercial communications as well as for the production, transmission and reception of popular culture. Elite cultures, high cultures, academic and scientific cultures, while obviously making use of these technologies, and occasionally featuring as content within them, are drowned in the high seas of business information systems and commercialized popular culture. No historic parallel exists for such intensive and extensive forms of cultural flow that are primarily forms of commercial enrichment and entertainment. This includes the explosive growth of international travel and mass tourism since 1945. Once again, this phenomenon has historic predecessors in the elite tourism of nineteenth-century Europe, but in scope and scale that era is dwarfed by today's industry.

Fourth, the dominant modes of cultural globalization have shifted. In the past imperial states, networks of intellectuals and theocracies were the key agents of cultural diffusion. In the contemporary world their role has been displaced by that of large media industries as well as by the greater flows of individuals and groups. MNCs are at the heart of these interconnected processes. Although large communications corporations are not unique to the last five decades – and we can trace the origins of international news agencies and publishers back into the nineteenth century, and those of international film exporters to the interwar era – their cultural reach and power is historically unparalleled (see Herman and McChesney, 1997). At a domestic level these corporations include publicly owned television, radio and telecommunications organizations, but as these are increasingly privatized and deregulated the field is more and more dominated by private corporations that are becoming increasingly trans-national (J. B. Thompson, 1990).

Fifth, the stratification of cultural globalization is changing rapidly. Since the advent of European modernity, cultural flows were primarily from the West to the rest, following lines of imperial control. In the contemporary world, the flows continue to be generated primarily in the West and in its more powerful cultural institutions – broadcasters, press agencies, music and film industries, universities, etc. Within the West the balance of cultural power has shifted away from Britain, France and Germany since the late nineteenth century and the pattern has been replaced by American dominance. However, flows have begun to be reversed, primarily through migration but also through other cultural forms shifting from South to North and East to West. Music, food, ideas, beliefs and literature from the South and East have been percolating into the cultures of the West, creating new lines of cultural interconnectedness and fracture.

Sixth, there is another significant shift in the historical form of cultural globalization that we should note. Culture is the medium through which individuals and collectivities organize and conceptualize their identity in time and space. There have been and continue to be a multiplicity of ways of conceiving the shape of the world. To speak of globalization is already to speak from a cultural discourse in which the world is a sphere, spinning in space. Neither the shape, nor the extent, nor the place of the earth in the universe have always been so conceived; the ways in which cultures have placed themselves within a broader cosmos, earthly and heavenly, have been highly varied. Few cultures prior to the European Enlightenment thought of the world as one whole and the people within it as a single generic humankind, above and beyond any sociological, biological or spiritual distinctions. It is from within that discourse that we can describe a particular form of the globalization of culture – the emergence and diffusion of ideas and beliefs about the globe and humanity itself. Even though most people remain rooted in a local or national culture and a local place, it is becoming increasingly impossible for them to live in that place disconnected culturally from the world in which it is situated (Dasmann, 1988).

7.5   Contemporary Cultural Globalization and its Political Impact

There are several difficulties in assessing the impact of cultural globalization on national cultures and identities. In the first place, we must entertain serious doubts about the object of change. If national economies are hard enough to define meaningfully, then national cultures are doubly so. What is Swedish or German culture, how can we chart its changes? Are we simply looking for changing cultural practices? Are we tracking beliefs and solidarities? Can we meaningfully gauge how Swedish the Swedes feel or how French the French? Even if we were able to do any of these things, could we track changes in the intensity of identification and relate it to shifts in cultural enmeshment? All of this line of argument rests on the assumption that there is in any case a definable, lived national culture. Yet we know that such an idea is, at least in part, an active ideological creation that masks profound cultural divisions of gender, race, class and region within a nation-state. Bearing these caveats in mind, what can we reliably conclude about the impact of cultural globalization on the political life of SIACS?

7.5.1   Decisional and institutional impacts: cultural flows and cultural autonomy

The least ambiguous element of contemporary cultural globalization has been the development of the infrastructure and institutions for the production, transmission and reception of cultural products and communications of all kinds. These have all become more global and transboundary in their reach in the last thirty years or so, though their ownership, control and use remain very uneven across and within countries. We can think about three overlapping and mutually reinforcing elements of these: an electronic infrastructure; a linguistic infrastructure; and a corporate infrastructure. The electronic element of the infrastructure includes the global diffusion of radio and television broadcasting; the spread of the technologies for producing and playing recorded music; and the global reach of telecommunications networks. The linguistic infrastructure of communication is bi- and multilingualism. In this respect, there can be no doubt that the spread of English as a medium of international communication is central. Finally, the corporate infrastructure provides the producers and distribution networks that exploit the technological and linguistic infrastructures by supplying content and product. The deepening of global markets for films, recorded music, news and television programming has been accompanied by the development of multinational culture industries, multinational telecommunication corporations and a variety of alliances and projects that link them to each other as well as to MNCs in computer, software and electronic hardware. To these shifts we can also add the massively expanded infrastructure of international travel. Combined, these infrastructures, irrespective of their cultural consequences or content, have made for large increases in the circulation of ideas, artefacts and images at global and regional levels. They allow for the movement of images and objects over enormous distances with greater intensity, volume and speed. They have made interaction between distant places cheaper and easier. They have also contributed to an increase in the symbolic density of social life. This has significantly altered the institutional context in which more local or national cultural projects of all kinds develop, and the costs and benefits of national policies of cultural autonomy or political control and censorship.

In terms of politics and the state, these global infrastructures of culture and communication have contributed to increasingly dense transnational elite and professional cultures; the formation of epistemic transnational elite communities; the formation of transnational political lobbies and alliances; the development and entrenchment of diasporic cultures and communities; an increasing openness of information, and increasing difficulties of censorship and information control for individual governments. The degree to which national cultural autonomy has been diminished in part depends on the kinds of cultural and information policies that governments have sought to impose. Totalitarian states, communist states and theocratic and right-wing military regimes have all attempted to implement a closed cultural policy in which foreign influences, products and ideas have been actively controlled. This may entail controls at the border through import bans of print and visual material, controls on the international use of telecommunications hardware, extensive censorship, travel restrictions and close management of educational curricula. This kind of policy is the most threatened by contemporary cultural globalization.

Satellite and other telecommunications technologies exceed the territorial control of nation-states. The Chinese and Burmese governments have, for example, found it impossible either to block transnational broadcasts or to control the sale and use of reception equipment. The Soviet Union and its East European satellites were unable to prevent the reception of Western radio and TV broadcasts or the import of foreign texts. The World Wide Web provides yet another channel through which citizens in such states can evade the information controls of government. Simultaneously, these channels make it more difficult for national governments to control 'bad news' from leaking out of the country. In other words, there has been a transformation in the context of national governments and in their capacity to manage cultural formation and development; the costs and benefits of control strategies have ineluctably changed.

SIACS, whose cultural ambitions are more restricted than those of authoritarian regimes, have tended to focus on strengthening domestic institutions and controlling external influence through regulation and trade politics. However, the intensity of the response may be more closely correlated with levels of elite cultural paranoia and the lobbying power of domestic culture industries than with any real erosion or transformation of national cultural identities. The French government through the European Union has sought to defend its own cultural industries by establishing a European directive that ensures 51 per cent EU output on national broadcast channels, and by preventing the WTO from dismantling its complex system of domestic subsidies, aids and ticket levies. At the level of language, France has conducted an endless battle to preserve and entrench the use of the French language – banning Franglais from official and public use, and establishing and reinforcing laws and institutions which preserve the purity and authenticity of the French language. The threat posed by processes of transnationalization and import penetration in the cultural industries, particularly the film and TV industries, has led France, Spain and Italy to a range of industrial and cultural policies intended both to stem the tide of imports and shore up domestic producers. Canada has attempted to control the degree to which US culture industries can take a stake in Canadian media and telecommunications industries – blocking some takeovers and contravening NAFTA regulations to do so. Trade negotiations in the early 1990s were bedevilled by US demands for a much freer market in cultural products, while many European nations argued for import limits, national quotas and extensive state aid to national cultural industries. These arguments have also been played out inside the Council of Europe and throughout the European Union.

A more substantial case for the cultural significance of transboundary or global cultural networks, organizations and flows has been made in other areas. Three examples have been dealt with at some length in the current literature. First, the case has been made for the existence and significance of a transatlantic black culture that links the thought and practice of black communities, whether they are in Africa, in North America or Latin America, in the Caribbean or in the wider diaspora of Western Europe (Gilroy, 1993). The efforts of the new social movements of the West, and increasingly of the South as well, are an additional example of transnational or 'third' cultural networks. In the women's movement, peace movement and above all in the environmental movement, cultural and intellectual networks of communication and discussion have been established between groups in many nation-states (see chapter 8). Transnational organizations linking them and facilitating flows of information and political mobilization have been established. Political cooperation and new types of campaigning and argument are evolving in the context of shared values and aims, helping to forge a distinctive transnational perspective (Dickenson, 1997). Finally, some researchers have argued for the existence of similar transnational networks and shared international cultures and frames of reference among otherwise disparate 'epistemic communities': scientists in different specialized disciplines, artists working in similar fields, and specialists of all sorts (E. Haas, 1990). All these developments raise questions about the impermeability of national culture and identity.

7.5.2   Distributional and structural impacts: popular culture and national identity

The vast majority of the artefacts and images circulating around the globe fall into the contested terrain of popular culture (Street, 1997). Across a range of cultural products and media there is ample evidence to suggest that the ratio of foreign to domestic has shifted towards the foreign. Of course, some states through insularity, government control, lack of resources or very robust domestic culture industries and traditions have managed to stay somewhat outside of this trend. For example, the power of the Indian and US film industries mean that they continue to dominate the vast majority of their domestic markets (Pendakur and Subramanyam, 1996; Ray and Jacka, 1996). The power of the Iranian state and the cultural hegemony of Islam ensure that home consumption in Iran is overwhelmingly domestic in origin. Nonetheless, the trends in these areas are clear. The overall global market in recorded music, television programming and broadcasting, feature film production and book publishing has seen a significant rise in foreign influences and icons.

The geography of these flows is complex. The ownership of culture industry MNCs is overwhelmingly Western and within that predominantly American. British, German, French, Dutch, Australian and Japanese corporations have a stake but often on the basis of ownership of American-based subsidiaries. The majority of export markets are controlled by these corporations. Thus there is a flow of imagery, genre and content mainly from the USA and some Western cultures to other Western states and most of the developing world. Where there are no indigenous mass audio-visual industries or they are very weak, these flows have dominated local consumption; they have even eaten into areas of consumption where domestic production has some foothold and strength. In some cases this has led to local producers being squeezed out of the market. However, while this kind of global production for local consumption has increased, corporations have had to adapt their structures and output to cater for the ingrained specificities of taste and interest in local markets and cultures. Moreover, there are many exceptions to the tendency of Western corporate dominance in this area. For example, Brazilian television has made significant inroads into Portuguese broadcasting (Tracey, 1988; Sinclair, 1996).

Of course, the extent of national enmeshment of individual countries in global and regional cultural flows and processes varies. In the context of our case study countries, the US is in a class of its own in terms of its domination of its own home market as well as its place in the international markets for information and cultural products. The UK, Japan, France and Germany have significant shares of their domestic markets, served by their own culture industries. These countries have been large enough to create

MNCs with export potential, although this has often been realized, as noted previously, through the purchase of American companies. The UK is assisted particularly by the use of English as a global language, but this has also made it vulnerable to US exports – a vulnerability highlighted in the film industry. Sweden, like many other small Western nations, has retained a significant presence in its own home markets, largely due to the specificities of language. But other than in popular music, it has enjoyed few successful cultural exports.

What is the impact on national identities and local cultures of the globally orientated production and distribution of popular cultural artefacts? The most that can realistically be claimed is that within the West there has been some degree of homogenization of mass cultural consumption, particularly among the young, and that it is spreading to the more affluent strata of the developing world, especially in East Asia and Latin America. In popular music, film and television a single product will be consumed in a multiplicity of places. There is also some evidence to suggest that this has, as a consequence, squeezed some domestic alternatives out of the market. The most obvious impact of US domination of, say, the UK film market is that it has become harder for UK film-makers to produce and distribute movies in Britain. However, the broader cultural impact of such a squeeze on British culture and national identity is rather more difficult to estimate. Whether the homogenization of consumption in the area of films has been translated into a homogenization of other cultural practices, beliefs and identities is difficult to assert. There is also evidence to suggest that after many decades of US commercial domination in popular culture, local and national alternatives are reviving.

The homogenization thesis has other weaknesses; it fails to take into account the ways in which cultural products are locally consumed, locally read and transformed in the process. First, it is evident that broadcasters and marketing strategists in the culture industries themselves are aware of the cultural variation and differentiation of the audiences to which they broadcast and that considerable adaptation on their part is required if viewing figures are to be maintained; this is true, for example, of MTV Europe which could not simply replicate the tone and content of its American parent (Negus, 1993). Second, the homogenization thesis assumes a rather too passive view of audiences and their capacity to read and reread programmes in the most unexpected of ways (Liebes and Katz, 1993; D. Miller, 1994; J. B. Thompson, 1995).

While the announcement of the eradication of national cultural differences seems highly premature, is it the case that national cultures remain robust and unsullied? There is considerable evidence to suggest that processes of national cultural fragmentation are at work in the contemporary world. One of the best indicators of this is the existence and political strength of devolutionist, regionalist or independence movements within many SIACS. The UK is faced by serious and sustained independence movements – in Scotland, Northern Ireland and Wales. Similarly powerful movements can be found in Italy (Legga Lombarda), in Spain (the Basque and Catalonian movements), in Canada (Bloc Québécois) and in Belgium (between the Walloon and Flemish regions). In the US there are many right-wing antistatist groups. In every case the territorial integrity and cultural unity of the nation-state is open to challenge on the basis of regional or local assertions of distinctive cultural identity and the need for a divided or separate political sovereignty. Outside the West, in countries where the idea of the nation-state, let alone a meaningful national culture, has often been wishful thinking, the situation is even more fragmented. However, it is not clear how far cultural globalization, challenging and eroding the hegemonic position of national sentiments, is itself a key factor in explaining the rise and strength of diverse successionist movements. Alongside forms of local resistance there have been more coordinated attempts to contest the flow of imported images with the aim of reinventing and reconstructing 'peripheral cultures'. In this respect technological shifts, including for instance the camcorder, have reduced the costs of production and so created new cultural spaces for 'alternative' TV channels and production. This is particularly true of TV organized by and for indigenous peoples in Canada and Australia, while the access TV tradition of some Western nations has also been stimulated (Downmunt, 1991).

Do such developments therefore suggest the emergence of complex mixtures and combinations of diverse cultural forms and practices that carry real cultural weight? The most obvious and historically long-standing of these hybrid cultures are immigrant cultures of all sorts. Despite conscious and unconscious attempts by host nations and immigrant communities towards assimilation, immigrant communities have rarely abandoned or lost all of their cultural inheritance or preserved it intact in a new situation. At the level of popular culture, what might at first sight appear to be processes of homogenization in fact display hybrid characteristics. No cultural message, no aesthetic artefact, no symbol passes through time and space into a cultural vacuum. The cultural context of production and transmission must always in the end encounter an already existing frame of reference in the eyes of the consumer or receiver. The latter involves a process of great complexity – simple notions of homogenization, ideological hegemony or imperialism fail to register properly the nature of these encounters and the interplay, interaction and cultural creativity they produce. However, it is not clear at all that these hybrid cultures and transnational communities have made significant inroads into mainstream national cultures and national identities.

7.6 Conclusion

For all the difficulties and constraints that SIACS now encounter in preserving a pristine, if mythic, national culture, or in controlling the flow of information and opinion within and across their borders, there is little sign as yet that these nationalist cultural projects are in terminal decline. In the end, Hollywood, Microsoft and AT&T are in the business of making money – not founding alternative centres of political identity and legitimacy. Yet the huge flows of information, people and imagery that circulate around the globe, crossing borders with impunity, have changed the context in which national projects of any kind must develop. The real threat to nationalist projects of all kinds is perhaps more likely to come from an incipient cultural cosmopolitanism that would challenge the idea of the nation as the primary political and cultural community and demand the relocation of power in institutions other than the national state (see chapter 1). But it has proved difficult to create an enduring multiculturalism within nation-states and an enduring cosmopolitanism within regimes like the EU.

Over the last forty years, Western Europe's political elites as well as the institutions of the EU itself have put considerable political capital and effort into the construction of a European identity (A. Smith, 1992; Leonard, 1998). On the one hand, as recently as 1997, 41 per cent of those sampled in EU states thought their country had benefited from EU membership, while 36 per cent thought their country had not benefited (Directorate General X, 1997). At the high point of Europe's public popularity in 1990, 47 per cent of the public sampled identified closely with Europe, although the figure has subsequently dropped. On the other hand, survey evidence reports that 97 per cent of Europeans have never had any direct contact with the EU and its various institutions, events, etc. (Leonard, 1998). It is hardly surprising, then, that additional research reveals that less than 5 per cent of those asked said that they were first and foremost Europeans; 45 per cent said that they did not feel any European component to their identity at all. At the same time, 88 per cent closely identified with their nation or region (Reif, 1993). For the EU this is a mixed picture. Yet if this is the best that can be managed after four decades of systematic effort in a region that possesses, for all its faultlines and geographical oddities, a sense of shared history and cultural inheritance and possesses transnational institutions of considerable political weight – how much harder will the task be at a transregional and global level?

8

Catastrophe in the Making: Globalization and the Environment

In the last three decades we have, all over the world, become familiar with an increasing litany of global environmental problems and threats. Environmentalism has become synonymous with a global outlook. In the sciences, radical biologists and ecologists have argued for conceiving the planet as an interdependent holistic ecosystem, be it the semi-mystic Gaia theory or the less prosaic spaceship earth; many less radical voices would accept that the entire planet is threatened by environmental changes whose origins and consequences are geographically widespread. Paralleling these debates, there has been an enormous growth in the number and scope of international institutions, laws and treaties that regulate the environment alongside the development of complex international alliances of environmental movements and organizations. Given our definition of globalization as social processes and interactions that assume interregional or transcontinental proportions, four qualifications are necessary in applying it to environmental questions.

First, not all environmental problems can be described as global, nor are all responses to environmental threats global. Many threats are highly localized in both their origins and consequences with little or no stretching of social relationships or movements of pollutants through space and time. Many forms of pollution, like photochemical smogs and the release of toxic heavy metals, have a small radius of action. Similarly, many forms of water pollution result from local or at least national sources. British beaches are predominantly polluted by British sewage. Los Angeles still swelters in its own cocktail of ozone. Minimata Bay was laced with mercury from local industrial plants. Second, although the existence of an unmediated nature is no longer tenable, the environment is not itself a social process in any simplistic or complete sense. Ecosystems are a complex mixture of flora, fauna and dynamic natural systems and cycles that interact with human social institutions and power networks. It is not possible to reduce an account of ecosystems, environments and environmental change purely to the language of the social sciences, or to describe a distinct form of environmental action in the same way that economic or political or cultural action can be described. Third, even if we were able to construct a model of the environment amenable to description in terms of our model of globalization, it would be the wrong focus. Our central concern is not the environment in general but environmental degradation in particular, and not social action or processes in general but social action or processes that either cause environmental degradation or respond to it. However, it is not altogether clear what is meant by environmental degradation. This points to a fourth problem: environmental degradation – for example, radioactive emissions – is often invisible. Such threats are often identified only through the use of sophisticated technologies and are only conceivable in terms of complex scientific models and languages. In short, the existence of environmental degradation and its consequences must always be actively constructed by human actors (Hannigan, 1995). To chart or measure the globalization of environmental degradation is simultaneously to chart or measure the construction of human perceptions and models of global environmental change (Taylor and Buttel, 1992; Yearly, 1996). Given that all models are open to contestation there is some obligation to be clear about one's own.

8.1   Globalization and the Environment

We take environmental degradation to mean the transformation of entire ecosystems or components of those ecosystems (though given the holistic quality of the former the two almost invariably merge together) whose consequences, whether acknowledged by human actors or not, have an adverse impact on the economic or demographic conditions of life and/or the health of human beings. In addition, environmental degradation includes processes explicitly acknowledged by human beings which in some sense offend, contradict or come into conflict with their aesthetic or moral values, irrespective of their practical or personal biological consequences. The decline in the numbers of Chinese pandas and their habitat, although of no immediate consequence to either local or international, economic or bodily well-being, can be classed as environmental degradation. For the loss of the panda comes into conflict with an interest in the preservation of a common environmental heritage and a recognition of a right to existence for non-human but sentient beings. Similarly, the decline of hedgerows and the micro-ecosystems they contain is of little direct consequence to the economic viability of the English countryside but is of enormous aesthetic, ecological and symbolic import.

This model of environmental degradation, albeit anthropocentric, directs our attention to the ways in which the interaction of natural and social worlds generates constraints, opportunities and problems for other forms of social action – be they political, military, ethical or economic. This must be combined with a sensitivity to the variable geographical reach of social processes that generate and experience environmental degradation. In this section, we will examine how the concept of globalization can be applied to the spatial character of the social origins and consequences of environmental degradation, and suggest how we might estimate the extensity, intensity, impact, etc., of these social interactions (see also the Methodological Appendix). In section 8.2, we sketch the historical forms that environmental globalization, and the responses to it, have taken, as an empirical check on claims that we are experiencing a historically unprecedented level of global environmental degradation. This is followed, in section 8.3, by a comparison of historical forms of environmental globalization. In section 8.4, we offer a more detailed analysis of the particular contribution of each of our six case study countries to global and regional patterns of environmental degradation and the threats that they consequently face. Finally, in section 8.5, we move on to consider what the impact of these processes is on the sovereignty and autonomy of SIACS.

8.1.1   Forms of environmental globalization

We shall chart the globalization of environmental degradation in two ways: first, by looking at the origins and consequences of distinct types of environmental problem, in a way that acknowledges the peculiar social differences generated by the transformation of different parts of ecosystems; and, second, by looking at the cultural and political processes that seek to describe and regulate those changes. Both can and do operate on global, regional, national and local scales.

Globalization and the environmental commons

While environmental degradation can be wrought upon highly localized and purely national environmental resources and ecosystems, it can also affect very widely shared resources and ecosystems. Indeed, without accepting all the implications of the homeostatic Gaia model, it is not unreasonable to suggest that the entire planet can be viewed as a single interrelated ecosystem or that significant parts of it constitute distinct regional or continental ecosystems. The environmental commons are those elements of the global ecosystem that are simultaneously used, experienced and shared by all and are under the effective jurisdiction or sovereignty of no one (Ostrom, 1990). The atmosphere and the climatic system are the best examples of this type of commons, although it could also be applied to the entire marine environment and global hydrological cycles and systems. The atmosphere and the climatic system are resources, essential for life, that immerse and exceed every state and society. It is inconceivable that anyone can effectively own the atmosphere and no one can be excluded from its usage, yet the consequences of any actions in specific and small locales can have impacts of a highly unpredictable and volatile nature all over the planet. The intrinsically global character of these common ecosystems means that spatially separated social actions and networks can become bound together in powerful ways.

For example, the historically and structurally ingrained Western predilection for the motor car and profligate energy use entails a very large release of greenhouse gases into the atmosphere and makes a significant contribution to global warming. It is not difficult to establish a complex but plausible chain of causation between Western driving habits, Western transport and energy policies and the changing agricultural fortunes of Bangladesh or sub-Saharan Africa and their internal politics. Decisions on public expenditure on sea defences and desertification measures are tied to, and dependent on, decisions made elsewhere about roadbuilding and energy efficiency. Politics is in effect 'stretched' and societies are entwined. Separate polities and societies are bound interdependently together behind their backs. As we already know, this kind of intersection between two polities is nothing new (see chapter 1). However, what distinguishes the contemporary problems of the environmental commons and makes the application of the idea of globalization useful is the unique extent of those interrelations, the increasing number of separate national polities and policy areas drawn into the expanding web of stretched relations, and the increasing intensity of global and regional interactions. Alongside the global extent of the atmospheric and climatic commons, seas and oceans provide examples of regional and more restricted commons.

Globalization, resources, demography and overspill

A second category of global environmental problems consists of the interlinked phenomena of demographic expansion and resource consumption. All environmental problems have a demographic dimension, for all other things being equal, more people means more pollution and resource consumption (WCED, 1987). Almost all contemporary population growth is occurring in the developing world. The environmental consequences of this will initially be felt in the societies experiencing rapid demographic change. However, as with the local pollution of the global and regional commons, there is a tendency for the consequences of those changes to spill over into the economics and politics of other nations. Similarly, the pool of global raw materials and resources will be affected by the accumulated impact of many local shortages, while separate national economies and industries could be affected by global shortages – reflected in global markets and prices for key commodities (Westing, 1986).

Rapid demographic growth is a key factor in explaining the increasing immiseration of sub-Saharan Africa and processes of desertification and soil decline. This has contributed to the growing economic problems of the region and its mounting international debts. Thus environmental problems in single African states have spilt over into the international politics of banking. The resolution of these international issues has involved political contests and struggles between Western governments and their financial sectors. In the future, the demographic and environmental squeeze on the South may contribute towards political instability and outward migration, both of which will affect a widening pool of other nations, internationally and domestically (Myers, 1993a, 1993b).

Another example of this type of global problem, whose consequences are ethical as well as economic and demographic, is the issue of biodiversity and species extinction. In this respect, environmental degradation is invariably local, for many species are confined to a small area either within one state or across a few adjacent states. However, the local environmental changes that then lead to extinction can be argued to have a moral, aesthetic and economic consequence for the entire planet. In the terminology of international law, species diversity and biodiversity constitute part of 'the common heritage of mankind' (see chapter 1).

Transboundary pollution and international economics

Transboundary pollution involves the transmission of pollutants through the media of air, soil and water from their point of generation or creation across political borders so that their environmentally degrading impact occurs in other legal jurisdictions. In addition to actual transboundary pollution, like acid rain or transboundary riverine pollution, we should also include perceived *threats* of transboundary pollution (Yearly, 1994). Most importantly, the siting and operation of nuclear power stations have created the risk of catastrophic levels of transboundary environmental degradation; a risk that was starkly actualized in the case of the Chernobyl accident. Another unintended threat with major environmental impacts is the movement of species from their own habitat to new ecosystems where their presence can radically disrupt the host community. The unintentional transfer of Pacific snakes to Guam via US army air transport is a good contemporary example of this. The result was that Guam was denuded of all bird life by the imported snake in fifteen years. In addition to these unintended side-effects of economic and social activity, we also examine transboundary movements of pollutants that are the immediate, intended and often legal result of economic exchange and production; for example, the export and import of hazardous wastes and the movement and relocation of highly polluting industrial plants.

Globalization, environmental politics and environmental knowledge

The final sense in which we can speak of environmental globalization or regionalization does not derive from the material extent, organization or form of environmental degradation and change, but from the spatial characteristics of the social institutions and processes that materially generate, interpret and attempt politically to control the environment. In short, the origins and consequences of global and regional environmental problems intersect with global and regional economic, political and cultural institutions and processes. An example of each shows how the idea of globalization can be usefully brought to bear on such phenomena.

In the case of economics, it can be argued that the steady diffusion of industrial modes of production from North to South – a form of globalization – has led to a massive increase in the total capacity of the global economy to generate environmental pollutants that threaten the global commons, such as the seas and the atmosphere. In political terms, it is clear enough that a plethora of institutions and treaties has been established over the last thirty years which encompass a very large number of states, place limits on domestic political and economic practices and lock national centres of politics and administration (such as departments or ministries of the environment) into global and regional networks of environmental monitoring, agenda building, policy formation and implementation. Finally, at a cultural level, the recognition and estimation of environmental degradation is clearly linked to an expanding transnational network of scientists and pressure groups whose arguments and analyses spread rapidly all over the globe, influencing purely domestic debates and environmental perspectives, as well as helping to forge a broader global consensus on the consequences of, and appropriate responses to, shared environmental problems (E. Haas, 1990).

We map responses to the globalization of environmental problems in four ways, we examine:

- cultural, intellectual and scientific networks that both track and expose global and regional forms of environmental degradation and are able to construct and disseminate models of global environmental interconnectedness;
- international and transnational political networks and organizations that seek to regulate environmental degradation;
- global and regional environmental institutions, laws, conventions and protocols seen in terms of their numbers, coverage and intrusiveness; and
- these two foregoing factors as they interact with, shape and determine the conduct of domestic political institutions, environmental movements and struggles.

Any of the four could have been considered in chapter 1 or in chapter 7 on culture. We have included them here because there is such a close causal interconnection between physical forms of environmental degradation, the ways in which they are culturally and scientifically identified, located, monitored and evaluated and the ways in which polities are mobilized in attempts to halt degradation and control it inside and beyond political borders.

8.1.2 Concepts

While we acknowledge the often spatially restricted character of environmental degradation, we argue that the framework specified in the introduction can usefully be applied to the spatial characteristics of the social origins and consequences of environmental degradation and environmental threats. We distinguish between three types of environmental problem: the global commons; the problems of demography, resources and overspill; and transboundary pollution both unintentional and intentional as well as actual or threatened. We also apply the measure of globalization to those political and cultural responses that seek to track and regulate environmental degradation. Global environmental degradation varies in its geographical coverage and we can differentiate the spatial origins and consequences or impacts of that degradation in terms of extensity, intensity, stratification and impact. Extensity, clearly enough, applies to the geographical reach of any particular form of environmental degradation – global, regional, national and local. Intensity is more difficult to calibrate, particularly for the degradation of the commons and for overspill effects which have no meaningful domestic comparator. But in the case of transboundary pollution an indicator of intensity would be the importance of domestically generated degradation relative to externally generated degradation. In the case of acid rain, for example, the relative weight of external to internally generated emissions would be a measure of the intensity of globalization or regionalization. Casual inspection of our narrative of environmental degradation in section 8.2 illustrates the geographical and material unevenness of both the origins of environmental problems and their consequences. Not surprisingly, there are many cases of global and regional environmental degradation which exhibit a basic asymmetry or hierarchy of power between polluters and polluted. Finally, the material and social impacts of environmental degradation can be broadly grouped under threats to human health, economic and demographic constraints, general costs and aesthetic-moral loss. Networks of global environmental knowledge and politics, like other infrastructures, can also be described in terms of their institutionalization.

8.2 Environmental Globalization in Historical Perspective

In sketching the history of global environmental change we ask two questions: Is the idea of the global environment or of global environmental problems a wholly modern one, or, as in the case of the international economy (see chapters 3, 4 and 5), is there evidence to suggest an earlier period of intensive global interconnectedness? Is the intensity of global environmental problems simply a reflection of a greater awareness and capacity to observe the environment or have there been real and profound shifts in the spatial form, quantity and consequences of environmental degradation? In this section, we focus on the global commons, environmental overspill and transboundary pollution alongside the development of transnational environmental movements and international institutions.

8.2.1 Globalization and the environment: from European expansion to the Industrial Revolution

Clearly environmental degradation is nothing new. We have ample evidence and accounts of premodern environmental problems. On the one hand, there are examples of environmental change caused by shifts in the natural cycles of climate and weather, like the medieval European little ice age, which contributed to continental demographic reversal (Lamb, 1977; Bryson and Murray, 1977; Utterstrom, 1988; Wigley et al., 1981). On the other hand, there are examples of environmental change caused predominantly by human activity: mammoths hunted to extinction by early human nomads, coal smoke in medieval London, deforestation and soil erosion in China, overpopulation, resource shortage and collapses of soil fertility in fourteenth-century Western Europe (Wilkinson, 1973; TeBrake, 1974).

William McNeill has constructed a global historical narrative around the interaction of human settlement and movement and the microbes and parasites that have stayed, moved and mixed among us (McNeill, 1976). Indeed, prior to the modern era the only forms of environmental changes during recorded human history to achieve global dimensions are those caused by the geographical shift and genetic mutation of pests and microbes. We have included some consideration of this kind of environmental change in our narrative, especially where movements in population at a global level are involved (see chapter 6). However, we would argue that the emergence and expansion of the peoples, institutions and practices of Western modernity significantly increased the capacity of human societies for environmental degradation, and that European expansion made a unique contribution to the environmental transformation of the planet.

With Columbus's arrival in the Americas the physical and ecological separation of the Eurasian land mass from the Americas was finally ended. The enormous social and economic importance of this was overlain by the most profound series of ecological transformations in both continental masses, though particularly in the Americas (Crosby, 1972, 1983; McNeill, 1976; Cronon, 1983). For alongside the institutions of modernity and colonial ambition, the Europeans brought a range of new micro-organisms, flora and fauna to the Americas. The consequences of these are well documented. Western micro-organisms fell on a vulnerable and unprotected indigenous population. The common cold, influenza, measles and a host of other viral and bacterial diseases totally decimated indigenous populations within a generation, leaving only 10 per cent of preconquest population levels. In the wake of such an epidemiological catastrophe, the social organization and economic practices of the indigenous populations crumbled in the face of militarily and logistically fragile European invasions (see chapter 2). This immediate demographic revolution was accompanied by the longer term transformation of many 'new world' ecosystems. Europeans introduced a variety of new plants and animals, especially the horse and cow, and in so doing began a long process of ecological change creating large grasslands for grazing and felling many indigenous forest areas. A similar fate awaited parts of Australia and New Zealand two centuries later. The return journey across the Atlantic of American species also provided important forces in shaping the environmental and social development of Europe. The potato, for example, became the staple crop of much of peripheral peasant Europe, transforming patterns of settlement and population growth. The environmental consequences of tobacco are scarcely smaller (Salaman, 1947).

This initial burst of transatlantic environmental change was surpassed in intensity by the subsequent transformation of European and then North American economies. Within Europe itself, but particularly England and the Dutch republic, the agricultural revolutions of the seventeenth and eighteenth centuries and the emergence of capitalist economic relationships for land, labour and products induced a further series of ecological changes. The combination of market incentives, higher investment and technological and practical innovations saw these agrarian economies thrive. But they were organic agrarian economies, ultimately dependent on the natural world for food, cloth, fuel, building materials and much of their transport. Economic and demographic growth led to a massive expansion of cultivated land and pasture (Skipp, 1978; Nef, 1977; Unger, 1984; Wrigley, 1988). Marginal ecosystems and some species were lost as swamps were drained, heathland and scrublands cleared and forests cut down. Many larger mammal species, denied their habitat and extensively hunted – like wolves and bears – were gradually extinguished from much of Europe or penned into the most inaccessible and inhospitable corners of the continent (Hoskins, 1977; Rackham, 1986).

Despite this expansion of cultivated land, raw material shortages developed in these economies, sending the price of fuel wood and other goods soaring; in the case of the Dutch republic the impact was great enough to halt and then reverse demographic and economic growth. However, the lethal combination of expanding demand, technological innovation and market pressures were most effectively unleashed outside Europe in the free-wheeling frontier capitalism of the western United States and in the unclaimed global commons of the polar regions, high seas and ocean islands. In the USA, in particular, the insatiable demand for cheap land, meat and wood saw the vast western plains and the dense ancient forests of the Great Lakes region transformed out of all recognition. By the mid-nineteenth century, as the forests were consumed and the prairies turned to extensive cattle grazing and intensive cereal crops, the American bison was eliminated (Cronon, 1991). Beyond the borders of this environmental juggernaut, Western demand helped spur the global hunting of seals, whales and fur-bearing animals, bringing many to the point of extinction (Fischer, 1963; Busch, 1985; Martin, 1986). At the same time, European and American economic demands combined with colonial expansion and control began to deplete rainforests in Latin America, Asia and Africa (Richards and Tucker, 1983).

However, it was within the societies of the West that the capacity for environmental degradation was once again ratcheted up. With the emergence of the Industrial Revolution and its radical shift in production technologies, power sources and raw materials, levels of environmental degradation and danger began to climb (Goldblatt, 1996). The dominant industrial sectors of the early waves of the Industrial Revolution – coal, oil, iron, steel and metallurgical industries, the new synthetic chemicals industries – generated old pollutants at unprecedentedly high levels and new pollutants of increasing toxicity and complexity (Wohl, 1983; Melosi, 1985; Evans, 1987). Combined with the obliteration of old ecosystems, beneath the vast urban conglomerates that developed around these industries, the intensity and speed of environmental degradation and the range of threats to human health rose. Nonetheless, the threats and dangers remained predominantly local in their impact and tolerated by the majority who lived with them (Tarr, 1985; Colten, 1986).

8.2.2 Global environmental degradation in the twentieth century

It is really only in the twentieth century, and the late twentieth century at that, that the environmental consequences of industrial production, combined with capitalist or state socialist economic organization, have been widely and actively registered as environmental degradation and extended their spatial reach beyond the local or the national. The clearest examples of the decisive shift in the extensity and intensity of contemporary environmental problems are those of global warming and ozone depletion.

Global warming, according to current scientific opinion, is caused by the build-up of a variety of gases (carbon dioxide, methane, nitrous and sulphur oxides, CFCs) in the earth's atmosphere which raise the capacity of the atmosphere to insulate the earth: as much sunlight and heat is reaching the earth as before, but less and less is allowed out. The theory of global warming is actually almost a century old, but it is only in the last two decades that the theory has been refined, a careful monitoring of global climate change has been conducted and a growing consensus has emerged that the mechanisms are sound and the evidence of the problem is reasonable, if not completely decisive (see Leggett, 1990; Nillson and Pitt, 1994; Rowlands, 1994; Young, 1994).

The consequences of global warming are phenomenally complex to calibrate. In the first place this is because the way in which an average increase in ambient global temperatures is actually translated into local temperature and climate change is very variable. Moreover, climate is more than just temperature, and the interaction of changing temperatures with winds, rainfall and pressure is impossible to predict in any very accurate way. Second, the response of other ecological systems to global warming is unclear. For example, it is argued that contemporary increases in carbon dioxide levels, which contribute towards global warming, will be counteracted by the capacity of the oceans to absorb the gas. Others argue that contemporary levels of deforestation, particularly in the tropical rainforests of South America and South East Asia, will radically diminish the capacity of the global environment to absorb carbon dioxide, thus accelerating global warming. Most complex of all, the increase in global temperatures could melt the polar ice caps and lead to large-scale rises in sea levels. This may in turn increase the absorptive capacity of the seas, thus slowing the process of global warming. Caveats aside, global warming is the clearest example we have of an environmental problem whose origins are global, covering not only the North but the South as well, and deriving from industrial processes as well as agricultural (and possibly natural) ones. Similarly, its consequences are global in scope. All continents can expect some kind of direct ecological shift in their climate and thus the flora and fauna that can survive locally. But given the enormity of the changes involved in many areas, including rising sea levels and rapidly declining soil fertility, most states and societies can also expect to experience the secondary effects of national and local social dislocation, migration and upheaval.

The depletion of atmospheric ozone has many parallels with global warming (Titus, 1986; Benedick, 1991; Parson, 1993; Rowlands, 1994; M. Miller, 1995). It is clearly a relatively recent problem as it is linked to the use of CFCs, whose widespread usage is no more than fifty years old. Although predominantly used in OECD states, these seemingly benign industrial chemicals had already spread to the developing world by the time the problem was discovered. Acting as catalysts of the atmospheric breakdown of ozone, their effects intensified by cold weather and winds in the polar regions, CFCs have thinned the stratospheric ozone layer. As a result, ultraviolet (UV) light from the sun, which is normally absorbed by ozone molecules, is reaching the earth's surface at higher levels. This appears to be linked to increasing levels of skin cancer, and diverse threats to many aquatic and terrestrial plants. Although these consequences are concentrated on and around the northern and southern poles of the earth, the volatile chemistry of ozone depletion and the variability of the earth's climate could easily mean they spread much further.

Processes of demographic change, levels of resource usage and threats to biodiversity also appear to be reaching a unique intensity, acquiring a greater global dimension. Historically, we have seen periods of overpopulation, resource shortages and species extinction. However, in the contemporary world there is good reason for thinking that the pace and geographical scope of all these forms of environmental degradation are increasing and expanding. On the demographic side it has taken somewhere around 10,000 years for the earth's population to reach its current level of around 5 billion. It will probably double within the next four to five decades. This represents an unprecedented leap in intensity and also in geographical scope. In fact rapid population growth will occur all over the planet outside the stable and ageing populations of Europe (Cipolla, 1978; WCED, 1987; UNFPA, *The State of the World's Population*, various years). The relentless spread of land cultivation that inevitably follows demographic explosion has eaten away at numerous ecosystems across the planet. As a consequence of this, more species than ever before, in more parts of the planet, are either extinct or under threat (National Science Board, 1989; World Resources Institute, 1993). Shortages of clean water and fertile land are beginning to emerge. Resource problems are complex to predict but we can be reasonably sure that increases in population, combined with the industrialization of many parts of the hitherto developing world, will generate some serious local shortages and place constraints on the resource consumption of individual nations.

As for transboundary pollution, there have been significant levels of acid rain and riverine pollution for as long as industries have been pouring wastes into rivers and as long as sulphur containing fossil fuels has been burnt. Where this has happened near borders there has necessarily been transboundary pollution. But as levels of pollution steadily rose through the twentieth century, the point was reached when the level of acid rain damage to forests and lakes became very visible. The long struggles to establish an international framework for lowering acid rain emissions in Europe and North America coincided with a contraction of some of the main polluting industries and technologies (coal burning for power, for example). So, in historical terms, there is a reasonable case for arguing that this form of transboundary pollution has peaked in the West; levels of sulphur dioxide production and river pollution seem to be falling. However, the progressive industrialization of the developing world and the introduction of fossil fuel burning for electricity production and transport have spread these forms of transboundary pollution, albeit at lower levels, to more countries and more borders (Yearly, 1994). The case of nuclear power and potential nuclear hazards is clearly a historical watershed in the scope and dangerous potential for catastrophic environmental degradation; and the last thirty years have seen an intensification of those risks as more and more countries have built more nuclear power stations. Moreover, the shifts in nuclear technologies have introduced complex systems of reprocessing and recycling which have in turn generated a large-scale and growing trade in nuclear waste. This has clearly added a new and important dimension to transboundary pollution and pollution threats. The international trade in nuclear waste has been paralleled by a rapid expansion in the international trade of other hazardous wastes in the 1980s (Greenpeace, 1993).

8.2.3   Global problems, global responses

In section 8.1 we argued that the political and cultural response to the globalization of environmental degradation can be mapped in four ways:

- the emergence and density of cultural, intellectual and scientific networks that both track and expose global and regional forms of environmental degradation;
- the emergence and density of international political networks and organizations that seek to monitor and regulate environmental crises;
- the numbers, coverage and intrusiveness of global and regional environmental institutions, laws, conventions and protocols; and
- the extent to which these two foregoing factors interact with, shape and determine the conduct of domestic political institutions, movements and struggles.

Below, we offer a short sketch of the history of these changes. (For the main sources on the history of international environmental discourses and politics see Dasmann, 1988; McCormick, 1989; Pearce, 1991; Hurrell and Kingsbury, 1992; Haas et al., 1993.) Our main contention in this section is that the history of environmental politics and discourse has followed a trajectory – although uneven and exhibiting a marked tendency to diminish in periods of economic recession – which is similar in pattern to the expansion and intensification of environmental damage and threats, such that it is reasonable to conclude that a global politics of the environment exists today (see chapter 1).

The postwar era has witnessed an increase in material global environmental problems and interactions as well as the development of an increasingly sophisticated set of scientific and moral discourses that seek to expose, monitor, record and assess those problems. Deep intellectual roots and significant cultural precursors can be found for these developments: debates over resource shortages and over population raged among nineteenth-century political economists; the theory of global warming was first proposed over a hundred years ago; and the material, aesthetic and moral impact of a rapacious and insatiable industrialism on the natural world has been the subject of critical attack for over three centuries (Passmore, 1974; Thomas, 1983; Pepper, 1984). Nonetheless, the postwar era has witnessed major advances in the technological capacity of science to record previously invisible forms of environmental damage, while the disciplines of climatology, atmospheric science, toxicology, epidemiology and biochemistry have provided more convincing accounts of their origins and consequences. This has been accompanied by a growing practical and moral discourse of global environmental interconnectedness and interdependence that has fed on diverse sources.

These cultural shifts have been accompanied by an institutionalization of dense networks of global environmental monitoring and interaction. Science, in particular, has always claimed universal status and individual scientists have long communicated with each other across borders. In the postwar era there has been a further globalization of scientific discourse and the scientific community. This has occurred because of the increasing ease of international communication and travel and the spread of scientific research and teaching to the developing world. In the environmental field, these scientific debates have been important catalysts in the political acceptance of environmental threats and an important component of the formation and institutionalization of international environmental organizations (P. Haas, 1992).

The moral and practical discourse of environmental interdependence has been germinated and propagated by the emerging networks of the global environmental movement. Once again, the environmental movement has many historical roots, but since the 1960s the scope, scale and form of its mobilization have been unique. In Northern Europe and North America the upsurge of new environmental arguments in the 1960s combined with receptive social groups to yield the diverse, transnational environmental movements of the 1970s and 1980s. Taking different paths in different states, drawing on distinctive traditions and resources, there was a common explosion of environmental activity: old conservationist and nature protection organizations grew, small local groups mushroomed in response to specific environmental threats, new and more radical NGOs, lobbying organizations and direct action groups emerged, and in Europe, Green parties were founded. In the 1980s and 1990s these developments spread to Eastern Europe and many developing states, where, overcoming unpromising political circumstances, organized environmental protest has emerged.

Despite the global proclivities of the movement, much of this activity has been local and national in its focus; the organizational resources and political spaces necessary for global political action have been more limited. States have generally sought to exclude international environmental NGOs and their ad hoc alliances and networks from international environmental negotiations and institutions. Where these groups have managed to gain some access, their power has been informal rather than formal, and they have usually depended on national electorates and publics to put pressure on individual governments. However, they have now established themselves as regular players in many fields of international environmental action; their presence if not their power at the Rio conference in 1992 (see below) was historic (Wapner, 1996). The coordinated response of European environmental organizations to the Brent Spar incident (in which Shell, with the agreement of the UK government, sought to sink an old oil rig at sea) indicates their significant organizational capacity.

At the core of this global swirl of environmental discourse and politics is the growing body of international environmental institutions and laws (see figure 8.1). Once again, there are historical precedents. In the case of rare species and the trade in exotic wildlife, the institutionalization of international environmental politics has a history of over a century. But as the pace of environmental globalization has soared and the power and influence of domestic environmental movements have expanded, so the global political response has also grown (see Hurrell and Kingsbury, 1992). The postwar era saw a number of early initiatives in the international environmental field. The first

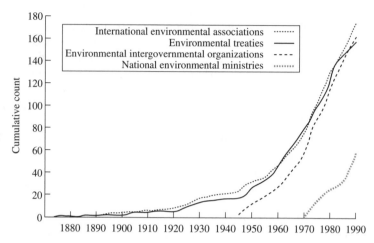

Figure 8.1 Cumulative counts of international environmental organizations and regimes, 1870–1990 (*Source:* Adapted from Meyer et al., 1997)

convention on the regulation of international whaling was signed in 1946 and early treaties on the international carriage of toxic substances, minor habitat protection schemes and some regulation of the international nuclear cycle were agreed in the 1950s and 1960s. However, it was only in the late 1960s and early 1970s that the density of international environmental regulation really began to increase. The seminal and symbolic moment of this transition was the 1972 Stockholm conference on the international environment sponsored by the UN Environment Programme (UNEP). This was the first occasion when multilateral agencies and national governments gathered to consider the whole panoply of shared environmental problems and the scope of the necessary response. While the actual practical consequences of Stockholm were rather more limited than the organizers had hoped, it set a precedent in environmental matters and established an agenda of action for the following decades.

Throughout the 1970s and 1980s, the regulation of international waters and the control of marine pollution became extensively institutionalized with the creation and signature of the London Dumping Convention (1972), the MARPOL convention on ship pollution (1978), the United Nations Law of the Sea (1982) and a multiplicity of regional seas agreements on cooperation and control of pollution (the Helsinki, Barcelona, Oslo and Paris conventions as well as the UN regional seas programme). In the field of wildlife protection, specific agreements were made on polar bears, seals and trade in internationally determined rare species, as well as on wetlands, migratory birds and the Antarctic ecosystem. Most dramatically, major conventions were signed on the international movement of hazardous wastes (the Basel convention in 1989), air pollution controlling the emission of CFCs (the Vienna and Montreal Protocols in 1985 and 1987) as well as a range of treaties regulating transboundary acid rain in Europe and North America.

Alongside the development of these international treaties and conventions, the European Union added another layer of international regulation and control of environmental policy. Although the EU had an environmental policy and directorate in the late 1960s, it was only in the 1970s that it initiated a programme of extensive work which began to impinge radically on the conduct of environmental policy in member states. So far the EU has focused on a number of areas bringing a range of directives to bear on water pollution and treatment, air pollution, minimum permissible standards for vehicles, and the disposal and treatment of waste. In addition, the EU has begun to be represented alongside member countries in international negotiations and in established international institutions such as the Oslo and Paris Commissions which regulate maritime pollution in the North Sea and north-east Atlantic (Haigh, 1990, 1992). Furthermore, within other regional arrangements, such as NAFTA, APEC, the Nordic Council, MERCOSUR, etc., environmental issues have become key bones of contention and the focus of regional cooperation and regulation.

In a reprise of the Stockholm conference, the intensive international diplomatic activity and rising domestic political concern of the 1980s helped generate the impetus for the 1992 Rio conference. Conducted under the auspices of the UNEP, and involving negotiations between almost every member state of the UN, Rio sought to establish the most far-reaching and comprehensive set of global environmental agreements ever arrived at and a significant programme of domestic and international action to meet international environmental targets. Included were conventions on biodiversity, climate change and greenhouse emissions, the fate of the rainforests and the establishment of international arrangements for transferring technology and capital from North to South for environmental purposes (UNEP, 1993). Progress on implementation, of course, has been less impressive. Nevertheless, Rio placed the environment firmly on the global institutional agenda such that the G7, the IMF, the World Bank and the WTO have all acquired a growing political interest in environmental problems.

8.3 Changing Historical Forms of Environmental Globalization

To return to the questions with which we began: Is the world experiencing material levels of environmental globalization and environmental degradation that are unprecedented? And if so, what exactly is new about the form and impact of contemporary environmental problems?

Prior to the advent of European modernity, the only very extensive forms of environmental change were created by the movements of microbes and pests to susceptible host populations and global climatic fluctuations – plagues and ice ages. On occasion, river valley ecosystems that stretched over large areas could be engulfed in collective environmental problems of soil loss and flooding. But premodern societies, whether agrarian or nomadic, were in general incapable of collectively transforming their environments much beyond their carrying capacity before overpopulation and disaster regulated their environmental appetite.

The fatal conjunction of Eurasia and the Americas in the sixteenth and seventeenth centuries set in train a series of global ecological changes and demographic shifts of immense intensity. These were accompanied, within parts of Northern Europe, by growing domestic environmental problems resulting from the rapid growth of organic economies, their increasing demands for resources and land, and their use of market mechanisms (see grid 8.1). Colonial agriculture and plantation economies began to

Grid 8.1 Key historical types and forces of environmental degradation

	Premodern Pre-1500	Early modern Approx. 1500–1760	Modern Approx. 1760–1945	Contemporary Approx. 1945 on
Key types of environmental degradation	Some global extinctions of species, especially large mammals and birds from overhunting Microbe movement leading to epidemics and population collapse Very localized emissions and wastes	Demographic and early ecological transformation of the Americas Rising resource shortage and land degradation under conditions of economic and demographic growth in advanced organic economies	Demographic and early ecological transformation of Oceania Some global extinctions of species Some contribution to cumulative impact of global warming Local resource exhaustion Agricultural transformation of the rural environment – forest loss, especially in some European colonies, etc. Urban air, soil and water pollution	Global warming, ozone depletion Marine pollution Deforestation, desertification, soil exhaustion Overspill and collective resource problems Acid deposition Nuclear risks Global biodiversity decline Hazardous wastes
Key forces of environmental degradation	Overpopulation, natural climate change, urbanization and poor agricultural practice Large-scale migrations, warfare and conquest	European ecological expansion Capitalist agrarian growth	European ecological expansion and colonial economic practice Capitalist industrialization Urbanization and concentration of industry	Western growth and consumption Socialist industrialization Industrialization of the South and demographic explosion New risks from nuclear, biological and chemical technologies

transform the landscape of the Americas, and intensive hunting, driven by European demand, led to the extinction of some species both in the Americas and in Siberia. Nonetheless, despite these loops of cause and effect between continents and economies, most environmental degradation caused locally, impacted locally. None of our three forms of environmental globalization – the commons, overspill and transboundary pollution – were of major consequence.

It is only with the advent of the Industrial Revolution in the West, from the late eighteenth century, that the collective power of humanity to generate environmental degradation really expanded. The transformation of energy sources and productive processes, combined with intense and partially regulated urbanization, altered the capacity of these economies for the creation of environmental hazards. Environmental degradation remained local in its impact – although industrial effluents began to creep by air and water courses out of cities and into their hinterlands. Global colonial expansion continued in this era but the capacity of European ecology to follow the European military machine into Africa and Asia was thwarted by their more robust immunological and ecological resources. There would be no parallel to the experience of 1492. Rather, it would require the power of Western capital and market demand to begin processes of environmental overexploitation in the colonies – deforestation, for example, can be traced back to the late nineteenth century in Java and India. Once again, global environmental degradation was limited in its impact by comparison with local and national impacts. But imperialism too generated the first attempts to identify, study, monitor and control local environmental impacts (Grove, 1997).

However, from the mid-twentieth century the picture changes (see grid 8.2). Capitalist economies in the West have been joined as agents of environmental degradation, by both southern industrialization and state socialist industrialization. The former massively increased the total volume of potential environmental problems as well as their geographical spread. The latter was distinguished by its unique capacity to be more environmentally problematic and myopic than the most rapacious capitalism (see figure 8.2 for the relative contribution of the former Eastern bloc to atmospheric carbon emissions). When these forces were combined with the immense transformative powers and ecological risks inherent in many modern technologies – new chemicals industries, mass transport systems dependent on fossil fuel, nuclear technologies – environmental degradation acquired a decisively global form (see figure 8.3 regarding CFC production in this era). No historic parallel exists for the contemporary levels of transboundary pollution, environmental commons problems and resource squeezes. Nor, unsurprisingly, is there any significant historical comparator for today's environmental movements, treaties and international agencies.

8.4 Stratification of Environmental Degradation and National Enmeshment

The enmeshment of any society in global environmental problems takes a number of interconnected forms. First, each country makes its own particular contribution to the creation of these environmental problems as a by-product of production and consumption. Second, each country is currently or potentially affected by a range of indirect environmental threats and risks produced by ozone depletion or climate change. Third,

Grid 8.2 Historical forms of environmental globalization

	Premodern Pre-1500	Early modern Approx. 1500–1760	Modern Approx. 1760–1945	Contemporary Approx. 1945 on
Extensity	Microbe movements provide only long-range form of environmental change	European expansion acquires transcontinental, transoceanic dimensions extending the reach of ecological changes	European expansion reaches Oceania; but unable initially to impact ecologically and demographically on Asia and Africa	Environmental degradation of the global commons crosses key thresholds – global warming and ozone depletion
		Conquest and colonization intensify demographic change, adding agricultural and landscape transformations in the Americas and Caribbean	Transformations in the Americas and Caribbean intensified	Sheer levels of global population and per capita consumption place collective pressure on land, resources and ecosystems with overspill risks
		Within societies, environmental degradation remains overwhelmingly local in its origins and consequences; some 'stretches' as organic economies grow, drawing resources from a wider area	Some localized deforestation under colonial auspices (India, Java, Malaya) and plantation-led ecosystem change in parts of Southern and Eastern Africa	Transboundary pollution – marine, riverine and airborne – acquires clear regional dimensions in industrialized areas: Europe and North America earlier in the century, increasingly now in Latin America and the Pacific Rim
			Capitalist industrialization and urbanization in West and agricultural development transform landscape and create intense local urban pollution	International trade in hazardous products and waste develops within the West, from Western Europe to Eastern Europe and from the North to the South
			Some transboundary pollution in industrializing areas	

Intensity	Degradation due to human action entirely local apart from long-range human and microbe movements – though potential for arrival of new diseases very large	Degradation overwhelmingly local beyond the great Atlantic demographic changes – but that process still required generations	In industrializing countries, local and national degradation more important than global and regional Outside the West, colonial relationships make a key contribution to local degradation	International trade in and diffusion of nuclear technology and risks spread to all continents Global risks and threats increasing relative to local and national threats
Velocity	Low	Major landscape and ecosystem transformations require generations	Major landscape and ecosystem transformations require generations, but industrialization raises the velocity of environmental degradation	International trade and technology transfer speeds spread of threats and risks Sheer voracity of modern economies and fragility of ecosystems speed the process of environmental degradation
Impact propensity	Potential break on population and agrarian growth from local resource shortages, price spirals, land degradation and land hunger	Demographic eradication of indigenous Americans Potential break on population and agrarian growth from local resource shortages, price spirals, land degradation and land hunger	Demographic eradication of indigenous Australians, Maoris Health and human impact concentrated in cities and by class in industrialized zones	Global and regional impacts and threats begin to outstrip local impacts, especially where domestic pollution has been diminished by political action, industrial change

continued

Grid 8.2 *continued*

	Premodern Pre-1500	Early modern Approx. 1500–1760	Modern Approx. 1760–1945	Contemporary Approx. 1945 on
Institutionalization	All regulation by custom, tradition, specific to each society	Most regulation by custom, tradition, specific to each society Some legal innovation to control urban pollution – limited	Very early forms of international regulation and political interaction – minor treaties	Growth of international environmental law, treaties and regimes Establishment of environmental agencies within the UN and other international organizations Growth of international environmental alliances between NGOs
Stratification	No explicit conscious hierarchy	Immunological and demographic power of the West dominant in Americas, and equalled in Africa and Asia	Immunological and demographic power of the West dominant in Americas and Oceania, and equalled in Africa and Asia Intense localized pollution in cities and manufacturing regions	Intense localized pollution in cities and manufacturing regions but with enormous variations between rich and poor societies Greater disparities globally in level of consumption and shifting relative contributions to global environmental problems

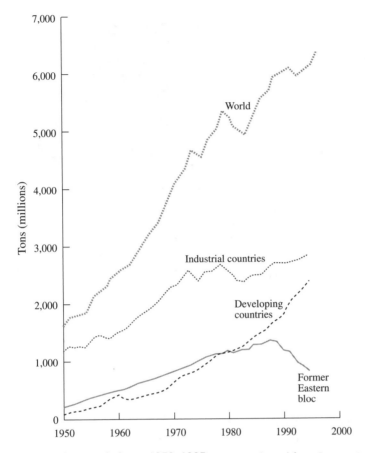

Figure 8.2 Global carbon emissions, 1950–1995 (*Source*: Adapted from Brown et al., 1996)

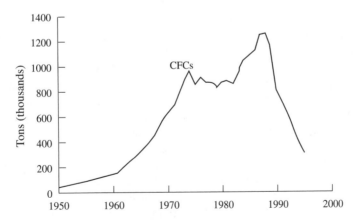

Figure 8.3 World CFC production, 1950–1995 (*Source*: Adapted from Brown et al., 1996)

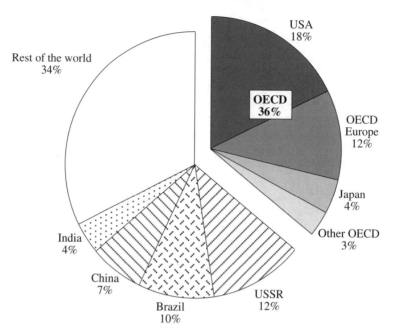

Figure 8.4 Contributions to annual net greenhouse gas emissions, early 1990s (rounded percentages) (*Source*: OECD, 1991a)

each country is currently or potentially affected by the secondary consequences of environmental degradation in neighbouring and distant states.

8.4.1 National enmeshment and the commons: global warming, ozone depletion and the marine environment

As contributors to the problems of climate change and ozone depletion, the differences between our six OECD countries are outweighed by their basic similarities as part of the bloc of Western industrialized countries who currently contribute over a third of global emissions (see figure 8.4), but contain less than 15 per cent of the world's population. In per capita terms, the OECD as a whole is contributing far more than its fair share of emissions. However, to view the matter in contemporary terms alone is to misjudge the issue, for both the greenhouse effect and ozone depletion are the product of cumulative global pollution. Molecules of gas released into the atmosphere, particularly CFCs, can persist for decades. Therefore, we are experiencing the consequences of past as well as present pollution. In historical terms, the West has produced the majority of the accumulated greenhouse emissions, which have been on the rise for well over a century. Similarly, despite a recent decline in use, the overwhelming bulk of accumulated CFC use has been in the West (see table 8.1). Thus some of the most significant costs of Western industrialization have been both deferred and externalized across the planet.

Table 8.1 Major CFC users, 1986–1994

Country or region	Use in tons		% change
	1986	1994	
China	46,000	90,900	+95
EC/EU	343,000	39,700	−88
Russia	129,000	32,600	−75
Japan	135,000	19,700	−85
South Korea	11,500	13,100	+15
Mexico	8,930	10,800	+21
Brazil	11,300	7,780	−31
Canada	23,200	4,850	−79
Australia	18,600	3,890	−79
South Africa	18,700	2,420	−87
United States	364,000	−91[a]	−100

[a] Indicates use of accumulated stock of CFCs.
Source: Adapted from Brown et al., 1997a

Shared Western culpability aside there are some significant differences between OECD countries. In terms of the overall contribution of individual economies, the US economy takes pride of place, generating almost half of all OECD greenhouse emissions during the late 1980s through the 1990s (OECD, 1991a). The USA accomplishes this with less than 5 per cent of the world's population. German, Japanese, British and French contributions are all substantial. Sweden with a population of only 8.5 million makes a very much less significant contribution. However, all these countries have a level of emissions per capita well in excess of the global average – this ranges from four times the global average per capita in the USA to around 50 per cent greater in Japan and Sweden.

The impact of global warming is highly unpredictable given the numerous effects that climate change and temperature change could produce, and the immense geographical variation of both (IPCC, 1990; Watson et al., 1995; Bruce et al., 1995). The most likely consequences, at the moment, appear to be radical changes in the agricultural productivity and potential of different areas, and a rise in overall sea levels leading to the submergence of many coastal and populated areas. The UK, for example, is threatened along its low-lying eastern coastal regions with serious loss of land (urban and agricultural) and rising sea levels. Japan and the US face similar problems, though none of these countries faces the potential catastrophes awaiting low-lying oceanic islands like the Seychelles or the reclaimed coastlines of the Netherlands. The impact of changing weather patterns is more difficult to predict, though once again it looks as if the West and Europe in particular will be less harshly affected than tropical and subtropical states, where weather patterns could render current agricultural practices unsustainable due to shifts in temperature and in patterns and levels of rainfall. Moreover, many developing states lack the financial and technological resources for conducting a managed transition of ecosystems and farming. For these reasons, the West is unlikely to be unaffected by the impact of global warming outside its own frontiers. Large rises in sea levels, the loss of heavily populated land and major reductions in agricultural productivity in the South could trigger extensive forms of social and polit-ical upheaval and dislocation. Combined with long-standing economic weakness and continuing demographic pressures, the internal stability of many states may be in ques-tion, levels of migration may rise and the already sharp conflicts over resources may become sharper still.

If the causes and economic benefits of atmospheric change are distributed inequit-ably, so too are the likely consequences. It is unclear as yet how the costs and con-sequences will be distributed; we are in the realm of scientific guess-work at this stage. However, a number of points can be made with some degree of confidence in relation to ozone. The main effect of ozone depletion is the formation of ozone holes. These have principally appeared at the North and South poles, with the atmospheric con-centration of ozone in these areas varying from season to season and year to year. Current orthodoxy argues that a 1 per cent loss of ozone leads to a 2 per cent increase in surface UV levels which in turn generates rather more than a 2 per cent increase in skin cancers (Titus, 1986). So far, most concern and research have focused on the southern hemisphere in general, and Australasia in particular, where increasing rates of skin cancers have been detected. However, the rate of northern ozone depletion is on the increase and the impact in North America and Europe is likely to escalate in the coming decades. Current levels of ozone loss vary according to pole and season but appear to be increasing in the range of 2–9 per cent ozone loss per annum (WMO, *Atmospheric Ozone*, various years). NASA scientists have estimated the loss to be on average 3 per cent a year over the 1980s, a figure which shows no sign of abating (Parson, 1993).

The environmental threats to the world's oceans and seas are multiple, intercon-nected and complex. They include the exhaustion of fish stocks and other marine fauna through overfishing; the impact of atmospheric change leading to rising sea levels; increasing threats of coastal flooding and erosion and shifts in ambient oceanic tem-peratures; the impact of oil and mineral extraction on marine environments; and, most importantly, the vast input of wastes into the seas and oceans, including nutrients, pathogens, oil, synthetic organic chemicals, radioactive waste, trace metals, solid wastes (both industrial and municipal), and plastic and other debris (Hinrichsen, 1990; Mitchell, 1993). It is important when considering marine environmental degradation to use the notion of globalization carefully. This is because a great deal of marine pollution is generated and experienced locally. Most obviously, local sewage production, even when there are long outflow pipes, pollutes local coastlines and beaches. Similarly, local industrial output and those pollutants that accumulate nationally along river courses wreak their main effects along a fairly narrow stretch of local coastline. However, over a sufficiently long period of time pollution can, and does, move through open marine expanses from country to country as well as polluting the common areas of seas. It is only in these cases that we can reasonably talk of the regionalization or globalization of marine pollution. Unfortunately, it is difficult to disaggregate statistics accurately in this way – the origins and destinations of different pollutants are notoriously hard to track – so only a fairly impressionistic picture of marine pollution in our case study countries can be drawn.

The USA has a quite distinctive pattern of marine environments. To the east and west it has very long seaboards – the Atlantic and Pacific. In the north, off the Alaskan coast, the USA shares the Arctic Ocean, while to the south lies the only significant regional, semi-enclosed sea on to which the USA borders, the Gulf of Mexico. It is here that international issues are most pressing for the USA as it shares the gulf with Mexico and the western Caribbean, all harvesting very large fish and shellfish catches from the sea. Pollution has increased sharply as petroleum extraction and distribution have risen, and coastal developments for residential and industrial use have escalated, especially in Florida. This has led to diminished fish stocks in the sea and local pollution hotspots that rebound on the tourism and retirement industries.

Japan, as an island, has an extensive marine hinterland; it borders the Pacific to the east and the semi-enclosed Sea of Japan to the west. Marine pollution levels rose rapidly in the postwar decades and peaked in the 1960s and 1970s when both heavy industrialization reached its zenith and the mounting consequences of pollution forced a minimal level of environmental regulation on the worst industrial culprits (OECD, 1991b). However, only minor improvements have been witnessed subsequently. That said, the vast majority of the environmental problems faced in Japanese waters are domestically generated rather than internationally transmitted. Intensive coastal development, major urban and industrial establishments on the seaboard and the very large levels of tanker-borne oil imports have caused most of the pollution in Japanese waters.

The European countries in this study have radically different lengths of coastline and access to common marine environments. (On European seas and pollution see P. Haas, 1990, 1993.) The most important regional seas for these states are the North Sea, the Baltic and the Mediterranean. These are heavily used and densely populated on much of their shoreline, though less so for the North Sea. In addition, the North Sea differs from the others in being much less enclosed. Both the Baltic and Mediterranean have only the narrowest of outlets to wide stretches of oceanic water and thus have a very slow turnover rate of water content, which ensures that pollutants remain in higher concentrations for longer than elsewhere. The North Sea receives the output of a number of important Northern European rivers as well as significant industrial and agricultural discharges. The same can also be said of the Baltic and the Mediterranean. They, in addition, have to face the problem of a mixture of developed and developing countries on their shorelines. This leads to radically different standards of pollution abatement, sewage treatment and discharge control into a shared resource and thus imparts a distinct political dynamic to the regulation of marine pollution.

8.4.2   National enmeshment and overspill: demography and resources

The exhaustion of mineral reserves and organic raw materials and the extinction of plant and animal species have been a preoccupation of environmentalists for over two decades. Of course, as argued in section 8.2, the practical problem of resource depletion and shortages has a long pedigree. We have ample evidence, both quantitative and qualitative, of severe resource shortages in premodern societies through both observers' accounts and the analysis of price statistics which reflect impending and actual shortages. However, it was in the early 1970s, with the publication of the Club of Rome's *Limits to Growth* and The Ecologist's *Blueprint for Survival*, that the finite nature of natural resources was brought firmly on to the environmental agenda (Meadows et al., 1972; The Ecologist, 1972).

The significance of resource shortages has, however, become more prominent in recent years because of the generalized importance of environmental issues, and for two more specific reasons. First, further research has revealed that the exhaustion of resources does not apply to inorganic raw materials alone. The irreplaceable tropical rainforests of the South have been disappearing at an unprecedented rate in the last fifteen years due to logging, agricultural change and large-scale infrastructure projects. Alongside the enormous importance of these forests for their indigenous populations, there are global consequences as well. Rainforest loss affects the world's climate (since rainforests are absorbers of carbon dioxide and producers of oxygen through photosynthesis) and it also effectively extinguishes a huge number of known and unknown plant and animal species. This loss has been accompanied by a more general sense of the diminishing biodiversity of the planet, led by the most obvious and emotive campaigns for the preservation of threatened large mammals – pandas, elephants, whales and big cats.

The second reason for increasing concern over resource shortage and its global implications is the remorseless logic of global population growth and the global spread of industrialization. Although the question of population growth has never left the environmental agenda, it has been given a decisive boost by the rapid industrialization – and therefore an expansion in resource consumption – of many parts of the developing world. The world is having to live with the prospect of, at best, a stabilized global population of over 12 billion people (UNFPA, 1994). This is nearly two and a half times today's levels. Moreover, this will be a population which lives overwhelmingly in industrialized societies. The passage of over a billion Chinese, as well as about another half a billion people on the Pacific rim, through a condensed industrial revolution poses the question of resource exhaustion with an urgency that never occurred to the original depletionists. All things being equal, a larger global population at a higher level of industrialization will mean more pollution and more resource consumption. Moreover, when questions of demographic growth are considered the concerns are not merely about raw material shortages that overspill into other countrys' politics but broader issues of social dislocation, mass migration and political instability. At present, it is impossible to assess accurately the extent to which raw material shortages, population growth and social and political dislocation will feed into each other. Rather than focusing on general predictions about the future, we have tried below to consider the broad enmeshment of the six case study countries in these ever more global issues.

These case study countries are all direct contributors to the problems of resource consumption and will all be directly and indirectly affected by global population growth, material exhaustion and political, economic and demographic spillovers. The scale of their enmeshment in these global resource shortages can be seen in their consumption of fossil fuels and other raw materials, their share of the global fish catch and their trade in endangered species and tropical rainforest products. The critical division on this issue is once again between North and South rather than differences between OECD countries. The evidence on almost any indicator one chooses to examine is stark. People in the OECD constitute 15 per cent of the world's population. In the next few decades this proportion will diminish further. In 1988 the OECD accounted for 51 per cent of total global energy consumption and, as previously indicated, a significant component of greenhouse emissions, CFC consumption and sulphur and nitrogen oxide emissions. The energy mix of Western economies is particularly skewed

Table 8.2 Natural resource consumption, United States and India, 1991

	US consumption	Indian consumption	US/India per capita ratio
Aluminium	4,137	420	34:1
Copper	2,057	157	45:1
Crude steel	93,325	20,300	16:1
Nickel	137	15	31:1
Phosphate rock	40,177	2,381	58:1
Coal	672,036	184,992	12:1
Petroleum	666,032	53,294	43:1
Natural gas (tetrajoules)	21,387,719	397,250	184:1
Pulpwood (1,000cm^3)	136,377	1,208	386:1

Units: 1,000 metric tons, except where indicated.
Source: World Resources Institute, 1995

Table 8.3 Relative levels of resource consumption in the industrialized and developing worlds, 1986–1990

	Industrialized countries	Developing countries
Fossil fuels (gigajoules per capita)	160.1	17.3
Aluminium (metric tonnes/100 people)	14.1	0.7
Roundwood (cubic metres per capita)	1.3	0.5
Beef and veal (kilograms per capita)	27.2	4.3
Cotton (kilograms per capita)	5.4	2.6

Source: World Resources Institute, 1995

to fossil fuels rather than to renewable wood and dung sources as in the non-industrial South (though the West also makes more use of nuclear fuel). While current depletion rates are important, it is essential to remember that past rates of resource use should be taken into account. Accordingly, we reach the present situation on the basis of even more inequitable usage rates between North and South over the last century. If we turn to other raw materials, such as ores and metals, we find an equal if not greater asymmetry of consumption (Westing, 1986; World Resources Institute, 1995). The data in tables 8.2 and 8.3 are particularly asymmetrical, drawing on the most resource profligate economy – the USA – and one of the least resource intensive countries – India – as well as showing the broader comparison of aggregate consumption rates in OECD and developing countries.

Given the small scale and unregulated character of the fishing industry in much of the world, as well as conscious efforts by many to elude regulation, estimates of the

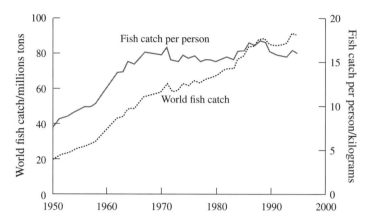

Figure 8.5 Global fish catch, 1950–1995 (*Source*: Adapted from Brown et al., 1997b, based on FAO estimates)

global fish catch must be treated with some caution. Food and Agricultural Organization (FAO) estimates (see figure 8.5) suggest that the total catch has risen from almost 60 million tons in 1970 to almost 84.5 million tons in 1990 (FAO, 1994; McGoodwin, 1990; OECD, 1991a; Peterson, 1993). Of that catch the OECD was responsible for 41 per cent in 1970, falling in relative terms to 37 per cent in 1988. However, given the much slower rate of population growth in the OECD over this period, the OECD's per capita consumption grew faster than that of the rest of the world. Within the OECD the Japanese are by some way the largest consumers of fish; with just over 2 per cent of the world's population they catch 14 per cent of the world's fish for domestic consumption. Equally large per capita consumers of fish are Norway and Denmark, with Spain and the UK just behind. Thus the OECD, alongside parts of the developing world, is rapidly taking the global fish catch to levels exceeding the FAO's estimation of a sustainable global annual catch and seriously depleting stocks in thirteen out of fifteen of the world's fishing areas (Ancharya, 1996). The fishing stocks most at risk include those in the Mediterranean, the Black Sea and north-west Pacific, while much of the Atlantic region teeters on the edge of unsustainable fish landings. As these traditional fishing grounds decline, the world's fishing fleets are operating in more and more distant oceans and threatening more and more marine species. When increasing levels of marine pollution and toxic accumulation in the marine food chain are taken into account, the prospects for global fish stocks are poor and the OECD is making more than its fair share of contributions to exacerbating the problem.

A similar story can be told for the use of forests in general and tropical rainforests in particular (Myers, 1986; Nectoux and Dudley, 1987; Hecht and Cockburn, 1989; Nectoux and Kuroda, 1989). Forests are an immense economic and ecological resource, above all for wood. Wood is a vital component of many industrial products and processes, as a source of fuel, paper and pulp-based products, and is a resource for joinery, shuttering and furniture. Ecologically, forests provide an enormous repository of genetic biodiversity and are an essential component in the global atmospheric and climate system, as we have noted. While there are local and national problems within the OECD, the ecological stability of Western forests is relatively high and systems of ecological and

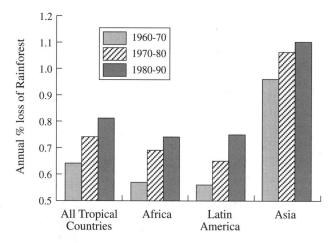

Figure 8.6 Estimated rate of tropical deforestation, 1960–1990 (*Source*: Adapted from World Resources Institute, 1997)

economic management are in place. In any case, the countries of the OECD had, for the most part, already cleared the majority of forest from their territory in earlier waves of industrialization. The greatest environmental pressures today are on forests in the developing world in general and on tropical rainforests in particular. While there are considerable domestic pressures forcing the pace of environmental degradation in developing countries and tropical forest regions, there are also considerable external pressures hastening the process – pressures to which all our case study countries contribute.

As usual, estimates are fairly speculative. FAO, for example, argued at the start of the 1980s that 16–18 per cent of the world's tropical rainforest would be lost over the next forty-five years. By the end of the decade this had risen to a 30 to 35 per cent loss by 2035. Annual rates of loss vary across the developed world, current estimates suggesting an annual loss of 0.33 per cent in Oceania, rising to 1.2 per cent in Asia (see figure 8.6). The OECD countries are helping to drive this process as the main importers of forest products from developing countries. Indeed, the OECD imports 73 per cent of the global total of wood products, while 90 per cent of its sandwood, pulp and paper requirements come from the South. OECD countries are also responsible for the import of the most expensive, rare and ecologically threatened hardwoods and tropical woods. But there are considerable variations within the OECD depending on patterns of domestic wood production and consumption: Japan and France have a predilection for tropical products, Sweden has a much more restricted appetite.

8.4.3 National enmeshment and transboundary pollution

The most significant transboundary pollution problems are acid rain and the movement of chemical waste along shared rivers. A further important threat and occasional reality is the wind-borne movement of radioactive elements released from nuclear

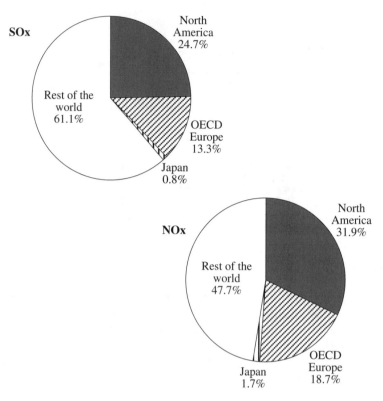

Figure 8.7 Global emissions of SOx and NOx, late 1980s (*Source*: OECD, 1991a)

installations as a matter of routine discharge or accident. We focus here on acid rain, hazardous waste and the nuclear industry.

Acid rain, which requires no physical connection between states to be transmitted, affects all six states (see Boehmer-Christiansen and Skea, 1991; Levy, 1993). Sulphur and nitrogen dioxides, generated by the burning of fossil fuels (mainly in power stations and combustion engines), are dissolved in atmospheric water to produce sulphuric and nitric acids. These acids are then carried by wind currents, often over considerable distances, and returned to the surface of the earth and sea in dry form, rain and condensation. Acid depositions have a major impact on lakes and rivers where they cause a shift in pH sufficient to directly kill off a very wide range of plant and animal life, as well as to release toxic metals from sediments. On land the most noticeable consequences of acid rain are the acidification of forest soils, and damage to trees. Acid depositions also affect urban areas, dissolving stone and brick.

In 1988 global emissions of sulphur dioxides totalled around 99 million tonnes. Of that total, 40 per cent was produced by OECD economies (see figure 8.7) which, as previously noted, constitute only 15 per cent of the world's population. However, in the next few decades it is likely that this imbalance will be equalized, as OECD nations stabilize or diminish their sulphur dioxide output and developing nations' industrialization programmes generate more. While 1970 levels of emissions were roughly correlated with the size of domestic economies, that correlation had ceased to be strong in the late 1980s as the UK and USA continued to be highly 'acidic' economies and our other four case study countries reduced their per capita and per unit GDP emissions of sulphur compounds through shifts in energy production and pollution regulation. Beyond the OECD it is important to note that the overwhelming majority of emissions came from just two sources: the former USSR and its successor states and China.

The transboundary emissions and depositions of each country are equally variable. Japan has experienced very little transboundary acid deposition and has been responsible for very little transboundary pollution of other areas. This is partly explained by the distance of Japan from mainland Asia and the prevailing winds and climatic conditions. However, there is a growing body of evidence to suggest that regional transboundary problems of acid rain are becoming more important in East Asia and the Pacific rim. As industrialization gathers pace and energy requirements soar, this densely populated region is beginning to experience a variety of cross-border flows of pollution. The devastating Indonesian forest fires of 1997 are indicative of such developments. These fires polluted cities as far away as Kuala Lumpur with dense smoke and smog and have provoked a regional response within ASEAN. The USA receives some acid depositions from Canada and Mexico and has experienced marked environmental degradation in the north-east. However, in international political terms it is worth noting that these depositions and the subsequent environmental damage are dwarfed by the US exports of acid rain to its northern and southern neighbours.

In Europe there are large differences between the foreign/domestic sources of acid rain (French, 1990). At the upper end of the range, the Netherlands, Switzerland and Austria received over 70 per cent of their acid depositions, in the late 1980s, from outside their borders. Sweden, Germany and France are in a more middling position with 58 per cent, 45 per cent and 34 per cent of depositions respectively coming from foreign sources. Finally, the UK is at the lower end of the scale, receiving only 12 per cent of acid depositions from overseas. All four European countries have contributed to the pollution of other states. The UK and Germany have been seen as particularly culpable in the pollution of Scandinavia, France and the Low Countries. In part the degree of foreign acid deposition as well as the overall level of depositions correlates with the enthusiasm of states for signing the various conventions on long-range transboundary pollution.

In what sense can we describe the nuclear industry and nuclear power generation as a contributor to the globalization of environmental risks and environmental pollution? First, we need to establish the types of risks and threats that nuclear power generation poses (see Kemp, 1992; Blowers and Lowry, 1991). These threats derive from the radioactive character of the fuel and by-products of the nuclear fuel cycle. The intensity and half-life of nuclear materials is variable but includes long-lasting and highly toxic materials (such as plutonium) whose radioactive emissions can make land useless and air unbreathable, and rapidly kill human beings, animals and plants for generations. Nuclear power generation is an immensely complex undertaking of which electricity production in a nuclear power station reactor is but one small part. In addition, uranium must be mined, processed, refined and delivered to power stations. Once fuel rods have been exhausted they must be removed and cooled. Depending on the type of nuclear reactor technology involved, used fuel can either be disposed of or it can be reprocessed. Reprocessing concentrates the plutonium generated as a by-product of nuclear reactions and this can then serve as the material basis of weapons manufacture or further power generation in fast breeder reactors. Even if this additional loop is placed into the fuel cycle, problems of final disposal remain. The wastes produced include both spent fuel and the water used in the cooling and storing of fuels, as well as the actual plants and machinery of the nuclear power cycle which become radioactive through use and proximity. Thus the environmental threats presented by nuclear power include the escape of radioactive materials into the environment; the emission of radioactive water and gases from refining, power and reprocessing plants; and the escape of radioactivity from low-level, medium-level and high-level nuclear waste. Finally, and most threatening of all, there is the potential problem of reactor malfunction, in which control is lost and a 'meltdown' is possible, leading to infinitely larger emissions of radioactive substances.

Given this risk profile we can describe a number of ways in which the nuclear industry contributes to the globalization of environmental degradation and environmental risk. First, the simple proliferation of nuclear technologies and installations to more and more countries increases the geographical scope and statistical likelihood of major nuclear accidents which are potentially global in scope. Second, this proliferation creates an increasing amount of routine low-level radioactive emissions which can and are borne by air and water across national boundaries. Third, the creation of large amounts of low-level nuclear waste has been dealt with in some countries by marine dumping and thus the spread of nuclear pollution to the global and regional commons. Finally, the storage and reprocessing of high-level nuclear waste is of such complexity and cost that only certain countries have been prepared and able to embark on the construction of the necessary facilities – in particular the UK and France. This has created an active and increasingly large-scale trade in nuclear waste reprocessing which both *localizes* nuclear risks, concentrating them from across the world into certain localities, and simultaneously increases global risks by transporting radioactive materials across very large stretches of ocean and land.

All six case study countries have civil nuclear industries, though the building of new stations has ground to a halt almost everywhere and in Sweden there is a timetable for the decommissioning of what reactors remain. Therefore, all six threaten their neighbours as well as their own citizens with the possibility of nuclear pollution of different kinds. This is particularly problematic for the Germans and the French with so many land borders in densely populated regions. Four of the six, to a greater or lesser extent, have been responsible for selling nuclear technologies and/or plant to other countries seeking to create a nuclear power industry. In this field, the Americans and the French have consistently led the field, though the British nuclear export drive has been limited only by the quality of the technology rather than the intensity of the effort.

In 1970 only 17 nations actually possessed operating civil nuclear power stations. Of these, the only nations outside the OECD core were the USSR, Czechoslovakia, East Germany and India. By 1976 the numbers had risen to 20 with the addition of operational stations in Argentina, Bulgaria and Pakistan. By 1980 the numbers had escalated again and the geographical diffusion of nuclear technologies, facilities and threats spread even further. Between 1976 and 1980 reactors came on-stream for the first time in Austria, Brazil, Finland, Hungary, Iran, South Korea and Taiwan, bringing the number of nuclear states to 27. By 1990 the peak of nuclear diffusion seemed to have passed with new reactor programmes in Italy and Iran ceasing and only a few new entrants to the civil nuclear club – Brazil, Mexico, South Africa (World Watch Institute, 1992). France and Britain are distinctive in that they alone have built commercial nuclear reprocessing facilities, Thorp in Cumbria and Cap La Hague in France. These plants are dependent for their medium- and long-term financial viability on large, long-term reprocessing contracts with German and Japanese energy utilities.

The final form of national enmeshment in global and regional environmental problems is transboundary pollution that derives directly from economic exchanges rather than from the unintended externalities of economic exchange, or from scarcity and overuse problems resulting from the economic exploitation of common resources. Three areas are significant. First, there is an international trade in hazardous waste products in which firms generate their waste in one country but export it abroad for final treatment or storage. Second, environmental degradation can result from the export of environmentally hazardous products across borders; often from countries where the sale of a product is banned for environmental reasons to countries where it remains legal. Pesticides and pharmaceuticals are the best examples of this practice (Paarlberg, 1993). Third, there are the environmental externalities of the internationalization of production in which the establishment of new or foreign subsidiaries or the actual movement of manufacturing capacity from one country to another is accompanied (and occurs for that reason) by large-scale pollution and waste production. However, the World Bank, in the only major survey of the issue, has argued that there is very limited evidence for suggesting a significant shift in the distribution and location of dirty industries from North to South or from strict to lax environmental regimes (World Bank, 1993). Although there has been a significant rise in the dirty industry composition of developing countries' output and trade, this is probably explicable in terms of their own indigenous industrialization. Where this is insufficient to account for shifts, it is more likely that differences in labour costs account for industry movements rather than the competitive advantage of laxer environmental standards (see chapter 5). In this section we focus on the international trade in hazardous wastes.

Any quantitative account of the international trade in hazardous wastes is beset by a number of significant problems (Davis, 1993; Greenpeace, 1993; OECD, 1994b). First and foremost, the definition of hazardous wastes is complex, varied and highly politicized. The capacity of modern societies to generate pollutants and distribute them across national borders has once again outpaced the capacity of state agencies to track and monitor their creation, distribution and consequences. Prior to the early 1970s, in most OECD countries regulatory frameworks for waste remained fairly primitive, failing to distinguish analytically or legally between the many different types of solid and liquid waste generated by productive processes and as a result of post-consumption disposal. It was only with the advent of a series of waste scandals in the 1970s that legal frameworks for describing toxic waste were created. It required the Love Canal incident in the USA or the BT Chemie scandal in Sweden to force the establishment of agencies that might track the production of hazardous waste and control its emission into the environment. As a consequence, the data available from national governments and international agencies do not go back much before the late 1970s. In any case, the data that do exist are far from properly comparable because the legislative and definitional frameworks for the control of hazardous waste varied so much.

In recent years strenuous efforts have been made by international agencies to create a common global list of agreed hazardous wastes around which properly compatible figures for the production of waste might be gathered. The types of waste usually classified as hazardous include waste oils, waste solvents after primary usage, metal products and scrap, PCBs from electrical components (especially capacitors), paint sludges and other heavy metal wastes and mercury compounds. Over the last two decades the regulation of hazardous waste disposal in OECD countries has become increasingly stringent and the costs of compliance have steadily escalated. A series of international treaties have effectively banned the dumping of hazardous wastes at sea and completely phased out the sea-based incineration option. On land, regulations governing the management of landfill sites have prevented many hazardous wastes from being stored in inappropriate sites. This has left recycling and land-based incineration options. However, the cost of using these methods has rapidly increased; all the more so in those countries with stringent regulation of land-based incineration. This combination of reduced options, tighter legislation, more stringent national regulation and increasing costs have been the main driving forces behind the establishment and profitability of the international trade in hazardous wastes.

Since the early 1980s two types of trade have developed. The first occurred within the OECD, the second between the OECD and the rest of the world, particularly Africa and Central and Eastern Europe. In the case of the former, a number of OECD countries have become importers of others' toxic wastes, which they have then reprocessed and/or stored. Britain and France have emerged as the main importers of toxic wastes and have expanded the number of incinerator facilities to cope with the demand, particularly from small countries who do not have sufficient technical facilities or home demand to establish expensive incinerator plants (Ireland, Norway) as well as from large-scale hazardous waste producers who face stringent and expensive domestic legislation (Germany and Switzerland). Sweden also falls into this category in that it provides some incineration services for Norway and Finland.

The second type of trade between the West and the East or between the North and the South is driven by the same kinds of factors as intra-OECD trade but is more profitable, often illegal and usually environmentally hazardous (Greenpeace, 1993). Both legal and illegal shipments of wastes have passed from all our case study countries to West Africa, Eastern Europe and parts of South East Asia. In the receiving countries it is not always the case that any kind of legal government permission has been given for the shipments. Nor is it always the case that wastes are correctly labelled. What appear to be innocuous products, speciality chemicals, products for recycling and reuse often turn out to be extremely dangerous and poorly packaged cocktails of hazardous wastes. These are rarely incinerated on arrival; rather, they are dumped on land or at sea with no proper forms of storage or surveillance and this in turn introduces enormous and lethal levels of pollutants into the local environment. However, with the exception of trade in 'recycled products', the UNEP Basel Convention, regulating the international trade in hazardous wastes, has made North/South and East/West trade in these products illegal.

8.5   The Contemporary Pattern of Global Environmental Change and its Political Impacts

It is not difficult, on the basis of the evidence presented in this chapter (and set out earlier in schematic form in grids 8.1 and 8.2), to draw a number of conclusions about contemporary patterns of environmental globalization. First, although environmental issues – local, regional and global – have a long history we can argue that contemporary forms of environmental degradation are more global than at any other point in human history and carry with them the most historically significant set of risks and threats to human life. That we view such a prospect from the dizzying heights of Western prosperity is causally related and a little ironic. Second, these threats and risks encompass the truly global (ozone depletion and global warming), the indirectly global (resource depletion and overspill effects), the more specifically regional (marine pollution) as well as bilateral, transboundary and purely national and local problems. Countries are differentially enmeshed in environmental problems at different spatial scales, which has differential consequences for levels of international environmental interests, activities and commitments. However, it is equally clear that we cannot read off environmental politics from international environmental enmeshment in any easy way. Domestic factors are essential in explaining how international environmental threats and commitments are translated on to the domestic political agenda and into domestic or international political action.

Third, while both environmental and political matters have undergone a substantial degree of globalization in the postwar era, we cannot grasp the progress of environmental degradation and the political response to it without looking at the globalization of economic affairs. In the economic sphere the origins and character of international environmental problems can, in part, be traced to a number of global phenomena. The global diffusion of industrialization from the West to the South and East massively increased the geographical reach of pollution, while simultaneously increasing the planet's overall capacity for resource consumption. Those patterns of industrialization, while bearing the imprint of specifically national and local causal factors, have also been shaped by the global diffusion of Western-inspired models of economic development (of both the right and the left).

In addition, the international economic institutions that have supplied some of the capital and infrastructure and much of the economic 'advice' for these developments – for example, the World Bank – have contributed to this trajectory of environmentally unsustainable industrialization (Schwartzman, 1986; Bank Information Centre, 1990). In the very weakest economies and most susceptible environments, these processes have acquired a vicious downward spiral of environmental degradation and economic retreat. Moreover, some of the already precarious industrializing economies of the South have been buffeted by the global economy as, for the last twenty years, raw material prices and export earnings collapsed and international capital markets closed off loans to some, or tightened the repayments screw on others. The causal path between these global economic constraints and the process of environmental degradation is complex. We can reasonably argue, for example, that the incapacity of large parts of sub-Saharan Africa to sustain a rate of growth to ensure that rapidly expanding populations maintain adequate levels of per capita consumption has been partly due to failures of national leadership along with dubious agricultural practices, which have led to the progressive ecological exhaustion of agricultural land. But we can equally reasonably argue that international economic constraints have played a part in bringing that about.

So what has been the impact of this historically unprecedented level of global environmental threats on the sovereignty and autonomy of SIACS? We would argue that global environmental risks and threats in the late twentieth century have significant decisional, institutional, distributional and structural impacts on SIACS. Indeed, they pose questions with greater clarity than almost any other form of globalization about the nature of the sovereignty and autonomy of even the largest and most powerful of the SIACS.

8.5.1   Decisional and institutional impacts: environmental politics and policy

One of the most powerful resources available to SIACS is their capacity to set the political agenda in the domestic arena through the occupation of state offices and the control of legislative programmes. That power is neither absolute nor uncontested, but it is considerable and particularly effective in excluding certain issues from mainstream debate. The growth of global environmental debates, movements and institutions ensures that whatever the condition of the domestic environmental movements, few states can completely exclude environmental issues from public debate or prevent their own environmental problems from being exposed; SIACS are particularly vulnerable in this respect. However, it remains the case that domestic environmental pressures have been the key force pushing for environmental regulation and control. International pressures on domestic policy agendas are not exclusively environmental. Given the causal origins of a problem like global warming, the primarily national politics of transport, agriculture, forestry and energy production have become increasingly shaped and constrained by international obligations and expectations. This is reflected in the transformation of some state institutions. Traditionally insular ministries such as transport and agriculture have acquired international departments, regular international contacts and transgovernmental networks.

However, while environmental globalization has shifted the balance of power in the formation of the political agenda, altered the range of political players to be taken account of by domestic politicians and changed the political and bureaucratic networks of significant parts of the national state machinery, it is not at all clear that SIACS have the capacity to enforce, regulate and monitor the kinds of environmental and economic change that these shifts have forced on them. It has taken over three decades for the environmental agencies of SIACS to acquire sufficient legislative, administrative powers, scientific expertise and staff as well as sufficient budgetary resources to monitor their own national environments. Among SIACS the unpalatable implications of many environmental policies for key groups of producers and consumers, and the enmeshment of problematic environmental practice with the basic routines of everyday life, are such that few governments, if any, have shown themselves willing to accept the political costs of policies – coercive or catalytic – which might bring economic and social practice into line with the requirements of global environmental sustainability.

8.5.2   Distributional and structural impacts: a global community of fate?

Significant pressures on SIACS emanate from collective environmental problems, international institutions and other states. These pressures vary enormously depending on the environmental enmeshment of different countries and their perceived interests. For leading environmental states international institutions have provided an instrument for forcing other states to assume standards as high as their own – thus minimizing the loss of international competitiveness that domestic environmental regulation might entail. Conversely, laggard states, although pursuing stricter standards than they might otherwise have done, have used these institutions as an instrument for achieving other foreign policy aims, deflecting domestic criticism and acquiring information and technology on best practice, and on occasion financial subventions, from richer states. Yet, in the face of unprecedented global ecological decline, the key question is whether international environmental institutions can practically deal with environmental problems and whether they can do so on a democratic basis. Normatively, if not practically, it is one thing to hand political power from national to international institutions, it is another to pass that power from democratic SIACS to undemocratic and unaccountable international institutions. At the very least we need to be clear about the political issues and trade-offs involved. Two examples illuminate these issues.

As far as practicality and efficacy goes, the history of ozone depletion and CFC regulation lies on the positive side of the balance sheet. The successive negotiations and protocols of the 1970s and 1980s enabled a common international framework for negotiations to emerge, and aided the establishment of a scientific consensus in the face of uncertainty. On the basis of this it proved politically possible to transform the production and consumption of CFCs, first in the West, and then through new financial mechanisms in the South. However, the speed of negotiations when measured against the pace of environmental degradation looks alarmingly sluggish and the relative simplicity of the politics of ozone depletion (few producers, possible substitutes, many non-essential uses) is unlikely to be replicated in other environmental contexts.

The case of global warming illustrates some of the reasons why international environmental institutions have so far been unable to provide durable solutions to many environmental problems. Agreement on the scope and scale of the environmental threat has been difficult to achieve. Similarly, there has been profound disagreement as to who has been responsible for creating the problem and the extent to which past contributions to global warming should be included in future calculations of redress. The implications of global warming in terms of both environmental costs and the costs of transforming major economic sectors like energy, agriculture and transport are so large that agreement on the distribution of those costs becomes complex and difficult. Different states and different economic sectors within those states have radically different interests which are not at the moment amenable to negotiation. Even where agreement on costs and threats has been possible, international institutions have neither the moral weight nor practical executive power to force compromises, extract significant concessions from participants or take independent action.

On all these counts nation-states can retain an effective veto through inaction and indecision should they choose to. No mechanism exists for forcing recalcitrant states into line. But even if this did exist, the democratic status of these processes and outcomes is debatable. Policy discussion and negotiations are invariably technical and decision-making largely unaccountable. Hidden within the vortex of international negotiations, national governments are rarely under significant domestic pressure from political parties or environmental campaigns. Though the space for environmental NGOs within these institutions is opening, it is still small. No meaningful mechanisms exist through which the opinions of national publics or the wider communities of environmental fate can be registered or tested. Yet in the face of such overwhelming collective global problems there is no issue on which the retention of state autonomy, or even state sovereignty, is so potentially counterproductive and the absence of public accountability so regrettable.

Environmental problems such as global warming, ozone depletion and resource consumption have generated an 'environmental community of fate' far bigger than any single nation-state. This point is enforced by the existence of transboundary pollution and environmental interdependency. The rightful scope of the contemporary political community and the extent of reciprocal obligations, responsibilities and rights appear no longer to be located at the level of a nation alone. It is clear that the geographical coverage of ecosystems and environmental degradation easily escapes the sovereign reach of even the largest SIACS. No state has the autonomous capacity to control the quality of its atmosphere, to prevent pollution arriving on the wind or, for that matter, to prevent all the negative consequences of its own environmental decisions travelling across the borders of others. Moreover, the traditional bastion of state sovereignty – military power – is worse than useless in protecting or extending the effective reach of national sovereignty despite the vital interests at stake. Indeed, it is not implausible to argue that the traditional concerns of international politics and traditional definitions of national security are being transformed (see chapter 2) (Myers, 1993b). The same can be argued on a more restricted geographical scale for problems of transboundary pollution, the regional commons and international economic externalities. It is not surprising, therefore, that having developed a multiplicity of treaties, institutions, agreements and programmes for developing collaborative solutions to these common threats, SIACS find that national sovereignty and autonomy are being renegotiated in the face of the globalization of environmental problems and politics.

Andrew Hurrell has usefully focused these debates by arguing that environmental globalization has three structural consequences for SIACS (Hurrell, 1994). First, the institutionalization of international regimes, treaties and organizations can place in question elements of the legal and normative sovereignty of SIACS, though it by no means guarantees their collective capacity to control environmental risks. Second, at a domestic level, whatever the intentions of politicians, the autonomous capacity of SIACS to deal with either local environmental problems or globally produced environmental problems may be insufficient. Both of which contribute to a third structural impact: in so far as the capacities of SIACS are insufficient for dealing with environmental problems, this poses distinct challenges to their domestic legitimacy. This is not to argue that the end of the nation-state is likely, but rather to recognize that the globalization of environmental risks is contributing to a fundamental shift in the nature and practice of state sovereignty and autonomy.

8.6 Conclusion

Contemporary patterns of environmental globalization, in many significant respects, are historically unprecedented. The optimists of the environmental movement claim that growing recognition of global environmental interdependence, and the moral rhetoric of the global environmental movement, are challenging the traditional locus of political legitimacy and the locus of political identification in the nation-state. Certainly, they can point to some real shifts in the terms of international political discourse on the environment. The road from Stockholm to Rio and beyond has seen real changes, while the capacity of environmental NGOs to mobilize domestic support for international environmental problems has increased considerably. However, there seems little evidence to suggest that these kinds of shift have as yet established deep roots in public life beyond the core supporters of environmental politics in the richer OECD societies. Similarly, there is considerable evidence to suggest that the incapacity of some governments to regulate environmental problems, and their tendency to promise higher standards of safety and environmental quality than they are capable of delivering, have contributed to a decline in public trust and confidence in SIACS. But then there are plenty of good reasons, which have nothing to do with the environment, for such an erosion in public legitimacy (Beck, 1992, 1995; Goldblatt, 1996). However, one thing seems beyond doubt: the capacity of environmental globalization to create potential risks and threats to SIACS greatly exceeds existing capacities to address them, and to construct alternative identities and effective international institutions at this time.

Conclusion: the Shape of Contemporary Globalization

Globalization is neither a wholly novel, nor primarily modern, social phenomenon. Its form has changed over time and across the key domains of human interaction, from the political to the ecological. Moreover, as the preceding chapters have sought to show, globalization as a historical process cannot be characterized by an evolutionary logic or an emergent telos. Historical patterns of globalization have been punctuated by great shifts and reversals, while the temporal rhythms of globalization differ between domains. In this concluding chapter we attempt to synthesize the discrete stories of previous chapters into a cumulative assessment of the contemporary global condition. In particular, we seek to address directly three questions raised in the introduction but which only now can be answered with any confidence:

- Does contemporary globalization represent a novel condition?
- Is globalization associated with the demise, the resurgence or the transformation of state power?
- Does contemporary globalization impose new limits to politics? How can globalization be 'civilized' and 'democratized'?

Historical Forms of Globalization: What is New?

Prior chapters have drawn variously on a fourfold periodization of globalization: premodern, early modern, modern and contemporary. In this regard, the narrative highlights four distinctive historical forms of globalization each of which reflects a particular conjuncture of spatio-temporal and organizational attributes. Although the initial populating of the planet by Homo sapiens occurred over many millennia and could be thought of as a form of globalization – in the sense that human beings spread from Africa and Eurasia to all the habitable parts of the planet – these processes formed sporadic global flows in contrast to enduring global relations or connections. Accordingly, we have not explored the prehistoric or pre-agrarian era at any length but rather have concentrated on analysing the dominant spatio-temporal and organizational features of four subsequent historical phases of globalization. By drawing together the main arguments and historical evidence of chapters 1–8, we can begin to codify the dominant features of premodern, early modern and modern historical forms of globalization as the prelude to identifying what is distinctive about its contemporary articulation.

Premodern Globalization

The premodern era covers, of course, an enormously long period that begins with the formation of distinct and separate centres of settled agrarian civilization in Eurasia, Africa and the Americas around 9,000–11,000 years ago. Over the next several millennia these and later civilizations developed the capacity to engage in the long-distance projection of power and even longer distance trade. This era is unified, in part, by the limits of globalization in all its many forms, for while there were significant social and infrastructural innovations in many areas – particularly in transport and communications – the scope for enduring global interactions was constrained enormously by available technology. Moreover, it was an era in which globalization was characterized, primarily though not exclusively, by interregional or intercivilizational encounters within Eurasia; Oceania and the Americas remained autonomous civilizations, while there were negligible direct or regularized networks or flows binding together the western (Atlantic Europe), eastern (South East Asia and Japan) and southern (Southern Africa) edges of the Afro-Eurasian land mass.

The key agents of globalization in this epoch were threefold: political and military empires, world religions and the migratory movements of both nomadic steppe peoples and farming societies expanding into populated but uncultivated areas. Long-distance trade between regions and civilizations constituted a fourth, but a somewhat less intense source of globalization at this time. The formation of empires and the extension of military power and enduring political relations over large distances can be traced back to Sumeria in the third millennium before Christ. The geographical extent, longevity, initial strength and coherence of imperial systems differed markedly, as did their efforts and strategies to institutionalize these relations (on empires, see chapters 1 and 7). For the most part, however, these empires represented extremely limited forms of globalization. Most remained quite small and localized for much of the era. Indeed, in some ways the most successful and enduring of these imperial civilizations came to form the basis of the regions between which subsequent global-level encounters occured: Indic civilization, Han China, the Latin Roman Empire. Alongside these imperial formations the era witnessed the emergence, expansion and stabilization of what have come to be known as world religions. Their universal messages of salvation, their capacity to cross and unify cultural divisions, their infrastructure of theocracies and widely circulating holy texts constituted one of the great episodes of interregional and intercivilizational encounters (see chapter 7). However, while their reach exceeded that of nearly all early empires, world religions remained initially confined to one or two regions or civilizations. The emergence of Islam in the sixth century CE was an exception to this; it can perhaps be thought of as the first globalized world religion.

A third key agent of globalization was the sporadic but devastating pattern of movement and conquest that emerged from the nomadic empires of the central Eurasian steppes. These movements included the Germanic peoples who conquered the Latin Roman Empire in the fifth century CE before settling in Western Europe and North Africa, and from the twelfth to the fourteenth century, the Mongols. Devastation, forced migration, conquest and plague tended to follow each wave of invasion. Indeed, this era closes with the dissolution and weakening of many of the long-distance connections established in the prior millennium, fractured as a result of the fourteenth-century crises of the pandemic Black Death and the destruction and final fall of the Mongol empires. While, of course, all these great movements left permanent traces, institutions and practices in their wake, the initial military impact of these nomadic expansions often outweighed their lasting cultural, economic and political legacies. By contrast the slower moving but inexorable expansion of farming peoples and polities into territories occupied by hunter-gatherers left deeper historical imprints.

Globalization, defined in this context as interregional and intercivilizational encounters, operated predominantly in this era through the domains of military and cultural power and human migrations – specifically, empires of domination, world religions, nomadic invasions and agricultural expansion, accompanied by the movement of human diseases. Political interaction in terms of institutionalized, regularized rule and authority was far more difficult to establish and operated over much smaller radii than either military or cultural power. Forms of economic globalization persisted throughout the period. These were, alongside the spread of Islam, the only forms of social interaction to achieve significant elements of global extensity. Compared with subsequent eras, globalization in the premodern period might be best described as a form of 'thin globalization' (see the introduction). The civilizations of Oceania and America remained separate from Eurasia and Africa. In fact, the civilizations of these regions remained pretty much separate from each other, as witnessed by the very slow or non-existent diffusion of domesticated crops and technologies. While some contacts, flows and relationships existed between Eurasia and sub-Saharan Africa, the desert proved almost as effective in separating these regions as the oceans were in separating them all from the Americas. Islamic culture, small camel-trading routes across the desert and trading contacts across the Indian Ocean brought African civilizations into contact with Eurasia. Within Africa itself the southern expansion of Bantu agrarian civilization created long-distance flows of people and the diffusion of languages, metallurgy and agricultural techniques (Curtin, 1984). Nonetheless, the overwhelming majority of interregional and intercivilizational contacts and relationships occurred within Eurasia. The majority of trading, cultural and military relationships were established between the Islamic lands of the Levant and Near East, the central Asian steppes, Indic civilization and China.

Quantitative measures of the intensity of global flows, relative to local and regional flows, and accurate estimations of the velocity of movements in this era are virtually impossible to generate. As argued above, the impact of sporadic encounters, especially where previously separate civilizations, environments, gene pools, etc., were joined for the first time, can appear much greater than more stable global interactions. In any case, military and political networks were unable to sustain relationships of regularized rule over truly global distances. Where it was attempted – for example, the early Islamic caliphate and the Mongol empires of the thirteenth century – such rule proved fragile. But in some instances cultural and economic networks were sustained over longer distances, as the trans-Eurasian and Indian ocean trades, and the cross-continental Islamic world illustrated. Their impact, however, was more diffuse and limited than that of military and political expansion. The reach of new religious ideas was significant, though the limits of their transformative power are illuminated at the geographical edges of the world religions; almost invariably they were forced to make large theological and ritual accommodations to local animistic practice (Islam in the Indian Ocean and the Sahel, Christianity in the Celtic periphery) or to the influence of adjacent world religions (Buddhism and Confucianism in China). Elite contacts and relationships, though thinner than these encounters, were more intense, providing channels for larger collective dialogues and the circulation of new ideas and technologies. The impact of economic networks was less diffuse. Trade, and income from trade, were of course vital to the well-being of many of the states and elites that organized or bestrode the major trade routes of the era. They also provided an important conduit for intercivilizational cultural contact and technology transfer. But the vast majority of the world's population remained, in economic terms, substantially unaffected by these flows.

The infrastructures of globalization in this era were incredibly variable and uneven. Some parts of the world remained untouched by them altogether. Many areas outside the metropolitan centres had only the barest interconnections with the metropole let alone other more distant centres of power. The size and scale of imperial systems determined, to a great extent, the reach of any given infrastructure: Roman or Inca roads did not, after all, extend beyond the respective empire's frontiers. Infrastructures of overland transport remained in many ways unchanged throughout the period. Once animals had been domesticated or tamed to provide transport – horses, elephants, oxen, camels – the speed and density of travel could only be increased by securing peaceable routes and maintaining limited roads. But roadbuilding technologies and supplies and logistics along land routes barely improved on Roman efforts over the whole period. Canals, even in China, remained in their infancy and the basic reliance of road transport on animal power confined its uses, for economic purposes at any rate, to the movement of valuable prestige goods; this was exemplified by the trans-Eurasian routes from East Asia to the Levant such as the Silk Road (Abu-Lughod, 1989). Maritime technologies and transport saw some developments and innovations. Networks of trade and movement could be established at a transoceanic level rather than merely across the small enclosed seas of the ancient world. Muslim merchants crossed the Indian Ocean on a regular basis and established networks along the west coast of Africa and in the islands of South East Asia (Chaudhuri, 1985, 1990). Successive developments in writing, printing and text storage meant that these fragile infrastructures could support increased interaction and exchange between cultures, but this remained limited to fragments of the theocratic, military and political elites and the merchant adventurers and travellers. Thus the velocity of regularized global flows was low; messages, merchandise, officials and orders could only circulate as fast as unmechanized transport could move them. Military flows could move slightly faster than most, but still only at a minimal velocity.

Almost no institutionalized forms of global or even interregional or intercivilizational regulation emerged in this era. There are elements of an emerging diplomacy in some regions, and systems of regularized intercivilizational tribute existed, especially between China and its domains. There was also some cross-cultural regulation achieved by the existence of a shared religious outlook and institutionalized church and theocracy across Christian and Islamic lands; though in both cases fragmentation into different religious orthodoxies and political units was considerable. Beyond this, interregional and civilizational encounters remained, for the most part, ad hoc and conflictual rather than institutionalized and regulated. It is important in this era to distinguish between the impact of global flows – often one-off encounters or engagements between civilizations or regions – and the impact of sustained relationships. The impact of initial flows such as external invasions, proselytizing world religions or the arrival of pandemics was often immense, resulting in the collapse or dislocation of existing states. Examples of these flows include the barbarian invasions of Latin Europe, the initial impact of Islam on south-western Asia and North Africa, the impact of the Black Death on Han China, and the spread of military technologies across Eurasia in the wake of the Mongol invasions. Where, in addition, these flows were followed by the settlement of outsiders, the formation of new political systems and new economic patterns and practices, the impact was longer lasting. The impact of more sustained relationships like trade was concentrated. Trade was crucial to the size of state incomes and the fortunes of trading cities and classes, and had some lasting influence in a few regions on domestic production. However, for the most part, most of the world's populations existed outside these economic interactions.

Early Modern Globalization, circa 1500–1850

The beginning of the sixteenth century is the conventional starting date for what has been called the 'rise of the West': the historical processes which produced the emergence and development of the key institutions of European modernity, the acquisition by European peoples of technologies and power resources that eventually exceeded those available to any other civilization and the subsequent creation of European global empires (McNeill, 1963; Giddens, 1990). We emphasize that our account of globalization is neither a retelling of conventional accounts of the rise of the West nor an account of world history. We recognize the opportunist rather than predetermined quality of Western expansion, as well as its often fragile character. We also recognize the degree to which European innovation and expansion was based on the importation and adaptation of Eurasian technologies rather than indigenous innovation alone. European expansion in this era was not truly global; it was overwhelmingly located in the Americas and Oceania. Europeans were able to defeat and conquer the empires and stateless societies of Oceania, North America and the Caribbean as well as the agrarian states of Mesoamerica and the Andes. However, their capacity to penetrate either Africa or Asia was very much more limited. Moreover, as this unequal pattern of global expansion suggests, power relations between Europe and its American colonies and the major states and civilizations of the Islamic lands, India and East Asia remained finely balanced for much of this era. Nonetheless, the creation of European empires in the Americas in the sixteenth and seventeenth centuries and in Oceania in the eighteenth and nineteenth brought these previously separate continents and regions firmly within the ambit of new and distinctive global relations. Alongside this a series of developments in the European and North American heartlands had simultaneously begun to create the social innovations that would transform, and intensify, this phase of globalization.

Globalization in this period was led by demographic, environmental and epidemiological flows between Europe, the Americas and Oceania. These were reinforced by more enduring political and military relationships and the formation of European global empires. New forms of economic globalization also began to gather pace, such as those initiated by the great trading companies (see chapter 5). By the mid-nineteenth century European peoples, empires, religions, flora, fauna and microbes had transformed the Americas and the Caribbean and were getting to work on Australia and the rest of Oceania. Thinly populated outposts had been established on the West African coast and in southern Africa. In southern Asia, the British presence in India was becoming more entrenched, while further to the east a thin European influence had established itself in the islands and archipelagos of South East Asia: the Spanish in the Philippines, the Dutch in Java, the Portuguese in Macau and Timor. Across the vast plains and tundra of Central Asia and Siberia, Russian presence and power steadily increased, reaching the Pacific coast.

Between these nodes of European empire ran the thickening sinews of global economic interaction, though in Eurasia, with the exception of the European capture of part of the spice trade, many interregional trading patterns remained for some time much as they had been before. Over time the European colonial corporations – like the Dutch and English East India companies – came to regularize many aspects of colonial trade and economic interaction, before their dissolution towards the end of this period and their replacement by colonial government. In the Atlantic the early bullion trades from the Americas and the triangular slave trade and associated trades between Africa, the Americas and Europe were at their peak in the sixteenth to eighteenth centuries. Indeed, for two centuries the Atlantic slave trade had been the core of transatlantic economic interaction, but by the end of this era it dwindled to almost nothing (see chapters 3 and 6). In its place there was emerging, in the wake of European and American industrialization, a more intense trade in raw materials, agricultural products and manufactured goods; this was accompanied by the evolution of international banking institutions and a small but increasing flow of capital investment from Britain into the Americas.

We argued above that in the premodern era the intensity of global flows and interconnections was generally low when compared to more local interactions and networks. Sporadic flows and the initial encounters between separate societies and civilizations could produce intense one-off interconnections, but the institutionalization and regularization of military and political power across continents were difficult and only sustainable on a regional, albeit often a large regional, basis. Economic and cultural networks were easier to sustain, but the interconnections were almost exclusively between elites. In the early modern era this pattern is generally reproduced, but in the context of a changing global balance of power and the European conquest of the previously isolated Americas and Oceania. Thus, while European military and technical power could be thrust at the societies of the Americas in a devastating transatlantic movement, European states were unable to maintain either de facto or de jure control over many of their colonial possessions. By the end of this era, the American colonies had broken with Britain, and most of Latin America had established independence from Spain and Portugal. Control over the Caribbean and Canadian remnants of these empires was limited. It is possible to argue that global economic interactions were becoming more intense – certainly for those states and societies most closely enmeshed with transatlantic trade and migration. The bullion shipments from the Americas to Iberia were of such a size that the monetary system of these states was overwhelmed (Braudel, 1984). While the definitive relationship between the slave trade, the plantation economies and European capital accumulation and industrialization has yet to be decisively resolved, it is clear that these global economic interactions had more impact than merely expanding the range of elite consumption and financing state expenditure

(Solow and Engerman, 1988; Blackburn, 1997). In north-western Europe new domestic industries and banking, trading and insurance companies and systems all arose on this wave of economic interaction.

For most of this era the infrastructures of globalization, both transport and communication, were based on technologies little different from those of the previous epoch. The spread of mechanized printing into Europe certainly aided the circulation and density of cultural exchanges. By the end of the era, railways, mechanized iron ships and advances in canal and road building were making interconnections over large distances easier. But none of these technologies had been extended much beyond the borders of a few core Western states. However, the expansion of European economies allowed all these technologies, particularly oceanic shipping, to be used more intensely than before. Military and political infrastructures decisively expanded their reach, stretching from Europe to the Americas and Oceania (see chapters 1 and 2). The formation of linked markets across the Atlantic and from Europe across Africa to the east was significant too in that it allowed European merchants gradually to evade the Islamic lands (see chapter 3). This was accompanied by the early transnational corporations such as the Dutch and British East Indies companies, albeit radically different in their structure and operation from contemporary MNCs (see chapter 5). But the velocity of flows within these more stable infrastructures of interchange and rule were still limited to the speed of the ship and the horse.

Once again, the degree to which these global relationships were institutionalized and regulated remained very limited. Within Europe an interstate system of diplomacy and reciprocal recognition was emerging alongside aspects of the multilateral regulation of interstate behaviour through developments such as the Concert of Europe. This European society of states also sought, incrementally and by various methods, to extend the 'standards of civilization' beyond Europe and its imperial outposts (Watson, 1992, 1997). Simultaneously, the reach of the institutions of the Roman Catholic church was greatly extended, though – as with the colonies and dependencies of European states – the potential of the centre to control the periphery meaningfully was very limited. The capacity of the peripheral outposts of European empires to operate without due attention to local circumstances and institutions was equally small.

As with the premodern era of globalization, initial contacts and solitary flows could prove devastating and transformative, while the impact of more sustained relationships was often less transparent or immediate. The initial arrival of Europeans in Latin America with their collection of Eurasian flora, fauna and microbes was a shatteringly important event for the indigenous peoples (see chapters 6 and 8). Longer term flows of migration to the Americas and from Russia to Siberia had less immediate effect but eventually resulted in profound demographic, ecological and political shifts in these regions. The impact of the slave trade on African societies varied as some societies collapsed or disintegrated while others thrived on collaboration. But the hinterland of the African continent remained closed to external influences. In Asia the impact of these global interconnections, outside of India, remained muted. The cultural, military and political strength of the main powers in the region remained sufficient for most of the period such that global linkages were minimized and had little domestic impact at all.

Perhaps the greatest impact of these global encounters was on Europe itself. Although the economic history remains disputed, it seems reasonable to argue that access to the wealth and surplus of the New World, the demographic relief provided by transatlantic migration, and the stimulus of interimperial rivalry all contributed to the development of new power technologies and institutions within Europe, forces that would be fully unleashed across the world in the second half of the nineteenth century.

In chapter 6, on migrations of people, we argued that for the greater part of human history centre and periphery and urban and rural provide a better model of thinking about political space than one clearly demarcated by fixed political borders. But during this epoch we see the emergence in Europe of new forms of territoriality and the emergence of the idea, if not always the reality, of fixed and demarcated borders enclosing a sovereign and autonomous state (see chapter 1 on state and border formation). The development of sovereign territorial states, and their relationship with nations, stretches across our eras of globalization (see chapter 7 on the early modern antecedents of nations, states and nationalism). But it is reasonable to assert that these processes did not become fully entrenched in Europe – let alone outside Europe – until the mid-nineteenth century. We pick up the story of state and border formation and its relationship to globalization below. It is this, as much as the new forms and the growing intensity of globalization, that marks a major shift between the early modern and modern eras.

Modern Globalization, circa 1850–1945

While the three and a half centuries prior to 1850 had seen the establishment of some extensive, and increasingly intensive, global networks and flows, predominantly under the control of European powers, the subsequent period witnessed an enormous acceleration in their spread and entrenchment. Within the West, the hundred years from the mid-eighteenth century had seen a whirlwind of structural economic and political transformation. European societies acquired, or began to acquire, industrialized capitalist economies, enormously advanced weaponry and naval technologies, and increasingly powerful state institutions. Exploiting these innovations, the reach of Western global empires, and thus also Western economic power and cultural influence, exploded. European power stretched into almost all of the areas of the globe it had found inaccessible (sub-Saharan Africa) or from which it had been actively excluded (East Asia): the scramble for Africa, the dismemberment of China, the colonization of much of North Africa and South East Asia and the opening of Japan all followed.

In the context of this enormous expansion of global political and military relations, the era saw very extensive, intensive and socially significant patterns of economic globalization – global trade and investment soared. The great transatlantic migrations from Europe to the New World peaked in a great surge of humanity before the start of the First World War. The decline of the slave trade opened up the possibility for enormous waves of indentured labour to leave Asia in search of work in North and South America and in European colonies in Oceania, Asia, Africa and the Caribbean. Cultural patterns and interconnections also intensified, as new technologies of communication and transport – railways and telegraph – were diffused and the threat and consolidation of European empire across the globe forced other societies into an unequal cultural encounter with the West. It was an era that also saw the beginnings of a new wave of international environmental interconnections as small-scale transboundary pollution began in Europe, tropical deforestation organized under imperial auspices gathered pace, and the global spread of industrialism and fossil fuel use began to transform, unknowingly at the time, the composition of the atmosphere. This era of intensified and multifaceted globalization was to be brought to a rapid and abrupt halt by the First World War.

The defining feature of this epoch was the political and military reach of European and American empires which achieved their furthest extent, creating a truly global network of interconnections, albeit fragmented by imperial rivalries. The British Empire was entrenched in the White Dominions, the Caribbean and India and spread to Burma, the Pacific Islands and outposts in China and across southern and eastern Africa. Similarly, the French expanded into Indo-China, took control of much of North Africa, and claimed parts of the Pacific and much of West Africa. The American Republic finally reached the Pacific coastline, closed the frontier and in a burst of almost effortless imperial expansion acquired the apparently barren state of Alaska from the Russians and annexed the Midway Islands in the north-central Pacific. Following the defeat of the Spanish in the war of 1898, American control extended to the Hawaiian Islands, the Wake Islands, Guam and the Philippines. In these respects, this was an era in which coercive forms of globalization acquired a truly global reach. Alongside these patterns of political and military globalization, an enormous network of international economic interactions and flows emerged that were genuinely global in their extent. Trade and investment rocketed to new historic levels, and despite significant economic flows between developed countries, most economic exchange was between imperial centres and the periphery. Similarly, migration patterns became more global as the transatlantic migrations grew; they were parallel, for example, to the massive Asian diasporas of the era that sent Indians to the Caribbean, Africa and the Pacific Islands, the Chinese to North America and South East Asia and the Japanese to Latin America.

Across a whole range of domains, the intensity of global relationships increased. This is clearest in the realms of trade, investment and migration. Trade to GDP ratios among developed countries and in particular economic sectors reached new peaks (see chapter 3). High levels of organized overseas investment were vital to the industrialization and infrastructural development of the US, parts of Eastern Europe, Scandinavia and parts of Latin America (see chapter 4). Absolute numbers of migrants and ratios of migrants to home and host populations were equally substantial (see chapter 6 on the transatlantic migrations and the Asian diasporas). Their economic impact was considerable. American industrialization thrived on incoming streams of cheap labour, while European industrialization was faster and more socially quiescent than it might have been, given the escape valve of migration for the poor, landless and unemployed. The intensity of political control over great distances also increased. The increased size, coherence and power of metropolitan states combined with faster transport and telegraphic communications allowed more systematic imperial policies to be pursued, though these remained weak by comparison to the degree of control and power states could achieve at home. The impact of cultural interconnections was also intense but quite different from that of earlier periods. For this period saw the circulation, diffusion and imposition of secular Western ideologies and discourses; earlier eras had been predominantly characterized by theological and religious discourses. As we argued in chapter 7, the impacts of Marxism, liberalism, nationalism and science, although fragmentary at first and concentrated exclusively on elite groups, would eventually significantly transform (though by no means extinguish) the cultures, identities and social practices of peoples all over the world.

Underlying this political, economic and cultural globalization was the development of new infrastructures of transportation and control which, combined with an international environment in which peace rather than war was the temporary norm, added considerably to its momentum. From 1850 to 1914 a wave of innovations began to link imperial systems together and to each other; railways and mechanized shipping were the technological key to this. Railways finally lifted the impediments and constraints of animal-based land transport. Bulk flows across land of agricultural and manufactured products – rather than merely a trickle of prestige goods – became economically feasible. Political and military control could be extended from coastal outposts into the interior of landlocked societies. The shift from sail to steam along with the construction of the Panama and Suez canals combined to reduce dramatically the distance and hazards of key oceanic shipping routes. The transport costs (and some of the uncertainties) of international trade and migration fell precipitously and volumes rose. While pigeon-based message systems had been used quite widely in Europe in the eighteenth and early nineteenth centuries, and some private international postal systems had been established there as well, global communication infrastructures were transformed both by the transportation revolution of the era and the creation of transoceanic telegraphy; an infrastructure that dramatically raised the velocity of communication. Political, military and economic elites with access to these networks were more closely and quickly informed about distant events than ever before. With the advent of mass literacy and a popular press in some societies, so also were sections of the public.

Unlike earlier eras, the modern period of globalization was characterized by a much greater level of institutionalization. Migratory flows, for example, were more systematically controlled by government and private agencies in both home and host countries, with more organized labour markets at work and more regular systems of transportation (see chapter 6). Economic interactions came to be governed by a developing set of international financial institutions – primarily multinational banks and, of course, the Gold Standard system; neither of these have parallels in any earlier era. In addition, a whole wave of international political institutions were developed to regulate common problems and concerns, including postal systems, navigation systems, weights and measures and telegraphic communications (see chapter 1; and Murphy, 1994).

In this era, the question of stratification is less ambiguous than before. The dominant powers of the world made and remade global interconnections, controlled the infrastructures that supported them and devised and controlled the institutions that regulated them. Among these Western states an uneasy balance of power and a shifting pattern of alliance and rivalry existed. Beyond the core of great powers, other states and societies were subordinated within these global networks but in different ways and with varying degrees of impact. The impact of global relations varied considerably across domains of interaction and with the differential involvement of states and societies in these domains. We have already discussed a number of them above, but the key impacts of the era include:

- Politico-military effects: many non-European states and elites declined or were destroyed. The threat of potential European domination also induced domestic modernization in some states which escaped direct colonization (Turkey, Japan, China).

- Trade and investment: economic growth and structural change were stimulated in core Western states, the path of economic development was decisively shaped in some colonies, and the means were provided for late industrial development in peripheral Europe and North and Latin America.
- Migration: demographic transformation was brought to the Americas and some European colonies, while Europe acquired a social safety valve.
- Culture: Christianity spread to parts of Africa and East Asia; Western secular ideologies and discourses circulated to the rest of the world – helping to stimulate the emergence of nationalist and communist movements, and a reconfiguration of traditional beliefs among elites.

This era of globalization was brought to a decisive end by the First World War. This may seem paradoxical, for the war involved immense imperial mobilizations by the French and British (see chapter 2). The war also saw powers in the Americas, Asia and Europe drawn together into the same conflagration. But from the perspective of globalization it was the fall-out of the war that had the most lasting impacts. In the decades after the war international trade, investment and production collapsed. Small revivals in the 1920s were undercut by the Great Depression of the 1930s. Although the impact of the Wall Street crash and the depression indicated the degree to which the world remained economically interdependent, the result was a fracturing of what was left of the global economy into imperial blocs. The Gold Standard system and patterns of free trade disappeared to be replaced by imperial preference and, in the case of the newly founded Soviet Union and the Third Reich, explicit economic autarchy (see chapters 3 and 4).

The interwar period did witness the emergence of some global political institutions and potential mechanisms of global governance – like the League of Nations – but, as with attempts to establish global economic institutions, these were undermined from the outset by imperial rivalry and later by the rising tide of autarchy and aggressive nationalism that swept across Europe and beyond. Outside the West the imperial and political structures of the era remained notionally in place, joined by an expanding Japanese imperialism in the East. But in all these imperial formations the spread of Western cultural discourses was helping to shape the forces and movements that would blow these imperial machines asunder. It would take the Second World War to sufficiently weaken Japan and the European powers that their global imperia could be finally dismantled. In their place arose a hegemonic USA which would establish the formal and informal structures of global governance alongside which a renewed wave of globalization, supported by new technologies and infrastructures of interaction, would cross a world dominated, not by amorphous empires, but by territorially demarcated nation-states.

Contemporary Globalization

In the period since 1945 there has been a renewed wave of global flows and interconnections. The impact of the Second World War, as well as subsequent events, have been sufficiently important that we can consider the postwar era as a distinctive historical form of globalization rather than as a return, as many sceptics suggest, to nineteenth-century patterns. Of course, in terms of the extensity of global linkages, the appearance is one of catching up; a return to the *status quo ante* of the classical Gold Standard era. But we argue that in nearly all domains contemporary patterns of globalization have not only quantitatively surpassed those of earlier epochs, but have also displayed unparalleled qualitative differences – that is in terms of how globalization is organized and reproduced. In addition, we argue that the contemporary era represents a historically unique confluence or clustering of patterns of globalization in the domains of politics, law and governance, military affairs, cultural linkages and human migrations, in all dimensions of economic activity and in shared global environmental threats. Moreover, this era has experienced extraordinary innovations in the infrastructures of transport and communication, and an unparalleled density of institutions of global governance and regulation. Paradoxically, this explosion of global flows and networks has occurred at a time when the sovereign territorial state, with fixed and demarcated borders, has become the near universal form of human political organization and political rule.

Contemporary globalization was shaped profoundly by the structural consequences of the Second World War: the defeat of the Axis powers, the exhaustion of the old European imperial powers, and the emergence of the US–Soviet Cold War which transformed the global power structure. Military power and military relations assumed entrenched and global proportions. The strategic space of geopolitics became truly global, and patterns of arms transfers, military technology transfers and alliance systems followed (see chapter 2). Simultaneously, a new world political order emerged based on the United Nations and its core institutions and agencies (see chapter 1). This global architecture of military and political relationships oversaw the disintegration of European empires and an immense wave of decolonization, independence and state formation across sub-Saharan Africa, the Middle East and North Africa, southern and eastern Asia and the Pacific. By the 1990s the basic political unit of the world was overwhelmingly the territorial nation-state, though it displayed considerable variations in internal coherence, strength and degrees of autonomy. With the end of the Cold War and the break-up of the Soviet Union, one of the world's last imperial structures gave way to a new mosaic of nation-states.

By the close of the twentieth century, empires, once the principal form of political rule and world political organization, had given way to a worldwide system of nation-states, overlaid by multilateral, regional and global systems of regulation and governance. Moreover, whereas previous epochs were dominated by the collective or divided hegemony of Western powers, the contemporary era can claim to have only a single potential hegemonic power: the United States. Yet, despite its potential for global hegemony following the end of the Cold War, the US has abandoned any pretensions to global empire or overt hegemony since its enormous structural power has remained deeply inscribed into the nature and functioning of the present world order. In this respect, the contemporary epoch is historically unique in so far as patterns of globalization, unlike earlier periods, are no longer associated with, or reliant on, the expansionary logic or coercive institutions of empire. This is not to argue that contemporary globalization is somehow more benign than in the past, but rather to acknowledge that its political shell and causal dynamics are quite distinctive. In part this is because new infrastructures and means of global surveillance and governance (political control) have transformed the terms on which, and mechanisms through which, the structure of global power relations is reproduced and contested.

Within this paradoxical structure of increasingly global political and military rela-tionships and increasingly demarcated, territorial nation-states, a wave of other types of globalization has characterized the era. Alongside the initial political and military institutions of American hegemony stand the economic institutions of the immediate postwar era collectively known as the Bretton Woods system. Combining regulated international financial transactions with extensive free trade and American overseas investment, this regime governed economic interactions in the West and beyond until its collapse in the early 1970s. However, unlike its interwar counterparts, the demise of the BWS did not lead to a phase of economic autarchy but, on the contrary, helped to unleash a period of even more intense economic globalization in which reformed BWS institutions have continued to play a major role. Both the OPEC oil crises and the massive influx of petrodollars into international banking institutions highlighted the increasingly global dimensions of economic interaction. The combination of these events with new communications infrastructures and a wave of neoliberal deregulation, initi-ally among core Western economies, encouraged an explosion of global trade, invest-ment and financial flows (see chapters 3, 4 and 5). While much of this has been conducted between the three centres of the advanced capitalist economies (North America, Asia-Pacific, Western Europe), there has been an increasing enmeshment of many other areas – particularly where industrialization has been successfully initiated.

Interestingly, alongside this more liberal world economic order tighter mechanisms of multilateral economic surveillance and regional supervision developed. In this regard, the intensification of economic globalization has been associated with an intensification of global economic surveillance, enhanced supervisory activity and the deepening of international regulatory activity, for instance through the WTO. The deregulation of national economies has been accompanied by new forms of regulation in the global domain. Yet these developments did not receive a boost while US hegemonic power was at its apogee, but while it experienced relative decline. In this context, the present era may be distinguished from the past in so far as the rhythm of globalization appears no longer to be correlated directly with the rise and decline of a single hegemonic power or bloc (Keohane, 1984a). Contemporary patterns of economic globalization reflect a cumulative tendency, in the context of new multilateral infrastructures of regulation and control, towards more self-organizing and market-driven arrangements, which tend only to receive overt political direction by a hegemonic power at times of crisis.

Contemporary globalization has also heralded a shift in patterns of global migration. For most of the three decades following the Second World War migrations had been from the peripheries of Europe and its ex-colonies to the labour-hungry economies of Northern and Western Europe. While these continued, albeit at a slower rate, after the slowdown in economic growth of the early 1970s, they were joined by new patterns of global migration. These included an explosion in refugee and asylum movements; Latin American and Asian migration to North America, and flows of labour from across the Middle East and South Asia to the newly enriched Gulf states.

The global spread of industrial production and consumption has combined with the eventual toxic returns on the West's industrial revolutions to create forms of environ-mental globalization that are unprecedented. The era of the Cold War, the UN and the global economy has been accompanied by a recognition of the massive transforma-tions being undergone by the global commons – in the climatic system, the atmosphere, the oceans and the polar regions. In addition, the degree of domestic environmental degradation has in many places risen to such an extent that the possibility of environmental overspill has increased and incidences of transboundary pollution, such as acid rain and the trade in toxic and nuclear wastes, have risen (see chapter 8).

As pollution and threats of pollution have crossed the newly minted borders in the postwar world with impunity, so have the new networks of global communications (chapter 7). The postwar era has seen the development of older technologies like undersea cables, radio and television, and older trades, like the international film and publishing businesses, as well the creation of new technologies such as satellites and computers. These have transformed the velocity and reach of cultural and social interactions of all kinds. Whereas the vast majority of cultural interactions in previous eras were elite to elite, the majority of postwar interactions have been through popular cultural media and artefacts; this has been accompanied by the emergence of unique transnational media corporations. These do have some precedents in the modern era's international news agencies and publishing houses, but their reach, diversity and power are of a different order (chapter 7). Reverberations from these changes have registered across economic, political and other domains of life as different forms of social power and social infrastructure intertwine with and are shaped by them. It is hardly surprising, then, that in a world of intensified globalization there have been the most significant historical attempts to regulate and institutionalize global flows and networks with a plethora of international laws, treaties, organizations, political networks and alliances, accompanying all of these different domains of interconnectedness (see chapter 1; on the environment see chapter 8).

Much of this book has examined the contours and character of different domains of globalization with a view to exploring their impact on the sovereignty and autonomy of nation-states; a summary of this is the task of the next part of the conclusion. In the remainder of this part, we confine ourselves to drawing out the main differences between the contemporary era and other periods of globalization, focusing on differences that are not merely quantitative but indicate significant transformations in the organizational form of globalization and its implications for social life.

In earlier eras when territory and sovereignty were less closely linked, core and periphery, metropole and colony were, as we have noted, useful models for describing political space. As such, many interregional and global flows transformed and extended those areas rather than necessarily crossing boundaries. Today, historically unprecedented levels of global flows and interconnections cross a world that is almost universally made up of nation-states. The near universality of the nation-state is paralleled by the extensity of globalization in nearly all domains. Environmental degradation of the global commons reaches, albeit unevenly, into every corner of the planet. The international trading system – particularly since the collapse of Soviet and East European communism and the opening of China – encompasses almost every state on the map (see chapter 3). Cultural products and technologies – like films and television programmes – circulate on every continent. No state is disconnected completely from global telecommunications networks. This pattern of interconnectedness is unique to the current era. That said, the enmeshment of different states and of different social groups within those nation-states, and their relative levels of control over those flows, remains highly uneven.

The intensity of global flows and interconnections relative to national and local networks remains variable across domains and states. Few states, like North Korea, have chosen to insulate themselves from these flows as far as is possible; though even

North Korea has not been able to sit entirely outside of geostrategic networks and regimes. Our case study material has been focused on a few core OECD states, which in some areas, in particular, gives an impression of rising intensity that is not always borne out in the rest of the world. Nonetheless, our evidence does highlight an increasing intensity of global flows in a number of areas. The intensity of global trading networks is generally on the rise both in terms of global trade in relation to world production and, for many countries, in terms of levels of trade in relation to national GDP. More sectors of Western economies are more dependent on exports for sales, and on imports for intermediate goods and parts. Moreover, these trends are unlikely to abate significantly as the Internet turns the corner shop into a potential global supermarket. The trading volume of the global currency markets relative to national currency reserves has intensified, as has the dependence of governments and corporations on international capital markets for raising investment funds. Levels of foreign direct investment may for a few countries still be less intense than at the height of the nineteenth century, but the complexity and extensiveness of networks of global production far exceed that of earlier eras; furthermore, among OECD states, the volume of national exports, employment, output and technology investment controlled by domestic MNCs and overseas subsidiaries is unprecedented (chapter 5).

The immense increase in global and regional interactions of all kinds has been supported by a series of transformations in the infrastructure of global interaction. We emphasize that the invention of some of these technologies is not sufficient by itself to account for their deployment, use and growth; but their contribution to both the increased volume and transformed character of contemporary globalization is undeniable. In terms of transport infrastructure the postwar era has witnessed the intensified use and global spread of older technologies like the internal combustion engine and railways. It has also seen the development of new forms of transport that are considerably quicker, or considerably more efficient, for moving bulk goods over long distances: jet airliners and containerized shipping, respectively. These have combined to increase massively the interaction capacity of separate states and societies. They have contributed to declining unit costs and diminished opportunity costs in crossing huge distances. As a consequence, these transport networks are more difficult for states or elites to monopolize or control and more open and accessible to bigger publics than in previous epochs: witness the expansion of global tourism, the inability of states to control migration fully or to prevent drug trafficking across international land borders.

A parallel set of factors is at work in the development of communication technologies and systems. The postwar era has again seen the fruition of older technologies like television, radio and telephony and the creation of new infrastructures such as fibre-optic cable, satellites and digitization. In addition, the contemporary era's cultural and communicative global infrastructure is distinguished from earlier epochs by the dominance of a single language – English – as a genuine global lingua franca among elites; the central role of private corporations in the production, regulation and transmission of culture, and the diminished role of churches and states; and mass publics as the audience for cultural exports rather than elites.

Whether global interaction networks are managed more benignly than they were through the imperial structures of the late nineteenth century is a moot point. What is certain is that the density and degree of the institutionalization of global flows and networks, the regularity and predictability of many connections and interactions, and the sheer volume of institutions and regimes of regional and global governance are unique. The enormous number of intergovernmental organizations, international treaties, international non-governmental organizations, etc., is primarily a postwar phenomenon (see chapter 1). Similarly, the pattern of stratification of contemporary globalization is quite distinct from that of earlier eras. In the first place, the enormous confluence of different forms of globalization has created variegated patterns of unevenness and hierarchy. In the domain of political and military affairs most of the contemporary era has been dominated by the bipolar world of the Cold War. This generated a very explicit hierarchy of powers – core allies, client states and notionally non-aligned states. In the aftermath of the Cold War, the global military hierarchy is uniquely dominated by the USA around whom a range of secondary powers have created a much more multipolar world. In the economic domain stratification has been predominantly between OECD and non-OECD states and within the OECD the largest economies – the G7 – have had the greatest control of the global networks and global infrastructures. With the collapse of Bretton Woods, the dominance of the USA in this sphere has again given way to a more multipolar world. In the last two decades, the industrialization of East Asia and Latin America, and the creation of global free trade networks have looked set – despite periods of economic turmoil – to rearrange the structure of power within global economic networks once again. Moreover, the old North–South hierarchy has given way to a more complex geometry of global economic and productive power relations – a new global division of labour (see chapters 3 to 5). North and South are increasingly becoming meaningless categories: under conditions of globalization distributional patterns of power and wealth no longer accord with a simple core and periphery division of the world, as in the early twentieth century, but reflect a new geography of power and privilege which transcends political borders and regions, reconfiguring established international and transnational hierarchies of social power and wealth.

In environmental terms, the stratification of global affairs takes on a different geography. On the one hand, the North/South, OECD/non-OECD divide describes the massively inequitable consumption of resources in the world, but the distribution of threats and exposure to risks is much more complex. Severe environmental problems, from ozone depletion to global warming, haunt nearly all corners of the earth, while many other environmental hazards – such as acid rain, toxic waste pollution and attacks on biodiversity – are unevenly spread (see chapter 8). Finally, in the realm of culture and cultural flows, the division of the world into the West and the rest that characterized the nineteenth century has endured to a considerable extent. However, the cultural flows and cultural infrastructures that have emerged are different in key respects. First, the old imperial networks of telecommunications have been eroded and replaced with private and more universal networks. Second, the role of the USA in the production and transmission of both elite and popular cultures is much more dominant than in earlier epochs. Finally, there have been some significant shifts in these flows as cultural identities, ideas, artefacts and popular cultural products have become more diverse.

In sum, although there exist important continuities with previous phases of globalization, contemporary patterns of globalization constitute a distinctive historical form which is itself a product of a unique conjuncture of social, political, economic and technological forces. Its fundamental features can be described in the following terms:

- *spatio-temporal* – the historically unprecedented extensity, intensity, velocity and impact propensity of global flows, interactions and networks embracing all social domains;

- *organizational* – the unprecedented institutionalization and organization of world-wide social, political and economic power relations through new infrastructures of control and communication. Globalization is far from being simply 'out of control' and is, on the contrary, the object of new forms of multilateral regulation and multilayered governance;

- *conjunctural* – the unique confluence of globalizing influences in all aspects of social life from the political through the ecological;

- *diverse modalities* – the growing significance of differentiated patterns of migration, cultural and ecological globalization alongside the enduring presence of military, economic and political aspects of globalization dominant in the late nineteenth century;

- *reflexivity* – a developing worldwide elite and popular consciousness of global interconnectedness reinforced by the globalization of communications infrastructures and the mass media industries. By comparison with the late nineteenth century, when globalization was defined as a coercive project of global empire-building or geopolitics, globalization today reflects the varied and self-conscious political or economic projects of national elites and transnational social forces pursuing often conflicting visions of world order;

- *contestation* – the growing awareness of globalization has encouraged its contestation in all spheres from the cultural to the military, as states, citizens and social movements seek to resist or manage its impacts. Moreover, the institutionalization of world politics has transformed the politics of contesting and managing globalization, which at the turn of the century was a purely internal imperial matter, into a global politics of agenda-setting, coalition building and multilateral regulation;

- *regionalization* – whereas the early twentieth century witnessed the expansion of global empires, the late twentieth century has experienced their dissolution and a significant regionalization of world economic, political, and military relations. But unlike earlier periods when empires and blocs sought autonomous development, contemporary processes of regionalization and globalization have become largely mutually reinforcing tendencies within the global political economy;

- *Westernization* – much of the history of globalization has been the story of Westernization and its contestation across the globe. Although still highly asymmetrical, contemporary patterns of globalization, whether in the military, financial, cultural, ecological, political or productive domains, by comparison with those at the turn of the century, have become less Eurocentric or Atlantic-centric;

- *territoriality* – globalization, as evident in the great political shifts discussed in chapter 1, has consistently contributed across the centuries to the drawing and redrawing of borders and political jurisdictions. But the reorganization of economic, social, cultural and ecological space implied by contemporary patterns of globalization, in the context of territorially fixed and exclusive political communities, challenges the territorial principle as the sole or primary basis for the organization of political rule and the exercise of political authority. Territory and territoriality thus remain as highly politicized as they were in the epoch of global empires, although today the 'threats' to the territorial integrity of the nation-state are no longer simply external or military; military power is no longer the sole, rational or effective instrument for resolving or managing many of the new cross-border challenges. Contemporary globalization is, accordingly, associated with a very different kind of politics of territoriality;

- *state forms* – different historical forms of globalization have been associated with quite different state forms. By comparison with the early twentieth century contemporary government is 'big government' in so far as states spend a significant proportion of the national income, employ significant numbers of people, and have wide-ranging responsibility not just for the management of the economy but also the security and welfare of their citizens. As a consequence, globalization has arguably a more visible political impact on SIACS today compared with the less interventionist and less welfare-oriented states of the pre-1914 era. Furthermore, the domestic politics of adjusting to, managing or mediating the impacts of global-ization (as with free trade) differ significantly now from that of the era of the imperial states of the late nineteenth century, although it is important not to ex-aggerate such differences.

- *democratic governance* – by comparison with previous epochs contemporary globalization unfolds against the backdrop of a global states system in which the majority of states claim to be democratic, but in which the democratic principle is only rarely extended to cover aspects of multilateral regulation and global govern-ance. Globalization today thus raises an entirely novel set of political and normative dilemmas which have no real equivalents in previous epochs, namely, how to com-bine a system of territorially rooted democratic governance with the transnational and global organization of social and economic life.

In short, contemporary globalization has some of the attributes of what in the intro-duction was referred to as 'thick globalization' (see pp. 21–7). This is especially so with regard to the extensity, intensity and velocity of political, economic and cultural flows and connections: see grids C.1 and C.2 (impact propensity is dealt with in grid C.3). If these trends continue to develop, alongside their growing institutionalization and organizational entrenchment they will increasingly bear the hallmarks of 'thick' global flows and interaction networks. However, the developmental trajectory of these pro-cesses remains uncertain because they depend both on a specific conjuncture of histor-ical circumstances and impacts which are complex and highly differentiated. In this respect, the present dominance of neoliberal globalization is not as secure as either many of its strongest proponents or its critics suggest. As the contagion effects of regional economic crisis in East Asia came to threaten global stability in the late 1990s, the limits to, and reactions against, the neoliberal project became increasingly trans-parent. Whether this crisis portends a further transformation – in Polanyi's terms a new 'double movement' – in the historical form of globalization remains to be disclosed. But several possibilities are manifest in the current conjuncture: from a shift towards a more highly regulated form of globalization, through a form of thin globalization (as protectionism, exclusionary regionalism and nationalism gain the upper hand), to a more predatory form of neoliberal economic globalization (see chapters 3 and 4).

Grid C.1 Key global flows and networks

	Premodern	Early modern	Modern	Contemporary
Key global flows and networks	Early imperial systems World religions Nomadic empires and agrarian expansion Plagues and pandemics Long-distance trade	Political and military expansion Europe and New World: demographic, environmental, epidemiological flows Development of European global empires New transatlantic economic exchanges	European global empires, military, political, cultural flows – geopolitics Global circulation of Western secular discourses and ideologies Transatlantic migrations, Asian diasporas World economy	Formation of Cold War and post-Cold War global military relationships, systems of regional and global governance and international law Pre- and post-Bretton Woods economic globalization: trade, financial markets, multinational production and investment, technology transfer Global environmental threats: global commons, interdependence, transboundary pollution New patterns of global migration Global spread of media MNCs, Western popular culture and discourses New global networks of communication and transport
States, borders and territories	All borders fuzzy and indeterminate Migrations and other movements tend not to be across borders but reshape political space; this continues into next two eras	Proto-nations and modern absolutist and constitutional states emerging in Europe First national revolutions towards the end of the period (France, USA) Kingdoms, empires and fractured overlapping 'sovereignty' still dominant forms in Europe, similarly outside of Europe	Nation-states develop in West and Latin America European and indigenous empires, and kingdoms dominant elsewhere	Nation-state dominant political unit Emerging regional units Multilayered governance

Grid C.2 Dominant attributes of historical forms of globalization: in sum

	Premodern	Early modern	Modern	Contemporary
Extensity	Majority of flows trans-Eurasian only, some interregional and intercivilizational	More global in some respects as America and Oceania more connected to Eurasia More interconnections between Europe and Middle East, and Africa too	Increasingly global: European empires bring East Asia and Africa more fully into global networks; East looks outwards Global economy spreads out from Atlantic triangle	Most key domains global. Some networks, relations truly global, such as global warming, some very nearly global, like trade
Intensity	Flows, intense but transitory Entrenched relationships, low intensity diminishing over distance	Flows, intense but transitory Entrenched political relationships remain low intensity: transatlantic empires fragment Intensity rising in transatlantic economies and other global economic linkages	New enduring political and military global empires and networks established Intensity in economic and cultural impact rises sharply	Very high in economic and environmental terms Culturally more intensive and pervasive in public domain Migration less intense than in earlier epoch but growing towards equivalence with it
Velocity	Low	Low	Medium	High for transport and communications, and in some cases instantaneous and in real time (television, financial markets) *continued*

Grid C.2 *continued*

	Premodern	Early modern	Modern	Contemporary
Infrastructure	Writing	European innovations and intensification of maritime technologies and navigation techniques	Railways	Flight
	Mechanized printing in some areas	Mechanized printing reaches Europe and then its colonies	Mechanized shipping	Telephony combined with computers and digitization
	Domestication of animals for transport	Establishment of European postal systems	Telegraphy, telephony	Global cabling
	Imperial peace – some road networks		Development and small use of internal combustion engine, radio, television	Global satellites
	Some advances in maritime technology and cartography			Internet
				Television, radio expanded
Institutionalization	Very low – ecumenes and tribute systems only	Very low – diplomacy etc. only	Medium, but increasing in some areas, especially economics, migration	High – all domains, many forms
Stratification	Within civilizations highly stratified engagement with long-distance flows – only metropolitan centres and metropolitan elites on key trade routes etc. closely linked to these flows and networks	Transatlantic networks dominated by European powers and colonies. Indian Ocean networks, increasingly controlled by Europe, but sharply contested by local societies and Islamic trading networks	Unambiguous European-American domination of global institutions and global networks. British Empire particularly powerful in context of global interimperial rivalry	Distinctive patterns of stratification in different domains of globalization. Political/military – most of era dominated by US–USSR Cold War; provides very clear hierarchy of power in these domains. Post-Cold War given way to more multipolar stratification

	Between civilizations – Islam, China, India – main nodes of global networks; Europe, Africa, South East Asia peripheral	Europe unable to penetrate/control interior of Asia and Africa Metropolitan centres and metropolitan elites on key trade routes etc. continue to be closely linked to global flows and networks, but some increase in areas of economies, polities, etc., influenced and shaped by global connections	Some non-European societies capable of greater resistance than others, some capable of indigenous modernization – Japan, Turkey	Economic stratification between and within societies. OECD countries dominant in terms of enmeshment and control, with balance of power shifting away from USA to other states. Rise of NIEs Cultural stratification, even more inequitable with US culture industries and English language dominant in global spread of popular cultures – though not uncontested Environmental stratification very sharp between North and South in terms of levels of consumption, but production of/and exposure to threats/risks unevenly spread
Modes	Coercive Religious/ideological	Coercive Imperial Religious/ideological	Coercive Ideological (increasingly secular) Competitive	Competitive Cooperative Ideological/cultural

The Demise, Resurgence or Transformation of State Power?

The distinctive attributes of contemporary globalization, as previous chapters have argued, by no means simply prefigure the demise of the nation-state or even the erosion of state power. Indeed, in all the domains surveyed, it is evident that in key respects many states, but most especially SIACS, have become more active, although the form and modalities of this activism differ from those of previous eras. Just as earlier historical forms of globalization were associated with particular kinds of state formation and transformation, so too in the contemporary epoch processes of globalization are closely associated with, although by no means the sole cause of, a transformation or reconstitution of the powers of the modern nation-state (conceived in terms of its functions, role, authority, autonomy and sovereignty). This is apparent in reviewing the extent to which contemporary patterns of globalization result in a confluence of decisional, institutional, distributional and structural impacts on SIACS which involve a significant renegotiation of elements of state sovereignty and autonomy. But before considering the issue of impacts, we need to address the prior, and related, issue of the principal driving forces underlying contemporary globalization, since this is central to any assessment of its cumulative consequences.

As the introduction observed, no single coherent theory of globalization exists although there are a variety of accounts which seek to identify its underlying causal dynamics. Any attempt to specify the driving forces behind globalization has to be carefully qualified in as much as definitive causal generalizations about socio-historical processes are inherently problematic (Giddens, 1984; Graham, 1997; McCullagh, 1998). Seeking to identify the primary causes of contemporary globalization necessarily involves a recognition that in accounting for processes of social change, the language of causality cannot be the same as that of deductive scientific enquiry. In analysing the driving forces underlying multifaceted processes of historical change, the emphasis is necessarily on the conjunction of tendencies and the factors which impede or fuel those tendencies. The relevant notion of cause here involves the idea of a conjunction of events, processes and conditions which together tend to generate a particular type of outcome (McCullagh, 1998, p. 178). Clearly, different historical forms of globalization may have quite distinctive causal paths in so far as the relative significance of different causal forces has varied between epochs. Thus, as we have seen, premodern and modern historical forms of globalization reflect a different configuration of globalizing tendencies. Whereas premodern historical forms of globalization tended to be dominated by migratory movements, military expansion, empire building and cultural/religious expansionism, modern globalization has tended to reflect the primacy of economic, political and military expansion. This is not to deny the contribution of other globalizing factors, but rather to argue that at different times some have been more causally significant than others.

Contemporary globalization is not reducible to a single causal process but involves a complex configuration of causal logics. These have been elaborated in previous chapters and embrace the expansionary tendencies of political, military, economic, migratory, cultural and ecological systems. But each is mediated by the late twentieth-century communications and transport revolution which has facilitated globalization across every domain of social activity and dramatically expanded – through the emergence of worldwide infrastructures for the movement of people, goods and symbols – global interaction capacity. It has also massively enhanced the intensity and velocity of global interactions while altering the impact of globalization, most especially in terms of its consequences for the distribution of power (Deibert, 1997).

What is especially notable about contemporary globalization, however, is the confluence of globalizing tendencies within all the key domains of social interaction. Thus it is the particular conjuncture of developments – within the political, military, economic, migratory, cultural and ecological domains – and the complex interactions among these which reproduce the distinctive form and dynamics of contemporary globalization. Accordingly, to explain contemporary globalization as simply a product of the expansionary logic of capitalism, or of the global diffusion of popular culture, or of military expansion, is necessarily one-sided and reductionist. That capitalism, in its many forms, has an expansionary logic is not in doubt; nor in question are the globalizing tendencies of the war system and certain cultural complexes. While analytically it is necessary to differentiate and assess historical patterns of globalization in each domain, this can lead to a partial and fragmented account. For to understand contemporary globalization fully requires an exploration of the conjuncture of globalizing forces and the dynamics of their mutual interaction. For instance, the contemporary pattern of trade globalization presumes the existence of global political, legal and financial infrastructures, while it simultaneously has financial, ecological, migratory, political, cultural and military consequences. The interactions between such processes tend to generate a systemic dynamic in so far as the totality of global flows, networks, interactions and interconnections involves a structural shift in the organization of human social affairs and exercise of power (Axford, 1995).

This structural shift or global transformation, however, should not be taken to suggest, as do some hyperglobalizers, that contemporary globalization is an irreversible or a linear historical process; in other words, that it has a fixed historical trajectory and is beyond political control. Globalization, as the arguments of previous chapters have pointedly emphasized, is not an automatic or self-reproducing process. Quite the contrary, what is distinctive about contemporary globalization is the magnitude and institutionalization of its political regulation at all levels and the plethora of social forces pursuing a defined global project, whether through the slogans of the global market or spaceship earth. Contemporary globalization is also a highly contested process since the infrastructures and institutionalization of global politics generate new arenas and mechanisms through which conflicts over the terms of global interaction are played out – from the corridors of the European Commission and dispute panels of the WTO to the alternative G7 summits of NGOs and annual meetings of the ILO. In this respect, contemporary globalization does not, as many hyperglobalizers argue, necessarily narrow the scope for political action and state initiatives but, on the contrary, may dramatically expand it, as the discussion in earlier chapters of the politicization and regulation of economic, cultural and ecological globalization suggests. However, arguing that contemporary globalization is highly politicized and regulated does not entail accepting the premises of the 'sceptical school' that globalization is effectively under the control of national governments (whether understood as state direction or acquiescence) and that the powers of the nation-state (defined in their widest sense) remain fundamentally unaltered. For the cumulative picture of impacts indicates the growing transformation of SIACS.

A summary of these impacts – their general tendencies or patterns – in relation to all the key domains of globalization is displayed in grid C.3. In respect of decisional

Grid C.3 Contemporary globalization: cumulative impacts on SIACS

	Decisional	Institutional	Distributional	Structural
Political domain	Shifting costs and benefits of domestic versus international/transnational political action	Rise of intermestic issues Multilateralism, regionalism and multilayered governance New arenas of political mobilization, action and authority – formation of elements of transnational civil society	Coalition building, political mobilization, diffusion of power and authority	Erosion of internal/external distinction Diffusion of political power and authority New regimes of sovereignty and autonomy Overlapping communities of fate Authority without territoriality Shift from government to governance
Military domain	Shifting costs and benefits of use of military force Military strategy and options change	Redefinition of national security as international security Cooperative security and defence Multilateralism	Transnationalization of military production New winners and losers Restructuring of defence industries, e.g. European champions	Questioning of war as a 'rational' instrument of national policy Post-military society Redefinition of defence and security politics
Economics: trade, finance, production	Changes to relative costs and benefits of different macroeconomic, industrial and sectoral policies and policy instruments	Deepening hold of global competition Growth of global and cross-border production networks	New global division of labour Shifting balance of power between national, international, industrial and finance capital	Altering balance of power between states and markets Trade specialization and changing

	Changing costs and benefits of interest rate and exchange rate management Tendency to convergence of fiscal policies – corporate taxation and incentives Decline of relevance of old-style interventionist industrial policy	Growth of multilateral economic surveillance and regulation New dilemmas of liberalization and deregulation vs state direction	Shifting boundary between tradable and non-tradable sectors Shifting benefits for skilled labour vs unskilled labour Wage competition across economies	industrial structures Decoupling of national and MNC performance Systemic risks
Cultural domain	Costs and benefits of national cultural policies alter Symbolic density creates problems for censorship	Changing context of the reproduction of national culture Future of national culture on agenda	Shifting balance between Western and non-Western cultures New social movements	Multicultural and polyethnic societies Erosion of cultural autarchy
Migration	New dilemmas of border controls vs surveillance Increasing costs of sealing borders	International controls necessary Migration as security issue	Differential patterns of employment and prosperity Labour market consequences different for skilled and unskilled groups	National identity and citizenship in question Emergence of multicultural and multiethnic societies
Ecological domain	Changing costs/benefits of domestic policy vs international action	Environmental issues firmly on global and national agendas Monitoring of environment	Transformation in the distribution of environmental goods and bads Biggest polluters don't always bear greatest costs Trade in hazardous waste – exporting the burden of environmental pollution	Overlapping environmental communities of fate – national, regional, global Capacity of states individually to deal with environmental problems, and legitimacy of state solutions, in question

impacts it is clear that globalization in many domains has altered the costs and benefits of policy choices, policy instruments and the balance between local, national, regional and global policy options. This is particularly evident in the economic and ecological domains where certain policy choices in respect of macroeconomic policy or environmental protection tend to become more costly (in a social as well as a monetary sense) while others become more attractive. Thus, for example, in a globalizing financial system expansionary macroeconomic policies for individual states may become very costly, since global financial markets tend to impose a risk premium on lending, particularly if such an expansion reinforces (or is perceived to reinforce) inflationary tendencies. Or, to take increased global ecological risks; as these become more politically visible the social costs and benefits of coordinated international action begin to tip the balance against the social costs and benefits of national inaction.

Contemporary patterns of globalization also generate significant institutional impacts in so far as they reconfigure institutional agendas and invite institutional innovation. Thus the emergence of a global trading system and the development of global production networks have made global competitiveness a new standard of national and corporate economic efficiency, and encouraged the reorganization of the state and private sectors to maximize national competitive advantage in the context of a global economic order. Similarly, globalization in the political domain has involved the internationalization of the activities of domestic bureaucratic agencies and, in the process, required the development of new modes of national policy coordination and bureaucratic organization to manage the internationalization of political decision-making.

Alongside these institutional impacts, contemporary globalization has significant distributional consequences. In the economic and productive domains it involves a new division of labour which shapes both the global and the domestic pattern of relative winners and losers from worldwide economic acitivity. But the pattern of economic stratification is not generalizable to other domains since the geographical patterns of global flows of capital, arms, pollution and people are, as previously noted, often quite different. The upshot of this is that globalization may accentuate existing social divisions within OECD societies while it also simultaneously creates new ones; the differential domestic impact of global migration and pollution appear to confirm this. In addition, the distributional impacts of globalization have important consequences for domestic politics and state power for they can trigger or reinforce the emergence of coalitions of social forces and/or the dissolution of pre-existing social bargains. This is evident, for instance, in respect of trade politics in which traditional protectionist coalitions appear to have lost ground as the social forces benefiting from more open national markets become more politically entrenched and more powerful, although not necessarily more numerous. Such distributional shifts may also contribute to underlying structural changes.

Contemporary globalization is associated with a reconstitution of state power among SIACS. As the cumulative consequences of globalization unfold, SIACS are undergoing a profound transformation as their powers, roles and functions are rearticulated, reconstituted and re-embedded at the intersection of globalizing and regionalizing networks and systems. The metaphors of the loss, diminution or erosion of state power can misrepresent this reconfiguration or transformation. Indeed, such language involves a failure to conceptualize adequately the nature of power and its complex manifestations since it represents a crude zero-sum view of power. It is evident from the preceding chapters that such a conception is particularly unhelpful in attempting to understand and explain the apparently contradictory position of SIACS under conditions of contemporary globalization. For while globalization is engendering a reconfiguration of state–market relations in the economic domain, SIACS and multilateral agencies are deeply implicated in that very process. Economic globalization by no means necessarily translates into a diminution of state power; rather, it is transforming the conditions under which state power is exercised. Moreover, in other domains, such as that of human migration, and the ecological and the cultural, SIACS have adopted a more activist posture, while in the political domain they have been central to the explosive growth and institutionalization of regional and global governance. These are not developments which can be explained convincingly in the language of the decline, erosion or loss of state power *per se*. For such metaphors (mistakenly) presume that state power was much greater in previous epochs; and, as Mann reminds us, on almost every conceivable measure SIACS are far more powerful than their antecedents (Mann, 1997). But so too are the demands placed on them. The apparent simultaneous weakening and expansion in the power of SIACS under conditions of contemporary globalization are symptomatic of an underlying structural transformation. This is nowhere so evident as in respect of state sovereignty and autonomy, which, as noted in the introduction, constitute core elements of the modern nation-state.

There are many good reasons for doubting the theoretical and empirical basis of claims that nation-states are being eclipsed by contemporary patterns of globalization. The position consistently taken in this volume has been one that has been critical of both hyperglobalizers and sceptics. We have sought to emphasize that while regional and global interaction networks are strengthening, they have multiple and variable impacts across diverse locales. Moreover, it is not part of our argument that national sovereignty today has been wholly subverted, even in regions with intensive overlapping and divided authority structures – such a view would radically misstate our position. But it is part of our argument that there are significant areas and regions marked by criss-crossing loyalties, conflicting interpretations of human rights and duties, interconnected legal and authority structures, etc., which displace – among SIACS especially – notions of sovereignty as an illimitable, indivisible and exclusive form of public power. Patterns of regional and global change are transforming the context of political action, creating a system of multiple power centres and overlapping spheres of authority – a post-Westphalian order (see chapter 1).

Neither the sovereignty nor the autonomy of states is simply diminished by such processes. Indeed, any assessment of the cumulative impacts of globalization must acknowledge their highly differentiated character since particular types of impact – whether decisional, institutional, distributional or structural – are not experienced uniformly by all states. Globalization, as we have stressed on many occasions, is by no means merely a homogenizing force. The analysis of the enmeshment of the six case study countries which runs throughout this volume highlights considerable variation between them, both within and across each of the major domains of globalization. Moreover, the impact of globalization is mediated significantly by a state's position in global political, military and economic hierarchies; its domestic economic and political structures; the institutional pattern of domestic politics; and specific government as well as societal strategies for contesting, managing or ameliorating globalizing imperatives (Hurrell and Woods, 1995; Keohane and Milner, 1996; Jessop, 1997; Mann, 1997).

The ongoing transformation of the Westphalian regime of sovereignty and autonomy has differential consequences for different states.

Political communities and civilizations can no longer be characterized as 'discrete worlds'; they are enmeshed in complex structures of overlapping forces, relations and movements which have diverse impacts on them. Clearly, these are structured by inequality and hierarchy, as we have seen. But even the most powerful forces among them – including the most powerful nation-states – do not remain unaffected by the changing patterns of regional and global flows and networks. It is rather that the nature of particular transformations and their impact on particular forms of political community vary. Two illustrations – from human rights law and interest rate policy – highlight these points.

Changes in the development of international human rights law have placed individuals, governments and non-governmental organizations under new systems of legal regulation. International law recognizes powers and constraints, and rights and duties, which have qualified the principle of state sovereignty in a number of important respects; sovereignty *per se* is no longer a straightforward guarantee of international legitimacy. One of the most significant areas in this regard is human rights law and human rights regimes, but it is also clear that such law and regimes have a variable impact. While in international law there has been a gradual shift away from the principle that state sovereignty must be safeguarded irrespective of its consequences for individuals, groups and associations, respect for the autonomy of the subject, and for an extensive range of human rights, varies across the world's major regions. In Europe practically all countries have now signed up to conventions which mean they are no longer free to treat their own citizens as they alone think fit. Human rights regimes also have a marked impact on domestic and foreign policy in the US – though none of this implies, of course, any consistency of implementation or application. Elsewhere, while the international legal direction may be clear, the costs and benefits of choices may lead to a very different weighting of priorities, for instance in many sub-Saharan countries such as Nigeria. Although there has been a shift from the weight granted to claims made on behalf of the interstate system in favour of those made on behalf of an alternative organizing principle of world order – in which an unqualified state sovereignty no longer reigns supreme – the outcome of this shift is still highly indeterminate and variable across regions.

Transformations in international law and human rights regimes impinge on the sovereignty of states but not yet, at least in terms of consistency of application, on the autonomy of all states. The de jure entitlement to rule may to an extent be transformed, but the de facto autonomy of the state may not yet be radically affected, due, of course, to weaknesses in enforcement mechanisms. A contrasting case can be developed by reflecting on financial globalization and its impact on macroeconomic policy. For this is an example of the radical impact of globalization not on sovereignty *per se* but on autonomy. The de jure entitlement to rule is not challenged fundamentally by financial globalization, but the de facto autonomy of states to establish and pursue their own policy preferences certainly is.

Financial globalization implies that national interest rates are determined largely in a global context (see chapter 4). This could lead in principle to a convergence in interest rates expressed in a common currency, and a convergence in real rates of return, although this cannot simply be assumed. Under a system of fixed exchange rates, governments must accept the interest rate necessary to sustain parity among currencies. Under flexible exchange rates, national authorities are free to choose (within market limits) their interest rates provided they accept the exchange rate consequences. In theory the existence of global financial markets offers national governments a new range of choice. For flexible exchange rates presume monetary autonomy: countries set their desired interest rate and the exchange rate moves to ensure interest rate parity with other countries. Governments in OECD countries at least have free access to global financial markets. Even if they are not able to borrow unlimited amounts at a given interest rate, the upward pressure on interest rates from government borrowing is much more muted than it would be (or was) in the absence of global capital markets.

Accordingly, it is hard to defend the view that financial globalization has simply shifted the autonomy of nation-states in one direction; globalization has not led to a simple increase or a simple decrease in the absolute autonomy or choices of states. But the costs and benefits of different policies have unquestionably been altered. For example, financial liberalization has made national authorities more reliant on interest rates as *the* primary tool of monetary policy, since capital controls, reserve require-ments, credit restrictions and other controls have become less effective and/or more costly as instruments of macroeconomic policy. At the same time control over anything but short-term interest rates has been weakened and in fixed or managed exchange rate regimes control of even short-term rates is largely dictated by the anchor currency and the risk premium required by the markets. The abandonment of capital controls and the scale of financial globalization have meant strict adherence to the monetary rules of the system and the anti-inflationary bias that this has often entailed. This bias has been sometimes accentuated by the way in which risk premia imply high interest rates for certain countries. The new initiative in Europe to establish EMU can be seen, in part, as reflecting a view that national autonomy in monetary policy has been so compromised that the only means of recovering it is at a European – regional – level.

Financial globalization raises several paradoxes for national economic policy. Short-term interest rates have become the prime tool of monetary policy as credit controls have become increasingly unworkable and reserve requirements can no longer be straightforwardly used as an active tool of monetary management. In several ways interest rates have become more important in the economy: credit levels are deter-mined by them, rather than by direct controls; liberalization and the growth of per-sonal credit have increased the effects of interest rates on household budgets and expenditure; and their effects on exchange rates, as well as investment decisions, are of major macroeconomic importance. However, while national authorities (outside EMU) may retain formal sovereignty in relation to the setting of short-term interest rates, in practice the range within which rates are set is severely constrained by global markets. Furthermore, even to the extent that national authorities are able to determine these rates, the effects of interest rate changes have become less predictable and control-lable. Accordingly, in contradistinction to the impact of changes in international law and human rights regimes, financial globalization does not necessarily entail change in de jure sovereignty, but it unquestionably transforms the regime of financial autonomy in which nation-states are embedded and, thus, their capacity to determine or imple-ment their own economic strategy.

In sum, traditional conceptions of state sovereignty and autonomy are being renegoti-ated and rearticulated within the changing processes and structures of regional and global order. States, moreover, are locked into diverse, complex overlapping political domains – what we earlier referred to as multilayered governance. Thus national sovereignty and national autonomy have to be thought of as embedded within broader frameworks of governance in which they have become but one set of principles, among others, underlying the exercise of political authority. The Westphalian regime of state sovereignty and autonomy is undergoing a significant alteration as it becomes qualified in fundamental ways. However, it by no means follows from this that the nature of this alteration is either straightforward or permanent.

New Limits to Politics?
Civilizing and Democratizing Globalization

While for many hyperglobalizers contemporary globalization is associated with new limits to politics and the erosion of state power, the argument developed here is critical of such political fatalism. For the evidence of previous chapters suggests that contemporary globalization has not only triggered or reinforced the significant politicization of a growing array of issue areas, but it has also been accompanied by an extraordinary growth of institutionalized arenas and networks of political mobilization, surveillance, decision-making and regulatory activity across borders. This has enormously expanded the capacity for, and scope of, political activity and the exercise of political authority. In this respect, globalization is not, nor has it ever been, beyond regulation and control. Globalization does not prefigure the 'end of politics' so much as its continuation by new means. The prospects for 'civilizing' and 'democratizing' contemporary globalization are thus not as bleak as some suggest. Yet this is not to overlook the profound intellectual, institutional and normative challenges which it presents to the existing organization of political communities.

Political communities are in the process of being transformed. Of course, transformation *per se* is not a new phenomenon. The history of political communities, as indicated in chapter 1, is replete with changing forms and structures, from empires to nation-states to emerging regional structures and organizations of global governance. One type of transformation has been of particular concern in this volume: the significant, albeit uneven, enmeshment of human communities with one another over time. Although the Roman Empire and the spread of Islam in the second half of the first millennium constituted formidable projections of power over space and time, it has only been in the last few hundred years that human communities have come into increasingly regularized contact with each other in nearly all regions of the world; the collective fortunes of human communities have become intertwined. This shift, and its implications for the project of civilizing and democratizing globalization, are the concern of this final part of the conclusion.

As repeatedly argued throughout the volume, we recognize today a confluence of changes across different social and economic realms which combine to create a uniquely extensive and intensive form of regional and global interconnectedness. This confluence of changes includes a number of developments which can be thought of as deep, indicative, structural transformations. These include the development of such phenomena as human rights regimes, which have ensured that sovereignty alone is less and less a guarantee of state legitimacy in international law; the internationalization of security and the transnationalization of a great many defence and procurement programmes, which means, for example, that some key weapons systems rely on components from many countries; environmental shifts, above all ozone depletion and global warming, which highlight the growing limits to statecentric politics; the revolutions in communications and information technology, which have increased massively the stretch and intensity of all manner of socio-political networks within and across the borders of states; and the deregulation of capital markets, which has enhanced the power of capital, particularly but not only financial capital, in relation to labour and the state.

These very significant changes are contributing to a transformation in the nature and prospects of political community. At the heart of this lies a growth in transborder or transboundary political issues and problems which erode the distinctions between domestic and foreign affairs, internal political issues and external questions, the sovereign concerns of the nation-state and international considerations. States and governments face issues like AIDS, BSE (Bovine Spongiform Encephalopathy), the spread of malaria, the use of non-renewable resources, the management of nuclear waste, diaspora cultures and the proliferation of weapons of mass destruction which cannot easily be categorized in traditional political terms, that is, domestic or international. Moreover, issues like the location and investment strategy of multinational corporations, the regulation of global financial markets, the development of EMU and the threat to the tax base of individual countries which arise from the global division of labour and the absence of capital controls all pose questions about the continued effectiveness of some of the traditional instruments of national economic policy. In fact, in all major areas of government policy, the enmeshment of national political communities in regional and global processes involves them in intensive issues of transboundary coordination and control. Political space in respect of effective government and the accountability of political power is no longer coterminous with a delimited national territory. The growth of transboundary problems creates what has been referred to here as 'overlapping communities of fate'; that is, a condition in which the fortunes and prospects of individual political communities are increasingly bound together (see Held, 1995, 1996; and see also Archibugi et al., 1998). Political communities today are locked into a diversity of processes and structures which range in and through them, linking and fragmenting them into complex constellations. Moreover, national communities themselves by no means make and determine decisions and policies exclusively for themselves when they decide on such issues as the regulation of sexuality, health and the environment; national governments by no means simply determine what is right or appropriate exclusively for their own citizens.

The assumption that one can understand the nature and possibilities of political community by referring merely to national structures and mechanisms of political power is clearly anachronistic. While it is a mistake to conclude from the seeming flux of contemporary interaction networks that political communities today are without distinctive degrees of division or cleavage at their borders, they have been shaped by multiple interaction networks and power systems over time and continue to be so at enhanced levels of intensity. Thus questions are raised both about the fate of the idea of the political community and about the appropriate locus for the articulation of the political good. If the agent at the heart of modern political discourse, be it a person, group or government, is locked into a variety of overlapping communities and jurisdictions, then the proper 'home' of politics and democracy becomes a difficult issue to resolve.

This matter is most apparent in Europe, where the development of the EU has created intensive discussions about the future of sovereignty and autonomy within individual nation-states. But the issues are important not just for Europe and the West, but for countries in other parts of the world, for example Japan and South Korea. These countries must recognize new emerging problems, for instance problems concerning AIDS, migration and new challenges to peace, security and economic prosperity, which spill over the boundaries of nation-states. In addition, the communities of East Asia, as recent developments show, are developing in the context of growing interconnectedness across the world's major regions. This interconnectedness is marked in a whole range of areas from the environment, human rights, trade and finance, to issues of international crime. There are emerging overlapping communities of fate generating common problems within and across the East Asian region. In other words, East Asia is necessarily part of the global order and is locked into a diversity of sites of power which shape and determine its fortunes.

Global transformations have affected our concept of the political community and, in particular, our concept of the democratic political community, which often gets split into the 'inner' and 'outer' spheres of political life. It is readily understood that the quality of democracy depends on rendering political decision-making accountable to citizens in a delimited political community. It is also understood, moreover, that the quality of democracy depends on more than merely the formal access citizens have to the public sphere and the polity – to public deliberation and decision-making. It is acknowledged today that the quality of democracy depends on the complicated processes whereby citizens gain or fail to gain access to the resources and procedures of the public realm – access that reflects a complex pattern of economic factors, cultural processes and social involvements. But it is still too rarely acknowledged that the nature, form and prospects of political communities are clouded by the multiplying interconnections among them. While more countries seek to establish national democracies, powerful forces affecting our social, economic, cultural and environmental welfare now transcend the boundaries of nation-states. Fundamental questions are raised about the meaning of democracy and citizenship in this context.

In existing liberal democracies, consent to government and legitimacy for governmental action are dependent on electoral politics and the ballot box. Yet the notion that consent legitimates government, and that the ballot box is the appropriate mechanism whereby the citizen body as a whole periodically confers authority on government to enact the law and regulate economic and social life, becomes problematic as soon as the nature of a 'relevant community' is contested. What is the proper constituency, and proper realm of jurisdiction, for developing and implementing policy with respect to health issues such as AIDS, narcotics, the management of nuclear waste, military security, the harvesting of rainforests, indigenous peoples, the use of non-renewable resources, the instability of global financial markets, and the management and control of genetic engineering and manipulation in animals and humans? National boundaries have traditionally demarcated the basis on which individuals are included and excluded from participation in decisions affecting their lives; but if many socio-economic processes, and the outcomes of decisions about them, stretch beyond national frontiers, then the implications of this are serious, not only for the categories of consent and legitimacy but for all the key ideas of democracy. At issue is the nature of a political community – how should the proper boundaries of a political community be drawn in a more regional and global order? In addition, questions can be raised about the meaning of representation (who should represent whom and on what basis?) and about the proper form and scope of political participation (who should participate and in what way?). As fundamental processes of governance escape the categories of the nation-state, the traditional national resolutions of the key questions of democratic theory and practice look increasingly threadbare.

The idea of government or of the state, democratic or otherwise, can no longer be simply defended as an idea suitable to a particular closed political community or nation-state. The idea of a political community of fate – of a self-determining collectivity – can no longer meaningfully be located within the boundaries of a single nation-state. Some of the most fundamental forces and processes determining the nature of life chances within and across political communities are now beyond the reach of nation-states. The system of national political communities persists of course; but it is articulated and rearticulated today within complex economic, organizational, administrative, legal and cultural processes and structures which limit and check its efficacy. If these processes and structures are not acknowledged and brought into the political realm they will tend to bypass or circumvent the traditional mechanisms of political accountability and regulation. For the locus of effective political power can no longer be assumed to be national governments – effective power is shared, bartered and struggled over by diverse forces and agencies at national, regional and global levels. In other words, we must recognize that political power is being repositioned, recontextualized and, to a degree, transformed by the growing importance of other less territorially based power systems. Political power is now sandwiched in more complex power systems that have become more salient over time relative to state power.

Accordingly, we are compelled to recognize that we live in a complex interconnected world where the extensity, intensity and impact of issues (economic, political or environmental) raise questions about where those issues are most appropriately addressed. If the most powerful geopolitical forces are not to settle many pressing matters simply in terms of their own objectives and by virtue of their power, then the current institutions and mechanisms of accountability need to be reconsidered. In fact, their reconsideration is already underway, both practically and intellectually. Indeed, it is possible to identify three broad schools of thought which represent, in their own ways, three overlapping projects for regulating and democratizing contemporary globalization. These three schools or projects are summarized in table C.1.

Implicit in liberal-internationalist thinking is an assumption that political necessity will drive forward the democratization and civilization of globalization. Avoiding global ecological crisis and managing the pervasive social, economic and political dislocation arising from contemporary processes of globalization 'will require the articulation of a collaborative ethos based upon the principles of consultation, transparency, and accountability. . . . There is no alternative to working together and using collective power to create a better [democratic] world' (Commission on Governance, 1995, pp. 2 and 5). In key respects, liberal-internationalism is a normative theory which seeks to transpose a weak form of domestic liberal democracy into a model of a democratic world order (I. Clark, 1989, p. 215). Its contemporary advocates, such as the Commission on Global Governance, are seeking to construct an ideal of 'democracy beyond borders' on the theoretical edifice of modern liberal democratic thinking.

While liberal-internationalism emphasizes the *reform* of existing structures of global governance, the radical project stresses the creation of *alternative* mechanisms of global social, economic and political organization based on certain republican principles:

Table C.1 Civilizing and democratizing contemporary globalization: a summary of three political projects

	Liberal-internationalism	Radical republicanism	Cosmopolitan democracy
Who should govern?	The people through governments, accountable international organizations and international regimes	The people through self-governing communities	The people through communities, associations, states, international organizations, all subject to cosmopolitan democratic law
Form of global governance?	*Polyarchy* – pluralistic fragmented system, sharing of sovereignty	*Demarchy* – functional democratic governance devoid of national sovereignty	*Heterarchy* – divided authority system subject to cosmopolitan democratic law
Key agents/instruments, processes of democratization	Accelerating interdependence, self-interest of key agencies of power in creating more democratic/cooperative forms of global governance	New social movements, impending global ecological, security and economic crises	Constitutional and institutional reconstruction, intensification of globalization and regionalization, new social movements, possible global crises
Traditions of democratic thought	Liberal democratic theory – pluralism and protective democracy, social democracy-reformism	Direct democracy, participatory democracy, civic republicanism, socialist democracy	Liberal democratic theory, pluralism and developmental democracy, participatory democracy, civic republicanism
Ethic of global governance	'Common rights and shared responsibilities'	'Humane governance'	'Democratic autonomy'
Mode of political transformation	*Reform* of global governance	*Alternative structures* of global governance	*Reconstruction* of global governance

Source: Adapted from McGrew, 1997, p. 254

that is, the self-government of communities in which the public good is to the fore (cf. Burnheim, 1986; Walker, 1988; Falk, 1995). The radical republican project is concerned to establish the conditions necessary to empower people to take control of their own lives and to create communities based on ideas of equality, the common good and harmony with the natural environment. For many radical republicans the agents of change are to be found in existing (critical) social movements, such as the environmental, women's and peace movements, which challenge the authority of states and international agencies as well as orthodox definitions of the 'political'. Through a politics of resistance and empowerment these new social movements are conceived as playing a crucial role in global democratization similar to the role of the (old) social movements, such as organized labour, in the struggle for national democracy. These new movements are engaged in mobilizing transnational communities of resistance and solidarity against impending global ecological, economic and security crises. Underlying these projects is an attachment to the achievement of social and economic equality, the establishment of the necessary conditions for self-development, and the creation of self-governing communities. Encouraging and developing in citizens a sense of belonging to overlapping (local and global) communities of interest and affection are central to the politics of new social movements as well as to the search for new models and forms of social, political and economic organization consonant with the republican principle of self-government. The radical republican model is a 'bottom up' theory of the democratization and civilizing of global order. It represents a normative theory of 'humane governance' which is grounded in the existence of a multiplicity of 'communities of fate' and social movements, as opposed to the individualism and appeals to rational self-interest of liberal-internationalism.

The third project, the cosmopolitan project, attempts to specify the principles and the institutional arrangements for making accountable those sites and forms of power which presently operate beyond the scope of democratic control (see Held, 1995; Linklater, 1998; Archibugi et al., 1998). It argues that in the millennium ahead each citizen of a state will have to learn to become a 'cosmopolitan citizen' as well: that is, a person capable of mediating between national traditions, communities of fate and alternative forms of life. Citizenship in a democratic polity of the future, it is argued, is likely to involve a growing mediating role: a role which encompasses dialogue with the traditions and discourses of others with the aim of expanding the horizons of one's own framework of meaning, and increasing the scope of mutual understanding. Political agents who can 'reason from the point of view of others' will be better equipped to resolve, and resolve fairly, the new and challenging transboundary issues and processes that create overlapping communities of fate. In addition, the cosmopolitan project contends that, if many contemporary forms of power are to become accountable and if many of the complex issues that affect us all – locally, nationally, regionally and globally – are to be democratically regulated, people will have to have access to, and membership in, *diverse* political communities. Put differently, a democratic political community for the new millennium necessarily describes a world where citizens enjoy multiple citizenships. Faced with overlapping communities of fate they need to be not only citizens of their own communities, but also of the wider regions in which they live, and of the wider global order. Institutions will certainly need to develop in order to reflect the multiple issues, questions and problems that link people together regardless of the particular nation-states in which they were born or brought up.

With this in mind, advocates of the cosmopolitan position maintain that democracy needs to be rethought as a 'double-sided process'. By a double-sided process – or process of double democratization – is meant not just the deepening of democracy within a national community, involving the further democratization of states and civil societies over time, but also the extension of democratic forms and processes across territorial borders. Democracy for the new millennium must allow cosmopolitan citizens to gain access to, mediate between and render accountable the social, economic and political processes and flows that cut across and transform their traditional community boundaries. The core of this project involves reconceiving legitimate political authority in a manner which disconnects it from its traditional anchor in fixed borders and delimited territories and, instead, articulates it as an attribute of basic democratic arrangements or basic democratic law which can, in principle, be entrenched and drawn on in diverse self-regulating associations – from cities and subnational regions, to nation-states, regions and wider global networks. It is clear that the process of disconnection has already begun as political authority and legitimate forms of governance are diffused 'below', 'above' and 'alongside' the nation-state. But the cosmopolitan project is in favour of a radical extension of this process so long as it is circumscribed and delimited by a commitment to a far-reaching cluster of democratic rights and duties. It proposes a series of short- and long-term measures in the conviction that, through a process of progressive, incremental change, geopolitical forces will come to be socialized into democratic agencies and practices (see Held, 1995, pt 3).

If globalization refers to those processes underpinning a transformation in the organization of human affairs, linking together and expanding human activity such that it encompasses frameworks of interregional and intercontinental change and development, then many of our most cherished political ideas – which formerly centred on nation-states – need to be rethought and recast. It is beyond the brief of this text to pursue these normative and institutional issues at any length. But if we live in a world marked by global politics and multilayered governance, then the efficacy of national democratic traditions and national legal traditions are fundamentally challenged. Whatever the precise specification of this challenge, it is surely based on the recognition today that the nature and quality of democracy within a particular community and the nature and quality of democratic relations among communities are interconnected, and that new legal and organizational mechanisms must be created if democracy and political communities themselves are to prosper. It would be wholly fallacious to conclude from this that the politics of local communities, or national democratic communities, will be (or should be) wholly eclipsed by the new forces of political globalization. To assume this would be to misunderstand the very complex, variable and uneven impact of regional and global processes on political life. Of course, certain problems and policies will remain properly the responsibility of local governments and national states; but others will be recognized as appropriate for specific regions, and still others – such as elements of the environment, global security concerns, world health questions and economic regulation – will be seen to need new institutional arrangements to address them. We need to refire our political imaginations so that we do not remain politically passive in the face of these regional and global shifts. There is every reason to believe that new political arrangements are not only a necessity but also a distinct possibility in the light of the already changing organization of regional and global processes, evolving political decision-making centres such as the European Union and growing political demands for new forms of political deliberation, conflict resolution and transparency in international decision-making. In this new emerging world, cities, national parliaments, regional assemblies and global authorities could all have a distinctive but interlinked set of roles within a framework of accountability and public decision-making. There is a choice and the choice remains ours to make.

Of course, whether the cultural traditions and resources exist to support the deepening democratization not just of nation-states but of the wider regional and global order is an open question (see chapter 7). Even though processes of globalization may be physically uniting the globe, we have seen that they are not necessarily engendering that sense of global community on which the legitimacy of global democratic governance would depend. Indeed, many thinkers argue that accelerating globalization merely intensifies and generates conflicts as the nations of the world seek to secure their interests in the 'global neighbourhood' (Bull, 1977). This fragmentation of the world into nations, regions, cultures and communities may inhibit the possibilities of a transcultural foundation for a global democratic politics. For example, in Asia-Pacific an 'Asian way' of democracy is championed, while in Africa indigenous democratic traditions and ideas of human rights are being reinvented. Growing nationalism and global inequalities reinforce cultural divisions and global fragmentation. Cultural relativism too, increasingly a hostage to authoritarian politics, undermines the basis of common agreement on democracy as a global ethic. There is no shortage of commentators who foresee that the contemporary international system must, and must always, be understood in terms of endemic conflict and inequality, albeit mitigated by fragile and limited attempts at global governance which lack the coercive means to ensure global order.

It would be easy to be pessimistic about the future of political communities, about the future of democracy, and about the prospects of attaining effective accountability in the context of the changing regional and global orders. There are plenty of reasons for pessimism; they include the fact that the fundamental political units of the world are still based on the nation-states while some of the world's most powerful socio-political forces escape the boundaries of these units. In reaction to this, in part, new forms of fundamentalism have arisen along with new forms of tribalism – all asserting the a priori superiority of a particular religious, or cultural, or political identity over all others, and all asserting their sectional aims and interests. In addition, the reform of global governance currently envisaged by the most powerful countries, for example the reform of the UN, is all too often focused on efforts to include other powerful countries, above all Germany and Japan. Such reform would consolidate the power of certain geopolitical interests but at the expense of many other countries which have some of the fastest rates of economic growth or some of the largest populations. This position is probably unsustainable in the long run.

But there are other forces at work which create the basis for a more optimistic reading of the prospects of political community and democratic politics. There are forces and processes, documented in all the chapters above, which are engendering a reshaping of political cultures, institutions and structures. First, one must note the emergence, however hesitatingly, of regional and global institutions and mechanisms of governance in the twentieth century. The UN is, of course, weak in many respects, but it is a relatively recent creation and it is an innovative structure which can be built on. The UN system, with its myriad of organizations, constitutes a resource which provides –

for all its weaknesses – an enduring example of how nations might (and sometimes do) cooperate better to resolve, and resolve fairly, common problems. In addition, the development of a powerful regional body such as the European Union is a remarkable state of affairs. Just over fifty years ago Europe was at the point of self-destruction. Since that moment Europe has created new mechanisms of collaboration, new instruments of human rights enforcement and political institutions in order not only to hold member states to account across a broad range of issues, but to pool aspects of their sovereignty. Furthermore, there are many regional and global transnational actors contesting the terms of globalization – not just corporations but new social movements such as the environmental movement and the women's movement. These are the 'new' voices of an emergent 'transnational civil society', heard for instance at the Rio Conference on the Environment, the Cairo Conference on Population Control and the Beijing Women's Conference. In short, there are tendencies at work seeking to establish new forms of public life and new ways of debating regional and global issues. These are all in the early stages of development, and there are no guarantees that the balance of political contest will allow them to develop. But there are also no guarantees that SIACS can be protected and nurtured in their current form. On the contrary, the processes of transformation described in this volume suggests that, at the very least, SIACS are being recontextualized, repositioned and to an extent transformed by regional and global processes. Our political institutions will have to change if some of our more cherished notions – a circumscribed political realm distinct from ruler and ruled, the rule of law, political accountability, social justice and a self-determining people, to name but some – are to retain their relevance and efficacy in the millennium ahead.

Methodological Appendix

This methodological appendix elaborates some of the assumptions underlying the treatment of statistical data and choice of case study countries.

Indicators of International Enmeshment

In order to assess the scope and depth of a state's enmeshment in the global system we developed a series of quantitative indicators of interconnectedness. These indicators are based on existing quantitative research work within international relations, international political economy, geography and sociology, and on official statistics. The construction of the indicators provided a unique opportunity for gathering empirical data on both global and regional levels of interconnectedness. It enabled comparisons to be made, across the six chosen country studies, of the relative significance of global, as opposed to regional, forces in structuring the environment in which the UK, Germany, France, Sweden, the US and Japan operate.

Five sets of indicators of enmeshment were developed in respect of key areas of state activity and the degree to which these are implicated in global or regional networks of interaction. These five sets of indicators consist of:

1 Politico-legal indicators. These include measures of the numbers and types of treaties and commitments obligating the state; participation in international governmental institutions; interaction with regional intergovernmental networks and structures, such as the European Union and the Organization of American States; the transgovernmental activities of domestic bureaucratic personnel; the international interactions of domestic political agencies, such as political parties, trade unions and business organizations.
2 Military indicators. These include measures of the proportion of defence expenditure and personnel allocated to alliance commitments; the arms trade and the extent to which the military is dependent on foreign technology and supplies; foreign penetration of the domestic arms industry; reliance on foreign operational military command and communication systems.
3 Economic indicators. These include measures of exports and imports; levels of inward and outward investment; levels of foreign debt and credit; enmeshment in global and regional financial markets; dependence on foreign technology of different industrial sectors; cross-border mergers, acquisitions and R&D cooperation.
4 Socio-cultural indicators. These include measures of the ethnic, linguistic and religious make-up of national populations; levels of international mail and telephone and electronic communications traffic; levels of exports and imports of cultural products; the proportion of media and communications industries owned and controlled by foreign corporate interests; dependence on foreign communications systems.
5 Environmental indicators. These include measures of the degree to which nations contribute to the problems of hazardous waste exports, ozone depletion, acid rain and global warming; the degree to which each nation currently suffers from these environmental threats.

Each of the indicator sets was generated as far as possible for our six case study nations: the UK, US, Germany, Japan, France and Sweden. Indicator sets were produced for various global time series, depending on data availability over various historical periods.

Choice of Country Case Studies

Several criteria were used in the choice of the UK, US, France, Sweden, Germany and Japan (from among all advanced capitalist states) as the primary empirical focus. In particular these six states exhibit differential characteristics essential to the comparative assessment of the impact of globalization and regionalization. Specifically the six states:

1   are all advanced capitalist states but with distinctive locations in the global power hierarchy;
2   have contrasting positions and roles in global and regional military, political and economic hierarchies;
3   have distinctive political systems and patterns of relations between state and civil society;
4   exhibit contrasting patterns of economic interaction in terms of the 'openness' of their economies;
5   experience distinctive sets of global and regional influences on state policy formulation and implementation;
6   have declared foreign policy orientations which differ along a continuum from independence to interdependence; and
7   demonstrate common as well as divergent responses to globalizing forces, that is, regional integration, multilateralism, unilateralism, etc.

It is this profile of similarities and dissimilarities which makes the selection of the UK, France, Sweden, Germany, the US and Japan a particularly useful test of the differential impacts of globalization on state autonomy and sovereignty in the advanced capitalist world.

Estimation of Foreign Direct Investment

The IMF (1993) defines FDI thus: 'Direct investment refers to investment that is made to acquire a lasting interest in an enterprise operating in an economy other than that of the investor, the investor's purpose being to have an effective voice in the management of the enterprise.' The same manual describes portfolio investment as 'long-term bonds and corporate equities other than those included in the categories for direct investment and reserves'. There are several difficulties in applying these definitions in practice.

The minimum proportion of stock held for foreign investment to constitute FDI on official definitions varies between 12 and 50 per cent of corporate capital in different OECD nations. This complicates the measurement of FDI in the situation where, for example, a company in country A owns 50 per cent of a company operating in country B, which then purchases 30 per cent of another company in country B. Thus the company in country A owns only 15 per cent of the third company and this may constitute FDI under the one country's definition but not the other's.

Available figures do not distinguish between gross and new levels of FDI, that is, they do not distinguish between capital and productive assets that merely change hands, and the actual creation of new capital or the scrapping of old. This makes for significant difficulties in establishing the broader economic consequences of FDI for a national economy. Simply aggregating FDI flows from balance of payments data can give inaccurate estimates of overseas holdings, since concerns also often fund their expansion through retained profits and/or borrowing. Some countries such as the US measure both the profits flowing from overseas affiliates back to the home country and those retained, but other countries do not and may underestimate expansion through retained profits or borrowing on capital markets. Finally, valuing investment stocks at historic values ignores changes in the current economic value of those stocks and tends both to understate their current value and to overstate the profitability of MNCs (cf. Kapler, 1997). Furthermore, FDI is only a very approximate measure of global production networks since it includes only those interfirm linkages based on direct investment as opposed to subcontracting or similar arrangements. Nor does it capture the magnitude of investment in multinational production since FDI flows account for only about 25 per cent of total investment in overseas production.

Measuring Environmental Degradation

Any attempt to view the globalization of environmental degradation and environmental politics in historical and quantitative perspectives is hampered by the peculiarities of environmental issues (Weale, 1992; Beck, 1992, 1995). *Temporally*, there can be substantial time lags between the acts that create or initiate processes of environmental degradation and the actual occurrence of environmental degradation. For example, contemporary levels of nitrates in British drinking water have been caused by the application of nitrogenous fertilizers some decades ago. This is because it takes many years for nitrogen compounds in the soil to work their way down to the water table. Similarly, it has been argued that the increasing concentrations of carbon, sulphur and nitrogen oxides in the earth's atmosphere are responsible for initiating global warming. If this is the case then the causal origins and specific acts that contributed to global warming have been taking place for the last hundred years or so and yet we may not have actually experienced the most severe adverse environmental affects to date. As noted in chapter 8, the temporal separation of cause and effect of environmental degradation is replicated by the separation of *spatial* origins and impacts.

A further peculiar quality of environmental degradation is its *cumulative effects*. The destruction of life in the Baltic Sea, for example, does not simply result from contemporary levels of pollution but the additive affect of both contemporary and past processes of pollution. The accumulation of heavy metals in the bodies of marine life over their whole lifespan illuminates this. The mixture of heavy metals that ultimately kills marine life in the Baltic is cumulative in a further sense: it is not one substance at one concentration that causes environmental degradation but a complex combination of substances that are produced at a multiplicity of sites, at a multiplicity of times, whose combined impact is greater than the sum of individual effects.

All three of the features described so far – the cumulative character and the temporal and spatial separations of effects – make the perception of environmental problems a highly complex affair. This complexity of perception is a fourth important feature of environmental degradation, for it can and regularly does occur 'behind our backs'. Of course, for a local population the process of desertification or deforestation will be obvious. But it may not be clear precisely what causal forces are at work in producing these effects or whether they are being experienced as a small part of a much wider process of environmental change. Many types of environmental degradation are much less accessible to everyday perception and sensation – the existence of and consequences of toxic metals in the bodies of animals, the tissues of plants, water courses and ultimately human beings can only be detected through very sophisticated and expensive biochemical tests and equipment. In the absence of a range of scientific disciplines and methods, many forms of environmental degradation would be experienced in due course – in terms of their impact on human health and well-being – but the actual process of degradation would remain unseen and inaccessible. Thus at the heart of the conduct of environmental politics and the estimation of environmental degradation is a complex technical and political process of the identification, location and naming of processes of environmental change.

However, once a problem has been identified and located, the politics of definition and measurement are unlikely to be over because the character of environmental politics is shot through with uncertainty (OECD, 1991c). First, the technical and scientific arguments describing environmental degradation, let alone the causal processes at work, are rarely uncontested. This is exacerbated by the temporal and spatial separations and the complex cumulative chains of environmental change described above. Second, while much environmental concern tends to focus on current forms of environmental degradation, by the same token it is orientated to the future as well, to what might happen. This implies a focus on the dangers and risks – the threat of nuclear plant meltdowns, of future trends in climate change, the likely impacts of diminishing ozone depletion, or the time frame of resource shortages.

How do these qualities affect the measurement of the origins, consequences and spatial organization of the environment and, thus, measures of the globalization of environmental issues? Perhaps most important in this regard is that there was limited systematic or government collection of any kind of environmental data until environmental issues became a significant political and public concern. Even if this issue were not a problem, the cumulative and uncertain qualities of environmental degradation render a number of possible quantitative measures of globalization and the environment somewhat limited. The multiplicity of sources of any one pollutant are such that it is almost impossible to track the spatial and temporal location of sources of pollution fully and accurately and to link them to their destination. Finally, given the often illegal and generally anti-social character of environmental degradation, a large amount of pollution and resource consumption goes unreported or underreported. Thus we must take all environmental data with a degree of scepticism. Nonetheless, there are reasonable grounds for thinking that there has in recent years been a significant expansion in the volume, scope, toxicity and consequences of environmental degradation.

Acknowledgements

Some sections of this book have been adapted from previously published material. The details of the original publication are as follows:

David Held, 'Democracy: from city-states to a cosmopolitan order?', in D. Held (ed.), *Prospects for Democracy: North, South, East, West*, Cambridge: Polity Press, 1993, pp. 13–52. An adapted version of a part of this essay informs section 1.3.1 of chapter 1.

David Held, 'The development of the modern state', in S. Hall and B. Gieben (eds), *Formations of Modernity*, Cambridge: Polity Press, 1992, pp. 71–119. Parts of this essay informed sections 1.1.1 and 1.1.2 of chapter 1.

David Held, 'The transformation of political community', in I. Shapiro (ed.), *Democracy's Edges*, Cambridge: Cambridge University Press, forthcoming 1999. A section of this essay helped shape the last part of the conclusion.

Anthony McGrew, 'World order and political space', in J. Anderson et al. (eds), *A Global World? Reordering Political Space*, Oxford: Oxford University Press, 1995. This essay informed the development of sections 1.2 and 1.3.2 of chapter 1.

Jonathan Perraton, David Goldblatt, David Held and Anthony McGrew, 'The globalization of economic activity', *New Political Economy*, 2, no. 2 (July, 1997). Chapters 4 and 5 drew on some material from this essay.

In addition, the authors and publisher gratefully acknowledge permission from the following to reproduce copyright material:

Cambridge University Press for map 2.4 adapted from 'Patterns of arms transfers, 1400–1700', in K. Krause, *Arms and the State: Patterns of Military Production and Trade* (Cambridge University Press, 1992).

Kogan Page Ltd/Earthscan Publications Ltd for figure 8.3 adapted from 'World CFC production', in L. Brown et al. (eds), *Vital Signs 1996–1997* (Earthscan, 1996), and figures 8.2 adapted from 'World Carbon emissions', and 8.5 adapted from 'World fish catch', both in L. Brown et al. (eds), *Vital Signs 1997–1998* (Earthscan, 1997).

HarperCollins Publishers for map 1.2 adapted from map 8 in P. Kennedy, *The Rise and Fall of the Great Powers* (Unwin Hyman, 1988).

MIT Press Journals for figure 8.1 from John W. Meyer, David John Frank, Ann Hironaka, Evan Schofer and Nancy Brandon Turna, 'The structuring of a world environmental regime, 1870–1990', *International Organization*, 51.4 (Autumn, 1997), copyright ©1997 by the IO Foundation and the Massachusetts Institute of Technology.

Myriad Editions for maps 2.1 and 2.2 adapted from originals in Michael Kidron and Dan Smith, *The War Atlas* (Pan, 1983).

OECD for table 3.9 adapted from OECD data in *Structural Adjustment and Economic Performance*, copyright © OECD 1987, and for figures 8.4 and 8.7 adapted from OECD data in *State of the Environment*, copyright © OECD 1991.

Oxford University Press, Inc. for table 1.1 from Craig N. Murphy, *International Organization and Industrial Change*, copyright © 1994 by Craig N. Murphy.

Polity Press for table 1.1 from Craig N. Murphy, *International Organization and Industrial Change* (Polity Press, 1994); table 1.2 from D. Potter et al., *Democratization* (Polity Press, 1997); and table C.1 from A. McGrew, *The Transformation of Democracy?* (Polity Press, 1997).

Routledge for data used in map 6.1 from A. Kenwood and L. Lougheed, *The Growth of the International Economy 1820–1960* (Allen and Unwin, 1989).

Sage Publications and the author for table 7.3 adapted from 'Book translations by country of publication . . .' in Göran Therborn, *European Modernity and Beyond* (Sage, 1995).

Stockholm International Peace Research Institute for figure 2.2 adapted from figure 8.1 in *SIPRI Yearbook 1998: Armaments, Disarmament and International Security* (Oxford University Press, 1998).

UCL Press Ltd for map 1.1 adapted from map in Jeremy Black, *European Warfare, 1660–1815* (1994).

John Wiley and Sons Ltd for maps 1.3, 2.3 and 3.1 adapted from maps in Tom Nierop, *Systems and Regions in Global Politics* (Wiley, 1994), copyright © John Wiley and Sons Ltd 1994.

World Resources Institute for figure 8.6 adapted from *World Resources 1996–1997* (Oxford University Press, 1997).

Worldwatch Institute for table 8.1 adapted from 'Use of chlorofluorocarbons and halons . . .', in L. Brown et al. (eds), *State of the World* (1997).

Although every effort has been made to contact copyright holders, the publishers apologize for any errors or omissions in the above and if notified, they will be pleased to make amendments at the earliest opportunity.

References

Abulafia, D. (1997) 'The impact of Italian banking in the late Middle Ages and the Renaissance 1300–1500', in A. Teichova et al. (eds), *Banking, Trade and Industry*, Cambridge: Cambridge University Press.

Abu-Lughod, J. (1989) *Before European Hegemony: The World System AD 1250–1350*, New York: Oxford University Press.

Adelman, H. (1995) 'The Palestinian diaspora', in Cohen 1995.

Akbari, A. (1989) 'The benefits of immigrants to Canada: evidence on taxes and public services', *Canadian Public Policy*, 15.

Akdogan, H. (1995) *The Integration of International Capital Markets*, Aldershot: Edward Elgar.

Albrow, M. (1996) *The Global Age*, Cambridge: Polity Press.

Allebeck, A. (1993) 'The EC – from the EC to the EU', in Wulf 1993d.

Allen, J. and Hamnet, C. (eds) (1994) *A Shrinking World? Global Unevenness and Inequality*, Oxford: Oxford University Press.

Alston, P. and Chiam, M. (eds) (1995) *Treaty-Making and Australia: Globalization versus Sovereignty?*, Sydney: Federation Press.

Altman, I. (1995) 'Spanish migration to the Americas', in Cohen, 1995.

Amendola, G., Guerrieri, P. and Padoan, P. (1998) 'International patterns of technological accumulation and trade', in D. Archibugi and J. Michie (eds), *Trade Growth and Technical Change*, Cambridge: Cambridge University Press.

Amin, S. (1996) 'The challenge of globalization', *Review of International Political Economy*, 2.

Amin, S. (1997) *Capitalism in the Age of Globalization*, London: Zed Press.

Ancharya, A. (1996) 'Aquaculture production rises', in Brown et al. 1996.

Anderson, B. (1983) *Imagined Communities: Reflections on the Origins and Spread of Nationalism*, London: Verso.

Anderson, K. and Norheim, H. (1993a) 'History, geography and regional economic integration', in K. Anderson and R. Blackhurst (eds), *Regional Integration and the Global Trading System*, Hemel Hempstead: Harvester Wheatsheaf.

Anderson, K. and Norheim, H. (1993b) 'Is world trade becoming more regionalized?', *Review of International Economics*, 1.

Anderson, M. S. (1993) *The Rise of Modern Diplomacy 1450–1919*, London: Longman.

Anderson, P. (1974a) *Passages from Antiquity to Feudalism*, London: New Left Books.

Anderson, P. (1974b) *Lineages of the Absolutist State*, London: New Left Books.

Anthony, I. (1993) 'Arms production and arms trade', in *SIPRI Yearbook 1993*, Oxford: Oxford University Press.

Anthony, I. (1994a) 'Current trends and developments in the arms trade', *Annals of the American Association of Political and Social Sciences*, 535.

Anthony, I. (1994b) 'The third tier countries', in Wulf 1993d.

Anthony, I. and Claesson, P. (1994) 'Arms production and arms trade', in *SIPRI Yearbook 1994*, Oxford: Taylor and Francis.

Appleyard, R. T. (ed.) (1988) *International Migration Today*, vol. 1: *Trends and Consequences*, Paris: UNESCO.

Appleyard, R. T. (ed.) (1989) *The Impact of Migration in Developing Countries*, Paris: OECD.

Archibugi, D. and Michie, J. (1997a) 'The globalization of technology: a new taxonomy', in Archibugi and Michie 1997b.

Archibugi, D. and Michie, J. (eds) (1997b) *Technology, Globalization and Economic Performance*, Cambridge: Cambridge University Press.

Archibugi, D., Held, D. and Köhler, M. (eds) (1998) *Re-imagining Political Community: Studies in Cosmopolitan Democracy*, Cambridge: Polity Press.

Armingeon, K. (1997) 'Globalization as opportunity: two roads to welfare state reform', ECPR Conference Workshop 12, Bern.

Armstrong, P., Glyn, A. and Harrison, J. (1991) *Capitalism since 1945*, Oxford: Blackwell.

Atalik, G. and Beeley, B. (1993) 'What has mass migration meant for Turkey', in King 1993a.

Axford, B. (1995) *The Global System*, Cambridge: Polity Press.

Bade, K. (1985) 'German emigration to the United States and continental immigration to Germany in the late nineteenth and early twentieth centuries', in Hoerder 1985.

Baily, M. and Gersbach, H. (1995) 'Efficiency in manufacturing and the need for global competition', *Brookings Papers on Economic Activity*, Microeconomics issue.

Bailyn, B. (1986) *The Peopling of British North America: An Introduction*, Harvard: Harvard University Press.

Baines, D. (1991) *Emigration from Europe, 1815–1930*, London: Macmillan.

Bairoch, P. (1989) 'European trade policies, 1815–1915', in P. Mathias and S. Pollard (eds), *The Cambridge Economic History of Europe, Volume VIII*, Cambridge: Cambridge University Press.

Bairoch, P. and Kozul-Wright, R. (1996) 'Globalization myths: some historical reflections on integration, industrialization and growth in the world economy', UNCTAD Discussion Paper 113, Geneva.

Balan, J. (1988) 'International migration in Latin America today: trends and consequences', in Appleyard 1988.

Baldwin, T. (1992) 'The territorial state', in H. Gross and T. R. Harrison (eds), *Jurisprudence, Cambridge Essays*, Oxford: Clarendon Press.

Ballance, R., Pogány, J. and Forstner, H. (1992) *The World's Pharmaceutical Industries*, Aldershot: Edward Elgar.

Bank Information Centre (1990) *Funding Ecological and Social Destruction: The World Bank and International Monetary Fund*, Washington: Bank Information Centre.

Banuri, T. and Schor, J. (eds) (1992) *Financial Openness and National Autonomy*, Oxford: Oxford University Press.

Barker, E. (1915) *Political Thought in England, 1848–1914*, London: Thornton Butterworth.

Barnet, R. and Cavanagh, J. (1994) *Global Dreams: Imperial Corporations and the New World Order*, New York: Simon and Schuster.

Barnet, R. and Müller, R. (1974) *Global Reach*, London: Jonathan Cape.

Bartlett, C. J. (1984) *The Global Conflict 1880–1970*, London: Longman.

Bartlett, R. (1994) *The Making of Europe: Conquest, Colonization and Cultural Change 960–1350*, London: Penguin.

Baylis, J. (1986) ' "Greenwoodery" and British defence policy', *International Affairs*, 62.

Beasley, W. G. (1995) *Japan Encounters the Barbarian*, New Haven: Yale University Press.

Beck, U. (1992) *Risk Society: Towards a New Modernity*, London: Sage.

Beck, U. (1995) *Ecological Politics in an Age of Risk*, Cambridge: Polity Press.

Beck, U. (1997) *The Reinvention of Politics*, Cambridge: Polity Press.

Beetham, D. (1998) 'Human rights as a model for cosmopolitan democracy', in Archibugi et al. 1998.

Beitz, C. (1979) *Political Theory and International Relations*, Princeton: Princeton University Press.

Bell, D. (1973) *The Coming of Post-Industrial Society*, New York: Basic Books.

Benedick, R. (1991) *Ozone Diplomacy: New Directions in Safeguarding the Planet*, Cambridge: Harvard University Press.

Bentley, J. H. (1993) *Old World Encounters: Cross-Cultural Contacts and Exchanges in Premodern Times*, Oxford: Oxford University Press.

Bentley, J. H. (1996) 'Cross-cultural interaction and periodization in world history', *American Historical Review*, 101, June.

Benton, L. (1996) 'From the world systems perspective to institutional world history: culture and economy in global theory', *Journal of World History*, 7.

Bergesen, A. and Fernandez, R. (1995) 'Who has the most Fortune 500 firms? A network analysis of global economic competition, 1956–1989', *Journal of World-Systems Research*, 1.

Best, G. (1980) *Humanity in Warfare: The Modern History of the Law of Armed Conflict*, London: Weidenfeld and Nicolson.

BIS (1997) *Annual Report*, Basle: Bank for International Settlements.

BIS (1998a) *International Banking and Financial Market Developments*, Basle: Bank for International Settlements.

BIS (1998b) 'Central bank survey of foreign exchange and derivatives market activity in April 1998', press release, Bank for International Settlements (www.bis.org).

Bitzinger, R. A. (1993) *The Globalization of Arms Production: Defence Markets in Transition*, Washington DC: Defence Budget Project.

Bitzinger, R. A. (1994) 'The globalization of the arms industry', *International Security*, 19.

Black, J. (1991) *A Military Revolution? Military Change and European Society 1550–1800*, London: Macmillan.

Black, J. (1994) *European Warfare 1660–1815*, New Haven: Yale University Press.

Black, J. (1998) *War and the World: Military Power and the Fate of Continents 1450–2000*, New Haven: Yale University Press.

Blackburn, R. (1988) *The Overthrow of Colonial Slavery, 1776–1848*, London: Verso.

Blackburn, R. (1997) *The Making of New World Slavery: From the Baroque to the Modern, 1492–1800*, London: Verso.

Bleaney, M. (1993) 'Politics and the exchange rate', *Economic Notes*, 22.

Blomström, M. (1990) *Transnational Corporations and Manufacturing Exports from Developing Countries*, New York: United Nations.

Blomström, M. and Lipsey, R. (1989) 'The export performance of US and Swedish multinationals', *Review of Income and Wealth*, 35.

Blomström, M. and Lipsey, R. (1993) 'The competitiveness of countries and their multinational firms', in L. Eden and E. Potter (eds), *Multinationals in the Global Political Economy*, Basingstoke: Macmillan.

Blomström, M., Lipsey, R. and Zejan, M. (1992) 'What explains developing country growth?', in W. Baumol et al. (eds), *Convergence of Productivity*, Oxford: Oxford University Press.

Bloomfield, A. (1959) *Monetary Policy under the International Gold Standard, 1880–1914*, New York: Federal Reserve Bank of New York.

Blowers, A. and Lowry, D. (1991) 'The politics of radioactive waste disposal' in Blunden and Reddish 1991.

Blunden, J. and Reddish, A. (eds) (1991) *Energy, Resources and Environment*, London: Hodder and Stoughton.

Bobbio, N. (1987) *Which Socialism?*, Cambridge: Polity Press.

Bobbio, N. (1989) *Democracy and Dictatorship*, Cambridge: Polity Press.

Boehmer-Christiansen, S. and Skea, J. (1991) *Acid Politics: Environmental and Energy Policies in Britain and Germany*, London: Belhaven Press.

Böhning (1991) 'Integration and immigration pressures in Western Europe', *International Labour Review*, 130.

Boltho, A. (1996a) 'Convergence, competitiveness and the exchange rate', in N. Crafts and G. Toniolo (eds), *Economic Growth in Europe since 1945*, Cambridge: Cambridge University Press.

Boltho, A. (1996b) 'Was Japanese growth export-led?', *Oxford Economic Papers*, 48.

Bond, B. (1984) *War and Society in Europe 1870–1970*, London: Fontana.

Bonturi, M. and Fukasaku, K. (1993) 'Globalization and intra-firm trade', *OECD Economic Studies*, 20.

Booth, K. (1991) 'Security in anarchy: utopian realism in theory and practice', *International Affairs*, 67.

Borjas, G. (1987) 'Immigrants, minorities and labour market competition', *Industrial and Labour Relations Review*, 40.

Borjas, G. (1990) *Friends or Strangers: The Impact of Immigration on the US Economy*, New York: Basic Books.

Borjas, G. (1993) 'The impact of immigrants on employment opportunities of natives', in OECD 1993a.

Borjas, G. and Trejo, S. (1993) 'The macroeconomic impact of immigration: review of the literature published since the mid-1970s', in OECD 1993a.

Borrus, M. and Zysman, J. (1997) 'Wintelism and the changing terms of global competition: prototype of the future', BRIE Working Paper 96B, Berkeley.

Boyer, R. and Drache, D. (eds) (1996) *States against Markets*, London: Routledge.

Bracken, P. (1983) *The Command and Control of Nuclear Forces*, New Haven: Yale University Press.

Braudel, F. (1982) *The Wheels of Commerce*, vol. 2 of *Civilization and Capitalism*, London: Collins.

Braudel, F. (1984) *The Perspective of the World*, vol. 3 of *Civilization and Capitalism*, London: Collins.

Breuilly, J. (1992) *Nationalism and the State*, Manchester: Manchester University Press.

Brodie, B. (1973) *War and Politics*, London: Cassell.

Broeck, J. van den (ed.) (1996) *The Economics of Labour Migration*, London: Edward Elgar.

Brown, L. et al. (1990) *State of the World: 1990*, London: Unwin Hyman.

Brown, L. et al. (eds) (1995) *Vital Signs, 1995–1996*, London: Earthscan.

Brown, L. et al. (eds) (1996) *Vital Signs, 1996–1997*, London: Earthscan.

Brown, L. et al. (eds) (1997a) *State of the World 1997*, Washington: Worldwatch Institute.

Brown, L. et al. (eds) (1997b) *Vital Signs, 1997–1998*, London: Earthscan.

Brown, S. (1994) *The Causes and Prevention of War*, New York: St Martins Press.

Bruce, J. et al. (eds) (1995) *Climate Change 1995: Economic and Social Dimensions of Climate Change*, Cambridge: Cambridge University Press.

Brunn, S. and Leinbach, T. (eds) (1991) *Collapsing Time and Space: Geographic Aspects of Communication and Information*, London: HarperCollins.

Bryant, R. (1987) *International Financial Intermediation*, Washington DC: Brookings Institution.

Brysk, A. (1993) 'From above and below: social movements, the international system, and human rights in Argentina', *Comparative Political Studies*, 26.

Bryson, R. and Murray, T. (1977) *Climates of Hunger: Mankind and the World's Changing Weather*, Madison: University of Wisconsin Press.

Brzoska, M. and Ohlson, T. (1986) 'Arms production in the Third World', in M. Brzoska and T. Ohlson (eds), *Arms Production in the Third World*, Oxford: Taylor and Francis.

Brzoska, M. and Ohlson, T. (1987) *Arms Transfers to the Third World 1971–1985*, Oxford: Oxford University Press.

Brzoska, M. and Pearson, F. S. (1994) 'Developments in the global supply of Arms', *Annals of the American Academy of Political and Social Sciences*, 535.

Bull, H. (1977) *The Anarchical Society*, London: Macmillan.

Burbach, R. et al. (1997) *Globalization and its Discontents*, London: Pluto Press.

Burnett, R. (1992) 'Dressed for success; Sweden from Abba to Roxette', *Popular Music*, 11.

Burnheim, J. (1986) *Is Democracy Possible?*, Cambridge: Polity Press.

Busch, B. C. (1985) *The War against the Seals: A History of the North American Seal Fishery*, Montreal: McGill-Queen's University Press.

Bustamante, J. (1989) 'Measuring the flows of undocumented immigrants', in Cornelius and Bustamante 1989.

Buzan, B. (1987) *Strategic Studies: Military Technology and International Relations*, London: Macmillan.

Buzan, B. (1991) *People, States and Fear*, Brighton: Harvester.

Buzan, B. (1998) 'The Asia-Pacific: what sort of region, in what sort of world?', in McGrew and Brook 1998.

Buzan, B., Little, R. and Jones, C. (1993) *The Logic of Anarchy*, New York: Columbia University Press.

Buzan, B., Waever, O. and de Wilde, Jaap (1998) *Security: A New Framework for Analysis*, Boulder: Lynne Reinner.

Cain, P. J. and Hopkins, A. G. (1993a) *British Imperialism: Crisis and Deconstruction 1914–1990*, London: Longman.

Cain, P. J. and Hopkins, A. G. (1993b) *British Imperialism: Innovation and Expansion 1688–1914*, London: Longman.

Callinicos, A. et al. (1994) *Marxism and the New Imperialism*, London: Bookmarks.

Cameron, R. and Bovykin, V. (eds) (1991) *International Banking, 1870–1914*, New York: Oxford University Press.

Cammilleri, J. A. (1990) 'Rethinking sovereignty in a shrinking, fragmented world', in R. B. J. Walker and S. H. Mendlovitz (eds), *Contending Sovereignties: Redefining Political Community*, Boulder and London: Lynne Rienner.

Cammilleri, J. A. and Falk, J. (1992) *The End of Sovereignty? The Politics of a Shrinking and Fragmented World*, Aldershot: Edward Elgar.

Cantwell, J. (1989) *Technological Innovation and Multinational Corporations*, Oxford: Blackwell.

Cantwell, J. (1997) 'The globalization of technology: what remains of the product cycle?', in Archibugi and Michie 1997b.

Capotorti, F. (1983) 'Human rights: the hard road towards universality', in R. St J. Macdonald and D. M. Johnson (eds), *The Structure and Process of International Law*, The Hague: Martinus Nijhoff.

Carlos, A. and Nicholas, S. (1988) '"Giants of an earlier capitalism": the chartered trading companies as modern multinationals', *Business History Review*, 62.

Carnoy, M. (1993) 'Multinationals in a changing world economy', in M. Carnoy et al. (eds), *The New Global Economy in the Information Age*, University Park: Pennsylvania State University Press.

Carr, E. H. (1981) *The Twenty Years Crisis 1919–1939*, London: Papermac.

Carus, W. S. (1994) 'Military technology and the arms trade', *Annals of the American Academy of Political and Social Sciences*, 535.

Cassese, A. (1986) *International Law in a Divided World*, Oxford: Clarendon Press.

Cassese, A. (1988) *Violence and Law in the Modern Age*, Cambridge: Polity Press.

Cassese, A. (1991) 'Violence, war and the rule of law in the international community', in D. Held (ed.), *Political Theory Today*, Cambridge: Polity Press.

Casson, M. (1995) *The Organization of International Business*, Aldershot: Edward Elgar.

Cassou, S. (1997) 'The link between tax rates and foreign direct investment', *Applied Economics*, 29.

Castells, M. (1996) *The Rise of the Network Society*, Oxford: Blackwell.

Castells, M. (1998) *The End of the Millennium*, Oxford: Blackwell.

Castles, S. and Kosack, G. (1985) *Immigrant Workers and the Class Structure in Western Europe* (2nd edn), Oxford: Oxford University Press.

Castles, S. and Miller, M. (1993) *The Age of Migration: International Population Movements in the Modern World*, London: Macmillan.

Caves, M. (1996) *Multinational Enterprise and Economic Analysis*, Cambridge: Cambridge University Press.

Ceckak, O. (1993) 'Czechoslovakia', in Wulf 1993d.

Cerny, P. (1990) *The Changing Architecture of the State*, London: Sage.

Chan, S. (ed.) (1995) *Foreign Direct Investment in a Changing Global Political Economy*, Basingstoke: Macmillan.

Chapman, K. (1991) *The International Petrochemical Industry*, Oxford: Blackwell.

Chase-Dunn, C. (1989) *Global Formation*, Oxford: Blackwell.

Chatterjee, P. (1986) *Nationalist Thought and the Colonial World: A Derivative Discourse?*, London: Zed Books.

Chatterjee, P. (1993) *The Nation and its Fragments: Colonial and Postcolonial Histories*, Princeton: Princeton University Press.

Chaudhuri, K. (1985) *Trade and Civilisation in the Indian Ocean: An Economic History from the Rise of Islam to 1750*, Cambridge: Cambridge University Press.

Chaudhuri, K. (1990) *Asia before Europe: Economy and Civilization of the Indian Ocean from the Rise of Islam to 1750*, Cambridge: Cambridge University Press.

Childers, E. (1993) *In a Time beyond Warnings*, London: CIIR.

Cipolla, C. (1978) *The Economic History of World Population*, Brighton: Harvester Press.

Clarence-Smith, W. G. (ed.) (1989) *The Economics of the Indian Ocean Slave Trade in the Nineteenth Century*, London: Frank Cass.

Clark, I. (1989) *The Hierarchy of States*, Cambridge: Cambridge University Press.

Clark, J. (1981) 'Land armament in France: the tradition of étatism', in B. F. Cooling (ed.), *War, Business and World Military Industrial Complexes*, London: National University Publications.

Clark, R. P. (1997) *The Global Imperative: An Interpretative History of the Spread of Mankind*, Boulder: Westview Press.

Clarke, C., Peach, C. and Vertovec, S. (eds) (1990) *South Asian Overseas: Migration and Ethnicity*, Cambridge: Cambridge University Press.

Clarke, M. (1992) *Britain's External Relations*, London: Macmillan.

Clausewitz, C. (1984) *On War*, Princeton: Princeton University Press.

Clegg, J. (1987) *Multinational Enterprise and World Competition*, Basingstoke: Macmillan.

Cohen, R. (1981) *International Politics: The Rules of the Game*, London: Longman.

Cohen, R. (ed.) (1995) *The Cambridge Survey of World Migration*, Cambridge: Cambridge University Press.

Colley, L. (1992) *Britons: Forging the Nation, 1707–1837*, New Haven: Yale University Press.

Colten, C. (1986) 'Industrial wastes in south-east Chicago: production and disposal, 1870–1970', *Environmental Review*, Summer.

Commission on Global Governance (1995) *Our Global Neighbourhood*, Oxford: Oxford University Press.

Commission on Neutrality Policy (1994) *Had There Been a War: Preparations for the Reception of Military Assistance 1949–69*, Stockholm: Statens Offentliga Utredningar.

Connca, K. (1992) 'Third World military industrialization and the evolving security system', in W. Sandholtz et al. (eds), *The Highest Stakes: The Economic Foundations of the Next Security System*, New York: Oxford University Press.

Connolly, W. E. (1991) 'Democracy and territoriality', *Millennium*, 20.3.

Connolly, W. E. (1996) *The Ethos of Pluralization*, Minneapolis: University of Minnesota Press.

Contamine, P. (1984) *War in the Middle Ages*, Oxford: Blackwell.

Cornelius, W. and Bustamante, J. (eds) (1989) *Mexican Migration to the United States: Origins, Consequences and Policy Options*, La Jolla: Centre for US-Mexican Studies, University of California.

Cörvens, F. and Grip, A. de (1997) 'Explaining trade in industrialized countries by country-specific human capital endowments', *Economic Modelling*, 14.

Cowhey, P. F. (1990) 'The international telecommunications regime', *International Organization*, 44.

Cowling, K. and Sugden, R. (1996) 'Capacity, transnational and industrial strategy', in J. Michie and J. Grieve Smith (eds), *Creating Industrial Capacity*, Oxford: Oxford University Press.

Cox, R. (1996) 'Globalization, multilateralism and democracy', in R. Cox (ed.), *Approaches to World Order*, Cambridge: Cambridge University Press.

Cox, R. (1997) 'Economic globalization and the limits to liberal democracy', in McGrew 1997.

Crawford, J. (1979a) 'Decisions of British courts during 1979 involving questions of public or private international law', *British Year Book of International Law*, 50.

Crawford, J. (1979b) 'The international law standard in the statutes of Australia and the United Kingdom', *American Journal of International Law*, 73.

Crawford, J. (1994) *Democracy in International Law*, Inaugural lecture, Cambridge: Cambridge University Press.

Crawford, J. (1995) 'Prospects for an international criminal court', in M. D. A. Freeman and R. Halson (eds), *Current Legal Problems 1995*, 48, pt 2, collected papers, Oxford: Oxford University Press.

Crawford, J. and Marks, S. (1998) 'The global democracy deficit: an essay on international law and its limits', in Archibugi et al. 1998.

Creveld, M. van (1989) *Technology and War: From 2000 BC to the Present*, New York: Free Press.

Creveld, M. van (1991) *The Transformation of War*, New York: Free Press.

Creveld, M. van (1993) *Nuclear Proliferation and the Future of Conflict*, New York: Free Press.

Cronon, W. (1983) *Changes in the Land: Indians, Colonists and the Ecology of New England*, New York: Hill and Wang.

Cronon, W. (1991) *Nature's Metropolis: Chicago and the Great West*, New York: Norton.

Crosby, A. (1972) *The Columbian Exchange: Biological and Cultural Consequences of 1492*, Westport: Greenwood.

Crosby, A. (1983) *Ecological Imperialism: The Biological Expansion of Europe, 900–1900*, Cambridge: Cambridge University Press.

Cross, G. S. (1983) *Immigrant Workers in Industrial France*, Philadelphia: Temple University Press.

Crystal, D. (1997) *English as a Global Language*, Cambridge: Cambridge University Press.

Curtin, P. (1969) *The Atlantic Slave Trade: A Census*, Madison: University of Wisconsin Press.

Curtin, P. (1978) 'Post-war migrations in sub-Saharan Africa', in McNeill and Adams 1978.

Curtin, P. (1984) *Cross-Cultural Trade in World History*, Cambridge: Cambridge University Press.

Curtin, P. (1997) 'Africa and global patterns of migration', in Wang 1997.

Dahl, R. A. (1989) *Democracy and its Critics*, New Haven: Yale University Press.

Daniels, P. (1993) *Service Industries in the World Economy*, Oxford: Blackwell.

Darby, M. and Lothian, J. (1983) *The International Transmission of Inflation*, Chicago: University of Chicago Press.

Dasmann, R. (1988) 'Towards a biosphere consciousness', in Worster 1988.

D'Aveni, R. (1998) 'Hyper-competition closes in', *Financial Times*, Supplement: Mastering Global Business, Part 2 (Feb.).

Davis, C. (1993) *The Politics of Hazardous Waste*, Englewood Cliffs: Prentice Hall.

Davis, E. (1991) 'International diversification of institutional investors', *Journal of International Securities Markets*, 5.

Deardorff, A. and Stern, M. (1986) *The Michigan Model of World Production and Trade*, Cambridge: MIT Press.

Deibert, R. (1997) *Parchment, Printing and Hypermedia*, New York: Columbia University Press.

De Jong, N. and Vos, R. (1995) 'Regional blocs or global markets? A world accounting approach to analyze trade and financial linkages', *Weltwirtschaftliches Archiv*, 131.

de Las Casas, Bartolomé (1992) *The Destruction of the Indies* (1552), Baltimore: Johns Hopkins University Press.

de Mello, L. (1997) 'Foreign direct investment in developing countries and growth', *Journal of Development Studies*, 34, no. 1.

Deng, G. (1997) 'The foreign staple trade of China in the pre-modern era', *International History Review*, 19, no. 2.

Derian, J. der (1987) *On Diplomacy: A Genealogy of Western Estrangement*, Oxford: Blackwell.

De Swann, A. (1991) 'Notes on the emerging global language system: regional, national and supranational', *Media, Culture and Society*, 13.

Deutsch, K. and Burrell, S. A. (1957) *Political Community and the North Atlantic Area*, Princeton: Princeton University Press.

Diamond, J. (1997) *Guns, Germs and Steel: A Short History of Everybody for the Last 13,000 Years*, London: Cape.

Diaz, B. (1963) *The Conquest of New Spain*, London: Penguin.

Dicken, P. (1998) *Global Shift* (3rd edn), London: Chapman.

Dickenson, D. (1997) 'Counting women in', in McGrew 1997.

Dinstein, Y. (1993) 'Rules of war', in J. Krieger (ed.), *The Oxford Companion to Politics of the World*, Oxford: Oxford University Press.

Directorate General X (1997) *Eurobarometer: Public Opinion in the European Union*, Report 47, Brussels: European Commission.

Dollar, D. and Wolff, E. (1993) *Competitiveness, Comparative Advantage and International Specialization*, Cambridge, Mass.: MIT Press.

Dominguez, K. (1993) 'The role of international organizations in the Bretton Woods system', in M. Bordo and B. Eichengreen (eds), *A Retrospective on the Bretton Woods System*, Chicago: University of Chicago Press.

Dominguez, K. and Frankel, J. (1993) *Does Foreign Exchange Intervention Work?*, Washington DC: Institute for International Economics.

Donnelly, J. (1993) *International Human Rights*, Boulder: Westview Press.

Donnelly, J. (1998) 'Human rights: a new standard of civilization?', *International Affairs*, 74, no. 1.

Dooley, M. and Isard, P. (1980) 'Capital controls, political risk, and deviations from interest rate parity', *Journal of Political Economy*, 88.

Dore, R. (ed.) (1995) *Convergence or Diversity? National Models of Production in a Global Economy*, New York: Cornell University Press.

Downmunt, T. (ed.) (1991) *Channels of Resistance: Global Television and Local Empowerment*, London: BFI.

Doyle, M. (1986) *Empires*, New York: Cornell University Press.

Dugard, J. (1997) 'Obstacles in the way of an international criminal court', *Cambridge Law Journal*, 56.

Dunning, J. (1988) 'Changes in the level and structure of international production: the last one hundred years', in J. Dunning, *Explaining International Production*, London: Unwin Hyman.

Dunning, J. (1993a) *The Globalization of Business*, London: Routledge.

Dunning, J. (1993b) *Multinational Enterprises and the Global Economy*, Wokingham: Addison-Wesley.

Dunning, J. (1997) *Alliance Capitalism and Global Business*, London: Routledge.

Ecologist, The (1972) 'Blueprint for survival', *The Ecologist*, 2.

Economist (1996) 'The coming global tongue', *The Economist*, 21 Dec.

Economist Intelligence Unit (1994) 'Military aerospace', *The Economist*, 333.

Economist Intelligence Unit (1995) 'Change at the checkout: a survey of retailing', *The Economist*, 334.

Eichengreen, B. (1992) *Golden Fetters: The Gold Standard and the Great Depression, 1919–1939*, New York: Oxford University Press.

Eichengreen, B. (1994a) 'History of the international monetary system', in F. van der Ploeg (ed.), *The Handbook of International Macroeconomics*, Oxford: Blackwell.

Eichengreen, B. (1994b) *International Monetary Arrangements for the Twenty-First Century*, Washington DC: Brookings Institution.

Eichengreen, B. (1996) *Globalizing Capital: A History of the International Monetary System*, Princeton: Princeton University Press.

Eichengreen, B. and Irwin, D. (1995) 'Trade blocs, currency blocs and the reorientation of world trade in the 1930s', *Journal of International Economics*, 38.

Eisenstadt, S. (1963) *The Political System of Empires*, New York: Free Press.

Emmer, P. (1993) 'Intercontinental migration as a world historical process', *European Review*, 1, no. 1.

EPAC (1996) 'Tariff reform and economic growth', Commission Paper 10, Economic Planning Advisory Commission, Canberra.

Ernst, D. (1997) 'From partial to systemic globalization: international production networks in the electronics industry', Working Paper 98, Berkeley Roundtable on the International Economy, University of California at Berkeley.

Evans, R. (1987) *Death in Hamburg: Society and Politics in the Cholera Years, 1830–1910*, Oxford: Oxford University Press.

Evans, T. (1997) 'Democratization and human rights', in McGrew 1997.

Fagan, B. (1990) *The Journey from Eden: The Peopling of our World*, London: Thames and Hudson.

Falk, R. (1969) 'The interplay of Westphalian and Charter conceptions of the international legal order', in R. Falk and C. Black (eds), *The Future of the International Legal Order*, vol. 1, Princeton: Princeton University Press.

Falk, R. (1970) *The Status of Law in International Society*, Princeton: Princeton University Press.

Falk, R. (1975a) *A Global Approach to National Policy*, Cambridge: Harvard University Press.

Falk, R. (1975b) *A Study of Future Worlds*, New York: Free Press.

Falk, R. (1990) 'Economic dimensions of global civilization', working paper prepared for the Cairo meeting of the Global Civilization Project, Center for International Studies, Princeton University.

Falk, R. (1995) *On Humane Governance: Toward a New Global Politics*, Cambridge: Polity Press.

FAO (1994) *Yearbook of Fisheries Statistics*, Rome: Food and Agriculture Organisation.

Fawcett, J. and Cariño, B. (eds) (1987) *Pacific Bridges: The New Immigration from Asia and the Pacific Islands*, New York: Centre for Migration Studies.

Feinstein, C. (1972) *National Income, Expenditure and Output in the United Kingdom, 1855–1968*, London: Cambridge University Press.

Feldstein, M. and Horioka, C. (1980) 'Domestic saving and international capital flows', *Economic Journal*, 90.

Fernández-Armesto, F. (1995) *Millennium*, London: Bantam.

Ferro, M. (1997) *Colonization: A Global History*, London: Routledge.

Fieldhouse, D. K. (1966) *The Colonial Empires: A Comparative Survey*, London: Weidenfeld and Nicolson.

Financial Times (1997) 'When capital collides with labour', *Financial Times*, 24 Oct.

Findlay, R. (1990) 'The "triangular trade" and the Atlantic economy of the eighteenth century', *Essays in International Finance*, no. 177, International Finance Section, Princeton University.

Fischer, R. (1963) *The Russian Fur Trade, 1550–1700*, Berkeley: University of California Press.

Fischman, B. C. and Moodie, M. L. (1989) 'Alliance armaments co-operation: toward a NATO industrial base', in D. G. Haglund (ed.), *The Defence Industrial Base and the West*, London: Routledge.

Fisher, J. (1989) *Mothers of the Disappeared*, London: Zed Books.

Fong, P. E. (1993) *Regionalisation and Labour Flows in Pacific Asia*, Paris: OECD.

Foot, P. (1965) *Immigration and Race in British Politics*, Harmondsworth: Penguin.

Ford, A. (1989) 'International financial policy and the gold standard, 1870–1914', in P. Mathias and S. Pollard (eds), *The Cambridge Economic History of Europe, Volume VIII*, Cambridge: Cambridge University Press.

Forsyth, M. (1992) 'The tradition of international law', in T. Nardin and D. R. Mapel (eds), *Traditions of International Ethics*, Cambridge: Cambridge University Press.

Fox-Genovese, E. and Genovese, E. (1983) *Fruits of Merchant Capital: Slavery and Bourgeois Property in the Rise and Expansion of Capitalism*, Oxford: Oxford University Press.

Frank, A. G. and Gills, B. K. (eds) (1996) *The World System*, London: Routledge.

Frankel, J. (1993) *On Exchange Rates*, Cambridge, Mass.: MIT Press.

Frankel, J. (ed.) (1994) *The Internationalization of Equity Markets*, Chicago: University of Chicago Press.

Frankel, J. and Chinn, M. (1993) 'Exchange rate expectations and the risk premium: tests for a cross section of 17 currencies', *Review of International Economics*, 1.

Frankel, J. and Froot, K. (1990) 'Chartists, fundamentalists and the demand for dollars', in A. Courakis and M. Taylor (eds), *Private Behaviour and Government Policy in Interdependent Economies*, Oxford: Oxford University Press.

Frankel, J. and MacArthur, A. (1988) 'Political versus currency premia in international real interest differentials', *European Economic Review*, 32.

Frankenstein, J. (1993) 'Peoples Republic of China', in Wulf 1993d.

Freeman, C. (1997) 'The national system of innovation in historical perspective', in Archibugi and Michie 1997b.

Freeman, G. (1979) *Immigrant Labour and Racial Conflict in Industrial Societies: The French and British Experiences, 1945–1975*, Princeton: Princeton University Press.

French, H. (1990) 'Clearing the air', in Brown et al. 1990.

Friedberg, A. L. (1991) 'The end of autonomy: the United States after five decades', *Daedalus*, 120.

Frieden, J. (1991) 'Invested interests: the politics of national economic policies in a world of global finance', *International Organization*, 45.

Frieden, J. A. and Rogowski, R. (1996) 'The impact of the international economy on national policies: an analytical overview', in Keohane and Milner 1996.

Friedmann, W. (1964) *The Changing Structure of International Law*, London: Stevens and Son.

Fukao, M. (1993) 'International integration of financial markets and the costs of capital', *Journal of International Securities Markets*, 7.

Fukao, M. (1995) *Financial Integration, Corporate Governance and the Performance of Multinational Corporations*, Washington DC: Brookings Institution.

Fukuyama, F. (1989) 'The end of history?', *National Interest*, 16.

Furnivall, J. S. (1948) *Colonial Policy and Practice*, Cambridge: Cambridge University Press.

Gagnon, J. and Unferth, M. (1995) 'Is there a world real interest rate?', *Journal of International Money and Finance*, 14.

Gansler, J. (1995) *Defense Conversion*, Boston: MIT Press.

Garcia, S. (ed.) (1993) *European Identity and the Search for Legitimacy*, London: Pinter.

Garrard, J. (1971) *The English and Immigration: A Comparative Study of the Jewish Influx*, London: Oxford University Press.

Garrett, G. (1996) 'Capital mobility, trade, and the domestic politics of economic policy', in Keohane and Milner 1996.

Garrett, G. and Lange, P. (1991) 'Political responses to interdependence: what's "left" for the left?', *International Organization*, 45.

Garrett, G. and Lange, P. (1996) 'Internationalization, institutions, and political change', in Keohane and Milner 1996.

Gellner, E. (1981) *Muslim Society*, Cambridge: Cambridge University Press.

Gereffi, G. (1994) 'The organization of buyer driven global commodity chains', in Gereffi and Korzeniewicz 1994.

Gereffi, G. and Korzeniewicz, M. (eds) (1994) *Commodity Chains and Global Capitalism*, Westport: Praeger.

Germain, R. (1997) *The International Organization of Credit*, Cambridge: Cambridge University Press.

Geyer, M. and Bright, C. (1995) 'World history in a global age', *American Historical Review*, 100.

Ghosh, A. (1995) 'International capital mobility amongst the major industrialized countries: too little or too much?', *Economic Journal*, 105.

Ghosh, B. (1996) 'Economic migration and the sending countries', in Broeck 1996.

Giddens, A. (1979) *Central Problems in Social Theory: Action, Structure and Contradiction in Social Analysis*, London: Macmillan.

Giddens, A. (1981) *A Contemporary Critique of Historical Materialism* vol. 1, London: Macmillan.

Giddens, A. (1984) *The Constitution of Society*, Cambridge: Polity Press.

Giddens, A. (1985) *The Nation-State and Violence*, vol. 2 of *A Contemporary Critique of Historical Materialism*, Cambridge: Polity Press.

Giddens, A. (1990) *The Consequences of Modernity*, Cambridge: Polity Press.

Giddens, A. (1991) *Modernity and Self-identity*, Cambridge: Polity Press.

Giddens, A. (1995) *Beyond Left and Right*, Cambridge: Polity Press.

Giddens, A. (1996) 'Globalization: a keynote address', *UNRISD News*, 15.

Gill, B. (1994) 'Arms acquisitions in East Asia', in *SIPRI Yearbook 1994*, Oxford: Taylor and Francis.

Gill, S. (1995) 'Globalization, market civilization, and disciplinary neoliberalism', *Millennium*, 24.

Gilpin, R. (1981) *War and Change in World Politics*, Cambridge: Cambridge University Press.

Gilpin, R. (1987) *The Political Economy of International Relations*, Princeton: Princeton University Press.

Gilroy, P. (1987) *There Ain't No Black in the Union Jack*, London: Hutchinson.

Gilroy, P. (1993) *The Black Atlantic*, London: Verso.

Gjerde, J. (1995) 'The Scandinavian migrants', in Cohen 1995.

Glebe, G. and O'Loughlin, J. (1987) *Foreign Minorities in Continental European Cities*, Wiesbaden: Steiner.

Glennon, M. J. (1990) *Constitutional Diplomacy*, Princeton: Princeton University Press.

Goldblatt, D. (1996) *Social Theory and the Environment*, Cambridge: Polity Press.

Golini, A., Gerrano, G. and Heins, F. (1991) 'South–north migration with special reference to Europe', *International Migration*, June.

Golub, S. (1990) 'International capital mobility: net versus gross stocks and flows', *Journal of International Money and Finance*, 9.

Goodhart, C. (1985) *The Evolution of Central Banks*, Cambridge, Mass.: MIT Press.

Goodman, J. (1997) 'The European Union: reconstituting democracy beyond the nation-state', in McGrew 1997.

Goody, J. (1986) *The Logic of Writing and the Organisation of Society*, Cambridge: Cambridge University Press.

Gopinath, P. (1997) 'Global production systems', paper delivered at the Conference on International Solidarity and Globalisation, Stockholm, 18 and 29 Oct.

Gordon, D. (1988) 'The global economy: new edifice or crumbling foundations?', *New Left Review*, 168.

Grabel, I. (1995) 'Speculation-led economic development: a post-Keynesian interpretation of financial liberalization programmes in the Third World', *International Review of Applied Economics*, 9.

Graham, E. (1996) *Global Corporations and National Governments*, Washington DC: Institute for International Economics.

Graham, G. (1997) *The Shape of the Past: A Philosophical Approach to History*, Oxford: Oxford University Press.

Gray, C. (1997) *Postmodern War*, London: Routledge.

Gray, J. (1996) *After Social Democracy*, London: Demos.

Gray, J. (1998) *False Dawn*, London: Granta.

Green, A. and Urquhart, M. (1976) 'Factor and commodity flows in the international economy of 1870–1914', *Journal of Economic History*, 36.

Green, N. (1985) '"Filling the void": immigration to France before World War I', in Hoerder 1985.

Greenpeace (1990) *The International Trade in Toxic Wastes: An International Inventory*, Washington: Greenpeace International.

Greenpeace (1993) *The International Trade in Toxic Wastes: An International Inventory*, Washington: Greenpeace International.

Greenwood, C. (1993) 'Is there a right of humanitarian intervention?', *The World Today*, Feb.

Gregorio, J. de, Giovannini, A. and Wolf, H. (1994) 'International evidence on tradables and nontradables inflation', *European Economic Review*, 38.

Greider, W. (1997) *One World, Ready or Not: The Manic Logic of Global Capitalism*, New York: Simon Schuster.

Grove, E. (1997) *Ecology, Climate and Empire: Colonial and Global Environmental History 1400–1940*, London: White House Press

Grugel, J. (1996) 'Latin America and the remaking of the Americas', in A. Gamble and A. Payne (eds), *Regionalism and World Order*, London: Macmillan.

Guéhenno, J. M. (1995) *The End of the Nation-State*, Minneapolis: University of Minnesota Press.

Gustavsson, P., Hansson, P. and Lundberg, L. (1997) 'Technical progress, capital accumulation and international competitiveness', in J. Fagerberg et al. (eds), *Technology and International Trade*, Cheltenham: Edward Elgar.

Gyory, M. and Glas, G. (1994) *Statistics on the Film Industry in Europe*, Brussels: European Centre for Research and Information on Film and Television.

Haas, E. (1990) *When Knowledge is Power: Three Models of Change in International Organisations*, Berkeley: University of California Press.

Haas, P. (1990) *Saving the Mediterranean: The Politics of International Environmental Cooperation*, New York: Columbia University Press.

Haas, P. (1992) 'Introduction: epistemic communities and international policy coordination', *International Organization*, 43.

Haas, P. (1993) 'Protecting the Baltic and North Seas', in Haas et al. 1993.

Haas, P., Keohane, R. and Levy, M. (eds) (1993) *Institutions for the Earth: Sources of Effective International Environmental Protection*, Cambridge: MIT Press.

Haggard, S. and Maxfield, S. (1996) 'The political economy of financial internationalization in the developing world', in Keohane and Milner 1996.

Haglund, D. G. (1989) 'Techno-nationalism and the contemporary debate over the American defence industrial base', in D. G. Haglund (ed.), *The Defence Industrial Base and the West*, London: Routledge.

Haigh, N. (1990) *EEC Environmental Policy and Britain* (2nd edn), London: Longman.

Haigh, N. (1992) 'The EC and international environmental policy', in Hurrell and Kingsbury 1992.

Hall, J. A. (1986) *Powers and Liberties: The Causes and Consequences of the Rise of the West*, London: Penguin.

Hall, J. A. (1996) *International Orders: An Historical Sociology of State, Regime, Class and Nation*, Cambridge: Polity Press.

Ham, R. and Mowery, D. (1997) 'The United States of America', in J. Dunning (ed.), *Governments, Globalization and International Business*, Oxford: Oxford University Press.

Hamelink, C. (1988) *Cultural Autonomy in Global Communication*, London: Longman.

Hamelink, C. (1995) *World Communication: Disempowerment and Self-Empowerment*, London: Zed Books.

Hamilton, K. and Langhorne, R. (1995) *The Practice of Diplomacy*, London: Routledge.

Hannertz, U. (1990) 'Cosmopolitans and locals in world culture', *Theory, Culture and Society*, 7.

Hannigan, J. (1995) *Environmental Sociology: A Social Constructivist Perspective*, London: Routledge.

Hanson, J. (1980) *Trade in Transition: Exports from the Third World, 1840–1900*, New York: Academic Press.

Hansson, P. and Henrekson, M. (1994) 'Catching-up in industrialized countries', *Journal of International Trade and Economic Development*, 3.

Harkavy, R. (1975) *The Arms Trade and International Systems*, New York: Ballinger.

Harkavy, R. (1989) *Bases Abroad: The Global Foreign Military Presence*, Oxford: Oxford University Press.

Harkavy, R. (1994) 'The changing international system and the arms trade', *Annals of the American Association of Political and Social Science (AAPSS)*, 535.

Harrigan, J. (1993) 'OECD imports and trade barriers in 1983', *Journal of International Economics*, 35.

Harris, G. (1990) *The Dark Side of Europe: The Extreme Right Today*, Edinburgh: Edinburgh University Press.

Harvey, D. (1989) *The Condition of Postmodernity*, Oxford: Blackwell.

Hassiz, R. (1985) *Trade, Tribute and Transportation: The Sixteenth Century Political Economy of the Valley of Mexico*, Norman: University of Oklahoma Press.

Hatzius, J. (1997a) 'Domestic jobs and foreign wages: labour demand in Swedish multinationals', Discussion Paper 337, LSE Centre for Economic Performance, London.

Hatzius, J. (1997b) 'Foreign direct investment, capital formation and labour costs: evidence from Britain and Germany', Discussion Paper 336, LSE Centre for Economic Performance, London.

Hawthorn, G. (1993) 'Sub-Saharan Africa', in Held 1993.

Hayek, F. A. (1960) *The Constitution of Liberty*, London: Routledge and Kegan Paul.

Headrick, D. R. (1981) *The Tools of Empire: Technology and European Imperialism in the Nineteenth Century*, Oxford: Oxford University Press.

Headrick, D. R. (1988) *The Tentacles of Progress: Technology Transfer in the Age of Imperialism, 1850–1940*, Oxford: Oxford University Press.

Hecht, S. and Cockburn, A. (1989) *The Fate of the Forest: Developers, Destroyers and Defenders of the Amazon*, London: Verso.

Helbling, T. and Wescott, R. (1995) 'The global real interest rate', in *Staff Studies for the World Economic Outlook*, Washington: International Monetary Fund.

Held, D. (1989) *Political Theory and the Modern State*, Cambridge: Polity Press.

Held, D. (1991) 'Democracy, the nation-state, and the global system', in D. Held (ed.), *Political Theory Today*, Cambridge: Polity Press.

Held, D. (1992) 'The development of the modern state', in S. Hall and B. Gieben (eds), *Formations of Modernity*, Cambridge: Polity Press.

Held, D. (ed.) (1993) *Prospects for Democracy: North, South, East, West*, Cambridge: Polity Press.

Held, D. (1995) *Democracy and the Global Order: From the Modern State to Cosmopolitan Governance*, Cambridge: Polity Press.

Held, D. (1996) *Models of Democracy* (2nd edn), Cambridge: Polity Press.

Held, D. and McGrew, A. G. (1993) 'Globalization and the liberal democratic state', *Government and Opposition*, 28.

Helleiner, E. (1994) *States and the Re-emergence of Global Finance*, Ithaca: Cornell University Press.

Helleiner, E. (1997) 'Braudelian reflections on economic globalization: the historian as pioneer', in S. Gill and J. Mittleman (eds), *Innovation and Transformation in International Studies*, Cambridge: Cambridge University Press.

Helpman, E. and Krugman, P. (1985) *Market Structure and Foreign Trade*, Cambridge, Mass.: MIT Press.

Hepworth, M. (1989) *The Geography of the Information Economy*, London: Belhaven Press.

Herbert, U. (1990) *A History of Foreign Labour in Germany, 1880–1980: Seasonal Workers, Forced Labourers, Guest Workers*, Ann Arbour: University of Michigan Press.

Herman, E. S. and McChesney, R. W. (1997) *The Global Media: The New Missionaries of Corporate Capitalism*, London: Cassell.

Herz, J. H. (1976) *The Nation-State and the Crisis of World Politics*, New York: McKay.

Higham, R. (1981) 'Complex skills and skeletons in the military industrial relations in Great Britain', in B. F. Cooling (ed.), *War, Business and World Military-Industrial Complexes*, London: National University Press.

Hines, C. and Lang, T. (1993) *The New Protectionism*, London: Earthscan.

Hinrichsen, D. (1990) *Our Common Seas: Coasts in Crisis*, London: Earthscan.

Hintze, O. (1975) *Historical Essays*, New York: Oxford University Press.

Hirst, P. (1997) 'The global economy: myths and realities', *International Affairs*, 73.

Hirst, P. and Thompson, G. (1996a) 'Globalization: ten frequently asked questions and some surprising answers', *Soundings*, 4.

Hirst, P. and Thompson, G. (1996b) *Globalization in Question: The International Economy and the Possibilities of Governance*, Cambridge: Polity Press.

Hobsbawm, E. (1969) *Industry and Empire*, London: Pelican.

Hobsbawm, E. (1990) *Nations and Nationalism since 1780*, Cambridge: Cambridge University Press.

Hobsbawm, E. (1994) *The Age of Extremes: The Short Twentieth Century, 1914–1991*, London: Michael Joseph.

Hobsbawm, E. and Ranger, T. (eds) (1983) *The Invention of Tradition*, Cambridge: Cambridge University Press.

Hodgson, M. G. S. (1993) 'The interrelations of societies in history', in E. Burke III (ed.), *Rethinking World History: Essays on Europe, Islam and World History*, Cambridge: Cambridge University Press.

Hoekman, E. and Karsenty, G. (1992) 'Economic development and international transactions in services', *Development Policy Review*, 10.

Hoekman, E. and Kostecki, G. (1995) *The Political Economy of the World Trading System: From GATT to WTO*, Oxford: Oxford University Press.

Hoerder, D. (ed.) (1985) *Labour Migration in the Atlantic Economies in Crisis*, London: Earthscan.

Hollifield, J. F. (1992) *Immigrants, Markets and States: The Political Economy of Postwar Europe*, Cambridge, Mass.: Harvard University Press.

Holsti, K. J. (1991) *Peace and War: Armed Conflicts and International Order 1648–1989*, Cambridge: Cambridge University Press.

Homze, E. (1967) *Foreign Labour in Nazi Germany*, Princeton: Princeton University Press.

Homze, E. M. (1991) 'The German military industrial complex', in B. F. Cooling (ed.), *War, Business and World Military-Industrial Complexes*, London: National University Press.

Hood, S. and Young, S. (1997) 'The United Kingdom', in J. Dunning (ed.), *Governments, Globalization and International Business*, Oxford: Oxford University Press.

Hoogvelt, A. (1997) *Globalisation and the Postcolonial World: The New Political Economy of Development*, London: Macmillan.

Hoskins, W. G. (1977) *The Making of the English Landscape*, London: Hodder and Stoughton.

Howard, M. (1981) *War and the Liberal Conscience*, Oxford: Oxford University Press.

Howard, M. (1984) 'The military factor in European expansion', in H. Bull and A. Watson (eds), *The Expansion of International Society*, Oxford: Oxford University Press.

Howard, M., Andreopoulos, G. and Shulman, M. (eds) (1994) *The Laws of War: Constraints on Warfare in the Western World*, New Haven: Yale University Press.

Howells, J. and Wood, M. (1993) *The Globalization of Production and Technology*, London: Belhaven Press.

Hu, W. (1992) 'Global corporations are national firms with international operations', *California Management Review*, 34.

Huebner, B. (1989) 'The importance of arms exports and armament cooperation for the West German defence industrial base', in D. G. Haglund (ed.), *The Defence Industrial Base and the West*, London: Routledge.

Hufbauer, G. (1991) 'World economic integration: the long view', *International Economic Insights*, 2, no. 3.

Hui, Ong Jin (1995) 'Chinese indentured labour', in Cohen 1995.

Hung, M. and Morencos, E. (1990) *World Record Sales, 1969–1990*, London: IFPI.

Hunt, E. (1994) *The Medieval Super-companies: A Study of the Peruzzi Company of Florence*, Cambridge: Cambridge University Press.

Hunter, L. and Markusen, J. (1988) 'Per-capita income as a determinant of trade', in R. Feenstra (ed.), *Empirical Methods for International Trade*, Cambridge, Mass.: MIT Press.

Huntington, S. P. (1991) *The Third Wave: Democratization in the Late Twentieth Century*, Norman: University of Oklahoma Press.

Huntington, S. P. (1996) *The Clash of Civilizations and the Remaking of World Order*, New York: Simon and Schuster.

Hurrell, A. (1994) 'A crisis of ecological viability? Global environmental change and the nation-state', *Political Studies*, 42.

Hurrell, A. and Kingsbury, B. (eds) (1992) *The International Politics of the Environment*, Oxford: Oxford University Press.

Hurrell, A. and Woods, N. (1995) 'Globalization and inequality', *Millennium*, 2.

Ichino, A. (1993) 'The economic impact of immigration on the host country', in Luciani 1993.

IDATE (1993) *Media and Cultural Industries*, London: Institut de L'Audiovisuel et des Télécommunications en Europe.

IFPI (1994) *The Recording Industry in Numbers, 1994*, London: International Federation of Phonographic Industries.

Ikegami-Andersson, M. (1992) *The Military Industrial Complex: The Cases of Sweden and Japan*, Aldershot: Dartmouth.

Ikegami-Andersson, M. (1993) 'Japan', in Wulf 1993d.

ILO/UNDP (1988)   *Agenda for Policy: Asian Migration Project*, Bangkok: International Labour Organization.

Imber, M. (1997)   'Geo-governance without democracy? Reforming the UN system', in McGrew 1997.

IMF (1988)   'International financial statistics supplement on trade statistics', *Supplement 15*, Washington DC: International Monetary Fund.

IMF (1993)   *Balance of Payments Manual*, Washington DC: International Monetary Fund.

IMF (1994)   *International Capital Markets: Developments, Prospects and Policy Issues*, Washington DC: International Monetary Fund.

IMF (1995)   *International Capital Markets: Developments, Prospects and Policy Issues*, Washington DC: International Monetary Fund.

IMF (1996)   *International Capital Markets: Developments, Prospects and Policy Issues*, Washington DC: International Monetary Fund.

IMF (1997a)   *Exchange Arrangements and Exchange Restrictions: Annual Report 1997*, Washington DC: International Monetary Fund.

IMF (1997b)   *World Economic Outlook: Globalization – Challenges and Opportunities*, Washington DC: International Monetary Fund.

IMF (1998a)   'Summary of reports on the international financial architecture', Washington DC (www.imf.org).

IMF (1998b)   *International Financial Statistics Yearbook*, Washington DC: International Monetary Fund.

IPCC (International Panel on Climate Change) (1990)   *Climate Change: The IPCC Scientific Assessment*, Cambridge: Cambridge University Press.

Irwin, D. (1993)   'Multilateral and bilateral trade liberalization in the world trade system: an historical perspective', in J. de Melo and A. Panagariya (eds), *New Dimensions in Regional Integration*, Cambridge: Cambridge University Press.

Isserlis, L. (1938)   'Tramp shipping cargoes and freights', *Journal of the Royal Statistical Society*, 101.

ITU (1993)   *Yearbook of Common Carrier Telecommunication Statistics*, Geneva: International Telecommunication Union.

ITU (1994a)   *Direction of Traffic: International Telephone Traffic 1994*, Geneva: International Telecommunication Union.

ITU (1994b)   *World Telecommunication Development Report 1994*, Geneva: International Telecommunication Union.

Jackson, J. (1989)   *The World Trading System*, Cambridge, Mass.: MIT Press.

Jacobs, M. (1991)   *The Green Economy*, London: Pluto.

Jacquemin, A. and Sapir, A. (1988)   'European integration or world integration?', *Weltwirtschaftliches Archiv*, 124.

Jasani, B. and Lee, C. (1984)   *Countdown to Space War*, London: Taylor and Francis/SIPRI.

Jenks, C. (1963)   *Law, Freedom and Welfare*, London: Stevens and Son.

Jervis, R. (1997)   *System Effects*, Princeton: Princeton University Press.

Jessop, B. (1997)   'Capitalism and its future: remarks on regulation, government and governance', *Review of International Political Economy*, 4.3.

Johansson, O. (1967)   *The Gross Domestic Product of Sweden and its Composition*, Stockholm: Almqvist and Wicksell.

Johnson, D. and Siklos, P. (1996)   'Political and economic determinants of interest rate behaviour: are central banks different?', *Economic Inquiry*, 34.

Johnson, K. and Williams, M. (1981)   *Illegal Aliens in the Western Hemisphere*, New York: Praeger.

Joll, J. (1984)   *The Origins of the First World War*, London: Longmans.

Jones, G. (1993)   *British Multinational Banking, 1830–1990*, Oxford: Oxford University Press.

Jones, G. (1996)   *The Growth of International Business*, London: Routledge.

Jones, R. J. B. (1995) *Globalization and Interdependence in the International Political Economy*, London: Frances Pinter.

Jonquières, G. de (1998) 'Rules for regulators', *Financial Times*, 2 Mar.

Joyce, J. (1993) 'The globalization of music: expanding spheres of influence', in Mazlish and Buultjens 1993.

Julius, D. (1990) *Global Companies and Public Policy*, London: Pinter.

Juselius, K. (1996) 'An empirical analysis of the changing role of the German Bundesbank after 1983', *Oxford Bulletin of Economics and Statistics*, 58.

Kaldor, M. (1998) 'Reconceptualizing organized violence', in Archibugi et al. 1998.

Kaldor, M. and Falk, R. (eds) (1987) *Dealignment*, Oxford: Blackwell.

Kapler, J. (1997) 'The theory of transnational firms: an empirical reassessment', *International Review of Applied Economics*, 11.

Kapstein, E. B. (1994a) 'America's arms trade monopoly', *Foreign Affairs*, May.

Kapstein, E. B. (1994b) *Governing the Global Economy: International Finance and the State*, Cambridge, Mass.: Harvard University Press.

Kapstein, E. B. (1996) 'Workers in the world economy', *Foreign Affairs*, 75.

Kearns, G. (1993) 'Fin de siècle geopolitics', in P. J. Taylor (ed.), *Political Geography of the Twentieth Century*, London: Belhaven Press.

Kegley, C. W. and Raymond, G. (1994) *A Multipolar Peace? Great-Power Politics in the Twenty-First Century*, New York: St Martins Press.

Kegley, C. W. and Wittkopf, E. R. (1989) *World Politics*, London: Macmillan.

Kelly, R. (1995) 'Derivatives: a growing threat to the international financial system', in J. Michie and J. Grieve Smith (eds), *Managing the Global Economy*, Oxford: Oxford University Press.

Kemp, R. (1992) *The Politics of Radioactive Waste Disposal*, Manchester: Manchester University Press.

Kennedy, P. (1988) *The Rise and Fall of the Great Powers*, London: Unwin Hyman.

Kenwood, A. and Lougheed, L. (1989) *The Growth of the International Economy, 1820–1960*, London: Allen and Unwin.

Keohane, R. O. (1984a) *After Hegemony*, Princeton: Princeton University Press.

Keohane, R. O. (1984b) 'The world political economy and the crisis of embedded liberalism', in J. H. Goldthorpe (ed.), *Order and Conflict in Contemporary Capitalism*, Oxford: Oxford University Press.

Keohane, R. O. (1995) 'Hobbes' dilemma and institutional change in world politics: sovereignty in international society', in H. H. Holm and G. Sorensen (eds), *Whose World Order?*, Boulder: Westview Press.

Keohane, R. O. and Hoffmann, S. (eds) (1990) *The New European Community*, Oxford: Westview Press.

Keohane, R. O. and Milner, H. V. (eds) (1996) *Internationalization and Domestic Politics*, Cambridge: Cambridge University Press.

Keohane, R. O. and Nye, J. (1977) *Power and Interdependence*, Boston: Little Brown.

Khan, L. A. (1996) *The Extinction of the Nation-State: A World without Borders*, The Hague: Kluwer Law International.

Kidron, M. and Segal, R. (1995) *The State of the World Atlas* (5th edn), London: Penguin.

Kidron, M. and Smith, D. (1983) *The War Atlas*, London: Pan.

Killick, T. (1995) *IMF Programmes in Developing Countries*, London: Routledge.

Kim, S. S. (1984) 'Global violence and a just world order', *Journal of Peace Research*, 21.

Kindleberger, C. (1967) *Europe's Postwar Growth: The Role of Labour Supply*, New York: Oxford University Press.

King, R. (ed.) (1993a) *Mass Migration In Europe; The Legacy and the Future*, London: Belhaven Press.

King, R. (ed.) (1993b) *The New Geography of European Migrations*, London: Belhaven Press.

King, R. (1995) 'Migration, Globalization and Place', in Massey and Jess 1995.

King, R. and Rybaczuk, K. (1993) 'Southern Europe and the international division of labour', in King 1993b.

Kitson, M. and Michie, J. (1995) 'Trade and growth: a historical perspective', in J. Michie and J. Grieve Smith (eds), *Managing the Global Economy*, Oxford: Oxford University Press.

Klein, B. S. (1994) *Strategic Studies and World Order*, Cambridge: Cambridge University Press.

Korajczyk, R. (1996) 'A measure of stock market integration for developed and emerging markets', *World Bank Economic Review*, 10.

Korten, D. (1995) *When Corporations Rule the World*, New York: Berett-Koehler.

Korzeniewicz, M. (1994) 'Commodity chains and marketing strategies', in Gereffi and Korzeniewicz 1994.

Krasner, S. (1983) *International Regimes*, Ithaca: Cornell University Press.

Krasner, S. (1993) 'Economic interdependence and independent statehood', in R. H. Jackson and A. James (eds), *States in a Changing World*, Oxford: Oxford University Press.

Krasner, S. (1995) 'Compromising Westphalia', *International Security*, 20, no. 3.

Krause, K. (1992) *Arms and the State: Patterns of Military Production and Trade*, Cambridge: Cambridge University Press.

Kravis, I. and Lipsey, R. (1992) 'Sources of competitiveness of the United States and of its multinational firms', *Review of Economics and Statistics*, 74.

Kritz, M. (ed.) (1983) *US Immigration and Refugee Policy*, Lexington: Lexington Books.

Krol, R. (1996) 'International capital mobility: evidence from panel data', *Journal of International Money and Finance*, 15.

Krugman, P. (1995) 'Growing world trade: causes and consequences', *Brookings Papers on Economic Activity*, pp. 327–62.

Krugman, P. (1996) *Pop Internationalism*, Boston: MIT Press.

Kulischer, E. (1948) *Europe on the Move: War and Population Changes, 1917–1947*, New York: Columbia University Press.

Kurzer, P. (1993) *Business and Banking: Political Change and Economic Integration in Western Europe*, Ithaca: Cornell University Press.

Kuznets, S. (1967) 'Quantitative aspects of the economic growth of nations: X. Level and structure of foreign trade: long term trends', *Economic Development and Cultural Change*, 15.

Lamb, H. H. (1977) *Climate: Past, Present and Future* (2 vols), London: Methuen.

Lash, S. and Urry, J. (1994) *Economies of Signs and Spaces*, London: Sage.

Latham, A. (1986) 'The international trade in rice and wheat since 1868: a study in market integration', in W. Fischer, R. McInnis and J. Schneider (eds), *The Emergence of a World Economy 1500–1914*, Wiesbaden: Steiner.

Laurance, E. J. (1992) *The International Arms Trade*, New York: Lexington.

Lawrence, R. (1994) 'Multinationals, trade and labour', Discussion Paper 4836, National Bureau of Economic Research, New York.

Lawrence, R. (1996) *Single World, Divided Nations? International Trade and OECD Labor Markets*, Washington DC: Brookings Institution.

League of Nations (1942) *The Network of World Trade*, Geneva: League of Nations.

Leamer, E. (1996) 'Wage inequality from international competition and technological change', *American Economic Review*, 86.

Lee, J. (1978) 'Migration and expansion in Chinese history', in McNeill and Adams 1978.

Leggett, J (ed.) (1990) *Global Warming: The Greenpeace Report*, Oxford: Oxford University Press.

Leifer, M. (1996) *The ARF*, Adelphi Paper 302, London: IISS.

Leonard, H. (ed.) (1985) *Divesting Nature's Capital: The Political Economy of Environmental Abuse in the Third World*, New York: Holmes and Meier.

Leonard, M. (1998) *Making Europe Popular: The Search for European Identity*, London: Demos.

Levathes, L. (1994) *When China Ruled the Seas: The Treasure Fleet of the Dragon Throne 1405–1433*, Oxford: Oxford University Press.

Levy, M. (1993) 'European acid rain: the power of tote board diplomacy', in P. Haas et al. 1993.

Lévy-Leboyer, M. and Bourguignon, F. (1990) *The French Economy in the Nineteenth Century*, Cambridge: Cambridge University Press.

Liebes, T. and Katz, E. (1993) *The Export of Meaning: Cross-Cultural Readings of Dallas*, Cambridge: Polity Press.

Light, I. and Bonacich, E. (1988) *Immigrant Entrepreneurs*, Berkeley: University of California Press.

Linklater, A. (1996) 'Citizenship and sovereignty in the post-Westphalian state', *European Journal of International Relations*, 2.

Linklater, A. (1998) *The Transformation of Political Community*, Cambridge: Polity Press.

Linklater, A. and MacMillan, J. (1995) 'Boundaries in question', in J. MacMillan and A. Linklater (eds), *Boundaries in Question*, London: Frances Pinter.

Lipsey, R., Blomström, M. and Ramstetter, E. (1995) 'Internationalized production in world output', Discussion Paper 5385, National Bureau of Economic Research, New York.

Lipson, C. (1985) *Standing Guard: Protecting Foreign Capital in the Nineteenth and Twentieth Centuries*, Berkeley: University of California Press.

Lithman, E. (1987) *Immigration and Immigrant Policy in Sweden*, Stockholm: Swedish Institute.

Liu, P. and Tanner, E. (1996) 'International intertemporal solvency in industrialized countries', *Southern Economic Journal*, 62.

Lloyd, P. (1992) 'Regionalism and world trade', *OECD Economic Studies*, no. 18.

Luard, E. (1977) *International Agencies: The Framework of Interdependence*, London: Macmillan.

Luard, E. (1990) *The Globalization of Politics*, London: Macmillan.

Lucassen, J. (1987) *Migrant Labour in Europe, 1600–1900*, London: Croom Helm.

Lucassen, J. (1995) 'Emigration to the Dutch colonies and the USA', in Cohen 1995.

Luciani, G. (ed.) (1993) *Migration Policies in Europe and The United States*, Dordrecht: Kluwer.

Lukes, S. (1974) *Power: A Radical View*, London: Macmillan.

McCann, D. (1995) *Small States, Open Markets and the Organisation of Business Interests*, Aldershot: Dartmouth Press.

McCormick, J. (1989) *Reclaiming Paradise: The Global Environmental Movement*, Bloomington: Indiana University Press.

McCullagh, C. B. (1998) *The Truth of History*, London: Routledge.

McEvedy, C. and Jones, R. (1978) *Atlas of World Population History*, Harmondsworth: Penguin.

McFail, M. and Goldeier, J. M. (1992) 'A tale of two worlds: core and periphery in the post-Cold War era', *International Organization*, 46.

McGoodwin, J. (1990) *Crisis in the World's Fisheries: People, Problems and Policies*, Stanford: Stanford University Press.

McGrew, A. G. (1988) 'Conceptualizing global politics', unit 1 in A. G. McGrew (ed.), *Global Politics*, Milton Keynes: Open University.

McGrew, A. G. (1992) 'Conceptualizing global politics', in McGrew and Lewis et al. 1992.

McGrew, A. G. (ed.) (1997) *The Transformation of Democracy? Globalization and Territorial Democracy*, Cambridge: Polity Press.

McGrew, A. G. and Brook, C. (eds) (1998) *Asia-Pacific in the New World Order*, London: Routledge.

McGrew, A. G. and Lewis, P. G. et al. (1992) *Global Politics*, Cambridge: Polity Press.

MacKenzie, D. (1993) *Inventing Accuracy: A Historical Sociology of Nuclear Missile Guidance*, Boston: MIT Press.

McKeown, T. (1991) 'A liberal trade order? The long-run pattern of imports to the advanced capitalist states', *International Studies Quarterly*, 35.

McNeill, W. H. (1963) *The Rise of the West: A History of the Human Community*, Chicago: Chicago University Press.

McNeill, W. H. (1976) *Plagues and Peoples*, New York: Doubleday.

McNeill, W. H. (1978) 'Human migration: an historical overview', in McNeill and Adams 1978.

McNeill, W. H. (1982) *The Pursuit of Power*, Oxford: Blackwell.

McNeill, W. H. (1995) 'The "rise of the West" after twenty-five years', in S. K. Sanderson (ed.), *Civilizations and World Systems*, Walnut Creek: Altamira.

McNeill, W. H. and Adams, R. S. (eds) (1978) *Human Migration: Patterns and Policies*, Bloomington: Indiana University Press.

Maddison, A. (1991) *Dynamic Forces in Capitalist Development*, Oxford: Oxford University Press.

Magnusson, L. (1994) *Mercantilism*, London: Routledge.

Malmans, K. (1982) 'Phonograms and cultural policy in Sweden', in K. Blaukopf (ed.), *The Phonogram in Cultural Communication*, Vienna: Springer-Verlag.

Mancini, G. (1990) 'The making of a constitution for Europe', in Keohane and Hoffmann 1990.

Mann, M. (1986) *The Sources of Social Power*, vol. 1: *A History of Power from the Beginning to AD 1760*, Cambridge: Cambridge University Press.

Mann, M. (1993) *The Sources of Social Power*, vol. 2: *The Rise of Classes and Nation-States, 1760–1914*, Cambridge: Cambridge University Press.

Mann, M. (1997) 'Has globalization ended the rise and rise of the nation-state?', *Review of International Political Economy*, 4.

Mansbach, R. W., Ferguson, Y. H. and Lampert, D. E. (1976) *The Web of World Politics*, Englewood Cliffs: Prentice Hall.

Marks, S. and Richardson, P. (eds) (1984) *International Labour Migration: Historical Perspectives*, London: Temple Smith.

Markusen, J. Y. and Yudken, A. (1992) *Dismantling the Cold War Economy*, New York: Basic Books.

Marston, R. (1993) 'Interest differentials under Bretton Woods and the post-Bretton Woods float', in M. Bordo and B. Eichengreen (eds), *A Retrospective on the Bretton Woods System*, Chicago: University of Chicago Press.

Marston, R. (1995) *International Financial Integration: A Study of Interest Differentials between the Major Industrial Countries*, Cambridge: Cambridge University Press.

Martin, J. (1986) *The Treasure of the Land of Darkness: The Fur Trade and its Significance in Mediaeval Russia*, Cambridge: Cambridge University Press.

Martin, P. L. (1991) 'Labour migration in Asia: conference report', *International Migration Review*, 25.1.

Massey, D. and Jess, P. (eds) (1995) *A Place in the World? Culture, Places and Globalisation*, Oxford: Oxford University Press.

Mazlish, B. and Buultjens, R. (eds) (1993) *Conceptualizing Global History*, Boulder: Westview Press.

Meadows, D. et al. (1972) *Limits to Growth*, London: Earth Island.

Melosi, M. (ed.) (1985) *Pollution and Reform in American Cities, 1870–1930*, Austin: University of Texas Press.

Meyer, J. et al. (1997) 'The structuring of a world environmental regime, 1870–1990', *International Organisations*, 5(4).

Meyrowitz, J. (1985) *No Sense of Place*, Oxford: Oxford University Press.

Michalet, C. A. (1997) 'France', in J. Dunning (ed.), *Governments, Globalization and International Business*, Oxford: Oxford University Press.

Millar, F. et al. (1967) *The Roman Empire and its Neighbours*, London: Weidenfield and Nicolson.

Miller, D. (1994) *Modernity – An Ethnographic Approach: Dualism and Mass Consumption in Trinidad*, Oxford: Berg.

Miller, M. (1995) *The Third World In Global Environmental Politics*, Milton Keynes: Open University Press.

Milner, H. (1989) *Resisting Protectionism: Global Industries and the Politics of International Trade*, Princeton: Princeton University Press.

Milner, H. V. and R. O. Keohane (1996) 'Internationalization and domestic politics', in Keohane and Milner 1996.

Minami, R. (1994) *The Economic Development of Japan*, Basingstoke: Macmillan.

Minford, P., Riley, J. and Nowell, E. (1997) 'Trade, technology and labor markets in the world economy', *Journal of Development Studies*, 34.

Ministry of Foreign Affairs (1971) *Development of Overseas Japanese* (2 vols), Tokyo: Ministry of Foreign Affairs.

Mitchell, B. (1975) *European Historical Statistics, 1750–1970*, London: Macmillan.

Mitchell, B. (1983) *International Historical Statistics: The Americas and Australasia*, London: Macmillan.

Mitchell, B. (1992) *International Historical Statistics: Europe, 1750–1988*, London: Macmillan.

Mitchell, R. (1993) 'International oil pollution of the oceans', in Haas et al. 1993.

Modelski, G. (1972) *Principles of World Politics*, New York: Free Press.

Montiel, P. (1994) 'Capital mobility in developing countries', *World Bank Economic Review*, 8.

Moravcsik, A. (1991) 'The European armaments industry at the crossroads', *Survival*, 33.

Morawska, E. and Spohn, W. (1997) 'Moving Europeans in the globalizing world: contemporary migrations in a historical-comparative perspective (1955–1994 vs 1870–1914)', in Wang 1997.

Morgenstern, O. (1959) *International Financial Transactions and Business Cycles*, Princeton: Princeton University Press.

Morgenthau, H. (1967) *Politics among Nations*, New York: Knopf.

Mörner, M. (1976) 'Spanish migration to the New World prior to 1810: a report on the state of research', in F. Chiappelli (ed.), *First Images of America*, Berkeley: University of California Press.

Morris, B. (1987) *The Birth of the Palestinian Refugee Problem, 1947–1949*, Cambridge: Cambridge University Press.

Morris, C. T. and Adelman, I. (1988) *Comparative Patterns of Economic Development, 1850–1914*, Baltimore: Johns Hopkins University Press.

Morse, E. (1976) *Modernization and the Transformation of International Relations*, New York: Free Press.

Moshirian, E. (1994) 'Trade in financial services', *World Economy*, 17.

Mowery, D. and Oxley, J. (1997) 'Inward technology transfer and competitiveness', in Archibugi and Michie 1997b.

Mueller, J. (1989) *Retreat from Doomsday: The Obsolescence of Major War*, New York: Basic Books.

Murphy, A. B. (1996) 'The sovereign state system as a political-territorial ideal: historical and contemporary considerations', in T. J. Biersteker and C. Weber (eds), *State Sovereignty as Social Construct*, Cambridge: Cambridge University Press.

Murphy, C. (1994) *International Organization and International Change: Global Governance since 1850*, Cambridge: Polity Press.

Myers, N. (1986) *The Primary Source: Tropical Forests and our Futures*, New York: Norton.

Myers, N. (1993a) 'Environmental refugees in a globally warmed world', *Bioscience*, 43.

Myers, N. (1993b) *Ultimate Security: The Environmental Basis of Political Security*, New York: Norton.

Narula, R. (1996) *Multinational Investment and Economic Structure: Globalization and Competitiveness*, London: Routledge.

National Science Board (1989) *Loss of Biological Diversity: A Global Crisis Requiring International Solutions*, Washington: National Science Foundation.

Neal, L. (1990) *The Rise of Financial Capitalism: International Capital Markets in the Age of Reason*, Cambridge: Cambridge University Press.

Nectoux, F. and Dudley, N. (1987) *A Hard Wood Story: Europe's Involvement in the Tropical Timber Trade*, London: Friends of the Earth.

Nectoux, F. and Kuroda, Y. (1989) *Timber from the South Seas: An Analysis of Japan's Tropical Timber Trade and its Environmental Impact*, Gland: WWF International.

Nef, J. (1977) 'An early energy crisis and its consequences', *Scientific American*, 237.

Negus, K. (1993) 'Global harmonies and local discords: transnational policies and practices in the European recording industry', *European Journal of Communication*, 8.

Neunreither, K. (1993) 'Subsidiarity as a guiding principle for European Community activities', *Government and Opposition*, 28.

Neven, D. and Röller, L. H. (1991) 'European integration and trade flows', *European Economic Review*, 35.

Newman, S. G. (1984) 'International stratification and Third World military industries', *International Organization*, 38, no. 1.

Nierop, T. (1994) *Systems and Regions in Global Politics: An Empirical Study of Diplomacy, International Organization and Trade 1950–1991*, Chichester: John Wiley.

Nillson, S. and Pitt, D. (1994) *Protecting the Atmosphere: The Climate Change Convention and its Context*, London: Earthscan.

Nishimura, S. (1997) 'International banking in China, 1890–1913', in A. Teichova et al. (eds), *Banking, Trade and Industry*, Cambridge: Cambridge University Press.

Noel, J. (1989) 'The Single European Act', *Government and Opposition*, 24.

Nolan, J. E. (1991) *Trappings of Power: Ballistic Missiles in the Third World*, Washington DC: Brookings Institution.

Noland, M. (1997) 'Has Asian export performance been unique?', *Journal of International Economics*, 43, nos 1–2.

Nordenstreng, K. and Varis, T. (1974) *Television Traffic: A One Way Street? A Survey and Analysis of the International Flow of Television Programme Material*, Reports and Papers on Mass Communication no. 70, Paris: UNESCO.

Nordlinger, E. (1981) *On the Autonomy of the Democratic State*, Cambridge: Harvard University Press.

Norman, H. and Runblom, H. (1987) *Transatlantic Connections: Nordic Migration to the New World*, Oslo: Universitetsforlaget.

Northedge, F. S. (1976) *The International Political System*, London: Faber.

Nugent, W. (1995) 'Migration from the German and Austro-Hungarian empires to North America', in Cohen 1995.

Obstfeld, M. (1995) 'International capital mobility in the 1990s', in P. Kenen (ed.), *Understanding Interdependence*, Princeton: Princeton University Press.

Obstfeld, M. (1996) 'Models of currency crises with self-fulfilling features', *European Economic Review*, 40.

Ochoa, O. (1996) *Growth, Trade and Endogenous Technology*, Basingstoke: Macmillan.

O'Doherty, D. (ed.) (1995) *Globalization, Networking and Small Firm Innovation*, London: Graham and Trotman.

OECD (1983) *The Internationalisation of Banking*, Paris: Organization for Economic Cooperation and Development.

OECD (1985) *Twenty-Five Years of Development Cooperation*, Paris: Organization for Economic Cooperation and Development.

OECD (1986) *Tourism Statistics*, Paris: Organization for Economic Cooperation and Development.

OECD (1987) *Structural Adjustment and Economic Performance*, Paris: Organization for Economic Cooperation and Development.

OECD (1991a) *Environmental Indicators: A Preliminary Set*, Paris: Organization for Economic Cooperation and Development.

OECD (1991b) *Japan: The State of the Environment*, Paris: Organization for Economic Cooperation and Development.

OECD (1991c) *The State of the Environment*, Paris: Organization for Economic Cooperation and Development.

OECD (1991d) *Taxing Profits in a Global Economy*, Paris: Organization for Economic Cooperation and Development.

OECD (1992) *Globalization of Industrial Activities*, Paris: Organization for Economic Cooperation and Development.

OECD (1993a) *The Changing Course of International Migration*, Paris: Organization for Economic Cooperation and Development.

OECD (1993b) *Germany: The State of the Environment*, Paris: Organization for Economic Cooperation and Development.

OECD (1993c) *Trade Policy Issues: Intra-Firm Trade*, Paris: Organization for Economic Cooperation and Development.

OECD (1994a) *The Performance of Foreign Affiliates in OECD Countries*, Paris: Organization for Economic Cooperation and Development.

OECD (1994b) *Transfrontier Movements of Hazardous Waste, Statistics 1991*, Paris: Organization for Economic Cooperation and Development.

OECD (1996a) *Globalization of Industry: Overview and Sector Reports*, Paris: Organization for Economic Cooperation and Development.

OECD (1996b) *International Capital Market Statistics, 1950–1995*, Paris: Organization for Economic Cooperation and Development.

OECD (1996c) *International Direct Investment Statistics Yearbook 1996*, Paris: Organization for Economic Cooperation and Development.

OECD (1997) *Communications Outlook*, Paris: Organization for Economic Cooperation and Development.

OECD (1998) 'How the OECD promotes the rule of law', Paris: Organization for Economic Cooperation and Development.

Offe, C. (1985) *Disorganized Capitalism*, Cambridge: Polity Press.

Ohkawa, K. and Shinohara, M. (eds) (1979) *Patterns of Japanese Economic Development*, New Haven: Yale University Press.

Ohlson, T. and Blackaby, F. (1982) 'Military expenditure and the arms trade: problems of data', *Bulletin of Peace Proposals*, 13.

Ohmae, K. (1990) *The Borderless World*, London: Collins.

Ohmae, K. (1995) *The End of the Nation State*, New York: Free Press.

Oliveira Martins, J. (1994) 'Market structure, trade and industry wages', *OECD Economic Studies*, no. 22.

O'Loughlin, H. (1993) 'Political geography of war and peace', in P. J. Taylor (ed.), *Political Geography of the Twentieth Century*, London: Belhaven Press.

Oppenheim, L. (1985) *International Law*, vol. 1, London: Longman.

O'Rourke, K. and Williamson, J. (1994) 'Late nineteenth century Anglo-American factor price convergence', *Journal of Economic History*, 54.

O'Rourke, K., Taylor, A. and Williamson, J. (1996) 'Factor price convergence in the late nineteenth century', *International Economic Review*, 37.

Osiander, A. (1994) *The States System of Europe, 1640–1990*, Oxford: Clarendon Press.

Ostrom, E. (1990) *Governing the Commons: The Evolution of Institutions for Collective Action*, Cambridge: Cambridge University Press.

OTA (1991) *Global Arms Trade: Commerce in Advanced Military Technology and Weapons*, Washington DC: US Congress GPO.

O'Tuathail, G. (1996) *Critical Geopolitics*, London: Routledge.

Paarlberg, R. (1993) 'Managing pesticide use in developing countries', in Haas et al. 1993.

Pacey, A. (1991) *Technology in World Civilization*, Boston: MIT Press.

Page, S. (1994) *How Developing Countries Trade*, London: Routledge.

Paine, T. (1987) *The Thomas Paine Reader*, Harmondsworth: Penguin.

Pakenham, T. (1992) *The Scramble for Africa*, London: Abacus.

Panic, M. (1988) *National Management of the International Economy*, London: Macmillan.

Panic, M. (1992) *European Monetary Union: Lessons from the Classical Gold Standard*, Basingstoke: Macmillan.

Paolini, J. (1994) 'The French case', in T. Taylor (ed.), *Reshaping European Defence Policy*, London: RIIA.

Papademetriou, D. G. (1991) 'South–North migration in the western hemisphere and US responses', *International Migration*, June.

Parker, G. (1988) *The Military Revolution*, Cambridge: Cambridge University Press.

Parson, E. (1993) 'Protecting the ozone layer', in Haas et al. 1993.

Passmore, J. (1974) *Man's Responsibility for Nature*, London: Duckworth.

Pattie, C. J. (1994) 'Forgetting Fukuyama: new spaces of politics', *Environment and Planning*, 26.

Pauly, L. (1997) *Who Elected the Bankers?*, New York: Cornell University Press.

Pearce, F. (1991) *Green Warriors: The People and the Politics behind the Environmental Revolution*, London: Bodley Head.

Pearton, M. (1982) *The Knowledgeable State*, London: Burnett.

Pendakur, M. and Subramanyam, R. (1996) 'Indian cinema beyond national borders', in Sinclair et al. 1996.

Pepper, D. (1984) *The Roots of Modern Environmentalism*, London: Routledge.

Perlmutter, H. V. (1991) 'On the rocky road to the first global civilisation', *Human Relations*, 44.

Perraton, J. (1998) 'What are global markets? The significance of networks of trade', in R. Germain (ed.), *Globalization and its Critics*, Basingstoke: Macmillan.

Perraton, J. et al. (1997) 'The globalization of economic activity', *New Political Economy*, 2, July.

Perroni, C. and Whalley, J. (1994) 'The new regionalism: trade liberalization or insurance?', Working Paper 4626, New York: National Bureau of Economic Research.

Peterson, M. (1993) 'International fisheries management', in Haas et al. 1993.

Petri, P. (1993) 'The East Asian trading bloc', J. Frankel and M. Kahler (eds), *Regionalism and Rivalry: Japan and the United States in Pacific Asia*, Chicago: University of Chicago Press.

Pfaller, A., Gough, I. and Therborn, G. (1991) *Can the Welfare State Compete?*, Basingstoke: Macmillan.

Phillips, J. R. S. (1988) *The Medieval Expansion of Europe*, Oxford: Oxford University Press.

Pieterse, J. N. (1997) 'Going global: futures of capitalism', *Development and Change*, 28.

Pinder, J. (1961) *European Community*, Oxford: Oxford University Press.

Pinder, J. (1991) *European Community: The Building of a Union*, Oxford: Oxford University Press.

Plano, J. C. and Olton, R. (1988) *The International Relations Dictionary*, Santa Barbara: ABC Clio.

Plasschaert, S. (ed.) (1994) *Transnational Corporations: Transfer Pricing and Taxation*, London: Routledge.

Poggi, G. (1978) *The Development of the Modern State*, London: Hutchinson.

Polanyi, K. (1944) *The Great Transformation*, Boston: Beacon Press.

Pomfret, R. (1988) *Unequal Trade: The Economics of Discriminatory International Trade Policies*, Oxford: Blackwell.

Porter, A. (1994) *European Imperialism 1860–1914*, London: Macmillan.

Porter, M. (1990) *The Competitive Advantage of Nations*, London: Macmillan.

Porter, T. (1993) *States, Markets and Regimes in Global Finance*, Basingstoke: Macmillan.

Portes, A. and Bach, R. (1985) *Latin Journey: Cuban and Mexican Immigrants to the United States*, Berkeley: University of California Press.

Potter, D., Goldblatt, D., Kiloh, M. and Lewis, P. (eds) (1997) *Democratization*, Cambridge: Polity Press.

Potts, L. (1990) *The World Labour Market: A History of Migration*, London: Zed Books.

Pringle, P. (1983) *SIOP: Nuclear War from the Inside*, London: Sphere Books.

Pugilese, E. (1993) 'Restructuring of the labour market and the role of Third World migrations in Europe', *Society and Space*, 11.

Qureshi, A. (1996) *The World Trade Organization: Implementing International Trade Norms*, Manchester: Manchester University Press.

Rackham, O. (1986) *The History of the Countryside*, London: Dent.

Ralston, D. B. (1990) *Importing the European Army: The Introduction of European Military Techniques and Institutions into the Extra-European World 1600–1914*, Chicago: Chicago University Press.

Ramstetter, E. (1998) 'Measuring the size of foreign multinationals in the Asia-Pacific', in G. Thompson (ed.), *Economic Dynamism in the Asia Pacific*, London: Routledge.

Ravenhill, J. (1998) 'The growth of intergovernmental collaboration in the Asia-Pacific region', in McGrew and Brook 1998.

Ray, M. and Jacka, E. (1996) 'Indian television: an emerging regional force', in Sinclair et al. 1996.

Redwood, J. (1993) *The Global Marketplace*, London: HarperCollins.

Reich, R. (1991) *The Work of Nations: Preparing Ourselves for Twenty-First Century Capitalism*, New York: Simon and Schuster.

Reif, K. (1993) 'Cultural convergence and cultural diversity as factors in European identity', in Garcia 1993.

Renard, J. and Litman, B. (1985) 'Changing dynamics of the overseas markets for TV programming', *Telecommunications Policy*, 9, no. 3.

Reynolds, C. (1981) *Modes of Imperialism*, Oxford: Martin Robertson.

Richards, J. and Tucker, R. (eds) (1983) *Global Deforestation and the Nineteenth Century World Economy*, Durham: Duke University Press.

Riemers, D. (1985) *Still the Golden Door*, New York: Columbia University Press.

Riley, J. (1980) *International Government Finance and the Amsterdam Capital Market, 1740–1815*, Cambridge: Cambridge University Press.

Rip, M. R. and Lusch, D. P. (1994) 'The precision revolution: the NAVSTAR GPS in the Second Gulf War', *Intelligence and National Security*, 9.

Ritz, M. (1989) 'International migration policies: conceptual problems', *International Migration Review*, 21.

Roberts, J. M. (1995) *The Penguin History of the World*, London: Penguin.

Robertson, R. (1992) *Globalization: Social Theory and Global Culture*, London: Sage.

Robinson, D., Buck, E. and Cuthbert, M. (1991) *Music at the Margins: Popular Music and Global Cultural Diversity*, London: Sage.

Rock, M. (1996) 'Pollution intensity of GDP and trade policy: can the World Bank be wrong?', *World Development*, 24.

Rodrik, D. (1997) *Has Globalization Gone Too Far?*, Washington DC: Institute for International Economics.

Rogowski, R. (1989) *Commerce and Coalitions: How Trade Affects Domestic Political Alignments*, Princeton: Princeton University Press.

Rohde, J. and Sandrat, H. H. von (1994) 'German defence and force structure planning', in T. Taylor (ed.), *Reshaping European Defence Policy*, London: RIIA.

Röling, B. (1960) *International Law in an Expanded World*, Amsterdam: Djambatan.

Rose, A. (1991) 'Why has trade grown faster than income?', *Canadian Journal of Economics*, 24.

Rose, A. (1996) 'Explaining exchange rate volatility', *Journal of International Money and Finance*, 15, no. 6.

Rosenau, J. (1980) *The Study of Global Interdependence*, London: Frances Pinter.

Rosenau, J. (1990) *Turbulence in World Politics*, Brighton: Harvester Wheatsheaf.

Rosenau, J. (1992) 'Governance, order and change in world politics', in J. Rosenau and E. O. Czempiel (eds), *Governance without Government*, Cambridge: Cambridge University Press.

Rosenau, J. (1994) 'New dimensions of security', *Security Dialogue*, 25.

Rosenau, J. (1997) *Along the Domestic-Foreign Frontier*, Cambridge: Cambridge University Press.

Rosenau, J. (1998) 'Government and democracy in a globalizing world', in D. Archibugi, D. Held and M. Köhler (eds), *Re-imagining Political Community*, Cambridge: Polity Press.

Ross, A. L. (1987) 'Dimensions of militarization in the Third World', *Armed Forces and Society*, 13.

Ross, G. (1995) *Jacques Delors and European Integration*, Cambridge: Polity Press.

Roudometof, V. and Robertson, R. (1995) 'Globalization, world-system theory, and the comparative study of civilizations', in S. K. Sanderson (ed.), *Civilizations and World Systems*, Walnut Creek: Altamira Press.

Rousslang, D. (1997) 'International income shifting by US multinational corporations', *Applied Economics*, 29.

Rowlands, I. (1994) *The International Politics of Atmospheric Change*, Manchester: Manchester University Press.

Rowthorn, R. and Wells, J. (1987) *De-industrialization and Foreign Trade*, Cambridge: Cambridge University Press.

Ruggie, J. G. (1982) 'International regimes, transactions and change: embedded liberalism in the post war economic order', *International Organization*, 36.

Ruggie, J. G. (1993) 'Territoriality and beyond', *International Organization*, 41.

Ruggie, J. G. (1996) *Winning the Peace: America and World Order in the New Era*, New York: Columbia University Press.

Ruigrok, W. and Tulder, R. van (1995) *The Logic of International Restructuring*, London: Routledge.

Rushdie, S. (1991) *Imaginary Homelands*, London: Granta Books.

Sabine, G. H. (1963) *A History of Political Thought*, London: Harrap.

Sabloff, J. and Lamberg-Karlovsky, C. (eds) (1975) *Ancient Civilization and Trade*, Albuquerque: University of New Mexico Press.

Sachs, J. and Shatz, H. (1994) 'Trade and jobs in US manufacturing', *Brookings Papers on Economic Activity*, 1.

Sachs, J. and Warner, A. (1995) 'Economic reform and the process of global integration', *Brookings Papers on Economic Activity*, pp. 1–95.

Safarian, A. (1993) *Multinational Enterprise and Public Policy: A Study of the Industrial Countries*, Aldershot: Edward Elgar.

Salaman, R. (1947) *The History and Social Influence of the Potato*, Cambridge: Cambridge University Press.

Salt, J. and Findlay, A. (1989) 'International migration of highly skilled manpower: theoretical and development issues', in Appleyard 1989.

Salt, J. and Ford, R. (1993) 'Skilled international migration in Europe', in King 1993a.

Sandel, M. (1996) *Democracy's Discontent*, Cambridge: Harvard University Press.

Sassen, S. (1996) *Losing Control? Sovereignty in an Age of Globalization*, New York: Columbia University Press.

Scharpf, F. (1991) *Crisis and Choice in European Social Democracy*, New York: Cornell University Press.

Schattschneider, E. F. (1960) *The Semi-Sovereign People: A Realist View of Democracy in America*, New York: Rinehart and Winston.

Schiller, H. (1969) *Mass Communication and the American Empire*, New York: Augustus Kelly.

Scholte, J. A. (1993) *International Relations of Social Change*, Buckingham: Open University Press.

Schön, L. (1986) 'Market development and structural change in the mid-nineteenth century – with special reference to Sweden', in W. Fischer, R. McInnis and J. Schneider (eds), *The Emergence of a World Economy 1500–1914*, Wiesbaden: Steiner.

Schwartzman, S. (1986) *Bankrolling Disasters: International Development Banks and the Global Environment*, San Francisco: Sierra Club.

Screen Digest (1996) 'World cinema and market shares: clarity in the confusion', *Screen Digest*, Sept.

Screen Digest (1997a) 'Europe's other channels: numbers double every three years', *Screen Digest*, Mar.

Screen Digest (1997b) 'Film production and distribution: a shifting balance', *Screen Digest*, May.

Screen Digest (1997c) 'World cinema market: start of the European fightback', *Screen Digest*, Aug.

Seecombe, I. and Lawless, R. (1986) 'Foreign worker dependence in the Gulf and international oil companies', *International Migration Review*, 20.

Segal, A. (1993) *An Atlas of International Migration*, London: Hans Zell.

Segal, G. (1994) 'China: arms trade policies and practices', *Contemporary Security Policy*, 15.

Sepstrup, P. (1991) *Transnationalization of Television in Europe*, London: John Libbey.

Shafer, J. (1995) 'Experience with controls on international capital movements in OECD countries', in S. Edwards (ed.), *Capital Controls, Exchange Rates, and Monetary Policy in the World Economy*, Cambridge: Cambridge University Press.

Sharp, J. (1991) 'Disarmament and arms control: a new beginning?', in K. Booth (ed.), *New Thinking about Strategy and International Security*, London: HarperCollins.

Shaw, M. (1991) *Post-Military Society*, Cambridge: Polity Press.

Shaw, M. (1997) 'Globalization and post-military democracy', in McGrew 1997.

Shepherd, W. (1994) *International Financial Integration*, Aldershot: Avebury.

Shimo, M. (1995) 'Indentured migrants from Japan', in Cohen 1995.

Silverberg, D. (1994) 'Global trends in military production and conversion', *Annals of the American Academy of Political and Social Sciences*, 535.

Simon, J. (1984) 'Immigrants, taxes and welfare in the United States', *Population and Development Review*, 10.

Simon, J. (1989) *The Economic Consequences of Migration*, Oxford: Blackwell.

Sinclair, J. (1996) 'Mexico, Brazil and the Latin World', in Sinclair et al. 1996.

Sinclair, J., Jacka, E. and Cunningham, S. (eds) (1996) *New Patterns in Global Television: Peripheral Vision*, Oxford: Oxford University Press.

Sinn, S. (1992) 'Savings–investment correlations and capital mobility', *Economic Journal*, 102.

SIPRI (1991) *SIPRI Yearbook 1991*, Oxford: Oxford University Press.

SIPRI (1998) *SIPRI Yearbook 1998: Armaments, Disarmament and International Security*, Oxford: Oxford University Press.

Sivard, R. L. (1991) *World Military and Social Expenditures*, Washington DC: World Priorities.

Skeldon, R. (1992) 'International migration within and from the East and Southeast Asian Region: a review essay', *Asian and Pacific Migration Journal*, 1.

Skinner, Q. (1978) *The Foundations of Modern Political Thought*, Cambridge: Cambridge University Press.

Skipp, V. (1978) *Crisis and Development: An Ecological Case Study of the Forest of Arden, 1570–1674*, Cambridge: Cambridge University Press.

Skons, E. (1993) 'Western Europe: internationalization of the arms industry', in Wulf 1993d.

Skons, E. (1994) 'The internationalization of the arms industry', *Annals of the American Academy of Political and Social Science*, 535.

Sloutzki, N. M. (1941) *The World Armaments Race 1919–1939*, Geneva: Geneva Research Centre.

Small, M. and Singer, J. D. (1973) 'The diplomatic importance of states, 1816–1970', *World Politics*, 25.

Smith, A. (1971) *Theories of Nationalism*, London: Duckworth.

Smith, A. (1990) 'Towards a global culture?', in M. Featherstone (ed.), *Global Culture: Nationalism, Globalization and Modernity*, London: Sage.

Smith, A. (1992) 'National identity and the idea of European unity', *International Affairs*, 68.

Smith, A. (1995) *Nations and Nationalism in a Global Era*, Cambridge: Polity Press.

Smith, A. K. (1991) *Creating a World Economy: Merchant Capital, Colonialism and World Trade, 1400–1825*, Boulder: Westview Press.

Smith, M. R. (1977) 'Military arsenals and industry before World War One', in B. F. Cooling (ed.), *War, Business and American Society*, London: National University Publications.

Smith, T. (1981) *The Pattern of Imperialism: The United States, Great Britain and the Late Industrializing World since 1815*, Cambridge: Cambridge University Press.

Smith, T. (1994) *America's Mission: The United States and the Worldwide Struggle for Democracy in the Twentieth Century*, Princeton: Princeton University Press.

Snow, P. (1988) *The Star Rafts: China's Encounters with Africa*, London: Weidenfeld and Nicolson.

Snyder, C. (1996) 'Emerging regional security co-operation in Europe and the Asia Pacific', *Pacific Review*, 9, no. 4.

Soete, L. and Verspagen, B. (1994) 'Competing for growth: the dynamics of technology gaps', in L. Pasinetti and R. Solow (eds), *Economic Growth and the Structure of Long-Term Development*, Basingstoke: Macmillan.

Solomos, J. (1993) *Race and Racism in Contemporary Britain* (2nd edn), London: Macmillan.

Solomos, J. and Wrench, J. (1993) *Racism and Migration in Europe*, Oxford: Berg.

Solow, B. and Engerman, S. (1988) *British Capitalism and Caribbean Slavery*, Cambridge: Cambridge University Press.

SOPEMI (1991) *Continuous Reporting System on Migration*, Paris: OECD.

SOPEMI (1992) *Trends in International Migration*, Paris: OECD.

Spear, P. (1990) *A History of India*, vol. 2, London: Penguin.

Staple, G. (ed.) (1991) *The Global Telecommunications Traffic Report, 1991*, London: International Institute of Communications.

Staple, G. (ed.) (1996) *Telegeography, 1996*, London: International Institute of Communications.

Steinmo, S., Thelen, K. and Longstretch, F. (eds) (1992) *Structuring Politics: Historical Institutionalism in Comparative Analysis*, Cambridge: Cambridge University Press.

Stone, J. and Lee, H.-H. (1995) 'Determinants of intra-industry trade: a longitudinal, cross-country analysis', *Weltwirtschaftliches Archiv*, 131.

Stopford, J. and Strange, S. (1991) *Rival States, Rival Firms: Competition for World Market Shares*, Cambridge: Cambridge University Press.

Stowsky, J. (1992) 'From spin-off to spin-on: redefining the military's role in American technological development', in M. B. J. Zysman and W. Sandholtz (eds), *The Highest Stakes: The Economic Foundations of the Next Security System*, New York: Oxford University Press.

Strange, S. (1996) *The Retreat of the State: The Diffusion of Power in the World Economy*, Cambridge: Cambridge University Press.

Street, J. (1997) *Politics and Popular Culture*, Cambridge: Polity Press.

Swan, N. et al. (1991) 'Economic and social impacts of immigration', a research report for the Economic Council of Canada, Ottawa.

Talbott, S. (1997) 'Globalization and diplomacy: a practitioner's perspective', *Foreign Policy*, no. 108, Fall.

Tanzi, V. (1995) *Taxation in an Integrating World*, Washington DC: Brookings Institution.

Tapinos, G. and de Rugy, A. (1993) 'The macroeconomic impact of immigration: review of the literature published since the mid-1970s', in OECD 1993a.

Taplin, E. (1994) 'Strategic reorientations of US apparel firms', in Gereffi and Korzeniewicz 1994.

Tarr, J. (1985) 'Historical perspectives on hazardous waste management in the United States', *Waste Management and Research*, 3.

Taylor, P. J. (1993) 'Geopolitical world orders', in P. J. Taylor (ed.), *Political Geography of the Twentieth Century*, London: Belhaven Press.

Taylor, R. and Buttel, F. (1992) 'How do we know we have global environmental problems? Science and the globalization of environmental discourse', *Geoforum*, 23.

Taylor, T. (1990) 'Defence industries in international relations', *Review of International Studies*, 16.

Taylor, T. (1994a) 'British defence policy', in T. Taylor (ed.), *Reshaping European Defence Policy*, London: RIIA.

Taylor, T. (1994b) 'Conclusions', in T. Taylor (ed.), *Reshaping European Defence Policy*, London: RIIA.

Taylor, T. (1994c) 'Western European security and defence cooperation', *International Affairs*, 70.

Taylor, T. and Hartley, K. (1989) *The UK Defence Industrial Base*, London: Brasseys.

TeBrake, W. (1974) 'Air pollution and fuel crisis in pre-industrial London, 1250–1650', *Technology and Culture*, 16.

Tesar, L. and Werner, I. (1995) 'Home bias and high turnover', *Journal of International Money and Finance*, 14.

Therborn, G. (1995) *European Modernity and Beyond: The Trajectory of European Societies, 1945–2000*, London: Sage.

Thiara, R. (1995) 'Indian indentured workers in Mauritius, Natal and Fiji', in Cohen 1995.

Thomas, K. (1983) *Man and the Natural World: Changing Attitudes in England, 1500–1800*, London: Allen Lane.

Thompson, G. (1998) 'Financial systems and monetary integration', in G. Thompson (ed.), *Economic Dynamism in the Asia-Pacific*, London: Routledge.

Thompson, G. (1998) 'International competitiveness and globalization', in T. Baker and J. Kohler (eds), *International Competitiveness and Environmental Policies*, Brighton: Edward Elgar.

Thompson, G. and Allen, J. (1997) 'Think global, then think again: economic globalization in context', *Area*, 29, no. 3.

Thompson, J. B. (1990) *Ideology and Modern Culture*, Cambridge: Polity Press.

Thompson, J. B. (1995) *The Media and Modernity*, Cambridge: Polity Press.

Tilly, C. (ed.) (1975) *The Formation of National States in Western Europe*, Princeton: Princeton University Press.

Tilly, C. (1990) *Coercion, Capital and European States, AD 990–1990*, Oxford: Blackwell.

Tilly, R. (1991) 'International aspects of the development of German banking', in Cameron and Bovykin 1991.

Tinker, H. (1974) *A New System of Slavery: The Export of Indian Labour Overseas*, London: Oxford University Press.

Titus, J. (1986) *Effect of Changes in Stratospheric Ozone and Global Climate*, Washington: Environmental Protection Agency.

Tracey, M. (1988) 'Popular culture and the economics of global television', *Intermedia*, 16, no. 2.

Trebilcock, M. (1996) 'Competition policy and trade policy: mediating the interface', *Journal of World Trade*, 30.

Triffin, R. (1960) *Gold and the Dollar Crisis*, New Haven: Yale University Press.

Tripp, C. (1995) 'Regional organisations in the Arab Middle East', in L. Fawcett and A. W. Hurrell (eds), *Regionalism in World Politics*, Oxford: Oxford University Press.

Ullman, R. H. (1989) 'The covert French connection', *Foreign Policy*, 75.

UN (1988) *Human Rights: A Compilation of International Instruments*, New York: United Nations.

UNCTAD (1993) *World Investment Report 1993: Transnational Corporations and Integrated International Production*, New York: United Nations.

UNCTAD (1994) *World Investment Report 1994: Transnational Corporations, Employment and the Workplace*, New York: United Nations.

UNCTAD (1995) *World Investment Report 1995: Transnational Corporations and Competitiveness*, New York: United Nations.

UNCTAD (1996) *World Investment Report 1996: Investment, Trade and International Policy Arrangements*, New York: United Nations.

UNCTAD (1997) *World Investment Report 1997: Transnational Corporations, Market Structure and Competition Policy*, New York: United Nations.

UNCTAD (1998) *World Investment Report 1998: Trends and Determinants. Overview*, New York: United Nations (www.unctad.org).

UNCTC (1983) *Transnational Corporations in World Development: Third Survey*, New York: United Nations.

UNCTC (1988) *Transnational Corporations in World Development: Trends and Prospects*, New York: United Nations.

UNCTC (1991) *World Investment Report 1991: The Triad in Foreign Direct Investment*, New York: United Nations.

UNDP (1994) *Human Development Report 1994*, Oxford: Oxford University Press.

UNEP (1993) *Report of the United Nations Conference on Environment and Development* (3 vols), New York: United Nations.

UNESCO (1950) *World Communications Report*, Paris: United Nations Educational, Scientific and Cultural Organization.

UNESCO (1963) *Statistics on Radio and Television, 1950–1960*, Paris: United Nations Educational, Scientific and Cultural Organization.

UNESCO (1980) *Many Voices, One World*, Paris: United Nations Educational, Scientific and Cultural Organization.

UNESCO (1988) *Statistical Yearbook*, Paris: United Nations Educational, Scientific and Cultural Organization.

UNESCO (1989) *World Communications Report*, Paris: United Nations Educational, Scientific and Cultural Organization.

UNFPA (1994) *The State of the World's Population*, New York: United Nations Fund for Population Activities.

Unger, R. (1984) 'Energy sources for the Dutch golden age: peat, wind and coal', *Research in Economic History*, 9.

UNHCR (1993) *Populations of Concern to UNHCR*, Geneva: United Nations High Commission for Refugees.

UNHCR (1994) *The State of the World's Refugees: The Challenge of Protection*, New York: Penguin.

Union of International Associations (1996) *Yearbook of International Organizations 1996–7*, Munich: K. G. Saur.

UN-TCMD (1992) *World Investment Report 1992: Transnational Corporations as Engines of Growth*, New York: United Nations, Transnational Corporations and Management Division.

Urry, J. (1990) *The Tourist Gaze*, London: Sage.

US Congress (Office of Technology Assessment) (1991) *Arms Trade 1991*, Washington DC: USGPO.

US Department of Commerce (1972) *Historical Statistics of the United States: From Colonial Times to 1970*, Washington DC: US Department of Commerce.

US Department of Commerce (1995) *Statistical Abstract of the United States*, Washington DC: US Department of Commerce.

Utterstrom, G. (1988) 'Climatic fluctuations and population problems in early modern history', in Worster 1988.

Varis, T. (1986) *International Flow of Television Programmes*, Reports and Papers on Mass Communication no. 100, Paris: UNESCO.

Vertovec, S. (1995) 'Indian indentured migration to the Caribbean', in Cohen 1995.

Vestel, P. (1993) *L'Industrie européenne de l'armament*, Brussels: GRIP.

Vilar, P. (1991) *A History of Gold and Money, 1450–1920*, London: Verso.

Vincent, J. (1986) *Human Rights and International Relations*, Cambridge: Cambridge University Press.

Vincent, J. (1992) 'Modernity and universal human rights', in McGrew and Lewis 1992.

Vogel, S. (1992) 'The power behind spin-ons: the military implications of Japan's commercial technology', in W. Sandholtz et al. (eds), *The Highest Stakes: The Economic Foundations of the Next Security System*, New York: Oxford University Press.

Vogler, J. (1992) 'Regimes and the global commons', in McGrew and Lewis et al. 1992.

Vos, R. (1994) *Debt and Adjustment in the World Economy*, Basingstoke: Macmillan.

Wagner, P. et al. (1991) *Social Sciences and the Modern States: National Experiences and Theoretical Crossroads*, Cambridge: Cambridge University Press.

Waldinger, R. et al. (1990) *Ethnic Entrepreneurs: Immigrant Business in Industrial Societies*, London: Sage.

Walker, R. B. J. (1988) *One World, Many Worlds: Struggles for a Just World Peace*, Boulder, Colo.: Lynne Reinner.

Walker, R. B. J. (1993) *Inside/Outside*, Cambridge: Cambridge University Press.

Wallace, M. and Choudhry, T. (1995) 'The gold standard: perfectly integrated world markets or slow adjustment of prices and interest rates?', *Journal of International Money and Finance*, 14.

Wallace, W. (1994) 'Rescue or retreat? The nation state in Western Europe', *Political Studies*, 42.

Wallerstein, I. (1974) *The Modern World-System: Capitalist Agriculture and the Origins of the European World-Economy in the Sixteenth Century*, New York: Academic Press.

Wallerstein, I. (1980) *The Modern World-System II: Mercantilism and the Consolidation of the European World Economy 1600–1750*, New York: Academic Press.

Walter, A. (1993) *World Power and World Money*, London: Macmillan.

Walters, F. P. (1952) *A History of the League of Nations*, London: Oxford University Press.

Waltz, K. (1979) *The Theory of International Politics*, New York: Addison-Wesley.

Waltz, K. (1993) 'The emerging structure of international politics', *International Security*, 18.

Wang, G. (ed.) (1997) *Global History and Migration*, Boulder: Westview Press.

Wang, S. (1978) *The Organization of Chinese Emigration, 1848–1888*, Beijing: Chinese Materials Centre.

Wapner, P. (1996) *Environmental Activism and World Civic Politics*, New York: State University of New York Press.

Ward, B. (1989) 'Telecommunications and the globalization of financial services', *Professional Geographer*, 41.

Ware, A. (1992) 'Liberal democracy: one form or many?', *Political Studies*, 40, special issue.

Watson, A. (1967) 'Back to gold – and silver', *Economic History Review*, 20.

Watson, A. (1992) *The Evolution of International Society*, London: Routledge.

Watson, A. (1997) *The Limits of Independence*, London: Routledge.

Watson, R., Zinyowera, M. and Moss, R. (eds) (1995) *Climate Change 1995: Impacts, Adaptations, and Mitigation of Climate Change: Scientific-Technical Analyses*, Cambridge: Cambridge University Press.

WCED (World Commission on Environment and Development) (1987) *Our Common Future*, Oxford: Oxford University Press.

Weale, A. (1992) *The New Politics of Pollution*, Manchester: Manchester University Press.

Webb, M. (1995) *The Political Economy of Policy Co-ordination: International Adjustment since 1945*, Ithaca: Cornell University Press.

Weber, M. (1951) *The Religion of China*, Glencoe: Free Press.

Weber, M. (1958) *The Religion of India*, New York: Free Press.

Weber, S. (1993) 'Shaping the postwar balance of power: multilateralism in NATO', in J. G. Ruggie (ed.), *Multilateralism Matters*, New York: Columbia University Press.

Weiss, L. (1998) *State Capacity: Governing the Economy in a Global Era*, Cambridge: Polity Press.

Weller, M. (1997) 'The reality of the emerging universal constitutional order: putting the pieces together', *Cambridge Review of International Studies*, Winter/Spring.

Wells, A. F. (1972) *Picture Tube Imperialism? The Impact of US Television on Latin America*, New York: Orbis.

Westing, A. (ed.) (1986) *Global Resources and International Conflict*, Oxford: Oxford University Press.

White, P. (1984) *The West European City: A Social Geography*, London: Longman.

Widgren, J. (1993) 'Movements of refugees and asylum seekers: recent trends in comparative perspective', in OECD 1993a.

Wigley, T., Ingram, M. and Farmer, G. (1981) *Climate and History: Studies in Past Climates and their Impact on Man*, Cambridge: Cambridge University Press.

Wildman, S. and Siwek, S. (1988) *International Trade in Films and Television Programmes*, Washington DC: American Enterprise Institute.

Wilkins, M. (1974) *The Maturing of the Multinational Enterprise: American Business Abroad from 1914 to 1970*, Cambridge, Mass.: Harvard University Press.

Wilkins, M. (ed.) (1991) *The Growth of Multinationals*, Aldershot: Edward Elgar.

Wilkins, M. (1994) 'Comparative hosts', *Business History*, 36.

Wilkinson, R. (1973) *Poverty and Progress: An Ecological Perspective on Economic Development*, New York: Praeger.

Williams, J. E. D. (1992) *From Sails to Satellites: The Origin and Development of Navigational Science*, Oxford: Oxford University Press.

Williams, P. (1994) 'Transnational criminal organizations and international security', *Survival*, 36.

Williamson, J. (1995) 'The evolution of global labor markets since 1830', *Explorations in Economic History*, 32.

Wilson, F. (1972) *Labour in the South African Gold Mines, 1911–1969*, Cambridge: Cambridge University Press.

Wilson, K. (1995) 'Refugees, displaced people and returnees in Southern Africa', in Cohen 1995.

Wohl, A. (1983) *Endangered Lives: Public Health in Victorian Britain*, London: Dent.

Wolff, E. (1997) 'Productivity growth and shifting comparative advantage on the industry level', in J. Fagerberg et al. (eds), *Technology and International Trade*, Cheltenham: Edward Elgar.

Wood, A. (1994) *North–South Trade, Employment and Inequality: Changing Fortunes in a Skill-Driven World*, Oxford: Oxford University Press.

Wood, A. (1995) 'How trade hurt unskilled workers', *Journal of Economic Perspectives*, 9.

Woodruff, W. (1966) *Impact of Western Man: A Study of Europe's Role in the World Economy, 1750–1960*, London: Macmillan.

Woods, L. T. (1998) 'Regional co-operation: the transnational dimension', in McGrew and Brook 1998.

World Bank (1992) *World Development Report, 1992*, Washington DC: World Bank.

World Bank (1993) *International Trade and the Environment*, Washington DC: World Bank.

World Bank (1994) *World Development Report 1994*, New York: Oxford University Press.

World Bank (1995) *World Development Report 1995*, New York: Oxford University Press.

World Bank (1997) *Global Economic Prospects and the Developing Countries*, Washington DC: World Bank.

WMO (1990) *Atmospheric Ozone*, Global Ozone Research and Monitoring Reports, Geneva: World Meteorological Organization.

World Resources Institute (1992) *World Resources 1992–1993*, Oxford: Oxford University Press.

World Resources Institute (1993) *Biodiversity Prospecting*, Baltimore: World Resources Institute.

World Resources Institute (1995) *World Resources 1994–1995*, Oxford: Oxford University Press.

World Resources Institute (1997) *World Resources 1996–1997*, Oxford: Oxford University Press.

World Tourist Organization (1991) *World Tourism Statistics*, Madrid: World Tourist Organization.

World Tourist Organization (1997) *World Tourism Statistics*, Madrid: World Tourist Organization.

Worldwatch Institute (1992) *The World Nuclear Industry Status Report, 1992*, London: Worldwatch Institute.

Worster, D. (ed.) (1988) *The Ends of the Earth: Perspectives on Modern Environmental History*, Cambridge: Cambridge University Press.

Wrigley, E. A. (1988) *Continuity, Chance and Change*, Cambridge: Cambridge University Press.

Wriston, W. (1992) *The Twilight of Sovereignty*, New York: Charles Scribners Sons.

WTO (1995) *International Trade*, Geneva: World Trade Organization.

WTO (1996) 'Participation of developing countries in world trade: overview of major trends and underlying factors', Working Paper 15, World Trade Organization, Geneva.

WTO (1997) *Annual Report 1997*, vol. 1, Geneva: World Trade Organization.

WTO (1998) 'Agreement on the Liberalization of Financial Services', http://www.wto.org.

Wulf, H. (1986) 'India: the unfulfilled quest for self-sufficiency', in M. Brzoska and T. Ohlson (eds), *Arms Production in the Third World*, Oxford: Taylor and Francis.

Wulf, H. (1993a) 'Soviet Union and successor republics: arms exports and the struggle with the heritage of the military industrial complex', in Wulf 1993d.

Wulf, H. (1993b) 'The US: arms exports and implications for arms production', in Wulf 1993d.

Wulf, H. (1993c) 'Western Europe: facing overcapacity', in Wulf 1993d.

Wulf, H. (ed.) (1993d) *Arms Industry Limited*, Oxford: Oxford University Press.

Yamamoto, T. (ed.) (1995) *Emerging Civil Society in the Asia-Pacific Community*, Tokyo: Japan Centre for International Exchange.

Yates, P. L. (1959) *Forty Years of Foreign Trade*, London: Allen and Unwin.

Yearly, S. (1995) 'Dirty connections: transnational pollution', in Allen and Hamnet 1994.

Yearly, S. (1996) *Sociology, Environmentalism, Globalization*, London: Sage.

Young, O. (1989) *International Regimes*, Ithaca: Cornell University Press.

Young, O. (1994) *International Governance: Protecting the Environment in a Stateless Society*, Ithaca: Cornell University Press.

Yü, Y. (1997) *Trade and Expansion in Han China*, Berkeley: University of California Press.

Zacher, M. (1992) 'The decaying pillars of the Westphalian temple', in J. N. Rosenau and O. E. Czempiel (eds), *Governance without Government*, Cambridge: Cambridge University Press.

Zacher, M. W. (1993) 'International organizations', in J. Krieger (ed.), *The Oxford Companion to Politics of the World*, Oxford: Oxford University Press.

Zegeye, A. (1995) 'Hunger, war and flight: the horn of Africa', in Cohen 1995.

Zelikow, P. (1992) 'The new Concert of Europe', *Survival*, 34, no. 2.

Zeppenfeld, W. (1979) 'The economics and structure of the record and tape industry: the example of West Germany', in H. Fischer and S. Melnik (eds), *Entertainment: A Cross-Cultural Examination*, Hastings: Communication Arts Books.

Zevin, R. (1992) 'Are world financial markets more open? If so, why and with what effects?', in T. Banuri and J. Schor (eds), *Financial Openness and National Autonomy*, Oxford: Oxford University Press.

Zimmern, A. (1936) *The League of Nations and the Rule of Law*, London: Macmillan.

Zlotnik, H. (1989) 'The concept of international migration as reflected in national data collection systems', *International Migration Review*, 21.

Zolberg, A. (1983) 'Contemporary transnational migrations in historical perspective', in Kritz 1983.

Zolberg, A. (1993) 'Are the industrial countries under siege?', in Luciani 1993.

Zolberg, A. (1997) 'Global movements, global walls: responses to migration, 1885–1925', in Wang 1997.

Zolberg, A., Suhrke, A. and Aguyano, S. (1989) *Escaping from Violence: Conflict and the Refugee Crisis in the Developing World*, Oxford: Oxford University Press.

Zurn, M. (1995) 'The challenge of globalization and individualisation', in H. H. Holm and G. Sorensen (eds), *Whose World Order?* Boulder: Westview Press.

Index

Page numbers in italics refer to tables or figures where these are separated from their textual reference.

Index by Zeb Korycinska